# TALK TALK

*The Midwest American Rock and Reggae Magazine*

# TALK TALK

*The Midwest American Rock and Reggae Magazine*
*Complete Editions 1979-1981*

Edited by Bill Rich

PRESS

Talk Talk
The Midwest American Rock and Reggae Magazine
Complete Editions 1979-1981 Edited by Bill Rich
Copyright © 2025 Talk Talk Publications
Talk Talk Publications P.O. Box 36 Lawrence KS 66044
All rights reserved


www.talktalkfanzine.com


Book design by Bill Rich, Tim Brown and Dennis 'Boog' Highberger
Book cover design by Bill Rich and Frank Loose

First edition First printed 2025
Arthole Press P.O. Box 1313 Lawrence KS 66044

ISBN 978-1-7346381-2-7
ISBN 978-1-7346381-3-4 (ebook)

Printed in the United States of America

# TABLE OF CONTENTS

Acknowledgements .................................................................................vii
Foreword ..............................................................................................viii
Prefaces .................................................................................................xi

Volume 1 No 1.......................................................................................2
Volume 1 No 2.......................................................................................8
Volume 1 No 3.....................................................................................14
Volume 1 No 4 ....................................................................................22
Volume 2 No 1.....................................................................................28
Volume 2 No 2.....................................................................................38
Volume 2 No 3.....................................................................................46
Volume 2 No 4.....................................................................................54
Volume 2 No 5.....................................................................................66
Volume 2 No 6.....................................................................................78
Volume 2 No 7.....................................................................................86
Volume 2 No 8...................................................................................102
Volume 2 No 9...................................................................................116
Volume 2 No 10.................................................................................136
Volume 2 No 11.................................................................................154
Volume 2 No 12.................................................................................168
Volume 2 No 13.................................................................................182
Volume 3 No 1...................................................................................198
Volume 3 No 2...................................................................................214
Volume 3 No 3...................................................................................246
Volume 3 No 4...................................................................................286
Volume 3 No 5...................................................................................318
Volume 3 No 6...................................................................................362

Talk Talk Tape Talk 1.......................................................................402
Talk Talk Tape Talk 2.......................................................................406

Index..................................................................................................410

# ACKNOWLEDGMENTS

A big thank you to my friend, Eric Schindling, who was the cofounder and early co-editor of Talk Talk. Several of us had sat around reading other fanzines and music magazines and thinking we could do something similar, but it was his initiative that got the first issue out.

Besides the contributing writers, reviewers and interviewers, it was the cover artists, photographers, and those doing typesetting and layout design that helped define what was created. It was all volunteer and it was not always fun.

The early issues were written by mainly Eric and I, often using additional initials. The style seemed to be using initials and not names. A chronological list credits the following: WB, VS, ET, Kenny Fulk, Rick Hellman, Marty Olson, Jim Schwada, JM, Eric Schindling, Bill Rich, DC, KD, EH, CH, II, NN, HM, U-Man, JTB, SMcB, Christopher Lucas, Steve Dibendetto, BI, JB, Mark Gilman, Bobs, Marc Burch, Scott Epsten, Dave Stuckey, Steve Kemp, Harold Thorn, Robin Kyle, Buzz Spencer, Sharon Maier, Mel Cheplowitz, Ivan Hough, Frank Loose, James Grauerholz, Mark Spencer, Blake Gumprecht, Andrea Rosenthal, Stephen Graziano, Rory Houchens, Dave Cade, and Tom Hoyt.

Photographers were Eric Schindling, Robin Kyle, Bill Rich, Brenda Haverkamp, Christopher Lucas, Patty Heffley, Chris Hunter, John Lee, Frank Loose, Doug Cunningham, Rick Schneider, Lowell Stewart, Nancy Schneider, Teri Bloom, Jo Stone, K Larson, Russ Battaglia, Kate Simon and Ugene Merinor.

Cover art credits include Nate Fors, Stakoff, Marty Olson, Bill Rich, Mark Schraad, Christopher Hunter, Rick Schneider, Christopher Lucas, John Lee and William Burroughs. Layout John Lee, typesetting by Joan McCabe Moore and design by Bill Rich.

For getting this all into book format, an enormous thanks to Tim Brown of Arthole Press, with assistance from Maggie Price. Boog Highberger of Arthole Press also assisted with indexing and project coordination.

*Bill Rich*

# FOREWORD

Johannes Gutenberg's invention of the printing press initiated a communications revolution, allowing information to be recorded, circulated, and read more widely and efficiently than previously possible. Though we often associate print technology with big important books—The King James Bible, the Shakespeare First Folio—throughout history the most vital printed agents of change were leaflets and pamphlets, "cheap print" in which people could circulate countercultural ideas and call for change. The Reformation, the American Revolution, the abolitionists, among others, were all engendered by the intellectual ideas spread by rebels using new print technologies to challenge dominant hegemonies.

Punk, too, was a print revolution. In the UK small, independently printed magazines—zines—like *Punk* and *Sniffin Glue* spread the anti-authoritarian ideas and aesthetics that spawned the Sex Pistols and the bands that followed them. In the United States, punk emerged as interlinking regional phenomena. Cities spawned local scenes with idiosyncratic artists, bands, and DJs. These scenes announced themselves with zines, which became regional calling cards; publications like *Subterranean Pop* (Seattle), *Touch and Go* (Lansing, Michigan), or *The Offense Newsletter* (Dayton, Ohio) created a communications circuit that promoted their hometown acts and let out-of-towners know where they could play when they came to town. At a time when formerly countercultural mags like *Rolling Stone* and *Creem* were turning into slick celebrity-obsessed public relations missives, zines were essential to documenting this new musical underground.

Founded in 1979 by Eric Schindling and Bill Rich, *Talk Talk* precedes a lot of the more famous American zines. Published in Lawrence, Kansas, it strove for a professional amateurism, generally eschewing the random cut-and-paste aesthetic of classic punk zines in favor of a cleaner layout, each issue with a proper copyright page neatly listing the editorial staff and contributors. Its reviews and features favored an enthusiastic but detached critical voice, speaking with a subtly subversive but accessible authority, offering a Midwest-nice window into worlds of music and culture beyond mainstream radio.

Appearing at a crucial moment in music history, *Talk Talk* punctured conventional perceptions of Kansas, and the Midwest generally. Its subtitle, "The Midwest American Rock and Reggae Magazine," revealed its great variety. "Rock" perfectly suits the Midwest—but here, rather than the 70s heartland likes of Bob Seger or REO Speedwagon that one might expect from the region, it championed XTC, The Clash, Iggy Pop. You can find reviews of early releases by The Cure, Siouxsie and the Banshees, New Order before they became icons of alternative music, as well as features on outré artists like Throbbing Gristle.

But "reggae"? Who would expect a Kansas zine to spend almost an entire issue covering Reggae Sunsplash '81 in Jamaica, or run regular features and reviews of reggae records? Rather than the forlorn black-and-white, tornado-damaged, all-American bucolic pastorale that Dorothy wanted to return to, *Talk Talk* communicated to the world that Kansas was a vibrant cultural outpost, creating its own art and music from the bricolage of underground artists around the world.

*Talk Talk* ran from 1979 to 1981, each year encompassing one series, keeping an impressively reliable publication schedule. It did not simply report on and to the Lawrence scene, it was embedded within it. Issues could include cover artwork from Thumbs's Marty Olson, photography from Get Smart!'s Frank Loose, reviews from Schloss Tegal's Rick "V2" Schneider, and other local musicians, artists, and photographers. Individual issues pulse with scene-sustaining places and people that are gone: The Lawrence Opera House, Kief's Records, long-lost bands like The Clean. Its third series, with Rich taking the reins solo, captured a local scene that, in part due to its own efforts, had exploded. Features on Abuse, Get Smart!, and new Lawrence resident William S. Burroughs were accompanied by flexidiscs, jump-starting the musical archive of Kansas postpunk. Although *Talk Talk* ended at the end of 1981, its energy continued through Fresh Sounds Records (home of The Embarrassment and Micronotz) and the massively influential *Fresh Sounds From Middle America* cassettes. *Talk Talk* and its offshoots were enthusiastically praised in publications across the US, in the UK, Germany, Australia. Because of its profound influence, *Talk Talk* must be recognized as the lodestar for Kansas's punk revolution, and a crucial record of American postpunk.

Zines are ephemeral by nature, cheaply made, not designed for posterity, but for capturing a particular moment and place in time. Paradoxically, this is what makes them essential historical documents. Collections like this one, gathering the contents of now-scarce issues of *Talk Talk*, are important history books, preserving the record of one of the most vibrant musical and cultural revolutions in Kansas and the US.

Francis X Connor
*Wichita State University*

*Eric Schindling and Bill Rich being interviewed by a local public television show Autumn 1980*

# PREFACE

*Rock & Roll destroyed my preconceived life plans.*

As a kid in the 60's, my dad would take some of us every Friday night to watch his bowling league. We had to sit for hours. There was an off-limits adult lounge that blared deep bass rhythms all night and the bowling alley air was a deep haze of cigarette smoke. We never knew what songs we were hearing, no vocals or melodies or treble clef notes. We listened to the vibrating bass lines and bowling balls hitting pins and read *MAD* magazines. I played trombone in the grade school band and took private lessons. In 7th grade, I was chosen to be in junior high stage jazz band, practicing before classes started for the rare performances. My brain was bass clef oriented, not so much melody or chorus. I thought in terms of underlying rhythms. At night, I was in my room listening to radio stations like KOMA in Oklahoma City and WLS in Chicago. I was always interested in learning about new bands. My small record collection was from a mail order club. I would read *Rolling Stone* sometimes, for news on music and also on the counter cultural movement.

In 1973, I came to college in the most liberal radical town in the Midwest, to a co-ed dormitory. I knew about politics and drugs and music, but not like Nate Fors, who was from my high school and the only one I knew in our dorm. Our first venture off campus was to the record stores. Nate had a massive record collection and instantly sought out and found some long-hairs with giant record collections like Mark Clifton and Eric Schindling. There was so much to learn about rock from these guys and others that I didn't have time to study chemistry, which I had to repeat but threw me off track for a continued scientific field of study. Music just filled more and more of my mind and time. I still kept some kind of focus on classes, finishing my degree in four years and starting a Psychology graduate program.

I was part of a circle of friends that included several groups of guys being roommates in different houses that got together to hang out and party, always with records on the turntable. When The Sex Pistols played in Tulsa, several carloads of us drove down there to be a part of it. A new local college radio station, KJHK, played lots of non-major-label new music. We still had one basic new record store in town, Kiefs, plus several chain stores 30 miles away in Kansas City. Besides the usual music magazines, we were obsessed with the new wave/punk pages of the *NME* from London. Some of us were pretty aware of new releases and new trends. And music was a hotly debated topic. There was some talk that we should put out our own fanzine. Eventually, it was Eric Schindling and myself who kept bringing it up. Eric worked at a copy store and would be able to slide some copying through on the sly. I worked on writing record reviews and thought that a handful of others were doing the same, but later found out no one else was doing so.

We set some deadlines to getting material to Eric. I had a typist for all my college graduate school papers who worked on some layout designs and she continued on to do all the typesetting for every issue that followed. I left Eric with my material and went out of town. Eric added a couple of pages and had Nate Fors draw a cover. Eric named it Talk Talk, after the 60's song and printed it up. A second issue was worked on and printed and we just kept working on more material. Eventually, others began to contribute. I took some classes on magazine design and photojournalism. I had a darkroom at my house and we used two campus darkrooms. John Lee started helping with the layouts at the Patterson, Theis & Lee Architects office. Later Craig Patterson bought some typesetting equipment and we generated all our own texts from there.

From time to time, some of us went to shows in Chicago. Our college roommate, Mark Clifton was now working at Wax Trax Records and had a place we could stay. I developed a long friendship with Jim and Dannie, Wax Trax owners. We started to do marketing by sending out copies to other publications and record labels and such, developing an emphasis on independent music, more punk and new wave oriented and later having a deep focus on reggae. I think our only original plan was to start a fanzine, not knowing what would happen with punk rock, which was evolving away. I just kept things moving along. Eric moved and we had less contact.

After I was labeled a music critic, I wanted to step back from criticizing to be supporting music. Flexi-discs of local bands seemed to be a fun way to do so. We did the Abuse and the Get Smart! flexi-discs and had the chance to do the Burroughs one. I wanted to create a new type of music and print fanzine. What we tried were cassette tape compilations with a booklet inside.

It became obvious bands needed the traditional album format still and eventually, *Talk Talk* evolved into the Fresh Sounds record label. There were several area fanzines starting, like *Alternative America*, *Bullet*, and *Blur* as well as the weekly or monthly newsprint ones like *The Note* and *The Pitch*. It didn't seem like *Talk Talk* was missed. The music scene flourished.

– Bill Rich September, 2024

# PREFACE II

One day I was at Bill Rich's house looking at his collection of English DIY zines and I told him we could do something like that. He said OK, we should do it! We got Nate Fors to do a cover and Bill and I wrote reviews. I printed everything up at Kinkos.

The name for the zine came from The Music Machine's song *Talk Talk*. Seven days from the time the idea was formed Bill and I were at his place again putting the first issue together. From there we got more people to contribute reviews. The primitive style became slicker. We put out buttons and flexi 45's. We started getting promo records from bands from around the world. It started out as a challenge posed and ended up as something special. *Esquire* magazine in their "What is Hip" issue named *Talk Talk* as the 5th hippest fanzine in the world! Who woulda thunk? LOL!

So now, over 40-something years later we've put together this collection. Hopefully people will find it an interesting view into a time and place that was filled with a new energy and a youthful rebellion. I hope it also shows that a couple of guys with an idea and not much else but desire can make something that can grow into a piece of history—the proof being that 40-plus years later this collection is being produced with eager support of fans that weren't alive when Bill and I first gave this baby its birth. I was proud of it when we first put it together and I'm proud that it's survived the test of time. I hope those who have discovered this collection enjoy themselves and maybe check out some of the bands mentioned that never made the Big Time! There were a lot of them... I hope they too might get appreciation.

Thank you to all of you who helped us put it out—wrote reviews, designed covers, contributed in every way. We also have to thank all the local bands and people who put the shows together. And thank all of you who had anything at all to do with the survival of the Music...

– Eric Schindling

# TALK TALK

*The Midwest American Rock and Reggae Magazine*
*Complete Editions 1979-1981*

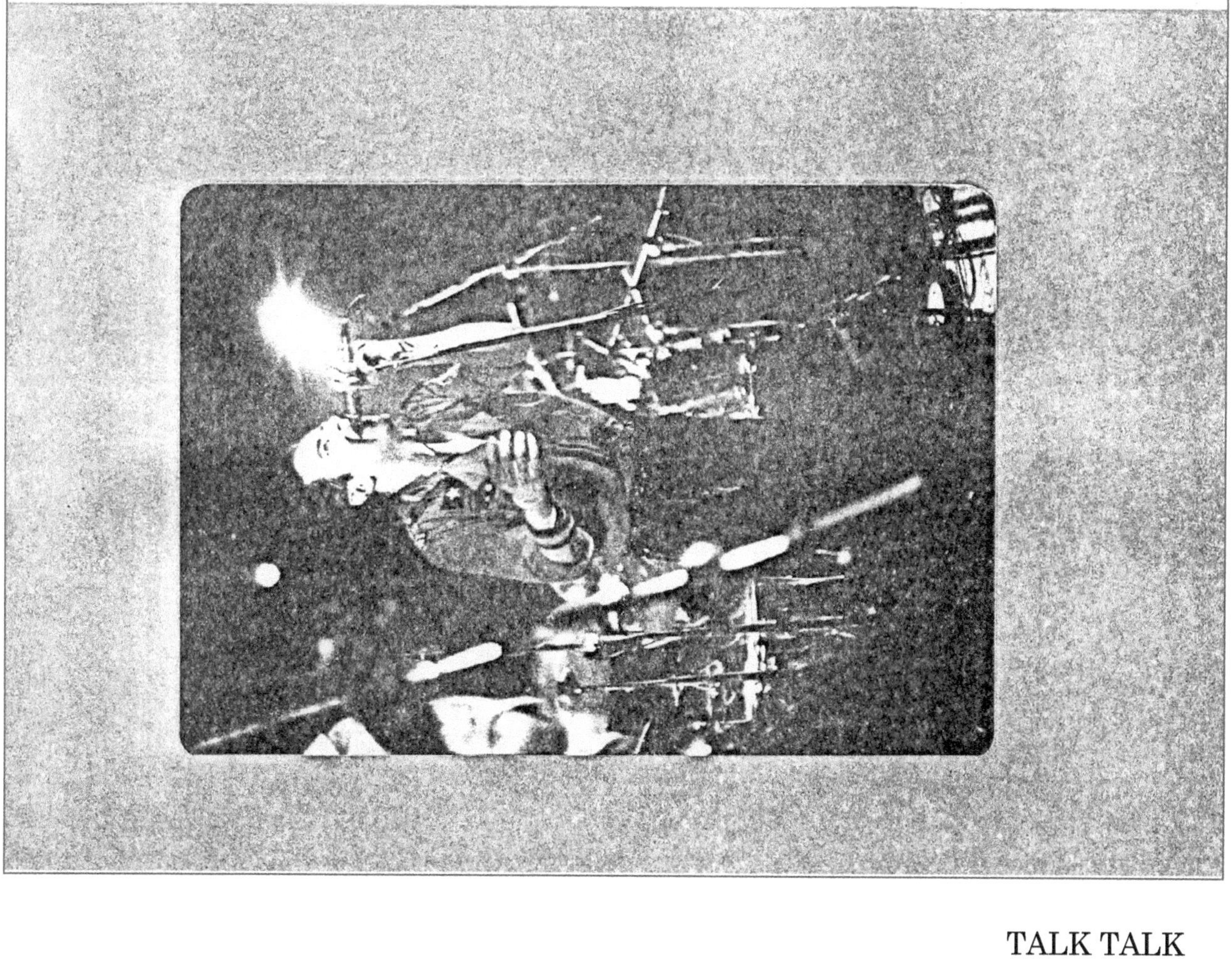

# Scenes
by ian noall

Recent press reports claim that the British scene is in a stage of "anything is possible." The English press frantically creates and destroys trends at faster speeds than music lovers can comprehend. Some of the current scenes include the British Mod revival, post-pop experimental music, and the still existing but declared dead punk movement and of course the standard catch-all, new wave.

Several new groups are definitely in the Mod tradition although others are marginal-Mod. The use of ska/blue beat/rock steady, generally early Jamaican roots rhythms, has increased. Of course England has always had their own reggae scene whether it be West Indian musicians or white rockers. It is the small record labels which have benefitted from this situation, particularly 2-Tone. Originally the private label of The Selector, the label has expanded to include The Specials (who are currently finishing the first album which is produced by Elvis Costello) and Madness. These three groups are currently on tour together, and considered three of the fastest rising groups of the year. In many ways, these bands combine the rock steady beat and rhythm with pop into unique blends. Interesting enough, Island has issued an album called "Various Artists: Intensified! Original Ska 1962-66." Check it out.

# Local Network

This issue of Talk-Talk will give you some information on local bands. Not everyone will agree on the opinions expressed; too bad.

1) Thumbs: A band that's been around a few years. Starting out rough but with loads of energy they've matured into a major musical force. Their sound is a cross section of *music*, covering the field, from soul to new wave. The mixture, because of superior writing is successful. An added note is that their first album will be out soon. I've heard the tape and it's great!

2) Regular Guys: This band follows the "New Wave" format fairly close, which does'nt mean they are'nt origanal. They know how to rock and since they've first formed their sound has improved. My only criticism is that they need a strong center focus. If they manage that they can be contenders. They will soon have a Ep out, watch for it.

That's all for now. In future issues we'll give you the low down on .....

.....Smart Pills, The Inevitable, The Embarassment, Terez-Terez, PBR and a great St. Louis group, Ray Miland.

## Import 45's

**The Undertones--You have my number** (Sire) Another Ulster band but with not the same ideology. While SLF vocalist has an emotionally packed, fast moving strain, the Undertones vocalist unleashes a unique warble. But don't let this influence you too much. The band has skyrocketed to stardom after a self-produced EP received the blessings of British DJ John Peel. Their debut album has recently been repackaged to include their single hits. If you didn't get the earlier album or the limited singles, this is your chance to get a superior product. This new single, however, is not on the album but definitely shows an improved band on their way up. Another album will be out soon. You should be able to find a good supply of their music. So do it.

**Public Image Ltd.--Memories** (Virgin) Two new PIL songs, similar to Death Disco and carrying on in their tradition. Whatever your opinion of the post-Rotten material has been, this single will probably confirm it. Personally, it's great!

**Stiff Little Fingers--Straw Dogs** (Chrysalis) Whether one calls it the war or the Troubles, living in Northern Ireland has strange effects on rock and rollers. SLF uses a hard hitting, strained energetic expression of hate and uncertainty of the environment. Their new single violently jabs at mercenaries--men of straw, while the B-side is You can't say crap on the radio. This band does not gloss everything over. Bitter people, you say? You bet and you can witness their involvement in the anti-racism movement which has resulted in concert violence in the worst of the Sham tradition. If you overlooked their first album (on Rough Trade) too bad. Rumored to be planning their first American tour soon, remember the name.

**The Members--Killing Time** (Virgin) The latest from these white reggae punks. What you might call concept packaging. The song is about killing time at the landromat with a washer on the cover. Real clever, aye? The B-side, entitled GLC, has a bit more of a grim political atmosphere. Good rhythms, good riffs and good hooks make it enjoyable to listen to.

## Import Albums

**Gang of Four--Entertainment** (EMI) A debut album by a relatively unknown (so far) band with two singles out. It has been described as an album-long burst of tense, hard, compulsive rock action with a stuttering pulse and machine gun rhythm guitar. While it might not be soothing music to knit by, those consumers looking for current new wave rock should check this out carefully and quickly.

**The Slits--Cut** (Island) Yet another debut album for this fall, but this all female group has been kicking around the punk scene for years. Finally vinyl-ized and marketed, the raw melodies and reggae riffs are packaged with a controversial cover which you must see and hear to appreciate. A surprisingly powerful record. The single from the album is Typical Girls b/w Heard it through the Grapevine. Hear it any way you can!

**Buzzcocks--A Different Kind of Tension** (UA) One of the top releases of the year, this third studio album presents some new sounds including an increase in influence of guitarist Steve Diggle and less emphasis on love songs. Try it. You'll fall in love.

**Sham 69--Hersham Boys** (Polydor) The long awaited third Sham album has finally been released. The band temporarily broke up this summer after consistent stage disruptions by the politically oriented groups of fans. After attempts at recording with Ex-Pistols Cook and Jones, Sham's man Jimmy Pursey united with his group to promote this album, while vowing never to play London again. The package includes a 12-inch single of Sham's classics. Several new songs in the Sham tradition along with some live sets make this album a must for all hungry Sham fans.

**Angelic Upstarts--Teenage Warning** (Warner Bros.) A few years ago the British stage was full of Sham-clones, basically a street-wise tough as loud singer/ spokesman backed by hard driving guitar, bass and drums. One of the few who have survived is the Angelic Upstarts (produced by J. Pursey). The Upstarts break into the vinyl world with an angry single--The Murder of Liddle Towers/ Police Oppression. Their debut album continues along this path being angry, but not offensive, with very powerful rebellious youth anthems.

If you like to dance... Tell Opera House Management that you wantNew Wave, Reggae and Rockabilly music more often and then don't make excuses about not going when they come to town....

## Reggae Albums

( Unfortunately only one album this time) next time lots!!!

**Bob Marley and the Wailers --Survival (Island)** The last few years have been a time of rising popularity for reggae. It has become easy to slag off Bob Marley. Finally, an album of new songs has been released. The question is has Bob become disco like some stars or has he become bland like others? The answer is Bob Marley shows himself as being just as relevant today as he was years and years ago. The roots sounds are definitely here with an emphasis upon Africa and struggling. Overdue for sure, but very welcome. The album will no doubt be a success adding momentum to the rasta revolt.

## Concerts

Nov. 4) Police/Fashon...Opera house

Nov 10) Thumbs/Secrets..."""""""

Dec 5 ) Buzzcocks !!!! same

Dec 6) Bob Marley...KU, Hoch aud.

Jan ?) XTC

6  TALK TALK

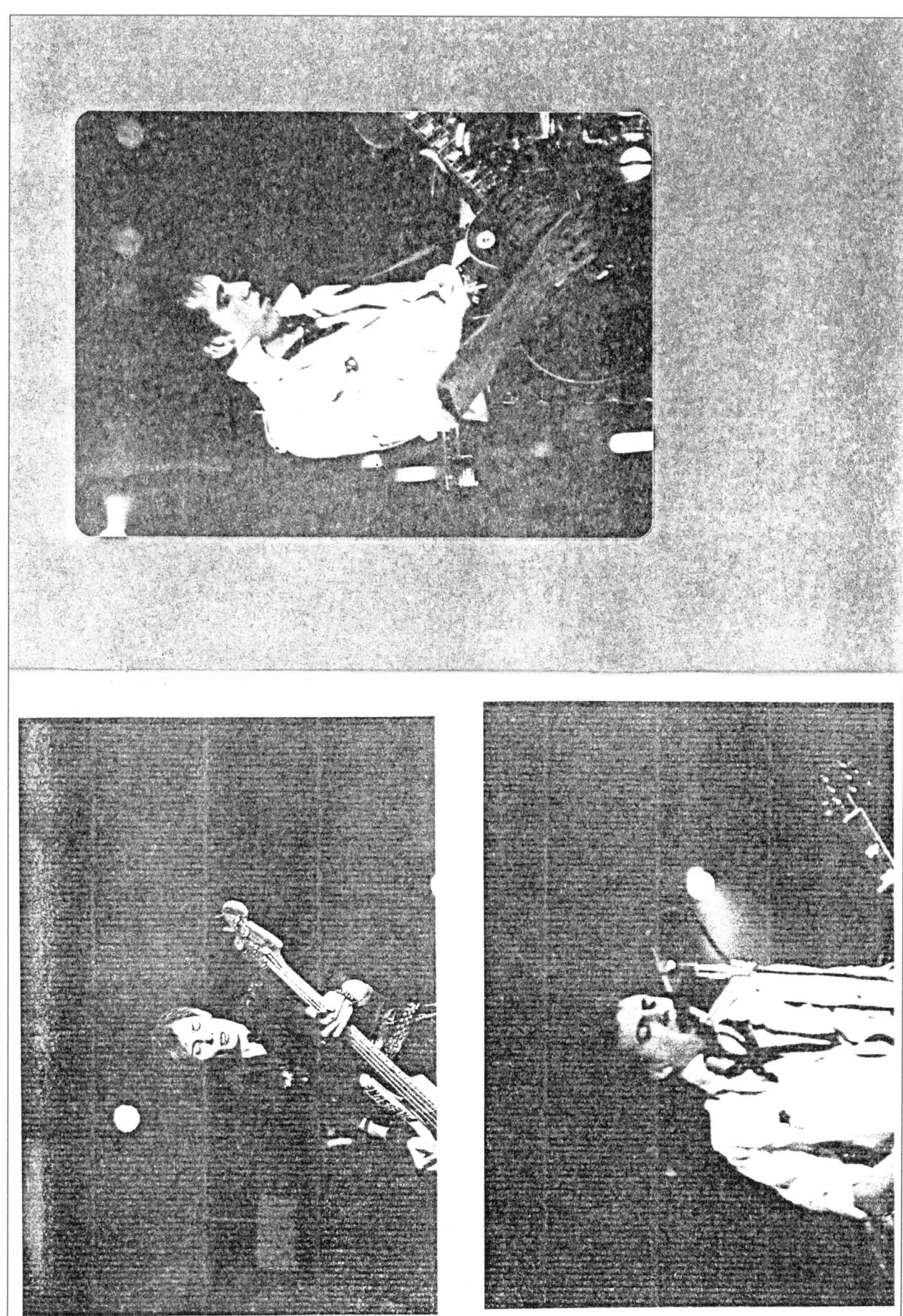

TALK TALK

TALK TALK

Issue #2

```
            Table of Contents

Local Scenes: Interview. . . . . . . . . . 3
The Hidden Force of the Revolutionaires. . 4
Live: Police/Fáshiön. . . . . . . . . . .  5
Album Reviews. . . . . . . . . . . . . . . 6
IRS Assistance . . . . . . . . . . . . . . 7
Singles Reviews. . . . . . . . . . . . . . 8
Live: Halloween Concerts . . . . . . . . . 9
More Reviews . . . . . . . . . . . . . . .10
Concert Schedule, In Town. . . . . . . . .11
```

The editors would like to state that the opinions expressed are not necessarily the opinions of the editors of Talk Talk but rather those of the writers.
                               The Editors
                                  ES/BR

---

Local Scenes: Interview with Miles Copeland

It was after the Police/Fàshiön concert that I ran into IRS Records head, Miles Copeland (Brother of Stewart, Police drummer). The following is the gist of the informal interview.

Talk Talk: Miles, I'm really glad you released the Fall album (Live at the Witch Trials) in America.
Miles Copeland: The Fall? Where'd you hear of them?
TT: They're one of my favorite bands.
MC: Really? Well there's another due out early next year. We're hopefully we'll be able to bring them over then. We're going to try bringing a few acts over in the spring. The Cure also have an album coming out in the spring--it will be the import with a few added songs.
TT: Like things off the first two singles?
MC: Right.
TT: What about the Siouxsie and the Banshees tour?
MC: Well, Siouxsie is pretty sick right now (in hospital with hepatitis) but we hope we can do it later. Of course, we're also getting the new Buzzcocks tour together.
TT: We're all waiting for it. By the way, how are the albums already released doing, as far as sales?
MC: Ok. Our biggest record is Root Boy Slim--He's a different type of artist than the other things we're releasing. But a lot of radio stations will play that and like it--it sorta opens the door for our other albums--say next time they get a batch of our records they might like two instead of one. (Someone asks why A&M was picked as distributor.) It all boils down to the fact that they're a record company with heart, the most human. They're willing to invest in and support an artist beyond the 1st album. They're about the most independent of the major labels. They sort of started out small like IRS.
TT: What other albums will be out?
MC: Like I said, The Cure. Klark Kent, Second Fall, John Cale.
TT: Is John Cale going to be on tour anywhere around here?
MC: I'm pretty sure--don't worry, he'll be around. And The Cramps are going to have an album out. How do you think they'd go over here?
TT: I'm afraid people aren't familiar with them, but if you think about bringing them you should get another act on the bill. Are you going to try and make the Lawrence area a regular stop?
(Continued on p. 7.)

## The Hidden Force of the Revolutionaires

One result of the new wave emergence has been the acceptance of musicians who have minimal instrument training. While the groups of today differ from the established traditions of musical expertise, they are similar in regard to having members playing guitars, drums and keyboards. That is the way rock and roll has been. But not so for reggae. Many reggae groups consist of a vocalist or several vocalists plus session players. The last few years have shown an increase in recordings coming from Jamaica. And it is well known that there are many talented studio musicians in demand. Seldom does one hear about any specific groups. One such group, which has been largely ignored, are the Revolutionaires, based at Channel One in Kingston. While looking through one collection of assorted reggae albums, it was discovered that the Revolutionaires, in mass or in part, played for 18 different reggae acts. To a large extent, the Jamaican sounds one hears today are actually various lead singers and the Revolutionaires.

The answer to the question of why session musicians are used so extensively lies in the nature of reggae rhythms. The heavy use of horns and percussion is an integral part of the sound known as reggae. This requires many musicians.

The basic makeup of Revolutionaires is Sly Dunbar, drums and percussion; Robbie Shakespeare, bass and rhythm guitars; Ansell Collins, keyboards and piano; Bartram (Ranchie) McClean, bass and guitars; along with many others occasionally, such as Rad (Duggie) Bryan on lead guitars, Eric (Tuffy) Lamont on rhythm guitars; King Sticky and Skully Simms on percussion; and, of course, the horns--Bobby Ellis on trumpet, Herman Marquis on alto sax, Tommy McCook on tenor sax, Vin Gordon on trombone, and Bongo Herman on Congo drums.

Based on liner notes, the above group comprises the Revolutionaires. Some of the musicians they play for include Jimmy Cliff, Peter Tosh, Bunny Wailer, Dillinger, I-Roy, Tapper Zukie, U-Roy, Culture, Burning Spear, Justin Hines, Gregory Isaaccs, Keeling Beckford, Toots and the Maytals, as well as lesser knowns including Israel Vibrations, Ijahman, Mighty Diamonds, Liaval Thompson, and Wailing Souls.

(Continued on p. 9.)

## LIVE: POLICE/FÀSHIÖN

Two British bands were at the Opera House on November 4. Because of Sunday closings of taverns, no age restrictions were imposed, allowing everyone to see Fàshiön and the Police. Of course the private club in the balcony was also packed. Although the ticket price ($7.50 at the door) seemed a bit high for these two three-piece bands, it is not often enough that the opportunity to see such shows occurs here.

Fàshiön opened to a full house, informing the audience they were from England not New York and playing material from the "Product Perfect" lp. The limitations placed on a band consisting of a guitarist, drummer, and bass player were overcome by a competent sound board man. They are a new, slick trio with a polished, black leather appearance. According to drummer Dïk, this was their last performance on the Police tour, having a west coast designation via Boulder.

Headlining the night were the Police, labelled as white reggae. About a year ago, when they first played at One Block West, your reviewer found himself pushed to the very front of the stage, six inches from Sting, on bass and vocals. Their show that night was very fresh and outstanding. At this return show, the band had retained their regular stage appearance with Sting in a jumpsuit and drummer Stewart Copeland in T-shirt and (Klark Kent) green gym shorts.

Guitarist Andy Summers was decked out in flashy garb and flashed superb sounds. His earlier experiences 15 years ago in a Mod band make him a heavyweight to the band, although only occasionally joining Sting in the limelight.

The show started with Next to You, So Lonely and Truth Hits Everybody from their first lp, Outlandos d' Amour, then moved to the second lp, Regatta de Blanc, currently No. 1 in the British charts, with Walking on the Moon. Hole in My Life was performed tight and stripped down. Following next were Death Wish, Bring on the Night with a long guitar solo, their hit Message in a Bottle, and The Bed's Too Big Without You. Their next selections were Peanuts, Roxanne, Can't Stand Losing You, Born in the 50's, and Be My Girl--Sally.

Their 16-song performance seemed to pass quickly. Their new p a system produced a loud, reverberated sound which combined with their hook-laden material. The Police are an energetic band. Their enthusiasm spread to the audience and provided for an enjoyable evening.

Album Reviews: Reggae Collections

Intensified: Original Ska 1962-66  Various Artists (Mango: MLPS9524)--Finally out, this collection of sixteen tracks is a must for those interested in the roots of today's reggae.  The musicians are listed together, making it hard to give the correct credits.  Lots of horns.  It definitely fills a gap linking reggae to calypso, jazz and the blues.

Rebel Music An Anthology of Reggae Music (Trojan: TRLD 403)--A double album collection of 28 songs by 22 artists from 1968 to 1976.  Chances are that at least half of the names are unfamiliar.  The variety of style presented expands the concepts of this musical form.  Very enjoyable listening.

Rockers  Various Artists (Island ILPS9587*)--A new film soundtrack.  The movie concerns a Jamaican drummer (Leroy "Horsemouth" Wallace) and his efforts to record and distribute--via motorcycle.  Similar in many ways to "The Harder They Come," with a comical presentation of the Rastafarian culture and life at the studio.
  The album contains 14 previously released songs--many being heavy hits.  To name a few:  Inner Circle's We a Rocker, Maytone's Money Worries, Junior Murvin's Police and Thieves, Peter Tosh's Steppin Razor, Jacob Miller's Tenement Yard, and Bunny Wailer's Rocker.  Other artists include Lee Perry, Mr. Isaaccs, Burning Spear, and Third World.  An album full of quality material.  This compilation is worthwhile to own and hear.  Don't know what the movie has to do with it.

Burning Spear  Harder Than the Best (Island ILPS9567)--A compilation of 12 of the best from the five studio lps out.  The last song:  Civilized Reggae is one of my favorites.  Four songs from the "Marcus Garvey" album, three from "Dry and Heavy" plus Man in the Hills, Social Living and more.  If you don't already own all previous releases, this is your chance to get familiar with the 'Spear, one of the top acts today.
(Continued on p. 10.)

I-Roy  The General (Virgin's Front Line:  FLD6002)--From one of the kings of dub, with a free dub album which is uncharacteristically plain background filler.  Dub without echoes?

## IRS Assistance

Good news for music lovers.  A new record label, International Record Syndicate (IRS) is releasing records of some of the top British bands on an American label with distribution by A&M Records.  Not only does this mean a reduction in prices, but more of a chance to see the releases one only gets to read about.  The big hits available so far include the Buzzcock's Singles Going Steady, The Fall's Live at the Witch Trials, Fashion's Product Perfect, Alternative TV's Best of ATV, Wazmo Nariz's Things Aren't Right, and Root Boy Slim and the Sex Change Band's Zoom.  Future plans include a repackaging of The Cure's Three Imaginary Boys plus singles, The Cramps, Klark Kent, John Cale, and a new Fall lp.
  Concert tours handled by Frontier Booking International (FBI) include the Human League, Steel Pulse, The Fall, John Cale, UK Subs, Buzzcocks, Iggy Pop, Police and Fashion.
  The formation of this record pressing and distribution network is a sign that the movement away from giant corporate control of the recording industry continues.  The punk rebellion and the new wave movement proved that self-production is possible.  But without the established business support, the new sounds were definitely on "limited supply."  IRS proves there are other ways to do things.  Americans now have opportunity to buy the records they want.

---

(Cont. from p. 3)
MC: We'd like to, but sometimes it's expensive.  If we could get another city interested in our artists, like Des Moines or St. Louis, it would be easy, but you're kind of isolated in a way here.
TT: Yes, we know.  Well, I hope you can.
MC: Yes, we do, too.
(At this point, Dik, Fashion drummer, was introduced to me and Miles went off to tend to Police business.)
--Read the Fashion interview next issue.
--Editors

Revolutionaires--Continued from page 4.

The Revolutionaires are also the talent behind much of the dub or version cuts using synthesized echo effects. They have several dub albums out. Interestingly enough, the Revolutionaires do not have a vocalist. Perhaps they feel that backing various vocalists is just as good as marketing under their own name. At any rate, their influence is becoming widespread and they continue to produce.

*********************************************

Live: Halloween Concerts

On Monday night, Oct. 27, Marty Olson (keyboard player for Thumbs) threw a Halloween Party. Besides costumes, beer and refreshments, there were three of Lawrence's best bands providing music: 11th Street Rhythm Method (for a brief reunion), The Regular Guys, and Thumbs.

11th Street started the evening, playing an entertaining mixture of R&B and funk that had the party crowd out of their seats and dancing. I had only seen them twice and am sorry they split. They were in top form. Next were the Regular Guys who provided plenty of great time fun, dance, music. Last but not least were my favorite local band, Thumbs, who pulled a trick out of the hat by playing exclusively cover versions (a rare event), including Eddie Cochran's C'mon Everybody, Animals' Got to Get Out of This Place, Searchers' When You Walk in the Room, and the Stones' Out of Time. They played with energy and style and provided a rocking finish to a great party.

Halloween Night at the Opera House, Pat's Blue Riddim Band performed three sets to a packed house. Concentrating on their reggae material, they presented a new sound. Minus the sax and with Bob Zohn on rhythm guitar, a different feel was given. The crowd had as enjoyable a time as the band, as usual.

Album Reviews (cont. from p. 6)
With no credits for the musicians given, this production could be made using old tapes with a voice track added. At times very mediocre. It could be worse, but it also could be much livelier. For those with mild tastes.

Culture International Herb (Front Line: FL1047)--Three herb-loving rasta vocalists supported by the Revolutionaires.

Import Singles

Sham 69--You're a Better Man Than I/Give a Dog a Bone (Polydor: POSP82)--The A-side is from the new lp and the B-side is the latest tune since reforming. A social statement from one of the top stars today. The theme on A, a Yardbird's song, is if you can judge others, you're better than I, with the flip concerns being frustrated at not getting what you want and being bought and sold. Strong resemblance to "Money," the lead cut on the lp.
Cockney Rejects--Flares 'n Slippers/Police Car--I Wanna be a Star (Small Wonder: Small 19)--A "Pursey at the controls" Ep, this band does not display as powerful a production as Sham, although the comparison is inevitable. Three original songs. If the lead singer had a lower-pitched voice, they would almost pass as Sham on an off-night.
The Specials--A Message to you, Rudy/Nite Klub (Two Tone: CHSTT5)--These two cuts from the forthcoming debut lp are instant classics of the ska/mod blend Two Tone has uncovered. The brilliant use of horns helps to establish a powerful presence for this nine-member group. You'll be hearing a lot more of them. The Selecter--On my Radio/

Too Much Pressure (Two Tone CHRTT4)--Connected so closely with The Specials (i.e., both on the previous Two Tone single, both releasing their first single followed by lps, touring together, etc.), they manage to show their personal style. On My Radio features female vocalist with rhythm of organ and cymbal. The flip is bebop roller coaster non-stop. This pressure's got to stop.
The Human League--Empire State Human/Introducing (Virgin: VS294)--As far as I can tell, this group uses no instruments, just synthesized sounds. This artform seems to be increasingly found everywhere, another glimpse into the sounds of the 80's.
The Mekons--Work All Week/ UKnown Wrecks (Virgin: VS 300)--The third single from a group fast becoming one of my favorites. The sound on this single reminds me of Gang of Four. On Unknown Wrecks, I could almost say that their lead vocalist is helping out. The structure is tighter, production better. A strong rhythm bass-drums dominate with guitar riffs here and there when needed. One of my top picks this month.
Junior Murvin--Cool Out Son, Joe Gibb--Cooling Out (Heavy Duty Records-JA)--This single made my day when I first (Cont. on p. 10.)

## Concert Schedule

| | | |
|---|---|---|
| Nov. 23 & 24 | Pat's Blue Riddim | Opera House |
| Dec. 5 | Buzzcocks/Ultravox | Opera House |
| Dec. 6 | Bob Marley and the Wailers/PBR | KU Hoch Auditorium |

## In Town

**Records**

Kief's Records  
2100 West 25th.  842-1544

Love Records and Tapes  
15 West 9th.  842-3059

**Concert Halls**

Lawrence Opera House  
642 Massachusetts  842-6930

Off the Wall Hall  
737 New Hampshire  841-0817

**Radio**

KJHK  91 FM  864-4747

---

(cont. from p. 9)--While not exactly new sounds, the ten cuts seem typical of current Kingston. The usual praises to JAH. Almost easy-listening mainstream.

Mr. Isaaccs (Micron-Canada: MICCAN009)--Popular in JA for a few years, but almost unheard of in America. GI is finally emerging. His hit "Slavemaster" can be found on the Rockers soundtrack lp. Seen in NY with Peter Tosh and Linton Kwesi Johnson, Mr. Isaaccs' music is a perfect blend of politics religion and soul. His voice reminds at times of Peter Tosh but smoother. Backup harmonies provided by the Heptones who blend in with the fine accompaniment of the Revolutionaires. This music carries a message but at the same time it holds a strong melody. Most of all though, you can feel the emotions put forth without feeling preached to. It's tempo, in time, just right. Hope you can find it.

(cont. from p. 8) bought it. Ever since hearing J. Murvin's lp "Police and Thieves", I've been waiting for a new release from this talented artist. The sound still deals with political subjects, still a Jamaican Curtis Mayfield. The backing track is a bit rougher, utilizing a sparser sound allowing the keyboards to rise above the mix, blending with the (dub) effect. A good dance song without the lyrical impact of the A-side.

More LPs----

UK Subs Another Kind of Blues (Gem Records: GemLP 100)--Seventeen original songs from a British band on the rise. It's easy to compare them with such diverse groups as XTC and Sham 69. The songs are sort of short, little, catchy things. Delivered with words yelled at times. Nice blue vinyl.

Penetration Coming up for Air (Virgin International: VI213l)--Their first American lp (they have an earlier one as import). Sorry to say their last, as they reportedly broke up last month. Nevertheless a good album--tapping on the rock and roll roots (some find them heavy metal--I cannot see it) with the strong voice of Pauline Murry. They have been around for a while, and their album along with their first and various singles make up a fitting epitaph for a great band that is no more.

Essential Logic--Lora Logic (vocals, sax) used to be a cornerstone of the now defunct X-Ray Specs and moved on long before they broke up to work on her own brand of music. This lp was long awaited but the wait was worth it. Also available: Arousal Burns and Quality Crayola Ep.

TALK TALK  13

TALK TALK

# TALK TALK

Issue 3 ............................ Free in Area
............................ $1.00 by Mail

The Midwest American rock and reggae magazine

## Table of Contents

News Items. . . . . . . . . . . . . . 3
Interview: Fàshiön . . . . . . . . . . 3
Live: Iggy Pop . . . . . . . . . . . . 4
Brian James Profile . . . . . . . . . 5
Reviews: Reggae Albums . . . . . . . . 6
Album Reviews . . . . . . . . . . . . 6
Local Music Update. . . . . . . . . . 8
Independent Labels. . . . . . . . . . 10

Opinions expressed are not necessarily those of the editors of Talk Talk.

The Editors
ES/BR

## News Items

The Clash are back in England after their successful American assault. A double lp "London Calling" with 18 songs is reported to be ready for release. Also their film, "Rude Boy" and a soundtrack album will be out early in the year.

The Ramones will release their next album, "End of the Century," after the Christmas rush.

The Jam have released their fourth lp, entitled "Setting Sons," hailed as the best one yet. Available in the U.S. in January.

Sham 69 will finally come to America with appearances in New York and Los Angeles. There are no other dates scheduled, so most fans will be overlooked for this premier and purely promotional show.

The Cure, formally a three piece band with two singles and an lp out, have changed bass players and added a keyboard player to become four piece and are currently regrouping their material.

The reformed Damned have released an album, "Machine Gun Etiquette."

Half of the Gang of Four were recently attacked, leaving vocalist Jon King with a fractured jaw, a flattened face resulting in loss of feeling permanently. Gui-

broken nose and tour dates have been cancelled.

Public Image Ltd. have released their second lp, marketed in a tin box containing three 12-inch 45s.

John Cale's new live lp, "Sabotage," will be released December 6.

## Interview: Fàshiön (Continued from Issue 2)

Talk Talk talked briefly with members of Fàshiön after their show with the Police. . . .

TT: How's your new album doing?

Dik: Okay. About as good as can be expected.

TT: Are you happy with the way it sounds? Your live sound is quite different. You didn't use the keyboards much tonight.

Dik: Well, we pretty well did everything on our own and I'm not sure we were ready to record, but when they came to us and said, 'Do you want to do an album,' we couldn't pass that type of chance up. We learned a lot.

(At this point, a Police fan, mistaking them for part of that group, began telling them how much he liked the Police. Fàshiön quickly exited.)

TALK TALK 15

## Live: Iggy Pop

Iggy Pop is in the middle of his American tour now. Concentrating on the coastal and northern areas, I caught the show in Chicago, the closest the tour came. Iggy looks very healthy, strong, and energetic. He came on hopping around the stage and previewed some of his smooth physical movements which have become one of his trademarks and are copied extensively by other performers.

The show opened with an old Stooges song, "Real Cool Time," which set the atmosphere. He moved into two new songs unreleased but quite familiar to the band, which includes assorted stars. On drums, from Berlin, Klaus Kruger. On keyboards and guitars, Ivan Kral, on loan from the Patti Smith Group which is taking a temporary break from performing. On bass, Glenn Matlock, of the Rich Kids and the original bassist for the Sex Pistols before the late Sid Vicious. On lead guitar, Brian James, originally the songwriter and guitarist of the Damned, who now has a new band, the Brains.

This group of musicians had been hand-picked by Iggy and have proved themselves to be a very successful lineup. Iggy has been

an underground superstar for years and continues to keep writing some of the best songs--both lyrically and musically. After ten years of singing some of the Stooges hits, his versions often vary in tempo and key. But this group of superb musicians played off the variations the others were picking up from Iggy's performance.

The mixture of old Stooges songs, recent songs, covers, and new material blended into a very enjoyable show. The night before they had played two shows at a club with an older audience seated at tables. Those daring to stand were quickly instructed to sit down by the numerous bouncers. The audience seemed unappreciative of the show, many being fans of the opening act, Scafish, a local group bordering on a form of outrageous pop.

The second night's show was held in a club in a suburban shopping center, where

## Brian James

### Profile

Over breakfast and a stroll along Lake Michigan, I had a chance to talk with Brian James and his travelling companion, Erica. Brian James was one of the creators of the early punk movement now in its fourth generation. He currently is the highlight of Iggy Pop's band playing lead guitar. The Stooges have been important to the evolving rock and roll scene, and Brian admits to growing up listening to them. Naturally, when the opportunity to go on tour opened, he joined. But there are no plans to release any material performed with Iggy. Too bad, because he makes the show successful. Brian wrote most of the Damned songs (the first punk band to release an album). The Damned played their first gig with the Sex Pistols, and now, Brian James is playing with Ex-Pistol bassist Glenn Matlock. In many ways, low-keyed Brian provided the quality sound and the rest of the Damned provided the madcap antics which defined punk. The Damned have reformed without Brian, and appear to have retained their image but not their earlier influence or impact.

"This is the first time I have backed a vocalist. I prefer to play my own songs." After completing the current tour, he will rejoin his new group, The Brains, who will be releasing a single, "Dancing on the Sand," available on Illegal Records. Brian pointed out that "there are many bands (including the Damned) who actually are not doing anything new. And the recent popularity of the 60's mod revival is another example of old, used trends resurfacing. The Brains will attempt to give new life to the new wave movement." Based on the past accomplishments of Brian James, they will. Be on the lookout. And pick-up his solo single, "Ain't That a Shame" and "Living in Sin"/"I Can Make You Cry," available on BJ Records in 7" and 12" as well as on the domestic IRS label.

Reviews: Reggae Albums

Steel Pulse  Tribute to the Martyrs (Mango: MLP59568)-- The second lp from this English reggae band of six black Britons. Steel Pulse have been very active in the Rock Against Racism movement. The Martyrs tributed include: Martin Luther King, Jr.; Malcolm X; George Jackson; Steve Bilko; and Marcus Garvey. While reggae is not always related to religion or race, in this case it is. This album reminds one of the black oppression and provides the skilled rhythms and chords of traditional reggae. Perhaps the tops in British reggae, Steel Pulse are doing more than their share in enlightening the world. (WB)

Front Line 3  Various Artists (Virgins Front Line FLB3062) --Ten songs from ten different groups. This is the third sampler of the newest Front Line releases. A very good assortment featuring Gregory Isaacs, Sly Dunbar, Mighty Diamonds, I-Roy, U-Roy, Culture and others. Worthwhile to have for those trying to keep informed on the barrage of Front Line releases. (WB)

Scratch on the Wire  Various Artists (Island: ILPS9583) --A Lee Perry-produced compilation of seven artists who are generally associated with the Upsetter himself. Lee Perry is legendary and this record shows the variety of sounds which he has created. Lots of overdub. (WB)

Joe Higgs  Unity is Power (1 Stop-Island: STOP1002)--I like this album. The way it fuses roots reggae with jazz and soul. It may be a bit too smooth for some. If you've never heard of or listened to Joe Higgs (shame on you) make amends now and listen to this fine lp from one of reggae's old masters. (VS)

Album Reviews

XTC  Drums and Wires (Virgin: V2129)--Possibly the best XTC album yet (their third). They do not seem to be hurt by the departure of keyboardist Barry Andrews. Their focus is tightened and refers to a more traditional rock sound (two guitars, bass, drums, with little keyboards). But there is nothing predictable about this band or this lp. It starts out with a great song, "Making Plans for Nigel," also the current single, and ends after an aural

Album Reviews (continued from p.6)

journey with "Complicated Game." The songs are all strong. The album is out in America with an added track ("Life Begins at the Hop"). (VS)

The Boomtown Rats  The Fine Art of Surfacing (Columbia: JC36248)--First off, this album has been a disappointment. Expecting something similar to the first two lps, there are many places where the sound appears ready to take off on new musical heights. But it doesn't. The mammoth hit "I Don't Like Mondays" is contained here. Area fans will remember their show (one of the best acts of that caliber, they should listen to the earlier Rats to tour in the midwest). If one expects a tour de force material and wait for the next attempt. Lead singer Bob Geldolf is destined to continue being a star and no doubt will use the changed shape of the Boomtown Rats to sustain himself, and at the expense of the American fans. (WB)

The Specials  Specials (Two Tone Records and Chrysalis Records Ltd.: CDLTT5001)--The much awaited debut album by one of the top new bands of 1979. Produced by Elvis Costello, this is sure to be a smashing hit. The Specials have a unique blend of rock steady and rock and roll. The five Britons and two West Indians, along with a roots horn section, play melodic and fast, with occasional Keith Richard chord stashes, and fast reggae enthusiasm, passing along their frenzied energy. (WB)

The Fall  Dragnet (Step Forward: SFLP4)--The Fall claim to put out material for those people who do not accept what is fed to them and have a taste for esoteric music with a good beat. They are accused of being formlessly repetitive, overbearingly earnest, distant, unaccomplished musicians. Their raw and abrasive sounds have been changed by personnel switches, and extensive experience. In this followup to last year's Live at the Witch Trials, their impact is just as powerful. They are still raw and abrasive. Founder and vocalist Mark Smith backed with keyboards, drums, bass, and two guitars shows an increase in intention and direction. Although the themes of the songs are undecipherably intense, the interchange with the melodic beat blends into enjoyable entertainment. (WB)

## Local Music Update

The Smart Pills, a Topeka-based three piece new wave band who played regularly in Lawrence until moving to LA last spring have broken up. Lead singer and guitarist, Get (Smart) has reportedly formed a new group and can be seen at the Whiskey A Go Go. Billing himself and the band as John Jones, a recording deal is being worked out. Two of the new band members are Warner's promo men, who first saw the Smart Pills when they opened for the Weirdos at the Troubador.

Regarding the rest of the Smart Pills, the bass player is playing in New York with some old friends and the drummer has returned home to Ohio. The Smart Pills will be remembered as a tight violent leather trio creating anthems such as "Yankee Doodle Boy" and "Person to Avoid."

So the Smart Pills will not be returning this winter as planned. Hopefully we will be hearing more soon.

---

The Regular Guys will be releasing their debut ep soon. On the National Recording Artist label, the cuts will be "It's A Secret," "Too Dumb," and "Leave," "I Forgot the Flowers."

---

The Thumbs will release their debut album very soon also. It's entitled "Thumbs" and is on Ramona Records.

---

The Inevitable, a Wichita-based four piece female group, have reformed since the bass player moved to Chicago. They stunned the Midwest by playing a concert at the State Boys' Reformatory last summer. Currently limiting their appearances to small clubs and private parties, it is rumored they will play in the area soon.

---

Another new wave Wichita group, The Embarrassment, who have been playing with The Inevitable, also plan to play in this area.

---

A local mystery group, Egg Hoover and the G.E. Three, are developing quite a cult following. Although it is reported that their original tapes have received heavy airplay in St. Louis, there is practically no information available on them. Rumored to be releasing more songs in the future, many are anxiously awaiting their next assault.

## Album Reviews

Madness One Step Beyond (Stiff: SEEZ17)--To many, Stiff made the "seez" of the year by signing Madness originally on Two Tone. This debut album rocks out, adding new material to their list of hits. The heavy emphasis on horns in the ska tradition, and lively tempo helps them carry on the emergence of white reggae. Dance to the music. (WB)

Pere Ubu New Picnic Time (Chrysalis: CHR1248)--At last, a new release from the U-Men. This new album, although a bit more melodic or structured than earlier material, continues Ubu's journey into nightmare and uncertainty. The familiar Ubu sound vortex is as disorienting and gripping as ever. Strange night noises and haunted house electronics drift throughout this dreamlike lp. In the midst of it, David Thomas' absurdist lyrics clearly showing Ubu's sense of humor. A band that can be scary and fun at the same time. Best songs are "Have Shoes Will Walk," "Small was Fast," "Jehovah's Kingdom Come," and "The Voice of Sand." This last song, with whispering vocals and sandstorm synthesizer, evokes images of the legendary Dutchman. This lp is awesome. (ET)

Adverts Cast of Thousands (RCA import: PL25246)--Over the course of their underrated existence, this band has released six singles and now two albums (their first single, "One Chord Wonder b/w Quickstep" was one of the early Stiff singles, released in 1977). Over the course of three years, they've changed, in some ways for the better and other times not. This new album finds them taking an anti-war, anti-mechanism stand. Their lyrics are laden with cryptic messages. Even the best song on the album, "My Place," speaks of the rot that has set in all around ("Here it is, all around me, my place"). They seem to be saying that we aren't going to exist if we don't start caring about the important things (and they aren't money or power in any form). Their first album is called "Crossing the Red Sea with the Adverts" and on the new album they quote the Book of I John. I don't want them to sound like "Christian Punks," but the Bible does hold a nice idea about Armageddon. Even the use of keyboards (a first with new member Tim Cross) has an epic sound to it (listen to "Television's Over"). The mixture of heavy organ and background chorus reminds one of an Italian Hercules movie. (VS)

# Independent Labels

In the past two years, the independent record label in England has emerged as an important source of immediate, vital, and relevant rock 'n roll. Records on these independent labels are among the best new music of the past year. While the major labels drag further and further behind the times, the minors--the independents--have burst forward and outward, launching such new, imaginative, and stimulating artists as Gang of Four, Joy Division, The Fall, Monochrome Set, Swell Maps, and many others; and, in fact, achieving chart success (in the UK) with records from such groups as Stiff Little Fingers (Rough Trade), The Specials, The Selector, and Madness (Two Tone). Led by rock 'n roll enthusiasts like Bob Last (FAST), Tony Wilson (Factory), Bill Crummond (Zoo), and Geoff Travis (Rough Trade), the independents are discovering new and innovative ways to do things and look at things. No longer is control of the music in the hands of the few major labels with their narrow-commercial point of view. The bands that create the music can now control the methods of presentation. The new labels say something about the times--they reflect the extent of decentralization, diversification, and flexibility of the new music.

What follows, then, is a buyer's guide to the best releases of these new labels. Though sometimes difficult to find, all of the records discussed in the following list are well worth your time, money, and attention.

ROUGH TRADE Based: London  Led by Geoff Travis

CABARET VOLTAIRE: 45s--"Extended Play" EP (RT 003); "Nag Nag Nag" (RT 018); LPs--"Mix-Up" (Rough 4).
Sheffield trio formed in '74. An electronic garage band --a psychedelic Kraftwerk. While their first release was a disappointment, their second single "Nag Nag Nag" is a must (one of the best of '79), with its perfect balance of punk attack and swirling, haunting electronic noise, all revolving around the title phrase. Don't pass this one by! Debut LP Mix-Up just released--should be great!

STIFF LITTLE FINGERS: 45s--"Suspect Device (RT 006); "Alternative Ulster" (RT 004); "Gotta Gettaway" (RT 015); LPs--Inflammable Material (Rough 1)
Belfast group formed in '77, swiftly gained popularity through the release of first single "Suspect Device" on the band's own Rigid Digits label (later re-released on Rough Trade). Musically, they're not too far away from the Clash, and like the Clash, their socio-political lyrics reflect and attack the violence and turbulence existing in their home environment. Powerful music and a powerful group led by gruff vocalist Jake Burns. Three killer singles and a strong LP make them a group to watch out for. Rumors of an upcoming U.S. tour.

MONOCHROME SET: 45s--"He's Frank" (RT 005); "Eine Symphonie Des Grauens" (RT 019); and "The Monochrome Set" (RT 028).
Described as pop art, this band has released three incredibly imaginative and witty singles to very little popular or critical acclaim. Led by a suavely deep-voiced Kevin Ayers' type vocalist called Bid, the Set play midtempo, jumpy, sometimes haunting songs with strong bass, jagged guitar attack and good melodies. The band is currently working on an album, which, if the singles are any indication, should be excellent.

SUBWAY SECT: 45s--"Ambition" (RT 007)
Led by singer/poet/songwriter Vic Goddard, Subway Sect were early participants in the punk movement, playing the legendary 100 Club Punk Festival, and, through their association with Clash manager Bernie Rhodes they appeared on the Clash's "White Riot" tour of '77. They released two singles, the first on Rhodes' Braik label, and this one "Ambition" on Rough Trade--both singles and group receiving much critical acclaim. Since the singles, Goddard has apparently dropped out of sight and an album recorded in '78 has yet to be released. Don't miss out on this fantastic single!

SWELL MAPS: 45s--"Dresden Style" (RT 012); LPs--A Trip to Marineville (Rough 2).
Swell Maps play basic rock 'n roll with all the wiring and machinery yanked out and left dangling with sparks flying everywhere. They disregard such things as production and tightness. Guitarist Jowe Head plays a guitar with the strings placed in reverse order. "Dresden Style" and A Trip to Marineville are garage rock brought to perfection. Important nonsense. Brilliant noise.

Product's Bob Last to document the progress and history of bands in the early stages of their careers, usually before they would normally be on record, and like any other magazine, an Earcom is a record of its time. Read/Hear it today, then tomorrow it's out of date. Two Earcoms have appeared so far--both filled with bright, youthful mutant pop that should not be missed. The first Earcom, "Youth," features two songs each from the Blank Students, the Flowers, the Prats, and Graph. Earcom 2, "Contradiction," features two songs each from Basczax, Thursdays, and Joy Division.

NEXT ISSUE: Manchester's Factory Records, Liverpool's Zoo Label, and London's Two Tone Records and Faulty Product. And in following issues I'll be discussing American independents, their importance, impact, and best releases. Stay Tuned!  --Kenny F.

Live: Iggy Pop (Continued from p.**4**)

the main floor was packed with wild fans who enjoyed themselves much more than the previous night's crowd. The band could sense this early on, and definitely gave a better performance. While Ig harrassed the dressed-up first crowd, he poured thanks on the second one. Quite a contrast. Once again, the godfather of punk proves that he is a force not to be forgotten.

RAINCOATS: 45s--"Fairytale in the Supermarket" (RT 013). Impressive all-girl trio led by Portuguese lead singer Ana, the Raincoats have used various drummers including Nick Turner--their first drummer, ex-101er Richard Dudanski (now ex-PIL), and finally recording this single with ex-Slits drummer Palmolive. Similar to the Slits in sound and instrumentation (though without the Slits' reggae based rhythms), Raincoats' songs--especially the B-side "In Love" and "Adventures Close to Home"--are more melodic; a cross between Patti Smith and the Velvet underground. Now, once again, drummerless, the Raincoats' future is uncertain, though an album recorded earlier this year should be out soon.

FAST Based: Edinburgh, Scotland  Led by Bob Last

HUMAN LEAGUE: 45s--"Being Boiled" (FAST 4). Giorgio Moroder meets the Ronettes. A Sheffield group that plays no instruments other than synthesizers, whose electro-comic pop single "Being Boiled" and enthralling live performances using interesting visuals (slides, films) along with their songs have gained them a reputation as one of the best new groups of the last year. Their subtly humorous techno-sociological lyrics blend perfectly with their innovative synthesizer music. The Human Leage take off where groups such as Kraftwerk, Devo, and Tubeway Army stop. Looney Tunes for the '80s!

GANG OF FOUR: 45s--"Damaged Goods"; EP (FAST 5). Counter-revolutionary disco. A powerful, intense, and exciting group on-stage and on-record, the Gang of Four are currently the cause of much favorable acclaim for their hard, rhythm-heavy musical approach and enlivening mental outlook. "Damaged Goods," their first release, contains some of their best (if not _the_ best) material, though a subsequent single and album on EMI are both excellent as well. Destined to be one of the most popular groups of the next few years.

EARCOM: No. 1--"Youth" (FAST 9A); No. 2--"Contradiction" (FAST 9B). Earcom--"ear-comic"--an aural magazine. Earcoms are instant 12" compilations of early recordings and demo-tapes of unsigned bands. Earcoms are an attempt by FAST

Everyone is aware of the terrible state of FM radio. One exception is the local college radio station. Many of the records and artists discussed in Talk Talk can be heard on KJHK-FM 91, throughout the afternoon and evening. Sunday shows include reggae from 2-4 p.m. and current English artist releases from 10-12 p.m. on the "England Rocks" show hosted by Kenny Fulk. The request line is 913-864-4747

BUZZCOCKS ARE COMING

December 5 the Buzzcocks will appear in town, along with Ultravox. They have a perfect blend of punk and pop. The lyrics are basically love oriented personal agonies. Four albums out and about ten singles. They established themselves quickly in the new wave. By successfully putting their own ep out, they paved the way for others. This is their second US tour. The top band to come to town.

Ultravox might not be as popular, but they have been around long enough for three lps, various singles, and various lineups. Their latest lp, "Systems of Romance," resembles Eno meets Magazine. They are one of the early synthesizer rock bands.

Wire 154 (EMI-SHSP4105)--Wire's third album almost needs a map legend enclosed because the entire feel of this record is that it deals with geography: mental, physical, emotional, and blends it into a musical motif. At times they sound like they've been influenced by Pink Floyd ("A Mutual Friend," a case in point) and then on the next song like Roxy Music ("Blessed State"). They seem to have the ability to span the range of musical styles in the sense that they can go from pop rock (i.e., "Mutual Friend") and then head off into left field with a song (if I can call it that) "Indirect Inquiries," which seems to be their version of white noise. (VS)

Jah Lloyd  Black Moses (Virgin's Front Line: FL1031)--Jah Lloyd the Black Lion, aka Patrick Francis, has been enrolled in the JA scene for many years. Most recently he has earned distinction as a producer and rub-a-dub lyricist, vocalizing over Revolutionaires' tracks at Channel One. This lp is well produced and concerns topics many artists write about ("Green Bay Incident," "Punk Reggae," "Rudy, Come Home," etc.). An interesting state of the art recording. (WB)

Hottest Hits (From the Vaults of Treasure Island) Various Artists (Virgin's Front Line: FL1034)--An album of re-released singles from 60s by virtually unknowns (Sensations, Melodians, Silver Tones, Techniques, Paragons). In general, this collection leans toward soul-oriented calypso, not exactly reggae but not ska or rock steady. This era of music covered was a turning point for reggae and Treasure Island filled an important role. (WB)

==================================================

Import Singles

Visage  Tar/Frequency 7 (Radar Record: ADA 48)--On first appearance, a new wave super-group, with members of Magazine, Rich Kids, and Ultravox fronted by an individual named Steve Strange. "Tar" lays its foundation on a disco drum-bass combo with outstanding sax. The B-side is heavily electro-music. Not a bad single but not a great one.

Pere Ubu  The Fabulous Sequel (Have Shoes, Will Walk)/Humor Me, The Book is on the Table (Chrysalis: CH52372)--The Fabulous Sequel, taken from the lp New Picnic Time is the best effort of Ubu to be pleasantly melodic and rocking.

22   TALK TALK

# TALK TALK

Issue 4 — Free in Area / $1.00 by Mail

The Midwest American rock and reggae magazine

## Table of Contents

Live: Bob Marley & the Wailers with
Pat's Blue Riddim Band. . . . . . . . . 3
Live: Ultravox and the Buzzcocks . . . . . 3
Import Singles Review . . . . . . . . . . 4
Album Reviews . . . . . . . . . . . . . . 5
Interview: Ultravox. . . . . . . . . . . 7
News Items. . . . . . . . . . . . . . . . 10

Opinions expressed are not necessarily those of the editors of Talk Talk.

The Editors
ES/BR

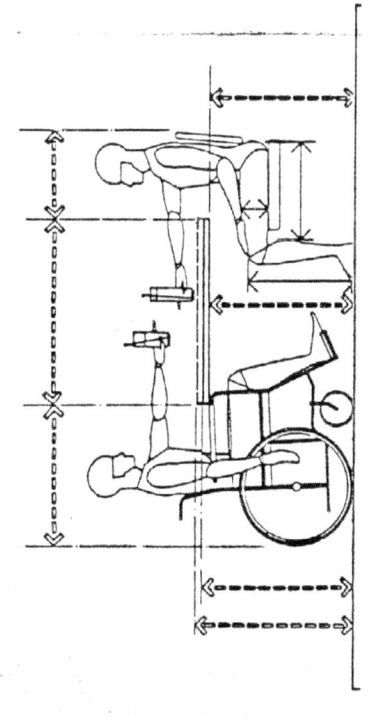

## Live: Bob Marley & the Wailers with Pat's Blue Riddim Band

At last, a reggae act actually came to the midwest without cancelling. There have been so many planned concerts that fizzled that most of those holding tickets almost assumed they would end up with refunds. But not this time. Bob Marley & the Wailers did show up and presented a show which will long be remembered. Along with the Barett brothers and the I-Two's, the ten-piece band showed the audience of 3,500 the style of reggae played live, complete with vibrating bass and Haile Selassie backdrop. The overall emphasis was similar to the live sound shown on "Babylon by Bus," drawing from the "Natty Dred" lp and the new "Survival." As one might have expected, the Rastafarian religious emphasis was evident. The lighting was very effective using the basic Jamaican colors of red, yellow and green.

Opening the evening was Pat's Blue Riddim Band, a locally-based reggae/funk group rooted more in JA than anywhere else. It appears that they were influential in arranging for the "Prince of Reggae" to show. And they played some very polished reggae which definitely pleased the fans.

It was most definitely the best concert that has been arranged by the University in years. The whole show went off very well. Hopefully, it will be taken as a sign that this area does appreciate quality reggae and in the future other artists will go beyond scheduling shows to actually appearing in this reggae-starved region.

## Live: Ultravox and the Buzzcocks

One of the early dabblers in the electronic sound that has become so popular the past few years, Ultravox provided an audience of over 500 their own mutated brand of music. Starting out the concert with "Hiroshima Mon Amour" off their second album, "HA!-HA!-HA!," they quickly had the crowd on their feet and at the stage. There was a new presence this tour, that of Midge Ure (formerly with Slick, Rich Kids, and Thin Lizzy for a brief stint). He proved an able replacement for John Foxx (ex-lead vocals) and Roger Simon (ex-guitarist). Instead of trying to be an imitator of Foxx, Ure provided the band with a stronger (some would say more pop) sound. Other songs they performed were "Life at Rainbow's End," "Satday Night in the City of the Dead," "I Want to be a Machine" featuring Billy Currie on a magni-

## Import Singles Review

**Arthur Kay:** Ska Wars/Warska Else's Train/I'm Cold (Friction Records: Nymph 001)--An enjoyable tune backed with a good dub version. Typical ska lyrics (rude boy, shanty town), typical rhythm, standard beat. Kay provides vocals, keyboards and bass with assistance of a drummer and guitarist. So it is not the live performance sound. But it is well produced.

**Angelic Upstarts:** Never 'Ad Nothing/Nowhere Left to Hide (Warner Bros.: K17476) --The Upstarts traditionally deal with unrest and injustices. Same for this single. The A side concerns an 18-year-old who wants some glory and gets shot, complete with a Ramonest hook and the usual powerful vocals. The flip is a fast moving, repetitive, "gotta keep running," number similar to the basic Upstart pattern set on the lp. Neither song is soothing or positive, but there is more than enough competitors who are.

**UK Subs:** C.I.D./Live in a Car--B.I.C. (City Records: PIN22)--Muted sounds, heavy metal guitar, fast & short. Three of the hit songs now available on the recent debut lp.

**The Cure:** Jumping Someone Else's Train/I'm Cold (Fiction Records: FICS5)--Two new doses of the Cure in their original three-piece form. Both pleasant listening, verging at times toward vacat (or sparse) backing instrumentals. But this single shows The Cure as still being one of the best new bands this year. The recent addition of a keyboardist should result in even a better band.

**Pretenders:** Brass in Pocket/Swinging London--Nervous But Shy (Real Records: ARE11)--Chrissie Hyndes' vocals on the A side make this 45 adult pop while the flip veers into bluessouthern fried.

**Cockney Rejects:** I'm Not A Fool/East End (EMI: EMI 5008)--This young rough band continue in their proto punk form. The loudly-shouted monotone lyrics add to the primativeness of this, the second Pursey-produced single of the Rejects. They continue their Steve Jones power chords and their typical punk 3 chord melodies. If anyone wondered whether this punk sound was still being used, check the Cockney Rejects out.

**Secret Affair:** Let Your Heart Dance (I-Spy Records:

## Album Reviews

**John Cale:** Sabotage/Live (Spy Records: SP004)--It has been a few years since John Cale has released an album. In that time he has put out an excellent EP (Animal Justice) and a throwaway (Disco Clone) and appeared on various other recordings. While many older artists like Cale (himself a member of the Velvet Underground, in case you forgot!) continue touring, recording and sustaining their positions; Cale has been interested in helping new, young developing talent. Many feel that this has been beneficial to the continuance of rock. So he does have a favorable reputation.
  This album was recorded live at CBGB's last summer and uses a backing band of unknowns. Some of the songs are a bit less exciting than others. The first song, "Mercenaries" is classic John Cale, sure to be a hit. "Captain Hook," a 14-minute opening for side two, is perhaps the most indulgent tune. Apart from "Walkin' the Dog," the remaining six songs are new originals. The sound is studio quality.

**The Jam:** Setting Sons (Polydor: POLD5028)--The fourth album from this three-piece band who have been the forerunners of the mod look and sound reemergence. The critics call it the best yet. It's also said that this album is Paul Weller's best, for he is the main force in the Jam. The theme involves three friends who grow apart and change, at least in five of the ten songs, all originals except the closing "Heatwave." The single, "Eton Rifles," has jumped to the top of the English charts. Although the musical style is familiar (aside from the use of strings in this version of "Smithers-Jones") the band begins to step away from the mod-cultist orientation.

**The Damned** Machine Gun Etiquette (Chiswick-EMI: CWK3011) --So they're still around, minus Brian James. But you know what? This album isn't bad. They may not be covering new musical ground, but they don't seem to care and the feeling is infectious. Without the central talent of James the rest of the band are relying more on each other and as a result the whole sound is more unified. Dave Vanian's vocals are especially improved, now meshing with the instrumentation instead of being mixed out front. All in all, a surprising effort from a band I had prematurely written off (sorry, boys, my mistake). Choice cuts are: "Love Song," "Smash It Up," and "Noise, Noise, Noise." --VS
(continued on p. 8)

## Live: Ultravox and the Buzzcocks (cont.)

ficent violin solo, "Slow Motion," "I Can't Stay Long," and "Quiet Men." They also premiered a few new songs, one of them "Attrax." When they left the stage, the audience wouldn't let them go and so they came back on for one last song, a rocker entitled, "King's Lead Hat," written by the producer of their first album, Brian Eno.

A lot of times a warm up band doesn't get the proper respect that they are due from a crowd waiting for the headline act (in this case the Buzzcocks) but they were appreciated.

The Buzzcocks, one of the best bands to come out of the English "New Wave" scene, lived up to their reputation. I'd seen them in Chicago in September but they played at a small, smelly basement bar with a crowd of mostly aging upper middle class pseudo punks wishing it was 1977 all over again who helped ruin the show (The Buzzcocks had said it was one of the worst nights of their career) and if it was as good as it was being "the worst," I could hardly wait to see them again. So came their debut at the Opera House.

They opened up their set with a powerful version of "I Don't Mind" off their first import album "Another Music" and also included on their first American lp "Singles Going Steady." It was followed shortly after with "Autonomy" and "Bad, Bad Judy." Before the evening was out they had covered numbers from every stage of their career. Other stand-outs were "Harmony in My Head" with Steve Diggle on vocals (he's becoming a stronger writer all the time), "What Do I Get?," "I Believe," and "Noise Annoys."

The group played with power. Steve Diggle on guitar all the while moving about, a perfect foil for the rest of the band's feigned nonchalant attitude. After they left the stage, the crowd screamed for more and before you knew it the Buzzcocks were back ripping into a searing rendition of "Breakdown" and then finishing up by an equally good version of "Boredom."

To sum it up, the Buzzcocks played fast, loud and had fun. I think I can say it was one of the best nights of Rock and Roll the Opera House has ever seen. --VS

## Interview: Ultravox

After their set, Talk Talk was lucky enough to get backstage and interview a couple of members of Ultravox. We were led to a small room, bare except for five chairs. There I was introduced to Warren Cann, drums, rhythm machine and vocals and Chris Cross, bass, synthesizer and vocals. Even though the surroundings seemed impersonal, the two gentlemen soon warmed things up with their friendly and gracious manner.

**Talk Talk:** How did you feel about the show tonight?
**Warren Cann:** We really enjoyed it, the crowd responded really well.
**TT:** I was a bit surprised by the encore number. Why "King's Lead Hat?"
**Chris Cross:** That's why we do it, to surprise people.
**WC:** Besides being a nice way to end up the set.
**TT:** Is Midge Ure with you now for good or is he only a temporary replacement.
**WC:** He's a permanent member of the band.
**CC:** He actually has been for about six months but we couldn' let on about it.
**TT:** Why not?
**WC:** Well, Midge was still tied up with some legal problems and he didn't want anybody to know that he was working on anything that might have prolonged the problem.
**TT:** How do you like working with him?
**CC:** Great, he's really good to work with. We personally feel he's a stronger singer than John was. Plus he can switch off from guitar to keyboards, which is a plus.
**TT:** Do you have anything ready for release with your new line up?
**WC:** Not yet; we plan to go out to the coast and pick up a label and start recording in February.
**TT:** So you haven't signed with anybody yet?
**WC:** No. We could have last January when we were dropped by Island . . .
**CC:** But we didn't think that would be fair.
**WC:** Exactly, we wanted to get everything straightened out with our inner problems.
**TT:** When did you get dropped by Island?
**WC:** December 31st, 1978.
**TT:** So that means you've never got support on any of your tours of America from them.
**CC:** Right.

(continued on p. 11)

## Album Reviews (cont.)

**Joy Division: Unknown Pleasures** (Factory Records: Fact 10)--More songs about alienation and uncertainty for the 80's can be heard on this debut lp from Joy Division. A popular UK band that remains faceless. The only credits given are words and music by Joy Division. The music is similar to the Monochrome Set, Ultravox, and the Tubeway Army. The singer is the most interesting part of the music. He sings in a kind of restrained monotone, hardly showing any emotion. Sometimes it sounds like he's trying to remember what it's like to be human; but like he says, "there's no room for the weak." This album's production is somewhat flawed, in that it seems muffled. The album cover looks like something from "Alien." A kind of topographic diagram. It's very sparse. Best songs are: "She's Lost Control," "Wilderness," "Insight," and "I Remember Nothing."

**Snakefinger: Chewing Hides the Sound** (Ralph: SNK7909)--Is this man the new wave Frank Zappa? Probably not, but the parallels are there. The humor, the wierdness--there's even some vocal resemblance, but that's as far as it goes. Phillip "Snakefinger" Lithman has a sound all his own and it's nothing like Zappa. Snakefinger employs a lot of double-tracked guitar leads over a minimal bottom composed of (is it a rhythm machine or is it) drums, percussion and various electronic sounds. Sometimes it comes out like middle-eastern prayer music, sometimes like 21st Century funk, and only occasionally approaches the balls-to-the-wall dissonant electronic onslaught of co-writers and producers the Residents. Altogether an eclectic and enjoyable album.

**Merton Parkas: Face in the Crowd** (Beggars Banquet: BEGA11)--The English music press would lead you to believe that the Merton Parkas are the worst thing to happen to modern music in years. The likes of New Musical Express and Melody Maker have blamed the Merton Parkas for singlehandedly causing the current Mod revival to remain simply that, a revival. Well, it just goes to show you, you can't always believe what you read. This is a very good album, and I would go so far as to say the Parkas are better than at least 75 percent of their fellow mods. Their near perfect blend of 60's Mod and Motown influences is an achievement few mod bands can (continued on p. 10)

## Import Singles (cont.)

**Secret Affair, Let Your Heart Dance** (I-Spy: SEE3)--Secret Affair are, for the moment, at the top of the heap of the Mod revival bands in England--enjoying much popular success and frequent critical acclaim. Unlike many of their contemporaries, their sound is based more in 60's Tamla/Motown than in 60's Mod. Their first single, the excellent mod anthem, "Time For Action," remains one of the best songs to come out of the Mod revival. "Let Your Heart Dance," though not quite living up to the first single, is still a good, very danceable song--with sax and guitar trading solos and a strong vocal from Ian Page. Look for their debut lp Glory Boys out soon--KF

that they're a six-piece band with two guitars and a sax. A thick, rich, dense production results in layer upon layer of sound, with guitar, sax and bass all melding into one to propell the song along at a fast pace. Singer Butler Rep, whose vocal style is somewhere between Jake Burns of Stiff Little Fingers and Jackie Leven of Doll by Doll, pours out lyrics like "I'm in love with Catholics," and "I'm in love with Frank Sinatra," and so on. Surely a counterpoint to today's tradition of bands condemning everything around them. Anyway, this is one of the best singles of the year, and the B side, "Pulse", is even better. --KF

**Protex: I Can Only Dream** (Polydor: 2059 167)--Ulster group Protex continue their string of Buzzcocks-like singles that began with "Don't Ring Me Up" (on Good Vibrations) and the brilliant "I Can't Cope." This is a bright, jumpy pop single with some nice hooks, and sooner or later this band is gonna' have a hit.

**The Psychedelic Furs: We Love You** (EPIC: EPC8005)--This single is fantastic! Can't tell you much about the group though, except

**Cult Hero: I'm a Cult Hero** (Fiction: FICS006)--Cult Figure are actually the Cure in disguise and "I'm a Cult Hero" is probably a Cure studio outtake. It's an enjoyable piece of silliness about being a cult hero ("I'm a Cult Hero, paid my dues . . . I'm a Cult Hero, got nothing to lose."). The sound is the same sparse 3-piece sound of the Cure's other material, but basically this is nowhere as good as any of their singles or album. --KF

**Snakefinger: Kill the Great Raven** (Ralph: RRWIL7907)--A funny single with a reggae beat, and nonsense lyrics (cont. on p. 10)

## News Items

Informed sources say the new Clash lp "London Calling," Public Image's "Metal Box," and a Sid Vicious live lp will hit Lawrence on December 19 or 20.

The debut lp from the Pretenders, led by vocalist Chrissie Hynde, will be released in January in the U.S. as well as England. The album is produced by Chris Thomas who will also produce the next Who album.

In yet another incident of meaningless violence, two members of Swell Maps, Jowe Head and Epic Soundtracks, were attacked outside Rough Trade Records in London. Epic Soundtracks suffered many severe cuts and bruises, and Jowe Head received three cracked ribs and a punctured lung.

There are rumors that Mayo Thompson may abandon his band, Red Crayola, and join Cleveland band, Pere Ubu, as replacement for guitarist Tom Hermann. Wichita all-girl group the Inevitable have broken up due to personal differences within the band. They might perform in the new year.

Egg Hoover and the G.E. Three are rumored to be in their studio, possibly recording new product.

## Import Singles (cont.)

about the "Great Raven" that looks for love and therefore must die, or something like that, and with a bit of Zappa influence here and there. Written and produced by Snakefinger and his San Francisco buddies, the Residents. Another hit for Ralph Records. Lots of Fun!

Lori and the Chameleons: Touch (Sire: SIR4025)--A picture postcard tour of Tokyo with a beat and the thrill of holiday romances all on one seven-inch single. A beautiful, funny song, told by Lori, of her vacation in Japan, the mysteries of the Orient, a motorbike ride through the streets of Tokyo with Japanese boyfriend Kato ("You Drive so Fast on Your Motorbike, the Lights Just Flash By"), and with a background chorus singing "Touch . . . Touch." It's all a brilliant, fun, and sensuous (like the Ronettes) fairy tale, and I think I'll put it on again.

## Interview: Ultravox (cont.)

WC: Chris Blackwell (Island president) told us we shouldn't even try to come here, that no one would like us. But it's proven just the opposite. We've been really well received.
TT: So you don't think you'll have any problem getting a label?
WC: No, new offers are coming in every day.
TT: Good. Thank you for your time.
WC: That's alright. We're not snobs; we don't mind talking to people, just as long as they're not idiots.
(With that thought, the interview ended.)

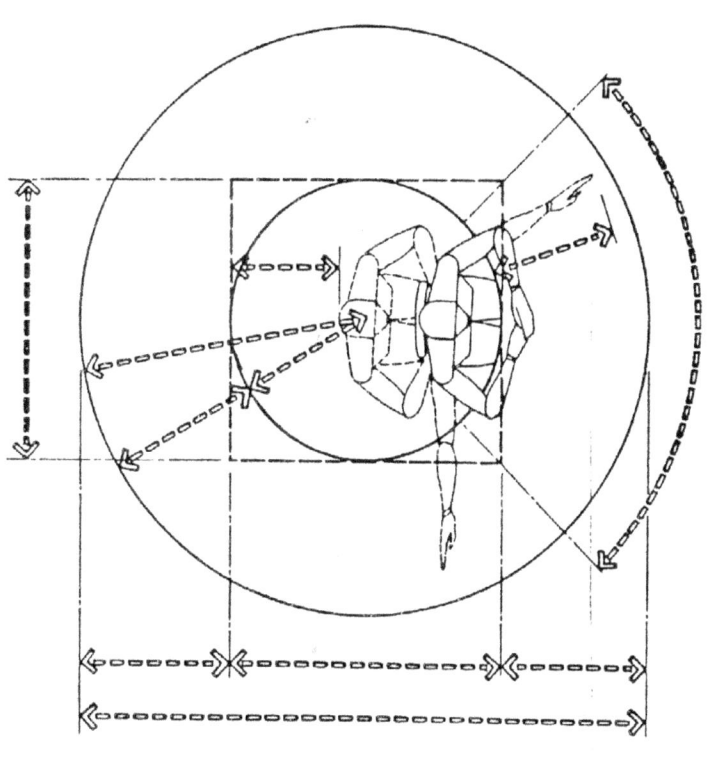

## Album Reviews (cont.)

claim. Mick Talbot's keyboards effectively fill out their basic guitar, bass, & drums sound. There are many sparkling songs here, plus an excellent cover of "Tears of a Clown." All in all a very enjoyable album. So

TALK TALK

| Vol. 2, No. 1 | January 1980 | $1.00 |

The Midwest American Rock and Reggae Magazine

Table of Contents

| | |
|---|---|
| The Clash--London Calling | 3 |
| Public Image--Metal Box | 4 |
| Raincoats, Dickies, Sid, etc. | 5 |
| The Buzzcocks | 6 |
| Single Reviews | 7 |
| Local Scene: The Clean | 9 |
| Top Singles | 9 |
| Top Compilation Albums/Top Albums (ES) | 10 |
| Readers Poll | 11 |
| Top Debut Albums/Top Albums (BR) | 12 |
| Reggae Reviews | 13 |
| Ultravox: Pics | 18 |
| Live: Thumbs | 19 |

Editors--Eric S/Bill R

photos by Robin K

Talk Talk Publications
Post Office Box 36
Lawrence, Kansas
66044
USA

Copyright 1980 Talk Talk Publications. All rights reserved. Not responsible for unsolicited material. Any opinion expressed is solely that of the writer and not necessarily that of the magazine.

## Clash

Talk Talk Vol. 2 No. 1/page 3

The Clash London Calling (CBS: Clash 3)--The long awaited Clash album is here--Produced by Guy Stevens (ex Mott the Hoople producer) it turns out to be in my opinion their most mature album. I do not say best-- because the first album and the new one are so radically different musically. While the first record set a standard for the "Punk" movement, on London Calling The Clash (still full of angry spirit) broaden their scope and in many ways pay homage to their R & B and Reggae influences.

While this album does not have the immediate impact of their first, on repeat listening, it builds its power and pretty soon you can find yourself moving to their brand new beat. For example, on "Wrong 'em Boyo" they approach a reggae influenced sound that could easily be played next to The Specials or Madness (two reggae-R & B bands). Basically, it is really hard to talk about this album. It is strange because for the first time they have other people involved in the playing--Micky Gallager on organ and the Irish Horns on brass--which gives them a fuller-bodied sound and really great help on the entire "soul" they were going for. As far as the band themselves, they play with vigor and style that they have never shown before. But, like I said, do not let the pleasant melodies fool you--the lyrical content is like a political science and history lesson combined. As for the music itself--it is great!! This is going to be my #1 album of the year. And for all those who cry--"The Clash are Dead (and surely there will be many) they are just fools who cannot allow a band to change. The Clash are nowhere near dead, as their album aptly illustrates.

## ALBUM REVIEWS

Public Image Limited Metal Box (Virgin Records)-- This release has received a lot of early attention due to its packaging. Its present form is three 12-inch 45's contained in a silver film cannister. The cost reflects the uniqueness. Just over an hour's worth of material; some old, some remixed, but most is new. No doubt it will be re-released on two discs in the UK or in the US soon. On this, the second PiL album, the band consists of vocals by John Lydon, formerly Johnny Rotten of the Sex Pistols; Keith Levine on guitar and drums; and Jah Wobble on bass and drums. Jeanette Lee and Dave Crowe are also listed, but what they do is a mystery. Public Image are into studio mixing and all members contribute to the final synthesized electro sound that results. In many ways, this "album" is a departure from their debut album, although the singles released in-between clearly show the trend. And they show up in alternative forms. For instance, "Memories," "Death Disco," and "And No Birds Do Sing" can be found on sides two and four. But so what? From the months PiL spend in the studio, there are new mixes and creations which they feel are great and should be released, so here they are. Side three is highly recommended, "Poptones" and "Careering." The lyrical impact could only be brought about through the vocals of Lydon. Of course the disco/reggae bass of Wobble is a trademark of the band. And Keith Levine's unique guitar work adds meat to the bones or framework that is set down. Public Image are not for everybody. They are hardly traditional. The facts are that they exist, they market their products and they influence. Whether the consumers like or dislike their sounds does not seem to have much of a motivational force on them. They continue experimenting, growing, and affecting the musical world. Lyrics on the back cover, as advertised in New Musical Express, November 24, 1979, page 39.

## ALBUM REVIEWS

The Raincoats The Raincoats (Rough Trade: Rough 3)--The first album by these four ladies. When compared to The Slits, another all female group, The Raincoats show several similar and several different points. Of course, the drummer, Palmolive, used to belong to The Slits, although she left before their album, "Cut," was made. One song, "Adventures Close to Home," appears on both Lps. Its arrangement is simpler here, which is one major difference in the two groups' sound. The Raincoats do not use the "wall of sound" approach so popular. At times the use of sharps and flats along with the violin creates an uneasy, queasy feeling. But even this can be enjoyable. Something that sets them apart, and also one of their strengths lies in the rollercoaster tempo. Their effective use of slow-downs and speed-ups, as well as their use of departing for a few measures, then reestablishing the earlier beat and melody gives their numbers added character. On Rough Trade Records, so the supply might be irratic. Remember the name and be sure to look at their future activities.

The Dickies Dawn of the Dickies (A&M Records: AMLE 68510)--The second album by these Californians. Evidently they are popular enough in England to have this record British-released. The Dickies are fun loving, as shown by their earlier covers of "Silent Night," "Eve of Destruction," and now, The Moody Blues' "Nights in White Satin." They prefer to play everything fast, and they buzzsaw through ten tracks. Those listeners who cannot keep up tend to dislike their sound. Those who can keep up want more. The Dickies have basically avoided the pop label. This album shows them continuing in their past traditions. They do show a higher degree of expertise in the use of instruments.

Sid Vicious Sid Sings (Virgin Records: V2144)--After the Sex Pistols broke up two years ago, bassist Sid Vicious played frequently in New York with different assortments of bands and with different levels of success. The album is a collection of live performances from this time. Although no musicians are credited, aside from Sid singing, (continued on page 16)

# BUZZCOCKS

When it was announced that the Buzzcocks would play in town, last month, Talk Talk arranged for an interview for this article. What did happen was running into half the band walking down the street (to buy a cassette player at a discount store), witnessing the soundcheck, receiving free passes (a first for Talk Talk, although tickets had been bought much earlier) admittance to the dressing room after the show, and drinking at the bar later. Far more numerous bits of information were disclosed than those which follow.

After the soundcheck, Pete Shelley exclaimed, "I don't give interviews. I can't add anything." The albums say more about the Buzzcocks than I can." Steve Diggle quickly added, "We each talk for ourselves." A few minutes later, those two left for an interview with the local university radio station. The remaining band members, Steve Garvey and John Maher talked me into giving them a lift to their new motel. The band had checked out of their original motel when, the restaurant refused to serve eggs after noon to the arriving roadies. (→ 15)

(→) Pete Shelley and Steve Diggle

# '45' REVIEWS

The Clash London Calling/Armagideon Time (CBS: 8087)--The title cut from the new lp (see review this issue), backed with the recent UK reggae hit of Willi Williams. Both show The Clash in top form and explain why The Clash are rated by most as the number one punk/New Wave group. It is made in Holland and they use an organ player. The band played these cuts on their last American tour a few months ago. Talking with Mick Jones, vocals and guitar, he kept stressing the group's dedication to early rock influences and originators. Their distinct techniques prove them to be roots oriented and also highly innovative and original. And also enjoyable.

4 Be 2 One of the Lads (dub version)/Ummbaba-One of the Lads (vocal) (Island: 12WIP 6530)--The rumors are that this is John Lydon's younger brother's band. The credits are scarce. It is produced by John Lydon and the sound is very much like Public Image Ltd. Available on 7- and 12-inch discs, the 12-incher has a remix of the title cut (the most PiL sounding by far). An interesting sounding release, no doubt a product of some of the long session tapings PiL is famous for.

Kidz Next Door What's It All About?/The Kidz Next Door (Warners: K17492)--Another example of a new band produced by an older famous brother. In this case, it is Jimmy Pursey who is producing Robbie Pursey (vocals, of course) and his young friends. These cuts are directed at an adolescent audience, both in terms of simple pop rhythms and lyrics (such as parents not letting me go out). Raw, young sound similar to other discoveries brought to you by the Sham man.

Delta 5 Mind Your Own Business/Now That You've Gone (Rough Trade: RT03)--Out of nowhere comes this single (Rough Trade's great at doing this). "Mind Your Own Business" starts out with a heavy bass line that is reminiscent of "Heard it Thru the Grape Vine"--and then it breaks into a female lead vocalist talking about people sticking their noses where they do not belong--Side two, "Now That You've Gone," is a love story of wierd sort. The best way (continued on page 8)

# '45' REVIEWS

(continued from page 7) to evaluate the Delta 5 is to say they sound like the Gang of Four meet The Slits but never trust comparisons --go out and find this single--you will not be disappointed.

Wire Map Ref./Go Ahead (Harvest: Har. 5742)--The A side is the most traditionally musical cut off their album (also the best cut). It has already been reviewed in a past issue. "Go Ahead" starts out with a heavy bass line--while in the immediate background there is an electronic ghost wailing away--a song has not set such a mood for me since "The Bogus Man" (any Roxy Music fans in the crowd?). The subject matter seems to concern commercialism-capitalism--what sells and why-- "ask--Go Ahead." Perhaps the best of the bands experimenting with electronics--this single just reinforces their position.

Joy Division Transmission/Novelty (Factory: Fac 13)--One of the many electronic bands, with deep bass and rhythm, haunting repetitive keyboards and deep vocals saying "dance, dance, dance to the radio" on the A-side. The B is similar, with more guitar chord progression. They are not really metallic noise. They ask "what are you going to do when the novelty is gone." This question remains to torment the trendies in this world, including this band. But Joy Division are tops in the synth-sound. This single is enjoyable to listen to.

UK Subs She's Not There-Kicks/Victim-Samething (Gem Records: Gems 14)--This Ep follows their album release and shows the band sticking with their basic formula. The lead song, by the Zombies, fits into this pattern. Their originals move along rapidly, energizing the listeners. It might be taking them a while, but the UK Subs are becoming a band popular with rockers and blues fans.

The Beat Ranking Full Stop/Tears of a Clown (Two Tone Records: CHSTT6)--The latest Two Tone discovery, not to be confused with the American band of the same name. The A side shows the band to be JA oriented and the flip is the cover so popular (?). Although it might be premature to love a group when only one song has been released, (→ 14)

## LOCAL SCENE: THE CLEAN

One of the newest young bands that is making the Lawrence scene is The Clean. They are a basic rock n roll, new wave oriented four piece--guitar, bass, drums, and keyboards. The Clean have recently changed with the bass player replacing the guitarist and a new bass player added. Their first gig featured covers of rock classics of the British Invasion period and new wave. Their latest performance showed a much improved band, performing eight originals. Although the band can be criticized for their present level of expertize (just normal things like occasional off key or off rhythm), The Clean are worth watching for. They do not have a large following, but they continue to improve. Try to catch them. The Clean. You will be hearing more.

## TOP 20 SINGLES

1 Slits - Typical Girls/Heard it thru the Grapevine
2 Clash - London Calling/Armigideon Time
3 Clash - Cost of Living Ep
4 Undertones - You've Got My Number/Talk about Girls
5 Buzzcocks - Harmony in my Head/Something Gone Wrong Again
6 Brian James - Ain't That a Shame/Living in Sin/...Cry...
7 Gang of Four - At Home He's a Tourist/It's Her Factory
8 Magazine - Rhythm of Cruelty/T.V. Baby
9 The Only Ones - You've Got to Pay/This Ain't All
10 The Fall - Rowche Rumble/In My Area
11 Iggy Pop - I'm Bored/African Man
12 Junior Murvin - Joe Gibb-Cool Out Son/Cooling Out
13 Pere Ubu - Fabulous Sequel/Humor Me/The Book is on the Table
14 Cure - Jumping Someone Else's Train/I'm Cold
15 Richard Hell - Boy with the Replaceable Head/I'm Your Man
16 X Ray Spex - Highly Inflammable/Warrior in Woolworth's
17 Members - Offshore Banking Business/Pennie in the Pound/
18 Cure - Boys Don't Cry/ Helga           Solitary Confinement
19 4-B-2 - One of the Lads/Ummbaba
20 Pretenders - Stop Your Sobbing/The Wait

## TOP COMPILATION ALBUMS

Intensified Original Ska 1962-66 - Various Artists
The Clash - US release (Lp + singles)
Buzzcocks - Singles Going Steady
Lee Perry - Scratch on the Wire
Rebel Music - Anthology
Desmond Dekker - Sweet Sixteen Hits
Burning Spear - Harder than the Best
Toots & the Maytals - Best of
Rockers - Various Artists (Soundtrack)
Hottest Hits - Various Artists (Treasure Island Vault)
The Great Rock & Roll Swindle

ƒƒƒƒƒƒƒƒƒƒƒƒƒƒƒƒƒƒƒƒƒƒƒƒƒƒƒƒƒƒƒƒƒƒƒƒƒƒ

## TOP ALBUMS

The Clash - London Calling
Gang of Four - Entertainment
Public Image, Ltd. - Metal Box
Graham Parker - Squeezing Out the Sparks
Linton Kwesi Johnson - Forces of Victory
Iggy Pop - New Values
Stiff Little Fingers - Highly Inflammable
The Mekons - The Quality of Mercy is not Strained
Wire - 154
Buzzcocks - Different Kind of Tension
Pere Ubu - New Picnic Time
XTC - Drums & Wires
Sham 69 - Hersham Boys
The Cure - Three Imaginary Boys
The Members - Chelsea Nightclub

---

Send to: Talk Talk Readers' Poll
Post Office Box 36
Lawrence, Kansas 66044

List your top ten albums of the year. Selections not limited to those listed. Results will be compiled and printed soon.

1) _____
2) _____
3) _____
4) _____
5) _____
6) _____
7) _____
8) _____
9) _____
10) _____

Name _____
Address _____

## TOP DEBUT ALBUMS

Stiff Little Fingers - Inflammable Material
The Slits - Cut
Gang of Four - Entertainment
Undertones - Undertones
Angelic Upstarts - Teenage Warning
The Cure - Three Imaginary Boys
The Specials - Specials
The Members - At the Chelsea Nightclub
Madness - One Step Beyond
Mekons - The Quality of Mercy is not Strained

## TOP ALBUMS

The Clash - London Calling
Sham 69 - Hersham Boys
Iggy Pop - New Values
Buzzcocks - Different Kind of Tension
Public Image Ltd. - Metal Box
The Jam - Setting Sons
Graham Parker - Squeezing Out the Sparks
Magazine - Second Hand Daylight
The Only Ones - Special View
Sex Pistols - Great Rock & Roll Swindle

## REGGAE REVIEWS

**Sly Dunbar  Sly Wicked and Slick** (Virgin Front Line: FL 1042)--This album has received a lot of flack already from some people who scream "sell out" because this album is not strictly a roots record. Sly Dunbar (Jamaica's top session drummer and the force behind the Revolutionaries, the top session band) is definitely slick but that is not necessarily bad. As a matter of fact, Sly succeeds quite well in blending reggae with a funk jazz fusion. His distinct drumming style and the strong backup help from members of the Revolutionaries keep the effort from falling apart (as recent inner circle albums have) when mixing roots music with other styles. Stand out cuts include a great version of "Sesame Street" (it got me dancing) and the funky "Dirty Harry." Another important fact about this album is that it is, for all intents and purposes, instrumental. (This will be good for all you amateur toastmasters out there.) So, listen to this record and find out for yourself how wicked Sly is this time around.

**Gregory Isaacs  Soon Forward** (Virgin International: VIFL 1044)--Once again, Mr. Isaacs comes through with a fine album. "Soon Forward." The backup men have been cranked up and Sly Dunbar's drums combined with Robbie Shakespeare's bass prove an unbeatable rhythm combination. Isaacs is usually a smooth singer but on this album he seems to have a spark that was missing last time around. His songs cover a range of subject matter. From Love to Lust to Revolution. In an earlier review I asked the question "Who is Mr. Isaacs?"; now we know, one of the growing forces in reggae. With his voice and the persuasive way he blends his music with the message he might soon be a force to be reckoned with. Like he says, he will be "Soon Forward." --VS

**Gladiators  Sweet So Till** (Virgin International: VIFL 1048)--One of the top groups around, the Gladiators have all the force on vinyl that Bob Marley has seemed to lack in recent years (although he is still great live). The music ranges from passive love songs (like the title cut) to songs of the evergrowing rasta revolution as in "Red, Green and Gold." With a persuasive beat, supplied by Leroy Horsemouth Wallace, the Gladiators move you, (→ 14)

# REGGAE REVIEWS

(continued from p. 13)
draw you into their songs. The vocal style is better articulated than many reggae groups and so the lyrics come across with all the impact that is intended. Sometimes the singing style reminds me of Marley's--smooth, but forceful--filled with all the passion of the third world. This lp is just one more example of the Gladiators' talent. If this band ever manages to get a decent U.S. tour together you can bet I will be there. --VS

Mighty Diamonds Deeper Roots (Back to the Channel) (Virgin International: VIFL 1045)--The Mighty Diamonds are back! With this, their third American release, they have (like the title said) escaped from their Americanized sound and returned to their musical roots. Their experience away from Jamaica must have been worthwhile because with this record they are at their peak. The vocals are stronger and the session band tighter. The songs even show a greater force, reflecting and conveying their conviction, as well as the sorrow and joy of the Jamaican people. Hopefully, those fans of reggae who were disappointed with the Mighty Diamonds last time around, will not ignore this excellent record. --VS

(continued from p. 8)
deserve serious attention. For sure they will soon become "in" with the trendies and end up successful.

The Pop Group We Are All Prostitutes (Rough Trade: RT023)--"Everyone has their price. . . we are the ones to blame." These thoughts to haunt you are the courtesy of the Pop Group. The flip is unnerving, with lyrics of British torture of Irish prisoners. This single has become popular, with many believing it to be the best so far. Maybe so. If the social statements are upsetting, take heart because both sides are short.

Rachel Sweet Baby, Let's Play House/Wildwood Saloon (Stiff Records: Buy 55)-- This single is great. The A side is an up tempo rockabilly number that gets your feet tapping and your fingers snapping. This girl has got a great voice and the backup band (I can hardly wait for the lp to find out who they are) is hot.

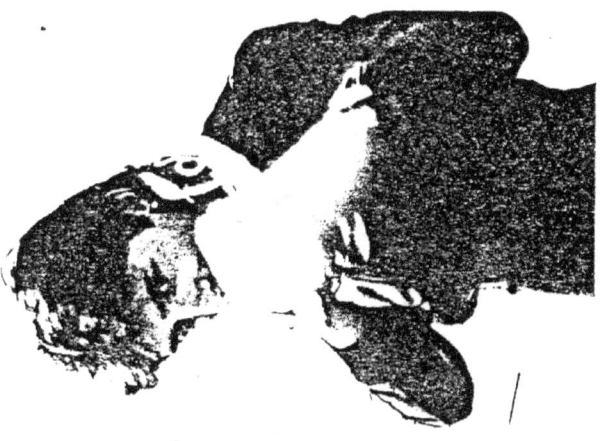

(↑) *John Maher, Pete Shelley and Steve Diggle*
(→) *Steve Garvey*

(continued from page 6)
The band is back in the UK now with plans to take several months off and concentrate on individual projects. Steve Garvey commented that he "wanted to go back to Spain." He also said he wanted to try his hand at writing (music for) commercials. Pete Shelley wants to market his solo lp which he and a rhythm machine created in less than an hour. When asked when he will start his own band, Steve Diggle replied that he plans to play apart from the Buzzcocks in this break time. But there are plans for the band to record an (→ 19)

# ALBUM REVIEWS

(continued from page 5)

it sounds like recordings from Max's Kansas City with the Heartbreakers. The quality is very poor, probably a combination of a drugged-out band, an inferior sound system, and violent audiences. The songs included versions of the Heartbreakers' "Born to Lose," "Take a Chance," and "Chinese Rocks;" Thunder's "Chatterbox;" the Stooges' "I Wanna' Be Your Dog," and "Search & Destroy;" the Monkee's "Stepping Stone," "Belsen Was a Gas," (cowritten by Sid & the Pistols); Eddie Cochran's "Something Else;" and two versions of "My Way--I killed the cat." There had been talk that a Sid Vicious album was planned. But the product does not begin to meet the expectations. Oh, well. Let us hope the newly-released movie, D.O.A., featuring the Pistols in America and Sid will be of higher quality.

The Boys  To Hell With the Boys (Safari: 1-2-Boys)-- After over a year of nothing, The Boys have a new (third) album and British tour. Giving no explanation about their absence, it seems they have been working on new arrangements. The band members remain the same, using two guitars, bass, piano, and drums. The results are pleasant enough. It is easy to subliminally forget until it ends. Occasionally their harmonies and progressions sound like their earlier material, but, overall, they have changed directions. But what have they changed to? And what have they changed from? Well, that is unclear. Someone else can tell you that. Maybe they are just getting older or trying for a part of the pop market. At any rate, if they get any more cutsie-sweet, maybe The Boys should hide out another year or two or three.

Fast Product  The First Year Plan (F1) and (EMI Records: EMC 3312)--This is a collection of six singles put out by Bob Last at Fast Records. Included are the first two Mekons singles, the first Gang of Four Ep, plus singles by 2-3 and Scars. It is a nice compilation of hard to obtain records previously available to only a few observant fans.

(continued on page 17)

# ALBUM REVIEWS

The Mekons  The Quality of Mercy is not strnen (Virgin Records: V2143)--Part Two of the Gang of Four Mekons collaboration: By this I mean I am sure these two bands influence each other (the back of this album has a picture of the Gang of Four)--Both bands use the conversation vocal style (--scatting back and forth) and the staccato rhythm--lead guitar--layering the sound--creating that frantic, at sometimes desperate, feel to their subject matter. Their songs are about everyday life--love-- urban decay--mental being--self pity → boredom →. Do not get me wrong, though, I have been a continuing fan of The Mekons and it is with great pleasure that I have listened to this album--it shows intelligence--humor-- and a sense of responsibility to its listeners. Also, when I compare them to the Gang of Four I do not mean The Mekons are copying another band's sound--quite the contrary, both bands have their separate musical identities even with their similarities. A point to stress is that The Mekons are more outfront melodically than the Gang of Four. This is an important album from an important group--Give it a spin. --VS

Secret Affair  Glory Boys (I-Spy Records: I-Spy 1)--There are some really good tracks on this record but at the same time there are some things that really bother me about this album. They are supposed to be one of the central bands in the Mod revivalist movement and at times I can see how that might be ("Time for Action" and a really good cover of W. Robinson's "Going to A Go-Go") but on the whole much of this record strikes me as The Rich Kids with horns. A year ago if they would have dressed differently they would have probably been labeled "Power Pop." Also, they put forth a lot of what some would call political diatribe. Only time will tell if what they sing about is really coming from their hearts or if it stops at their throats (actions are bigger than words). To sum it up, "Glory Boys" is not a bad record but it is not the definitive Mod revivalist album many people have been waiting for. Maybe next time. --VS

BUZZCOCKS (Continued from p. 15)

experiment to be entitled "Soundcheck." Manager Richard Boone explained how, in warmups and soundchecks, the band throws out riffs and tries new approaches (some of which might turn out). So they will be trying to combine some of these sessions for release on their New Hormones label. By spring, we should see the Buzzcocks back in action and back in America.

===========================================================

LIVE: THUMBS    *Off the Wall Hall*--*December 27/28, 1979*

Thumbs are one of the most interesting bands around. They continue to write good, solid songs that have influences from Dylan to Elvis C. to Smokey Robinson to Patti Smith, with a touch of a garage band in their heart. So why is it that they do not get proper support from the local audiences? The only answer that I can think of is that since what they do is hard to pin down everybody writes them off as a band that is either too "punk" or too "pop." (They are in good company, though, because The Only Ones have alot of the same problems.) Even though the crowd was shamefully thin, 17 the first night and about 50 the next, the band played with vigor and professionalism. They did a cover of Neil Young's "Hey Hey, My My (Into the Black)," with Martin Olson (usually on keyboards) playing bass along with Karl Hoffman and Dee Dee Mosier (new drummer) supplying a strong percussive force. Both nights they played two hours of solid Rock n Roll with some other highlights being "Rags to Rags," "Inch or Two," "Art History," and one of my favorites "The Last Word," complete with a searing guitar break by Kevin Smith. Steve Wilson's vocals have improved over the course of two years and those two nights he was in top form. Bounding across the stage, supplying energy when needed. (Sometimes he does not have enough control but it was not a fault these nights.) To sum it up, Thumbs are the best band in this part of the Midwest. Their album will be out at the end of January and hopefully when they move on they will have fond memories of the area. But if they do not get more support, I would not blame them if they do not.    --DP

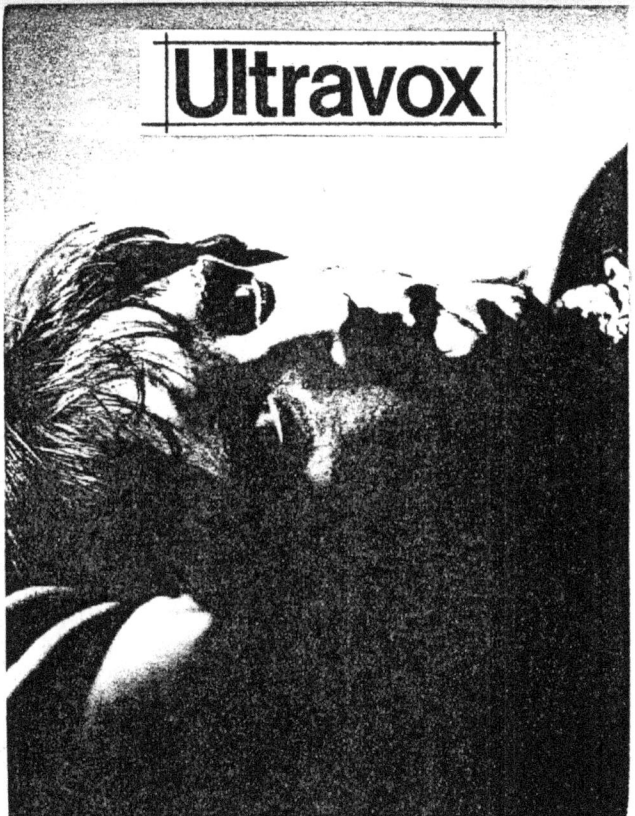

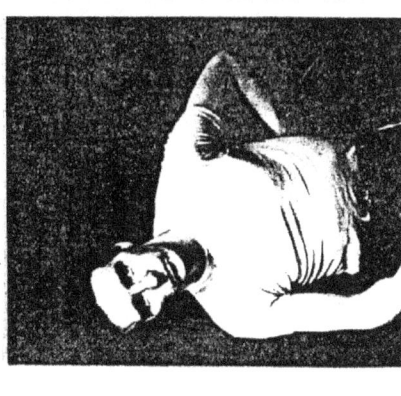

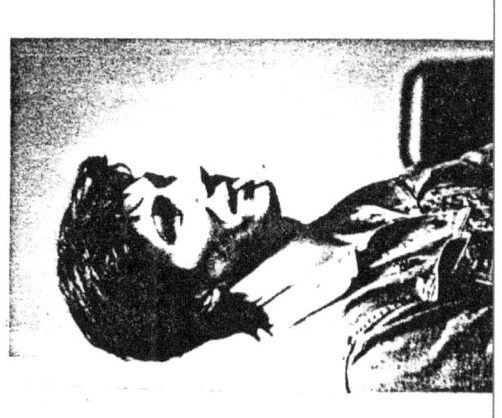

*Ultravox: Chris Cross (↑), Warren Cann (←), Midge Ure (↓). No pic: Billy Currie.*

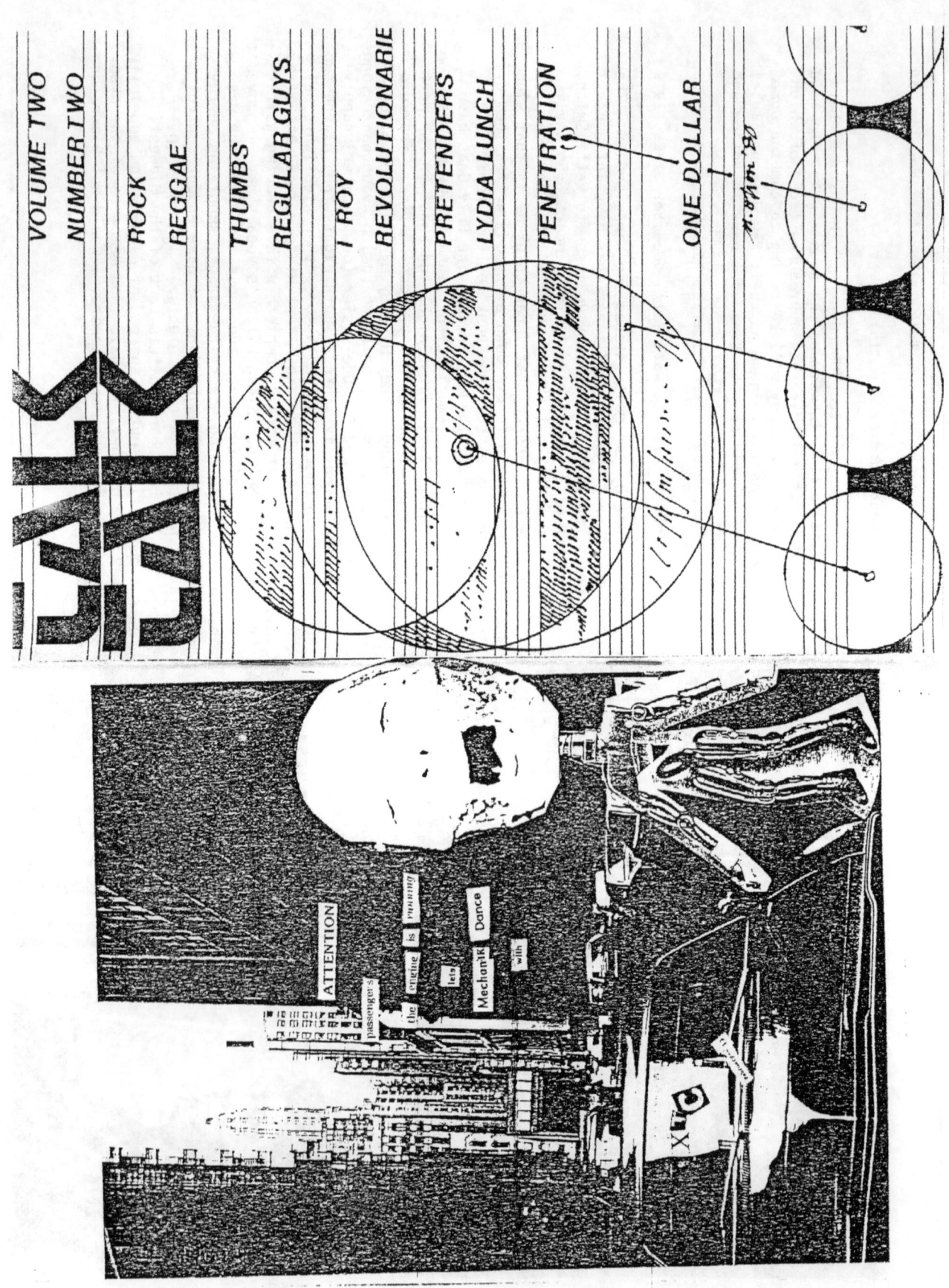

# TALK TALK

Vol. 2, No. 2   February 1980   $1.00

The Midwest American Rock and Reggae Magazine

## Table of Contents

Album Reviews: Thumbs 3
Graham Parker, 20 of Another Kind, The Clash 4
Ramones, Penetration 5
Reggae Reviews: I Roy, Prince Jammy, Earth & Stone 6
Revolutionaries, Upsetters, Rico 7
Single Reviews: Regular Guys, Madness, John Foxx, Mo-dettes 8
Local Scene: Record Stores 9
More Single Reviews: Flowers, The Human Switchboard, Echo & the Bunnymen 10
More Album Reviews: Lydia Lunch, Pretenders 11
This Heat 12
Live: The Regular Guys 13
Corrections and Additions and News 13
Readers Poll Results 15

Editors: Bill R. and Eric S.
Contributors: VS, WB, ET, RH, MO, JS & JM
Photos: by Robin K. and Bill R.

Talk Talk Publications
Post Office Box 36
Lawrence, Kansas
66044
USA

Copyright 1980 Talk Talk Publications. All rights reserved. Not responsible for unsolicited material. Any opinion expressed is solely that of the writer and not necessarily that of the magazine.

## Thumbs

Talk Talk Vol. 2. No. 2/page 3

**Thumbs** Thumbs (Ramona Records: RR1)--From out of the real Midwest comes one of the most promising bands around. Now, after three or so years, they have put out an album and their live performance is almost caught on vinyl. I say almost because at the present moment they have a new drummer that I wish could have played with them on the album. Aside from the wish that the drums could have been beefed up a bit, I have no complaints about this fine record. Side one starts out with a more romantic version of a real upbeat song, "Sweet and Wild," but the new version is as strong as the old, reflecting a growing up of the band. Kevin Smith on lead guitar is in fine form as usual and Steve Wilson's vocals are lended a new strength with the recording medium. Karl Hoffman (bass) and Marty Olson (keyboards) prove that this band is not just one (→ 12)

*Thumbs: Live*
*Pictures by Robin K.*
*Steve Wilson, vocals →*

*Karl Hoffman, bass, and*
*Kevin Smith, guitar ↓*
*Not pictured: Marty Olson*
*and Dede Mosier.*

## ALBUM REVIEWS

<u>Graham Parker & the Rumour</u>  High Times (Vertigo: RJ-7633) --A Japanese released greatest hits collection. The 12 songs have all been previously released, but never this lineup. The cuts are: Soul Shoes/Heat Treatment/Pouring it All Out/Stick to Me/White Honey/The New York Shuffle/ Hey Lord, Don't Ask Me Questions/That's What They All Say/ Protection/Hold Back the Night/Discovering Japan/and I Want You Back. It comes with a lyric sheet in both English and Japanese.

Graham Parker has put out several albums in the last few years. He is often overlooked when artists are credited for their influence upon the new wave. His style of rapid rhythm spitting-out of syllables with the expertise backing by the Rumour has been picked up by many others who have gained in popularity. Part of the reason why he has not achieved a larger superstar status has been his albums. Although, in general, they contain great songs, there have also been some losers. He has fared well with singles, both studio and live, whether available on Lps or not. For these reasons, this collection is a worthwhile addition to the Parker discography. There is not a bad cut included. The only other way to get such a collection is by making a tape yourself. The chances are slim that this will be released on an American label. (I must admit that this is the first Japanese import I have bought.) Try to find it or have your record store order it. High Times is sure to become an enjoyable collector's item.

<u>20 of Another Kind Volume Two</u> (Polydor: POLX 1)--Twenty songs by 15 groups which represent quite a mix of the many influences evident in 1979. For example: The Jam, Sham 69, Gary Numan, The Cure, Protex, Patrik Fitzgerald and Purple Hearts. It is a good compilation.

<u>The Clash Bootleg Lp</u> (A Fashion Mall Production)--Studio outtakes and parts of the Capitol Radio Ep. Different versions of early songs. Side one is Polydor tapes produced by Guy Stevens in 12/76. Side two is CBS tapes recorded winter 77/78. Best surprise is "One Two I Got a Crush on You" and "Pressure Drop." Always glad to find additional material from this excellent band.

## ALBUM REVIEWS

<u>Ramones</u>  End of the Century (Sire: SRK 6077)--It has been well over a year since these boys put out an album and recently rumours have abounded about what the Ramones would sound like with Phil (Mr. Wall of Sound) Spector producing them. A brief look was given fans with the sound track album "Rock N Roll High School" (the title track of the film is included on this record). To understand this record and the way it sounds, we must first understand where the Ramones are at the present time. This is their fifth album and they need a hit off it in order to keep progressing and if this album does not produce a hit their future might be shaky. The second factor is that they have to maintain their own integrity, while pleasing the bland tastes of American music company moguls and DJs. To say this album will fill the requirements is hard. It has all the earmarks of a hit, but who knows whether this album will get the airplay and backing it deserves. This is a good record and should not be a disappointment to anyone. Side one goes way back with a radio show intro, urging us to rock and roll with the Ramones and then bursts out with "Do You Remember Rock 'N' Roll Radio?," a song that takes me back to Mott The Hoople's heyday. They do a standout version of "Chinese Rocks," an old tune that Dee Dee cowrote with some others. The album is still full of the Ramones humor, but there is a maturity present that was started with their last Lp, "Road to Ruin." Johnny's guitar playing is still superb, and with this album the snide remarks that "the Ramones do not know how to play anything over three chords" can not even be heard. To say I love this album would be wrong, but I sure do like it one hell of a lot. Long Live Rock 'N' Roll and the Ramones.

<u>Penetration</u>  Race Against Time (1979 Clifdayn LTD)--Where this album came from and who is responsible for it may be a mystery for a while. Packaged in a cheap, almost bootleg style, jacket, it gives only song titles and basic dates. Hopefully, Pauline & Company are getting royalties for this. Penetration were one of my long-time favorites and their break-up was something that was sad to see. There is no side one or two, just demo and live but both sides are high quality recordings. The demo side (→ 11)

# REGGAE REVIEWS

I-Roy Cancer (Virgins Front Line: FLX4001)--One problem reggae fans encounter is not knowing or being able to find out what an artist is doing or has done. This album came out before I-Roy's latest, The General, but was not announced. Too often reggae artists receive inadequate promotion or publicity. At least there seems to be more material released in 1979 than earlier, even if one does not know it until it is seen.

The title refers to the Zodiac Cancer, with a crab being on the cover. But the appreciation of Roy Reid grows on this ten-cut disk. The musicians are the top Jamaicans. As one might expect, some of the riffs and blends are well known I-Roy classics. You almost expect his booming voice to filter in. But it never does. Perhaps this makes the record more pleasant or pleasurable for some. When the labels start promoting their reggae artists, I-Roy will certainly lead the way in American appreciation of reggae.

Prince Jammy Presents Kamikazi Dub (Trojan: TRLP174)-- Lloyd James, aka Prince Jammy, has been the most sought after technical engineer in Jamaica for mixing studio-recorded tracks into the final pressing. For this dub album, the tracks were laid down by the finest studio musicians anyone could hope for. The melodies float in and out, vibrating and echoing in a manner which only Prince Jammy could develop. As usual, no vocal track is used.

Earth and Stone Kool Roots (Cha Cha Music: CHADLP007) --Earth and Stone are Albert Bailey and Clifton Howell on vocals, backed by Channel One Studio's super session musicians. It is a double album, with the second record being a remixed version of the first record. The high pitched, close harmonies of these two are the highlight and also the low point. There are no dates on this album. The liner notes suggest it was recorded in the late 70's, probably released about a year ago. All the songs are originals.

Revolutionaries Sounds Vol. 2 (Ballistic Records: UAK 30237)--This album is a compilation of masterful dub remixes by the Revolutionaries, JA's premier session men. All the stars are here, all grooving relentlessly. The mix is as smooth and muscular as the playing, moving in and out, echoing with fluid grace. The album is about 90 percent instrumental, replete with heartmassage bass, rocksteady drums and cutting guitar. This record is so good, it is bad, mon.

Upsetters Double Seven (Trojan Records: TRLS 70)-- An old record from the Upsetters (1976) but a record that was sure to have been missed by a lot of people. Lee Perry is the mainstay of the Upsetters, producing all their albums and toasting on the majority of the tracks. The album is one long trip with a mixture of dub, roots, and reggae meeting soul. The first cut on side two is an excellent, energetic version of the old Sam & Dave song, "Soul Man." There's also selections that feature U Roy, I Roy and David Isaacs, which add to the quality of the festivities. This record is just another example of Lee Perry (also known as The Upsetter) and The Upsetters' capabilities, something never in doubt.

Rico Rodrigues Man From Wareika (Blue Note: BN-LA 819H)--This is an older album, recorded in 1976 in Jamaica. Rico is the top trombone player around. He was important in the 60s during the ska period of Jamaican music. Lately he has been involved with new English bands, like the 2-Tone groups, reestablishing himself as a master musician. This album features his smooth trombone and other horns, with all compositions and arrangements by Rico. The backing band is the best group of studio musicians possible. And the results are classic. Rico has developed his own style of slide trombone mixed with muting techniques. The tempo of this album is semi-slow. There are no vocals, except for the last song, which is performed by a different group of musicians. In many ways, this album can be appealing to a variety of tastes and ages. In fact, your parents might enjoy it as much as you. Rico is in high demand nowadays. This is one of his few solo efforts and demonstrates his talents.

TALK TALK 41

## SINGLE REVIEWS

The Regular Guys (National Recording Artists: 36708).-- The debut single by one of the hometown bands. This 33-1/3 Ep contains four original songs. It was recorded last fall. The songs are It's a Secret/Leave/Too Dumb and I Forgot the Flowers. Two are written by the lead, John O'Dell, and the other two by Mark Gilman, who is no longer with the band. At times, heavy on harmonies and short guitar breaks. Not really repetitive, but close. The production and sound is excellent; very clean, very distinct. As with most recording, the musicians sound different during a live performance. The Regular Guys sound better than this nowadays, but they used to sound like this. They deserve praise for this Ep. A job well done.

Madness My Girl/Stepping Into Line (Stiff Records: BUY 62)--Madness are one of the top new sounding bands, as Talk Talk readers no doubt know. The A-side, My Girl, has been released on their debut album. The B-side is new, and shows the band to be capable of new sounds while still keeping in their set style of fast moving, dancing, rhythmic reggae. It comes complete with a picture sleeve featuring the band members and a new Rude boy drawing. It seems this band is just beginning to get the breaks they deserve. It is good to see.

John Foxx Underpass/Film 1 (Virgin Records Ltd.: VS318) --This is the first release of John Foxx since leaving Ultravox. The A-side is a synthesizer-based vocal-less composition that tends to easily draw the listener in. The flip reestablishes Foxx as an important vocalist-writer as shown in early Ultravox recordings. An album is following and should be available soon.

Mo-dettes White Mice/Masochistic Opposite (Rough Trade: Mode 1)--Another four-piece female group with a fantastic sound. Comparisons to other bands won't be made. Their sound can be surprisingly complex in parts. Sure to become popular, at least in the current wave of cult-followings. Plus enjoyable. (→ 10)

## Local Scene

Being a music magazine, *Talk Talk* informs the readers of certain facts and opinions on the local, national and world scenes. Today's rock & roll listener can become easily overloaded by the sheer number of possible different songs, bands and albums. And the variety is growing with new rock sounds developing continually.

A major problem is availability and exposure to the interested (and semi-isolated) fan. This article will discuss most of the better record stores in the local area which the reader should be aware of as important outlets of recorded music.

If you are interested in new material, both domestic and import, Kiefs Records and Tapes in Lawrence at 25th & Iowa is your best bet. Kiefs is by far the largest and most current record shop within a (too many) hundreds of miles radius. They stock all categories, including rock, jazz, soul, classical, and easy listening. In addition to a large number of domestic and import albums, Kiefs is the main source of New Wave singles. They may not have the most complete selection, because what they get in goes quickly. If they do not have something you want, they can usually order it if it is still available. Besides retailing to the individual, Kiefs is also the source for about 50 smaller record stores. That is quite a volume.

One such smaller store is Better Days Records, located in downtown Lawrence, 724 Massachusetts. They get several copies of most releases and keep abreast of the current scene, aside from stocking a great selection. If you find yourself downtown and do not want to waste the time and gas to go to Kiefs, in the southwest section of town, Better Days is the place to check out.

Love Records & Tapes, also downtown Lawrence at 15 West 9th, is the local used record shop. They buy and sell at constant prices. There is a wide assortment of vinyl here. New materials come and go quickly. New stock is kept separate for a few days, for all the regulars to check through. Love is also the only source for rock & roll posters.

The scene in Kansas City is constantly changing. Budget Tapes & Records have just moved away from their 45th and Main store, which was one of the tops. Taking over (→ 10)

# Local Scene

(Continued from page 9)

the No. 1 spot is Pennylane Records at 4128 Broadway. They have just moved into their new and bigger shop. The Reggae selections seem to be the largest in the KC area at the moment, with plans made for expanding it.

Close by is Love Records at 39th and Main (not connected with Love in Lawrence). They are a vinyl specialty shop, where one can find old and obscure records at various prices. They have changed, also. An upstairs balcony has been developed and is loaded with 45's of all kinds. As might be expected, this is where the collectors go.

# SINGLE REVIEWS

(Continued from page 8)

Flowers Confessions/Life After Dark (Fast Product: POP 001)--Not much information out about these people. The female vocals bring Lene Lovich to mind. A good single. They appear on Earcom 1 and Fast's Mutant Pop lp.

The Human Switchboard Prime of My Life/In My Room (Square Records: Sq-One)--The Human Switchboard are a two-man and one-woman band from Ohio, playing drums, guitar, keyboards, and vocals. They are engineered on this record by Paul Hamann of Pere Ubu fame. The A-side is a catchy number, like the Boomtown Rats on the choruses and the Contortions on the guitar breaks. The B-side is a Lou Reed/Sister Morphine-Stones dirge. But comparisons are odious, eh? The Human Switchboard sound like a band with a lot of potential breadth and depth. A good single--not earthshaking, but give them a chance.

Echo & the Bunnymen The Pictures on My Wall/Read It In Books (Zoo Music: Cage 004)--A debut single from a new UK band and the first time I played it, I was ready for more. The A side is a blend of 60's psychedelia and New Wave electronics, complete with acoustic power chords. The B side is more of this basically acoustic music with an Eno-like percussion running throughout.

# ALBUM REVIEWS

(Continued from page 5)

starts out with "Duty Free Technology," followed by an excellent, fast-paced version of "Firing Squad." As a matter of fact, there is not a bad song on this album. Pauline Murray's voice is strong and clear (if you want a comparison, try a mixture of Poly Styrene and Sandy Denny).

Lydia Lunch Queen of Siam (ZEA Records: ZEA 33006)--This woman is supposed to be Queen of "No Wave." She formed Teenage Jesus and The Jerks, along with James Chance (aka James White) and immediately managed to put out some of the most amazing music around. Her Teenage Jesus work was typified by her screeching guitar work and vocals accompanied by a bass and snare drum (there was a saxophone for a while). It came as quite a surprise when I put this album on, expecting something along the lines of Teenage Jesus, and getting instead something that at the first few listens seems totally unlike Lydia's previous work. What I found was a very musical album that could be the next step in blending rock with avant garde jazz. None of the present fusion stars have put out a record that even comes close to the quality and daring of Lydia Lunch. This album takes us back to the seedy side of the 50s. My favorite tune: "A Cruise to the Moon" is the big band jazz sound that makes you think of New York City and all the sleaze of old Film Noir movies and Sinatra and Sammy Davis, Jr. All in all, this record will probably be overlooked by many people who hated her other work. It will be a shame for them to miss this album which is already up there as my No. 1 album of the month.

Pretenders Pretenders (Sire Records: SRK 6083)--The debut album from one of the better groups around. This record is exciting, funny, serious and strange. Chrissie Hynde is a Detroit girl who went over the big water to seek her fortune and found it with this band. Her vocals cover the gamut of emotions. They are strong and . . . well, sexy. This record has something for everybody, good clean pop, like "Stop Your Sobbing," and dirty, raw power, as in "The Phone Call." The American release includes five songs off their first three singles, available as imports only. (→)

## ALBUM REVIEWS

(Continued from page 11)
**This Heat** *This Heat* (Piano Records: This 1)--Charles Hayward, former percussionist with Quiet Sun, has released this debut Lp with a new group, with Charles Bullen on guitars, tapes, and clarinet and Gareth Williams on keyboards, bass and tapes, along with Hayward on percussion and vocals. This entire Lp was recorded in a cold storage building called the Workhouse. This is not a jazz rock fusion Lp. It is a first attempt at creating a new sound. The studio is used as an instrument. There is a lot of multi-track recording; 24 tracks to be precise. This Heat has applied both Brian Eno's and Robert Fripp's theories of musicmaking to good use. A studio masterpiece, proving that all sound can be music. Best songs are: "Testcard I and II, Not Waving," and "Twilight Furniture."

§§§§§§§§§§§§§§§§§§§§§§§§§§§§§§§§§§§§§§§§§§§§§§§§§§§§§

(Continued from page 3) **Thumbs** person's front but a group effort that works. Some people might describe this record a sort of mutated R&B but when you listen to songs, such as "Inch or Two" or "Rags to Rags," you forget about labels and just enjoy yourself. "In The Family" is a funny story of a young man and the problems faced because of his girlfriend's parents, church, holidays, and the family. Thumbs are a band with roots and each member is an individual with something to say. Their music manages to bring back flavors of every musical period of rock and roll's history and they do it well. This album is one that I will still play a long time from now.
*Thumbs: Marty Olson, Karl Hoffman, Steve Wilson, Dede Mosier, and Kevin Smith. Photo by Bill R.*

LIVE: **REGULAR GUYS** *Lawrence Opera House--Jan. 15, 1980*

I had not seen the Regular Guys in quite a while, in November I think, and certainly not with their new lineup (Mark Gillman supposedly split the group to go do some solo work). John O'Dell has brought his sister, Carolyn, in for a few appearances (she may be a semi-regular for a bit) and added the guitar work of David Stuckey. The new lineup is (I am happy to report) working out quite well. The band members are playing together and have a more powerful stage presence. Dave Stuckey seems to have added a punch where needed. Their drummer, John Chiarello, has a more powerful role, with his steady beat, and Brad Reid on bass filled his spot nicely, but I would rather see him back on guitar (I like John O'Dell's bass work). Their sound is cleaner and, with the addition of Carolyn's vocals, they just sound overall good. The band opened with a fast and loud version of an old Smart Pills song, "Yankee Doodle Boy," that at times shook their PA. Other highlights of the night were an Undertones song, "You Got My Number," and several originals, such as "Survival, Kindness, Dr. Simon," and "Without You." If the Regular Guys keep up their present pace and maintain a good working rapport, they will definitely be heard from in the future. January 15th proved that point quite well.
--VS

==================================================
CORRECTIONS AND ADDITIONS AND NEWS

Last issue, Local Scene incorrectly explained a change with the Clean. Actually, the original guitarist now plays bass. The old bass player is no longer with the band and a new guitarist has joined.

In addition, the band now goes under a new name, which is The Youth System. More details next issue!

XTC will be supported by Wazmo Nariz at the Opera House February 13.

## Top Albums of 1979
## Readers Poll Results

Gang of Four--Entertainment!
The Clash--London Calling
Iggy Pop--New Values
Graham Parker--Squeezing Out the Sparks
The Slits--Cut
The Undertones--The Undertones
Public Image Ltd.--Metal Box
Wire--154
Pere Ubu--New Picnic Time
Stiff Little Fingers--Inflammable Material
XTC--Drums & Wire
Linton Kwesi Johnson--Forces of Victory
Sham 69--Hersham Boys
The Members--Chelsea Nightclub
Elvis Costello--Armed Forces
The Specials--The Specials
Buzzcocks--Singles Going Steady
Magazine--Secondhand Delight
Buzzcocks--A Different Kind of Tension
Talking Heads--Fear of Music
Devo--Duty Now for the Future
Roxy Music--Manifesto
The Jam--Setting Sons
Bob Marley--Survival
Angelic Upstarts--Teenage Warning
The Only Ones--Special View
The Cure--Three Imaginary Boys
The B-52's--The B-52's
The Mekons--The Quality of Mercy is Not Strnen
Intensified: Original Ska 1962-66
Lee Perry--Scratch on the Wire, Sex Pistols--R
'n R Swindle, Lene Lovich--Stateless, Cars--Candy
O, Squeeze--Cool for Cats, Joe Jackson--Look
Sharp, Bowie--Lodger, Madness--One Step Beyond,
Ramones--Road to Ruin, The Pretenders, John Cale
--Sabotage, Red Crayola--Soldier Talk

---

--Coming Soon--

The Best of
Talk Talk
Volume 1

Highlights of the
first four issues.

$2.00 a copy

First time offered

Available by Mail

Order today!

Talk Talk Publications
P.O. Box 36
Lawrence, Kansas   66044

Please send me:

____ copies of the next issue @ $1.00

____ copies of Vol. 1. Collection @ $2.00

____ subscriptions to the next six issues @ 5.00

Total enclosed by check or money order ____

Name _____

Address _____

TALK TALK   45

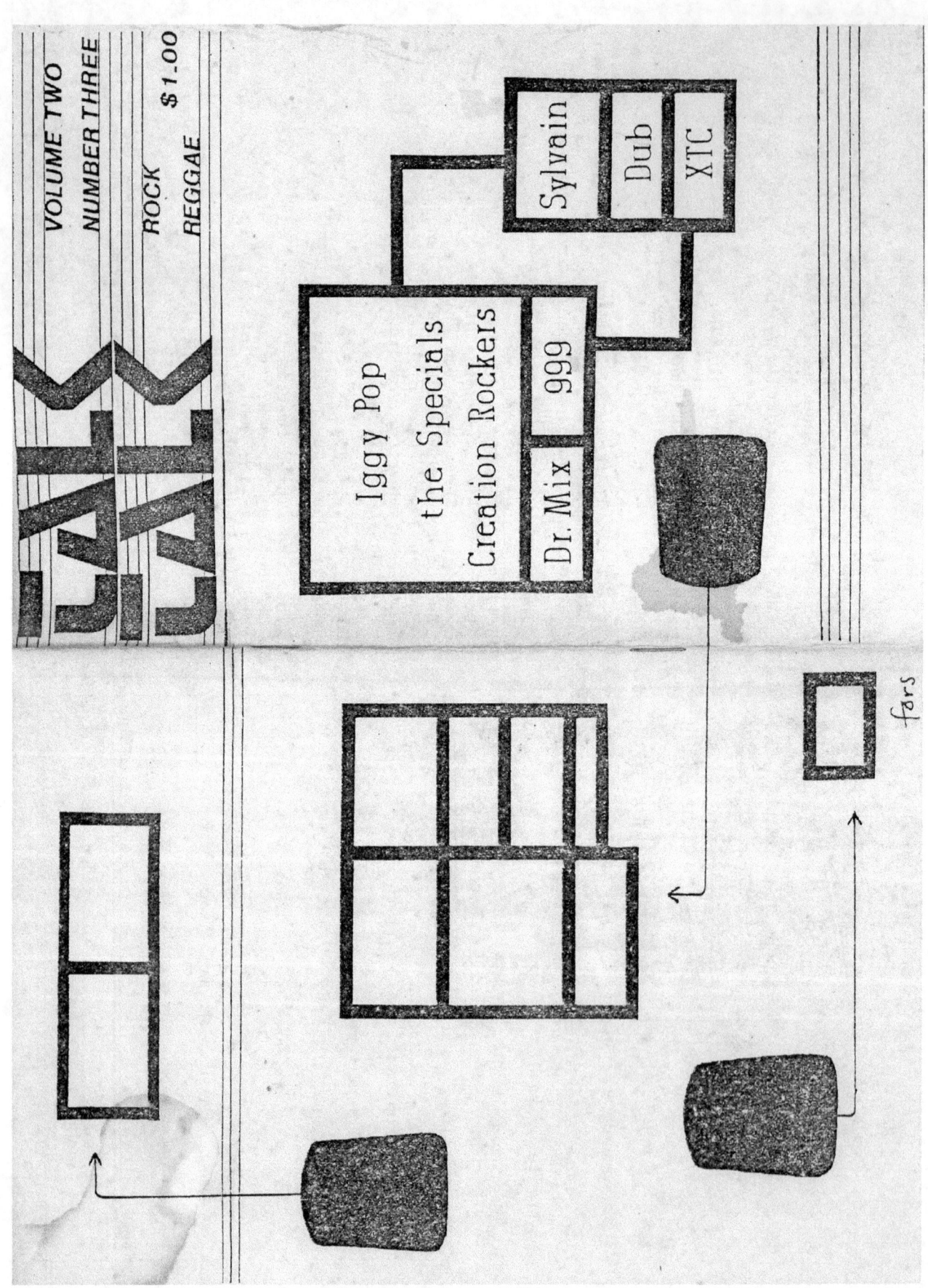

TALK TALK

Vol. 2, No. 3      March 1980      $1.00

The Midwest American Rock and Reggae Magazine

Table of Contents

XTC                                                          3
Album Reviews: Iggy Pop, John Foxx                           4
Sylvain Sylvain, Nine Nine Nine,                             5
Durutti Column                                               5
Reggae Reviews: Revolutionaries Dub                          6
Dennis Brown                                                 7
Creation Rockers, David Isaacs                               8
Single Reviews: The Clash, The Specials                      9
Killing Joke                                                 9
Local Scence: Record Stores                                 10
Single Reviews: Tom Robinson, Lene Lovich                   11
Album Reviews: Dr. Mix                                      13
Single Reviews: Cabaret Voltaire                            14
Album Update and Concert Schedule                           15

Editors: Bill R. and Eric S.
Contributors: VS, WB, BR, ET
Cover: Nate Fors

Talk Talk Publications
Post Office Box 36
Lawrence, Kansas
66044
USA

Copyright 1980 Talk Talk Publications. All rights reserved. Not responsible for unsolicited material. Any opinion expressed is solely that of the writer and not necessarily that of the magazine.

---

Talk Talk Vol. 2 No. 3/page 3

# XTC

XTC Live/Opera House, Lawrence, Kansas February 13, 1980

One of the best bands to come out of England in the past few years played in town and lived up to their reputation of quality (Sounds like a beer commercial). Opening up for XTC were a mediocre act that has gained some cult status of late, Wazmo Nariz, which some people in the crowd enjoyed. But there was no mistake who the crowd was there for.

XTC appeared during a recorded version of "Bushman President" off their "Making Plans for Nigel" single. The band then picked up their instruments and ripped into an excellent version of "Beattown" and kept up the pace with slightly altered renditions of "Life Begins at the Hop", "Mechanicc Dancing" and "Reel By Reel". The newest member of the band, David Gregory, fit in nicely and added to the sound texture with some excellent guitar and keyboard work. At times vocals were indecipherable but overall the vocal strength of both Andy Partridge and Colin Moulding were outstanding and the percussion work of Terry Chambers left nothing to be desired. The band supplied the audience with an extra treat in the form of a scratched-film show consisting of basic white light in different geometric forms. The use was tasteful and effective. Other highlights of the evening were "Complicated Game", "This Is Pop", "Are You Receiving Me", "When You're Near Me" and "Crowded Room". They also premiered two new songs (neglecting to mention the titles). They played about 20 selections and came out for two encores. (The second one was "Science Friction", an obscure song available on the 3D Ep and "Live at the Hope and Anchor Club" Lp.) XTC in the course of the evening covered material off all three of their albums and several singles and Ep's and provided the Opera House and all within with a wonderful time that will be hard to match by very many bands in the USA or England. XTC set a standard of quality and I plan to see them again whenever I get the chance.  --ES

---

XTC arrived in town via the traveling van, in the middle of the ten-week American tour. After Lawrence,

## ALBUM REVIEWS

**Iggy Pop Soldier** (Arista: AB4259)--Once again Iggy demonstrates that he is still a major force in today's musical world. After last year's Lp, New Values, it appeared hard to follow up such an excellent work. It seems that the Ig has pulled it off once again. Part of the secret lies in his constant changing lineup of talented musicians. This album used the band of Europeans from his last English tour. It includes Glen Matlock on bass, Ivan Kral on guitar and keyboards, Klaus Kruger on drums, Steve New on guitar, and Barry Andrews on keyboards.

Iggy Pop is by far one of the greatest songwriters around. Of these 11 new songs, Iggy wrote five, co-wrote with Matlock three, one with Bowie, and one with Andrews, plus one Matlock original (perhaps the poorest cut). It starts off with "Loco Mosquito," which makes you glad to be alive. Iggy says it best, "I got some energy to burn. It makes me jumpy and nervous." If you ever have seen Iggy live, you know how much he zips around the stage. Like a loco mosquito. "Take Care of Me" is another excellent song. These two cuts make the album. Of course there are others equally as great. The organ adds a new sound to Iggy's work. The vocals remind me of the raw strain evident on Kill City. Very fast paced, like a shot of adrenaline. I do not know what the "critics" think of this product, but I know it will provide a lot of people with good, enjoyable rock and roll. --BR

**John Foxx Metamatic** (Virgin: V2146)--John Foxx used to be the lead vocalist for Ultravox and is supposedly one of Gary Newman's (Tubeway Army) main influences. Metamatic is John's first solo work and it carries on certain trends that he first started to employ in Ultravox; the electronic textures and his understated smooth vocal style. Unfortunately, Metamatic seems to lack certain important items that Ultravox had. For one thing the full sound and mood layers that his old band produced are missing. Where Ultravox could evoke certain emotions with most of their songs (fear, alienation, etc.), Foxx only manages to pull it off on two or three songs (which do not make an album), such as "No-One Driving", "030", and "Plaza". This album can only be called (+ 13)

## ALBUM REVIEWS

**Sylvain Sylvain Sylvain Sylvain** (RCA: AFL 1-3475)--The first solo record from the ex-New York Dolls' guitarist. This could easily be classified as "pop oriented rhythm and blues." It is uplifting and fun listening. A single he put out last year with his band, The Criminals, was similar sounding. Sylvain has been playing extensively the last few years, mainly in New York clubs with The Criminals. They never got their big break. Finally Syl began working on this Lp with different musicians. He is reportedly rehearsing now with a new band. No doubt they will continue to be a dance band, as Syl has a knack for playing fast rockers. But there is also a slower, jazz style evident on this record. In short, a mixture of musical tastes, with something for everyone.

**Nine Nine Nine The Biggest Prize in Sport** (Polydor: PDI -6256)--What, these guys are still around? This band gained recognition three years ago for releasing singles on green vinyl, when it was still unique to get colored vinyl. This is their third album. A collection of the first two Lps was released in the US last year. But this product contains 12 new tunes, very similar to the past and distinctly 999, as evidenced in the high-pitched voice of Nick Cash, with two guitars, bass, and drums. A fifth face has joined the boys as a second drummer. The graphics that 999 use have always been exceptional and once again they set high standards for record packaging. Their musical style probably turns some listeners off, but overall, the band deserves credit for their continued existence. They have their act down pat. They remain just far enough off the pop-mainstream style that it is doubtful 999 will ever branch out but will remain a cult-band. And I would hate to be confronted by their followers en masse.

**The Return of Durutti Column** (Factory Records: FACT 14) --A most unusual group, Durutti Column creates an almost indescribable sound mixture of guitars, bass, drums, and synthesizer (plus other electro-tones). It comes packaged with a sandpaper sleeve. Maybe to warn the uninformed potential buyer that they are a rough lot. No vocals. Much of the sound is various guitar solos done light and eerie. It all sort of blends together. --WB

# REGGAE REVIEWS

The Revolutionaries
Guerilla Dub (Burning Sounds: BS 1028LP)
Culture Dub (Sky Note: SKYLP16)
Satisfaction in Dub (Flames Records: LAP005)
Goldmine Dub (Greensleeves Records: GREL4)
Jonkanoo Dub (Cha Cha Music: CHALP5)

Five dub albums with the Revolutionaries currently available (in England). They all are from the late 1970's, so they are not real new releases, but very important anyway. Each has been marketed by a different company. Several producers and several recording studios were used, including Channel One, King Tubby's, and Treasure Isle. Although each were recorded in Kingston, Jamaica, they all were marketed in London.

So, what is Dub and who are the Revolutionaries? Neither is easy to explain. Basically, dub is a remix of recorded tracks. The bass and drums are brought out to establish the rhythmic flow. The guitar tracks are echoed in and out and keyboards and horns pop in and out. Sometimes vocals filter in for brief attacks. The synthesized sounds hardly resemble the original cut. The psychedelic effect which results is definitely an aural experience. And although dub is not so dialectical, this technique is by no means exclusively confined to reggae. It extends from old acid-rock groups to modern synthesizer groups, no doubt influenced by present-day electronical wizardry. But dub-reggae seems to be the most exciting display for the mixing technicians.

The Revolutionaries are a loose-knit group of Jamaicans who record in studios, reportedly getting only a day's wages for playing and receiving no royalties or even credit for their creations. But this does not stop them from continually producing some of the heaviest sounds around.

These five albums no doubt include different players, but almost certainly drummer Sly (→ 11)

# REGGAE REVIEWS

Dennis Brown Words of Wisdom (Laser Records:LASL1)
Live at Montreaux '79 (Laser Records: LASL5)

Two UK releases from 1979 which show the superb vocals of Dennis Brown. Words of Wisdom is a Joe Gibbs production, recorded at his JA studio and contains compositions of Gibbs, with numerous super-session musicians. Laser Records is a new label, distributed by WEA, which began last fall, with Brown and Gibbs being the major artists. Whether it is a characteristic of Dennis Brown or Laser Records is uncertain, but both of these albums are surprisingly long--around an hour each. In today's market, that is long! Dennis Brown has been around for some time. He is not a household name in the U.S., but he has proven himself a major reggae singer and influence.

One of his many songs on the Rebel Music Lp is "Money in My Pocket (But I Just Can't Get No Love)" from 1972. New versions are contained on both these albums. The live version, which was recorded at the Monreaux Jazz Festival in Switzerland, is one of the highlights. Both lps open with "So Jah Say," a powerful number. Bob Marley does a similar version on Natty Dread. All have the lines "Not one of his seeds shall sit in the sidewalk and beg bread, not one of his seed shall be a living dead. So Jah say, no no no. No let him down."

As you might guess or expect, Dennis Brown is a devoted Rastafarian. Yet this theme is not so upfront or preachy to be offensive, as certain artists sometimes get. But the religious message is definitely there.

Other songs on the new studio album also performed live include "Ain't That Loving You" and the title cut, "Words of Wisdom," which says "Take heed Jah people and live upright." That leaves 14 more cuts for comment. In general, the studio album shows the mastery of Joe Gibbs and the high quality of Jamaican artists.(→ 11)

## REGGAE REVIEWS

Creation Rockers Vols. 1-6 (Trojan Records: TRLS 180-185)--There have been a lot of collection albums coming out nowadays which proves that reggae music is finally starting to be noticed. This set of six records may not be the definitive reggae collection (with all the old music around that would be almost impossible) but it is the closest thing to it yet. Each record starts out with an early ska tune and moves forward, through rock steady and into present day reggae. Some of the artists are recognizable, such as The Wailers, Augustus Pablo, Big Youth, I Roy, U Roy, and the Maytals but for the most part these artists are presented with obscure songs that would almost be impossible at times to find. The gist of these albums though are filled with obscure artists of the past, like The Interns and their great song, "Mr. Chatterbox" and "Guns Fever" by an old ska artist, Baba Brooks. As I said before each album stands on its own feet as a future classic. Other songs that are great on this fine collection are "Pope Paul Dead & Gone" by Trinity, "Mr. Fire Coal-Man" by The Wailing Souls, and "Better Days" by Carlton & The Shoes. Unfortunately, none of these records supply any background information on the history of the artists. If Trojan decides to put these marvelous albums into a second pressing, I hope they correct this (the only, as far as I am concerned) shortcoming. Again, if you have a hard time finding these records around here (and I am sure you will), write Trojan Records for a catalogue because this collection is not to be missed. --VS

David Isaacs & Jah Thomas Just Like A Sea/Version (Attack Records-Tack 13)--This single is able to represent two of the major forces that are going on in reggae music today. David Isaacs is a soulful, sweet singer that probably was heavily influenced by mid-60's American Black radio. He starts out the song sailing above the powerful back beat (the drummer sounds like Sly Dunbar). The song is at first a straightforward love song ("My Love is Like the Sea") but about halfway through it changes abruptly, from the soul style into a heavy dub mix with Jah Thomas toasting above the backing track. Like all reggae, this single (→ page 9)

## SINGLE REVIEWS

The Clash London Calling-Armagideon Time b/w Justice Tonight (version)-Kick It Over (version) (CBS Records: 12-8087)--This month's Clash review from a No. 1 Clash fan and a dub enthusiast. The A-side of this 12-inch single is the same as earlier singles. The B-side is Armagideon Time-dub versions produced by The Clash. This reggae cover is an excellent song. The alternative mixes show an additional side to the band. Very forceful, very energetic. A must for Clash fans, reggae fans, and dub addicts. --BR

The Specials A.K.A. Live Too Much Too Young/Guns of Navarone/Long Shot Kick the Bucket/Liquidator/Skinhead Moon Stomp (2 Tone Records: CHST7)--Five live songs from the newest craze to hit England (and America). This EP is marred a bit by the tape quality. But it demonstrates that this band performs as well as their records. Their revitalization of ska-influenced dance music has probably affected more concert goers and record buyers, bringing life back into bored youth. --BR

Killing Joke Nervous System/Turn to Red (Island: WIP 6550)--This single is arresting. The first time I put it on my turntable I fell in love with it. The sound is (here go some comparisons) between that of The Cure and PiL. Side one is a song called "Nervous System" and it is carried along by a almost funky instrumental track while the singer croons along in a throaty, talk-sing style. The second-side of this gem, "Turn To Red" starts out with a heavy bass, line that is interrupted by a Keith Levin-style guitar line. The use of electronics and dubbing is heavy as the song progresses. If this group can continue to put out products of this quality they should be a major group on the scene in a very short time. I hope an album follows soon. --VS

David Isaacs & Jah Thomas (continued from p. 8)--will probably be hard to find, if all else fails try ordering it through Trojan Records, it is worth the trouble. --VS

# Local Scene

Last month's column looked at six record stores, including Kief's, Love Records and Better Days, all of Lawrence, and Budget, Pennylane and Love Records in Kansas City. This month's column will look at a new store in KC, Rock Therapy. Also included will be World Records, in Topeka. Somehow Talk Talk has never mentioned their favorite store, WaxTrax in Chicago. It is not that the local area stores are not recommended, of course.

Since last issue, a new record store has opened in Kansas City. The name is Rock Therapy and the address is 7511 Troost. It might not be the most central or accessible location, but it definitely is well worth the effort to go check out. Rock Therapy has an assortment of old and new rock and reggae albums and singles. There is also a mixture of other categories, such as rockabilly and 60's. It opened February 1 and looks to be very promising as a primary source of records.

On the western edge of the local area is Topeka, about half an hour from Lawrence. A used record store which opened in the fall is World Records, at 615 West 6th. They carry a wide assortment of rare and collectable albums and singles, plus they offer a search service to find the records wanted. World Records is also the reported hangout for the new-wavers and bands such as Special Ed and Abuse, to name a few.

The greatest source for the latest records is, unfortunately, quite a distance away. Of course, reference is to WaxTrax Records in Chicago. Located at 2449 North Lincoln, this store has the hits before you even know they are out. They also carry oldies. If you ever find yourself close to Chicago, be sure not to miss going to WaxTrax. --BR

# SINGLE REVIEWS

Tom Robinson Never Gonna' Fall In Love...(Again)/Getting Tighter (EMI: 2967)--The A-side presents a different, disco-sounding Tom Robinson with the Voice Squad doing a song co-written by E. John. The Tom Robinson Band plays a Hot Peaches tune on the flip, maybe their last ever recording. Since they disbanded several months ago, Tom has formed a new band, Sector Twenty Seven. Shortly after the free TRB concert last summer in Kansas City, it was reported that Tom Robinson would put out a gay-oriented disco single. I guess it finally happened. The lyrical themes for both involve social and personal problems of a gay-oriented individual. "Getting Tighter" is by far the better of these distinctively different cuts. TRB was a fine band who put out two good albums and had many fans before they decided to split up. And supposedly, things are going better and they like it better now. The now band which Tom has developed is totally different. S27 are reportedly "hoping to explore newer musical directions." So if you feel disappointed with this new single, remember that this is not the way Tom Robinson sounds these days.  --WB

Lene Lovich Angels/The Fly (Stiff Records: Buy 63)--The single from the forthcoming album. "Angels" features Lene's wide-ranging and sounding voice; her typical style. The B-side is basically a continual chant and timed synthesizer backing. Maybe there is some message behind it all. Maybe the Angels watching over Lene know. --WB

(Continued from page 6) backed by Duggie and Tuffy on guitars and probably an assortment of other session artists.

The 48 cuts included on these Lps all seem to be different, which might be wrong, but they are all at least each a unique mix. Credit should go to the engineers and also to the band, The Revolutionaries. --WB

(Continued from page 7) The live album demonstrates reggae crossover to jazz. No matter what group of musicians with which Dennis Brown works, his smooth and identifiable vocal-style provides for pleasant listening. --WB

## ALBUM REVIEWS

(Continued from page 4) self-indulgent. John Foxx does have talent but I am sad to say that it does not shine through nearly enough on this record. Metamatic will probably gain a cult following along with the overrated Gary Newman, meanwhile I will go put on "Systems of Romance" and hope that John Foxx fares better on his next outing. --VS

Dr. Mix and the Remix Wall of Noise (Rough Trade: Rough 6)--An interesting debut album from another Paris-based band, or is it aliens doing cover versions of such rockers as: Grey Lagoons, No Fun, Supermen, Sister Ray, as well as a couple of oldies by the Seeds. This was probably done in a studio by a couple of nameless lifeforms. After being remixed and subjected to heavy industrialization, the majority of the songs lost a lot of their lyrical intensity. It's as if the words are there simply to add to the wall of noise effect that the doctor has created and it is a monster. The cutting guitar, insect droning vocals, the sense of not-of-this-world that this album creates are quite a feat. The only let down is that there is no original material, it is all covers. But then again there is nothing like the sounds on this Lp; they are different. --ET

XTC (Continued from page 3) the band played at Norman, OK, then on to Texas. Next to California, for a series of already sold out shows. Earlier in the tour, they set the record attendance at Hurrah in New York. After the west coast, they head north to Canada and then eastward.

In trying to talk with the band, we found Andy Partridge before the show, who agreed to an interview. When asked if he minded being taped, he thought it would be a good idea because then "*you would be sure to get things right.*" Given a choice of listening to the new Iggy Pop album on a little cassette deck, he wanted to listen to Iggy. On the subject of Barry Andrews (ex-XTC writer and keyboardist), he said, "*The last time I saw him he came down and brought Iggy with him...but that was quite a while* (→ 14)

---

If You Missed It
The First Time
Here Is Your Chance

The Best of
Talk Talk
Volume 1

A Compilation of the
First Four Issues.

$2.00 a copy

Order Today!

Or Subscribe!

Talk Talk Publications
P.O. Box 36
Lawrence, Kansas 66044

Please send me:

___ copies of Vol. 2 (circle choice)   @ $1.00
___ (circle choice) No. 1 2 3 4        @ $1.00
___ copies of Vol. 1 Collection        @ $2.00

___ subscriptions to next six issues   @ $5.00

Total enclosed by check or money order  $ _____

Name _____

Address _____

# SINGLE REVIEWS

Cabaret Voltaire  Silent Command/Chance versus Causality (Rough Trade: RT035)--This is the third single released by this Paris-based band, featuring bass, guitar, tapes, and electronics. With each new release they seem to get better soundwise and this is their best effort so far. The A-side is a metallic dub track with plenty of echo and underwater sounding vocals is one of the most interesting things they have done. The French-speaking robot voice and taped effects that float in and out should appeal to the machine in all of us. The B-side is an extract from a soundtrack for a film entitled, "Chance vs. Causality." Upon first listening, it sounded like Pere Ubu, with a buzzing rhythm dominating the foreground and a wailing, almost haunting guitar off in the distance. It is definitely mood music, similar to the Eraserhead soundtrack. Reminiscent of Henry walking through his bleak and oppressive neighborhood from work and the only thing he has to look forward to is staring at the walls surrounding him. What could be more fun?  --ET

(Continued from page 13) ago, even when we were together in the band we weren't really social outside. You know you can hear Barry all over this (referring to Iggy's new record). He probably does all the sax work, too." We then asked about his Solo record, The Lure of Garbage. "No, not 'Garbage'. Those people at MM (Melody Maker) got it all wrong, and please don't call it my record. It's just that I did all the mixing and production on it so everybody told me to just put my name on it. Actually, the album has two names, The Lure of Salvage, not garbage, and Take Away. It's basically a remixing of old XTC songs. It ought to be really interesting. There're all sorts of weird things on it, vocals sort of here and there. Also, there is an old song that was an outtake from our White Music album called 'Refrigerator Blues', but you won't recognize it because you never could have heard it because it's never been on a record. The title isn't even the same. It ought to be out the 14th of February. What day is this anyway?" Told it was the 13th, he replied, "Really? We've been on the road so long."
(To be continued with photos in the next issue.)

---

Several important records reviewed in past Talk Talk issues have now been released on American labels. Besides being lower in cost, they are easier to find. Often, different songs or mixes are contained on the domestic releases. The following is a partial list of these new lps.

The Clash--London Calling (EPIC: 36328)
The Jam--Setting Sons (Polydor: PD1-6249)
The Undertones--The Undertones (Sire: SRK6081)
The Members--At the Chelsea Nightclub (VI: 2120)
The Specials--The Specials (Chrysalis: CHR1265)
XTC--Drums and Wires (Virgin: VA 13134)
Buzzcocks--A Different Kind of Tension (IRS: SP009)
The Slits--Cut (Antillies: AN 7077)
Sham 69--Hersham Boys (Polydor: PD1-6245)
The Boomtown Rats--The Fine Art of Surfacing (Columbia: JC 36248)
The Dickies--Dawn of the Dickies (A&M: SP4796)
Madness--One Step Beyond (Sire: SRK 6085)
Ramones--End of the Century (Sire: SRK 6077)
Wire--154 (Warners: BSK 3398)
Iggy Pop--Soldier (Arista: AB4259)

************************************************
*                                              *
*               Concert Schedule               *
*                                              *
*Pat's Blue Riddim Band           March 7, 8*
*       Lawrence Opera House                *
*Iggy Pop                           March 26*
*       Lawrence Opera House                *
*Nine Nine Nine                     March 29*
*       Lawrence Opera House                *
*                                              *
************************************************

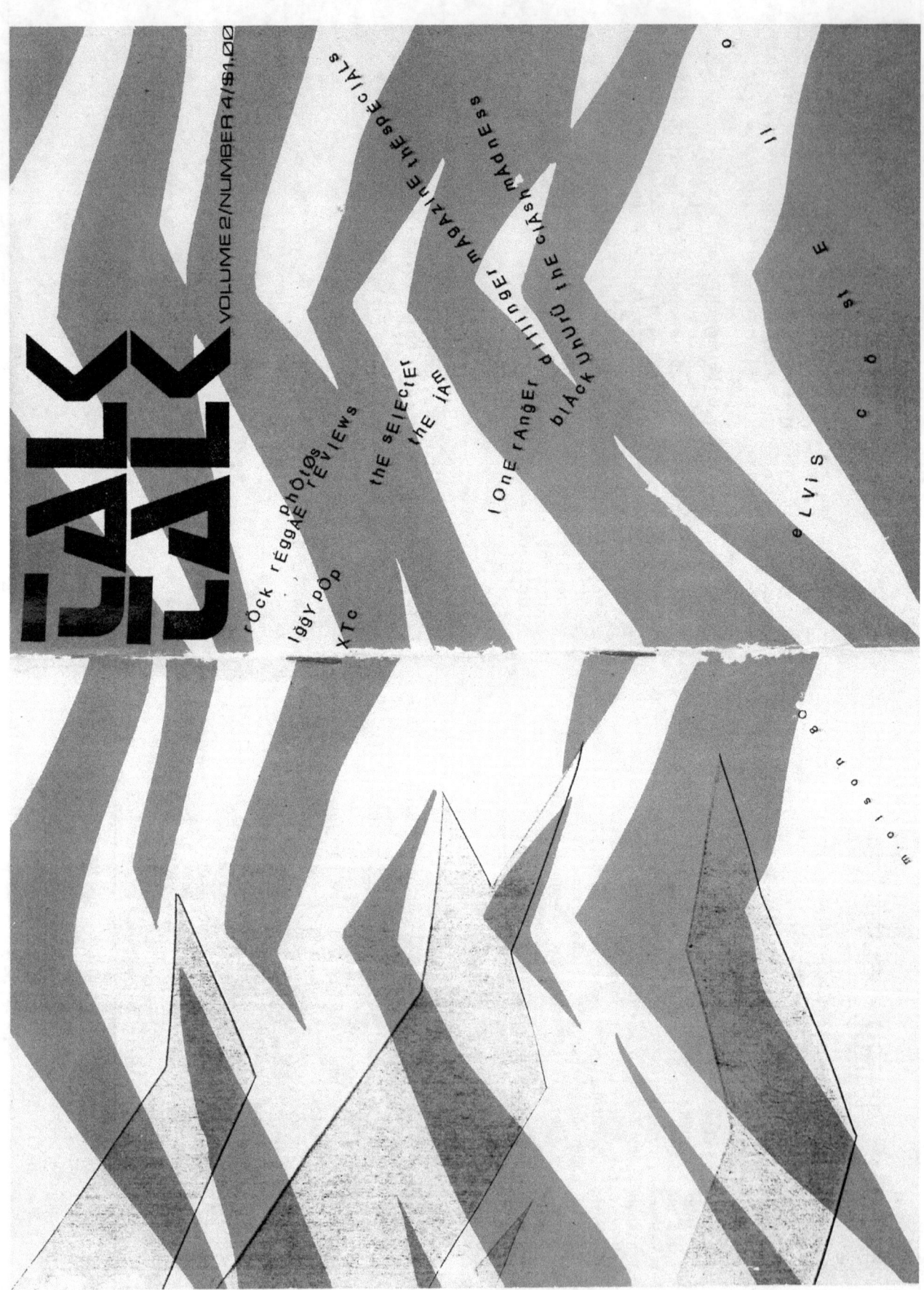

# TALK TALK

Vol. 2, No. 4    April 1980    $1.00
The Midwest American Rock and Reggae Magazine

| | |
|---|---|
| Album Reviews: Elvis Costello, Selecter | 3 |
| N.O. Experience Necessary, Mr. Partridge | 4 |
| Concert Reviews: New Orleans, Iggy Pop | 5 |
| Specials | 7 |
| Lene Lovich, The Jam | 8 |
| Madness | 9 |
| The Clash | 10 |
| Interview and Photos: XTC | 11 |
| Single Reviews: Elvis, Magazine, Stiff Little Fingers | 14 |
| The Tea Set, Cockney Rejects, Silicon Teens | 15 |
| The Fall, MI-Sex, Chelsea | 16 |
| Reggae Reviews: Dillinger, Lone Ranger, Black Uhuru, Joe Gibbs & the Professionals | 17 |
| Reggae Singles: Dr. Alimantado, Big Youth, Dexy's Midnight Runners, UB40, Barry Brown, N Kojak, Dillinger | 18 |
| Black Uhuru, Cairo, Gregory Isaacs, Prince Far I | 19 |
| The Jam Photos, News and New Talent | 20 |
| Album Reviews: U.K. Subs, Squeeze, Original Mirrors, Orchestral Manoeuvers in the Dark | 21 |
| Cabaret Voltaire, Moebius & Plank, Bukowski | 22 |
| Local Scene and Concert Schedule | 23 |

Editors: Bill R. and Eric S.
Contributors: VS, WB, ES, BR, ET, DC, RH, JM, KD
Photos: Robin Kyle and Bill Rich
Cover: Martin Olson

Talk Talk Publications
Post Office Box 36
Lawrence, Kansas
66044
USA

Copyright 1980 Talk Talk Publications. All rights reserved. Not responsible for unsolicited material. Any opinion expressed is solely that of the writer and not necessarily that of the magazine.

## ALBUM REVIEWS

Elvis Costello and the Attractions Get Happy (F Beat Records: XXLP1)--It has been almost a year since Elvis put out his last record, Armed Forces, and a lot has happened to him in that time. He has produced a record for "The Specials" and got knocked down by country girl Bonnie Brammlet for making a sarcastic remark. So what could his fans be expecting in the way of music? Well, what one should expect from the "King"--an Album that is his strongest work since "This Years Model."

There are 21 songs on his new Lp and every one of them is a jewel. What we get with Get Happy is a record that is highly personal. The big C has grown up on us over the past few years and a new-found strength and maturity is evident.

The Attractions as well have gotten better over the year's sojourn and prove to be one of the best band in the business. Their playing is tight and economical. Elvis might be the central focus of this album but the band are his perfect foil. My advice is to Get Happy and turn up the volume on your stereo and have a good time.
Pick cuts: "I Can't Stand Up for Falling Down," "New Amsterdam," "The Imposter," and "I Stand Accused." --VS

The Selecter Too Much Pressure (Two Tone Records: TT5002) --This is the best record to come out under the Two Tone banner. The Selecter have a sound unique unto themselves. Whereas The Specials and Madness share a similar sound, Selecter breaks away from the form. Also where the other two bands are either all white or with a couple of blacks, The Selecter is all black with the exception of Neol Davies, who is white. They also have a female vocalist (Pauline Black) who helps the band establish an even stronger separate Identity.

The whole feeling of this record comes closer to the roots in the musicianship. They also care about their social surroundings and are not afraid to put forth their viewpoints in song. I could go on and on about this album but will not. What I will do is say that whereas The Specials and Madness are getting the major notices at the moment I feel that The Selecter have the best chance for becoming one of the most important bands to emerge in quite a while. Get them while they are hot!
Choice cuts: "Three Minute Hero," "Everyday," (+ 4)

## ALBUM REVIEWS

(Continued from page 3)
"Too Much Pressure"...What the hell, the whole album!--VS

N.O. Experience Necessary Various Artists (Oblique Records: PB001)--A group of New Orleans-style punks got together to compile an album of original new wave songs. They advertised in the newspaper and knew the local scene enough to develop a product superior to most compilation attempts. Of course, among the 12 songs by eight bands, there are some throw aways and some outstanding cuts. The Mechanics, who perform two numbers, are the most accessible, with catchy, quick, pop sounds. They are a four-piece band together about a year, who also have an Ep out. The Contenders' two cuts show a polished sound, at least some power chords.

I guess that most of these bands are not really a part of the current scene--some leaving for NY, others for the West. So if you were to go to N.O. expecting to hear these sounds, you would have to search hard. With this album available, more new sounds surface. It is good to see that new scenes continue to develop. Even if punk is dead, and new wave has been assimilated and electro-pop is taking over, there are still many small geographic pockets on this earth which continue to act and react as they please, disobeying the media's commandments. Congratulations, N.O. We all need more. --BR

Mr. Partridge Take Away/The Lure of Salvage (Virgin: V2145)--This is the XTC dub record built around remixed tracks with new lyrics. The sound is pretty much different and unique. The concept was used earlier on the 2nd album, Go To, which was accompanied by the Go + version. But this record uses a more detailed stripping or altering. Since their debut, White Music, Lp, XTC have been a major influence on the rock scene. Many groups attempt to duplicate their vocal style, rhythm patterns and complexities with varying levels of success. The band, and, to a certain degree Andy Partridge personally, are establishing themselves among the leaders of experimentation with their rhythmic strategies expanding the possibilities of rock music. It is easy to get caught off-guard by these sounds. But even that can be fun.--BR (→ 21)

## CONCERTS

Little Queenie & the Perculators 2/16, Tipitinas, New Orleans

A pre-Mardi Gras party featuring one of the most popular N.O. groups at one of the "in" clubs. Warming up were a local combo with a blind singer/guitarist, backed by piano, bass, drums, and three saxes. Little Queenie began about 4 a.m. playing their brand of Calypso jazz.

Alligator Ball 2/17, New Orleans

When buying tickets to this giant jam session featuring the best of N.O. musicians, it was discovered that Iggy Pop, who was opening his American tour here, was to make an in-store appearance.

Back at the Alligator Ball, a benefit for Prof. Longhair, the music continued all afternoon and into the evening, when most of the musicians had other shows to play. The names are too numerous to mention, the sounds basically homegrown blues and jazz.

Iggy Pop 2/18, Ole Man Rivers, New Orleans

The afternoon before the show, about 50 fans gathered to see Iggy, who was accompanied by guitarist Ivan Kral and manager Dennis Sheehan. Iggy talked freely for several hours, focusing on the new Lp, Soldier, the tour and himself.

At the show, The Normals opened. They are a local group who have been playing in New York lately. Their half-hour, non-stop set was composed of original, intense, and interesting material. Their strength is the ability to switch singers and styles by the line-up of two guitarist/vocalists with bass and drums.

Iggy had earlier said, "not to come to the show unless you are a gambler," because the band had not exactly developed the desirable style for the tour. (→ 7)

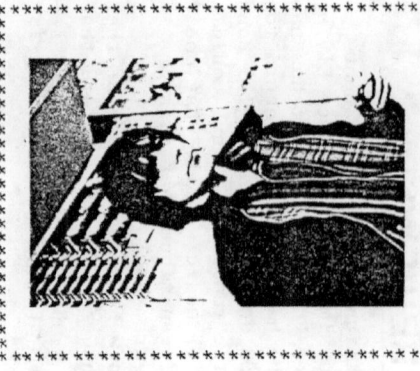
*Iggy Pop*

# CONCERTS

(Continued from page 5)

The personnel were drummer Klas Krugger, bassist Billy Rath and Robert Dupree and Ivan Kral on guitars. No keyboards at all, noticeable especially since the new Lp uses more keyboards than any previous release.

The show was a mixture of old songs, some from Soldier, and five new ones. There was no focus on any past stage, if anything, it showed a new stage. The older songs used new arrangements and the new ones were enjoyable. The crowd demanded two encores and wanted more.

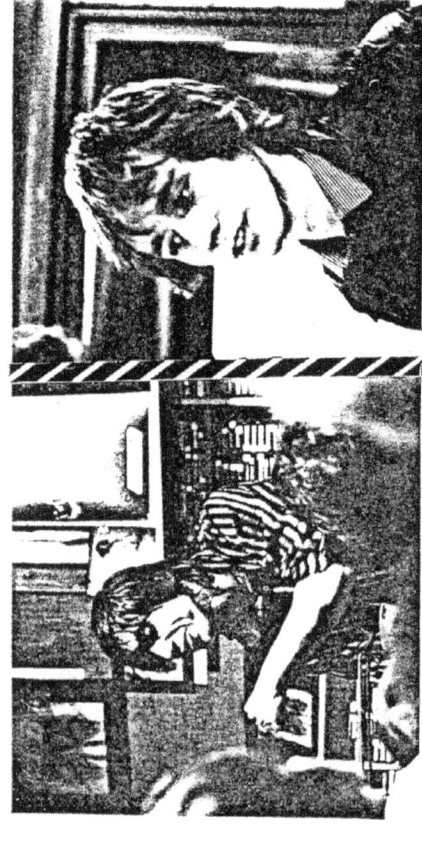

*Iggy Pop and Ivan Kral.*

The Specials with Rico 2/21-22, Beginnings, Park West, Chicago

The Specials have received a lot of praise for their approach to music and concerts, and I might add it is well deserved. It is impossible to convey the enthusiasm and excitement this group puts out, which quickly spread to the audience, who danced away on the packed floor. The combination of vocalists Neville Staples from Jamaica and English Terry Hall, along with Jerry Dammers on keyboards, two guitars, bass and drums is very powerful. Their live performance is much better than their excellent recordings. With the addition of horns, an extra punch was thrown in, something most artists cannot accomplish (→ 8)

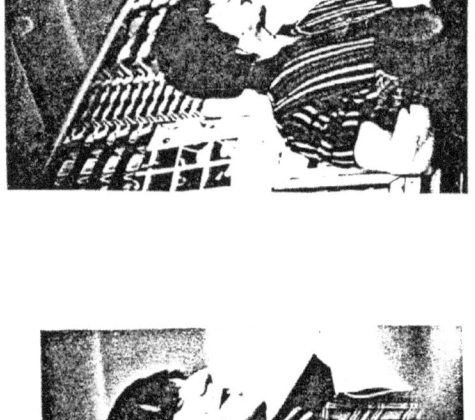

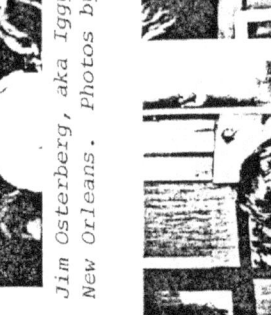

*Jim Osterberg, aka Iggy Pop, visits Leisure Landing in New Orleans. Photos by Bill Rich.*

# CONCERTS

(Continued from page 7)

The stage filled several times with fans dancing to the ska sounds. At one point, a guitar was given away to the best dancer; another time, one was smashed to bits. Jerry Dammers jumped into the crowd occasionally and everyone left soaked with sweat and memories of how much fun a concert should be.

Lene Lovich 3/15, Park West, Chicago
  Lene Lovich gained exposure and a following by dressing in a variety of ancient clothing styles and using a warbling vocal style. On tour promoting her new album, the crowd expected more than she and her band gave. At least she could have been arty enough for one costume change. Instead, we got her saxaphone. The crowd went crazy while her hits were played. But basically, the songs all sounded the same. A bit pretentious and boring perhaps, but this is rock & roll and her performance was better than most. For example, the warmup attempt by Bruce Wooley and the Camera Club. My only comment is that maybe they can develop better songs in the future, along with more assured stage presence.

The Jam 3/7-8, Park West, Old Chicago, Chicago
  The Jam just made an across-the-board sweep of musical polls as the best band, musicians, song writer and album. They remain the model for "mod" revivalists, although their sound is not totally "mod," whatever that implies. It is amazing how a three-piece group can have such full sounds. Their three albums are all of superior quality. Their live sound is almost magical. At times the bass and guitar rhythm is totally different than the vocal rhythm, something not exactly easy to do successfully or continually.
  The second show was an all-ages show, important because many of The Jam's fans are not 21. They played very expertly and the crowd loved them. The songs were mainly from singles and Eton Rifles, the 3rd Lp, and included their new single, "Going Underground." Another excellent show which was actually much better than I had anticipated. (See photographs, page 20.)

*Chas Smash, vocals, footwork; Mark Bedford Bedders, bass; Lee Thompson, sax.*

Madness 3/2, Park West, Chicago
  Madness, who had an early Two Tone single and were the first to come to America, have a unique style and show. Their "nutty" attitude is evident in their stage antics, such as head knocking fights. They use two vocalists and a saxaphone, along with guitar, bass, keyboards and drums. Chas Smash has taken a more involved part with the performance as second vocalist to Suggs, both of whom sing and dance like there was no tomorrow. By the end, they invited the crowd to skank around the packed stage. (And the dance floor was still packed more than ever.)

*Bedders; Chris Foreman, guitar; Dan Woodgate, drums; Graham McPherson "Suggs," vocals.*

# CONCERTS

**The Clash** 3/10, Motor City Roller Rink, Detroit

On this last show of a brief, seven-city tour, The Clash played a benefit for Jackie Wilson, a 60s star who is now lying at the brink of death, penniless. Joe Strummer said that when The Clash heard that Wilson could not afford to keep his life support machines running, they wanted to do something. (Something more than Ted Nugent, who timely appeared at their dressing room before the show. "Get a haircut" is what the band told him, refusing to let him come on stage. A good move by The Clash, although "the Nuge" can somehow draw giant crowds. Well, let him give a benefit show himself.)

Opening acts for the evening were Mikey Dread, the famous Jamaican DJ, and Lee Dorsey. The show was DJed by Britain's own Scratchy. Then Mikey Dread took over the controls. Beginning with some outstanding but basic dub, he progressed to singing to the melodies and rhythms assembled on tape. The cuts included some from his previous recordings and some new ones. The crowd was completely caught off-guard and hostility grew. Of course, this type of presentation is not the customary rock show. But Mikey Dread put on a tremendously awesome show in spite of the reaction.

Lee Dorsey was an important figure in the early 60s, with several Motown oriented hits. He was well received by the crowd. He moved around quite a bit, although recovering from two broken legs from a motorcycle accident. His big single, "Working in a Coal Mine," was an anticipated highlight.

The Clash opened with "Clash City Rockers" and "Brand New Cadillac." Micky Gallagher joined in on keyboards for the rest of the show, starting with "Safe European Home," and moving to the new Lp with "Jimmy Jazz," "London Calling," "Guns of Brixton" and "Train in Vain." During the whole show, different members sang, as on their recordings. Mick Jones and Paul Simonon performed some solos. This variety of vocalists and styles added to the enjoyment. They moved into a set of older tunes, including "Protex Blue," "Hammersmith Palais," "I Fought the Law" (with Pearl Harbor jumping onto stage), "Spanish Bombs," "Police & Thieves," "Clampdown," "Stay Free," "Wrong Em Boyo," "Complete Control," and ending with "Garageland." Mikey Dread accompanied the band on the encore of (→ 20)

# XTC

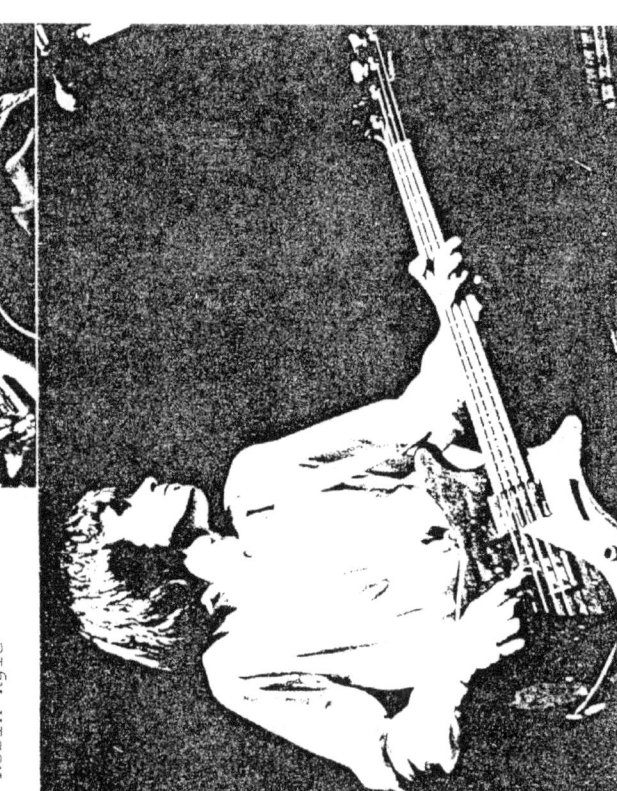

(Continued from last issue) When asked what he does to keep busy while on the run, Andy Partridge explained that he likes to read books of facts. "Facts are wonderful things." He asked if we could get him a copy of The Ticket That Exploded by William Burroughs. Instead, we gave him Roosevelt After the Inauguration, a Burroughs book he had not seen before.

*Andy Partridge →*
*Colin Moulding ↓*
*Pix: Robin Kyle*

TALK TALK

# XTC

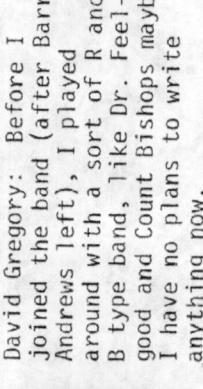

Clockwise: Colin Moulding → Andy Partridge, Colin Moulding, Terry Chambers → Andy Partridge, Colin Moulding → David Gregory, Terry Chambers

Photos by Robin Kyle

David Gregory: Before I joined the band (after Barry Andrews left), I played around with a sort of R and B type band, like Dr. Feelgood and Count Bishops maybe. I have no plans to write anything now.

Terry Chambers: We are on a long bus tour of America. I really like it. America's different naturally because of its size but we have had a really good time over here. A lot of people in England do not realize that whatever happens to America is bound to affect us.

Colin Moulding: Do they actually shoot at you, if they don't like you in Texas?

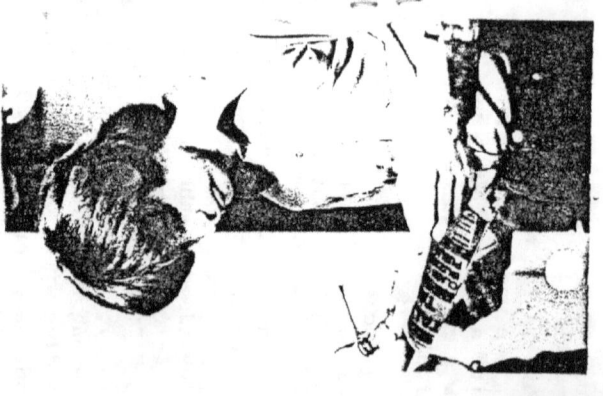

After the show, a video crew burst into the dressing room and asked to film a while and talk to the band. They set up and it was learned they were from a sick K.C. radio station, which has begun a short concert show on TV. When Colin Moulding, XTC's bass player and vocalist/writer asked the interviewer why their records were not played by the station, he was told they play them at home. "Probably got them for free," Moulding retorted. Several people repeated the fact that the local radio station, KJHK, has been playing XTC for quite a while now.

# SINGLE REVIEWS

**Elvis Costello and the Attractions I Can't Stand Up For Falling Down/Girls Talk** (F Beat: XX1)--This single is a must. The A side is an old Sam & Dave song (does anybody remember them? If not, go out and look them up.) which applies to what Elvis has gone through in the past year. It's exciting and at the same time it reaches you on an inner level.

Now the B side is a song that outdoes the other two versions on the market (Dave Edmunds & Linda--who?--Ronstadt). It does not move as fast as the other two but the music (slow and twisted) gives it a more sinister meaning. If you have the album, then get the single or vice-versa. --VS

**Magazine A Song From Under the Floor Boards/Twenty Years Ago** (Virgin: VS321)--Another single from one of my favorite bands. This time they pull a fast one and slip in something totally unexpected. On the first listening of this single I was too quick to judge it in the context of what they had done before. It was a mistake because this single ranks right up there with the best things Magazine have done. "A Song From Under the Floor Boards" is a cold statement of a survivor in a cold today. The lyrics will chill you, but at the same time it does give hope. (At least there are survivors.) The music is as important with Barry Adamson laying down one of the most infectious pieces of bass work that I have heard in a long time. An added irony is that the song even faintly reminds one of The Beatles.

The B side is even harder to adjust to. The synthesizer work of Dave Formula reminds one of a scream of some damned thing from the nether regions. All in all, a great buy. Look for their 3rd album which will be out soon. --VS

**Stiff Little Fingers At the Edge/Silly Encores, Autumn 79** (Chrysalis: CHS 2406)--The boys from Ulster have made a comeback. This single definitely proves that they are still a vital force in Rock and Roll (I never had any doubts). The vocals are not quite as raw but the playing still has the punch. The B side is a bit slower, kind of an old pub song and a Christmas greeting. It may (→ 15)

# SINGLE REVIEWS

(Continued from p. 14) not be for everybody's tastes but, then again, nothing is. Not the best thing they have done but a move in the right direction. --VS

**The Tea Set Parry Thomas/ Tri-x Pan** (Waldo Records:PS 006)--Nice picture sleeve, interesting sound. The lyrics of "Parry Thomas" are reminiscent of the old Hot Rods to Hell epic songs that were popular in the late 50s and early 60s in America (at that time it was cool to die in a fast car). But the structuring of the music and the vocals fits nicely into the stream of modern music, coming out of England nowadays. Slightly electronic in sound but infectious. The B side, "Tri-x Pan," is a silly little song (almost a commercial) for Tri-x Pan-- nothing important to say but a nice way of saying it. The Tea Set are a good pop band (nothing wrong with "good pop"), which I hope to see more of in the future. --VS

**Cockney Rejects Bad Man! New Song** (EMI: EMI5035)-- Sham 69 with more energy (is that possible?). The Cockney Rejects are one of the few bands that carry the sound of 1977 (nostalgia time) and make it fresh. The vocals are screamed out at you (you can almost see the finger waving in your face). Co-produced by the Sham Man himself (J. Pursey), these boys are survivors (rumors have it that their new album is really a knock-out)--the single is fast, loud and hard to stand still to, a good sign for this day and age. We may never get to see them live in this area so the records will have to do. --VS

**Silicon Teens Judy in Disguise/Chip 'n Roll** (Mute Records: Mute004)--"Judy in Disguise" was originally done by John Fred and His Playboy Band. It was a great dance tune then and the Silicon Teens still do a good job of it. They manage to retain the purposeful stupidity and good time feeling of the 60s version, but at the same time restructure the instrumentation (they are basically a keyboard band). It is nice to see a band that go the electronic way but do not take the gloomy, sensitive artist "pose" that is so prevalent among the rank and file electronic rock followers. The B side, "Chip 'n Roll," was penned by Carry Least, the (→ 16)

## SINGLE REVIEWS

(Continued from p. 15) Teens producer, and is a straight fun time tune that just carries on like a merry-go-round--good things from the Silicon Teens. --VS

The Fall Fiery Jack/2nd Dark Age Psykick Dance Hall (Step Forward Records: SF 13)--The Fall used to be the darlings of the British Rock press but after a series of personnel changes (they change all the time) the praise turned to criticism (mostly unfounded). Mark Smith (the only original member) seems to be the target of the irate critics. It seems that his ego is the central focus of the trouble. This new single (three songs) may be the best thing they have released with the exception of the brilliant "Bingo Masters Breakout" and "PsychoMafia." They still retain their old sound (heavy rhythms and a sneering vocal) but The Fall have built upon it. A clearer overall sound helps and the lyrics (still dealing with the state of mankind) have been able to emerge a bit more; so the full implication of the songs comes through. The Fall have some disturbing and important things to say. --VS

MI-Sex Computer Games/Wot Do You Want (CBS Records: SCBS7985)--This band hails from Australia and this is their 2nd single. Something about them bothers me. It could be that this single just is not exciting. The A side is pleasant electronic fluff with a supposed "sinister" message about mankind being dominated by machines. Well, it does not come across. The flip is even more disturbing because it smacks of MOR rock with the required synthesizer thrown in so we know they are a techno-rock band. MI-Sex promise a lot but fulfil little. --VS

Chelsea No One's Coming Outside/What Would You Do (Step Forward Records: SF 14)--Poor Chelsea, they try so hard that you have to admire them. They have been around so long. Their 1st album was panned by the critics (I like it) and you hardly hear anything about them--they just seem to put out something every now and then. Their new one follows their same pattern; angry vocals and a Jam-like backup instrumentation. The lyrics deal with the political and social situation in England. They tread the line between becoming good and staying alright. --VS

## REGGAE REVIEWS

Dillinger Funky Punk (IF Records: 67273)--Dillinger has been one of the top DJ to emerge in recent years. This time out he uses a funk approach to broaden his power base. The reggae roots are still present, but not as up-front as usual. The beat is comparable to Dury's "Rhythm Stick"--a fast moving tempo. Although some of the verses might be a bit shocking, the album is quite lively and enjoyable. Rock to the music. --WB

Lone Ranger Barnabus Collins (GG Records: GG0021) On the Other Side of Dub (Studio One: SOC 5454).--One of the stars from last summer's Jamaican festival was The Lone Ranger, a DJ/toastmaster who has had several hit singles. The title cut, "Barnabus Collins," demonstrates the versatility of this artist (and the Revolutionaries). While both albums are filled with new sounds and approaches, I prefer Barnabus Collins. It is reported that he has signed a major contract, so we can expect to hear from The Lone Ranger in the coming months. --WB

Black Uhuru Showcase (D-Roy Records: DRLP 1003)--The Black Uhurus are currently the most popular group in Jamaica. They are three Jamaican males backed by the Revolutionaries. This is a debut album, featuring some of their recent hits, such as "Guest Who's Coming to Dinner," "Leaving to Zion," and "General Penitentiary." They have a fantastic sound, good harmonies, sure to become even more developed and established. Look for them. They have a string of impressive singles out also. --WB

Joe Gibbs & the Professionals African Dub-Chapter 4 (Joe Gibbs Music Inc.)--The latest in the series of dub Lps created at Gibbs Recording Studio. Although these ten tracks probably have been released in their earlier form, it all sounds new to my ears. If you have not been converted to dub yet, this is the record for you. And if you have, do not miss this. A superior effort. Good as background music or as a loudly vibrating force. --WB

## REGGAE REVIEWS

Dr. Alimantado It Cold In A Babylon/Nat King Cole-Bob Marley (Isda Records: ISDA SUS11)--Two toaster greats from the best dressed chicken in town. A good mixture of classic reggae guitar, floating bass, complex drumming, occasional echo and female backing vocals. --WB

Big Youth Progress (Nichola Delita)--In which Jah Youth continues his string of great discs. Possessor of arguably the best voice in reggae, the Youth has written nine of the ten tunes here, the highlights being "Red Dress Lady" (it is as funky as it sounds) and "Stepping Out of Babylon," a pretty tune featuring Rita Marley and Marcia Griffiths on backup vocals.

Big Youth continued to grow musically in the somewhat restrictive format of reggae. On Progress he works in horn charts that are unique and fit in well with his dubwise vocalizing. Superb backing from the usual JA session cats makes this a roots triumph for Big Youth. --RH

Dexy's Midnight Runners Dance Stance/I'm Just Looking (Oddball Productions: R6028)--The first single by new ska (?) band gaining popularity with support acts for Two Tone tours. Heavy use of brass carries them through. These are sort of soul songs--maybe--at least a unique sound. --WB

UB40 King/Food for Thought (Graduate Records: GRAD6)-- I hear they are great live--in fact, supposedly the best new reggae (not earlier era ska) band to emerge in England. On this, their first release the mood is pretty laid back. Too laid back for me. --WB

Barry Brown Mafia/Version (State Line)--One of the hottest things on the chart. Barry Brown sings about the Mafia with an excellent version. A bit basic perhaps but still very catchy. --WB

N Kojak Penetentiary/Version (N G.P. Rock/Version (N Kojak)--A superb song. Not going to the pen, great bass line, repetitive lyrics. The version really trips out. N Kojak is a great singer/artist who produces quality vinyl and deserves better distribution. --WB

Dillinger Disco Tek/Version (Gussie Productions)-- The expected Dillinger-type lyrical roll, not (→ 19)

(Continued from p. 18) exactly pro-disco. A very outstanding flip side. This instrumental features an organ, probably Ansel Collins. The guitars move in and out. The bass and tambourine set the stage and it all follows. Try to find this one. --WB

Black Uhuru Guest Who's Coming to Dinner/Version (Taxi)--One of their hit singles. Produced by Sly and Robbie. The lyrical harmonies are outstanding. Very crisp and clear. Uses one of those unsyncopated drum rolls. The version is excellent! Three Chicago reggae record stores were playing it when I was recently in them. --WB

Cairo I Like Blue Beat/Versian (Absurd Records: Absurd 7)--A lot of sax from this Manchester band. Good use of early ska techniques. Almost so sophisticated that it makes you wonder where they are coming from. At least it is quality work. --WB

Gregory Isaacs Rock On/Dennis Brown and Dillinger Jah Is Watching/Hustling (Ziggy Observer: FDP001)-- Quite a powerhouse combo of the cream of vocalists. The backing band plays a quite similar melody but the vocal styles of these three Jamaicans completely take over. --WB

Black Uhuru Shine Eye/D-Roy Band Licking Stick (D-Roy: DRD015)--("Shine Eye" features Keith Richard on guitar, but you can hardly hear or notice it. Good harmony progression. The flip features the organ of Ansel Collins in an instrumental rocker. --WB

Prince Far I Free From Sin (Trojan: TRLS175)--More Prophecy and Jah Praise from the gravel-voiced toaster Michael Williams, aka Prince Far I. One of the most distinctive voices in Reggae, the Prince delivers a tight album with the help of top JA Session players like Chinna Smith, Bobby Ellis, and Deadly Headly, with guitarist Sowell adding violin on a couple of tracks (violin?). Themes range from Rasta righteousness ("Free From Sin," "I and I Are The Chosen One") to the requisite reefer anthem ("Don't Deal with Folly") delivered with gruff delight by the Prince and anchored on the rocksteady percussion of Bongo Herman and Ras Millinack. Essential! --DC

# ALBUM REVIEWS

(Continued from page 4)

U.K. Subs Live Kicks (Stiff Records: Mail 1)--A poor attempt at representing the energy this powerful band generates. It was recorded in 1977 at the Roxy, before any demos or singles had been cut. Most of the 11 songs are available on their debut LP and various 7-inchers in vastly superior forms. The 25 minutes here are a flat, one-dimension sound with hardly any audible guitar (or enthusiasm), almost characteristic of many Roxy club concert recordings. Pass it up if you must, there is sure to be some new material out soon rather than more historic audio failures. --BR

Squeeze Argybargy (A&M Records: AMLH64802)--The 3rd album from this five-piece pop group. The opening tune, "Pulling Mussels (From the Shell)," is the highlight. Overall, the album is very tight and planned. The changing arrangements and use of three vocalists result in a more defined sound-image. It seems the looseness of earlier hits ("Cool for Cats," "Take Me, I'm Yours," and "Up The Junction") is gone at least on this Lp. Rather than concluding that they have become too cute for their own good, I hope that this exercise in rigidity has not overtaken their live performances. --BR

Original Mirrors Original Mirrors (Mercury: 9102039)--The debut album from a relatively new band. Very modern, up-to-date approach, drawing from all the current pop gimmicks. Probably appealing to too many. Electronic heavy metal at times. The whole album seems to move quickly along, including their cover of "Reflections." Talented musicians. --BR

Orchestral Manoeuvers in the Dark (Din Disc: DID2)--Paul Humphreys and Andy McCluskey are The Orchs. Their shows were unique, using backing tapes, no lead guitar, and combining "rhythm programming" with percussion, keyboards, bass and vocals. These ten songs, including "Electricity" and "Red Frame/White Light" from their singles, cover a wide variety of styles. Many fans and critics believe them to be the most creative of the new barrage of electronic music. Definitely they are perfectionists. --BR

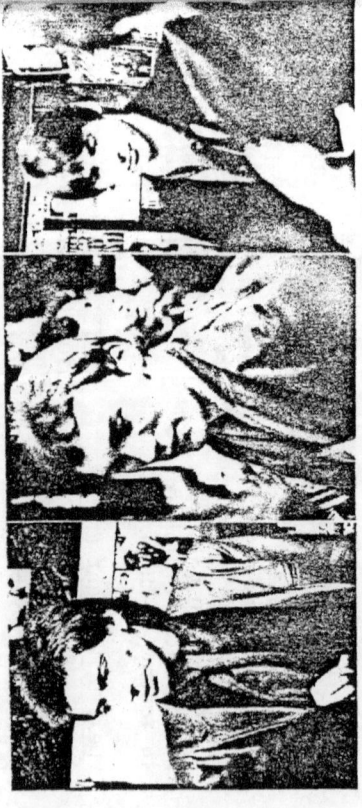

*The Jam at WaxTrax in Chicago. Photos by Bill Rich. Bruce Foxton-bass, Rick Buckler-drums, Paul Weller-guitar.*

(Continued from page 10) "Armagideon Time." Next was "English Civil War," "Tommy Gun" and "London's Burning." Some people left before the second encore which included "I'm So Bored with the USA." Although Joe Strummer's talking voice was gone and Topper Headon is recovering from an arm injury, these conditions were not evident in their performance. The Clash demonstrated the versatility and power which have helped them retain their high level of respect. If they are not the only band that matters, they are certainly one of the few who do matter. Their next tour, beginning in July, should bring them closer to the midwest--maybe even to Lawrence.

There are some reggae bands in Chicago. Two very different ones are The Skanking Lizzards and The New Era Band. I saw The Skanking Lizzards at the Cubby Bear, across from the Cub's Stadium. (Are they more than just white realtors who get together to play Wailers songs?) They did seem to "get into" the music they played.

The New Era Band might have formed in Chicago, but they are Jamaicans with experience. Currently recording their 1st album, they draw on cover versions for their live show. Chances are good that they will appear close soon. (More in future issues.)

New Talent Dept. Chicago seems to be bursting with bands. Epicycle are a young group of three modish guys with singles out. They can be seen at various clubs.
The Imports (aka Voids) are the newest talent to (→ 23)

## ALBUM REVIEWS

Cabaret Voltaire  LIVE YMCA 27/10/79 (Rough Trade: Rough 7)--Imagine faceless robots filing into a dank Y-gym to a metal heartbeat, and a droning percussion with an almost pagan sound to it and you have the opening of this live Lp. Where was this concert held? In what dimension? From the first track, "untitled," on it is an introduction into the bleak, metal and non-human world of the Cabaret Voltaire. The entire Lp has a frightening soberness to it, as if it were some kind of techno-ritual and there is no escape. Even the audience seems to understand what is occurring and respond with applause...they understand.

The lyrics are cold, sometimes revealing, as they drift through the electric vortex created by these robots. This is probably the closest we will ever come to a visitation from Cabaret Voltaire in this part of the universe. It is the music the machines make. It is just one song after another; sorry, no boring and overlong guitar or drum solos on this live album. This one is for us from the outer limits. Best songs: "Untitled;" "Nag, Nag, Nag;" "Expect Nothing;" and Baader Meinhof." --ET

Moebius & Plank  Rastakraut Pasta (Sky: 039)--A collaboration between two or Brian Eno's many cohorts; Moebius (half of Cluster) and Connie Plank (musician and producer/engineer of Ultravox, Liliental, and the Eno/Cluster Lps). Moebius's ambient approach to music and Plank's rock orientation creates an Lp with a variety of rhythmic textures. The engineering techniques are effective dub-wise. Echoing Deutsch vocals are drone-toasted across some tracks. Traces of Skysaw float in and out, building in intensity and then fading away; and what a heavy bass played by H. Czukay that sets the cogs in motion! Is it German-Techno-Dub, or Lee Perry in the 25th Century?--ET

Charles Bukowski  Bukowski Reads His Poetry (Takoma Records: TAK7073)--He is a dirty old man. He will tell you himself. He drinks his beers two at a time and enjoys his women the same way. He is also an author and poet, who has turned half a life spent among society's rejects into volume of the most incisive, despairingly funny prose ever written. He has style and as he says, "I've met more dogs than men with style--and very few dogs have style."
--DC

emerge. They are a four-piece with a 15-year-old singer, a 12-year-old drummer, 17-year-old guitarists (all brothers) and a 17-year-old three-string bass player. Their sound goes beyond British punk, with influences of Magazine, PiL and the Buzzcocks.

Reports from Denver say The Vague really rock out. They sport a lineup of two 14-year-olds and two 13-year-olds

## Local Scene

Even though the Lawrence area has not been a hive of overt activity the past month there are several items of interest to report. First off, the Lawrence Opera House, the main spot recently for virtually all big name new wave activity, is at the moment in a state of financial distress. So in the next few weeks those interested should show as much support as possible for the Opera House, by attendance at some of the local bands' shows and especially at the Iggy Pop and 999-Dickies show (those of you thinking about going to the Todd Rundgren show should forget about it). We at Talk Talk cannot begin to stress the importance of the Opera House to the music scene in this area. So get out there and help keep national new wave acts coming to Lawrence. Also they have started to show films there and one of the first held was that classic reggae film, "The Harder They Come," starring Jimmy Cliff and the music of some of the finest musicians coming out of Jamaica. After the movie Lawrence's own reggae-funk band, PBR (Pat's Blue Riddim) did a couple of sets. Their playing on this occasion was not particularly inspired but this writer caught them two nights later and they were much livelier. The Opera House is trying to get "Rockers," the new, acclaimed reggae film. The Wichita group, The Embarrassment, opened for John Cale in Tulsa last month. Look for: Abuse, Special Ed, Vomitones, and Fizz The Tab. Betty Two's, a new music club at 42nd & Troost in KC, will open soon. --ES

CONCERT SCHEDULE

March 26   Iggy Pop            Opera House
March 29   999-The Dickies     Opera House
April 12   Regular Guys-Abuse-Vomitones   Expo East Hall
                                          Topeka

TALK TALK   65

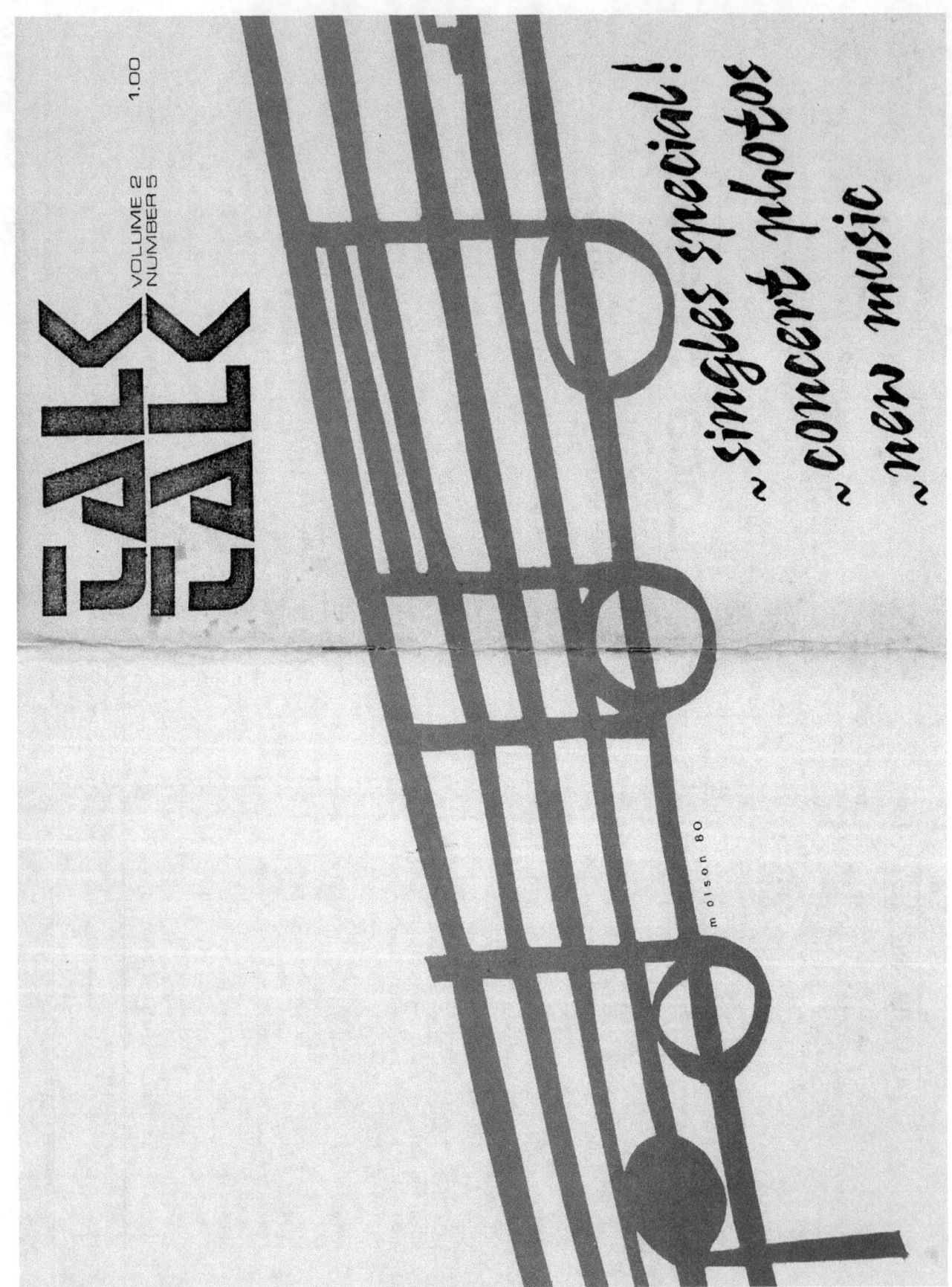

# CONCERTS

Talk Talk Vol. 2 No. 5/page 3

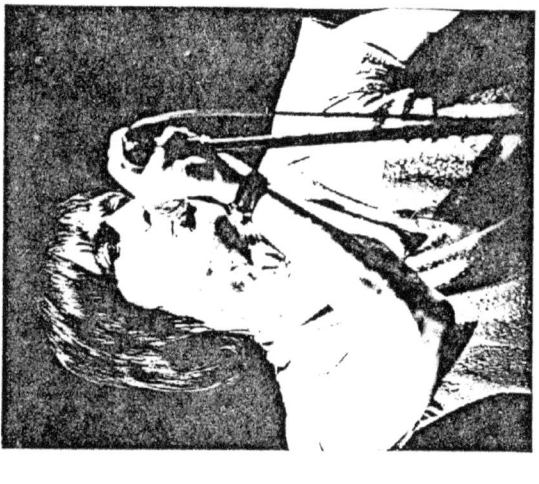

## IGGY POP
3/26, Lawrence Opera House

Iggy Pop is no stooge. After 13 years on the road in the U.S. and Europe, his hard driving rock and roll attack and sinewous psychodramatic delivery remain as distinctive and powerful today as they were ahead of their time in 1967.

Iggy (aka James Osterberg) may be the "Grandfather of Punk" but his recent Lawrence appearance gave new meaning to the phrase "not getting older, getting better." Iggy powered through an hour-long set that left the 600 or so in attendance screaming for more.

From his opening recitation of the Lord's (over)

---

## TALK TALK

Vol. 2, No. 5          May 1980          $1.00

The Midwest American Rock and Reggae Magazine

Concert Reviews: Iggy Pop. . . . . . . . . . .3
Album Reviews: Cockney Rejects,
  Stiff Little Fingers, The Cure . . . . . . .5
Concert Reviews: Nine Nine Nine and The Dickies . .6
Reggae Reviews: Barrington Levy, Trinity,
  Dennis Brown. . . . . . . . . . . . . . . .8
Single Reviews: The Beat, Madness, Dexy's,
  Bodysnatchers, Holly and The Italians . . .9
The Clean . . . . . . . . . . . . . . . . . .10
Single Reviews: Earcom 3, XTC, Bodies. . . . .11
Nine Nine Nine. *Photos by Brenda Haverkamp.* 12
Single Reviews: The Jam, Magazine, UK Subs,
  The Slits, The Teardrop Explodes . . . . .14
The Dickies . . . . . . . . . . . . . . . . .17
Reggae Singles: Linton Kwesi Johnson, X•O•Dus,
  Trinity, Toots, Burning Spear, Tappa Zukie 18
Single Reviews: John Foxx, The Mekons, Bauhaus, 20
Fad Gadget, Factory Sampler. . . . . . . . . .22
News and Views. . . . . . . . . . . . . . . .23

Editors: Bill R. and Eric S.
Contributors: VS, WB, ES, BR, ET, EH,
  CH, DC, RH, II, KD, JM
Photos: Robin Kyle, Brenda Haverkamp, Bill Rich
  Cover: Martin Olson

Talk Talk Publications
Post Office Box 36
Lawrence, Kansas
66044
USA

Copyright 1980 Talk Talk Publications. All rights reserved. Not responsible for unsolicited material. Any opinion expressed is solely that of the writer and not necessarily that of the magazine.

## ALBUM REVIEWS

<u>Cockney Rejects Greatest Hits Vol. 1</u> (EMI: ZONO 101)--The ultimate Punk Rock album of 1980. As you recall, the Rejects put out two singles last year (included in the 14-song Lp) spearheaded by Jimmy Pursey. He claims that this is the record Sham 69 should have put out but did not or could not. Some say they are better than Sham because they mean it. The Rejects certainly play with a force most acts never develop. They are a punk band and the fans can yell-along with the lyrics. Although their shows have a violent tinge, they claim to offer fun. But back to the album...it is well produced, the songs are excitable, and the quick pace never lets up. One cut even has a toaster intro. The Cockney Rejects are not the Son of Sham. They are going places and are one of the best youthful street bands to emerge recently. A good debut album, with promise for the future.--CH

<u>Stiff Little Fingers Nobody's Heroes</u> (Chrysalis Records: CHR 1270)--The second album from this group and while it does not have the immediate impact of the first, it still is a strong showing from one of the most promising bands around.

The major difference between their first Lp and this one seems to be production. On Nobody's Heroes, the sharp edges seem to have been honed away, leaving a smoother product. Now do not get me wrong. I like this album, more with every listening, and after such a powerful debut it would be hard to follow it up. The final consensus is that this Lp is still one of the finest of the new year and I will be looking for their next product in the future (hopefully soon).

Choice cuts: "Doesn't Make it All Right," "Wait and See," and "Tin Soldiers."--VS

<u>The Cure Boys Don't Cry</u> (Friction: PVC7916)--This is the first domestic release from the English boys. It contains their three singles, some cuts from their English Lp, and one new song. A good packaging job. Their earlier Lp has remained hard to get. Finally a compilation has been made available. The Cure are one of the best bands around. They use the basics--guitar, bass, and drums. They have recently added a keyboardist, and an Lp of new material is due for release soon, meanwhile, pick this one up. --BR

## CONCERTS

(Cont. from p. 3) Prayer through his quoting from <u>Hamlet</u> and patented snake dancing, The Ig proved himself a performer without peer (comparisons with Jagger be damned).

Musically, he drew heavily from his recent <u>Soldier</u> Lp, firing out "Take Care of Me," "Conservative," and "Loco Mosquito" like a man possessed. Oldies like "Sister Midnight" had the crowd swaying in delight, as did my favorite "Five Foot One," from his <u>New Values</u> album. (→ 21)

*Iggy Pop →*
*Michael Page, bass, Rob Dupree, guitar, Doug Bowne, drums, Iggy Pop, Ivan Kral, guitar and keyboards ↓*
*Photos by Robin Kyle*

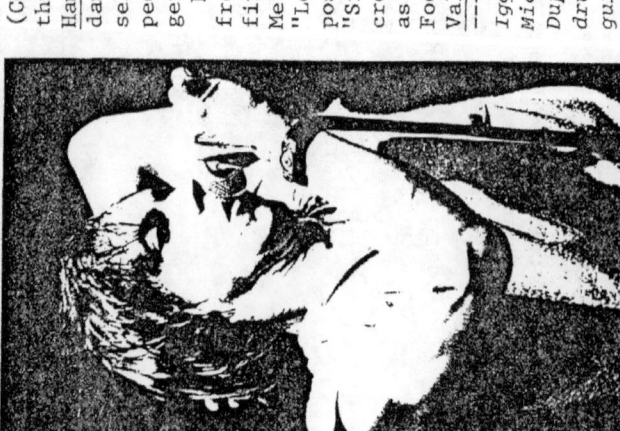

# CONCERTS

Nine-Nine-Nine with the Dickies 3/29, Lawrence Opera House

This show was an unknown factor for me. From the English press I had read, both bands were not supposed to be anything special. After the show, I did not think those who slagged these two bands knew what they were talking about.

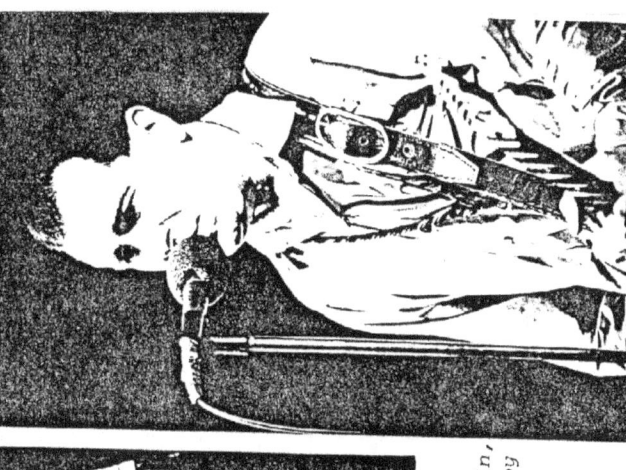

*Guy Days↑  Pics by Robin Kyle*
*Nick Cash→*
*Jon Watson, Pablo LaBritain, Nick Cash, Guy Days, Pic by Brenda Haverkamp↓*

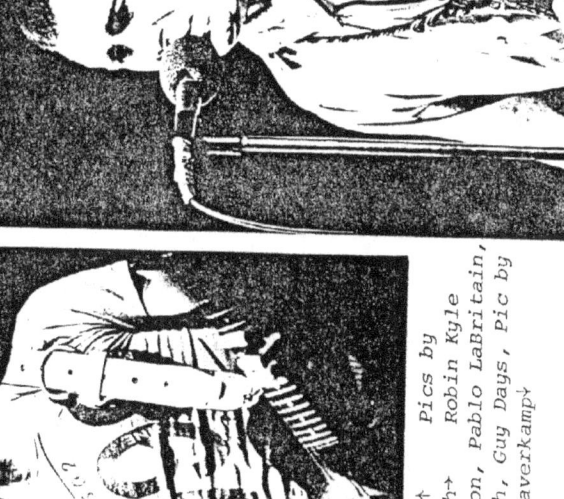

# CONCERTS

(Cont. from p. 6)

The Dickies opened the show announcing that "We're Punk Rock" to the cheers of the crowd. During their 45-minute set, they played fast, loud and with a high energy-tongue in cheek persistence that kept their fans dancing. Each song was like a burst of M-16 fire aimed at taking prisoners of the people who had thought of them as just another three-chord band. Included in their set were several of their hits off their first two albums and several Ep's-singles. Particular highlights were their covers of the Moody Blues' "Nights in White Satin," and the "Banana Splits Song."

The Dickies may not change the world of music with their brand of Ramomisque pinhead Rock but they will provide a good time to those who come to enjoy themselves and is not that what Rock and Roll's all about anyway?

The second part of the evening was a fitting topper--the icing on the cake, so to speak! The crowd, warmed up by the Dickies, were bouncing around the main floor waiting for 999. The wait was not too long and well worth it because when the band did take the stage they literally took the house by storm. Nick Cash's snarling vocals came across much better live than on vinyl. His singing live came from deeper down-- closer to the heart--so together with the music hitting the crowd like a sledgehammer. This was the post- "punk"--"New Wave" promise of powerful, intelligent Rock n Roll being fulfilled.

Live, Nick Cash left the meat of the guitar-playing in the capable hands of Guy Days. But occasionally he would pick up his telecaster (he could play as well as he sang). Overall they never let up on their energy level, hopping all over the stage in a musical frenzy. Jon Watson, especially, stood out with his crewcut pate and gaunt features (just from his looks I would not want to leave him alone with any little girls) and in the background, setting the pace, was drummer Pablo LaBritain. This is the first major tour he had been on with the band since his accident over a year ago (he got drug behind a van and shattered his arm).

In the course of the performance, 999 ran through about two-thirds of their new album, The (→ 19)

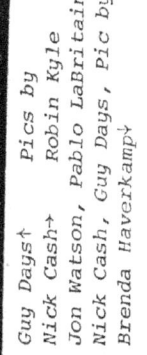

## REGGAE REVIEWS

Barrington Levy Englishman (Live and Learn Prod.: JL 003)--An album which is very hard to come by but well worth the effort. This is much stronger than Levy's last, "Bounty Hunter." Prince Jammy has engineered a beautiful combination of bluebeat and very rockers. The bass (Errol Holt) is slow and thick but much softer than "Bounty Hunter," the voice is bright and covered, creating a sheen which enhances rather than detracts from the album. And what an album! With Holt are Earl (Chinna) Smith, Ansel Collins, and Carlton Davis playing together flawlessly, song after song. No filler. Barrington's songs are all very hot and his singing tops them. Very fast roots and very slow roots come together to create poverbial reggae. --II

Trinity Rock in the Ghetto (Trojan: TRLS170)--A very strong, though short, album from Trinity, a singer in the style of Roy Beckford. Trinity is, however, much mellower and with Linval Thompson's high, bright production the album seems safe, but it is very deadly. The song, "Rock in the Ghetto," flows along easy but catches you by surprise about the time the roto-toms dub in double time. Lots of quiet hooks. "Pope Paul Dead and Gone" begins as a tribute to the Pope and his immediate successor (Thank God they found a new, improved, longer-lasting Pope) and ends accusing Paul of tricking the people with false hopes. At one point, his cries turn to laughter, "Rasta, give praises!" In fact, "Rock in the Ghetto" is Trinity's answer to false and unrealistic hopes; an attempt to make ghetto life musical and, perhaps, meaningful. "Try to sweat up your brow, you must be brave." --II

Dennis Brown Joseph's Coat of Many Colours (DEB Music: DEB 9523)--The latest album from this talented artist opens with "Slave Driver" by Bob Marley and then moves into eight originals, ending with "Man Next Door" by John Holt. It was recorded in various Jamaican studios with an assortment of quality musicians--as one would expect from Dennis Brown. He plays some guitar himself this time, besides adding his smooth vocals. This Jamaican pressing has also been released on the English Laser Records label, adding to its accessibility. He is currently on a British tour promoting this release. --WB

## SINGLE REVIEWS

The Beat Hands Off...She's Mine/Twist and Crawl (Go Feet: FEET 1)--This is the second release of this group --the first on their own label. They are a six-piece --three black, three white, male band. Saxa, the 50-year-old Jamaican saxophonist, blends in well with both musical styles The Beat use--the happy energetic and the intense metallic. Their constant 4/4 rhythm (Oh?) is dependable and familiar, but also might limit their future. The band consider themselves to be calypso-punk fusion, not ska. "Hands Off" concerns three males telling each other to leave a girl alone. It moves fast. The flip features good toasting. This single is also available on a 12-incher in extended length. Get one or both! --CH

Madness Work Rest and Play Ep (Stiff: BUY71)--This four-cut EP begins with a remix of "Night Boat to Cairo," on the Lp. "Deceives the Eye" is an involved tale of past sins, shoplifting, with a good, full, fast moving sound. On side two, "The Young and The Old" is a rollercoast dittie and "Don't Quote Me On That" is influenced by the attention and misrepresentation the press creates. Good vocal echoes. A good record from the rockingest sound around. --BR

Dexy's Midnight Runners Geno/Breakin' Down The Walls of Heartache (EMI: R6033)--The second single from this band finds them sticking to their full brass and multi-harmony routine. They use a fast and steady beat which might seem basic in places. Their Stax-soul orientation separates their sound from the ska-pack. --WB

The Bodysnatchers Let's Do Rock Steady/Ruder Than You (Two Tone: CHSTT9)--This is the first release from the latest ska band. If you know that this female group is just developing, you might be less critical of their attempt. But maybe that is not a good enough excuse. It seems pretty normal sounding, very repetitive and derivative, as one might expect. --CH

Holly and the Italians Tell That Girl to Shut Up/ Chapel of Love (Oval Records: OVAL 1016)--Holly and Company accompanied The Selector on a recent tour in England. The crowd was not very (→ 20)

# THE CLEAN

The Clean. Photo by Bill Rich
Mark Waltrip, Jay Francis, Todd Kitchen, Shawn Kelly
*Drums     Guitar    Bass, Vocals  Keyboards, Vocals*

**Shawn:** The earliest tales of the Clean ... all we played were the Beatles, Stones, and Who. That was like a year and a half ago. Everybody else joined later.
**Todd:** I joined in June or July.
**Shawn:** And Jay joined in about October and Mark in September. We have kept the same lineup for the past five months.
**Todd:** I'd just moved to Lawrence and saw an ad in a record store: Guitarist wanted for rock and roll band. I brought my guitar and amp to the house. At the time Shawn was in Hawaii, so it was just me and Chuck Mead.
**Shawn:** Of the Fizz Tabs now.
**Todd:** Yeah. There were a couple of others, drum and bassist. Then Shawn came back and joined the band or rejoined the band. We played the Elks Club. The drummer couldn't keep a steady beat. So we got rid of him and got Mark. We played at Off the Wall Hall for a handful of people. Chuck was playing bass and I was playing the guitar. Then Chuck quit, Jay joined and I switched to bass. And it's been the same ever since.
**Jay:** I've been in and out of The Clean since it began. I met Shawn in high school. (Continued on p. 15)

## SINGLE REVIEWS

**Earcom 3** (Fast Product: Fast 9)--Side 1. USA:NoH Mercy: My favorite tracks on this compilation. The band consists of a lead female vocalist and a drummer. It is hard biting and moves along like Gangbusters faintly reminiscent of old Teenage Jesus and The Jerks.
Side 2. Britain:Stupid Babies: Two cute novelty pieces that are fun to listen to every now and then but I seriously doubt anything will come of them (maybe Lawrence Welk needs a child act?).
From Chorleg: A haunting number that reminds me of PiL. Bass guitar and percussion with vocals and echo effect. Simplistic but effective.
Side 3. W Germany:Deutsch Amerikanisch Freundschaft: More metal machine music from the Germans. This cut makes me think that they still suffer from war guilt. Oppressive but listenable.
Side 4. USA:The Middle Class: Hoy, Hoy minimalistic punks. Songs that are short and almost powerful. They could go somewhere, or then again . . . Earcom 3 is not as successful as #2 but good to have around. What will 4 be like? --VS

**XTC Wait Till Your Boat Goes Down/Ten Feet Tall** (Virgin: VS322)--Can Andy Partridge do no wrong? Another tune from XTC's main songsmith and another winner. This one is a slower number, a bit reminiscent of "Life is Good in the Greenhouse." Andy's distinctive vocals are the highlight here as he slides uncannily from pitch to pitch over a backing track that sounds, in turn, like Jamaican dub and the Beatles. It is a synthesis that few can make work, but Partridge makes it look easy. --RH

**The Bodies Art Nouveau/ Machinery** (Waldo's Records: H5007)--An excellent single from a relatively new band. These boys seem able to mix the current trend of heavy electronic with a fine blend of traditional Rock n' Roll. Their message is depressing --about alienation, and the death of the world. Negative attitudes seem to be in fashion nowadays. I just hope to see more of their band. This single is strong, but what of their other material? Buy this if you can and remain open, they might take things by storm. --VS

# NINE NINE NINE

Nine Nine Nine formed in 1977 when the Punk movement was beginning to expand and also became more defined thanks to Malcolm M. The scene was much different and young then. When asked to categorize their sound, Nick Cash explained, "We think of ourselves as playing new music, not punk or new wave or power pop."

When they broke into the business, from hit singles and unique performances, their fans were the punks. The band has stayed basically the same--hard driving guitars and drums.

999 has a new single coming out this month. The B side includes two live cuts.

"The English press seems to care more about your politics than your music."

"The mod revival? It's come and gone. The media is flogging it out."

On the American scene: "We haven't found the coasts so different from other areas. We notice certain regional similarities."

# SINGLE REVIEWS

The Jam Going Underground/ The Dreams of Children (Polydor: POSP113)--The A-side is a strong song in The Jam tradition with added orchestration. "The public wants what the public gets," sings Paul Weller angrily/intensely. The B-side is a bit slower. The best thing about this release is the added live single of "Away From the Numbers," "The Modern World" and "Down at the Tube Station at Midnight." Very good versions and a valued addition to anyone's record pile. --CH

Magazine Thank You (Falettinme Be Mice Elf Agin)/The Book (Virgin: VS328)--An eerie cover of the Sly Stone favorite backed with a spoken story. A different approach from most releases for sure, showing Devoto and Co. continuing in their unpredictable arty manner. The new album should follow soon, likely with surprises. --CH

UK Subs Warhead/The Harper-Waiting for the Man (Gem: GEMS 23)--The throaty moans of Charlie Harper inform us the end is near with deep drums and occasional guitar licks. He plays a haunting harp on the flip before launching into the Lou Reed classic. --CH

The Slits In The Beginning There Was Rhythm/The Pop Group Where There's A Will There's a Way (Rough Trade: RT 0039)--The Slits are a very atypical group. Their Cut LP showed a customary song format in use. But these girls do not play as such live. As with this tune, they flow along with occasional guitar chords, repetitive drum patterns, whine/wail vocals and minimal layering. Their main concern is rhythm, as this song relates. They actually just warm you up for the flip side. The Pop Group display a lot of rhythm, too. This cut is one of their more melodic attempts, with a great funk feel. Their militant ideologies can almost be ignored. A good release from Rough Trade. Maybe it will not be enjoyable to everyone's ears. It is to mine. --WB

The Teardrop Explodes Treason/Books (Zoo Music: CAGE008)--An acoustic-sounding quartet in the vein of Echo and the Bunnymen (both are on the Zoo label). The Teardrop has a more direct approach to their music, however, no vocal harmonies and a bigger punch musically (→16)

---

# THE CLEAN

(Continued from page 10)
Shawn: I forced him to buy his first guitar, for ten dollars.
Jay: Then I bought a Les Paul and was immediately in the group. I was thrown out because I couldn't keep a blues change. Then I joined again, I've been kicked out about three times. I knew if I just kept working at it, I could do it.
Mark: I met Todd and he mentioned the band he was in needed a drummer. Within a week, I was playing. When we played Off the Wall Hall, I wasn't so gung ho on it. After Chuck quit, we got Jay and started practicing and came up with some new songs. Every new song I heard I didn't like, I couldn't get the drum parts. But then they evolved and changed with time. The final product that we've been working with since seems a lot better than they did at first. I think we're a lot more definite now because we've got some original material and confidence.
Shawn: It's important to note that we had no original material at all before the form we're in now. Nothing ever came together.
Todd: Shawn and Jay are the songwriters. But my influences are evident. Some of the songs Shawn would just come down and say, "here's the whole song" and show it to us and Jay would usually tape record something. They usually change.

TT: Have you played outside of Lawrence?
Shawn: We haven't had any opportunity to...
Todd: We'd like to. We don't want to stay in Lawrence at all. We'd like to play other places and we will.
Mark: Money kind of limits us.
Todd: We've been trying to build up money for the band. Instead of paying everybody, we keep a common fund so we can make posters and so we can get tapes to show our material.
TT: So what else do you guys do besides "The Clean"?
Todd: We're part of the local scene. We're all KU students, some with jobs.
Shawn: We're part of the local scene. We take ourselves serious, but not too serious. We feel like we're a band to contend with.

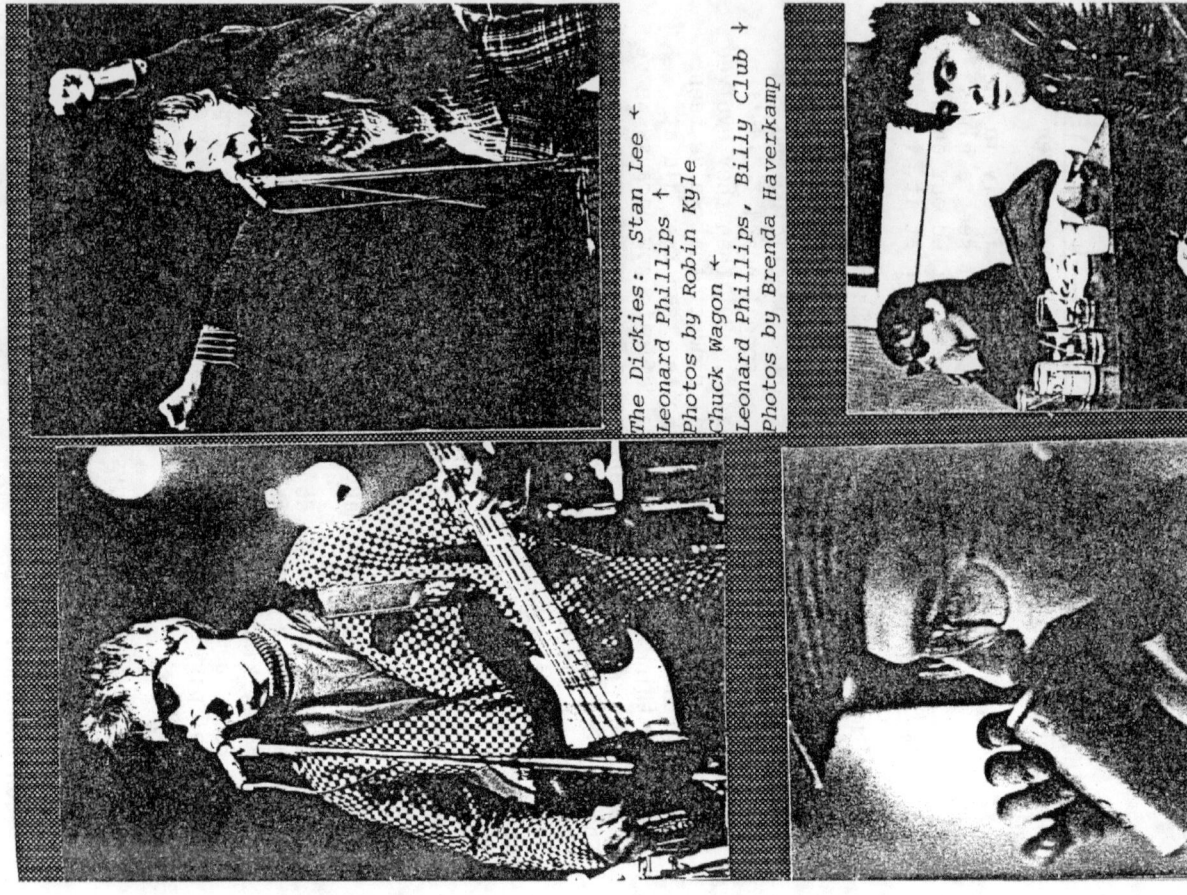

*The Dickies: Stan Lee +
Leonard Phillips +
Photos by Robin Kyle
Chuck Wagon +
Leonard Phillips, Billy Club +
Photos by Brenda Haverkamp*

# SINGLE REVIEWS

(Cont. from p. 14) separate these two bands. The 60's plastic keyboard sound and acoustic guitars create flashbacks of psychedelia. The lead vocalist sounds very much like David Bryne, as he sings about lies and lost love. The B side is a puzzler, a rendition of Echo and the Bunnymen's "Read It In Books." The credits for this song are Ian McCulloch (one of the Bunnymen) and Julian Cope (of Teardrop). My question: Is Julian Cope Echo? --ET

Deutsch-Amerikanisch Freundschaft Gewalt/Kebab-Träume (Rough Trade: Mute 005)--D.A.F. is a five-man band from the BDR, who have recently moved to the UK and signed with Mute (Rough Trade). This is their debut single, since the release of Earcom #3 on which they also appear, doing "Ich und die Wirklichkeit." D.A.F. is a band with a political message, you could almost label them Marxist. The A side, Gewalt (violence) begins with a synthetic cacophony of electric tension, anonymously droning bass and heavy breathing, like that of someone fleeing. The drums come crashing in and then it is a psychedelic blitz. Over the sonic guitar attack, lead vocalist Gabi Delgado Lopez shouts, "Gewalt!" This song seems to capture the violence of RAF, IRA, or even a police attack. It demonstrates the force or violence that rival political factions use to get their messages across. The B side, "Kebab-Träume" (detente) is a song with references to the DDR and the Soviet Union. The refrain is "Deutschland, Deutschland alles ist forbei" (In Germany it is finished). D.A.F. reflect on the economic, social, and political troubles of the BDR. D.A.F. has a very interesting sound and it is due to each member of the band. Ludwig Hass's synthesizer is used sparingly but effectively. Michael Kemner's bass has a bouncy, jew's-harp sound to it. Wolfgang Spelmann on guitar is comparable to the amphetamine-style of Mayo Thompson. Robert Görl is on drums and Gabi Delgado Lopez is the lead vocalist. If you have not guessed by now, the vocals are in German. This is Teutonic rock and roll at its best. Das ist alles. --U-Man

# REGGAE SINGLES

Linton Kwesi Johnson De Black Petty Booshwah/ Straight to Madray's Head (Island: WIP6554)--A new LKJ single with an echo-filled flip side version. The song uses a basic progression utilizing about five chords and notes. I am unsure of the exact nature of the story Linton tells, but he does not "side with the oppressor when the going gets rough." It could become an anthem of the struggle. Seen.--WB

X•O•DUS English Black Boys/See Them A'come (Factory Records: FAC11)--I have not heard of these guys before seeing this 12-inch...on Factory no less! They keep a good reggae rhythm, especially the upbeat guitar. The lead vocals are real smooth and the backing harmonies blend in softly. Both songs are soft and soothing--not sweet soul. A good release. --WB

Trinity Owner Fi De Yard (Crystal Records)--Produced and co-written by Derrick Harriott. Great percussion and Trinity's dark, lusty voice are featured on this JA single. Derrick's recording of Trinity is mellower than, say, Linval Thompson's production of Trinity's latest album, "Rock in the Ghetto." Good somnambulistic ganja-rock. --II

Toots and the Maytals Chatty, Chatty/Turn It Up (Island Records: WIP6544) --This new single from Toots and the boys just reaffirms that he is the best vocalist in reggae music today. After an uneven album, Pass the Pipe, Toots' direction seemed unsure. But, now with these excellent roots tunes he is back on the right track. Rocking and carrying the listener along. It is hard to sit still with this single on the turntable. --VS

Burning Spear Roots Mix (VP Records: 45)--A dubwise remix of two Winston Rodney movers, "Institution" and "Natural," Roots Mix drips with dread. If only they would reissue "Lion" in a similar fashion! --D Cool

Tappa Zukie Revolution/ Version (Stars)--The theme is the time for revolution is here. The vocal style is the usual and the backing track floats in and out. A nice approach. --WB

# CONCERTS

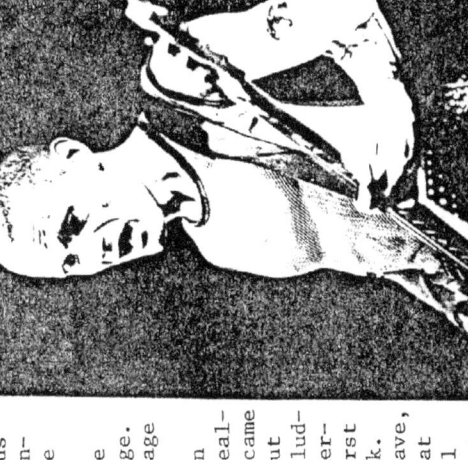

*Nick Cash, Guy Days ↑, Jon Watson → Pix by Robin Kyle*

(Continued from p. 7)

Biggest Prize in Sports plus a few oldies. Nick Cash invited the crowd to join the band on the stage during "Homicide" and the audience was only too happy to oblige. After the band left the stage their crowd made it clear they would not stand for an end to the festivities. Realizing this fact, the band came back for not one or two, but three sets of encores, including a great version of "Emergency," which was their first hit single a few years back. They finally took their leave, promising to return and that they were going to tell all their mates in England to come to Lawrence. It was a fitting end to a fantastic evening. One I hope will be repeated-- the sooner the better!

# SINGLE REVIEWS

(Cont. from p. 9) responsive, i.e., hostile, at times so Holly and The Italians dropped out. How anybody could be stupid enough not to appreciate this single, let alone the band, is beyond me. Holly and The Italians are a great band and "Tell That Girl to Shut Up" beats out anything The Pretenders have ever done (their closest comparison). This single rocks, moves--makes you want to move. Get it --get it--get it... --ES

John Foxx No-One Driving/ Glimmer/This City/Mr. No/ Metal Beat (Virgin: VS338) --This double single is better than his album. Ideas are compressed. Presented in a single format, each song shows a strength, a cohesive whole that was lacking from the album. Fluid music for those who want to grow out of the pablum of Gary Numan. Worth the trouble. John Foxx may make it on his own yet (even if part of this reminds me of "Tangerine Dream"). Strange, cold, lonely--perfect for a rainy night. --VS

The Mekons Teeth/ Guardian/ Kill/Stay Cool (Virgin: SV

101)--This double single set should dispel all notions that The Mekons are just Gang of Four clones. The Meeks arrive at a different sound this time out with the addition of a violin to the mix. It is not a scratchy, Raincoats-type of violin, but long, flowing solos that command the listener's attention. The best song of the four here is "Kill," with its funky rhythm and anguished vocals. There are a lot of parallels to the sound on this record (PiL, Ubu, etc.) but the Mekons have a habit of progressing in leaps and bounds and I doubt if they will sound this way for too long. --RH

Bauhaus Dark Entries/Untitled (Axis: AD3)--The third release from one of my fave bands. The A side originally appeared, although not in its entirety, on their first release, the 12-inch Bela Lugosi's Dead Ep (Small Wonder Records: teeny 2). Bauhaus are able to create a nervous kind of interplay between the guitar and drums and then spice it up with an occasional bass line. The lyrics show some dada influence and capture the essence of loneliness and the need for (→ 22)

# CONCERTS

(Cont. p. 4)

The band assembled to replace the original tour band includes some of the rockingest musicians around. The veteran of the scene is Ivan Kral, who switches from guitar to keyboards. For this show, his amps were too low. Rob Dupree, ex-Mumps, played lead guitar. The rhythm section included drummer Doug Bowne, who can be heard on the new John Cale live Lp and bassist Michael Page, recently with Chubby Checkers and Syl Sylvain's The Criminals. A good lineup that worked well with Iggy.

The music scene in Lawrence has been particularly jumping of late. The fact that a hot talent like Iggy Pop would come here at all is a statement about the persistence of hard core Rock-starved Midwest fans. The standard has been set-- demand no less and support live music in Lawrence.

*Iggy Pop photos by Robin Kyle.*

## SINGLE REVIEWS

(Cont. from p. 20) physical love. "Any lay suffices his dollar green eye." The B side is also catchy. A grating sandpaper guitar fading in and out and a solitary slapping percussion. In the midst of this, a voice cryptically speaks of a pocketful of posies!?

Fad Gadget Ricky's Hand/ Handshake (Rough Trade: Mute 006)--According to sources this is the second release from another kitchen band in the tradition of Crash Course in Science and Egg Hoover and the GE 3. Fad Gadget is basically a one-man band, Frank Tovey to be precise. On this single, he is accompanied by Daniel Miller on synthesizer and B.J. Frost doing a Choir Girl Effect. This single uses only synthetic sound sources. Tapes, synthesizers, and a Black and Decker V8 Double Speed Electric Drill are the credited instrumentation. The A side is a song explaining the hazards of blenders and the B side is kitchen-dub leftovers of the A side. The production technique separates each of the gadgets so that they can be individually heard. The sounds of tomorrow's kitchen today. --EH

Factory Sampler:Joy Division/Durutti Column (Fac 2) --Two previously unreleased cuts: "Digital" and "Glass" are on the A side. It is a rougher sounding Joy Division that is caught on this vinyl disc. The musical emphasis is placed on the seemingly electric drums and a resonant bass. The lyrics are delivered in a restrained monotone, giving them an alien feel. This is some of Joy Division's best material to date. The B side features the Durutti Column's "No Communication" and "Thin Ice." This is a continuation of the melancholy sounds of Vinny Reilly's guitar. The most interesting thing about this material is that unlike previous work, this stuff has vocals (provided by Colin Sharp). The lyrics are spoken rather than sung. They deal with social paranoias and attitudes towards the modern world and its current trends. It is a condemnation of the masses and their mediocrity. "There's a lot of strange people out there; a lot I wouldn't want to meet." To some this may be judgemental. I like it. --U-Man

## NEWS & VIEWS

*This issue is dedicated to the memory of the great late Jacob "Killer" Miller, who died in a car wreck March 23 in Kingston, Jamaica. As lead vocalist in Inner Circle, formed in 1973 with the Lewis brothers, his songs were social statements about life in the Jamaican ghettoes. He was an influential artist who helped shape the development of reggae.*

---

Duchamp-Duchamp, a young KC band with lots of energy, played Hashinger Hall last week. At times their inexperience showed through but give them time.

---

Andy's Club South (4707 Troost, KC) had their grand opening last week featuring The Regular Guys. The club could become the only place booking new bands. Remodeling is occurring, and Andy, the owner, wants to give it a chance (money = success). This weekend, The Embarrassment, from Wichita, will make their KC premiere. And the next week, Thumbs are scheduled. Credit and congratulations go to Sum Thing Tu Du Productions, run by Craig and Pam Travitts, who are putting a lot of energy into this. Go and check it out.

---

33 1/3 Management, operating out of Topeka, is a new concert promotion company. Their first big show is April 12 at the Expo Hall at the Topeka State Fairgrounds with three to five bands, including The Regular Guys, Vomitones, and Abuse. They offer a much-needed service and want to work with other local bands.

---

It is benefit time in Lawrence, with the Opera House staging fund-raising shows to obtain capital to remain in business. It seems the banks do not want to renew/extend notes because the whole area might be leveled so a shopping mall can be developed. Off the Wall Hall, which is a couple of blocks away, faces a similar threatening future. Last week, they held a "No Mall At All" benefit to help finance some of the opposition forces. If either of these venues close, the area will suffer a serious setback. Hopefully, everyone will realize this and become involved before it is too late.

# TALK TALK

Vol. 2 No. 6  Special Summer Mini-Issue   $.50

The Midwest American Rock and Reggae Magazine.

TALK TALK

Editors:
Bill Rich
Eric Schindling

Contributors:
Rick Hellman
Jim Schwada
Plus: ET,
Daddy Cool,
VS, WB, CH,
KD, JM

Photography:
Robin Kyle
Bill Rich

Cover:
Mark Schraad

## Table of Contents

Album Reviews:
  Public Image Ltd. . . . . . . . . 3
  Photo: Iggy Pop . . . . . . . . . 4
News and Views . . . . . . . . . . 5
Reggae Reviews:
  Tappa Zukie, Mikey Dread. . . . . 6
  U-Roy, General Echo . . . . . . . 7
Local Scene: The Regular Guys . . . 8
Single Reviews: Selecter,
  Decorators, Ludas . . . . . . . .10
  Monochrome Set, Undertones, Love
  of Life Orchestra, John Cale. . .11
  Members, Richard Hell, Joy
  Division, Delta 5 . . . . . . . .12
Live: The Embarrassment . . . . . .13
Album Reviews: MX-80 Sound. . . . .13
Live: Thumbs. . . . . . . . . . . .14
Live: Abuse . . . . . . . . . . . .15

All contents copyright 1980 by Talk Talk Publications, PO Box 36, Lawrence, Kansas, 66044. All rights reserved. Any opinion expressed is solely that of the writer and not necessarily that of this publication. Subscription rate is $6.00 for six months. All articles, reviews and photos submitted for editorial consideration are welcome. Not responsible for unsolicited material. Address all correspondence to Talk Talk Editors, PO Box 36, Lawrence, Kansas, 66044.

---

Talk Talk Vol. 2 No. 6/page 3

# ALBUM REVIEWS

Public Image Ltd. Nubes and Recorded in Paris (Bootlegs) --There are currently a couple of unofficial recordings of live performances of PiL going around. Nubes is from a London show in 1978. The other one only states "Recorded Live in Paris when nobody was looking." They both concentrate on songs from the first album, Public Image, which still have not been released domestically. As one might expect from bootlegs, the quality is very bad, probably a result of using portable recorders. The important thing about these records is that they document the crowd reaction to PiL at a time when the band was trying hard not to be "pop stars," but rather to be anti-rock and roll.

Public Image Ltd. is a hard band to understand. The press has tried to explain, categorize and shelf them. The media attention of the Sex Pistols unavoidably focused on John Lydon and his musical activities. And from the beginning, PiL have been attacked. Their strange, unfamiliar electro-blends often alienate the masses, the recordings are musically and conceptually intricate. Their dedication to the studio results in a unique layered sound. The bass is deep and the guitar rhythm danceable. Lydon's lyrics are the highlights of the records.

Their second LP, Metal Box, released in the U.S. as Second Edition, shows the band moving to higher levels of expertise. The band has not really changed (except for the numerous drummer changes). But the media's attitude has. Nowadays, everyone loves these guys--basically for the same reasons they were hated. The critics have been trying to label PiL and influence the public's interpretation of their music. The band rarely perform. But finally they have begun an American tour. In preparation, John Lydon and Keith Levine were interviewed to death by all types of media personalities. Their shows have produced mixed feelings of enjoyment, torture, and boredom. It seems to make no difference to the band. They continue their dedication to this style and musical approach, which probably results in a greater impact than any other possible action. Just as the Pistols influenced the new music movement, Public Image offer an alternative approach to rock and roll. Many bands have been affected. John Lydon and company remain a force to contend with. --BR

# NEWS & VIEWS

The prize for the best unreleased Iggy Pop song goes to "One For My Baby," currently available only on bootleg recordings, such as the double live Heroin Hates You. The first three sides are a radio-broadcasted Pasadena show from late November, 1979 using the 79 tour band of Kral, Kruger, Matlock and James. The fourth side is a 1977 French show with the Sales brothers.

The song is a slow melodic blues influenced number, something which the Ig will probably sing when he plays cabarets in the very distant future. (When asked recently how long he planned to continue playing, he replied, "until I'm 80." We hope so.

Iggy has been resting in New York in recent weeks, following the end of his US tour. He plans to return to England soon, with his band, for more work.

*(Photo by Robin Kyle)*

The American television networks have recently shocked a lot of rockers by finally covering some of the major acts. Dick Clark's American Bandstand had on Madness and The Jam. Saturday Night Live had The Specials and Friday had The Clash. Plus, other shows have used videos of groups like The Dickies and Iggy Pop, to name a few. Why the sudden change? The watchful critic must be suspicious of such trends. Of course, there have always been the usual rock acts on the tube but it seems things are beginning to move.

Of the recent live shows, Madness gave Dick Clark a sample of their "nutty" antics and The Jam appeared bored. The Specials were a huge success—more stage action than Americans are used to being fed. And what could have been the best, The Clash, turned out to be the worst technical failure to date. The variety show they appeared on is basically an insult to humans, and one might have guessed that the production (sound quality, camera angles, stage set-up) would be substandard. But the band played very well. Where will it all lead? Dunno, but the networks are beginning to offer an alternative to their usual trash.

## REGGAE REVIEWS
## Blasts from the Past

Tappa Zukie: Living in the Ghetto (Stars: WF 543)--mon, this place is a mess." This is how Tappa Zukie starts out the title track on this intense Lp. Tappa Zukie and his music goes beyond Jamaica, beyond religion. He is concerned with people and their welfare. The rising above the negative attitudes and environments that keep people enthralled. It is not like he hits you over the head with his message but amidst the infectious rhythms and echoes he gets the point across. He is for the betterment of all people and why he has not gotten more recognition and a solid record contract in the States yet just goes to show that the money moguls are as tight-fisted as ever when it comes to reggae music. I hope you can find this album. I promise you, you will not be disappointed. (Distributed by Roots Music, 7747 Pembrooke Pine, Miami, FL, USA). --VS

Mikey Dread: Dread at the Controls (Trojan: TRLS 178) --This album is not exactly new, but it is good and therefore worth reviewing. Dread at the Controls was released late last year but it proves that he is perhaps one of the most innovative of the newer dub stars on the scene. Those who saw him on the recent Clash tour were impressed by the effort he made to really explain what reggae music is all about. In doing so, he hoped that with understanding there would be a deeper and wider appreciation (you do not have to agree with the religious aspects of reggae to enjoy the music).

Dread at the Controls carries the listener along with the heavy beat and the smooth over-dubbed vocals. The masterful craftsmanship that helps make this album a must for any reggae fan in part must go to the musicians that play on this album. The Revolutionaries are here, as well as a handful of others who comprise Jamaica's top session men. The rhythms make you want to get out of your seat and start moving your feet. A perfect album to play on the hot summer days ahead. --VS

## REGGAE REVIEWS
## Blasts from the Past

U-Roy Version Galore (Virgin International: FL 1019)--Fans of the distinctive reggae style known as "Deejay" will rejoice at the reissue of this classic lp by the master, U-Roy (Ewart Beckford). Author of the monster hit "Chalice in the Palace," U-Roy's manic rapping over taped instrumental "Versions" set the style for such DJ stars as Dillinger, Big Youth, and the ubiquitous I-Roy. "Version Galore" is an example of his early, ska influenced technique, a relaxed and thoroughly enjoyable groove. Check out "Your Ace from Space," "True Confession," and the title track "Version Galore" for a taste of DJ style at its best. --DC

General Echo Rocking and Swing (Manzie: DRSLP 001)-- This album is the first for General Echo, who is a Jamaican DJ popular with the dance hall scene. In the late 70's, he was reaching a peak with the local Jamaicans, so the General began recording. He helped change the style from soul or rock-steady to reggae, an important step in the history of reggae music. General Echo's main contribution to this recording is in the lyrical tone of the words he has written to accompany the rhythm tracks. His style can be compared with many toasters. Yet there are distinctions such as his usual four-note range and smooth delivery. This is a Channel One product. So the Revolutionaries plus others are some of the main track-layers. And, as usual, the music is exceptional. The rhythms seem to be different, not the typical tunes everyone seems to use. It sounds new and refreshing. --WB

# Local Scene

*The Regular Guys are one of the top local bands, playing frequently in Lawrence, Topeka and Kansas City. Earlier this year they released a four-song Ep. Talk Talk recently questioned the band which resulted in the following.*

Talk Talk: It seems that your lineup changes a lot.
John Odell: We like to keep a fluid makeup. It keeps things interesting. Brad is moving away. But The Regular Guys will continue to perform in one incarnation or another. We are going to focus on private parties and small bars. If we get the occasional big gig, we will do it. This summer is basically a time to write and get our thing together for a major assault by next fall.
TT: How does Mark Gilman fit in The Regular Guys now?
John O: He is a real source of inspiration to the rest of us. Mark is a great songwriter and we want to retain him in at least that capacity.
Brad Reid: And as an occasional guest lead vocalist.
John O: Right, as somebody who can be considered part of the band even if he doesn't play with us.
TT: So after Brad leaves, are you planning to become a three-piece?
John O: We might do that. We might try to add a keyboard player.

*The Regular Guys • Photos by Bill Rich*
*Dave Stucky, John Chiarello, Brad Reid, John Odell*
*John C. drums. Others share lead, bass and vocals.*

# Local Scene

*John Odell reading Talk Talk*

TT: How much material do you have now?
John O: When you talk about the basic, standard three 45-minute sets, we are about half covers and half original. We would rather do two sets of our own and one set of good time rock and roll. That's what we are working towards.
TT: How about your songs? Is anyone else writing now?
John O: Dave and I have another real hot one in the can. We wanted to write something a little more hard-edged and less "pop"-y. That one we will be playing soon.
Dave Stucky: Compared with other bands I've been in before, this has come a lot easier. The song John and I wrote, "Boulevard Blonde," we just did it one time at practice.
John Chiarello: I've been in a lot of bands and this has been the closest-knit one I've been in. And it's also the most fun band. I think that's why we have been kind of successful.
John O: From an outsider's view, it looks like a constant state of flux with people coming and going like Carolyn and Mark. At the same time, the core band is a real solid thing. That is why we can allow people to come and go. And that is why the band will remain. It is something bigger than any of us individually.
TT: What are your recording plans?
John O: I have a few things up my sleeve that haven't been worked out with the band yet. It will probably remain that way until we go into the studio. We won't perform them until it's recorded. Most of the stuff from our last record were first takes, basically. We can go in and run through it. Luckily, we have the kind of personnel who can work like that. It really helps to have John Chiarello, an excellent drummer.
TT: Will you use the same studio?
John O: No, we're going to a new studio. The last one was Chapmans. This time we're going to Sound Recorders. It's probably going to be self-produced by the band. We want to get a good, competent engineer, too. We are shooting for August.

82  TALK TALK

# SINGLE REVIEWS

The Selecter: Missing Words/Carry Go Bring Come (Two Tone: CHS TT10)--The first side of this single is on the album and was reviewed a few issues ago, so I do not have anything to add to the subject except to say it is an appropriate choice for a single. The flip is another matter altogether. The song itself was on the album but the main difference here is that "Carry Go Bring Come" is live on this 45. This version should dispell some nasty notions people seem to have about Pauline Black's voice not fitting in with this particular brand of music. On "Carry Go Bring Come," her voice blends in perfectly with the rest of the band's efforts. She is a good singer and I suspect that those who put her down might be suffering from some form of latent (dare I use the word) chauvinism. Who says a woman cannot sing this form of music as well as a man? I will allow for time to get used to it because The Selecter's sound is different in many ways than their other Two Tone brethren. But this single proves that live The Selecter are great, so, when they show up near you do not dare miss them. --ES

The Decorators: Twilight View/Reflections (New Hormones Productions: Org 5) --Pop for the eighties. "Twilight View" is a love song that carries one along with the rhythm and a lilting sax part. A song you would play for your girlfriend over the telephone. "Reflections" is more of an uptempo rocker but still retains the quality of the first side. These five boys are moving in a dangerous field but one that needs intelligent music like this. They manage to make good songs and avoid clichés. I wish them luck. --ES

Ludas: The Visit (New Hormones: Org 4)--This is a four-song, 12-incher. Ludas is a three-piece English band. The female vocalist adds to the sparce, jazz-like instrumentation. I am not totally sure what they are doing but the band sounds like they are attempting a jazz-fusion (but fusion with what?). The girl's voice reminds me of a mutated Flora Purim (who?). Not for everybody--I'm not sure yet if it is for me. Time will tell. --VS
(Continued on p. 11)

The Monochrome Set: The Strange Boutique/Surfing S.W. 12 (Dindisc: Din-18)-- I am not sure if I even halfway understand what these guys are trying to do. But it is some form of techno-electro-new music. The conceptual background goes right past me. This must be their fourth single or so, and an album is expected very quickly. These two cuts are not as good as "He's Frank," one of my all-time favorites. I like them better with each play. --CH

The Undertones: My Perfect Cousin/Hard Luck Again (Sire: 4038)--The latest from my fave Irish group does not have quite the punch of their last release, "You've Got My Number." The A side concerns teenage rivalry with a good beat and enthusiasm. The B side is repetitive, basically an instrumental ("Hey, Hey, Hey, ... Hard Luck" being the only words). But it is done in good style. The single ends with a mini-song--"Don't Want to See (You Again)." Well, I'd like to see them again! Also, their new album has been released already. I would like to see it, too. --WB

Sham 69: Tell the Children/Jack (Polydor: POSP 136)-- Two new anthems from these punks. The themes have something to do with spreading the word before things fall apart. Sham seem to have reverted to their earlier angry approach. You could probably live without this one, if you had to. --CH

Love of Life Orchestra: Extended Niceties/Beginning of the Heartbreak (Lust/Unlust Music: JMB 227)-- This is an interesting experiment featuring Peter Gordon and David Van Tieghem, plus assorted others, including David Byrne. Gordon does all keys and reeds. The A side is at times similar to a Sanford and Son theme revisited. Funky Jazz influenced. The end of the B side has a chorus sounding like Yes, of all things. But it seems that there is still some action in New York. --WB

John Cale: Mercenaries/Rosegarden Funeral of Sores (Spy Records: IR 9008)--This is the follow-up single to the Sabotage/Live album. "Mercenaries" is a different recording than the Lp's version. Some of the rough edges have been removed, resulting in a better (→ 12)

# CONCERTS

**The Embarrassment Live:** Andy's Club, April 4-5

This Wichita band's debut in the area was at times fantastic, and at other times weak-kneed. At their best, they build up an intense texture of sound that is reminiscent of Wire and The Mekons. They are developing strength and direction, which shows that with continued effort they can become one of the best bands to come out of the midwest in recent years. Some of their problems actually stem from their adventurous attitude. They build a song to such a peak that they have a hard time ending it and so it loses its power and flounders. Also, at times, the lead singer goes on verbal tirades, whether this is from being or acting drunk or a natural part of his stage presence is at the moment a mystery to me. Aside from this criticism, I found him to be a most engaging singer, fitting the flow of the music perfectly. Yes, The Embarrassment are a band that at the moment seem to be in a state of change. At worst, they are uneven; at best they are a band that are paving a path to the top. I wish them the best. (An added note: This show was the last to be held at Andys Club. The venue changed to 4719 Troost.) --VS

ʃʃʃʃʃʃʃʃʃʃʃʃʃʃʃʃʃʃʃʃʃʃʃʃʃʃʃʃʃʃʃʃʃʃʃʃʃʃʃʃʃʃʃʃʃʃʃʃʃʃʃʃ

**MX-80 Sound:** Out of the Tunnel (Ralph MX 8002)--This is not an easy album to listen to. It is challenging in the same way as a later King Crimson album or soem of the stuff by the labelmates, The Residents. MX-80 Sound is full of rough edges and harsh textures that do not sit easy on the ears, but reward repeated listenings. There is a pop sensibility underlying all the seeming chaos here. The group uses only guitar, bass, drums, and saxophone and they get some very interesting sounds from that line-up. Kind of like the first Roxy Music album with the vocals competing with the instruments to be heard. Best cuts: "It's Not My Fault" and "I Walk Among Them." --RH

# SINGLE REVIEWS

(Continued from page 11) cut. "Rosegarden" is an experimental, studio creation featuring Cale on vocals, bass and piano, accompanied by a rhythm machine. It could have blended in well on the album, although some listeners might be put back by it. But then there are a lot of tense people in regard to being "ready for war." --CH

**The Members:** Romance/The Ballad of John and Martin (Virgin: VS 333)--With this single, The Members might make a stab at regaining their title of the best white-reggae group. The title cut exhibits reggae guitar chops and the vocals flow along the underlying rhythms. The flip is a rocker--no reggae connections evident. Their second album should be available soon. From the quality of this release, I would say that they are on an improved progression. --WB

**Richard Hell:** Don't Die/Time; The Neon Boys: That's All I Know (Right Now)/Love Comes In Spurts (Shake Records: SHK101)--This is probably the last Richard Hell and the Voidoids single which will be put out. The flipside contains old (1973) songs with Hell, Tom Verlaine, and Billy Ficca, before they became Television. Hell takes credit for inventing punk rock. He considers these Neon Boys' cuts to be the first modern punk bands recorded. His influence cannot be denied. This is a worthwhile single, containing historical sounds, as well as the latest recordings. --CH

**Joy Division:** Atmosphere/Dead Souls (Sordid Sentimentale: SS 33002)--This is a limited edition French release which is outstanding because of the color folder packaging. The accompanying text is a bit of extreme rambling. Two previously unrecorded tracks are contained here and both are excellent cuts in the Joy Division tradition. These songs might be released domestically, so keep an eye out. The band is working on their second Lp and plan to tour the US soon. --WB

**Delta 5:** Anticipation/You (Rough Trade: RT041)--This is the second release from these guys and girls. The female vocals show similarities with the Raincoats, Slits, or Kleenex. --CH

# CONCERTS

Thumbs; LIVE at The Plaza East--4/18/80

The first concert/dance at the newly renovated Plaza East. Well actually it was not quite renovated. The promoters were forced to leave their original bar due to circumstances beyond their control; so, instead of letting the new music scene go down the drain they quickly switched venues and managed to pull it off.

Now, Plaza East does not have a New Music audience. As a matter of fact, they view the new crowd with suspicion and at times hostility. That is not to say that every one of the old crowd were down-home rednecks but just let us say the reaction I had Friday night was amused paranoia. Thumbs played that Friday night with an animation and excitement that I had not seen in quite a while. Kevin Smith (guitar) was an epitome of this feeling. His manner and playing held an aggressive edge that sometimes gets buried. The entire band projected an energy that had the crowd out of their seats, leaving their drinks on the table and dancing away. At times the intense atmosphere would literally explode into fights. At the back of the bar drinks were spilt and during the course of the evening a pitcher was smashed over somebody's head.

# CONCERTS

(Continued from page 14)
But this seemed in some ways natural and not really threatening. (It was pretty threatening where I was.--Ed) Thumbs fit in perfectly. Putting out three great sets that included three or four new songs ("New Twist," for example) and a newly-arranged Van Morrison medley.

This was a great evening of Rock 'n Roll, just affirming the fact that Thumbs are still the best band in this area.

Abuse Live: The Downliners Club, April 25-26

The Downliners Club is the basement club located beneath Plaza East at 4719 Troost. It is still in a state of renovation, but the atmosphere bodes good things for the future of New Music in the area.

Abuse were the first band to play at the Downliners Club and in many ways they were the appropriate choice. They are like a midwest Heartbreakers in sound and style. Playing with a raw enthusiasm that carries across to the audience, it was no surprise that they had the crowd dancing. Abuse are a fairly new band and this did show up in their performance (They learned a third set in a week so they would be able to play this show.). Their momentum at times was seriously slowed by minor technical flaws (guitars out of tune and a little too much chatter between songs). During the course of their three sets, they performed songs by The Stooges ("I Want to be Your Dog") and several by Johnny Thunders ("Chinese Rocks"). Despite the flaws, I really enjoyed them and if they just get the chance they could go far and provide a much needed musical alternative to this area and beyond. --VS

---

Good News! The Opera House appears to be back on its feet. The benefit week held last month was successful. They made their back mortgage payments just barely. Although they continue to operate on a low budget plan, major acts will continue to be booked.

Don't miss The Selecter, May 6. It should be an excellent show!

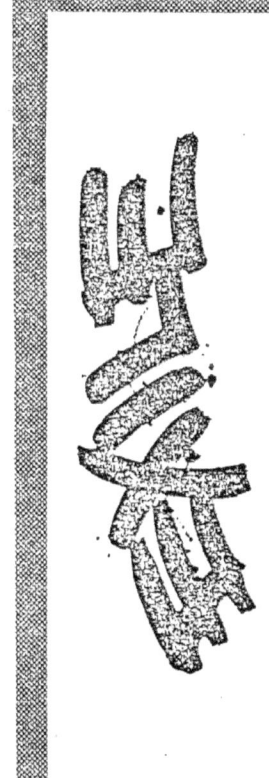

RECORDS AND TAPES
GUARANTEED USED ALBUMS AND TAPES
We also carry a large selection of posters and t-shirts. Bring your good used albums in for cash.
OPEN 7 DAYS A WEEK

15 W. 9th St. Lawrence, Ks.       7222 W. 75th St. Overland Park, Ks.
(913) 842-3059                              (913) 384-2499

TALK TALK

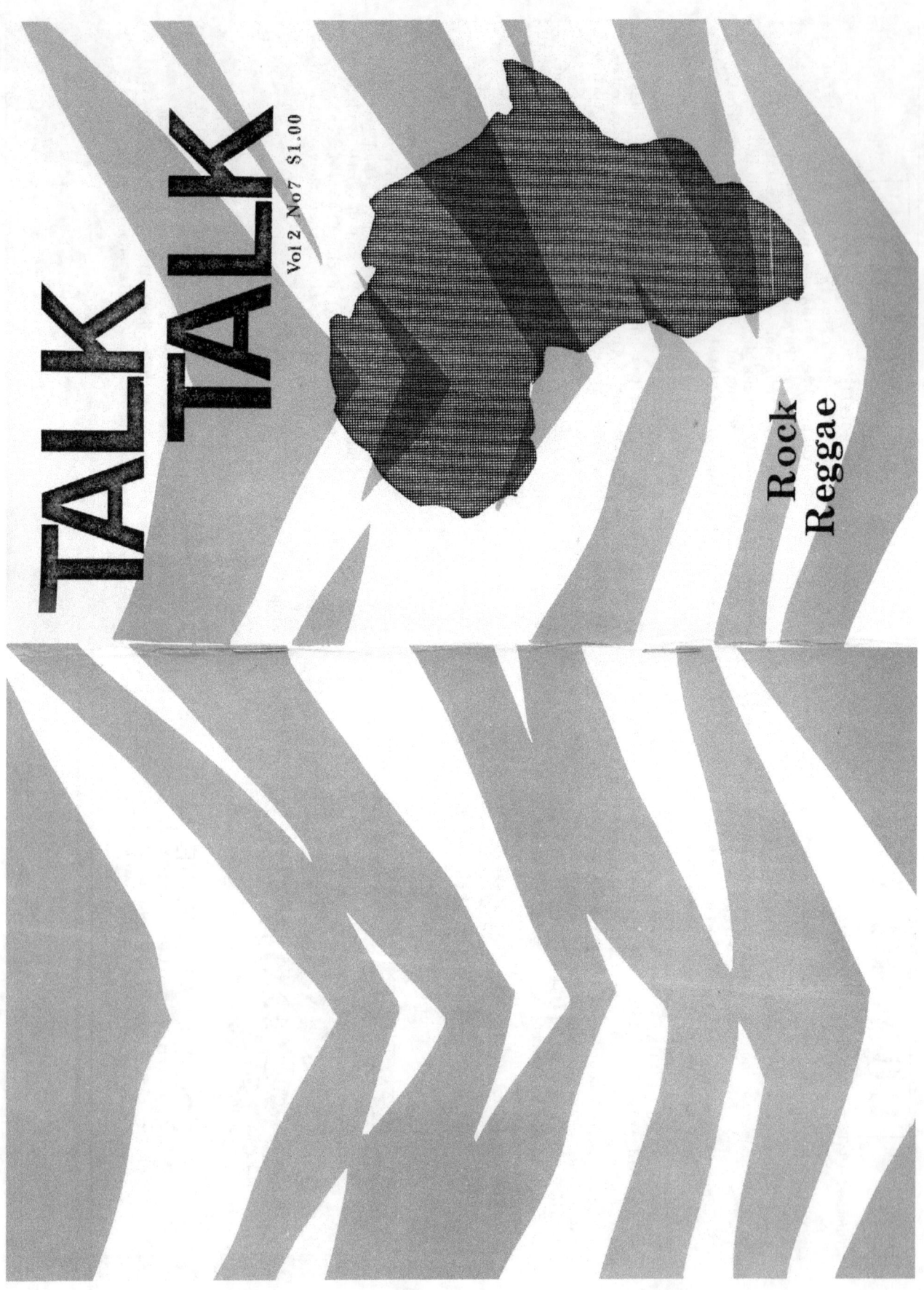

# TALK TALK

Vol. 2 No. 7     June, 1980     $1.00

The Midwest American Rock and Reggae Magazine

## TALK TALK

**Editors:**
Bill Rich
Eric Schindling

**Contributors:**
Rick Hellman
Jim Schwada
The U-Man
Daddy Cool
VS, WB, NN
KD, JM

**Photography:**
Robin Kyle
Chris Lucas
Patty Heffley
Bill Rich

**Cover Design:**
Martin Olson
**Layout help:**
John Lee

### Table of Contents

Live: Toots & The Maytals,
  Third World . . . . . . . . . . . . 3
  The Tourists. . . . . . . . . . . . 4
Album Reviews: Tourists,
  The Pop Group . . . . . . . . . . . 5
Interview: The Tourists . . . . . . 6
Album Reviews: Only Ones, Slits,
  Cure, Glaxo Babies, Chrome,
  Tuxedo Moon . . . . . . . . . . . 7-8
Concerts: Moderns, Mi-Sex, Imports. 9
  New Era Reggae Band . . . . . . . .10
Reggae Reviews: Sly & The Revolu-
  tionaries, Blackbeard, Scientist v.
  Prince Jammy, Jah Wobble. . . . . .11
  Toots & The Maytals, Burning Spear,
  Linton Kwesi Johnson. . . . . . . .12
Live: The Selecter . . . . . . 13-15
  Public Image Ltd. . . . . . . . 16-19
  Blue Riddim Band. . . . . . . . . .20
  The New Irish Movement. . . . . . .20
Reggae Reviews: Intensified Vol. 2,
  Club Ska '67. . . . . . . . . . . .21
  Clint Eastwood, Third World . . . .22
Single Reviews: Gang of Four, Cure 24
Album Reviews: Bad Manners, Psyche-
  delic Furs, Magazine. . . . . . . .25
  Angelic Upstarts, UK Subs, Fall . .26
  Cabaret Voltaire, Monochrome Set. .28
Live: Squeeze. . . . . . . . . . . .29

All contents copyright 1980 by Talk Talk Publications, PO Box 36, Lawrence, Kansas, 66044. All rights reserved. Any opinion expressed is solely that of the writer and not necessarily that of this publication. Subscription rate is $6 for six months. Articles, reviews and photos submitted for editorial consideration are welcome. Not responsible for unsolicited material. Address all correspondence to Talk Talk Editors, PO Box 36, Lawrence, Kansas, 66044.

## Third World/Toots and The Maytals    June 3
### The Uptown Theater

Toots and The Maytals opened the show with a warm version of "Pressure Drop," from his Funky Kingston album. It was not as energetic as I wanted but supposedly Toots is tired of the song. He soon came out with "Funky Kingston" and drew it out into a sing-along. You could tell he was happy (playing around with the crowd and moving like James Brown in his heyday, doing the splits, etc.). Of course, Toots was not the only part of the show as shown by The Maytals with their warm harmonies. The band was hot this night, supplying the energy needed for Toots to spark off of. All in all, a lot of people were exhausted after they danced their way through "Monkey Man" and a really exceptional finale, "Reggae Got Soul." This first part of the double bill was no warm up act. Toots and The Maytals were a great evening in themselves.

After a short break filled with recorded reggae, Third World hit the stage. This group of musicians are one of the most popular reggae bands around and after seeing them I can see why. Third World opened their searing set with a fiery version of "One Cool Vibe." Soon after, they had ripped through "1865 (96 Degrees In The Shade)," in which they indulged themselves in a fantastic dub session. Following this they moved into "Third World Man" and then, slowing things down a bit with a soulful "Now That We've Found Love." The blood pressure picked up again with other songs from their five albums. Third World supplied all the ingredients for Kansas City to cook with and from the looks of the crowd the reggae recipe was a success! All those involved with this show should be proud of themselves and then get on the stick to get more acts of this sort and calibre. This area is ready and overdue for our regular dose of reggae. Toots and The Maytals and Third World just whetted our appetites for things to come.

*Next issue:*
             *photos*
               *and*
             *Interview*

# ALBUM REVIEWS

**The Tourists:** Reality Effect (Epic Records: JE36386)--
The second record from The Tourists proves to be a much stronger effort all the way around. While their first record (available at this time only on import) was a strong debut, it did suffer from a thinness in sound. In particular, "Blind Among the Flowers" comes across much fuller--giving it the emotional punch that was only hinted at on their first Lp. It is really hard to label this band. One could easily dismiss them as a "pop" band but that would be foolish and unfair to the band. On listening to this record, it is easy to pick up some musical influences, such as their folk roots which give them their clean sound. It may sound strange but if anything they remind me of some old San Francisco bands, the acoustic meeting the electric. This album does not have a weak moment on it. Ann Lennox and Peet Coombes are hauntingly good on vocals and the out front bass of Eddie Chin and drumming by Jim Toomey are largely responsible for the improved sound. Dave Stewart's guitar-playing is tasteful and forceful, soaring in and out of the proceedings. Yes, this is a good album and The Tourists combine their different musical influences well. Not to be dismissed as just another pop album, it is much more. Give it a listen and see what I mean. Fave cuts: "I Only Want to Be With You," "Blind Among the Flowers," and "Fools Paradise." --ES

**The Pop Group:** For How Much Longer Can We Tolerate Mass Murder (Rough Trade: Rough 10)--The Pop Group have always taken a stance on enlightening the world on social injustice. For many, this is a turn-off. But not for me. In fact, this album is one of my new favorites. The lyrical message is quite forward with songs on forces of oppression, robbing banks, starving millions, and on. The music resembles a punk-funk fusion. The vocals, sometimes chanted, screamed or sung, are similar to The Contortions, with the flaring saxophone. A great sound from a great group. It is not pop pablum but rock with feeling and conviction. --BR

**The Tourists:** May 1st Lawrence Opera House

It would be dishonest to say I was looking forward to this show. To my surprise and pleasure, the performance they gave was tight and rocked out with energy that I had not expected.

The set began with "Don't Get Left Behind" and continued to build. By the time they got around to "Blind Among the Flowers," a good portion of the audience was packed around the stage.

Ann Lennox's stage presence brought to mind Chrissie Hinde of The Pretenders. Both women carry an aura of strength and vitality. Ann's voice was able to match the songs, covering the emotional gamut, expressing love, rage, and frustration. (→30)

*Peet Coombes and Dave Stewart.* *Pics by Robin Kyle.*

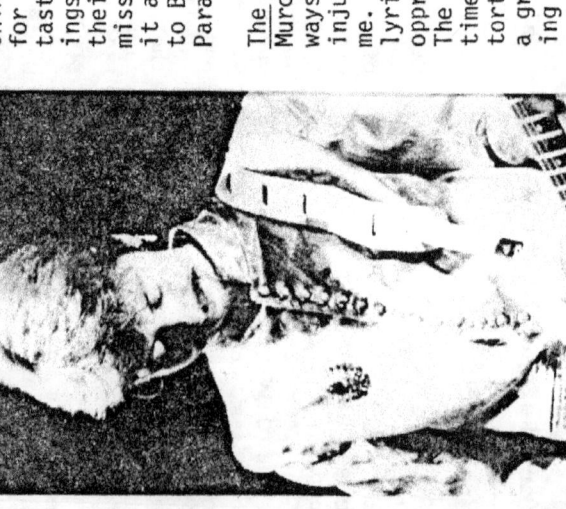
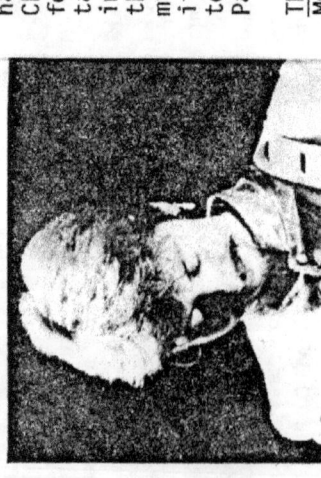
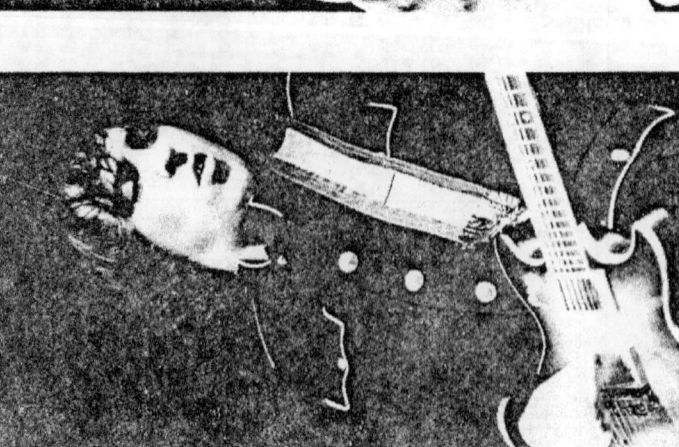

*The day The Tourists were in Lawrence, Talk Talk made a few phone calls\* and managed to get an interview with Ann Lennox and Dave Stewart. The interview took place in their hotel room. \*Thank you, Paul Bailey.*

Talk Talk: So, how long does your tour last and how far are you into it?
Dave Stewart: Actually, we're about halfway through it. After this show we head south...I think...Tulsa, and then over to the coast. The total tour is supposed to last seven weeks.
TT: How do you like America so far?
Ann Lennox: It's quite nice actually, even though you can't get a proper perspective seeing it as we do. But on the whole the audiences have been good. Last night we played in Nebraska, at a really small town, but the place was packed. We had a lot of fun.
DS: Yes, Annie got quite wild (both laugh).
TT: Has your new album done well so far?
DS: Well, it's really too soon to tell. It's only been released a short time, but the signs are good and this tour will help it I'm sure.
TT: I hear a lot of people call you a pop group, but how do you feel and how would you describe yourselves?
AL: Well, there's nothing wrong with pop groups. And we admit it does bother us to be labelled. Labelling is always bad because it tends to cut one off (→27)

*Ann Lennox
Pic by Robin Kyle*

## ALBUM REVIEWS

The Only Ones: Baby's Got A Gun (CBS Records: CB271)-- The third effort from this vastly underrated band, it is also the first time they have used an outside producer. I am not sure what they think of this album but I have found it to be their most complete and strongest effort to date. The ideas and styles they have worked with on earlier records seemed to jell under the production guidance of Colin Thurston. This album moves. The drums are more upfront and John Perry's guitar playing seems to have taken on a new edge. Also The Only Ones have added the singing abilities of Pauline Murray (ex-Penetrations) to the mix. The two songs she is featured on are "Me And My Shadow" and "Fools" (The latter being perhaps one of my favorite songs on the album and the A side of their new single.). Recently some critics have slagged this Lp as boring and not fit for anyone other than cretins. To say that about this album is stupid at best and shows the reviewers' own ignorance. To sum it up, Peter Perrett and Co. have put out one of the best records of 1980. Give it a listen and see what I mean. --VS

The Slits: Y Records (Dist. by Rough Trade)--This album is for Slits fans only. It shows the girls like a lover sees their mate. Sometimes they look like hell while at other times they radiate. But it is not just the physical beauty one is interested in, it is the whole picture: how they move and the everyday activities that endear them to you! That is how this record is. The Slits are bitchy, coy, funny and serious on this odd mish-mash of an album. Their rhythm is still there, as well as their individual quirks. I find it interesting and enjoyable. But isn't love close to S&M at times. --VS

The Cure: Seventeen Seconds (Fiction Records: FIX004) --A second album from these feverishly productive boys and like most second Lps, this one shows some change or refinement. Besides the obvious additions of Matthieu Hartley on keyboards and replacing Michael Dempsey with Simon Gallup on bass, this record is more "atmospheric" than their debut Lp, Three Imaginary Boys. Seventeen Seconds is like being lost in some legend-haunted (→31)

## ALBUM REVIEWS

**Glaxo Babies: Nine Months to the Disco** (Heartbeat Records: HB2)--The debut Lp from one of my favorite bands and for those of you expecting things like "Who Killed Bruce Lee?" and "Christine Keeler" forget it. This album takes some getting used to. The Glaxo Babies have changed their sound drastically. This record is similar to the Pop Group or PiL. There is a lot of heavy bass, jazzy sax and very few comprehensible vocals (most of them are treated in some manner), the guitar's presence is also not as prevalent but this is not a bad record. The songs have strange titles: "Maximum Sexual Joy," "The Tea Master and the Assassin," and "Dinosaur Disco Meets the Swamps-Stomps." This is a new direction for the Glaxo Babies. I like it. So pick it up and dance to it or something! --UM

**Chrome: Red Exposure** (Beggars Banquet: BEGA 15)--The fourth album from this two-man band, who are the source of inspiration for Doctor Mix and the Remix. But, whereas the Dr. interprets past earth songs, Damon Edge, Helios Creed and occasional accompaniment by John L. Cyborg perform their own alien compositions. Current events are a favorite topic. Chrome no doubt intercept radio and TV transmissions from deep space and from this compilation of information compose songs with titles like: "Jonestown," "Eyes on Mars," "Static Gravity," and "Rm. 101." Everything from televisions, rhythm buzz, distortion units and reverse guitar is used in creating Chrome's sound. A case study of TV as culture. --UM

**Tuxedo Moon: Half-Mute** (Ralph Records: TX8004-L)--The debut Lp from this popular SF band and yet this record is quite different from their previous material. Tuxedo Moon is now made up of Steven Brown on saxes, vocals, and electronics; Blaine Reininger on violins, vocals, guitar, electronics; and newcomer Peter Principle on bass and further electronics...gone are Winston Tong and Victoria Lowe. The album opens with a pseudo jazz piece entitled "Nazca" but once it has blown over the record takes off. This album shows Tuxedo Moon's influences ranging from jazz greats, The Velvets, Roxy Music, The Residents, (→27)

## CONCERTS

**The Moderns    May 24**
**Off the Wall Hall**

This four-piece band hails from Wichita, Kansas. Their set consisted of a few Talking Heads songs mixed in with other covers and some originals. At times their lead singer came off a bit too much like some game show host. But overall the band played well and the sound was good. Even though they are still a bit rough, I would recommend you see them if you get the chance. They will be playing at the Downliner in Kansas City June 6 and 7.

**Mi-Sex    May 5    Tuts, Chicago**

On the strength of a hit single, "Computer Games," and the following debut album, this Australian band got a U.S. tour together. I expected them to be less polished live and they were. For instance, some of the synthesized sound was absent. But Mi-Sex played tight and expertly. They did some new songs from the forthcoming second album which will probably not be much of a movement away from their developing style. But it might. So be on the lookout for these guys.

The Imports at the Lucky Number, Chicago

If The Imports had begun in England three years ago, they would probably be releasing their third album by now. Instead, they originate from Chicago in 1980. For what its worth, you could probably call them punk. They only play originals and they have quite a few. Their sound is basically minimal with the line-up of guitar, bass, drums and singer. The four members are in high school but manage to practice and play all the time.

The Imports are gaining quite a following. When you see them you will become a fan, too!

*The Imports:*
*Joe Stuell-bass*
*Alex Dale-drums*
*Tom Krug-vocals*
*Ben Krug-guitar*
*Photo-Bill Rich*

# CONCERTS

The New Era Reggae Band is a collective effort of six Jamaican musicians and several managers and coordinators. Brought together several months ago, in Chicago, their following is growing in the midwest. It is very rare to find a reggae band in America, but this band is opening new doors for the future reggae explosion which is bound to occur before too long. Booking the band in Babylon is not the easiest thing. But manager Bob Swire has arranged future shows at Off the Wall Hall.

I recently saw The New Era Band several nights in Chicago. The band has a wide-ranging performance, based on the pure, basic roots reggae form. The lineup is simple--keyboards, bass, guitar, drums, and two vocalists. Junior Braitwaite is well known from his early days with The Wailers. He wrote "It Hurts to be Alone," the first Wailers hit, and sings on that song and on "Simmer Down." His voice is similar to Marley's and he sings on several Wailers songs that the band cover. Aswad Greggori, the (→23)

*Aswad Greggori (vocals, percussion), Bunny Martin (drums), Chris Rose (bass), Tony (rhythm--no longer with band), Junior Braitwaite (vocals, percussion), Gregory Banns (rhythm and guitar), Donny Johnson (keyboards).*

# REGGAE REVIEWS

Sly and the Revolutionaries Black Ash Dub (Trojan: TRLS 186)--A great new dub album by the masters themselves. This is the latest Trojan release, recorded at Channel One and produced by Jah Thomas. The titles are all drug-related, but the main lyrics are just "Version." Of the ten cuts, a few are recognizable from somewhere. The basic sounds and chords are vintage Revolutionaries, making Black Ash a welcome addition to any collection. --WB

Blackbeard I Wah Dub (EMI-More Cut: RDC 2002)--Dennis Bovell, producer of The Slits and The Pop Group, is Blackbeard. His regular band is Matumbi, but his real genius shows up in the studio work. This dub album, highly praised in the music weekly trade mags, is mainly a solo project. As a rhythm guitarist, Bovell tends to emphasize that aspect when compared to other dub styles of heavy drums and bass. On an earlier (1978) album, Strictly Dubwise (UA-LBR1013), Blackbeard created a similarly outstanding album's worth of dub in the mellow subdued style. But I Wah Dub is full of surprises. It may space you out some, but you will not fall asleep or take it off. --WB

Scientist v. Prince Jammy Big Showdown 1980 (Greensleeves: GREL 10)--This recording is a dub style contest at King Tubby's between two of the great mixers--Prince Jammy and the Dub Scientist himself, Dennis "Blackbeard" Bovell. The band is the Roots Radics Band, which includes Errol H. H., Carlton Davis, Ansel Collins, Bo Peep, and Chinna Smith. The ten cuts are divided between the two "boxers" into Rounds. With five cuts each, it must be a tie. But the decision is yours to make. So listen and judge for yourself. --WB

Jah Wobble  The Legend Lives On...Jah Wobble in "Betrayal" (Virgin: V2158)--"Great, Fantastic, Funny...Wild" (VS Talk-Talk magazine). Jah Wobble the legend carries on in the perfect Ying to PiL's Yang. The man has always been a self-proclaimed genius and with this record he proves he is right! The album starts out with "Betrayal" and moves quickly into Fats Dominoe's hit "Blueberry Hill," of course Wob does not let the song go by unaltered. (→31)

## REGGAE REVIEWS

Toots and the Maytals: Just Like That (Island: ILPS9590)--After last year's disappointing Pass the Pipe, many reggae fans and music critics dismissed Toots and the boys as "nothing happening." Well, Jamaica's answer to Otis Redding is back, with an Lp that qualifies as one of the best reggae releases of the year. Just Like That is Toots and the Maytals at their most soulful, a bright, rollicking sound, refreshingly free from the sometimes impenetrable Jah praises that are many reggae artists' stock in trade. No dire spiritual/political pronouncements here--just good danceable music--reggae got soul, indeed! --DC

Burning Spear: Hail H.I.M. (RDC 2003)--While certain reggae artists tone down their sound in an effort to become commercially successful, Winston Rodney, the famed Burning Spear, has stuck to the roots and may triumph in spite of it. Hail H.I.M., Spear's latest effort, is full of fire and thunder--invocations of Rastafarian idols ("Follow Marcus Garvey") and cries of revolution ("Cry Blood Africa"). Burning Spear has produced some of the finest music ever to come from Jamaica. Hail H.I.M. is an excellent example of reggae music as social protest. --DC

Linton Kwesi Johnson: Bass Culture (Island: ILPS 9605)--Speaking of protest, British poet/singer Linton Kwesi Johnson has just released his third Lp, and like his powerful Forces of Victory, Bass Culture is mainly concerned with the lot of the Black working class in industrial England. Johnson, whose songs are often poetry written in Jamaican/West Indian patois ("It Noh Funny" is a classic example) has a sound that, while rooted in the classic dub tradition, often approaches the fringes of avant-gardé jazz. It is no accident that he has chosen as sidemen British jazz trumpeter Dick Cuthell and harmonica wizard Julio Finn, who learned his trade at the knee of saxman Ornette Coleman. Singing/talking in an ominous voice, Johnson creates images of Black men harrassed, jailed, and killed by the British government and right wing groups. His angry, yet restrained, attitude adds odd melancholy to the album's only "love song" ("Lorraine") and reaches its peak with the haunting "Two Sides of Silence." (→ 31)

The Selecter Live at the Lawrence Opera House May 6

This was a high energy, skanking show from one of the best bands around. After a hot warm up set by the Blue Riddim Band (a local soul, ska and reggae group), The Selecter came on like gangbusters. Pauline Black chided and charmed the audience while Gap took credit for the other part of the vocal excitement. Desmond Brown (keyboards) in particular stood out in a bright red pullover. In accordance with his Rude Boy image, he (at one point) ran out from behind his organ and started a mock fight with Gap. During the course of their set they covered songs off their debut Lp, Too Much Pressure, and the highlights of the evening came with "Three Minute Hero," "Carry Go Bring Come," and with their encores, "James Bond" and with the Blue Riddim Band "Madness." All in all it was a fantastic show that I am sure made many converts for Selector.
Arthur "Gaps" Hendrickson, Compton Amanor, and Desmond Brown. Photo by Chris Lucas.

"Two Tone is basically The Specials and The Selecter, which is 14 people. So it is a bit like a small record company having 14 A & R men permanently out on the road looking for other bands. At the moment, it has had sort of a 100 percent chart success. We have had ten hit singles.

"When people talk about a revival, what they really mean is somebody comes along and takes exactly what there was in the early '60s and copies it. So they are wrong and I suggest that they get themselves together and actually listen to the record, instead of making vague statements."

"There is nothing 'revivalist' about what we do. We've taken the basic ska rhythm, which came from the early '60s, which is really just an offbeat dance rhythm. And the rest of us have various influences, ranging form rock to reggae, some punk influences as well, which we have just incorporated into that basic dance thing...and hence you've got The Selecter's music."

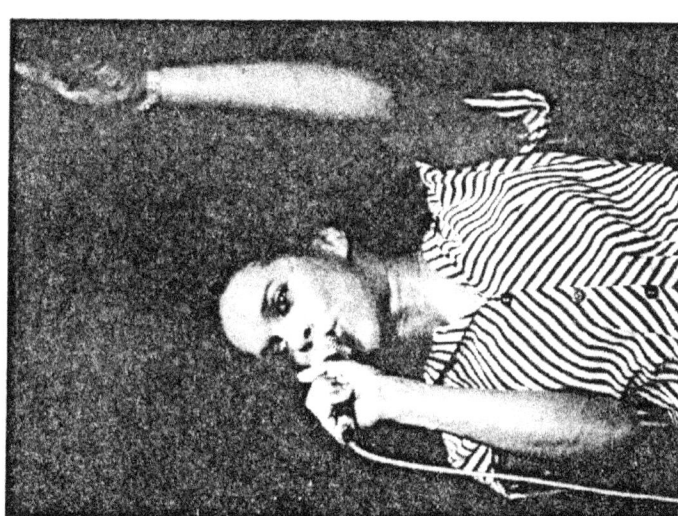

On the movement:
"It has had a positive effect. If you're busy dancing, which the audience usually is, there isn't time to thump the person next to you."
--Pauline Black

*Comments from radio interview, KJHK.*
*Pauline Black by Robin Kyle.*
*Neol Davies by Chris Lucas.*

TALK TALK 93

# PUBLIC IMAGE LTD.

↳Keith Levine, guitar; John Lydon, vocals; Martin Aitken, drums; Jah Wobble, bass. Photo by Bill Rich.

↳Keith Levine and John Lydon. Photo by Patty Heffley.

May 1          Chicago

Public Image Ltd. have a reputation of being a studio band. But their American tour showed them to be competent live musicians. I caught the show in Chicago, where they performed outstandingly to a packed house. They opened with "Careering," which brought the whole crowd out of their padded theater seats and onto their feet for the hour the band played. The whole floor shook from the bass lines layed down by Jah Wobble. The percussion work of Martin Aiken provided layers of rhythms which allowed Keith Levine to experiment and show off his style of guitar licks. But the focus of the crowd was on John Lydon. There is still a part of Johnny Rotten in his performances, evident as he stalked the stage and crooned and wailed through songs from the first and second albums, including "Poptones," "Attack," "Swan Lake," "Memo-

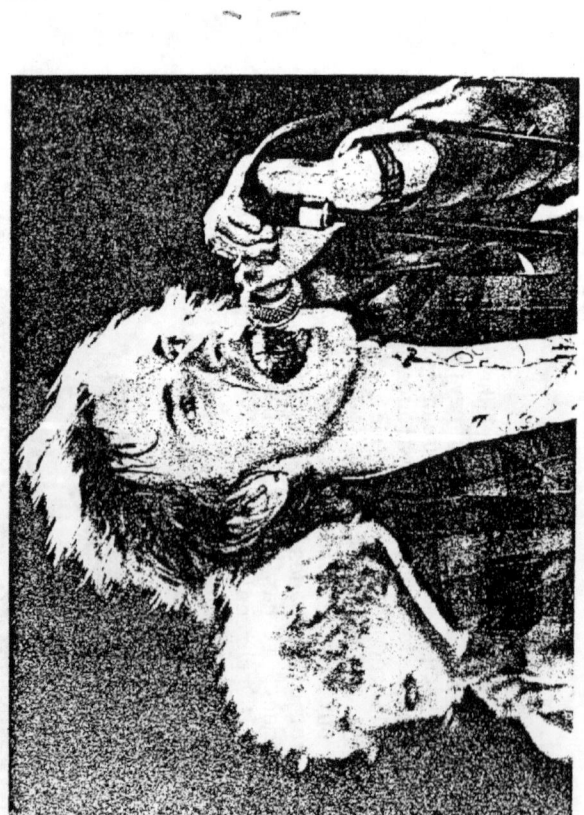

ries," and "Bad Baby." Earlier on, Lydon stated, "Throw money," wrap the silver in bills." The stage became covered with material. Yet no one was injured or hit. Perhaps the fact that no alcohol was served kept the crowd from being too aggressive. Anyway, Lydon proceeded to pick up everything for the remainder of the show, usually squatting, looking at the assortment on the floor. After spending $10 for a ticket, what one got was watching Lydon ask for money and collecting it all. That is the major criticism of the show, although the shortness of it was a bit disappointing.

The band ended their set with "Public Image," which ends with "good-bye." And so ended the show. No encore. And while the show had been very outstanding, Chicago wanted more. But everyone had to settle for what had been witnessed.

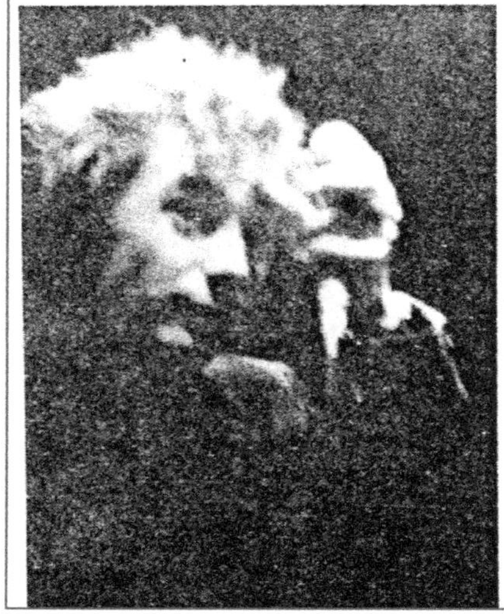

Public Image Ltd. (clockwise)
Levine, Lydon and Aitkens by
Bill Rich
Jah Wobble by Chris Lucas
Lydon in NY and in Chicago
by Patty Heffley
Lydon by Bill Rich

The Blue Riddim Band with Black Uhuru--
Off-the-Wall Hall                    May 27

Well, it started out as the 2nd No-Mall-At-All Ball, but it ended up a hot reggae jam session, featuring members of Black Uhuru singing in front of local boys, the Blue Riddim Band.

The first set was all the Blue Riddim Band as the place filled with hippies, Rastas and other assorted types, all skanking to the beat. During the break, one member of Black Uhuru told me he thought the Blue Riddim Band were the best reggae band in America. That these guys are without a contract is yet another example of the chauvinistic, idiotic policies of the major record companies.

Meanwhile, back at the dance, things were heating up and finally two of the singers from Black Uhuru took the stage. With the Blue Riddim Band laying down the funk, the Jamaicans toasted away in fine reggae tenor. All five songs they did together flowed like honey, like Channel One had been dropped in Lawrence for the night or something.

Cannot wait to see these guys when they return as headliners (sometime this summer), says the manager of the Hall). Then we will see if the town hippies will show up for a real Jamaican reggae band... --RH

The New Irish Movement (The Outcasts, Rudi, The Moondogs, Shock Treatment, The Vipers, Big Self) Good Vibrations Records: Got 17, 12, 1, 10..Energy NRG 1)--Reading through the English newspapers about the only Irish band you hear about are The Undertones and it is true they are a great band, with two fine albums under their belt. But the sad part of it is that The Undertones came from the same place that these other bands did and, while The Undertones moved on and receive all the praise, there are still things going on in Northern Ireland. I do not really know that much about the history of these groups, but of all of them The Outcasts and Rudi are the two strongest. The Outcasts' "Self Conscious Over You" is a fast paced song with a clean energetic sound. Rudi's Big Time and I-Spy singles show that they hope to be the new Undertones but with their own identity (similar but no copy-cats). The Moondogs are reminiscent of the early 60's invasion (→31)

## REGGAE REVIEWS

More Intensified Vol. 2: Original Ska 1963-67 Various Artists (Island: IRSP 3)--Put on your pork pie hats and dancing shoes because this is a record you cannot sit still when listening to. Island has dug into their vaults for this exciting second part to their first release, Intensified Ska. There are less vocals on this collection, which allows the full Ska style to perk. The dates on this record range from the earliest efforts of The Maytals in 1963 doing "Six and Seven Books of Moses" to 1967 with one of my favorites on the album, Sir Lord Comic's classic "The Great Wuga Wuga." With reggae gaining new popularity it is important that Ska come forward, too, for it preceded reggae and in many ways is a good introduction to the novice listener to this form of music. It is more instrumentally based, which allows one to appreciate the music without having to get involved with the Rastafarian religion. After listening to Ska a while, hopefully, the novice will be able to accept the religious aspects of the songs and see the music as a whole. It is a sad thing that some of these classic and talented artists have almost faded into oblivion. But with the advent of the renewed interest in reggae perhaps artists such as Desmond Dekker, Lord Brynner and Stranger Cole will come out of the past and shake the world with their talents and get people dancing as their older songs do on this great record. --VS

Club Ska '67 (Island Records: IRSP4)--Island does it again. Following Intensified 1 and 2 is this reissue of a 1967 gem. Included on this record is the classic Baba Brooks tune "Guns Fever," complete with ricocheting bullets on the over dub and "Guns of Navarone," The Skatalites' premier song (Incidentally, this would be a perfect film score for a Japanese horror film). This record is just full of the Ska and Rock Steady hits that you never could hear on U.S. radio. Each selection is well worth having and just begs to be played on your turntable and danced to over and over again. So introduce this record to Babylon and hear and enjoy the sweet, funny, danceable sounds of Club Ska '67. A must for reggae fans and music lovers alike. --VS

## REGGAE REVIEWS

<u>Clint Eastwood</u> Sex Education (Greensleeves: GREL 11)--Clint Eastwood is considered the top new DJ. His style is similar to Dillinger and I-Roy. On this album, he toasts over tracks laid down by the Roots Radics Band. Besides being the latest Greensleeves release, this album is probably the first one Clint Eastwood has released. He has had Jamaican singles out...and, as usual, they are hard to find. Reggae fans should be able to get Sex Education from the normal distribution system or am I dreaming again? Of the ten cuts, "Lend Me One of Your Girlfriend" is a classic, demonstrating the dj's characteristics, including phrase repetition in a slightly minor key with high gulping yelps in between. The melody flows in and out, creating a very pleasant experience. He gets an "A" for this.
--WB

<u>Third World</u> Arise in Harmony (Island: ILPS 9574)--I have to admit on the onset that these guys are not my favorites. But they have done a good job at bridging the gaps between the primative island image of reggae and a more commercial disco-influenced Western world. These six guys are definitely talented and good at what they release. It seems they are moving away from the latest fling with disco. As always, the extensive harmonies produce their easiest to identify trademark. --WB

## CONCERTS

dreadlock vocalist, is a Peter Tosh double in looks and style. The drummer, Bunny Martin, besides being one of the hottest session drummers a while back, is a master of Ketta reggae, the early one-drop beat with nothing mixed in and chanting vocals. He sings on the Burning Spear covers. Donny Johnson, on keyboards, is the Rude Boy of the group. He provides the occasional echo. Greg Bann's guitar provides both the reggae rhythm and lead. He was involved in the Jamaican scene from which Inner Circle developed. The youngest member is bassist Chris Rose, who resembles Robbie Shakespeare in holding the bass high on the chest and bopping his head--at times like the "nutty" Madness.

These guys are quite a combination. Their performance is authentic reggae, played the way only Jamaicans can.
--BR

TALK TALK highly recommends...

**NEW ERA REGGAE BAND**
from Chicago
Fri. & Sat. JUNE 13 & 14
$3.50 • 9:00pm.
One original Wailer
All from Jamaica
On tour in U.S.
for only 4 months!

**Off the Wall Hall**
737 N.H.
Lawrence, Ks.

RECORDS AND TAPES
GUARANTEED USED ALBUMS AND TAPES
We also carry a large selection of posters and t-shirts. Bring your good used albums in for cash.
OPEN 7 DAYS A WEEK
15 W. 9th St. Lawrence, Ks.    7222 W. 75th St. Overland Park, Ks
(913) 842-3059                  (913) 384-2499

## SINGLE REVIEWS

Gang of Four Outside the Trains Don't Run on Time/ He'd Send in the Army (EMI Cat. No. Z1)--More spare and stinging rock and roll from the Gang of Four. This single finds the group in a position not much different from their excellent first album of last year.

The A side is uptempo funk that would have been right at home on Entertainment. Andy Gill's nervous guitar riffing leads the way here but it seems like everything's up front; the slithery bassline, Hugo Branham's athletic drumming. In fact, the only thing that's the least bit smothered are Jon King's vocals. That's not an aid to understanding the indirect lyrics, but who said you had to understand the words to like a song anyway?

The B side is a bit of a departure for the Gang. They have taken the sparse sound they have come up with to its extreme. Never was there more space between the instruments and never have they used the resultant tension better. The song nearly stops in the middle, but Gill's ineffably right guitar licks get it going again.

For all its good points though, this single just has the air of a follow-up about it. We will have to wait and see how much farther the Gang of Four can take a sound that seemed so fresh a few months ago. --RH

The Cure A Forest/Another Journey By Train (Fiction Records: FICSX 10)--A new bass player, the addition of keyboards and the release of this 12-inch single, and The Cure are off with another great work. The A side is very atmospheric, creating a feeling of being lost in the Black Forest or wandering amidst the haunted moors. Melancholy vocals, the jangily guitar and especially the keyboards add to the effect. The keyboards, used in an ambient way, create an illusion of a foggy and mystical time-lost environment. I really like the addition of this new instrumentation to The Cure's line-up. The keyboards complement their sound rather than bolster it. The B side shows how tight they are instrumentally as they take what could almost be a fragment from "Jumping Someone Else's Train" and turn it into a song. "Another Journey By Train" captures the crisp vitality of The Cure. --UM

## ALBUM REVIEWS

Bad Manners: Bad Manners (Magnet Records: MAGL 5033)--Hey, Hey Fatty Fatty. Let's all of us dance to dis fine record. Bad Manners were almost a Two Tone band and their approach to the Ska style is definitely unique and I find it tastier than cornbread. They call their style Ska 'n B to show that their roots are not just in Ska but also in the old tradition. Their lead singer "Fatty Buster Bloodvessel" looks like an overgrown Curly of The Three Stooges but his voice hits the mark. This is a nine-piece band with a full horn section that is put to full use on "Here Comes The Major," "King Ska/Fa," and the totally R&B "Caledonia." These boys are fun to listen to and fun to dance to so what else is required? With this band, nuthin'. So put it on your turntable and enjoy yourself. --VS

The Psychedelic Furs: The Psychedelic Furs (CBS Records: CB 271)--The debut album from what may become one of the most important groups on the scene today. On this album they capture the feel of early Roxy Music and (dare I say it) David Bowie. They are an intelligent band, skirting the trends and coming out with music that has a message. Like The Talking Heads, they deal with the problems that face the world and individuals. While Butler Rep's vocal style takes getting used to, after a while one realizes that his voice is the only one for The Furs. Vince Ely's drumming supplies the forceful back beat that is so integral to the band's sound. As a matter of fact, this band plays so well together it is uncanny. I could go into a slow and steady dissection of the songs, but I will not allow myself to go off on an intellectual tangent. Simply put, this record should be heard more than once. --VS

Magazine: The Correct Use of Soap (Virgin: V2156)--This album will grow on you. Devoto and company have reached a happy medium with this (thier third) album. On first listening, the Lp seemed a little disappointing. Both the A sides of the singles were included (something that originally was not supposed to happen). But I decided to give the disk a second chance and slowly I started to realize how different and how strong this record was in comparison to the last two efforts. Every instrument is in (→27)

## ALBUM REVIEWS

**Angelic Upstarts: We Gotta Get Out of This Place** (Warner Brothers: K56806)--The second album from one of the few bands carrying out the punk tradition. The title track is the old hit done quite well--also the only cover they perform. Maybe this Lp is not as hot as their debut which was in the top albums of 1979 in our poll. They sound about as rough as always. There are few places these guys are not banned from in England because of skinhead violence. But, over here, we can listen to their records and get energized all the time. It sort of grows on you. --NN

**UK Subs: Brand New Age** (RCA Gem: GEMLP106)--The UK Subs are another of the (remaining) few punks who put out good material, like this album. Fast paced, racing guitars, pounding beats are all prolific. Fourteen songs, with several from the recent singles (which you probably missed anyway) make it a worthwhile buy. About the only gimmick involved is clear vinyl--for the brand new age. Their first Lp, as you remember, was in blue vinyl and entitled Another Kind of Blues. --NN

**The Fall: Totale's Turn's (It's Now Or Never)** (Rough Trade: Rough 10)--Mark Smith and other Fall members have put out an excellent live album. Those who are familiar with the band and do not like them will not change their minds after listening to this Lp. But those of us who have followed The Fall's career will find this a long-awaited product. It is really amazing that The Fall sound almost identical live, as they do on their studio releases. Some might call it a dull repeat but there are enough variances in percussion, vocals and guitar-playing to erase that thought from mind. This is the third re-lease from Rough Trade's bootleg-like packaging (the first being Cabaret Voltaire). Mark Smith's voice still carries that raw-edged whine that can drive people up the wall and the band still plays in that almost disjointed style. This record shows the band covering some old tunes, such as "Fiery Jack" and "In My Area," plus a few new songs, like "Cary Grant's Wedding" and "New Puritan." One thing for sure is that no one can stay in the middle of the road when it comes to The Fall. One seems to either love (→27)

from other groups. We like to play to different kinds of crowds.
DS: Yes, the English press tried to label us--said some nasty things.
AL: But, hopefully, they're finished with that.
TT: Are you going to do some more recording soon?
AL: Yes, after this tour we'll start work on our next album. I also think our first album is going to be re-leased over here soon.
TT: That one was recorded in Germany.
DS: Right.
TT: Also, are you touring with any one group on this tour?
DS: No, usually we get a local band to open for us. Most of them are God awful heavy metal.
AL: But it's the audience we care most about. They're important to us. I think we'll have a good time tonight.

(from p. 26) them or hate them. I for one am one of the league of the former. --VS

(from p. 8) and Pere Ubu. In fact, a number of the songs bring "Dub Housing" to mind. The most amazing thing about this record is the violin technique of Blaine Rein-inger. It has a very classical sound to it. Imparticular-ly, the song "Volo Vivace" is reminiscent of (shall I say it?) the plucking technique of Shostakovitch. This is a captivating record from a promising American band. It has got a nice cover, too, for a domestic product. --UM

(from p. 25) its place, a perfect mesh of power and sound, and Devoto's lyrics and voice compliment the entire proceed-ings. In the past Magazine might have been Howard Devoto's child. Since the beginning, though, and most apparent now, the band is now a working unit and Howard an important part. No one member is in charge and the balance that they have achieved with this record just makes the listener greedy for more. Fave raves: "Philadelphia," "Sweetheart Con-tract," and "I Want To Burn Again." --VS

## ALBUM REVIEWS

Cabaret Voltaire: Three Mantras (Rough Trade: Rough 7) --An album of cultural prayer from one of my fave bands? I was leery from the start when I discovered that there are only two songs on the album. The A-side, the Western Mantra, is a rather drawn-out electronic piece, with very few interesting moments. There is some Doctor Mix-type guitar work and bizarre vocals referring to red shirts and open doors. What does it all mean? The B-side is obviously entitled the Eastern Mantra. (The west is best?) This side is grating and tedious. Is this what the hostages hear in Tehran? A distorted Arab transistor radio, complete with marketplace sounds and an incessant droning that sounds like, "We know Eno," or some such nonsense. Three Mantras is Cabaret Voltaire's most self-indulgent work. Are they expounding on their beliefs, utilizing forms of ancient music or what? This lp is not nearly the quality of their previous material such as: the Live YMCA lp or any of their three singles. If you want religious tracts, switch to CBN. --U-Man Wiley

The Monochrome Set: The Strange Botique (Dindisc: Did4) --I love this album. Any band that can take influences as diverse as Eno, Elvis Costello, Lou Reed, Lee Perry and surf music and make it work is o.k. by me. The Lp leads off with an altered version of "The Monochrome Set," the group's self-titled single of last year. It is a nice dub treatment with a strong drum track that really adds something to the original. Other highlights include Lester Square's wonderful guitar work on the instrumental "Etcetera Stroll." His fluid, jazzy style is like a breath of fresh air. It is not power pop, punk, dub or anything else, it is great. The titles alone are worth the price of this album..."The Lighter Side of Dating" (a mover), "The Puerto Rican Fence Climber" (a Beatlesesque slow tune), and "Martians Go Home" (!!). The whole album abounds with wit (snotty though it is) and cool playing behind Bid's reedy vocals. This is a record that brings back half-forgotten memories from the recesses of your youthfully impressionable mind. You know--where have I heard that lick before? In the end, it does not matter. Just enjoy this album. --RH

Squeeze May 2 "Grad Night" Worlds of Fun

Normally, Squeeze could have drawn an enthusiastic crowd in K.C. or Lawrence, but due to the fact that admittance that night was restricted to high school seniors, most of their fans were excluded. However, Squeeze made the best of a bad situation and presented an enthusiastic and lively show composed mainly of songs from Cool for Cats and Argy-Bargy. Starting off with "Slap and Tickle," Squeeze made it clear that their main intent was to get people up and out of their seats. Squeeze deserve the "I Can Play Faster Than Elvis Costello" award for their up-tempo performance. Their live set is definitely more high energy than their studio work.

Squeeze found the young audience to be quite a challenge. Vocalist Glenn Tillbrook commented on the differences between American and British audiences. It seems that in Britain, your peer group dictates your musical taste, Mods do not listen to ska and skinheads do not listen to pop, but Glenn feels that Squeeze transcends this phenomenon and appeals to diversified audiences with great success. However, in America they have had difficulty breaking into the mainstream.

*Jools Holland. Pic by Robin Kyle.*

Squeeze has survived some of the music business' more irritating quirks. On American tours they are constantly mismatched with their audiences, the Grad Night show being a perfect example. In Britain, they have had hit singles, but that number one spot has eluded them. They are trying for it again with their latest single, "Another Nail in My Heart." Through all this Squeeze has maintained a delightfully fresh and unaffected outlook toward their music and life, and continue to win fans. --PM/RK

*Glenn Tillbrook*
*Photo by Robin Kyle*

But just because she was the focal point did not mean that the rest of the band were sluggards. Peet Coombes, vocals and guitar, provided some nifty punches and he is an integral part to The Tourists' sound. The entire band acted as a unit, from Dave Stewart on guitar, Eddie Chin on bass, to Jim Toomey on drums. After three strong encores, The Tourists left the stage, leaving behind some new fans and reaffirming their status with their old followers. It was a fine show that they could be proud of. --ES

```
THE DOWNLINER
(below Plaza East)
    4719 Troost
    K.C., Mo.
   816-753-9368

   MAY 30-31
     Abuse

   JUNE 6-7
   The Moderns

   JUNE 13-14
    The Clean

   JUNE 20-21
   The Jumpers

 Coming soon:
    Thumbs
   Fools Face
 The Embarrassment

     Open
  Tues. & Thurs.
    7 to 1
    Be 21!

Brought to you by
Sum-thing-tu-du
  Productions
```

(from p. 7) place, with the cry of the Lorelei tormenting your plight and then, from inside, comes a cry of despair. Best songs: "Play for Today," "Secrets," "In Your House," and "Side II." --UM

::::::::::

(from p. 12) "How indeed can there be a silence when our hearts beat out a sonorous beat meeting the beating drums of our African past, and our eyes shed solid tears of iron blood that fall on concrete ground... How can there be calm when the storm is yet to come?" --DC

::::::::::

(from p. 20) sound but rougher and therefore enjoyable (the closest thing to pop). Of the other three (available on an Ep from Energy), The Vipers are my preference, but all three are good and worth having. Hopefully, in the future Talk-Talk will be able to give you more information on the strong and exciting music scene in Northern Ireland. --ES

::::::::::

(from p. 11) The music behind the lyrics is "The Suit" from PiL's Metal Box. This is perhaps the best solo album of the year. Don't take my word though. Go out and get it. --VS

Talk Talk Vol. 2 No. 8/page 3

B. Rich

B. Rich

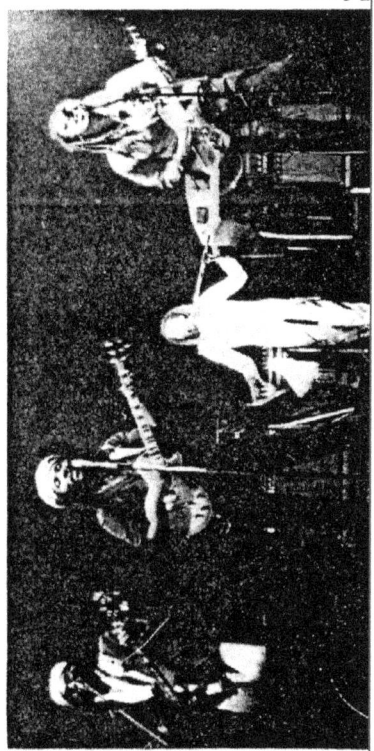

C. Lucas

# TALK TALK

Vol. 2 No. 8     July 1980     $1.00

The Midwest American Rock and Reggae Magazine

TALK TALK

Editors:
Bill Rich
Eric Schindling

Contributors:
U-Man
VS, HM
WB, CH, NN

Photography:
Robin Kyle
Christopher Lucas
Bill Rich

Cover Design:
Nate Fors

Layout:
John Lee
Bill Rich

Typesetting:
Joan M. Moore

Live: The New Era Reggae Band                               4
Album Reviews: Pop Group, Pink
  Military, Pylon                                           5
  Members, Undertones                                       6
Single Reviews: Clash, Mikey
  Dread, Cockney Rejects, Magazine,
  Embarrassment, Holly and The
  Italians                                                  7
  MnM's, Subway Sect                                        8
Live: Debs, Regular Guys,
  Embarrassment                                             9
Album Reviews: Beat, Sharp
  Cuts, Peter Gabriel                                      10
  Toots                                                    11
Photos: Toots and The Maytals                              12
  Third World                                              14
  Blue Riddim Band                                         18
Reggae Reviews: Big Youth,
  Collections                                              19
Single Reviews: Throbbing
  Gristle                                                  20
  Specials, Guns For Hire,
  Originals, Bad Manners, Flowers                          21
  Susan Springfield, Drinking
  Electricity                                              22
  Album Reviews: X, Deaf Club                              23
Live: New Era                                              25
  Blue Riddim, Thumbs                                      26

All contents copyright 1980 by Talk Talk Publications, PO Box 36, Lawrence, Kansas, 66044. All rights reserved. Any opinion expressed is solely that of the writer and not necessarily that of this publication. Subscription rate is $6 for six issues. Articles, reviews, and pix submitted for editorial consideration are welcome. Not responsible for unsolicited material. Address all correspondence to Talk Talk Editors, PO Box 36, Lawrence, Kansas, 66044.

## Album Reviews

The Pop Group We Are Time (Ys: Rough 12)--What could be better than two Pop Group albums? The answer is three Pop Group albums. We Are Time is an odd assortment of outtakes, promo tapes and live material and when it is put together it stands as strong as anything they have done on vinyl. This band are on top of the world situation and their political message is carried by a funk bass and drum section with that soul, scat guitar weaving its way throughout. The band acknowledge influences by The Last Poets (check out their four albums on Blue Thumb if you can still find them) and Parliment-Funkadelic. As a whole this record is actually more accessible than their previous releases. It is an admirable Lp from the most (my personal favorites I admit) important group on any scene today. When most groups are sinking into the post-punk quagmire, The Pop Group stay loyal to their cause, to bring to the people a music with a message. Listen and learn. There are no favorite songs at the moment, they are all good. --VS

Pink Military Do Animals Believe in God? (Eric's Records: Eric 004)--The question is "Do Animals Believe in God?" and from the sound of this album I would say yes. As a matter of fact this strange band must like animals an awfully lot, because they use animal noises on almost every track, almost like a separate instrument. Pink Military have put out a solid album that rivals Souxie and the Banshees and Pere Ubu for total wierdness. From the very first track, "Degenerated Man," they bring on the sound of the jungle. The entire feeling of this album is perfect for an evening of reading and what book would I recommend? Why Joseph Conrad's Heart of Darkness. Just keep flipping the album over until you are done with the book, for maximum effect. --VS

## Single Reviews

Pylon Cool/Dub (Pylon Records: Pylon 001)--Out of the same great south that The B52's come from (Athens, GA) come Pylon, perhaps the best American group at this moment. On "Cool" the band starts out with a funky, funny rhythm line that builds until their lead vocalist burst out with the opening stanza. The chorus, "Everything is cool,"(→24)

## The New Era Reggae Band

June 13 and 14 Off The Wall Hall

Reggae, reggae, reggae. These two evenings were a much needed shot in the arm for Lawrence reggae fans. The New Era Band proved that they are an exciting, explosive group that can take a crowd and get them up and dancing. Every member of the group is a skilled professional. They played together with an intensity that lacks in many unrecorded bands that at the moment have to make their living from playing small clubs. They play reggae music as it should be played, with conviction. The bass work of Chris Rose was a deep hall-shaking growl that hit you in the chest and then sank down. Bunny Martin's drum playing set the pace, while Gregory Banns' single guitar filled in the sound so well that at times I had to wonder how he could sound so good. Characteristically, (→25)

C.Lucas

B. Rich

## Album Reviews

The Members 1980--The Choice Is Yours (Virgin: V2153)-- With this second album, The Members re-establish themselves as one of the top white-reggae bands. Lots of special guests play, including trombonist Rico, Dick Cuthell, and Joe Jackson. Vocalist Nicky Tesco displays excellent syncopation, complimented by great rhythm guitars and brass. The album opens with an instrumental offering a preview of things to come. The lyrical content of most of their numbers are based on everyday situations, such as quitting a job, love and romance, airports, police, gangs, and so on. "Romance" was an earlier single, and "Flying Again" has just been released as an A-side of an interesting package (V5352), which has a three-song B-side including "Disco Oui Oui", a soul version of "Love In A Lift," and a new version of "Rat Up A Drainpipe," both redone excellently. It is a "more for your money" Ep and has different sounds than the album--at least in some ways.

The second side of the album opens with "Normal People" featuring guitars building up to frenzied peaks. Tesco smoothly chants, "They say the meek will inherit the earth." Believe that for what it's worth. I say the normal people were there first." The drumming really carries it all across. Next is a cover version of the Larry Wallis song, "Police Car." Originally performed on the Live Stiff album, it could have launched Wallis' career. But I guess it did not. It is a great song, but The Members' version has different stresses. Luckily, that is the only cover they do. The next cut is closest to a title track. "Clean Men" deals with the elections and voting and features good brass again. The last two cuts drag on at times. Even judged from the overall excellence of this release, the poorer cuts still rank over most of the flooded market. Yes, competition is harder these days. The Members will get this. After all it is 1980-- The Choice Is Yours. --BR

The Undertones Hypnotised (Sire: SRK6088)--It took me a few times playing this before I became h..y..p...I'm hypnotised! The second album from these Irish boys shows them expanding their teenage lament style away from (→24)

## Single Reviews

The Clash Bankrobber Mikey Dread Rockers Galore --UK Tour (CBS-German import) --These two new songs are the flip of "Train in Vain." Produced by Mikey Dread, The Clash move away from the guitar emphasis. The keyboards (and synth) are up-front, along with Strummer's singing about a bankrobber who never hurt anyone, but just took money. The bass and drums coast along with a background humming. Sort of a sad ballad actually but something expected of a bankrobber song maybe.

Mikey Dread takes the rhythm track and takes over at the controls for his "Rockers Galore" cut. He gives a good reggae rap, explaining his style and his feelings of being on the latest Clash tour. At the first few listenings, it does not sound like a Clash song, but the same vocal backing track and rhythmic beat is evident, although completely changed. The band had said they wanted to work with Mikey. Hopefully, a lot more songs will be released. According to press interviews, The Clash have quite a bit of new material partially finished, with plans for another double lp package by early Fall. We will keep you informed on the progress. --BR

Cockney Rejects The Greatest Cockney Ripoff/Hate of the City (EMI: Z2) Bubbles (EMI: Z4)--The two latest singles from these punks finds The Rejects maintaining their roots. For those unfamiliar, they play basic punk with Stinky Turner yelling/singing, thrashing bass and guitars, steady drumming. Songs are repetitive riffs and the tone is angry. About the subject matter--I wonder what the great ripoff was or has it ended yet? "Bubbles" is the old one--"I'm forever blowing bubbles." Stinky leads with the pack repeating him. Why did they choose this one? Beats me. Even if the flip is untitled, the packaging is fantastic. I still like these guys, even if they get a bit ridiculous sometimes. --NN

Magazine Upside Down/The Light Pours Out of Me (Virgin: VS334)--Devoto and Co. score big again with this release. "Upside Down" is similar to their latest style. The B-side is an alternative version of the song on the first album, not officially released before. This must be the third (→24).

## Single Reviews

<u>The Embarrassment Patio Set/Sex Drive</u> (Big Time Records: BT 001)--An independent single from the heartland of America, Wichita, Kansas. I like this group and I like this 45 even though it has a few problems--the main one being the vocal mix is slightly too high. Both songs have a powerful driving force to them and an individuality that marks the band as one with great talent. When this single is on the turntable, make sure you turn up the volume on your stereo for maximum effect. Which means that first you have to buy it, right! (Available and worth the dollar-fifty from The Embarrassment, 641 Woodlawn, #14, Wichita, KS, 67208) --ES

<u>Holly and The Italians Miles Away/It's Only Me</u> (Virgin: VS34)--The second single from Holly and The Italians is not quite as power-packed as the first classic, "Tell That Girl To Shut Up," but a fine 45 nonetheless. Holly still shows up her closest sister in styles band, The Pretenders. "Miles Away" is a smooth song that builds in intensity but the B-side is the standout for me. Sex Pistols fans will recognize the "Submission" rhythm line and those who like Holly singing really gutsy will find this side particularly tasty. Be on the lookout for the album and the promised American tour. --HM

<u>MnMs I'm Tired/Knock Knock</u> (Quark Records: Void 1A).--This single is my favorite of the month. The MnMs are a fast paced pop group that takes me back to the early 60s sound of Leslie Gore. Marcy Marcs' voice is perfect for the lighthearted songs that this single presents. She is energetic and has a sense of humor that comes across on vinyl. Paul Collins, of the (American) Beat, writes or co-writes both songs and from the sound of it, he should break up his band and take his place alongside Marcy somewhere. --HM

<u>Vic Godard and Subway Sect Split Up The Money/Out of Touch</u> (MCA Records: MCA585) --It has been a long time since Vic has put out anything and now the phantom of the original Punk scene has made his comeback. Both of these songs are gems that should not be passed (→22)

Live: The Debs/The Regular Guys   June 7   Off The Wall Hall

It was a muggy Saturday night with the humidity running high. I had heard a few positive things from reliable sources about The Debs but I decided to take a look-and-see attitude. I knew they were an all-girl band from Springfield, MO. What I wanted to know was how good they actually were. I expected to have a good time watching the show, even if these four girls were not that capable. Fortunately, I found The Debs to be more than capable. To put it mildly, they were great!

From the first song, I knew that I was not watching some ragamuffin outfit, but a dedicated band that could take a song like Blondie's "Rip Her To Shreds" and give it their own unique sound. The audience was not blind to this fact either, which they aptly proved by literally dancing their heads off. After a too-short set, The Debs left and soon The Regular Guys took the stage and, as on previous occasions, delivered an exciting display of rock 'n roll. This was a great evening which will be repeated in July (18 and 19, I think). --ES

Live: The Embarrassment   June 20   The Spot,   Wichita, KS

The Spot is not too wide, but a fairly long bar that is known for its shuffleboard tables. It is one of the few places in this culturally-starved town that is open to bands that play artistically-daring music. The crowd on Friday night was fairly good-sized but at times throughout the band's three sets, people would get up right in front of them and play pool. I felt sorry for the band because without a doubt The Embarrassment are one of the finest bands around and with the present musical direction they should be recognized. The last time I wrote about them, I still thought they had a long way to go, particularly with musical control and the jelling of their diverse ideas. This time, though, they showed me they had come a long way in a short time. During the course of the evening, they performed a few covers from Iggy to Michael Jackson and, in particular, a fine, funny and mutated version of "Stairway to (→20)

## Album Reviews

The Beat <u>I Just Can't Stop It</u> (Go Feet Records: Beat 001) --The long awaited album from one of England's top new groups is finally out and the promise of the singles has been fulfilled. (Unfortunately, a couple of songs from those singles are on the Lp.) The Beat are impossible to classify because they cover a scope of feelings and styles. One of the big surprises of the record is the cover of "I Can't Get Used to Losing You," a song that I first heard performed by that suave guy himself, Andy Williams. But this record is full of hits that are just aching to be put on the turntable and danced to. The Beat are the perfect in-between, balancing themselves perfectly between the politics of The Specials and the nutty sound of Madness. What else can I say, I love their sound and love their sax. Go Feet is right. Faves: "Mirror In The Bathroom," "Big Shot," and "Noise In The World." --VS

<u>Sharp Cuts</u> (Planet Records: P6)--Ten American bands perform one song each for this studio compilation album. They are all fairly new, fairly unestablished groups, representing various musical tastes. Standouts include Single Bullet Theory, The Fast, and The dB'S. Interesting sounds. Check it out. --CH

Peter Gabriel <u>Peter Gabriel</u> (Mercury Records: SRM 1-3848) --The third Lp from Mr. Gabriel and possibly his best work to date. Not since "The Lamb" has he written such intense lyrics. He has dropped the theatrical gimmickry and concentrated on his lyrics and delivery. The spirit of the age is captured on this record and that feeling is dread...the floundering of the human race in these complex times. He attacks the false sense of security that the masses have been lulled into. Gabriel is able to orchestrate or fully develop his ideas; and with the help of people like: Robert Fripp, Morris Pert, Larry Fast, and Phil Collins, a dynamo of feeling is created. Atlantic declared this record commercial suicide and dropped him from their label, fortunately Mercury was quick to snatch him up. Two singles are included on this album, "No Self Control" and "Games Without Frontier." My personal fave is "Biko," a litany to the African martyr. With PG3, Peter is at last on his way. --UM

B. Rich

## Toots

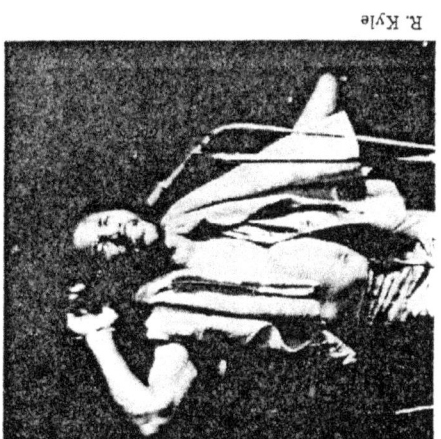

R. Kyle

Toots: We're going to sing tonight. We've been here once. Maybe not in this place. But we have been here (K.C.) before.

TT: Right. You were with The Who in 1975. How was that show?

Toots: It was terrible. A terrible show.

TT: What happened to you the two years before <u>Pass the Pipe</u>?

Toots: We had stopped touring. Just writing music and doing recordings. We have a new album now. And we're working on another. We'll have a good show tonight.

# Toots and the Maytals

Frederick "Toots" Hibbert has been the leader of The Maytals, the strongest Jamaican vocal trio, for over 15 years. Along with Jerry Mathias and Raleigh Gordon, Toots and The Maytals have had more affect upon the history of reggae music than any other group, except perhaps The Wailers. Toots is credited with inventing the term "reggae." Of course, they were important in other forms of Jamaican music, having ska hits and rock-steady hits, while also working with some of the classic producers of those eras.

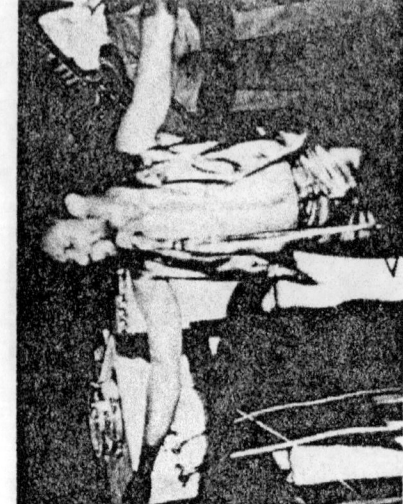
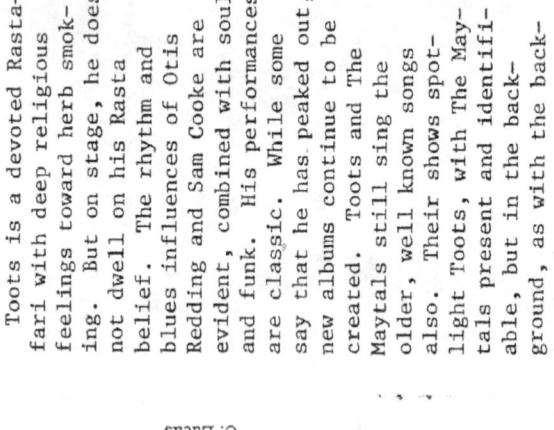
B. Rich

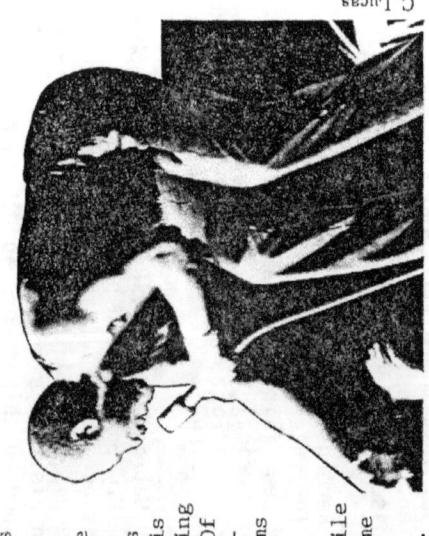
R. Kyle

Toots is a devoted Rastafari with deep religious feelings toward herb smoking. But on stage, he does not dwell on his Rasta belief. The rhythm and blues influences of Otis Redding and Sam Cooke are evident, combined with soul and funk. His performances are classic. While some say that he has peaked out, new albums continue to be created. Toots and The Maytals still sing the older, well known songs also. Their shows spotlight Toots, with The Maytals present and identifiable, but in the background, as with the backing band.

*Winston Wright, Raleigh Gordon, Toots Hibbert, Willie Lindo, Jerry Matthias, Paul Douglas*

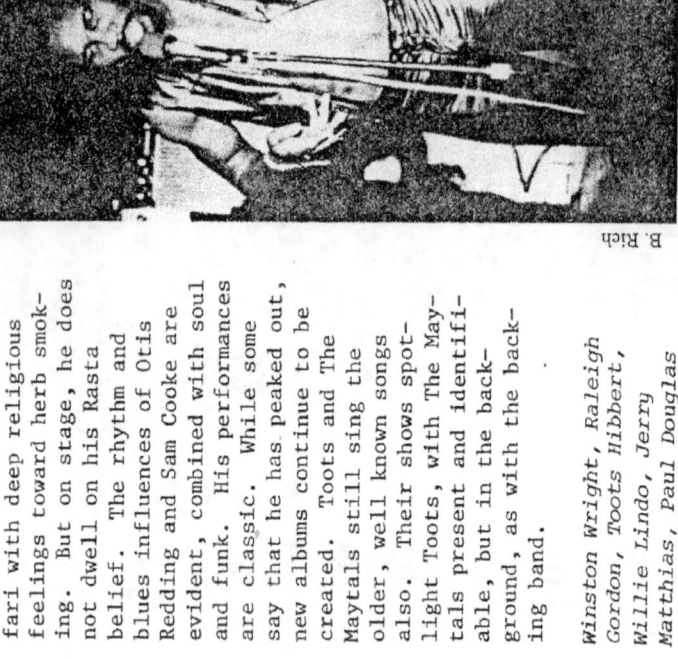
C. Lucas

C. Lucas

# Third World

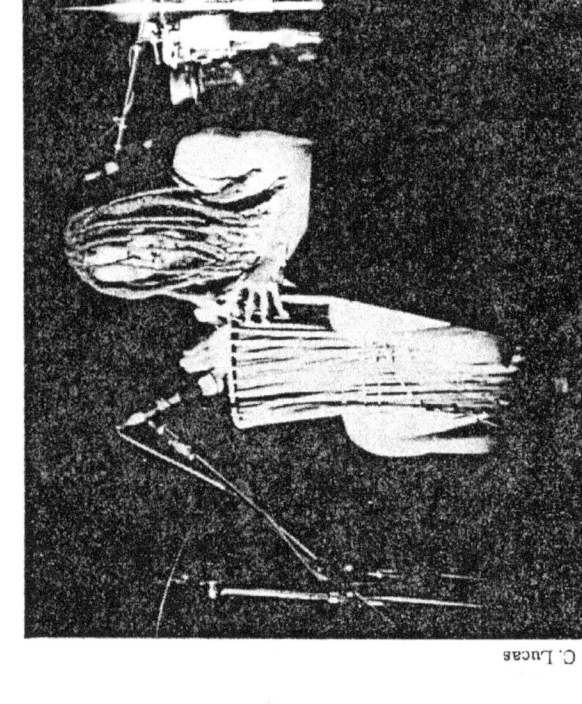
C. Lucas

June 3  The Uptown Theater

Clockwise: Willie Stewart, drums

Bunny "Rugs" Clarke, rhythm guitar; Richie Daley, bass; "Ibo" Cooper, keyboards; Cat Coore, lead guitar

"Carrot" Jarrett, percussion

Willie, Richie, Rugs, Ibo, Cat, Carrot

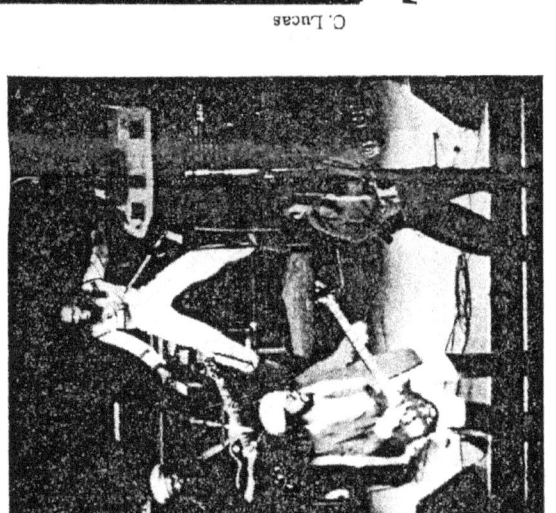
B. Rich

R. Kyle

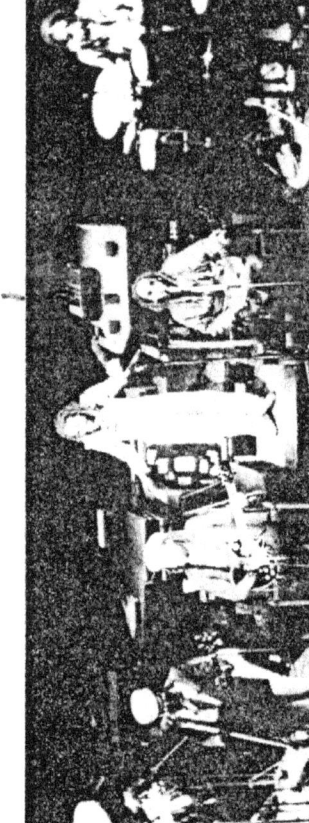
Rich

# Interview:

*Before the show, Talk Talk visited with Bunny "Rugs" Clarke, rhythm guitarist and vocalist.*

TT: What are you going to do after the tour is over?
Bunny: We're working on our plans. We plan to go to Africa. And we plan to come back to America. We want to go to Brazil. Our album, Journey to Addis, is doing real well there. They are turning on to music...reggae music. Sunshine music.
TT: You have about 31 people with you on tour?
Bunny: 35. We have mobile homes, a couple of buses and trucks. We move from bus to hotel. We spend a lot of time on the bus, most of the time. Last night we did 580 miles. A long pull (from Texas)...We did a movie, should be coming out soon. (Prisoner In The Street)
TT: You were in Rockers (the film)?
Bunny: No. They just used the music, "Satta Amasagana." We weren't in the film, just soundtrack.
TT: And what's your movie to be?
Bunny: It's a 35mm color filmed in Jamaica last February. It's an hour and a half. We have some concerts in it from Paris and Jamaica.
TT: Do you do songs from all the albums?
Bunny: We play from all five. We are promoting five albums really. A lot of people who might not turn on to Arise In Harmony might with Journey to Addis, 96° or The Story's Been Told. So we're promoting all of that.
TT: What about your disco influences?
Bunny: Disco is not a music. Disco is a word. It's not a music. It's a name.

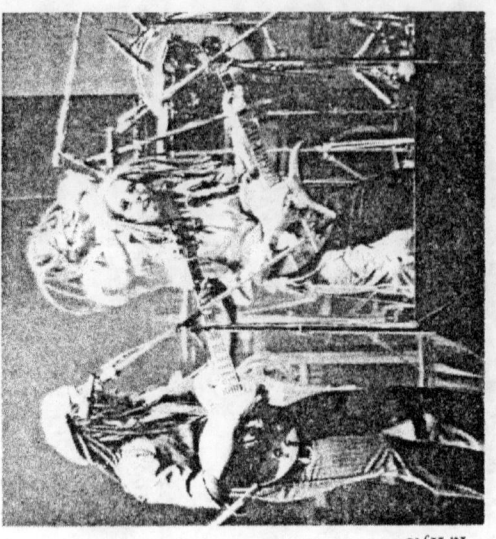

R. Kyle

# Third World

*Opposite: Rugs*
Rugs, Carrot, Cat
Cat
Richie

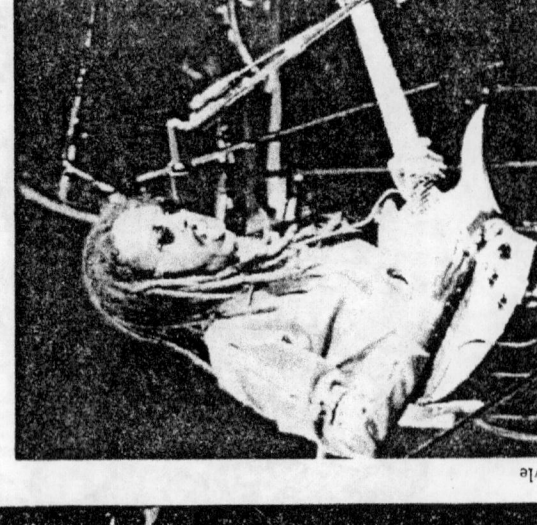

# Blue Riddim Band

Lawrence is lucky in having a top reggae band based here. If it sometimes seems to you that no good shows are scheduled for weeks, you are bound to find The Blue Riddim Band breaking the monotony associated with this isolated area.

They are a versatile group, having members who can switch instruments quite successfully. In fact, sometimes they could be several different bands by the lineups. The Blue Riddim Band is basically a reggae band. They play some reggae covers, as well as originals. The reggae rhythms are at times used for departure into soul and blues and funk. But they are a popular dance band, too. The dance floors are always crowded when they take the stage. Sometimes the band gets so involved that they play half the night with the crowds continually getting larger.

The Blue Riddim Band have many influences. But they are an original. They have recently been polishing up an album's worth of tracks. When it hits the streets, you can be sure that their (→26)

B. Rich

June 21 Centennial Park -- Pat Pearce, keyboards; Bob Zohn, guitar/vocals; Steve McLane, drums; Scott Korchak, vocals/trumpet; Jack Blackett, saxophone; Andy Meyers, bass; and Steve Prince, guitar.

# Reggae Reviews

<u>Best of Big Youth Everyday Skank</u> (Trojan: TRLS 189)--Trojan finally has compiled the best hits of Big Youth, one of the earlier and most outstanding Jamaican toasters. This album covers his career from 1972 to 1977. Big Youth originated many of the current DJ sound effects and used the current rhythms going around. He is well known for getting people to dance and twist and skank all over. Listen to this and skank away. --WB

Various Artists <u>Monkey Business</u> (Trojan Records: TRLS 188)--Yet another fine collection from Trojan. This package seems to be a mix of ska and rock steady. Some of the tunes are not that rare, as in the case of Desmond Dekker's "007 Shanty Town" and The Maytals' "54-36." For the most part, the contents of this record would take a while to track down. Particular jewels include two of the Lee Perry-produced songs, "Tighten Up" and "Return of Django." The latter one containing some very tasty sax work. The Pioneers' classic "Long Shot (Kick the Bucket)" is also included, as is the hilarious "Birth Control" by Lloydie and The Low Bites, who are known for their bawdy lyrics. To sum it up, this collection is a must for any man, woman or child who finds their reggae appetite growing by the day. <u>Monkey Business</u> is indeed a satisfying treat. --ES

<u>Duke Reid Golden Hits</u> (Treasure Isle: TILP003)--Twelve songs are included on this album which salutes one of the older producers. Duke Reid was quite a force in the early 60's and brought many artists into the limelight. Most of the cuts are unfamiliar to me and they help to round out the reissued beginnings of reggae. Most are the easy-listening type of songs soothing to listen to. --WB

Various Artists <u>Hottest Hits Vol 2</u> (Treasure Isle: TILP 002)--This excellent collection is a follow-up to last year's From the Vault compilation and it carries the Treasure Isle tradition to a new generation of music fans. The songs use brass and have some sweet sounding harmonies. Maybe they could be classed as post ska, early rock steady pop. Artists featured include Alton Ellis, Sensations, Melodians, Techniques, Phillis Dillion, Freddy McKay, (→24)

**TALK TALK**

(from p. 9) Heaven." Their performances of originals had me out of my seat and dancing between the tables. Finally, near the end of their third set, they played "Patio Set" and "Sex Drive," the two songs from their first 45, and the versions surpassed the ones captured on vinyl. Yes, The Embarrassment have come into their own and they should be proud that their hard work and talent set them way above the majority of bands the large domestic companies are passing off as "New Wave." Somebody should send an A&R man down to check them out. If they do not, it is their loss. --ES

Throbbing Gristle Zyklon B Zombie (Industrial Records: IR003)--This single recorded in mono is transmogrifying, as it takes the listener from the comfort of his room and into the gray world of industry. The A-side is directed at keeping the "zombie" worker in line. He must fill his quota and after a hard day at the plant; after handling toxic materials all day...five days a week, he and his fellow workers are rewarded. The industrial drones shower, washing the body of chemical residues (in technical terms: the foam down); but the mind still corrodes and what of the internal systems? Finally, in the (→24)

## Single Reviews

The Specials Rat Race/ Rude Buoys Outa Jail (Chrysalis: CHSTT11)--"Rat Race" was about the only song unreleased which The Specials performed on their recent U.S. tour. The sound on this recording is more tinny than usual. But they keep their social relevance standard up by putting down those who work for the rat race. The flip starts out with a harmonica solo, then the fast frenzied pace takes over. It is an enjoyable, light song fitting in with the other side to make this a single to own. --WB

Guns For Hire I'm Gonna Rough My Girlfriend's Boyfriend Up Tonight/I'm Famous Now (WEA: KOW6)--This four-piece outfit got caught up in the ska movement. I believe this is their first release. They fit in with the rest with the guest harp player. No brass used. The basic beat offers no surprise. --WB

Arthur Kay's Originals Play My Record/Sooty Is A Rudie (Red Admiral: NYMPH 002)--The second release on Nymph has taken awhile to reach the midwest. The first, "Ska Wars," offered hope for the then infant ska rebirth. This one is a Rude Boy's delight. Good horns and a steady beat keep you bouncing. It may be a joke for all I know. --WB

Bad Manners Lip Up Fatty/ Night Bus to Dalston (Magnet Records: MAG 175)--This group considers themselves to be Ska and Blues and this single shows it. "Lip Up Fatty" is on their album, which was reviewed last issue. The B-side is worth the price of the single. It is an upbeat horn-band song which utilizes all styles that these guys touch. Bad Manners have not received the attention the Two-Tone/ ska bands have, but they deserve it. I have a feeling their time will be coming soon. --ES

The Flowers Ballad Of Miss Demenaour/Food, Tear Along (Pop Aural: POP003)--What more can be said of this fine band. Strong smooth haunting tunes with seductive vocals. Not quite as good as their last effort but still a head above most of their peers. This is all worthless criticism anyway, as you will either like it or not regardless of what I say. But get it, okay? --VS

---

Talk Talk, KJHK, Bomp and The Lawrence Opera House Present

Stiv Bators and the

# DEAD BOYS

with

TESTORS

Lawrence Opera House
7th Spirit Club
642 Mass. St., Lawrence, Ks. (913) 842-6930

July 9
$3.50 advance
$4.50 at door

## Album Reviews

X Los Angeles (Slash Records: SR-104)--I cannot really rave on and on about this record. X has a strong West Coast following. I find the vocals to be boring and hard to listen to--hardly any variance in notes or tone. There is some good guitar work. The fast pace is a strong point. Ray Manzarek plays organ and produces the recording. X might be stars in their genre and it might be a triumph to have this album finally out. But, like their style on the Yes LA lp, it is easy to avoid picking this one out to play. However, you might like it. --NN

Can You Hear Me? Music From The Deaf Club (OPTIONAL: OPT-LP001)--A live album from a "happening" San Francisco club featuring Dead Kennedys, K.G.B., The Offs, Mutants, Pink Section, and Tuxedo Moon. This is a diverse section of the "California scene" bands which seems to think the only musical movement is with the West Coast. I do not agree with that attitude in general. But on to this album... Overall, these recordings are surprisingly good quality. Pink Section are my favorites. The Dead Kennedys come across well, also. This release shows that the big record companies are not needed, a healthy sign. --CH

---

Talk Talk Publications
P.O. Box 36
Lawrence, Kansas 66044

Please send me:

___ copies of Vol. 1 Collection    @ $2.00 _____

___ copies of Vol. 2 (circle choice)    @ $1.00 _____
    1  2  3  4  5  6  7  8

___ subscription to next six issues    @ $5.00 _____

Total enclosed by check or money order    $ _____

Name _____

Address _____

---

## Single Reviews

(from p. 8) over. "Split Up The Money" is almost Kinks-like in sound and the flip, "Out of Touch," is a great fun, twisted, almost R&B-sounding tune that proves Vic is brave and talented enough to buck all trends at all times. Maybe that is why he has been passed over for so many years. Maybe now MCA will put up enough backing and get an Lp out. That would be something worth waiting for. --ES

Susan Springfield The Tenant of the Room (Doe Records)--To be honest, I am not really all that crazy about her voice but the music is great, bringing to mind old Television. I never heard her with The Erasers but her guitar playing is fine. I even think she could be a good singer, if she would decide to approach the vocals a little more straight-forwardly. This 4-song Ep is not a must, but she shows promise. --VS

Drinking Electricity Shaking All Over/China (Pop Aural: Pop 004)--Radiation must have leaked out of a French reactor and into their Champagne. But I love it and so will you. (→24)

---

THE DOWNLINER
(below Plaza East)
4719 Troost
K.C., Mo.
816-753-9368

June 27-28
REGULAR GUYS
THE METHOD

July 4-5
ABUSE

July 11-12
THUMBS

July 18-19
THE NUKES

July 25-26
FURIOUS CHILD

August 1-2
THE DEBS

Open
Wed. to Sat.
7 to 1
Be 21!

Brought to you by
Sum-thing-tu-du
Productions

*Aswad Greggori, vocals/percussion; Chris Rose, bass; Donny Johnson, keyboards; Bunny Martin, drums; Greg Banns, guitar*

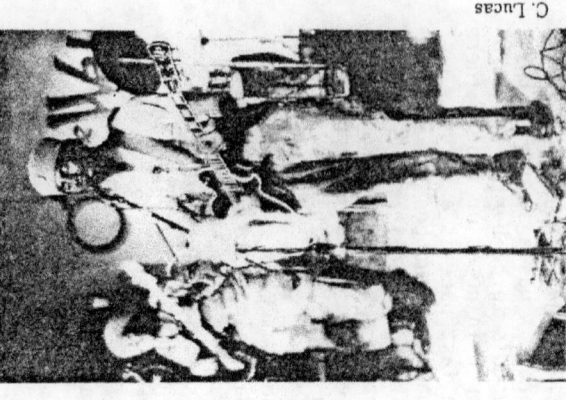

*Chris and Greg*

(from p. 6) the raw power evident on last year's debut. Their concern with girls and love comes across in cheery, poppy songs. Their version of "Boardwalk" is enjoyable. A lot of different sounds have been created by The Undertones. A great band and a great album. --CH

(from p. 7) single, ending the series of one a month until the album, but it did not make it out until after the Lp, reviewed last issue. --CH

(from p. 22) This old classic has been done to death but this band makes it sound fresh. Usually, "Shaking All Over" has been done from the macho viewpoint. Now a woman gets a chance at the song and she sings it so well that it will melt your strength from your limbs. "China" is straight electronics. Nowhere near as good as "Shaking" but interesting enough to make me search out their next product. --VS

(from p. 4) reggae uses both rhythm and lead guitars. With only one guitar for both rhythm and lead, other instruments become important in filling out the sound. While this was going on behind them, Donny Johnson moved and grooved and provided sound effects and tasty keyboard effects, while Aswad Greggori sauntered across the stage with microphone in hand and dreadlocks in his eyes.

During the course of both shows, they covered songs by Bob Marley and The Wailers, as well as Toots and The Maytals, Burning Spear, and Inner Circle.

The crowds both nights were good, which proves that this part of the country is ready for more reggae. The New Era Band supplied a quantity of it and I will be glad to see them come back. --ES

(from p. 20) distance the 6 o'clock commuter whistles and on to home, where it starts all over again. The B-side, "United," is more of this workers' lot trip. The workers are compelled to love their jobs; work towards higher production and risks. As the foreman says, "You can't stop the growth." --UM

(from p. 19) and Joya Landis. Overall, this album is sort of laid back with pleasant sounding varieties that are sure to please. --WB

(from p. 5) is something that I find myself muttering in my weak imitation falsetto. The flipside has a frenzied lead and rhythm section. Fast paced, intricate and tight. --HM

---

**Have A Heart**

This elegant crystal heart, to hang or wear, is yours FREE with every 2 pairs of fine imported crystal earrings you order. But hurry. OFFER LIMITED.

Each is cut to reflect endless sparkles and soft glows. Posts are hypoallergenic.

A. Faceted Globe  B. Shooting Star  C. Smooth Crystal Ball

A and B colors: Rose-green, Blue, Crystal-clear C colors: Blue or Crystal-clear.

Each Pair $4.00 p.p.

For complete line of beautiful crystals to hang or wear send for FREE CATALOG.

LOVE THEM OR MONEY BACK

TO ORDER: Specify A,B or C and color choice. Send Check or Money Order to:

LOCOMOTIVE, P.O. Box 8352, Prairie Village, KS. 66208
(913) 381-6732

**ROCK THERAPY**
7511 TROOST K.C.,MO.
816-333-8006

RECORDS
NEW & USED
BUY
SELL
TRADE

REGGAE
NEW WAVE
ROCKABILLY

**RECORDS AND TAPES**
**GUARANTEED USED ALBUMS AND TAPES**
We also carry a large selection of posters and t-shirts. Bring your good used albums in for cash.
**OPEN 7 DAYS A WEEK**

15 W. 9th St., Lawrence, Ks.   7222 W. 75th St., Overland Park, Ks
(913) 842-3059                 (913) 384-2499

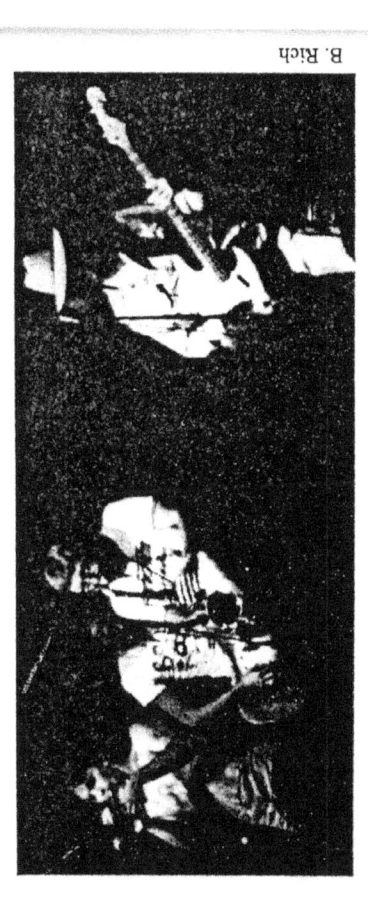

B. Rich

*June 13 Lawrence Opera House*
*Scott Korchak, Bob Zohn, Jack Blackett, and Andy Meyers.*

(from p. 18) fame will grow. Hopefully, they will remain in the area and continue providing their fans with their sounds.

=============

B. Rich

*Thumbs at The Downliner*
*Kevin Smith, guitar; Dede Mosier, drums; Steve Wilson, vocals; Karl Hoffman, bass; and Marty Olson, keyboards.*

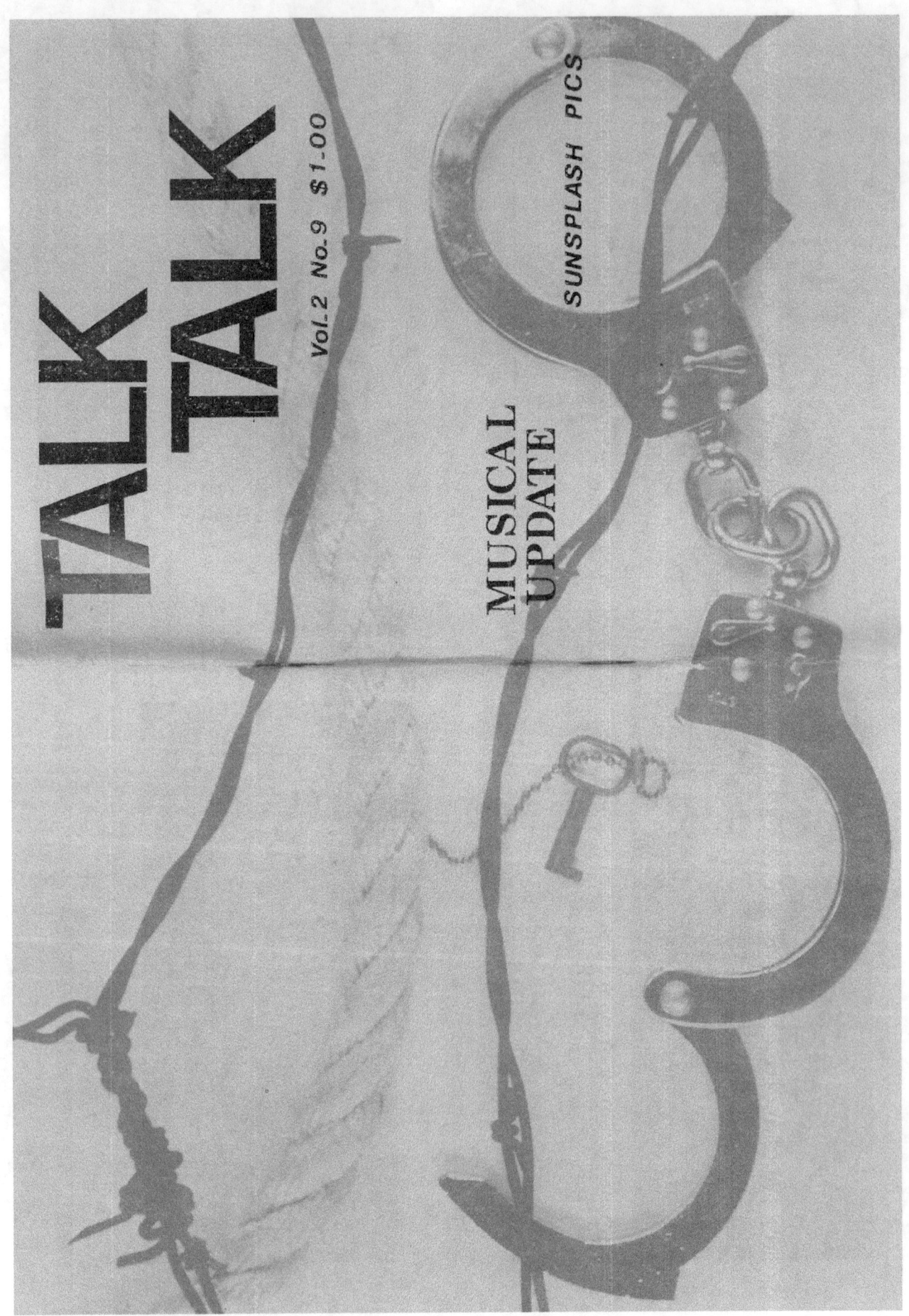

# TALK TALK

Vol. 2 No. 9    August 1980    $1.00

The Midwest American Rock and Reggae Magazine

**TALK TALK**

| | |
|---|---|
| Interview: Jake Burns........ | 3 |
| Album Reviews: Sham 69, Vic Goddard and Subway Sect..... | 5 |
| Reggae Reviews: Bob Marley, Sly and Robbie, Basement 5..... | 6 |
| Concerts: Undertones | 7 |
| Single Reviews: Ultravox, Modettes, Section 25, Joy Division | 8 |
| John Foxx, Echo and the Bunnymen, Siouxsie and the Banshees..... | 9 |
| Concerts: Debs, Regular Guys, Peter Gabriel............ | 10 |
| Traxx | 11 |
| Reggae Sunsplash III....... Exclusive coverage with photos Kingston, JA Update on the | 12 |
| Reggae Center | 28 |
| Concerts: Skeletons......... | 31 |
| Single Reviews: Glaxo Babies Slits, Young Marble Giants, | 32 |
| Du Champ.................. | 33 |
| Album Reviews: Joy Division, Colin Winski............. | 34 |
| Reggae Reviews: Jimmy Cliff, Steel Pulse, Capital Letters,. | 35 |
| Album Reviews: DAF........ | 36 |
| Feelies.................. | 37 |

**Editors:**
Bill Rich
Eric Schindling

**Contributors:**
U-Man
Rick Hellman
Jim Schwada
VS, WB, DC
Plus JFB, SMcB

**Photography:**
Robin Kyle
Christopher Lucas
Bill Rich

**Cover Design:**
Mark Schraad

**Layout:**
John Lee
Bill Rich

**Typesetting:**
Joan M. Moore

All contents copyright 1980 by Talk Talk Publications, PO Box 36, Lawrence, Kansas, 66044. All rights reserved. Any opinion expressed is solely that of the writer and not necessarily that of this publication. Subscription rate is $6 for six issues. Articles, reviews, and pix submitted for editorial consideration are welcome. Not responsible for unsolicited material. Address all correspondence to Talk Talk Editors, PO Box 36, Lawrence, Kansas, 66044..

---

Talk Talk Vol. 2 No. 9/page 3

# Interview

*On Thursday, July 10, Talk Talk had the pleasure of having a telephone interview with Jake Burns, lead vocalist and guitarist of Stiff Little Fingers. The following is an approximate account of the conversation. (Thank you, Mike at Chrysalis.)*

Talk Talk: Jake, this is Eric....
Jake Burns: Hello, Eric, this is Jake (laugh).
TT: Why are you in New York, is the band about to start a tour of the States soon?
JB: No, actually, there are only two of us over here, our manager is with me. What we're trying to do is set up some kind of tour for the fall. So the major purpose of this trip was to check out some possible venues. To see what places might be good to play at.
TT: Have you had any luck?
JB: Not yet, we've only been to a few places so far.
TT: How about Hurrahs?
JB: Yes, we've been there, last night, I think. Are you familiar with the place.
TT: Yes...
JB: Well, what did you think of it?
TT: Actually, I didn't like it very much. It was way too slick. Sort of a place that upper middle class kids go to act punk or trendy.
JB: That's it exactly. It sort of reminds me of The Music Machine in England. I don't like that place either. But the really funny thing is that at Hurrahs there was some awful band and the singer was putting on an English accent. It had us rolling!
TT: Well, have you found anywhere that might suit you?
JB: There is one place that looks promising...The Ritz, I think.
TT: So, was there any truth to the rumor that you were going to go on tour in the U.S. earlier this year?
JB: Yes. We were originally lined up to go on a tour of the States with The Who. They had asked us, but then they didn't get back in touch till it was, well about a week before their tour started and we had, by that time, set up a show at a festival in Scotland.
TT: That is interesting. There were some stories that you were somehow going to bring some members of the (→4)

## Interview

JAKE BURNS INTERVIEW (from p. 3) IRA with you.
JB: Really? What nonsense. It's funny to hear that, though. Some people try to associate us with some political groups, but we're not interested in doing that. What we sing about is that certain conditions exist and people killing each other and that's a stupid waste. We don't have any solutions except just stop the killing.
TT: In association with that, do you have any trouble playing in Ireland?
JB: We don't have any trouble. We would like to play some of the smaller cities, but right now, after I get back to England we're supposed to start a new tour.
TT: There is talk of a live album.
JB: That's right, it should be out to coincide with our American tour. We'll be recording it at two places in England on this upcoming round of shows. It will consist of some material off our first Lp. You might say it will be aimed in a way at the American market, because they've never released our first album over here. But it won't be soft. As a matter of fact, it will probably sound a lot rawer.
TT: That sounds promising. One other thing and then I will let you go. On Nobody's Heroes you cover a Specials song, "Doesn't Make It Alright," why that song and do you have any connection with The Specials?
JB: Well, we're friends with the band and if you've seen them live you'd notice that that particular song is really powerful. But on their Lp it sort of has a, how would I put it?
TT: A thin sound.
JB: Yes, that's the word, the critics called it shallow, but thin is a better word because it's in the production. The song isn't shallow at all. So, we decided to do it our way.
TT: That was really nice that it followed one of my favorite songs, "Bloody Dub."
JB: You like that, good. The critics in England thought we put it on as filler, like we had to stick something on so we came up with that. But it just isn't true. I really like that song.
TT: Well, when you tour the States, look for me.
JB: Really, let us know you're there. Hope to see you soon...

## Album Reviews

Sham 69 The Game (Polydor Deluxe: PolD 5033)--Hailed and reviled, that has been the lot of Jimmy Pursey and Sham 69. At the birth of punk they were in the forefront of the movement. The critics hailed them as equals of the Sex Pistols and The Clash. Unfortunately, increased violence at concerts and the release of a fair but not earth-shaking Lp hurt their image and soon the press turned their back on Sham 69 in search of newer things. Surprisingly enough, though, Sham 69 have held on and each of their followup works showed the band to still be strong. I have to admit I find all their albums to be unevenly but the last two, Hersham Boys and in particular The Game to be their strongest, most cohesive efforts to date. By now the English press have put out despairingly bad reviews of The Game but for the most part the bad press is wrong. Where they find heavy metal, I find a return to the heavy Detroit guitar sound of such great bands of the past as MC5 and The Stooges. Perhaps in this new influx of thinking man's mood rock (e.g., Joy Division, Wire, Echo and The Bunnymen) people tend to sneer at Sham 69 but they would be wrong to sneer for in doing that they show themselves to be in league with a petty intellectualism that has no traces in the working class, the world of Rock and Roll, which has its roots in the oppressed and poor and not art school snobbery. For a fact Sham 69 are not the only band that counts but Jimmy Pursey and Co. do care and on their new Lp they show they can play their own brand of music with energy. So, yes, it is worth having once you get by the awful cover (sorry, Jimmy)
--VS

Vic Godard and Subway Sect What's The Matter Boy? (MCA Records: MCF 3070)--Finally it is here. After three years or more Vic Godard has released his debut Lp and it is as good as I was expecting it to be. You might say that this album might throw you for a loop in the modern age of techno-rock popularity. Vic takes us back to a sparce, acoustic sound that has the flavor of dark, smoke-filled clubs. Men with sunglasses and berets and women with straight hair and black, tight slacks. If anybody has seen Orpheus by Cocteau, they will understand. At different times and on different tracks we get a (-37)

## Reggae Reviews

**Bob Marley and the Wailers** Uprising (Island: ILPS 9596) --These ten new songs by Bob Marley provide another step on the progression of The Wailers. While the last album, Survival, developed the idea of historical oppression in society, Uprising has a message for the individual that although things might not get better in the world, people can still exist and improve. The opening cut, "Coming In From The Cold", has the thoughts "when one door is closed, don't you know another is open." "Real Situation" is lyrically bleak, saying, "it seems like total destruction the only solution, and there ain't no use, no one can stop them now." From my perspective, I do not think the situation is quite so fatalistic, but then I do not have the Third World experience shaping my thoughts and activities. And I agree that Marley's message is all too realistic in terms of both worldwide failure and inner-soul reliance. The last song, "Redemption Song," features Marley playing acoustic guitar and singing all alone. "Emancipate yourselves from mental slavery. None but ourselves can free our minds." The melody is soft and simple, which is similar to the overall album's sound. Although expertly produced, there is not a reliance on studio effects. The voice of Bob Marley is upfront, along with the rhythm sounds. Great harmonies and a lively feeling. --BR

**Sly and Robbie** Gamblers Choice (Taxi Records)--The Channel One stars once again shine. This album is vocalless except for the last track featuring Sly scatting nursery rhymes and personal feelings to a steady beat. My favorite cut, especially since Sly sings so little although his drumming can be heard on thousands of recordings. In many places, they sound like Public Image played in 4/4 time. The consistent rhythm is hypnotic. Gamblers Choice is a great album to add to your Revolutionaries collection. --WB

**Basement 5** Silicon Chip/Chip Batty (Island: 10WIP 6614) --Something different from this English reggae (?) band. The throaty growl of the lead vocalist reminds me of a black John Cooper-Clark meeting John Lydon. The background musicianship relies heavily on an outfront (→37)

## Concerts

**The Undertones** Detroit Punch & Judy Theatre June 28

You would think rock 'n roll fans in Detroit, birthplace of The Stooges, MC5, and other bands at the roots of the same musical movement The Undertones now lead, would turn out in respectable numbers for one of the rare American performances by this amazing young band. But, an error in the Detroit Free Press regarding the time and place of the show bolstered attendance up into the middle-200's and undoubtedly left more than a few Undertones fans cursing the Free Press and the sounds of New York's Boyfriends at Bookie's, downtown. Undaunted by the size of the crowd, The 'Tones displayed energy rivaled only by The Ramones as they covered most of the material from their Ep, two albums, and all six singles. Feargall Sharkey made faces like an inquisitive bird at the audience whenever he was not projecting his unmistakable warble over the addicting guitar interplay of brothers Dee and John O'Neill. The sparce crowd at this posh suburban theatre made their appreciation known by pelting the band with wads of paper, dollar bills, and potatoe bread, and bringing them back for three encores. The Undertones created a night never to be forgotten by anyone lucky enough to find the gig. --JTB

**Ultravox** Sleepwalk/Waiting (Chrysalis: CHS 2441)--A new release from the revamped electric boys featuring: Billy Currie, Chris Cross, Warren Cann, and Midge Ure. The A-side is atypical of an Ultra-V tune, a fast-paced electric ditty interspersed with Currie's violin and Cann's electronic percussion. The B-side (which should have been the A-side) starts with an intro sounding like Eno or Cluster. A very pleasant, almost organic piece that picks up quite rapidly with Cann's very crisp drumming. Midge Ure displays his guitar playing ability, besides some of his best singing to date. All I can say is that Midge Ure is at last comfortable with his role in the band and has cast off the stigma of simply being a replacement for John Foxx. This single is produced by Conny Plank, she has produced previous material for them as well as other electronic groups. An album entitled Vienna is on the way. --U-Man

## Single Reviews

**Mo-Dettes Paint It Black/ Bitta Truth...Twist and Shout (Deram: Det R1)**--Another offering from the girls who brought you "White Mice." This cover of the classic Rolling Stones could have been a tired cover, but The Mo-Dettes approach it with a sly grin and a heavy rhythm line that reminds me of the darkest Africa of an old Popeye cartoon. The flip side, "Bitta Truth," shows that they still write well and The Mo-Dettes style is becoming more defined. There is an extra added goodie in the form of a one-sided flexi disc with the old classic, "Twist and Shout," done with a tinny sound and a sense of fun that does the original proud. All in all, a welcome offering from one of the up and coming stars on the horizon. I want more. --VS

**Section 25 Girls Don't Count/Knew Noise/Up to You (Factory: Fac 18A)**--You say you like PiL? You think Joy Division are the greatest thing since sliced bread? Then you will probably enjoy the new single by Section 25 on Factory Records. No, not Sector 27, Tom Robinson's new band, this is Section 25, a group firmly entrenched in the sparce funky style pioneered by PiL and a few other English bands. This is dreadrock and it has got nothing to do with Rastafarians or dope. The vocals are suitably screamed in the best Lydon style and the backing track is nicely rhythmic. The three songs here have a palpable beat and, because of length restriction or good sense, never have a chance to get boring. All in all, an auspicious debut for Section 25, so get it right away or be condemned forever as un-hip!--RH

**Joy Division Love Will Tear Us Apart/These Days plus... (Factory Record: Fac 23)**--By the time you read this, you should know that Ian Curtis, the band's lead vocalist and a great talent, is dead. In his wake he leaves two excellent new 45 releases and the Joy Division's second Lp. His legacy to us with the band is a great one. For this Ep is perhaps the best thing Joy Division has done. The mixed irony of "Love Will Tear Us Apart" is almost too much to bear. The song has perhaps the most spry melody of any of their work, yet the (→33)

**John Foxx Burning Car/ 20th Century (Metal Beat vs 360)**--This single sounds a lot like stuff taken from his debut album, Metamatic, a lot of steam pipe percussion and violin with very simplistic lyrics. It could get old fast. I could never understand why John Foxx went off on a solo career. Perhaps so he could imitate Gary Numan, who was imitating him. The B-side is a lot more of this electronic hand clapping stuff with siren sounding synthesizers and all the while Mr. Foxx tells us it is the 20th century. There is a great bass line that runs through this song and some clever background effects. But I, as well as most of us, know what time it is...it is almost the 21st century to be more precise. --U-Man

**Echo and the Bunnymen Rescue/Simple Stuff (Korova Records: KOW 1)**--With the addition of a drummer, replacing their tape recorder (the Echo of the band), The Bunnymen have further electrified and intensified their sound. No longer is it as thin or hollow sounding due to their once seemingly acoustic oriented sound. But make no mistake, their first single, Books/ Pictures, was not bad. In fact, it was the very sparceness of their sound that captured my attention. Now they do not have to be as oblique and haunting, with a full complement of talented musicians, they can be uninhibited and really show what they are made of. This single proves my point. Be on the watch for their debut album entitled Crocodiles. --U-Man

**Siouxsie and The Banshees Happy House/Drop Dead-Celebration (Polydor: POSP 117) Christine/Eve Black-Eve Whit (Polydor: 2059 249)**--When personal problems caused a split among the members of this band in the midst of their last UK tour, many thought that the brief history of Siouxsie and The Banshees was finished. Yet Siouxsie and (sole Banshee) John Severin continued on, first with members of The Cure accompanying them and now John McGeoch (guitarist for Magazine). It is his guitar playing on both of these singles that helps to make these four songs some of Siouxsie's best material "Happy House" is a song about living in an asylum where everyone is happy. It is here that one (→32)

# Concerts

The Debs with The Regular Guys   Off the Wall Hall   July 19

It was a warm (very hot actually) welcome that greeted The Debs this Saturday night. Off the Wall Hall was filled. The beer flowed and sweat shimmering bodies were gyrating on the dancefloor as The Debs let loose with their own fine brand of Rock and Roll. By mixing rockabilly, soul, and fairly new music they provided something for everybody.

Their version of "Black Slacks" was a success as was their dancefloor shaking encore of "You Can't Sit Down." This four-piece all girl girl band were loved. Unfortunately, I am afraid that many view them as an oddity (being an all girl band) which is wrong because when they are on stage they have an intense presence that goes beyond gender. They play with a fervor lacking in too many bands. The Debs are another example of a midwest band that should be picked up by a major label. It is indeed sad to see so many worthless bands picked up and then hear the record industry moan about lack of sales. If anybody has any sense they should bet an A&R man to see The Debs. (→31)

Peter Gabriel   Chicago   June 26

Things may change in this world, but Peter Gabriel is still Peter Gabriel, at least he was in Chicago on June 26. Even though he has discarded the costumes and musical styles of old, his personality remains, making him one of the most interesting, if not strange, solo artists around. His concert centered around his new album, which he performed almost in its entirety, although such old favorites as "Solsbury Hill," "Moribund the Burghermeister," and "Mother of Violence" were also performed. His new band, consisting of David Rhodes on guitar, Tony Levin on bass, Larry Fast on keyboards, and Jerry Marotta on drums and assorted percussion, is not as polished as bands Gabriel has performed with in the past, the harder edge they gave Gabriel's music fit right in. The lighting and staging of the band was almost stark, as he used white television lights for most of the songs. Gabriel also threw in two as yet unreleased songs: "I Go Swimming" and "Milgram 23/64." Both of these were lyrically simplistic and (→31)

# Concerts

Traxx  Live  Off The Wall Hall   July 5

It was hot, very hot. So far the great Heat Wave of 1980 has claimed over a thousand lives. On this night I felt as if I would become one of the statistics. Traxx are a fine band. They had the crowd forgetting about the heat and swaying to the music. They are more of a Burning Spear type band, which means they play slow and steady and sing many praises to Jah. I found them satisfying but I wish they would have used their keyboards more. I think that would have picked up their sound a bit. They were steady and another fine addition to the local music scene that seems to be thriving and wanting more reggae nowadays. I hope to see them again when the temperature is down around 90 degrees. --ES

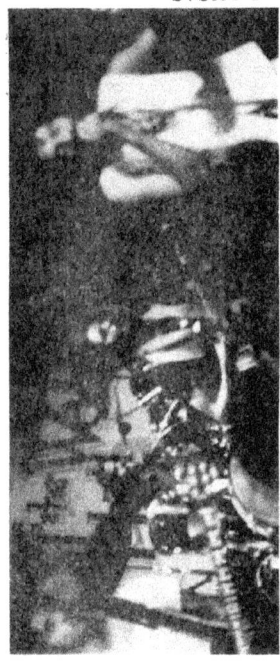

C.LUCAS

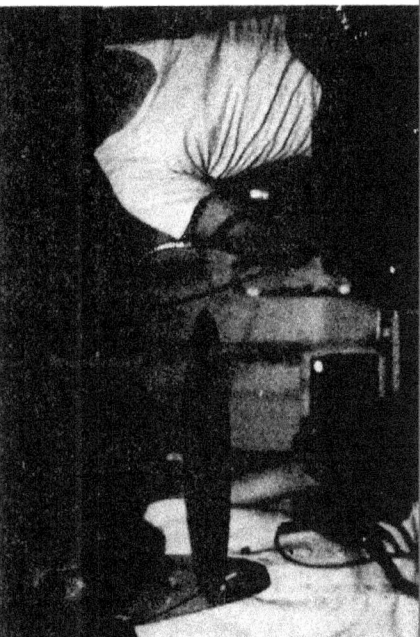

C.LUCAS

# Reggae Sunsplash III

Text and Photos by Bill Rich

Reggae Sunsplash III, Jamaica's International Music Festival, was staged in Kingston in early July. The annual event was moved from Montego Bay to the city in a return to the roots, where reggae developed. Kingston has problems similar to other large cities. But more importantly, it is the home of the legendary recording studios and reggae artists who have put Jamaica on the map. Many feel that reggae is the music of the 80's and will soon mushroom into popularity. Sunsplash III was a showcase of about 30 acts which certainly have been and continue to be major influences in the continuation of reggae.

The highlights of the Festival were four nights of concerts held outside under the stars. Headlining the first night, Wednesday, July 2, was Peter Tosh. His performance was perhaps the best, although other acts excelled. Sunsplash began with the dub poet, Oku Onaru. He recited/chanted a few of his works, then he was accompanied by his four-piece band for some more songs. It was a memorable, well received performance expressing the anguish caused by injustice.

After a lengthy break, Word, Sound and Power took to the stage. Featuring the great duo, Sly Dunbar on drums and Robbie Shakespeare on bass, they provided the backing music for the remainder of the evening. Jimmy Riley came out and sang a few songs. Then The Tamlins took over. They are a vocal/percussion trio with several recent hits which they slickly presented along with an encore before turning the stage over to The Black Uhuru. They sang several of their many hit singles and the title cut from their new (→14)

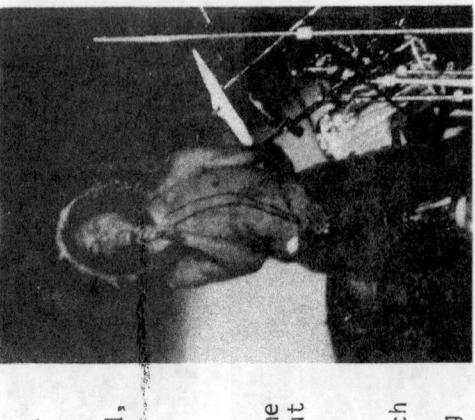

Peter Tosh

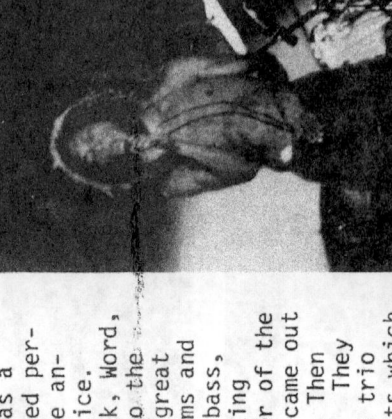

Oku Onaru

Black Uhuru

# Sunsplash

(from p.13) Mango Lp, "Sinsemillian". Michael Rose bounded across the stage, reacting to the crowd's roar. After an encore they left and the band took a break to prepare for the superstar, Peter Tosh. Wearing oversized baggy pants, a black and green dashiki, a turbin, and sunglasses, The Mystic Man danced to centerstage with his spliff in hand. He sang some of his well known hits and along with Wood, Sound and Power provided an extremely intense performance. The Tamlins provided some backing harmonies. At one point, Tosh began preaching about the injustices inflicted upon Rastafarians. He had a message to the people to change their ways. He was serious, not joking, and the continual laughter from the crowd upset him. Perhaps this crowd response was shaped by the evening's M.C., who had tried to be comical and entertaining --night club style. Reggae music is the only music with spiritual ingredients, which can heal a sick nation, said Tosh, before continuing his show. The night ended with the encore number "Buck In Ham Palace."

Robbie Shakespeare and Sly Dunbar

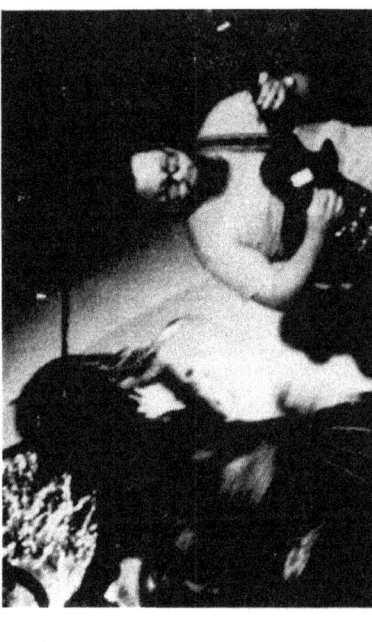

The Tamlins and Peter Tosh

Robbie Shakespeare, Peter Tosh, Mikey "Mao" Chung

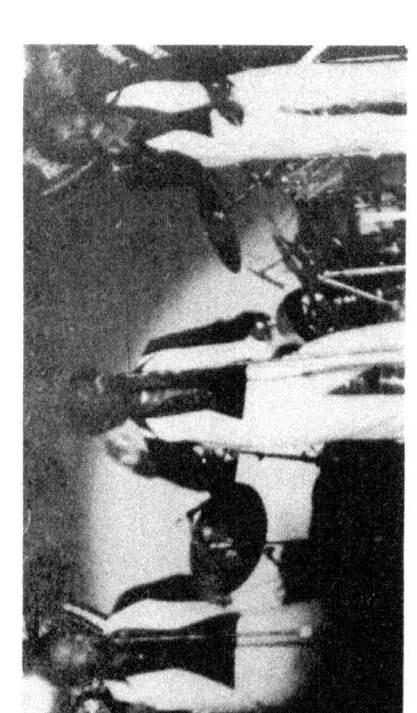

The Tamlins

# Sunsplash

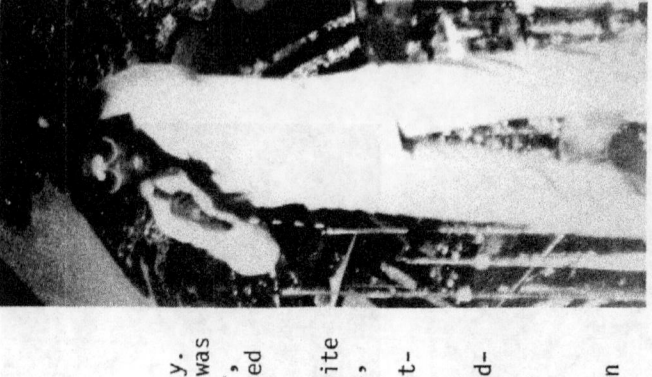

Trinity

We The People

Bob Andy

The second evening began with a predominately white rock band from Ocho Rios, Native. The three guitarists switched to drums and percussion at times backed by bass, drums, and keyboards. It was more rock than reggae oriented. Although a little out of place, they excelled with some good instrumental numbers and harmonies.

After a set change, Infinite Sensuality appeared. This seven-piece group: of two keyboardists, guitarist, sax, bass, drums, and vocalist, played a while then they were joined by Bob Andy, who sang many of his numbers. As the master of easy rhythm, he set the tone for this evening of slower rhythm.

Next Lloyd Parks and We The People began. Their sound employed a brass section of trombone, trumpet, and saxophone with harmonica, keyboards, drummer, singer, and the outstanding bass of Lloyd Parks. Trinity came out after a few songs for a brief appearance. The crowd demanded more and received it. Carlene Davis followed, singing some of her originals and Wailers' songs. Delroy Wilson followed her. Then General Smiley and Poppa Michigan, a new young dj duo, sang a few of their recent hit songs as the crowd went crazy. It was quite late when it was announced that the headliner, Burning Spear, had not arrived in Jamaica yet. Ken Boothe ended the evening with his smooth sounds. There was quite a range of styles that night, from the opening rock influences to smooth songs to scatting. An hour power outage proved to heighten the audience's anticipation about midway through the night. The crowd, significantly smaller than the sold-out opening night, remained calm and patient, perhaps a reflection of the slow paced Jamaican society.

# Sunsplash

Sunsplash crowd

Delroy Wilson

Ken Boothe

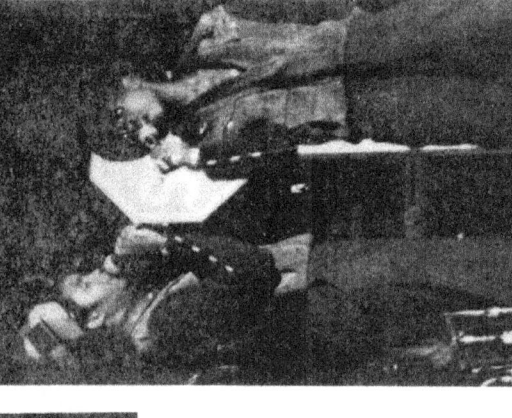

General Smiley and Poppa Michigan

# Sunsplash

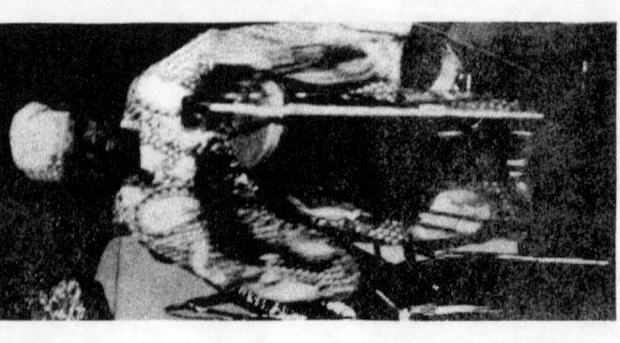
Bongo Herman

Ansel Collins
Kiddus I

The third evening opened with a new inexperienced group, Sagitarius. Their line-up included guitarist, bassist, drummer, and a brass section of trombone, trumpet, and saxophone. They were joined by a four-man vocal group, reportedly all doctors and featuring the best tenor around. The focus was on tight harmonies and high register notes.

Bongo Herman appeared in African dress to beat rhythms along with another bongo player. This unique musical form receives little attention or interest in today's civilization. His performance was accompanied by a young female dance team grooving to his beats.

Up next was Kiddus I and his band featuring two keyboards, bongo player, drummer, two guitars, bass, and vocalist. Theirs was a very polished sound. After their set, a four-piece male dance group, Shade, danced to four recorded songs.

Zap-Pow played a lengthy set, covering a lot of their older material with keyboards, drums, percussion, two guitarists, bass, saxophone, and trumpet.

After a short break, the stars of the evening came out. The Revolutionaries were in fine form as they played some instrumentals before being joined by Culture and the Mighty Diamonds.

On this evening, the band was composed of Ansel Collins on keyboards, Willy Lindo on guitar, Doug Bryan on rhythm guitar, Ranchy McClean on bass, Sticky Thompson on skins, Michael Richardson on drums, and Harry Fehant on bongos.

Culture featured Joseph Hill, although the other two members of this important trio were outstanding. Hill provided the most energetic movements of the evening. They performed for some length with Hill giving comments between each song, asking for peace. The crowd demanded more and Culture played an extended encore. (→22)

## Sunsplash

(from p.21)

The Diamonds took the stage. They performed some of their hits and new material, providing a fitting end. This evening of Sunsplash had been dominated by high male harmonies, slick stage movements, and coordinated dress, showing some soul influence in the diversified Jamaican Reggae scene.

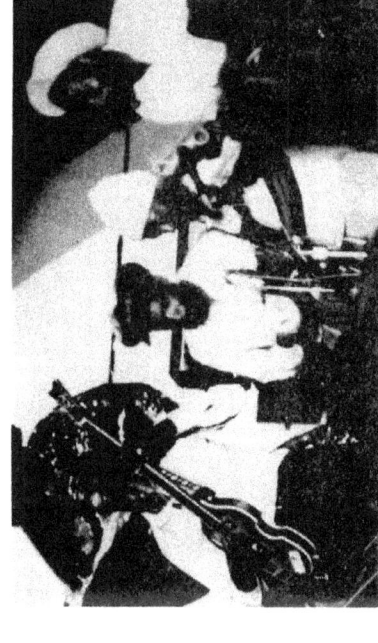
Revolutionaries

The Mighty Diamonds

Zap-Pow

Joseph Hill of Culture

# Sunsplash

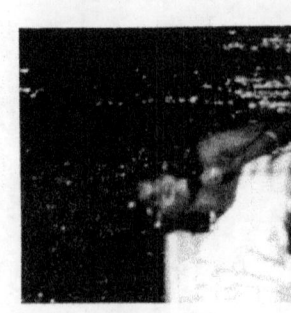

Carlene Davis

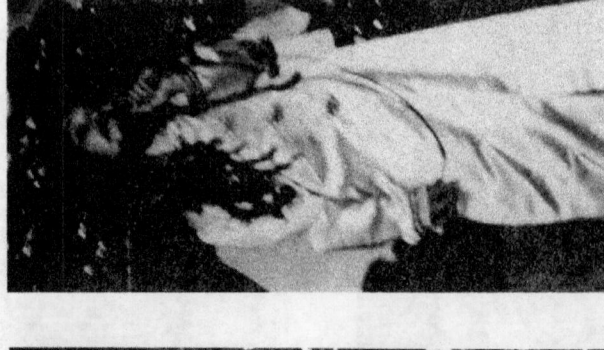

Michael Smith

I Kong

Barrington Levy

The final night of Sunsplash opened with the poet, Michael Smith, accompanied by two bongo drum players. Although outstanding at times, his extended use of a throaty moan-wail became a major barrier for the audience who had been waiting patiently for the show.

Lloyd Parks and We The People came out soon and played some instrumentals before being joined by the next three artists. Carlene Davis bounded on stage for a repeat performance of Thursday's show. Then I Kong, an African-Chinese Rasta in oriental dress, appeared with a pipe and four assistants to smoke a little to begin his performance.

Barrington Levy was up next, and the crowd went wild. He sang a few of his hits plus an encore. His fine voice does rival that of the great Dennis Brown, the headliner this evening. During the set change, Prince Edwards told his off-color jokes. The next set featured The Revolutionaries backing Sugar Minott and Leroy Sibbles (of The Heptones). The Revolutionaries were in fine form again and carried the artists across to several encores.

We The People set up for the final acts of Sunsplash. First, General Smiley and Poppa Michigan provided another dose of their special duo-dj style, which has made them the tops. The crowd wanted more and more. Finally, they had to stop. It was after 3 and Dennis Brown hopped on stage as the crowd roared and the front became even more packed. He sang songs from older Lps and recent releases. His outstanding performance was a fitting end for the final evening of Sunsplash and the finale of a great series of concerts which will long be remembered as the Reggae showcase.

Talk Talk Vol. 2 No. 9/page 27

# Sunsplash

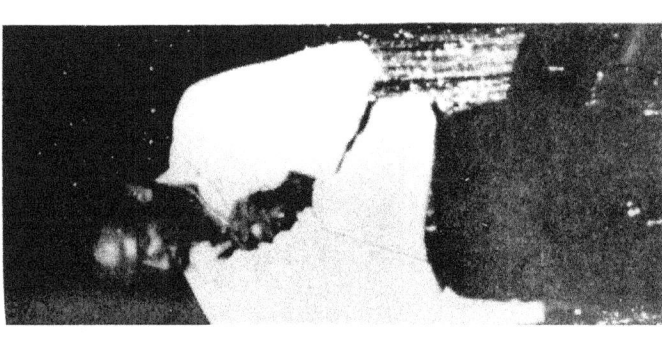

Dennis Brown ←

General Smiley and Poppa Michigan →

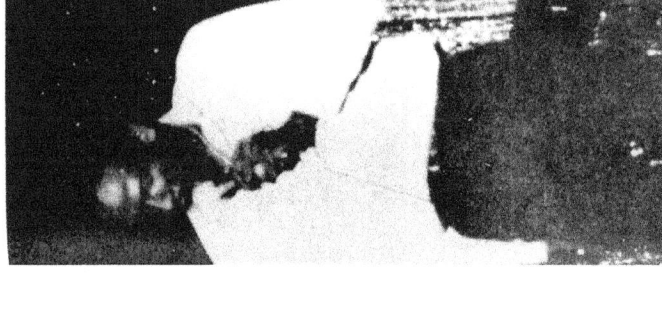

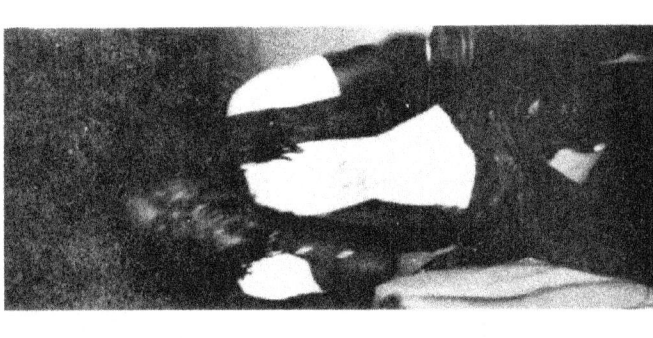

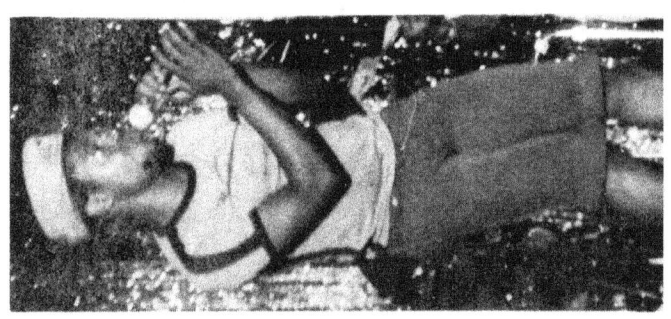

Talk Talk Vol. 2 No. 9/page 26

Sugar Minott w/ actors. Below – Sugar Minott, Leroy Sibbles

## Kingston, Jamaica

"Jamaica is at war, you know," said my taxi driver. "The two political parties are fighting each other. But you don't have to worry. They can tell you are a tourist and won't bother you." Maybe, but if you are not a supporter of one party, you must be an enemy. Everyday, handfuls of people are shot or machetted to death or burned out. Poverty, hunger, and injustice are highly visible, and the resulting crime is on the increase. Jamaicans will point out that their problems are worldwide, especially in large cities. Some say other places are worse, and point to Iran. While this is undoubtedly true, the fundamental difference is that Jamaicans want to remain a democracy—"Ballots not bullets" can be seen sprayed on buildings. Current problems and the upcoming Jamaican elections are making Kingston a very tense city. But being the home of reggae, the music continues with recording studios as busy as ever.

Stopping at Channel One Studio, I found a session going on with Sly and Robbie, along with Earl Lindo, Pablo and Skully, working on an album, "Prince Junior Tops The World", produced by Stewart Chin of Black Ovation. Sly Dunbar and Robbie Shakespeare are personally responsible for a new barrage of reggae flooding the world.

At Joe Gibbs Recording Studio, I met N Kojak, a young vocalist who is still trying to launch a career, as many other Jamaicans. He brought me into the control room where Errol Thompson, the chief engineer, and his

## Kingston, Jamaica

assistant, Oswald Palmer, were mixing a tape.

The scene at Tuff Gong was different. A record store is in one end, where the clerk was singing over a PA playing a rhythm track. In another part of the building, the small studio was busy with a horn section rehearsing. There were many people roaming around here everytime I came by—both white tourists and Rastas.

I went by Prince Buster's Records and talked to the Prince. With the recent Ska revival, the Two Tone phenomena and groups such as Selecter and The Beat covering old Prince Buster songs, there has been a worldwide interest in what the man is doing. The Prince has recently started singing again, with the ten new tracks finished and 26 more planned. He had quit singing for a period because he (→30)

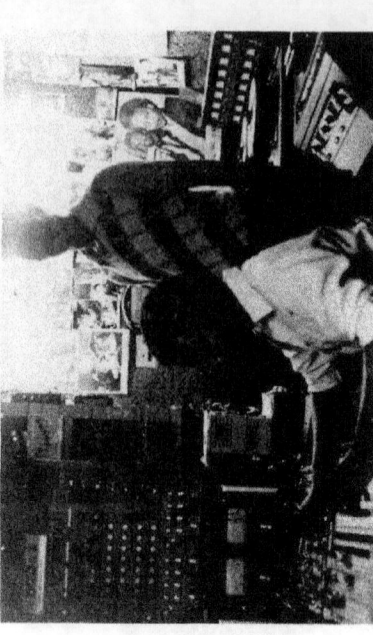

N Kojak
Errol Thompson and Oswald Palmer
Opposite: Abandoned construction project, Kingston, JA

# Kingston, Jamaica

was studying Islam. But there were too many things he felt did not apply to his life and he decided to begin recording again. In this period, he had been involved with music, helping others to be produced but never singing. He is still with the same manager and is working on a deal with Arista who are very interested in him. "I have some new beats. Sometimes you can tell a hit when you hear it. I think I have some good hits," he said. Later he added, "Last night at least a thousand rounds were fired on this street. It is like Chicago in the 20's. Lots of fighting. They were just driving down the street shooting and everyone was running. But you are safe in front of my store. Not down the street or at night."

There is talk that musicians are planning to leave Jamaica for a safer environment. Most agree that reggae in the 80's will take over the world. Byron Lee's Dynamic Sounds Studio is remodeling their studio and claims to be the only ones expanding. Their focus is not reggae, anyway. What the future holds for reggae is unclear presently. But since reggae is all about peace, love, and justice, it seems that this musical form will continue to grow and increase in importance.

*Prince Buster*

# Concerts

(from p.10) Now with all this ballyhoo I bet you thought I forgot about The Regular Guys. Well, I have not and cannot, they too are another fine example of this area's music. At times their performances can be uneven but this was not the case on July 19th. As a matter of fact, it was perhaps the best show I have seen by them in a while. From the very first chord leading into "Yankee Doodle Boy," I knew I was in for a grand time. For the length of their two sets, I was finding myself moving to their beat. Once again, they prove themselves to be a hard working, hard playing band. The Debs and The Regular Guys are a powerful one-two combination that will knock you out. --ES

(from p.10) more rock than some of his other pieces. Gabriel proved himself to be the showman of old, dancing and gyrating across the stage and at times teasing the audience for their passivity. The concert was not a duplication of the album, but rather an amplification; songs like "And Through The Wire" and "Intruder" were more uptempo and harder, while songs like "Not One Of Us" and "Lead A Normal Life" were more haunting and eerie. The climax of the show was "Biko," done with much feeling and ending the show. Three encores followed: "In the Air," "Here Comes the Flood," and "D.I.Y.," the last coming after the houselights had gone up. Random Hold opened the show, with rather mechanical music and bleak music they set the tone for the evening. In all, the concert re-affirmed Gabriel's unique ability to entertain in cerebral fashion. --SMcB

The Skeletons Live   The Lawrence Opera House   July 18

What promised to be a great evening turned out to be just a fair one. The Skeletons sound like they are a really fine band. On this night though, they just could not get the spark going. Maybe it was the oppressive heat and the sparce crowd (due in part to the heat). Nevertheless, this band is of professional quality (you might recognize them from being Steve Forbert's backup band). Over the course of the evening, they performed songs of their own as well as a bevy of covers. Their style is (→37)

## Single Reviews

(from p. 9) starts to notice the changes in sound. That continuous chainsaw guitar is no longer, instead a refined, more sombre sound is created. Siouxsie's voice still has that Valkyrie quality to it. The B-side, "Drop Dead-Celebration", has that familiar dirge-like tone to it. It is a litany to many of Siouxsie's fans or groupies, perhaps hangers-on (if you will). In so many words she tells them to drop dead or get lost...the stinking little worms that they are, but nonetheless it is still a time for celebration. "Christine", the A-side of the second single is a somewhat psychedelic sounding song about a girl who is transformed into a strawberry girl (?) and a turtle, among other things. With John McGeoch playing on acoustic guitar, this song has the feel of early Bowie (circa Ziggy). "Eve White"/"Eve Black" is also in that familiar Banshee vein, with Siouxsie giving us some of her most nerve rending wails. This is a song about split personalities. Each Eve is fighting for dominance. One of them wants out, but which is stronger? The picture sleeve for the "Christine" single is rather Freudian. One blindfolded and bikini-clad beauty gnaws on a huge strawberry or is it a piece of meat? Red fluid runs down her arm as she satiates herself. Her twin, on the other hand, is busy holding up a bunch of bananas. All due to a hormonal imbalance, I suppose. --U-Man

Glaxo Babies Shake (the Foundation/She Went to Pieces (Heartbeat: Pulse 8)--The A-side is taken from their debut Lp, Nine Months to the Disco, and is almost an exact rendition of the song. The guitar and bass interact well together. This is a great dance number. The B-side is new material recorded live on 28-3-79 and is dedicated to the modern fashion hounds (?). This one sounds a lot like the Pop Group in its musical frenzy. A crazed guitar and elephantine sax seem to battle it out and accentuating it is frenetic bass while the lead singer shouts the title. For a live recording, it is a little muddled but still it is a look at them outside the studio. --U-Man

## Single Reviews

(from p. 8) message of doom is still with us as the title so aptly puts it. If any single is worth having at the moment it is this. The new album will be in soon and after that what will happen to this (a landmark, groundbreaking) band, only the future can tell. One thing for sure is that their name is turning out to be an appropriate one. --VS

The Slits Man Next Door/Version (Y-Rough Trade: RT 044)--This new offering from The Slits has the girls doing a John Holt tune (look him up in your reggae history books) and they change it to fit their style. Personally, I find the version of "Man Next Door" preferable to their so-called straight cover of it. It still is typical Slits (if anything they do can be called typical). All and all a single worth having. Lots of nice Dub effects used wisely and, of course, their enchanting vocals. Hope a new album is on the way. --VS

Young Marble Giants Final Day, Radio Silents/Cakewalking, plus... (Rough Trade: RT043)--More mutated folk-rock from one of my favorite bands. If you like a clear, clean voice then you will love Allison Statton's style, sort of like a clean cut Nico. As for the rest of the band...Philip and Stuart Moxam play the instruments and you will not find a drummer on this Ep or their album and they get along quite nicely without one. The music has a heavy bass sound to it and a chilling carnival organ. The last song, not listed on the sleeve could have been included in the soundtrack for The Shining. Friends of mine who usually hate my taste are surprised by this band. --VS

DuChamp Rain/What You Say? D-(GrimpTimusic Records: 1050)--The one DuChamp concert I saw was pretty dire, which makes this single something of a surprise because it is quite good. The A-side takes the basic beat of Pere Ubu's "Modern Dance" and stretches it out while vocalist Bi Scanlan improvizes nicely. Scanlan shows good range and phrasing which was not evident in concert. The B-side is good, too. Kind of Talking Heads-meet-The Rolling Stones funk riff. The playing is together and the songs hold your interest. --RH

## Album Reviews

Joy Division Closer (Factory Records: Fact 25)-- The cover of this, Joy Division's, second and probably last album is a fitting epitaph. It is a reproduction of The Passion Play. It shows mourners weeping over the dead body of a Christ figure. The album is their most powerful and emotion moving work. The music weaves in and out of your consciousness, as if it is part of a dream movement. Two of the most immediately striking songs are "Atrocity Exhibition," with its chilling lyrics, talking of people deriving pleasure from torture, and "Decades," the final track, which has such a hauntingly beautiful melody that it brings my heart up into my throat. So this is an end to a chapter in Joy Division's book of Genesis. The band is reportedly going to change their name and go on...life goes on... --VS

Colin Winski Rock Therapy (Takoma Records: TAK 7083)-- Yeeow! I like this record. Colin used to be in a real hot rockabilly outfit called Ray Campi and His Rockabilly Rebels. Since then he has flown out on his own and does he fly! The first good sign was when I found out this record was on Takoma, home of John Fahey and The Thunderbirds. From the first moment, this record hit my turntable I could sense it was a winner. You will not find much of anything to make you think here. Colin Winski's music should be taken for what it is, good, rollicking fun that starts your toes tapping and rear end wiggling and will not let you stop moving until the tone arm lifts off the record. Colin Winski succeeds where others (like Robert Gordon) fail. So, if you like good solid rockin' music that you can dance to, then you need a session with Colin Winski's Rock Therapy. --VS

## Reggae Reviews

Jimmy Cliff I Am Living (WEA Records: K99089)--What a great voice. What a great cover, with Jimmy staring out at you like the eternal rude boy. Unfortunately, the record as a whole is disappointing. I will not say it is a total failure because there are moments on this record that really shine. "All The Strength We Got" is perhaps the best cut on this Lp and it is recorded in Jamaica. Which brings me to a point that I am sure has been brought up before; why does not Jimmy Cliff record in his own country more often and utilize the fine musicians that at the moment abound there? Jimmy's main problem is that he is too smooth for his own good and as an example look who arranges the horns on this album, none other than Mr. L.A. school of easy listening Tom Scott! So come on, Jimmy, your last album was a move in the right direction, move back to your roots, musically. At this time, when reggae is starting to finally take a foothold, we need Jimmy Cliff, but not in his present form. --VS

Steel Pulse Caught You (Island Records: ILPS 9613)--First let me say that I like this band. I have never been one of the many that have criticized them to death. Their first Lp was my favorite reggae album of the year. Their second record did not quite match their first but that often happens after stunning debuts. Unfortunately, their third album, Caught You, is a major disappointment, not because of the material like many feel, but the way they present it. Their smooth harmonies are inappropriate on a song like "Harrassment" and "Drug Squad." Instead of leaping into the song with a heavy rhythm and vocal growl to express their dilemmas and stands, they choose to play softly, assuming maybe that this might be their ticket to success. My greatest fear is that this album will be considered such a dismal failure that Island (which seems to be a very fickle label) might drop them and that would be a shame. Steel Pulse can really burn as is shown more recently on their 12-inch single, "Sound System." As much as I like the band and have faith in them, I cannot recommend this album. Maybe next time. --VS

# Album Reviews

Capital Letters Headline News (Greensleeves: GREL7)-- Another band from the burgeoning U.K. reggae scene, Capital Letters combines political awareness with a driving beat reminiscent of another U.K. band, Steel Pulse. Headline News, the band's first Lp, is a cooker from start to finish with the subject matter of their songs ranging from "Herb" (their hit U.K. single "Smoking My Ganja") to everyone's favorite insane despot "President Amin", all delivered with faultless harmony by vocalists Danny McKen and George Scarlett, with backup by Pauline Spence and Pauletta Hayden. Also worthy of mention is the inventive percussion work of Rodrick Harvey and Wenty Stewart, with special assist from "dub" whoever that might be. My pick is "Daddy Was No Murderer." --DC

Deutsch Amerikanische Freundschaft Die Kleinen und Die Bösen (Mute Records: STUMM 1)--At last an album from DAF and what an album it is. There are 19 songs on this record, each a manifesto performed in a somewhat nursery rhyme form. Their sound is similar to DEVO and the Gang of Four, but then again it is quite different altogether. The synthesizers (performed by C. Haas) are bouncing little sonic rhythms that are constantly in flux (from a fluid, almost hypnotizing drone to electronic chaos). The Jews-harp sounding bass and a slashing almost spastic guitar fit right in, accentuating the vocals. And speaking of them...they are not really sung, rather they are shouted. DAF make great use of the guttural almost angry nature of the German language. At times it is reminiscent of Nazi oratorios in its degree of frenzy. In fact this record could be an aural attack. DAF could be a terrorist group, who are conducting their war through commercial venues. The 19 songs deal with politics and sex. Politically they are apolitical. Their very name, DAF, is a parody of banners found draped on the Berlin Wall proclaiming Soviet and German friendship. DAF attack both the East and West. They think that the very idea of nationalist zeal or pride is a joke and a recurring one at that. Life in the technological society of BDR is also jibed at. This record is not for everyone but if you are willing to expand your horizons, give it a listen. --U-Man

# Album Reviews

(from p. 5) variety of sounds, from jazz to blues to folk, but all with one style. Vic Godard has come up with an album that he can be proud of and it is a strong contender for the Lp of the year. --VS

The Feelies Crazy Rhythms (Stiff: Use 4)--Crazy Rhythms, The Feelies' debut album, gives us a minor-league Talking Heads with little of the Heads' incisive lyrics or startling music. Not that The Feelies do not excite at times, it is just that those moments are few and too far between here. When the band tries a more traditional pop song like "The Boy with the Perceptual Nervousness" or their re-make of the Beatles' "Everybody's Got Something to Hide (Except Me and My Monkey)" they seem to do best. Most of the tracks, though, are simply repetitious. Some artists, like Van Morrison or Winston Rodney, are able to reveal new things about a riff through repetition, but The Feelies do not quite cut it. They have a strong drummer and their approach to the guitar is quite interesting, employing acoustic and surfer-style electric. It is just that the passion of, say, David Byrne is not there. Maybe that is not a fair comparison, but with the Heads-like cover shot and song titles, The Feelies invite it. --RH

(from p.31) that of Rockabilly meets the surf scene. Hopefully, they will be back, when the conditions are better (cooler and more people). --VS

(from p. 6) bass and some electronic trickery. It would be easy to compare Basement 5 to PiL but they are not heading the same direction and the resemblance is only superficial. With this 10-incher, Basement 5 join the ranks of socially conscious people like Dennis Bovell and LKJ. A good beginning. I hope their efforts will continue to be this good. --VS

Talk Talk Vol. 2 No. 9/page 38

Talk Talk is now available at the following record stores across America.

Exile Records   15 W. 9th St., Lawrence, Kansas
            and   7222 W. 75th St., Overland Park, Kansas
Better Days Records   724 Massachusetts, Lawrence, Kansas
Rock Therapy   7511 Troost, Kansas City, Missouri
World Records   615 W. 6th St., Topeka, Kansas
Wax Trax Records   2449 N. Lincoln, Chicago, Illinois
            and   638 E. 13th Ave., Denver, Colorado
Rough Trade   1412 Grant Ave., San Francisco, California
Leisure Landing   5500 Magazine, New Orleans, Louisiana
Ninety Nine Records   99 MacDougal St., New York, New York

Also available by mail.

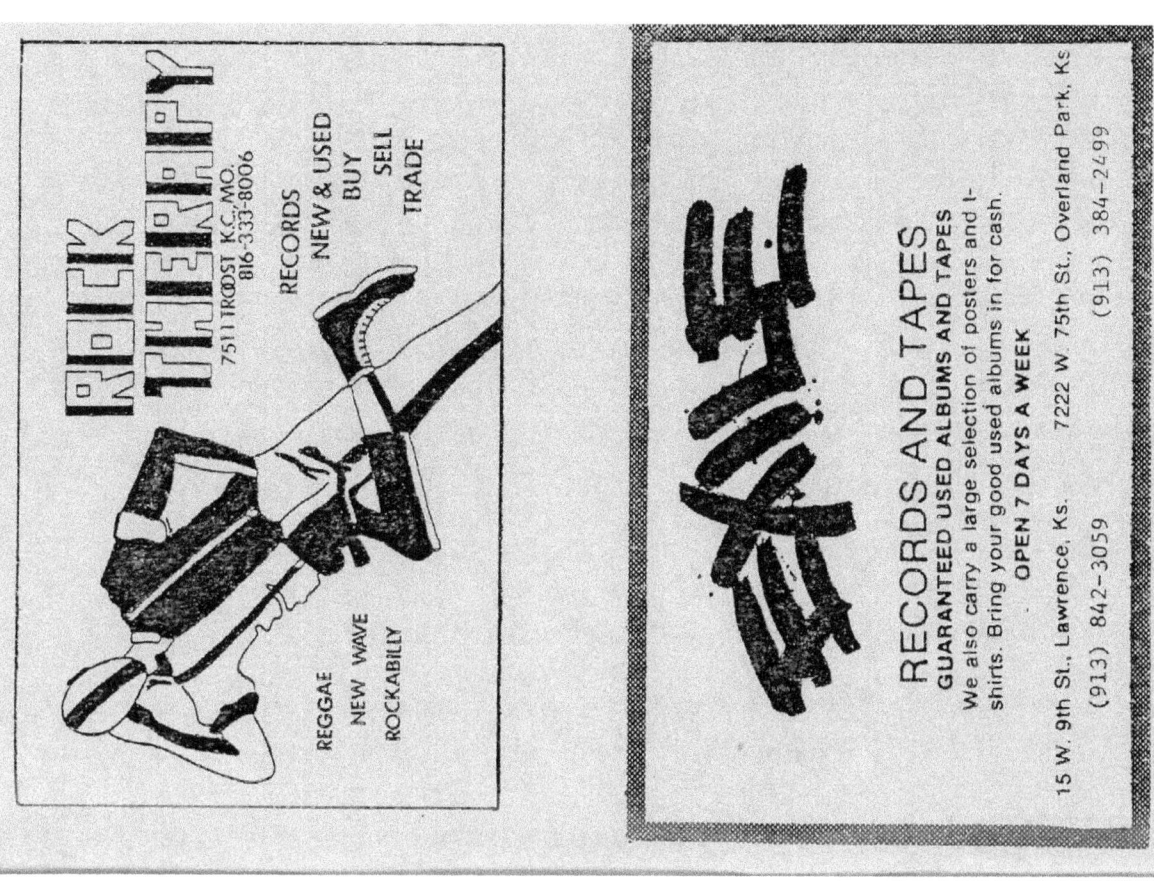

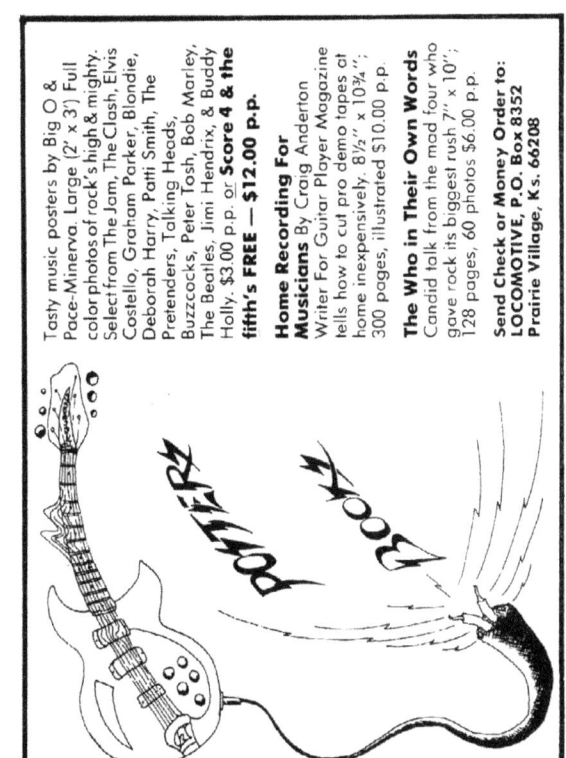

Tasty music posters by Big O & Pace-Minerva. Large (2' x 3') Full color photos of rock's high & mighty. Select from The Jam, The Clash, Elvis Costello, Graham Parker, Blondie, Deborah Harry, Patti Smith, The Pretenders, Talking Heads, Buzzcocks, Peter Tosh, Bob Marley, The Beatles, Jimi Hendrix, & Buddy Holly. $3.00 p.p. or **Score 4 & the fifth's FREE — $12.00 p.p.**

**Home Recording For Musicians** By Craig Anderton Writer For Guitar Player Magazine tells how to cut pro demo tapes at home inexpensively. 8½" x 10¾"; 300 pages, illustrated $10.00 p.p.

**The Who in Their Own Words** Candid talk from the mad four who gave rock its biggest rush 7" x 10"; 128 pages, 60 photos $6.00 p.p.

Send Check or Money Order to: LOCOMOTIVE, P.O. Box 8352 Prairie Village, Ks. 66208

TALK TALK   135

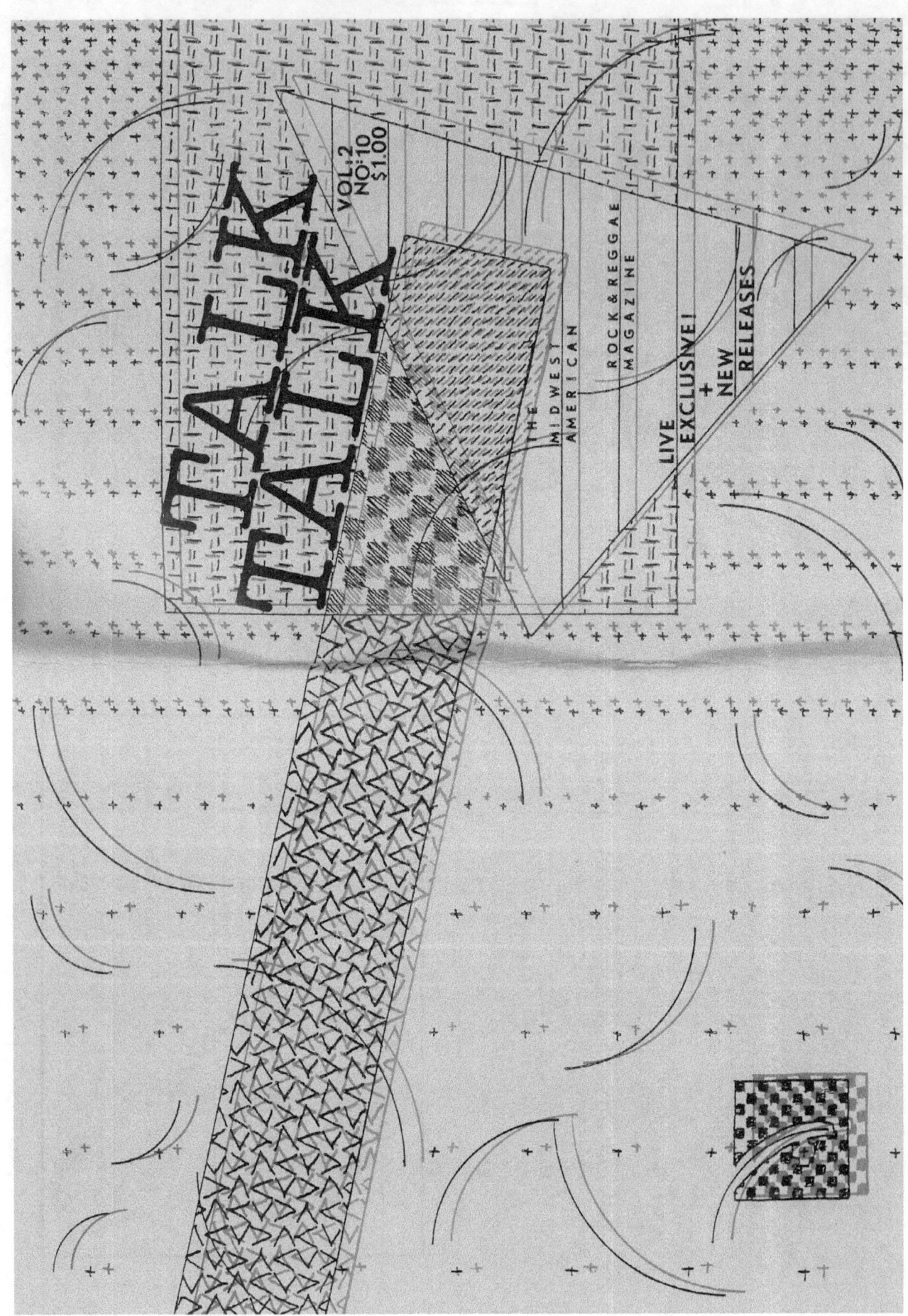

# Dexy's Midnight Runners

Talk Talk Vol. 2 No. 10/page 3

CHRISTOPHER LUCAS

CHRISTOPHER LUCAS

Live Hurrah  August 24 New York

Eight men searching for New York soul at Hurrah? "There are 20 people feeling the intensity of the soul, and eight of them are up here on stage," exclaimed Kevin Rowland, lead singer of the Dexys Midnight Runners, during their first show in America. These sweatless soul workers, dressed in Longshoremen's garb, blew their way through an evening of songs. At first they (→4)

↑Al Archer, guitar; Andy Growcott, drums; Kevin Rowland, vocals
←Guitarist/vocalist Kevin Rowland

---

## TALK TALK

Vol. 2 No. 10   September 1980   $1.00

The Midwest American Rock and Reggae Magazine

TALK TALK

Editors:
Bill Rich
Eric Schindling

Contributors:
U-Man
Rick Hellman
Jim Schwada
Christopher Lucas
Steve Dibendetto
Plus: VS, WB, DC
NN, BI, JB

Photography:
Chris Hunter
Robin Kyle
Christopher Lucas
Bill Rich

Cover Design:
Martin Olson

Layout:
John Lee
Bill Rich

Typesetting:
Joan M. Moore

Concerts:
Dexy's Midnight Runners. . . . . . .3
Thunderbirds. . . . . . . . . . . .7
Interview: Throbbing Gristle. . . .8
Reggae Reviews: Black Uhuru,
  Prince Far-I. . . . . . . . . . 12
  Lee "Scratch" Perry. . . . . . .13
Album Reviews: Jah Wobble,
  Dexy's Midnight Runners,. . . . 14
  Dome, Echo & The Bunnymen. . . .15
  Pere Ubu . . . . . . . . . . . .16
  Cabaret Voltaire . . . . . . . .17
Concerts: The Cramps. . . . . . . 18
Single Reviews: Bauhaus,
  Monochrome Set, Bow Wow Wow,
  Brian Brain, The Fall. . . . . .22
  Stiff Little Fingers, Joy
  Division, Comsat Angels. . . . .23
Reggae Reviews: Roy Reid,
  Desmond Dekker . . . . . . . . .24
  Growling Tiger . . . . . . . . .25
Concerts: Magazine. . . . . . . . 26
Single Reviews: 4" Be 2",
  Mekons, David Bowie. . . . . . .30
Concerts: The Debs. . . . . . . . 31
  Abuse, . . . . . . . . . . . . .
  New Era Reggae Band. . . . . . .32

All contents copyright 1980 by Talk Talk Publications, PO Box 36, Lawrence, Kansas, 66044. All rights reserved. Any opinion expressed is solely that of the writer and not necessarily that of this publication. Subscription rate is $6 for six issues. Articles, reviews, and pix submitted for editorial consideration are welcome. Not responsible for unsolicited material. Address all correspondence to Talk Talk Editors, PO Box 36, Lawrence, Kansas, 66044.

## Dexy's Midnight Runners

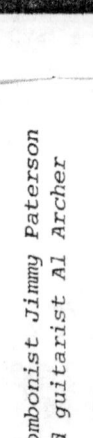

(from p. 3) startled the crowd with a song sounding like a happy birthday ditty (old soul cover). Wasting no time, they got down to business playing most of their debut album, Searching for the Young Soul Rebels. The hottest number was "Geno," which burst upon us after a long improvisation of steady riffs between the drummer and lead guitar player (while the bass player changed his second broken string of the night). The burst was provided by the horns, which played as well as any top Motown section.

Outside, while escaping the warmup act, I found the boys arriving in taxis. Offering a cigarette, I spoke to Jeff Bailey (tenor saxophone) about this show and the current music scene in Britain. Asking what kind of bands open for them in Britain, Jeff said, "Mainly local funky unknowns," adding that they might bring an opening act next time to the States. Bringing up the subject of other bands, Jeff replied between drags on his cigarette, "They are too many little bands in England not doing anything new or original." Asking about two of my favorites, Joy Division and Public Image Ltd., "Like Joy Division but they are not well received in England, PiL are laying (→6)

*Drummer Andy Growcott*
*Vocalist Kevin Rowland*
↑

*Trombonist Jimmy Paterson and guitarist Al Archer*
↓

*Tenor saxophonist Jeff Bailey and alto saxophonist Steve Spooner*
↓

*Photos by Christopher Lucas*

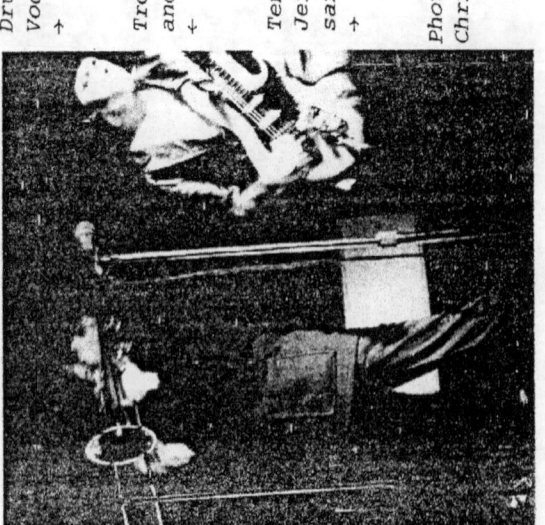

## Dexy's Midnight Runners

(from p. 4) too low, not performing enough or doing anything." Jeff went on to say, about the Dexys, "This show is to find a record company interested enough in us to release our record in America." After New York, the band is heading to Europe for their first European tour, then maybe back to the States. I told Jeff to hit the Midwest, maybe Chicago. A third taxi came, containing Kevin Rowland and the band headed for the dressing room.

The Dexys are a band with an image as honest as The Ramones' and soul feelings all of their own. --CL and SD

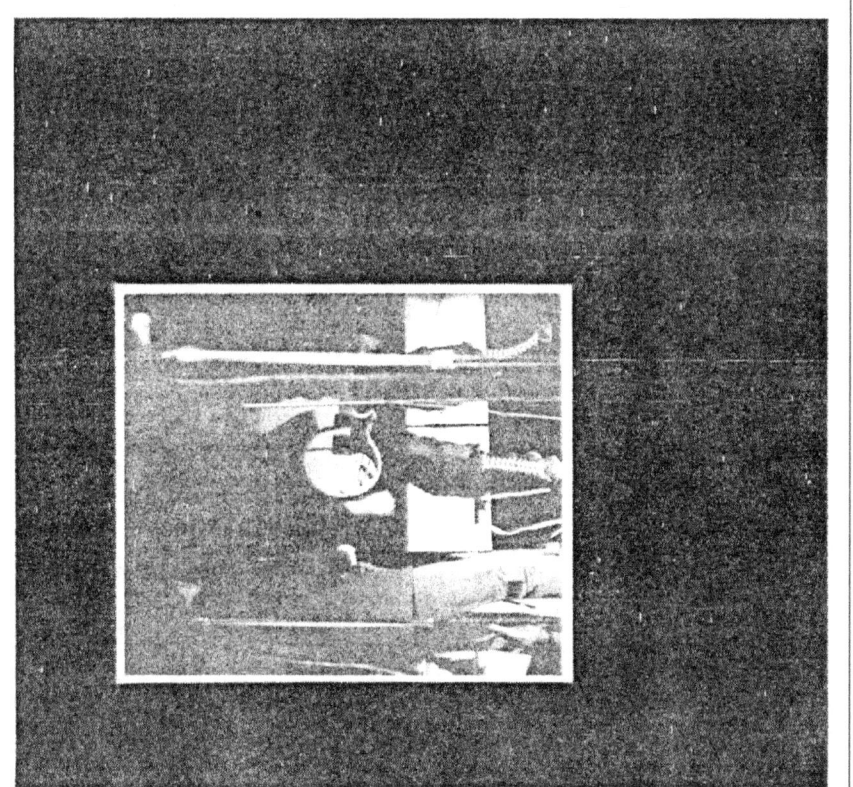

## The Thunderbirds

Live: August 12  Lawrence Opera House

Austin Texas' premiere blues quartet, fronted by harp wizard Kim Wilson, powered through an hour and a half of material from their first two Takoma/Chrysalis releases, "Girls Go Wild" and "What's the Word?" Despite an atrocious sound system, the T-Birds ably demonstrated why they are at the forefront of the "blue wave" contingent of bands like The Nighthawks, The Cobras, and George Thorogood and The Destroyers.

In an interview with KJHK, Wilson, whose prowess with a harmonica has made him the idol of aspiring harp players everywhere, spoke encouragingly about the vitality of blues music and the reception the T-Birds have gotten from Rock 'n Roll fans, especially in England, where they opened a tour with Dave Edmunds, Nick Lowe, and Rockpile.
--DC

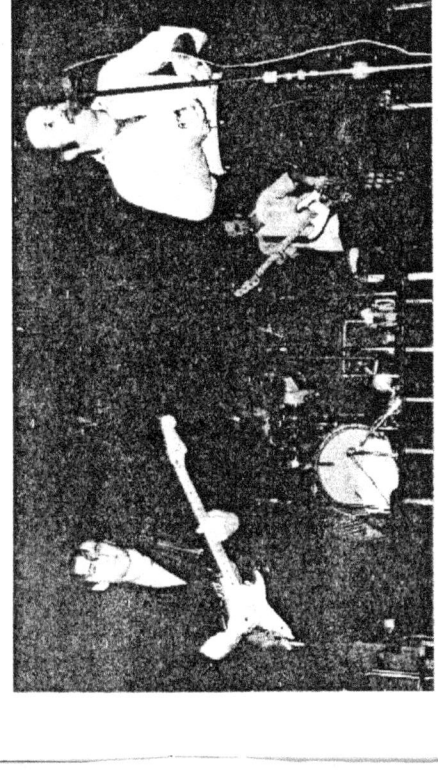

*The Thunderbirds. Jimmy Vaughn, guitar; Kim Wilson, vocals and harp; Evan Christina, drums; and Keith Ferguson, bass. Photo by Chris Hunter.*

# Throbbing Gristle

*Throbbing Gristle are pioneers whose unorthodox approaches to a rock concert have helped spawn the electro-synth sounds currently bursting into the music world. Two of the four members were recently in Lawrence working on a project. The following is the first half of a radio show they did with the conclusion next month.*

Marc Burch: Welcome to London Calling at KJHK. We are talking with...
Peter Christopherson: Peter Christopherson of Throbbing Gristle and...
Genesis P. Orridge: Genesis P. Orridge of the cracking voice of Throbbing Gristle.
MB: Why are you here in Lawrence?
P: We are here to collect and gather together some tapes that are located here in the archives of William Burroughs Communications. The operator of that organization is James Grauerholz, who's helping us assemble some tapes of William Burroughs for an album that is coming out on Industrial Records, hopefully in the fall.
M: Are you having any dates while you are here?
G: Not while we are here because the logistics of coming to America are quite complicated with customs, bonds, and all types of work permits. Unless you have got a straight big record company behind you it is very, very hard to actually make it across. But maybe next year. We have been invited by various people, mainly ourselves, but hopefully soon we will come up with somebody who knows how to operate that and we'll do not many but maybe four shows.
M: Industrial Records is pretty small, but more and more seems to be coming out.
G: We are Industrial Records, along with the other two members of Throbbing Gristle. We formed the record company because we wanted things done right and it seemed to us that no other record company in England would do it. So in '76 we set up Industrial Records, which was...the first, would you say?
G: Basically the first.
P: More or less the first of the new English independent labels. And it just sort of grew kind of accidentally on purpose.
M: You don't consider yourselves a rock band?
P: Right.
G: We don't consider ourselves at all. No, not musicians, not a rock band, not aiming to have a career, not aiming to keep making records.
P: Or money.
G: Or money.
P: I don't know how we do it. I think of it as an enigmatic agent provocateur.
M: Your first single was Zycon b Zombie. I didn't know what Zycon b was until...
P: There's a picture on the cover. Most people don't pick up on that.
M: Extermination gas used during WWII, right?
G: That's right, yeah.
M: You guys seem to dwell on morbid subjects.
P: We do?
M: What do you have cued up now?
P: We have a casette of a live concert we did in some year or other about three years ago. It has never been played on the radio and it is far more abstract than the things we just played. We wanted people to get the idea of what TG might sound like if we actually get over here and do some things. It has no title.

M: You were telling me you went out to the demolition derby. Did you have a good time out there?
P: It was great. We made some recordings; shortly to be released on Industrial...no, ah...we had a good time.
G: It was fab.
P: Gen enjoyed seeing the cars get....
G: I love anything where things get destroyed. I loved it. I wish they all could have blown up as well.
M: Were there any fires?
G: They kept putting them out. Really annoying...they had all these firemen rushing out spraying carbon dioxide on all the time.
(The casette is turned on.) M: What kind of recorder? It's pretty nice.
P: It's ok.
G: If you can hear it on a hi fi it sounds really good then. You can even hear the mud hitting everybody. We're going to play some more.
P: This is the second of the two so far unreleased singles.
G: Is it? No, it's not. It's not. Nope. Nope. You're wrong. This is from Central Barrical London, which was a derelict school run by Spanish anarchists. We did a concert on a Sunday afternoon at three o'clock on a very, very cold day, burned part of the room before people got in. We showed a film on castration and then we played this concert. Several people fainted...At the film.
P: Well, it might have been because of the playing. This section is a duet between me and Sleezy, which is Peter here. It is kind of the battle of the bands between the feedback violin and a distorted tape machine.

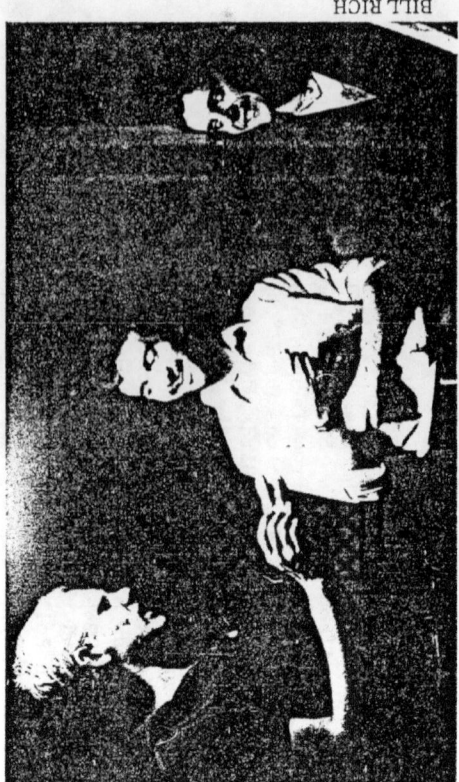

*James Grauerholz talks with Peter and Genesis.*

# Throbbing Gristle

PC: More than 80 percent of the material we release is recorded live.
MB: Do you like to perform live?
PC: Yeah, it is very different in some sense from recording in a studio.
SG: I know you probably get a wider range of audience reactions than probably any band I can think of. What have been some of the stranger audience reactions?
GP: There was a girl at the London Filmmaker's Coop--we did a benefit for them and she had a spontaneous orgasm. Her friend told me. This girl next to her suddenly started wriggling and moaning and saying it was fantastic and explained what had happened. I was trying desperately to find out exactly at what point in the concert it had happened because we keep a casette of each gig and we could have worked out exactly what sounds made it happen. We could have then followed her around the street playing the casette. Then we have had people pass out. We get a lot of people describing sensations much more like taking a very strong drug or a religious experience. They tend to use a language of sort of brain damage, not musical.

↤*Peter Christopherson*
↧*Genesis P. Orridge*
↦*Peter and Genesis*
*Photos by Bill Rich*

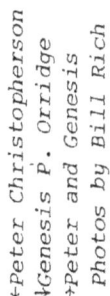

PC: Remarkably, because something about our music that one would think would cause extremely negative reactions, violent reactions in audiences tends to have quite the reverse affect, especially with the kind of people you would expect to be rather violent people, like in England they have skinheads and various violent factions. In fact, rightly or wrongly, our music tends to have a very pacifying affect on these people.
GP: Yes. It's true actually. The people who get most violent are students and intellectuals who find it is too uncouth and alien to them --like they have literally run into a brick wall or demolition derby. They just panic, they can't handle it because they can't make a logical analysis of what is taking place because so much of it is instinctive. They just get brainstorms quite literally and they are the ones who freak out.
SG: There are sounds and frequencies that have physical effects and there are some that are illegal to broadcast. Have you fiddled around with anything like that?
GP: Yes, we have. We try to use everything that everyone who is...
PC: I don't see why the authorities and people in control positions should be the only ones to have fun with the technology that is available these days.
MB: It should be open to the masses.
GP: Yes, use mass culture to generate an immunity to the kind of techniques that might be used. That's what we do. We never do anything to an audience that we have not tried out on ourselves first.
PC: Yes, and we are standing there in front of the speakers ourselves anyway. We're getting it first, so it is not like an "us and them" situation. A joint research thing.
GP: When we play, it is more like a live sound laboratory, rather than just a concert. But we have had examples like Chris Carter, our electronic whiz kid and I amplifying very high frequencies in our studio and all the objects in the room started moving and then we started to see criss-cross patterns in the air and he got tunnel vision and our clothes were moving, although there was no actual wind. And we lost all sense of balance and started falling over. It was very strange.

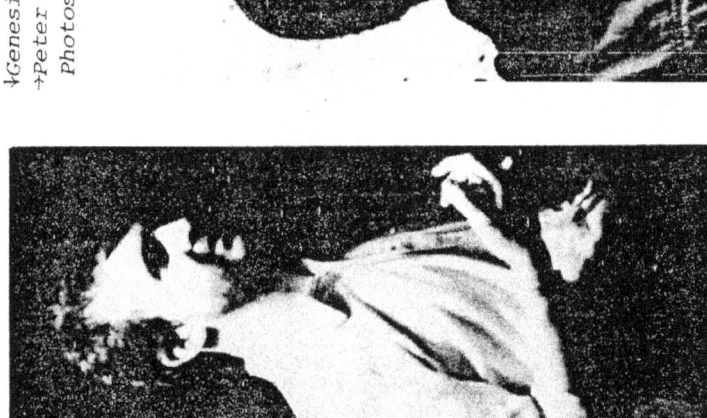

TALK TALK

## Reggae Reviews

Black Uhuru Sinsemilla (Mango Records: MLPS 9593)--On this, their first American, Lp (their third Lp to date) Black Uhuru continue on their pilgrimage. The purpose now being to conquer the USA and bring their message of Jah to the people and of course sell records. Sinsemilla is a strong effort. Part of that strength lay in the fact that their backup band is composed of the best reggae musicians around at the moment. Yes, Sly Dunbar and Robbie Shakespeare produce this album as well as lending their great talent as the knock down rhythm section behind Black Uhuru's vocals. As a matter of fact, the tune, "Happiness" (the Lp's first track) has the same music as "Strapper Lee Rap," a composition on the latest (as far as I know) album by Sly and Robbie, entitled Gamblers Choice. Well, enough of praising the band. The voices of Michael Rose, Puma Jones and Derrick Simpson are Black Uhuru. On this record they enthrall the listener with their harmonies and strong individual vocals. They bring to us an understanding of the way, life and soul of the oppressed. They sing of their environment with Ganja and the importance of it to their spiritual way. Also, as on "No Loafing (Sit And Wonder)" they show that the Rasta man is not a lazy man, as so many people who do not understand them try to portray. Yes, this album might help bridge the gap between the music of our country and Jamaica. It will be a hard road though, but this record shows that they have already started the journey and are making their way. --JB

Prince Far-I And The Arabs Cry Tough Dub Encounters Chapter III (Daddy Kool Records: DKLP15)--The Prince is back and on this record (his best dub Lp to date) he still shows us that he is in fine form. From the very first track, "Plant Up," to the very last, "Mansion Invasion," the Prince entertains us and lifts our spirits. The use of electronic on this record is especially surprising. In the liner notes that came with it, we are told that members of The Slits, PiL and The Flying Lizards all lend their talent to this album. This is perhaps one of the best crossover records of the year. Taking the wonderful gruff voice of Far-I's and putting behind it a strange mixture of sounds and ghost noises we have a record (→34)

## Reggae Reviews

Lee "Scratch" Perry The Return of Pipecock Jackxon (Black Star Liner: BSLP 9002) Africa's Blood (Trojan: TBL 166) The Best of Lee Perry and "The Upsetters" (Jet Star: PTLP 1023)--A new outpour of Lee Perry records is happening. His latest album of new songs comes from Holland, where "Scratch" was working this spring. The Return of Pipecock Jackxon shows a milder side of the dub master. "Bed Jammin," the 11-minute opener, features Perry singing along with backing female chorus and continuous "rockers" rhythm. It is somehow uplifting and mystifying and also my favorite Lee Perry song since the Scratch on the Wire Lp of earlier Lee Perry song this year. Side 1 continues with a short instrumental and ends with an energetic offering of praise to Jah. The second side gets bogged down too often. The sketchy press I have seen mentions that Scratch left before the album was finished and Black Star put the finishing touches on it and quickly marketed it for all us hungry Upsetter fans waiting. In other words, it could have been better, maybe, if Lee Perry had been the one to put the final mixes through. Consequently, the usual dub techniques which identify his works are not as evident. But maybe he will be able to work more with the cuts and create even better sounding material. That is something to look forward to or dream about. Trojan has released Africa's Blood with 14 tracks produced by Lee. There are no dates or credits, making it hard to place this period other than the fact it sounds earlier on a gut-level feeling. The Best of... states, "these recordings are among the first and considered the best of Lee Perry. All his original imagination went into these works because he had them stored up for years." His style has changed in the ten years he has been producing. Also out are a series of 12" Disco mix 45's on Black Ark, distributed by Black Star Liner of Holland which are worth finding. The songs have probably been released earlier in the standard mix. But the extended remix results in new songs. "Cane River Rock" uses the reggae rhythm to simulate chopping of cane with bubbling water fading in and out...one of Scratch's mediums to work with. The flip has "Dread Lion" almost totally foreign to the earlier versions, followed by a ska-oriented tune with trombone. The second release is his earlier single, "Baffling Smoke Signal," with "Captive." The third is a Heptones disco dub, the highlight being "Mr. (→33)

## Album Reviews

Jah Wobble V.I.E.P. (Virgin: VS 36112)--"The" Jah Wobble is with us again. Bringing with him an almost Lp from what was supposed to be the taping session for a single. Also on the heel of this record is a report that he has split from PiL. Whatever happens he will always be around and a major talent. On this new record he takes two mutated versions of "Blueberry Hill" (from the already weird version on his first Lp, Betrayal) and serves them up on a twelve-inch platter. But that is not all. Included on this record are other Dub mix downs and an almost new track of other works by him. The joy of this record is that he can take already released material, play with it and then serve it up as something new within ten weeks of his first long player and that it works. As a matter of fact, parts of this record come off stronger than Betrayal. Supposedly, Keith Levine (PiL guitarist) is unhappy that the Wob decided to cannibalize certain tracks from PiL sessions and use them on a solo effort. No matter what Keith's feeling on the end product, I, for one, am happy that Jah Wobble got both these records out. --VS

Dexy's Midnight Runners Searching For The Young Soul Rebels (EMI: PCS 7213)--The Dexy's are a prime illustration of an up and coming band's progression. Since last year, they put out two singles followed by this album. It is a strong debut, showing the band to be quite skilled soul musicians. They stand apart from rock bands by the emphasis on two saxes and trombone. The guitars, bass, drums and keyboards also shine through. Their live shows are reportedly quite moving (see review, p. 3, of their first show outside of Britain). Sometimes grouped with the ska movement, and they have done Two Tone tours, they are very soul oriented. After being built up and torn down by the press, the Runners now refuse to do interviews. Their method instead is to take ads out which express their feelings. One was a copy of the album sleeve, and in another, they explain that they do not want people to imitate their dress. Regarding the search for the young soul rebels, the band explains that they have found them and they are the band. Although, basically a move to prevent cult fads from centering on (->34)

## Album Reviews

Dome Dome (Dome 1)--Welcome to the outer limits, folks! B.C. Gilbert and Graham Lewis of Wire have come up with a dandy new slice, entitled Dome. It would seem Wire are now defunct, but Gilbert and Lewis carry on with sounds that recall some of that band's stranger efforts. The two play all guitars, synths, percussion, etc., and they do an excellent job of it. The sound is, for the most part, thin, but veers in interesting directions, focusing here on a voice, there on the percussion and back to the guitars, against a backdrop of atmospheric keyboards. There are a lot of comparisons that come to mind when listening to this album--Red Crayola, Lydia Lunch, Mr. Partridge, Pere Ubu--but Dome is right out there on the fringe with the best of them. And just to further confuse the issue, the full-tilt weirdness is relieved by one song at the end of side one. "Rolling Upon My Day" is as pretty and haunting a pop tune as Wire ever managed, and they had some good ones. All together, Dome is a remarkable album that recognizes musical boundaries and surmounts them before your ears. --RH

Echo and the Bunnymen Crocodiles (Korova: KODE 1)--Is there a psychedelic revival going on? Well, this debut Lp from one of Liverpool's newest bands makes one think that there is. I mean, it is as if one was swept back a few years into those hallucenogenic daze that were, but was able to take along some of today's technical know-how. This is not a retrogressive thing at all, rather it is a re-evaluation of a style. It is clearly evident who their influences are once this record is heard. There are ten tracks on this album, three of them are taken from their singles: "Pride, Pictures on My Wall," and "Rescue," but they are somewhat slower and moodier versions. Jangling guitars, a stark percussion and bass tandem, and occasional keyboards give these sons of the white rabbit one of the best sounds around. It hits right in the pleasure center; then again it could be the fall-out affecting our milk. Best songs: "Monkeys, Crocodiles" and the entirety of side 2, especially the "Day in the Life" type finale... you must listen carefully. --UM

TALK TALK 143

## Album Reviews

Pere Ubu The Art of Walking (Rough Trade: Rough US-4)--So Ubu has undergone yet another incarnation, their fourth since their inception. Gone is Tom Herman, the lead guitarist, and in his place is Mayo Thompson (of the Red Crayola). His position is multi-purpose: he plays guitar and organ, sings both lead and backing vocals, and composes. Two of his compositions "Loop" and "Horses") are on this Lp. Yet there is something a little bit different about this record. Could it be that this Lp has an almost (choke) religious message to it? Well, it does. The majority of the 11 songs on this fourth Lp seem to have religious connotations. Even the title, Art of Walking, is evidence of this. After all, it is a miraculous thing to stand erect and move about defying gravity...moving one foot in front of the other. "Hey, what do you know I'm going somewhere!," David Thomas shouts. This praise of life's small things continues with "Go." References to Jah are made, who blesses the everyday things and the small details that tend to get overlooked. This song catches Ubu in top musical form. "Rhapsody in Pink" features DT telling us how he spent his day underwater as a big pink ball. This is a tale of too much fun and then suffering for it. "Let this be a lesson to you." "Arabia" is a continuation of this with its references to the ants that save the little things and the grasshoppers who just want a good time, as they jump in the pool. This lesson is learned by DT because he never saw the things under his big fat feet. Once again we learn from the small things...it all does add up. "Miles" sounds like it should have been on Pere Ubu's second Lp, Dub Housing. Is it a ghost explaining the benefits of home, "There's no place like home cause it's homey," or is it a tribute to Miles Davis, with its squeaking horn played by Scott Krauss? "Misery Goats," with its happy bouncing bass, is a warning to worriers. Herd 'em up, Tex. Side 2 opens with the first of Mayo Thompson's compositions, "Loop," a rather strange one about getting there (?). He sings lead vocals on his works and his voice fits right in to the Ubu structure, especially with David Thomas backing him. Ubu gets a little funky with "Rounder" and Allen Ravenstine displays some of his most ferocious synth playing. It could almost be a machine gun attack. (→17)

(from p. 16) This one deals with the anxiety of success and how it can lead to failure. The title track of this record could very well be "Birdies," a song about the simple act of walking. Pere Ubu does The Tin Drum in "Lost in Art." David Thomas beats his drum chaotically and shouts repeatedly to his phantom audience, "gimme, gimme, gimme!" In the background, a matinee organ and electronic snoring; could it be the response of the audience. Eventually, he is deserted, frantically he calls them back. "I didn't mean it," he mumbles. Is this a statement on music and musicians today? A parody of themselves? Whatever it is, it is a classic. Mayo Thompson's second song follows this and is entitled "Horses." This could be one of the best western themes since the Magnificent Seven. Actually a lover waits impatiently at his phone during this one. But it is the desperation of it all created by the music. There is forlorn whistling, galloping guitar and tweeting birdie synths that help to create the image of Pa Ubu Cowboy. The last song on this Lp, "Crush This Horn," is Ubu the broken vacuum tube radio and the struggle to tune in a marching kazoo band or is it the wailing sax of King Curtis. It is only Ubu or is it UFO surveillance. But truthfully, this is Ubu's best Lp to date and with the addition of Mayo Thompson Ubu will go far. --UM

Cabaret Voltaire The Voice of America (Rough Trade: Rough 11)--The most cohesive album that Cabaret Voltaire has released to date. The only thing that irks me is the title, this is not the voice of the US today, it is more like America in the mid-50's. In fact, this record could almost be a ghost transmission...a radio broadcast that has no origin. From the very beginning of side one, the title track, a school authority of some kind is busy lecturing a group of students about a rock concert assembly. He is busy giving them a list of thou shalt nots and threatens them with detention hall in Room D, as soon as he is finished, the electronic tension of Cabaret Voltaire ensues. The ten songs actually seem to have structure and definite endings, instead of meandering and clumsy closings found in a lot of their stuff. Best songs: "Voice of America," "Damage Is Done," "Kneel to the Boss," "News from Nowhere," and "Messages Received" with its mention of euthanasia is my raver. --UM

# The Cramps

Live: July 31      Lawrence Opera House

After a brief set by the Kansas City band, The Jumpers, there was a long break (approximately 50 minutes) before the crowd was treated to the starting drum roll of Nick Knox. What followed was a high energy show that either left the crowd wanting to leave or wanting more. I knew what was in store when Lux Interior hit the stage, full of energy, ready to take on anything pitched his way. Dressed in low riding black leather pants and pointy-toed boots, with a mop of dark hair that partially hid his face, he stalked the stage area, growling and shouting out whatever song the band arranged. In a period of an hour, he managed to gyrate his way through most of the cuts off The Cramps' first album, Songs The Lord Taught Us. Visually he reminded me of a young Iggy Pop. Their playing was a verbal and audio assault on the concert goers. By now everyone knows that Brian Gregory left the group in order to fill religious commitments. In his place and adding her own style is a short, black-haired woman by the name of Julian. She might not be as frightening as Brian, but her playing leaves nothing to be desired. Listening to her makes me impatient to hear her record with the group. Once the next album is out, I am sure people will stop moaning about the loss of Brian Gregory, because this girl is a full-fledged Cramp. On the far side of the stage, Ivy stood, bringing up the rhythm with searing guitar lines. Her heavily made up face catching the light in such a way that it lent it a deathly pallor. Behind it all was Nick Knox, beating away on his drums, setting the pace. He looked a bit like Robert DeNiro, which only helped the dread. The songs they covered were all familiar, from my favorite "TV Set" to "Garbage Man." In the end, they came back for an encore that included both "Surfin Bird" and "The Bird Is The Word." After this The Cramps left the stage, leaving behind them screaming fans and broken equipment.

CHRIS HUNTER

# The Cramps

After The Cramps' show I was lucky enough to get a word with the band. They seem to have the reputation of being a difficult band to interview and when I walked in and found Lux Interior in a fetal position on the floor my hopes were not up.

"Hello," I said, looking around the room and seeing all the members of the band lounging about. "I'm from Talk Talk and we are supposed to do an interview and get some pictures."

"Oh, yeah. Come on in," Lux replied, sitting up, bleary-eyed. "Have a seat anywhere." I sat down in the closest chair. "Except that one," he added, motioning to the chair I just sat in. "It's all wet."

"That's okay," I replied, "so am I. So," I continued, "Julien, you used to be with a band called The Mad?" No reply. "How do you like being Brian Gregory's replacement?" At this time I knew that my foot was firmly in my mouth. For all I got as a reply was an icy stare. "Well," I continued hurriedly, "where does your tour go from here?" (→21)

## Interview

(from p. 20) "Tulsa, I think," Lux answered, as he stared into space, his hands folded neatly in his lap, "and after that we go out to LA to do the Urggh show."

"I heard you have a new single out."

"That's right," Lux said.

"It's called Drug Train," Ivy added. "It will be the flip to Garbage Man. We're also working on our next album."

"When will that be out?"

"Oh, around October. We start recording it after this tour."

"Back to 'Drug Train,' wasn't that supposed to be included on your Lp?"

"No," Ivy stated flatly. "It was listed on some covers that I.R.S. printed without our permission. They sent out about a thousand and then told us, 'Whoops, we don't know how it happened.'"

"Did you know," I questioned, "that your promo sheet calls you the Punk ABBA?"

"It figures," Lux added. "You'd think they have better ways to keep themselves busy. Do you know what they were into awhile ago?"

"Pyramids," Ivy shot in with a grin.

"Julian seemed to fit in without any trouble at all."

"Yeah, we're really happy with her," Lux beamed. "It was getting to the point that we couldn't work with Brian anymore and then he just up and left in the middle of the tour. Julian used to come to all our shows in New York, so she knew the material and we liked the way she played in The Mad. It wasn't like we grabbed her out of thin air. We're all excited about recording the next album with her."

At this time, we asked The Cramps to pose for a few pictures. After that Ivy and Julian were run out of the room by Nick who was tossing a serrated bread knife at the couch, trying to make it stick. Lux just stood up and smiled.

The Cramps: Poison Ivy Rorschach, Julien H., Nick Knox, Lux Interior.

CHRIS HUNTER

## Single Reviews

Bauhaus Terror Couple Kill Colonel/Scopes (4AD Records: AD7)--Well, you can throw me down and sit on my face, if this is not one of the best singles of the year, bar none. Bauhaus go PiL one better with this record, merging their hypnodrone bass lines and psycho guitar work with an inspired hook. Singer Peter Murphy screams the title phrase like some insane headline-mantra is wracking his brain and he exorcises the demon to our delight and amazement. "Scopes" is a short, choppy tune that would not sound out of place on an early Wire album. Like Wire, Bauhaus display hints of a pop sensibility then mask it again in a web of avant-garde weirdness, to the benefit of both styles. Even the dub version, "TC KCZ," is interesting and different enough, I suppose, to warrant inclusion here. This 45 shows Bauhaus with a new-found vigor that feels good on them. I await their first LP with high hopes. --RH

The Monochrome Set 405 Lines/Goodbye Joe (Dindisc: DIN 23)--The A side is a fast moving instrumental with guitar running up and down and the bass plucking along. It goes by quickly and is the kind of song hard to recall. The B side is from their fantastic album. The Set continue to be one of the more versatile sound producing bands around. --BI

Bow Wow Wow C'30, C'60, C'90, GO (EMI: 5088)--The newest of M. McClaren's push for the home recording market. This sounds like a high school cheerleader's poor try. My copy has a double A side--no telling how the B side turned out. No great loss, though. --NN

Brian Brain Another Million Miles/Personality Counts (Secret: SHH 105)-- Not much to this one. After the recent Public Image Ltd. tour of the U.S., drummer Martin Atkins parted company and formed this group. For their first attempt, they should have done something different. But what? Atkins can do more, I think. --NN

The Fall How I Wrote Elastic Man/City Hobgoblins (Rough Trade: RT048)-- Another fine effort by the band that everybody seems to love or hate. When this single first hit my turntable, there were either moans or compliments. (→23)

(from p. 22) Understandably The Fall might be the most misunderstood group recording at the moment. This single will not help their reputation. Those who like them will be impressed with "How I Wrote Elastic Man," with the repetitious rhythm lines and familiar screech, whine vocals. The message can be seen in earlier works by them. Gloom is like a laughing monkey on your back. But, what the hell, you can still dance to it. The flip, "City Hobgoblins," is a rock 'n roll song for the working class. It is uptempo with a strong r&b bass and drum combination. More accessible to the masses. Maybe it will make it to Billboard magazine's disco 100 chart. Do not laugh, stranger things have happened. --ES

Stiff Little Fingers Back to Front/Mr Fire Coal-Man (Chrysalis: CHS 2247)--This is a great single. "Back to Front" is a powerful new song that should silence the band's detractors. In fine form, SLF deal with the racist mentality of our time. Then on the flip, they bring an old Clement Dodd reggae song to the masses. It is a fitting song that deals with the truism that "The Man Who By The Gun Now." The song was originally intended to speak to the youth of Jamaica but SLF take it and place it in an international setting. They also prove with this song that they can make their own form of Anglo Reggae work for them without sounding derivative. Yes, this 45 makes me anxious for the live LP that is promised out in October. --VS

Joy Division She's Lost Control/Atmosphere (Factory: FACUS 2)--From the vaults at Factory comes this fine single. "She's Lost Control" was a cut off their first album, Unknown Pleasure, but this single is a definite remix and is as good as the original. At times, though, I get a chill listening to it. It is as if Ian is singing to us from the grave. The flip, "Atmosphere," was on the hard to get and very expensive "Sordid Sentimental" single and it was thoughtful of Factory to release it here. It is a fine and haunting tune that shows the band in their best form. Well worth looking for. --VS

The Comsat Angels Independence Day/We Were (Polydor: 2059 257)--This band reminds one of Echo and The Bunnymen, The Teardrop Explodes (→33)

## Reggae Reviews

**Roy Reid Whap'n Bap'n** (Virgin: V2164)--This latest release from the great dj known as I-Roy shows a bit of progression. Speaking of DJ's, it seems that the earlier American '50's east coast developers never get credit for beginning the "rhythm talk over"--then more of a passive announcer selecting tracks compared to today where the tracks used are often written for the deejay. Perhaps 20 or so years ago, the emphasis was more soul and the beginning of funk--at least funk talk. On this album, Roy Reid has two distinctive sounds--reggae and funk. The musicians are even divided into the two sections. The funkier cuts remind me of the famous U.S. old timer disc jockey, Jocko Henderson, and similar to the style of Sly Dunbar in talking. So that is the main reason I prize this album. But the real reason I bought it was because of the producer--Dennis Bovell. Almost everything he works with is worth the money. And this is a good example of why. Bovell plays bass, organ, guitar and guitar synth as well as co-writing most of the tunes with Roy Reid. Sometimes I-Roy sings, other times he sort of chants along. Although his vocals are the focus, the backing musical sounds, rhythms, and brass harmonies blend together to give a full sounding musical experience bound to keep you bopping or jumping. Lively music for sure--no praises to Jah or herb to get caught up in. Just pure I-Roy sounding better than ever. You owe it to yourself to check out his blend of reggae and funk. No jive, man. --WB

**Desmond Dekker Black and Dekker** (Stiff: SEEZ 26)--Years have gone by since Desmond Dekker and the Aces released the classic "Israelites." It was an early reggae hit, around 1968, which was the first reggae which the masses listening to AM experienced. Then Desmond sort of faded away. Early this year, Stiff had him re-record "Israelites" and the project grew to this album. A nice story, eh, for his comeback? Unfortunately for everyone, it is a major disappointment. What happened? Whoever produced this should be shot. Let's see someone who knows the music in charge. Backed by various musicians, mainly white British rockers (where are Sly and Robbie when (→25)

## Reggae Reviews

**Growling Tiger, High Priest of Mi Minor Knockdown Calypsos** (Rounder: 5006)--If you have always associated Calypso music with drunken surfers limboing endlessly through bad beach movies, you will be surprised, and delighted, by Rounder Records' Knockdown Calypsos. Calypso, which originated on the island of Trinidad, has always been party music. During its "Golden Age" in the 20's and 30's, performers with titles like the Lord Executor and Atilla the Hun added to the dancing beat lyrics which were topical, amusing, political and sometimes raucous. Servicemen stationed in Trinidad during WW II brought back with them a taste for this roots music, and several watered-down Calypsos became commercial hits, "Rum and Coca-Cola" being the most famous. Last year Rounder Records, a small Massachusetts folk and blues label, found and recorded one of the original Calypso masters, Growling Tiger. Tiger, an ex-prizefighter, who was the first man crowned "King of Calypso" in Trinidad in the 30's, had not recorded in over a decade, and the resulting Lp Knockdown Calypsos is a masterful comeback both for the artist and his music. Backed by the "Trans-Caribbean All Star Orchestra" (featuring master percussionist Candido), The Tiger growls his way through ten original tunes, which are as fresh today as when they were first written in the 30's--as seen in this wry passage from "Money Is King":

"If you have money an' things goin nice
Any woman will call you honey and spice.
If you can't give her a dress, one new pair of shoe,
She'll say she have no uses for you."

Check out the Growling Tiger and let Knockdown Calypsos knock you out. --DC

(from p. 24) we need them?) The highlight of this record is the singing. Desmond's voice is as good as ever. Why didn't they get a band that could relate to the feelings of the songs. I am glad that he is finally getting the recognition deserved. But the result of this disappointment night be Dekker's disappearance for another ten years. If you want to listen to him, buy the Trojan release, Sweet Sixteen, a greatest hits collection, and patiently wait for a real record to someday emerge. --VS

# Magazine

Live  Tuts,
August 19  Chicago

On their third US tour, Magazine have established themselves as a band with an intellectually abstract seriousness. They are used to playing small packed clubs with the show at Tuts no different. The crowd was packed tight and enthusiastic as Magazine played selections from their latest Lp, The Correct Use of Soap. The new guitarists played sparingly behind the keyboards and bass. Howard Devoto sang along but Barry Adamson on bass was the star, despite problems with his (rented) amps. I asked him after the show if the media and fans were giving Magazine members more attention than the earlier periods of Devoto devotion. "No, not really, yet," he stated with a nervous laugh. That will continue to change.

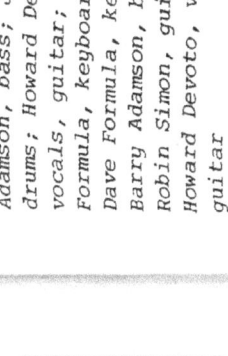

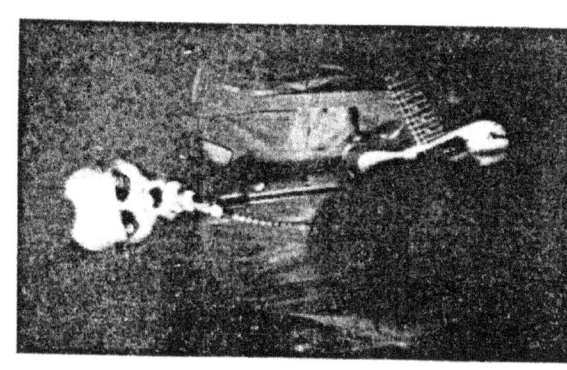

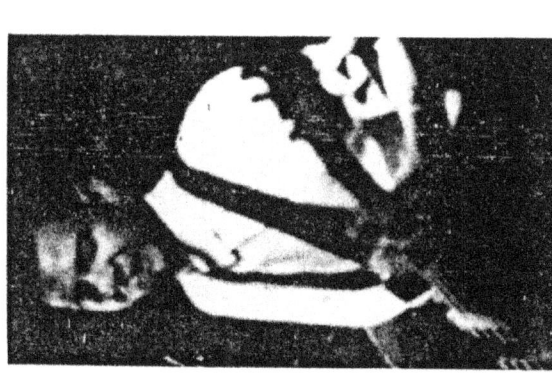

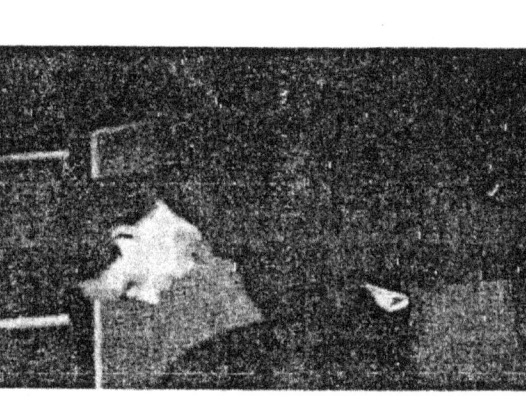

*Magazine from left: Barry Adamson, bass; John Doyle, drums; Howard Devoto, vocals, guitar; Dave Formula, keyboards. Dave Formula, keyboards. Barry Adamson, bass Robin Simon, guitar Howard Devoto, vocals, guitar Photos by Bill Rich*

# Interview: Magazine

*Following the concert, Magazine remained in the dressing room as the local opening band prepared for another set. Drummer John Doyle, having received the most rest in the day, acted as spokesman.*

TT: Do you think the band has been overlooked or fading out of the public?
John Doyle: Only from the fact of avoiding commerciality, avoiding the banal. We just prefer to stand on the outside and observe what's going on inside the general media. We prefer to be outside these influences. Anything that comes out of our MUSIC is devoid of those banalities that go on in that circus.
TT: How do you do that?
JD: By avoiding influences....never trying to freeze the people that are involved in that side. Music comes from personal experiences as opposed to experiences in the rest of the music world. We are not affected by other musicians or whatever else is happening in the music scene. We keep apart from that.
TT: Did you used to have blonde hair?
JD: No. The first drummer did. I'm the second drummer. I joined after the first album.
TT: How is it going with John McGeoch (guitar and saxophone) gone?
JD: We see a new influx of fresh ideas. As the name "Magazine" implies, it is like a totally changing format. I mean you never see the same Magazine twice. John decided to leave because he wanted to broaden his horizons. Working with Siouxie and the Banshees, he probably realized he could be doing different things.

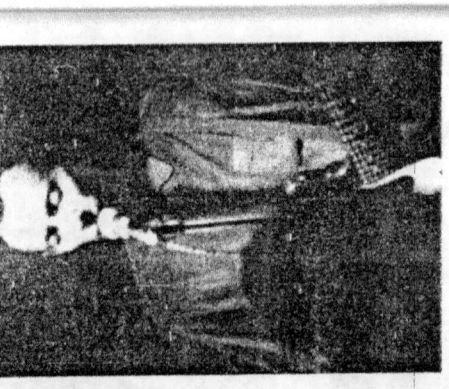

TT: It seems that the whole tempo of the songs are concentrated on the drums now. With John gone.
JD: We have new material, Robin at the moment is standing in John's shoes--what he is playing is what John played. We have not made any changes in our material for Robin. He is just fitting in with us. The new material is probably more rhythmically based. At the same time, there is always an underlying constant rhythm with most of our music. Now things have been simplified on top of the layers. If you want to talk about the keyboards or guitar or bass or vocals. It has been modified--well, not modified, but the layers have been lessened for more immediacy. We try to delineate between all the musical instruments. We are getting more and more involved with melody in songs. And that shows in all instruments as opposed to just one instrument. Barry plays melody on bass, he follows the melody and layers it and also keeping the rhythm. It is more of using everybody as a whole to create the full picture.
TT: So what is in the future for Magazine? The same sort of track or progression?
JD: It is not a matter of progression, just changing. We don't set any foundations. We don't build from the same thing. What ever ideas that come up they are totally fresh from what has gone down before. We don't take anything from our precious music. The only influences we take are from each other.

←Barry Adamson
Howard Devoto
↑John Doyle

TT: How is it going with Virgin?
JD: OK. We do basically what we want to do. We have a lot to say in what we release and publicity and artwork. We will be starting work on new material when we finish this tour. We're going to Australia and New Zealand from Los Angeles August 26 for three weeks. We have already written some material with Robin. We tried a different approach when we auditioned him as opposed to saying, "OK, this is what we play, can you play it." We decided to try and write some new material with him to see what it was like to work with him, from that angle. We got a few ideas.
TT: What is going on in Great Britain now?
JD: The usual. It is always a fashion. And fashions go out very quickly. So, unless you are prepared to keep changing with fashion, you have got to remain outside. Unfortunately, it is now becoming a trend to stay outside, which is possibly where we might attract a few more people. We all hate the imagery involved in being a rock 'n roll band. We do what we do in a minority field. We either play music or we don't.

## Single Reviews

**4" Be 2" Frustration/Can't Explain (WEA: K 18290)**--Contrary to popular belief, this is 4" Be 2"'s second single (the first was released on Virgin last winter). Part of the notoriety of this band comes from the fact that John Lydon produces them and has a brother in the band. Their first single sounded like a PiL clone but I am happy to say that on this new effort of theirs they have finally started to sound like themselves. Unlike PiL, they are a rock band and "Frustration" is a fine song that deals with that exact same thing. The flip side is the old Who song "Can't Explain" and where it would be hard to compare it to the original, I can say that they do it justice and include tasty sax riffs throughout. An added note would be to mention that the picture sleeve was supposedly done by a friend of theirs in jail. The back photo might be upsetting because it tends to make one believe that these lads might be sexist as possible. Oh, well, we will find out...will we not? --VS

**The Mekons Snow/Another One (Red Rhino Records: Red 7)**--They are back! The Mekons have returned. After being dropped by two record labels, they have found a third that not only released this 45 but promises to have a new Lp out soon. This band has never been known to rest on past laurels and this single is no exception. Those who are looking for something like "Teeth" will be disappointed because The Mekons are, it seems, in constant motion. "Snow" is a slow, haunting number and, like its flip "Another One", they both rely on an eerie synthesizer to carry the songs across and make them sink in, like nails in a coffin. I do not know what the album will be like but if this single is any hint, it will be worth it. Yes, I like The Mekons. --VS

**David Bowie Ashes to Ashes (RCA: BOW 6)**--Everybody wants to be a clown, including our Mr. Bowie, but instead of your typical bozo, he chooses to be a European burlesque clown. The jacket of this single shows Bowie the clown in various stages of dressing or undressing and inside the single there are more of these xerox art stamps. There are four sets, so collect them all. "Ashes to Ashes" is a litany to the many incarnations Bowie has used throughout his (→30)

## The Debs

*The Debs at Off the Wall Hall, August 20
Kris, Katie, and Terry*

*Peggy, Terry, Kris, and Katie*

**Live: Abuse    August 19    Off The Wall Hall**

On this particular night their sound system made Abuse sound like so much mush. They did manage to overcome this problem with sheer energy and a dedication to what they were doing.

During the course of the evening, they covered a variety of old hits by the likes of The Heartbreakers (not Tom Petty's) and Iggy Pop. An added surprise came in the form of five new songs that went over well with the dance-crazy crowd. For a three-man band, they managed to overcome some of the limitations that type of structure imposes.

Part of their strength comes from the fact that they are enthusiastic about what they do and are dedicated enough to stick through whatever problems may come their way. Their only long range restriction might come from the fact that they might admire certain "Famous" bands a little too much and restrict themselves to a certain sound instead of fully realizing their own potential and developing, as they mature as a band, their own style. I do have high hopes for them though and they are worth catching if they ever make it to your area. --ES

**Live: New Era Reggae Band   August 25**
**Off the Wall Hall**

On their return performances, The New Era Reggae Band displayed a more personally developed style than their earlier appearances. They have added new arrangements and performed several originals. The band plans on recording some of those this month, meaning their material will finally be available on vinyl. New Era has also added another guitarist, although he still is not worked in totally quite yet. It is bound to add to their sound. The musicians are all multi-talented. Most of the vocals are divided amongst them all, with the lead vocalist and the drummer still the main singers. For those looking for live reggae, The New Era Band are among the tops. Be sure to check them out next time. --WB

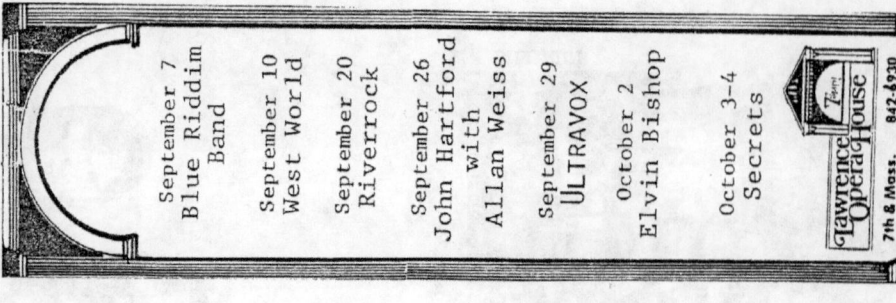

Lawrence Opera House
7th & Mass.    842-6930

September 7    Blue Riddim Band
September 10   West World
September 20   Riverrock
September 26   John Hartford with Allan Weiss
September 29   ULTRAVOX
October 2      Elvin Bishop
October 3-4    Secrets

Lee Perry (from p. 13) President." The fourth release is Max Romeo's "Norman," Lee Perry and The Full Experience doing "Disco Devil" and Jah Lloyd's "Earth is the Lord." Finally it seems that Scratch is getting some well deserved exposure for his efforts and successes both as an artist in his own right and as a genius producer. --WB

The Comsat Angels (from p. 23) and possibly Joy Division (to drop a few names) yet there is something about their sound that sets them apart. With just guitars, bass, and drums they manage to create a catchy sound. The lyrics to Independence Day deal with the work/leisure ethic and the inability of people not being able to separate the two or are simply incapable of doing either. "I can't relax 'cause I haven't done a thing and I can't do a thing 'cause I can't relax." Never has it been said so obviously or simply. The B-side, "We Were," is a dirge-like instrumental, that sounds vaguely like the closing to Roxy Music's "For Your Pleasure," with its driving percussion and the sense of distance that is created. An album is due out soon.--UM

**ROCK THERAPY**
7511 TROOST K.C. MO.
816-333-8006

RECORDS
NEW & USED
BUY
SELL
TRADE

REGGAE
NEW WAVE
ROCKABILLY

**RECORDS AND TAPES**
GUARANTEED USED ALBUMS AND TAPES
We also carry a large selection of posters and t-shirts. Bring your good used albums in for cash.
OPEN 7 DAYS A WEEK

15 W. 9th St., Lawrence, Ks.   7222 W. 75th St., Overland Park, Ks
(913) 842-3059                 (913) 384-2499

David Bowie (from p. 30) career, with references made to Maj. Tom especially. It is also a track from his soon to be released Scary Monsters Lp. The B-side is "Move On," which is taken from The Lodger. This is one of Bowie's better singles in some time. --UM

Dexy's (from p. 14) their existence. This move also demonstrates that they are serious about themselves. Their songs are emotional vehicles using almost-whiney vocals and layered brass. The resulting sounds are unique to this band. Dexy's will continue becoming more and more successful, no doubt. A welcome departure from the current corporate rock garbage overloading the scene. --WB

Prince Far-I (from p. 12) that begs to be played over and over. My only complaint is that I wished I knew who played what on each song. On one track where I recognize the background singers (The Slits), they put to words what I hope Prince Far-I will do with this new and great record of his and that is "Shake The Nation." --ES

**THE DOWNLINER**
(below Plaza East)
4719 Troost
K.C., Mo.
816-753-9368

September 5-6
THE EMBARRASSMENT

September 12-13
ABUSE

September 19-20
THUMBS

September 26-27
THE DEBS

October 3-4
THE MODERNS

Open
9 to 1
Be 21!

Brought to you by
Sum-thing-tu-du
Productions

TALK TALK

# TALK TALK

Vol. 2 No. 11    October 1980    $1.00

The Midwest American Rock and Reggae Magazine

## Table of Contents

Concerts: The Beat..............3
Interview: The Beat.............7
Concerts: The Downliner,
  The Clean....................9
Album Reviews: Ultravox,
  Swell Maps..................10
  B-52s, James Chance.........11
Single Reviews: The Beat,
  Madness, Selecter, Dexy's...12
Interview: The Blue Riddim
  Band........................13
Concerts: The Embarrassment...14
  The Aagarnes................16
Single Reviews: The Body-
  snatchers, The Swinging Cats,
  Bomis Prendin, The Cramps...17
Reggae Reviews: Bob Marley,
  Gregory Isaacs, Rock Against
  Racism, Third World.........18
Interview: Throbbing Gristle,
  Part 2......................19
Corrections...................25
Single Reviews: Pauline
  Murray......................26

TALK TALK
Editors:
  Bill Rich
  Eric Schindling
Contributors:
  Rick Hellman
  VS, WB, NN
Photography:
  Robin Kyle
  Christopher Lucas
  Bill Rich
Layout:
  John Lee
  Bill Rich
Typesetting:
  Joan M. Moore

All contents copyright 1980 by Talk Talk Publications, PO Box 36, Lawrence, Kansas, 66044. All rights reserved. Any opinion expressed is solely that of the writer and not necessarily that of this publication. Subscription rate is $6 for six issues. Articles, reviews, and pix submitted for editorial consideration are welcome. Not responsible for unsolicited material. Address all correspondence to Talk Talk Editors, PO Box 36, Lawrence, Kansas, 66044.

## The Beat

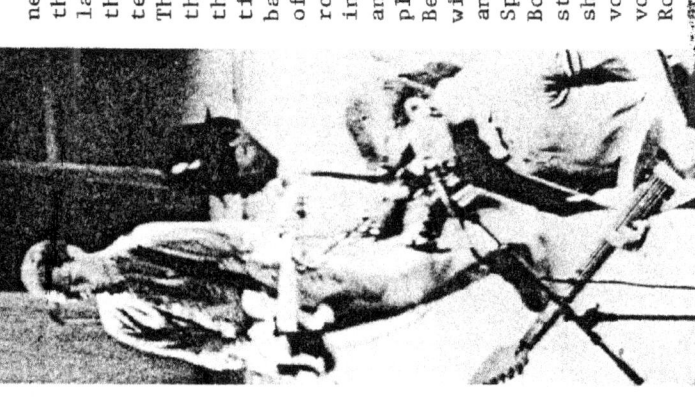

*David Steel*
*Saxa*
*David Wakeling*

Live Sept. 12
Uptown Theater, KC, MO

The Beat are one of the new groups benefitting from the ska-dance craze in England. In their second year, they are performing an extensive North American tour. The crowds have been loving their shows and this evening the reception was enthusiastic. The Beat are a dance band who play with a vigor often missing from today's rock and roll bands. Drawing tunes from their album and three singles, they played an hour set. The Beat have been associated with the Two Tone movement and comparisons with The Specials have been drawn. Both bands employ a lot of stage movement. The Beat's shows focus on guitarist/vocalist David Wakeling and vocalist/toaster Ranking Roger. Guitarist Andy Cox and bassist David Steel are constantly on the move—dancing, jumping, and running around the stage as the heavy, steady beat of drummer Everett Martin keeps everything going. The great alto saxophonist, Saxa, blows on and on, pulling it all together. And in the corner, the unknown member of the band, the keyboard player, Blockhead. Since he (→4)

# The Beat

(from p.3) was not on their recordings, he often is ignored and not given credit. His additions to the songs add further fullness to the sound so popular. When they return to the studio, hopefully this winter, the keyboards will be included and The Beat will be recognized as a seven-piece dance band.

Although their new material is not as abundant as one might desire, they do have plenty to play. It was said that the crowd was so exhausted from the show that later in the evening their reception to the next act was less enthusiastic.

ROBIN KYLE

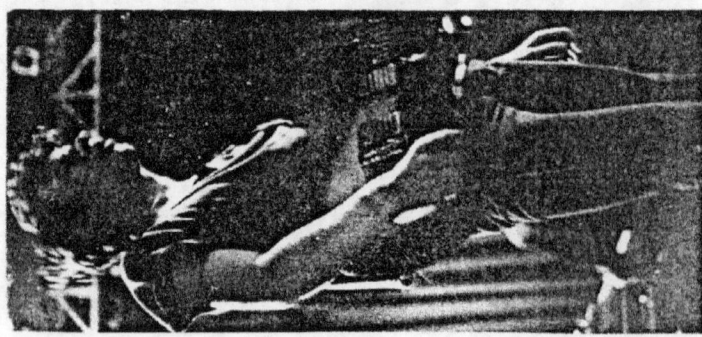

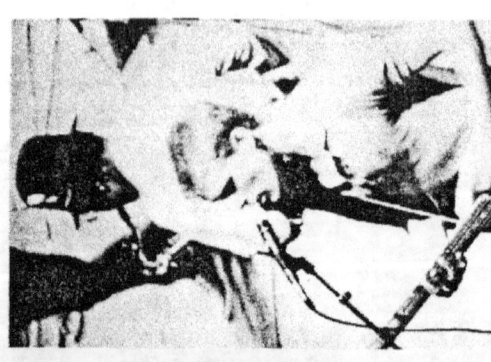

↑*Andy Cox, guitar*

→*Saxa, saxophone and David Wakeling, vocals/guitar*

*Opposite page: Saxa*

# The Beat

↳Ranking Roger amplifys Saxa as David Wakeling continues on.

↳David aka Blockhead at keyboards

↳Andy Cox, guitar
David Steel, bass
Ranking Roger, vocals
David Wakeling, guitar

Photos by Bill Rich

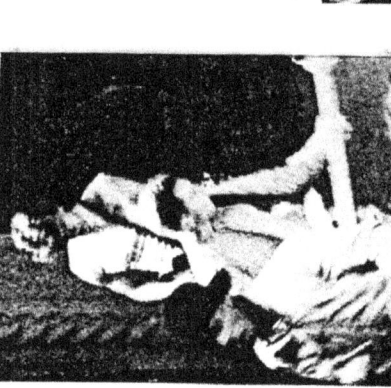

## Interview

*Before their show in Kansas City, we spent the afternoon with The Beat to get their perspective.*

David Wakeling: These are the first ever sit-down gigs we have done.
Rankin Roger: Ever. We have played four shows. We've been in America one week. Everett, you want to come do this interview? (He enters.) The whole tour is about six weeks long. We open for The Pretenders about another week.
Roger: I came to America and it's all supposed to be flooded with funk and I've not heard any funk since I've come here.
Everett Martin: You have not listened to the radio.
Roger: I expected to go out and see funk bands...
TT: What about new material, besides the single?
David Steel: We've got about four new songs.
TT: What do you think about the whole labelling aspect of Two Tone and ska revival?
David S.: I don't think anyone in America knows what Two Tone is anyway.
TT: Oh, you would be surprised.
Roger: Everybody calls us a ska band and it is obvious that we're not a ska band.
David S.: Most people don't know what ska is....We do about two ska songs. If you like something, you shouldn't try to copy it, you should try to make something different of it.
TT: So you do not really set yourselves apart from that whole movement?
David S.: We did come up around the same time in Coventry (where The Specials and The Selecter originated).
TT: How did you organize your label (Go-Feet, distributed by Arista in England, Sire, in the U.S.) so quickly?
David S.: It was quite easy. We released "Tears of A Clown" on Two Tone and had every English record company bumping around us. So we asked for our label and they had to give it to us if they wanted us.
TT: What kind of crowds do you draw?

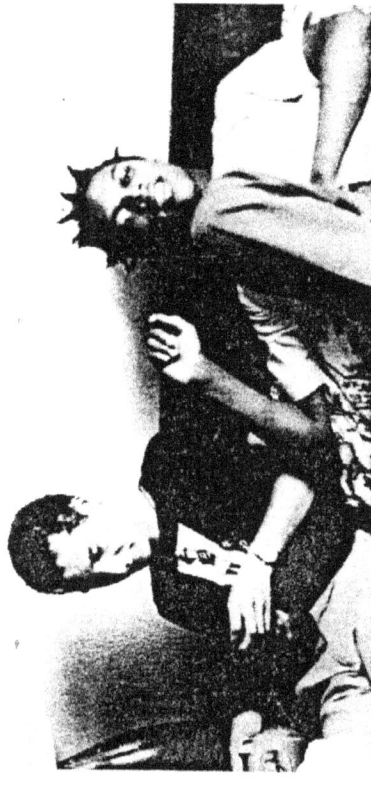

*David Steel and Ranking Roger relaxing and talking.*

## "The Beat"

**David S.:** In England, we get a lot of English people. Much more than over here. We get more Americans here....At first when we started we used to get these Two Tone people--lots of black and white clothes.
**Roger:** When we first started we got a lot of students, before Two Tone. You get little guys in beards coming in and sneaking into the corners, wondering what it is all about.
**Roger:** A few hippies.
**David S.:** A lot of hippies are into reggae.
**TT:** So you are not too against being associated with Two Tone and ska revival-type bands, right?
**Roger:** We don't mind the association. It is just the revival aspect of it.
**David S.:** I don't think people here really know what The Specials are and what we are.
**TT:** So who is Bob Sargent (producer)?
**David S.:** You know the John Peel Show? Well, he does the radio sessions. We were doing one for him and needed a producer quick. So the next day.....
**TT:** So it sounds like you have some preconceived prejudices about America.
**David S.:** Oh, gosh. The thing is the only Americans we see are idiot politicians and Starsky and Hutch. So that's the impression in England you get of America. All we get on the news is how wonderful America is and how nasty Iran and Russia are. It tends to put you on Iran and Russia's side.
**David W.:** They keep telling you so often that you think somebody is trying to get a message across.
**David S.:** I don't know. We thought we would come and see what it is like. If we hate it we will never come back again and if we like it we'll come again.
**TT:** How long have you been planning to come here?
**David S.:** It's all happened so fast. We haven't planned it really. A year ago in October 3 was the last pub gig we have played. So it has all happened since then.

*The Beat. Everett Martin, drums; Ranking Roger, vocals; David Wakeling, vocals, guitar; David Steel, bass; Saxa, saxophone; Andy Cox, guitar; and Blockhead, keyboards. In the far left top corner, manager John Mostyn looks on.*

## The Downliner

Readers of Talk Talk no doubt are familiar with The Downliner in Kansas City--if not from going there at least by seeing the concert schedule in each issue. Located in the basement of a bar, it is more primitive than plush. There have been a lot of good shows there. If you have not checked it out yet, plan to do so soon. September has been a busy month there. The Embarrassment played to a packed house (that translated to about 200 maximum). They had been there earlier, although their Lawrence debut did not occur until recently. September 12 saw a packed to the outside crowd following The Beat and The Pretenders (both of whom showed up and stayed that evening also), while Hitler's Youth, a new four-piece, black leather punk band beat out fast, short, and furious originals. The next evening, Abuse, from Topeka, had the crowd in their control as this young three-piece performed one of their best shows I have witnessed. September 19 and 20 brought the old favorites, Thumbs, back to the stage. And celebrity time again as The Kinks appeared after their show to take in some of the real Kansas City night life. The Debs, from Springfield, Missouri, returned last week with KC's own DuChamp. And more "events" are planned. Do not miss it! --BR

## Live: The Clean   September 25   Off The Wall Hall

Although it was an early fall, chilly night, the large and loyal groups of followers of The Clean filled the dance floor on the first song, warming the hall. I missed the opening act, Fred's Wallet, but heard they showed an improved form. And speaking of improvements, The Clean demonstrated great strides in development of their musical performance. This was the second public appearance of the new lineup with Jim Slocomb on drums. Their show included new material, as well as some covers and their earlier songs. Shawn Kelly had a looser, more in control, presence with his keyboards more upfront than I recall from seeing this band the past year. Todd Kitchen throws out the bass lines as easily as walking, it seems. Dressed in military garb with Old Glory draped around, The Clean enter (→23)

BILL RICH

# Album Reviews

Ultravox  Vienna (Chrysalis: CHR 1296)--Ultravox have always been frontier-breakers. Their early use of synthesizers helped a whole new scene to emerge. But they never seemed to receive much support or acclaim. At one point, they were considered dead. After their third album, the band regrouped with Midge Ure. They did extensive touring, and played in Lawrence last winter. Vienna is the first release since the lineup change and shows a strong and versatile band. This album should be their vehicle to the top. Ultravox seem to have perfected the blend of electronics and the usual drum, bass, guitar, keyboard band sound to give an even further example of how it can be done. Well, I do not really know how it was done but it shows how it can sound. And the sound is the important thing. Some bands have such a steady, distinct sound that one could listen to a few measures and recognize the name. I find that this album has so many different approaches to constructing tunes that often I fail to recognize it as the same album. Produced by Connie Plank, this is one of the outstanding releases of the year. --BR

Swell Maps  In "Jane From Occupied Europe" (Rather/Rough Trade: ROUGH 15)--After finishing this album, Swell Maps decided to break up. I have read that they were together eight years, but their first big exposure came with last year's debut album, A Trip to Marineville. They also have a handful of singles out and probably will release more. These guys believed in the home recording do it yourself, creative sound school of thought. Sometimes the beat just goes on and on and the mind wanders and rambles along with it. At times, the album could be very irritating, at others soothing. Could they play these things live? I guess they could try but Swell Maps captured an unduplicable effect. Critics call them erratic, brilliant, scrappy, fragmented, tedious, moody, uplifting, muted, self destructed by random noise. It is probably all true at times. So, if you are interested or bored, pick this one up and see how you rate it. --NN

# Album Reviews

B-52s  Wild Planet (Warner Bros.: BSK 3471)--Fie on all who said the B-52s' first album was a fluke, a one-shot comic book-record! Wild Planet is an excellent follow-up to an excellent debut LP, a tough thing to manage, as Devo or Lene Lovich would tell you. The riffs on Wild Planet are just about as hot as the ones on the first Lp, but what they lack in incendiary guitar leads, they make up for with a fuller sound (courtesy Rhett Davies) and tighter ensemble playing. Not to say there are not some terrific melodies here--"Devil In My Car" and "Quiche Lorraine" are immediate favorites and "Give Me Back My Man" is a poodle put-on worthy of Frank Zappa himself. The album does have some shortcomings, though--some sound-alike parts from the first album--but overall the B-52s show a lot of growth on the two rather short sides. With their first album still hanging in there at number 98 in the Rolling Stone Hot 100, who knows? Wild Planet may sell big. It is too bad they could not have gotten it out in time to help us through the sultry summer of '80, though. --RH

The B-52s:  Central Park, New York, August 25, 1980.

James Chance-Contortions  Live Aux Bains-Douches (Invisible: SCOPA 10008)--This album was recorded live in Paris in May. If you are a Contortions and James Chance fan, you should get this one. Otherwise, maybe something a little more subdued would be better. It starts out with Michael Jackson's "Don't Stop Till You Get Enough" with a good trumpet keeping it together. "I Danced With A (→23)

# Single Reviews

Featuring ska/dance band releases

The Beat Best Friend/Stand Down Margaret (Dub) (Arista/Go Feet: FEET 3)--"Best Friend" is a follow up release to their debut album. From the beginning chords, it is easily identified as the sound of The Beat, who furiously run through the story and song. On the B-side, an overdub has been constructed of the "Whine and Grine" album version. The subject is the Prime Minister, and it is doubtful that she will stand down no matter what The Beat plead. It is a good version, which shows once again that The Beat can successfully produce dub and extended versions of their material. --WB

Madness Baggy Trousers/The Business (Stiff: BUY 84)--The A-side is an upbeat, unexciting, danceable number with upfront vocals and rhythm keyboards. The bass line is quite versatile and strikes me as more developed than earlier. "Baggy Trousers" recalls growing up and messing around with mates. "The Business" is an instrumental with plenty of buildups and peaks. It is sort of an Eastern-influenced, slow progression. Music to pass out by. --WB

The Selecter Train to Skaville/The Whisper/Street Feeling (Chrysalis: CHS125l)--This 12-inch 45 has the band playing the classic Ethiopians song in extended form. It is a great song, superbly done. The flip features two Selecter tunes. "The Whisper" is a moving, energetic number with vocalist Pauline Black in fine form. "Street Feeling" was on their first album but does fit in nicely here. The band have recently parted company with Two Tone and have dropped their dreadlocked bassist and keyboardist. So this might be the final release with the old line-up. They will probably continue on strong. --WB

Dexy's Midnight Runners There, There My Dear/The Horse (EMI: R6038)--The soul-influenced brass and vocals shine out on this release--their third single and the first since the album. The B-side is a fast horn-laden instrumental that ends too soon. --WB

# Blue Riddim Band

*Lawrence's premier reggae group, The Blue Riddim Band, are now operating out of Chicago. They were recently back in town and played several shows to enthusiastic audiences. We talked to drummer Steve "Duck" McLane before they left again to get a historical perspective on the group and its members.*

Talk Talk: How long have you all been together?
Steve McLane: In various forms, over 13 or 14 years, going back to high school and playing in soul bands--me and Scott and Andy and Howard have played together since then. And since then, in all different combinations in all kinds of bands; jazz, country, r & b.
TT: And how long have The Blue Riddim Band been together? Three years?
Steve: No, two years this August.
TT: I remember an earlier form--The Rhythm Function? That was your first name, right. Then you went to Pat's Blue Riddim?
Steve: Yes. Same rhythm section, we just added horns.
TT: You recorded an album for Mango?
Steve: Yes. It will be a miracle if it ever comes out.
TT: So did they give you money or did Blackwell hear you play?
Steve: No, he never heard us. Just word of mouth. He managed to hear that it was something to record. So we did. Five originals, two or three ska covers, a couple of New Orleans covers. We don't play much New Orleans stuff live, but we're really interested in it. We have enough ideas for materials for about 20 bands. Two years ago we played about half r & b, one tenth ska, and two or three calypso tunes, and maybe 30 percent reggae. Now we play 60 to 70 percent (reggae) and 25 percent ska and two funk tunes. It is always changing.
TT: What about Robert Zohn?
Steve: He was in Rhythm Function and then went to Florida after it broke up. We were a couple of years ahead and actually played steady in Kansas City, something you can't do even today, unless you are a top 40 disco, country western, pop group. He recorded some and came back when Howard and Jack had to exit for a while. And it all worked out for the better and made the band real strong. Now Jack is back and Howard will be soon.
TT: So you are moving to Chicago tomorrow?
Steve: Well, yes. We will be based out of there. Moving?--We are taking the blender, soup pans, winter coats. If you want to call that moving. There isn't room for too much else. Eventually we want to be based out of New York. We want to go to Jamaica in January and record. We want to get some tracks together on our own, regardless of what Mango/Island does. There was never any contract.

(→24)

# The Embarrassment

Live: September 19,20  Off The Wall Hall

*Brent Giessmann, drums*

*Ron Klaus, bass*
*John Nichols, vocals*
*Bill Goffrier, guitar*

*Photos by Christopher Lucas*

Out of the flatlands of Kansas comes The Embarrassment. From their formation in the summer of 1979 until the present, they have constantly been shifting their sound. When I last saw them at The Spot (a Wichita bar), they had taken enormous strides in their development. Now in late September they make their debut in Lawrence. Due to my own lack of a timepiece I missed all but their last three songs on Friday night. But, on the 20th I caught their second set and was not disappointed. Their sound has the unique ability to be tight and driving yet loose all at once. Also, their sound man should be congratulated. I do not know how he did it but somehow he had the band loud, but clear, unlike so many shows I have been to at The Hall. Yes, The Embarrassment are a band to be reckoned with. With their ever-developing (→16)

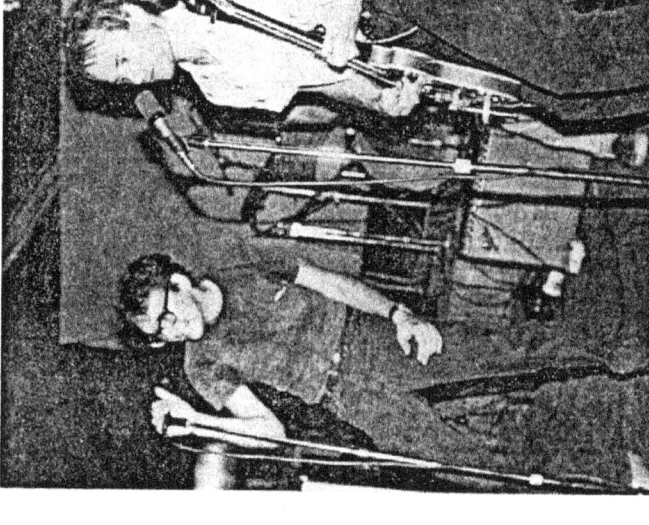

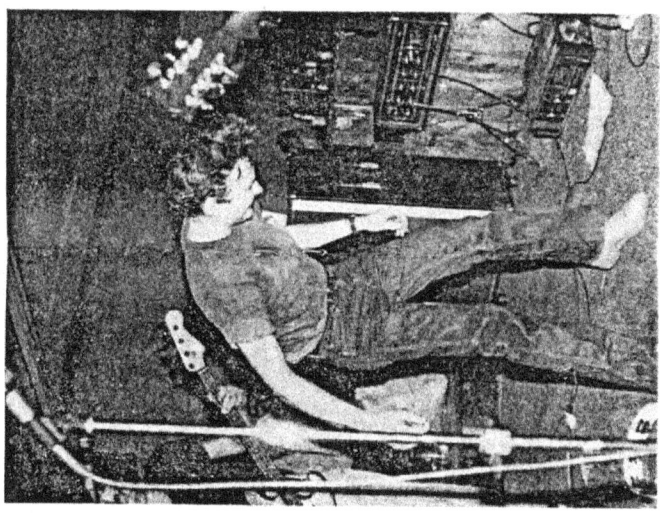

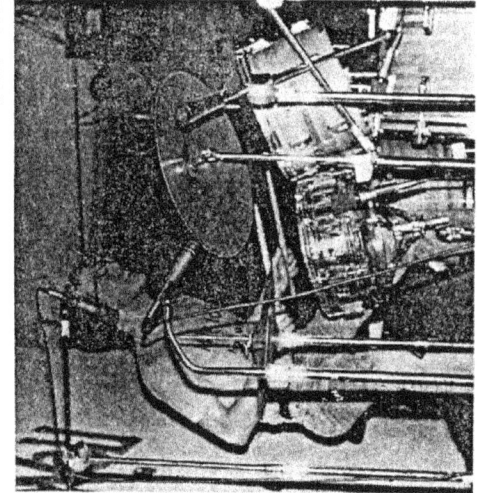

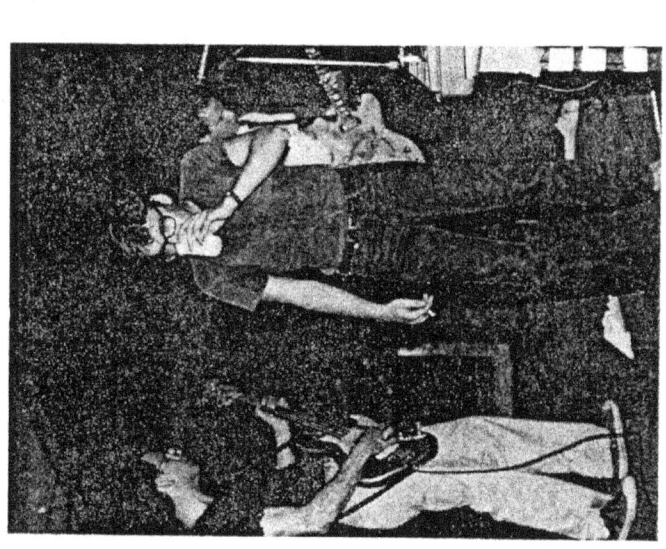

## The Embarrassment

(from p. 15) style and obvious influences (Velvet Underground, Wire, Gang of Four), they had the audience dancing throughout their set. The only thing I wished they would do was announce song titles. The Aagarnes opened the (→26)

The Aagarnes. Jim Rosencutter, guitar. Alex Erickson, vocals; Eric Cale, bass. Britt Rosencutter, drums; Sara Bagby, rhythm guitar. Photos by Christopher Lucas.

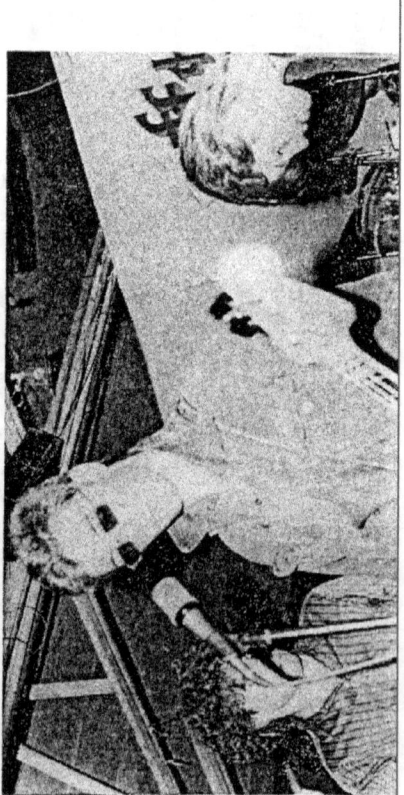

## Single Reviews

The Bodysnatchers Easy Life/Too Experienced (Two Tone: CHSTT12)--The second release from this female dominated band shows sweet harmonies backed with the customary ska rhythm. Overall, the sound moves more towards rock steady or lovers' rock. Speed up, please! --WB

The Swinging Cats Away/Mantovani (Two Tone: CHS TT14)--The latest Two Tone discovery sound like they fit into the label's history. Produced by Jerry Dammers himself, The Swinging Cats will probably get lost when the black and white checkered movement is crunched. Although sounding very derivative, look for this band. They can play. --WB

Bomis Prendin Phantom Limb (Artifacts Records: 1980)--What a nifty idea! A less-than-an-album but more-than-a-single 9-inch flexidisc, and for the going price of $3. Which, nonetheless, would not be worth it unless the music therein was as interesting--even arresting--as it is on Bomis Prendin's "Phantom Limb." Bomis Prendin leads this four-person outfit through some intriguing changes on the 13 short songs here. Some are pastoral instrumental passages and others feature rolling waves of electronic sound topped with robotic vocals. On some tunes, Bomis Prendin sound like The Residents with the annoying rough edges of their sound trimmed off--which still leaves lots of interesting ground to cover. Besides, how can you not like a guy who writes lines like these in "Monster Zero":
Calling Nick Adams!
Calling Fuji!
Calling Godzilla!
Calling Rodan!
The Nippon papparazzi flash
The army holds their fire
The leader of the X-men speaks of peace
Oh, what a liar.
Bomis Prendin will probably never be picked up by a major label, so get "Phantom Limb" while you can. --RH

The Cramps Drug Train/Love Me/I Can't Hardly Stand It (Illegal Records: ILS0021) --Well, this one probably will not win The Cramps any new fans, but those familiar with their unique brand of psycho-billy should get off on this three-song set. "Drug Train" was cut when Bryan Gregory was still with the group, and they show no musical incompatibility (→25)

## Reggae Reviews

**Bob Marley and The Wailers** One Drop/One Dub (Tuff Gong)--The A-side is taken from the Survival album and is one of the more traditional Wailers songs. The message is strong Rastafarian theology--"I know Jah never let us down." The I-Threes' vocals fade in and out occasionally. The bass line is upfront at times. Marley floats in--"give us the teachings of his majesty, we don't want no devil philosophy" and then pops up again towards the end. The big question is why are there not any Wailer dub albums out? At Tuff Gong, versions are made of almost all records, so why not make them more available by collecting them on an album or more? Bob Marley will be in Kansas City for two shows October 20. But at $15 a show, many fans will not be there to see it. I guess it is one way to exist in Babylon.  --WB

**Gregory Isaacs** Tune In/Version (African Museum)--Mr. Isaacs' voice is as clear and light as always. The continual reggae basic rhythm flows here with horns faintly mixed in. From all the special echoes on the A-side, you might think the flip side would really space out. And it does. Try to find this one. Or look for some of the compilation albums he has out with a new release on the way. --WB

**Rock Against Racism** Various Artists (Virgin: RAR1)--Not a strictly reggae album, this live collection of greatest RAR concerts. Steel Pulse's "Jah Pickney," Matumbi's "All Over This World (Money)," Aswad's "Sons of Criminals," Barry Ford's "Rebel" demonstrate the working collusion of reggae and "punk" bands in their efforts to oppose racism. White English groups like The Members, Mekons, Gang of Four, Clash, Elvis Costello, and Stiff Little Fingers also contribute some important cuts. A good record bound to be treasured with time. --WB

**Third World** Prisoner In The Street (Island: ILPS 9616)--Many things could be said about this release. As their first live album, it carries across quite successfully the feeling of a Third World performance. The production is outstanding. It is the soundtrack from the film of the same name. They play some of their top tunes (→25)

## Interview: Throbbing Gristle

*Last issue contained Part One of an interview with half of the English group, Throbbing Gristle, who were recently in Lawrence. Genesis P-Orridge and Peter Christopherson appeared on KJHK's "London Calling" program, a weekly import record show hosted by Marc Burch. In the conclusion of this interview, they talk about creating their music, their ideas, current plans, and their nightmares.*

SG: Isn't it actually all done with mirrors? Didn't you guys used to use mirrors on stage?
GP: Yeah, that's another one. We use any toys we can get hold of.
MB: You use films.
GP: Well, we got a--Peter's got a computer now as well, an Apple computer which he puts through a WahWah and fuzzbox and an echo deck.
PC: Clarinet, too. As far as we know, we are about the only group--certainly the only group in Britain--using computers like on stage and improvising with them, actually using them as an instrument.
MB: I've read that there is a Japanese band that is starting to do that now.
PC: There are several groups who use, just to be technically briefly, they use what is called a CMI, which is a machine made in Australia by a firm called Fairline, which reproduces the frequencies in a digital manner. But I don't do that. What I'm doing is a bit more interesting in the sense that, ah, maybe I shouldn't go into that.
MB: Do you consider yourselves laymen when it comes to technology or scientists?
GP: Not when it comes to technology. Peter and Chris are very, very well versed in technological developments. Peter Gabriel actually asked for advise on what kind of drum machines and computer synths to get from us. And Public Image actually got the same synth...a lot of groups in England come and watch us play and ask us about our equipment. And when we decide to dole out they decide whether to come and get it.
PC: Sounds like we're pushing our...
GP: No, it's true. It is what they have said, you know. All we are doing is quoting their own remarks. Even Robert Fripp has said that he listens to our records and it gave him a lot of new ideas. So it is kind of acknowledged in Britain that we have quite a lot of knowledge in that field. But when we actually use it, we use it like idiots, you know. We kind of abuse it in every way we can think of, to find out what it might do that nobody expects.
PC: Unlike a lot of people, I don't think we are awed by technology. I think technology is something you have to understand but you just have to use it for your own whims and enjoyments.
MB: It is a tool.
PC: Right, it is a tool.
GP: It's a toy. We literally play with it in the child's sense and we think, well now we have this wonderful thing, what can we do to mess it up and make it sound stupid or wierd or strange. We try to mangle everything, which is why people think we are a synthesizer group when actually we are mainly guitars and violins and straight instruments. But we process them all so much that even we can't always tell who's doing which noise.

Cabaret Voltaire, Public Image, Orchestral Manoeuvres...

# Throbbing Gristle

MB: Tell us about the way you collect tapes.
PC: Tapes that we use are more like an instrument. The way I use tapes live is that I have a box that has three auto reverse car cassettes made by Clarion and there are three track heads on them because they are automatic reverse and customized so that the keyboard operates any of the twelve tracks simultaneously. So it is like instantly I press a key and get whatever is on the tape. So if I have three tapes that have normal, regular notes on them I can use it like a melotron or alternatively, if some of the casettes have noises like dogs barking or people screaming or operations or anything like that, I get that noise when I press the key. Now, in terms of the kinds of tapes that I use, these can be from more or less any source, but normally they are from the kind of things that have a lot of emotional charge to them or a lot of scientific interest. Where I get these tapes from again is very varied. Some of them, I actually record myself, normally biaurally, just like walking down the street or outside the pub if there is a fight or outside a hospital and some are recorded from broadcasts that you can receive on radio, legal and illegal, and some I make myself using technologies usually used by private eyes and police agencies and things like that--better not say too much about that. For example, a lot of the recordings on the D.O.A. album are made of mercenaries without their knowledge using this kind of technology. As I said before, I don't see any reason why that technology should not be put to some good use rather than worrying if your chemical markets are the same as your competitors', I think that is boring.
SG: Peter, if you don't mind my asking, could you tell us about how much your albums cost to record?
PC: It varies very greatly. Our first album was recorded on a portable casette machine and so I guess there was about three hours of tape used, so it would be about $15. The last album was recorded in our studio in about an hour, but we did hire an eight-track machine for that, so I would guess about a thousand dollars for that. The singles we just did, we hired a machine that Paul McCartney just used to record his latest album and we mixed in a proper studio and stuff like that, so the two singles cost more than anything ever cost put together. It varies. We use the technology that seems to be appropriate for the project we are actually working on at that particular time. We haven't got thousands and thousands of dollars so it is pointless to spend money we don't have in order to record an album that sounds like the Eagles. I'm not interested in doing that.
PC: After a while a lot of the performances that we did tended to be in artistic kinds of environments like galleries. We got, after a while, very depressed at the fact that most of the people who were coming to see us were the people to whom it didn't really make any difference. Because of the performances we did in the end, the ICA got some incredible press, lunatic press from the British press, which is really organized to sell newspapers. It was condemning us as the wreckers of civilization.
GP: Well, that was a member of Parliament, actually, who went into print on the first page saying we are the wreckers of civilization something which we have been trying to live up to ever since. We were discussed in Parliament and by the Cabinet, the government and the foreign office. So it got quite interesting. This was before the Sex Pistols as well.
GP: Yes, much before.
MB: How long has Throbbing Gristle been around then? Since '74?
GP: Since Adam and Eve. Oh, you mean the group? Sorry, I misunderstood. Since September 3, 1975.
GP: I was just saying that I was being stared at very nastily by a very large Skinhead who had all stitches and cuts on his face and I was convinced he was about to leap up and kill me because he didn't like what we were doing and just when it finished he rushed up and grabbed my arm and said that was expletive great man, expletive great. And I thought, well that's all right. I'm alive for another day. Sometimes you feel very relieved that people don't assassinate you on the spot.
SG: Could you fill us in a little more on the William Burroughs album you have coming out on your label?
PC: We are assembling an album from tapes in the archives of William Burroughs Communications, which is here in Lawrence. Mostly tapes which were of experimental work done with the famous cutups that were originally done in the late '50s and early '60s.
SG: It is Burroughs reading?
PC: It is some readings but it is also a whole bunch of all sorts of stuff cut together to produce a totally new entity in itself. It would be unreasonable of us not to say that to some extent what I do with tape is based quite a lot on the techniques that were pioneered by these guys a long time ago. And so we have come here to assemble some of the original, the real thing.
MB: What is your role in this James?
PC: James Grauerholz, come to the microphone.
James: Well, I merely live here.
PC: That's not quite true. He's the...
GP: Come on, tell him the story, James. We've got to make you famous, too.
James: The story of how I first came into possession of these fabled tapes. Well, it has got very little behind it. They were simply handed to me, by a man in a dark trenchcoat....and nothing underneath as I found out later.
GP: And you are overseeing this with great patience.
MB: Are you the producer?
JG: No, not really. Not yet.
PC: I'd say he is the Executive Producer.
JG: Yeah, right.
PC: I'm not sure this album has a producer at all.
GP: I don't think even William is sure who the producer is now.
JG: We can't identify half the voices. And voices seem to appear that weren't even recorded.

## T.G. Interview:

SG: When is this coming out?
CO: Hopefully, October or November.
PC: It is a Christmas album basically what we are doing.
GP: Yeah, Gristle-mas.
MB: Gristletoe.
GP: It is for all the moms and dads to groove to instead of Andy Williams. Although he might even be on there, too.
PC: I don't think so.
GP: Perry Como.
PC: Pere Ubu.
SG: I've got one final question. What is your worst nightmare?
GP: Worst nightmare. The psychological nightmare I have is about being abandoned by somebody I don't want to be abandoned by.
PC: See you later.
GP: I have a terrible nightmare about very, very grossly fat women making advances to me sexually. That freaks me out totally. And I don't like flying in airplanes. But that's just like real life. Especially the small plane we came from Kansas City to Lawrence in. It was terrifying, absolutely terrifying.
PC: I enjoyed it. I had a good time.
GP: Yeah, but you like to be frightened.
PC: Yeah, I think maybe that protects me against it. I have a recurring nightmare about tape getting mangled up in a tape recorder. I can't explain that really. Apart from that, maybe my nightmares are all so terrible I forget them in the morning. I always have this fantasy that something terrible happened to me when I was a kid--like when I was six and it was so awful that my brain kind of shut it off and one day I will remember what it was and freak out.
JG: And wake up feeling refreshed.
GP: Your entire body is refreshed and alert.
PC: And everyday is a new threat.
GP: I'm not frightened by physical things. It is all to do with emotional stability.
JG: Other peoples'?
GP: No, mine being threatened by other peoples'. I don't like the idea of being completely alone and isolated and sitting there for the next 40 years thinking why did those rotten people go and leave me on my own, what have I done wrong, where have I failed and all that.
JG: Like a thin Spectervoice?
GP: Yeah, why have they left me alone? It's not fair.
SG: Well, on that upbeat note...
MB: Thank you, Peter. Thank you, Genesis, thank you, James, everybody else, thanks.
GP: And all the spirits of the universe, man.
MB: One love, peace.

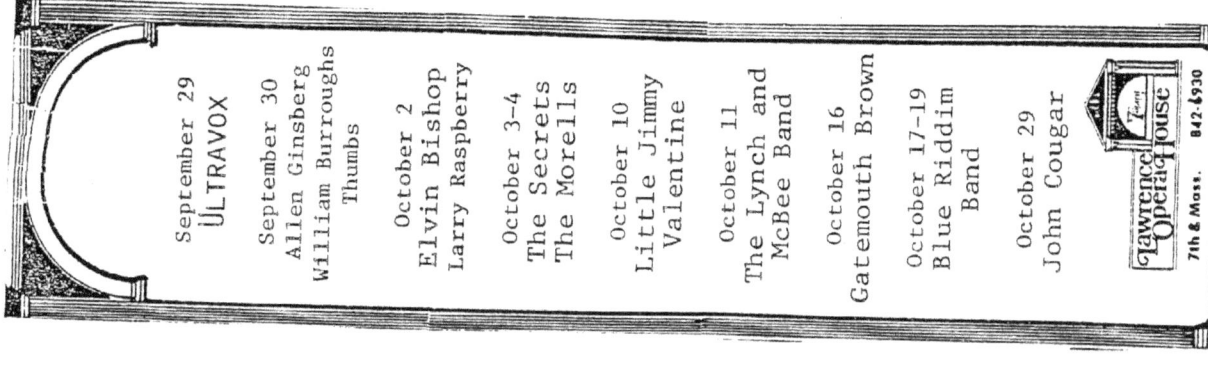

Lawrence Opera House
7th & Mass.      842-6930

September 29
ULTRAVOX

September 30
Allen Ginsberg
William Burroughs
Thumbs

October 2
Elvin Bishop
Larry Raspberry

October 3-4
The Secrets
The Morells

October 10
Little Jimmy Valentine

October 11
The Lynch and McBee Band

October 16
Gatemouth Brown

October 17-19
Blue Riddim Band

October 29
John Cougar

---

(from p. 11) Zombie" and "My Infatuation" follow with a more familiar sound before launching into James Brown's "I Feel Good." Chance is either screamsinging or blowing away on his saxophone with the band barely audible. Side 2 opens with "Almost Black" followed by "King Heroin." Next is "Put Me Back In My Cage." Closer to the end, it finally seems to pick up again with the concluding "Contort Yourself." Overall, a mixture of old songs and songs that seem to have been created for Chance. An interesting addition to the no wave jazz products already available. --NN

The Clean (from p. 9) into a new definitive hardness. The progress shown by guitarist, Jay Francis, definitely adds to the impact they have. Many times a band peaks early but continues to gain in acceptance and success. I think that The Clean are going places. Their songs should be available on vinyl and they should be playing at more shows. Let us hope that the future will include such steps. --BR

TALK TALK   165

Corrections: Photography credits for last issue's Magazine concert should have included Marc Burch. Sorry about that. Issue 9's Sunsplash review had captions for Dennis Brown and Leroy Sibbles photos reversed.

The Cramps (from p. 17) here. The A-side is a mover and well sung by Lux Interior. The songs on the B-side are a bit more experimental with Lux again in good voice. --RH

Third World (from p. 18) here--"96° In The Shade"/"Now That We've Found Love," "Third World Man," to name three. I still think that Third World have a mass appeal factor which introduces reggae to current musical acceptance. It is a different approach than The Wailers', but as important. --WB

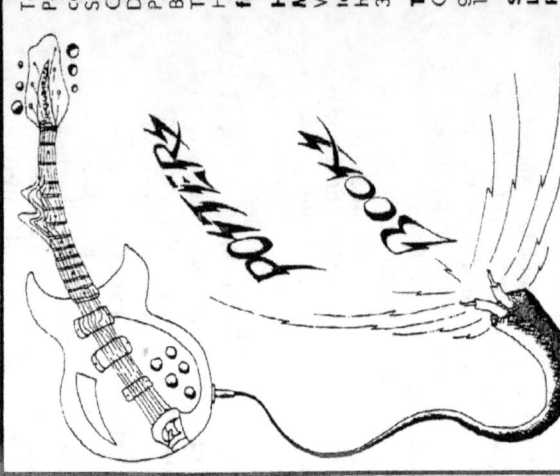

Tasty music posters by Big O & Pace-Minerva. Large (2' x 3') Full color photos of rock's high & mighty. Select from The Jam, The Clash, Elvis Costello, Graham Parker, Blondie, Deborah Harry, Patti Smith, The Pretenders, Talking Heads, Buzzcocks, Peter Tosh, Bob Marley, The Beatles, Jimi Hendrix, & Buddy Holly. $3.00 p.p. or **Score 4 & the fifth's FREE** — $12.00 p.p.

**Home Recording For Musicians** By Craig Anderton Writer For Guitar Player Magazine tells how to cut pro demo tapes at home inexpensively. 8½" x 10¾", 300 pages, illustrated $10.00 p.p.

**The Who in Their Own Words** Candid talk from the mad four who gave rock its biggest rush 7" x 10", 128 pages, 60 photos $6.00 p.p.

Send Check or Money Order to: LOCOMOTIVE, P.O. Box 8352 Prairie Village, Ks. 66208

# Interview: The Blue Riddim Band
(from p. 13)

TT: So the tapes belong to you?
Steve: No, they belong to them because they paid for them. They probably would be glad to sell them. I don't know what they want to do.... We have had it off and on about six times.
TT: Do you see any major changes in direction for the band?
Steve: Right now, the way Jamaican music is evolving is almost towards American funk. There is some with a straight "oomph oomph bup." We are going to get into more of that, plus more of the old stuff, kind of keep our roots balanced out. Plus we are going to work up a Motown thing and a Stax thing, a medley of three tunes. Just because it is music, ancient music now, but it is the best.
TT: Have you noticed in the past year getting more support, since reggae has started to get its second wind?
Steve: Oh, for sure. The new wave people have definitely made a difference in the acceptance of the ska. Pretty soon people will be ready for every Skatalite tune ever made. I would someday like to see the Skatalites or Soul Syndicate get the recognition they deserve...maybe go on the road with them. That would be slick.
TT: The band is set up for a tour now?
Steve: We've been playing Madison, Milwaukee, Minneapolis, Bloomington, Detroit, Ann Arbor, Canada, whatever, just a scoop around the north.
TT: Who writes your songs?
Steve: It's overall. Bob Zohn comes up with all the lyrics, and changes. And the band embellishes on it with horn parts and breaks and turnarounds and whatnot.
TT: And David, the Rasta. How did he come about joining?
Steve: He came up to Lawrence for the Bob Marley concert and saw us on the show and made the connection. Then about nine months later we played Wichita and he came around before the show, introduced himself and then just started bringing his drum around. It was kind of a natural evolution.
TT: Is he going to Chicago with you?
Steve: Yes.
TT: Is Pat?
Steve: Yes. It is hard to pick up the roots and pull them out but it is happening. Plus this DJ we are working with up there is as good as any DJ I have heard on record. His name is T-Jacks. He might come back with us next time.
TT: Do you have any dates lined up already?
Steve: We have the next two months booked.
TT: And you will be back in Lawrence October 18 and 19. That will be good.

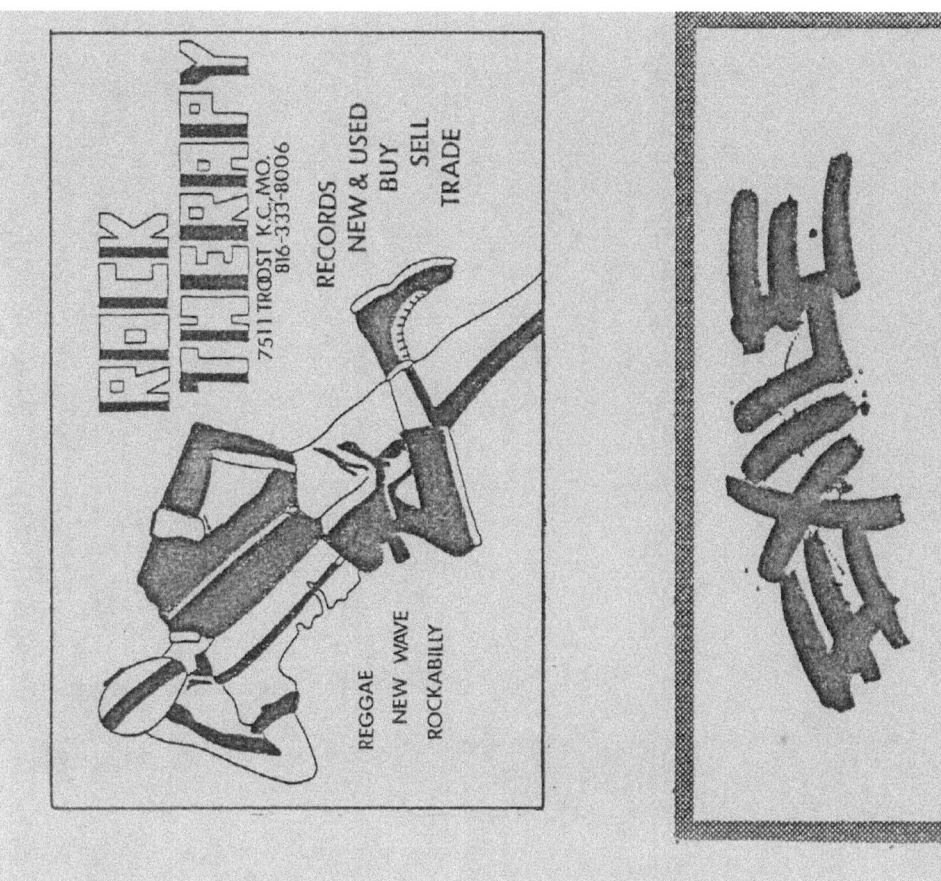

Pauline Murray and the Invisible Girls Dream Sequences 1 & 2 (Illusive Records): IVE 1)--A good song from Pauline Murray, late of Penetration, but this business of including an ever-so-slightly altered "version" of the same song as the B-side has got to stop, especially as this single goes for $3.50. With the Invisible Girls backing her and Martin "Zero" Hannett producing, Pauline has achieved a sound that is more refined than that of her old band but still uses her beautiful voice to good advantage. By George, it has even got a hook and her sustained notes will still send chills up your spine, but better to wait for the forthcoming album, on which this will doutless be included. Better yet, tape it from a friend. --RH

The Embarrassment (from p. 16) evening with a half-hour set of oldies, including "Pushing Too Hard" by the Seeds. They were asked to come back again. But I do not know when The Embarrassment will be back again. I hope it will be soon. --ES (They are finishing new demo tapes. Their single, "Patio Set/Sex Drive" is available for $1.50 from 641 Woodlawn, #4, Wichita, 62208)

THE DOWNLINER
(below Plaza East)
4719 Troost
K.C., Mo.
816-753-9368

October 3-4
THE MODERNS

October 10-11
THE TUNES

October 17-18
BROWN & LANGRER

October 24-25
THE CLEAN

In November
THE NUKES
DUCHAMP

Open
9 to 1
Be 21!

Brought to you by
Sum-thing-tu-du
Productions

TALK TALK

TALK TALK

Vol. 2 No. 12   November 1980   $1.00

The Midwest American Rock and Reggae Magazine

**TALK TALK**

Editors:
Bill Rich
Eric Schindling

Contributors:
Rick Hellman
Jim Schwada
The U-Man
Christopher Lucas
VS, DC, WB

Photography:
Robin Kyle
Christopher Lucas
Bill Rich

Cover Design:
Nate Fors

Layout
John Lee
Bill Rich

Typesetting:
Joan McCabe Moore

### Table of Contents

Concerts: Ultravox................3
Album Reviews: The Clash,
  Monochrome Set................6
  Glaxo Babies..................7
  Siouxsie and The Banshees,
  Talking Heads.................8
  Dead Kennedys, Kurtis Blow....9
Single Reviews: SPK, In Camera,
  The The, Bush Tetras.........10
  Glenn Branca, Liliput,
  Echo and The Bunnymen,
  The Professionals............11
Concerts: Burning Spear........12
Reggae Reviews: UB 40,
  Soul Syndicate, Earl Zero,
  Toots and The Maytals........16
  Jimmy Cliff, Bunny Wailer,
  Derrick Laro and Trinity,
  Rico Rodriguez...............17
Interview: William S. Burroughs
  and Allen Ginsberg...........18
Concerts: Burroughs, Ginsberg,
  Thumbs.......................24
Album Reviews: James Brown.....25
  Prince Far I.................26

All contents copyright 1980 by Talk Talk Publications, PO Box 36, Lawrence, Kansas, 66044. All rights reserved. Any opinion expressed is solely that of the writer and not necessarily that of this publication. Subscription rate is $6 for six issues. Articles, reviews, and pix submitted for editorial consideration are welcome. Not responsible for unsolicited material. Address all correspondence to Talk Talk Editors, PO Box 36, Lawrence, Kansas, 66044.

Talk Talk Vol. 2 No. 12/page 3

# Ultravox

Live: September 29       Lawrence Opera House

Ultravox...They played here last year on a shoestring-budgeted tour. Without a label, they plowed across the USA, leaving fine performances behind them. The only thing that hurt them last time was old material having to be reworked to fit Midge Ure's style of singing. This time, though, they were the headliners and it showed. The sound system was fairly good and they brought quite a bit of equipment with them, light, computers, and synthesizers, with a new record label and material from their newest album. Tonight their (→4)

*Midge Ure adds feeling during "Vienna". ↓Chris Cross, Warren Cann, Midge Ure, Billy Currie. Photos by Christopher Lucas.*

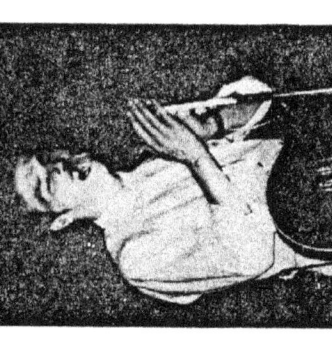
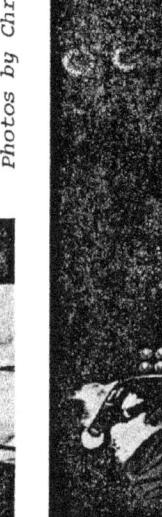
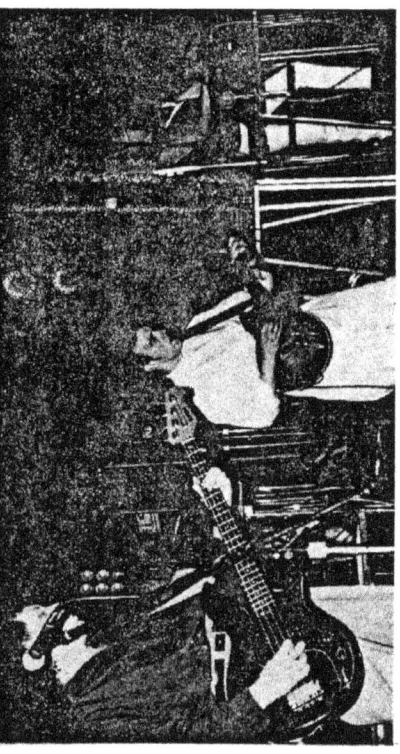

# Ultravox

set was tight and flashy, with Midge Ure shaking his hips, dressed in a white suit with fashionable baggy trousers, looking similar to Bryan Ferry. Why then did I have questions about this show? Maybe it was the fact that they were a little too slick. I mean I enjoyed myself and all that, but my memory kept flashing back to a year before when they were on their own with less flash and maybe a little more flesh. Some of the songs that stood out were good solid versions of "Mr. X" and "Vienna" (the title track from their new album) and an outstanding reworking of "Hiroshima Mon Amour" that had an electronic instrumental part in it that reminded me of Throbbing Gristle. The band played for a little more than an hour and came back and did an encore that featured Eno's "King's Lead Hat." Once again, though, the feeling came back to me that they performed this song with more desperation and energy the year before. All in all, though, it was a good show, though not a great one.

Opening the evening were Brown and Langrehr, a St. Louis duo. Their choice of drums and guitar creates a sparce sound. --VS

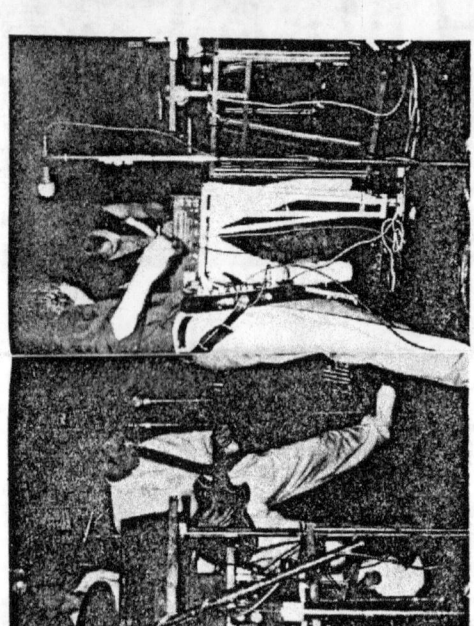
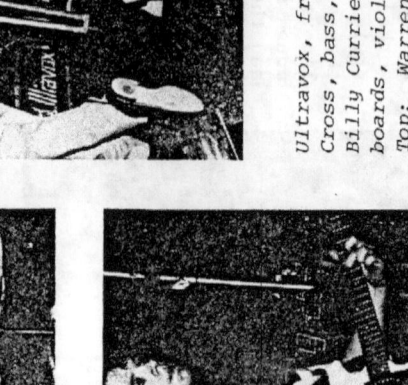

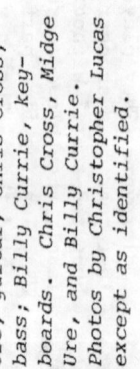
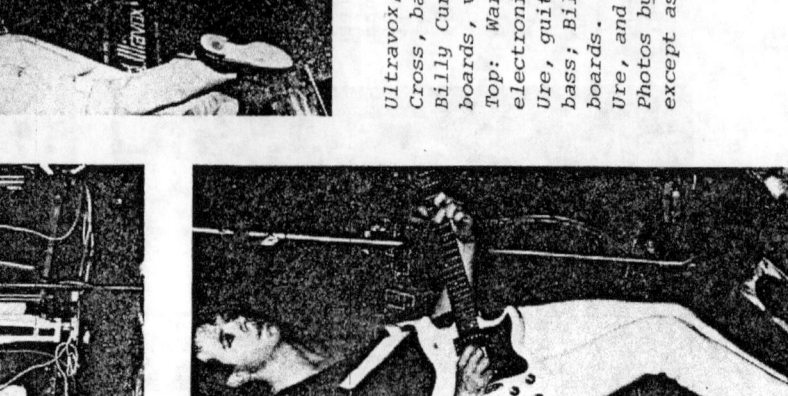

Ultravox, from left: Chris Cross, bass, synths, vocals. Billy Currie, synths, keyboards, violin, guitar. Top: Warren Cann, drums, electronic percussion; Midge Ure, guitar; Chris Cross, bass; Billy Currie, keyboards. Chris Cross, Midge Ure, and Billy Currie. Photos by Christopher Lucas except as identified.

## Album Reviews

The Clash Capital Crisis
Clash on Tour
Blackmarket Clash (Epic:4E36846)--Two bootleg recordings currently surfacing are necessary additions for the Clash fan. Clash on Tour, live in Paris 1977-78, has a date of 9-29-77 for side one with their early songs. The second side, recorded 10-16-78, contains selections from their first album. "The Tommy Guns Live" is what the label says. As far as the fidelity of the recording, I have bought worse ones. But not many. If you have not heard the boys do The Ramones' "Blitzkrieg Bop", that is how they ended this one.

Capital Crisis is a double record bootleg recorded in March, 1980 at the Capital Theater. Again the fidelity is low but the band sound a lot more together for this show. The bulk of material is from London Calling and Give Them Enough Rope. Mikey Gallagher is present on keyboards. The momentum continues building, making the listener wish they were there--or that they had a better recording!

On the legitimate side of clash releases, Epic Records have added class to their 10-inch Nudisk Ep concept of more than a single, less than an album packaging by finally including a decent band--in this case, an excellent band. As far as new material goes, only one new cut, the instrumental ending side one, is included. And it is probably the poorest thing on the disc. It is a fine collection and covers early material as well as their latest, "Bankrobber", and some extended versions. Of the three releases reviewed here, the new 10-incher is definitely the best for the money and listening pleasure. --WB

The Monochrome Set Love Zombies (DinDisc:DID8)--Four months after their debut Strange Botique, The Monochrome Set offer a companion release. The two go together quite well and this record adds to their credibility of being the best modern pop band. The vocals of Bid sweep up, down, and sideways along the guitar work of Lester Square. The band has changed a little since their early Rough Trade singles. Maybe a bit slower than before but the sound remains heavily layered. No more Bob Sargent, as Alvin Clark is the producer. The A sides of their two latest singles, "405 Lines" and "Apocalypso" are here, along with eight new ones. --WB

## Album Reviews

Glaxo Babies Put Me On the Guest List (Heartbeat Records: HBM 3)--This second Lp from the Glaxo Babies is a compilation of unreleased material, as well as material taken from their first Ep, This Is Your Life (12 Pulse 3), the "Shake" single (Pulse 8), and some unavailable singles. Since their start in '77, they have gradually progressed in sound and this record captures this progression. From the first song on to the last, the music moves from rock to a more funk-oriented Pop Group kind of sound. However they are not quite as grating or blatant. Best songs: "Avoiding the Issue", "She Went To Pieces", "Burning" (with its sonic bass and sax attack), and "The Puppet Patrol." They do a dub version of "Who Killed Bruce Lee", compare it to the version on the TILY Ep. This album is a great insight into the history of the Glaxo Babies. And for those of you craving even more GB material, they have just released a four-song Ep, Limited Entertainment (Rough Trade: Y6). This is much more socio-politico-oriented stuff than the above. The back of the jacket states the purpose of the Glaxo Babies. "We use entertainment to forget; they maintain their power." Even the record label itself has quotes from Mrs. Thatcher and Andy Young referring to infringement on essential liberties and the state of intelligence technology. But on with the musical aspect. The A-side, "Limited Entertainment"/"Dahji": "LE" is a materialistic anthem that expounds on the work ethic, with a refrain "sell your soul for a pot of gold." This song has a very funky rhythm, the bass of Tom Nichols and guitar of Dan Catsis really get this one jumping. The second song, with its synths, high-pitched sax, and percussion that sounds like rainfall, gives this a third world sound. Beneath it all, a driving bass and drifting voices. This could almost be Pere Ubu or Hare Krishnas. The B-side: "There'll Be No Room For You In The Shelter"/"Permission To Be Wrong" is the best side of this Ep. "TBNRFYITS" is a song about the acceptance of the nigh-inevitable WW3 or world holocaust. Like the Pop Group, the Glaxo Babies make sure to spread the guilt and name the names. The funniest line is "I've never seen a Russian in my life." "PTBW" is a slow, haunting piece, like a walk down death row. I am making my decisions for you. --U-Man

## Album Reviews

Siouxsie and the Banshees Kaleidoscope (Polydor Deluxe: 2442 177)--An album of successful experimentation, as Siouxsie and the Banshees incorporate other instruments into their music. Each member displays their musical talents on this, their third and best Lp. John McGeoch and Steve Jones (stand in Banshees) on guitars. Jones plays lead guitar on three songs: "Clockface", "Paradise Place", and "Skin." McGeoch plays guitar, sax, and some synth on four songs: "Christine", "Happy House", "Hybrid", and "Desert Kisses." John Severin and Budgie, besides their usual instruments (basses and percussion), get to toy with pianos and electronix. While Siouxsie, besides some of her most sensual singing, plays a variety of instruments ranging from acoustic guitar, bass, and melodica to camera, and finger cymbals. This record is much more atmospheric than any other of their records. It is not nearly as death-oriented as the previous two Lps; especially the dirge-like "Join Hands." Included on this record are the A-sides of the two recently released singles, "Happy House" and "Christine." Every song on this Lp seems to have some essential element that just will not allow the listener to be distracted. Best songs: "Desert Kisses", "Lunar Camel", "Red Light", and "Paradise Place." --UM

Talking Heads Remain In Light (Sire: SRK 6095)--Talking Heads are not the flashiest band to come down the punk/wave pike, but they may be the best. Their fourth Lp (and third produced by Eno), Remain In Light, is another giant step in the Heads' creative process. The band has been expanded, the lyrics are more obtuse than ever and Byrne has embraced the punk/funk movement. It all adds up to a stunning experience and leaves me slavering for the upcoming Byrne/Eno excursion. Side 1 consists of three rather long songs, of which my fave is "The Great Curve." All three center on Byrne's now-familiar voice and surround it in a frenetic mix of funk riffs and more traditional T. Heads sounds. Even some Bowie and Fripp inflections can be heard here and there. I do not know exactly why, but this Lp reminds me of none so much as "Heroes." The Eno connection is apparent, but the sheer breadth of influences synthesized is Talking Heads. --RH

## Album Reviews

The Dead Kennedys Fresh Fruit for Rotting Vegetables (Cherry Red:BRED10)--"Mellow out or you will pay"--"The fuhrer in California Uber Alles. Welcome to the private world of The Dead Kennedys, a world we all belong to, a world with chemical warfare, corrupt politicians, drafts, and just plain unaccountable ways to die. The music is full of high speed chords from the guitar, a thumping rhythm that, along with Jello Biafra's voice, form a tension hard to find in today's American music. On the album there are a few unneeded tracks, more instrumental breaks would make Biafra's sick voice more perfect and less tedious. For those people who see The Dead Kennedys as just another late punk band from LA, watch out for the "suede denim secret police" and listen to the record. --CL

*Sorry we do not have any pictures of The Dead Kennedys. Here is one of a dead horse. Photo by Christopher Lucas.*

Kurtis Blow Kurtis Blow (Mercury:SRM 13854)--This young New York "rapper" has received high acclaim for his first Lp. His vocal style is based on the Deejay rap in the vein of Jocko Henderson and Strapper Lee. Some people like it, others hate it. Side one has an outstanding beginning with "Rappin' Blow" and "The Breaks". Once these raps get into your head, watch out. They will remain forever. --WB

## Single Reviews

Surgical Penis Klinik (SPK) Slogan/Factory (Industrial Records: IR011)--An ode to psychopaths, mass murderers, and revelers in violence everywhere. The trollish inquisitors giggle at the electronic agony; the gift they bring a sensual experience in pain. They scream in demon voices, "therapy for violence" continually. The drill press, the chainsaw, the disintegration ray, whatever...the buttons are pushed, the levers pulled. Death and comedy. Only mutants, misfits, and video babies could appreciate this.--UM

In Camera Final Achievement/Die Laughing (4 AD: AD8)--The debut single from another of the so-called existential or neo-psychedelic bands. The A-side, though a bit slow-paced, is still a good piece. The B-side is vastly superior. What starts out as an almost Joy Division-sounding instrumental transforms into something more apocalyptic. This one has a more desperate feel to it, with the lead singer screaming in his rather strange nasal tone, "the horror!" and at the close a fatalistic laugh. Some joke.--UM

The The Controversial Subject/Black & White (4 AD: AD10)--I love the name of this band, it is so ordinary yet enigmatic. This single owes a lot, no doubt, to the production of Bruce Gilbert and Graham Lewis (of Wire, Cupol, and Dome). They manage to create the sound that one associates with those two: sparse percussion that sounds ever so distant, screaming airplane guitars, and weaving synths. Both songs on this single are incredible; perfect examples of minimalism, ambiguity, and ethereal weirdness. Here is one that will spend a lot of time on the turntable.--UM

Bush Tetras Too Many Creeps/Snake Crawl/You Taste Like The Tropics (99 Records: 99-02)--Pat Place (former Contortionist) plays guitar on this great single. "Too Many Creeps" is a song about exactly that. I am sure in New York creeps abound and I wonder if the song might not also be referring to good old Jimmy White-AKA-Chance? The flip is equally good with a sound that reminds me at times of Lydia Lunch. I know this is a short review but the single speaks for itself. Go out and get it.--VS

## Single Reviews

Glenn Branca Lesson No. 1/Dissonance (99 Records:99-01)--Glenn Branca has a winner here with this exceptional Ep. At times, he sounds like he listened to every Fripp-Eno Lp and then took his own warped sensibilities and came up with this recording. Both tunes are repetitious but this is what Eno calls ambient music. Fabrics and textures being drawn up out of the rhythm and making your own mind work. A promising work from this new artist and record label. --VS

Liliput Split/Die Matrosen (Rough Trade:RT 047)--LiLiput, formerly Kleenex, have this new single out. The B-side sounds like their old selves. High vocals and choppy but lovable rhythms. The A-side has a sweeter melody and a lilting sax in the background. It is nice to know that these girls are still around and putting out fine music. --VS

Echo and The Bunnymen The Puppet/Do It Clean (Korova: KOW 11)--Think about Echo and The Bunnymen. I mean, what kind of name is that for a rock and roll band? A little wimpy-sounding maybe, but, as depicted on the cover of their first single, this is a muscular hare, indeed. Besides, I have always had a soft spot for psychedelia. That is such a poor tag, though, for the so-called psychedelic revival going on. There is no gimmick about Echo and The Bunnymen, no substitute for impassioned singing and playing. "The Puppet" moves along smartly, propelled by a strong bass line and McCulloch's incantory vocals. Like many of the songs on the first album, the words themselves are secondary to how they are sung, thereby allowing the feeling to be more directly transmitted. Kind of like The Cure's last album, but more agitated. And to top it off, the chorus of "Do It Clean" suggests The Bunnymen might have been a great garage band in a different time and place. So, buy this single and get hoppy! --RH

The Professionals One Two Three/White Light White Heat, Baby I Don't Care (Virgin:VS 376)--The meat of the Sex Pistols, guitarist Steve Jones and drummer Paul Cook prove to be as powerful as before. Each song has a different sound; "1,2,3" is an original Cook'n Jones tune worth listening to."White Light" has been done better numerous times. --WB

# Burning Spear

**Live: The Uptown
October 20 Theater**

Burning Spear is Winston Rodney. He is, perhaps, one of the foremost spokesmen for his Rastafarianism in the world today. His albums consist of pleas for unit among all men and praises to Jah. At The Uptown Theater, unfortunately, Burning Spear never seemed to be able to build up the energy level that was needed to get the entire crowd involved. Part of the fault lay with the sound system which has no bottom end at all. So some of the heavier numbers lost almost all of their force. This problem is not unique to just this show. The Uptown Theater's sound system is not made for rock or reggae but rather for jazz so the same problem will probably haunt every show held there. Another factor for a weak show might be the fact that the Uptown Theater's security guards had earlier in the evening thrown out the percussionist of The Burning Band because he was not wearing a stage pass. The entire security force at The Uptown have been known to be overtly hostile and violent in the past (→14)

*Burning Spear and The Burning Band*

*Winston Rodney*

*Linden Davis, Keyboards
Elias Rodney, Percussion
Anthony Bradshaw, Rhythm Guitar
Winston Rodney, Vocals
Nelsen Miller, Drums
Michael Wilson, Guitar*

# Burning Spear

(from p. 12) and from all reports that were heard they were in that very form this night. A third factor about the evening which had nothing to do with Burning Spear was the fact that another fine reggae band, Soul Syndicate, were advertised to play but our sources show that the band had never intended to be there. The promoters, who knew this, did not tell anyone and so on the night of the show The Blue Riddim Band opened. Now, I liked their set fine, but what I did not like was the fact that the promoters knew all along that The Soul Syndicate were not going to be there yet they let people believe that up to the very end. Well, once all the negative factors are exposed and realized, I can now say that even though I considered Burning Spear's performance not up to my expectations, I still enjoyed them. Winston Rodney's voice alone could carry off the whole deal. His back-up musicians were solid and he did give us an hour of his brand of reggae. Burning Spear's music is in some respects more roots oriented than say Bob Marley's. But for conviction and power, Winston Rodney might have the edge.--VS

CHRISTOPHER LUCAS

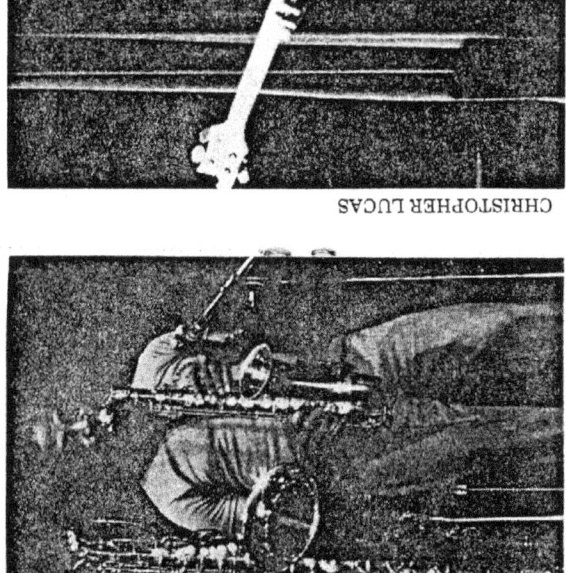

CHRISTOPHER LUCAS

BILL RICH

Far left:
Herman Marcus
Saxophone
Left:
Sidney Gussine
Bass
Below:
Linden Davis
Keyboards
Elias Rodney
Percussion
Anthony Bradshaw
Rhythm Guitar
Winston Rodney
Vocals
Nelsen Miller
Drums
Michael Wilson
Guitar
Herman Marcus
Saxophone
Sidney Gussine
Bass

## Reggae Reviews

UB 40 Signing Off (Graduate:LP2)--Very pleasant Lp by UB 40, an interracial group of Reggae Rockers from England. Lots of tenor sax and melodica with a vocalist who reminds one very much of Stevie Wonder. Only the second release by Graduate Records, a small label out of Birmingham, England, there is a lot of music here. Both a 33 1/3 disc and a 12-inch 45, containing new material and both sides of their single "Food for Thought" and "I Think It's Going to Rain Today"--not as-rockin' as Capital Letters or as repetitious as Steel Pulse, UB 40 is a welcome addition to the U.K. Reggae scene--check out their version of Billie Holiday's "Strange Fruit", a biting indictment of racial violence in the American South, the updated version of which is just as eerie and ironic as the original. --DC

Soul Syndicate Was, Is, and Always (Epiphany:3020) Earl Zero Visions of Love (Epiphany:3010)--A couple of eminently forgettable Lps from San Francisco's Epiphany label. The Soul Syndicate are a group of studio musicians who have backed up just about everybody in the business. Unfortunately, their own albums have lacked. Was, Is, and Always presents a group of old classics ("Guns of Navarone", "Tonight", "Just Another Girl") done up without the drive or interest of the originals--the one saving grace being "The Soviets are Coming", a reggae version of Dave Brubeck's classic jazz standard "Take Five." The Soul Syndicate can be heard to slightly better advantage backing guitarist/vocalist Earl Zero on his latest Visions of Love, but even the addition of session superstar Augustus Pablo does not help raise it above a mediocre level. Better luck next time, Dreads. --DCool

Toots and The Maytals Live At The Palais 29-9-80 (Island:TOOTS1)--A masterpiece by one of the greatest in the world of reggae. With a special promo gimmick of having this record in the store the day after the show, it could have been disaster. But the (→26)

## Reggae Reviews

Jimmy Cliff Satan's Kingdom/Version (Sunpower Records)--This is what Jimmy Cliff should be sounding like on Lps. The production of this single is vastly superior to that of his recent albums. Here we find Cliff's vocals as powerful and sweet as ever as he talks about the temptations of evil and Bablyon. The mix is heavy on the bass, which helps his voice and the general dread of the song. Why Jimmy Cliff does not get an album of this quality out is a mystery to me. But it is good to know that Jimmy Cliff is still capable of putting out quality records. It would seem if he just keeps his next record production out of the U.S. of (Babylon) A., he should have no problem.--VS

Bunny Wailer Crucial/Togawar Game (Solomonic Records)--The heaviest Dreadmaster has a fairly new single out and it is every bit as good as anything he has come up with so far. Bunny, rumor has it, lives in the outback of Jamaica, working his magic and waiting for the time when Jah brings an end to Babylon. The music is a fairly melodic dub style, with Bunny's vocals over the mix. On "Crucial", he talks about how things are getting better and this is an important time to get motivated because the times are "Socially crucial and Crucially crucial." The flip, "Togawar Game", is about the pulling of the poor against the rich in a Tug of War game with a nice horn section playing beneath the vocal mix. All in all, a fine single from Bunny. Now, if a major label would pick up on him...--VS

Derrick Laro & Trinity Don't Stop Till You Get Enough (Joe Gibbs 12" 45).--Okay, okay, call me a snob if you want--before this single came out I would have scoffed at the idea of enjoying Michael Jackson (at least anything past "I Want You Back"). This is the type of thing that should be playing in discos across the country...a classic along the lines of Dillinger's "Cokana In My Brain." Don't stop...Don't stop...Don't stop...Go Deh! --DCool

Rico Rodriguez Sea Cruise/ Carolina (Two Tone:CHSTT15)-- A nice little instrumental release from the famous trombonist. Both songs seem to float along. As expected, the emphasis is the trombone playing a melody as percussion and bass beat out rhythms. --WB

ROBIN KYLE

# William S. Burroughs

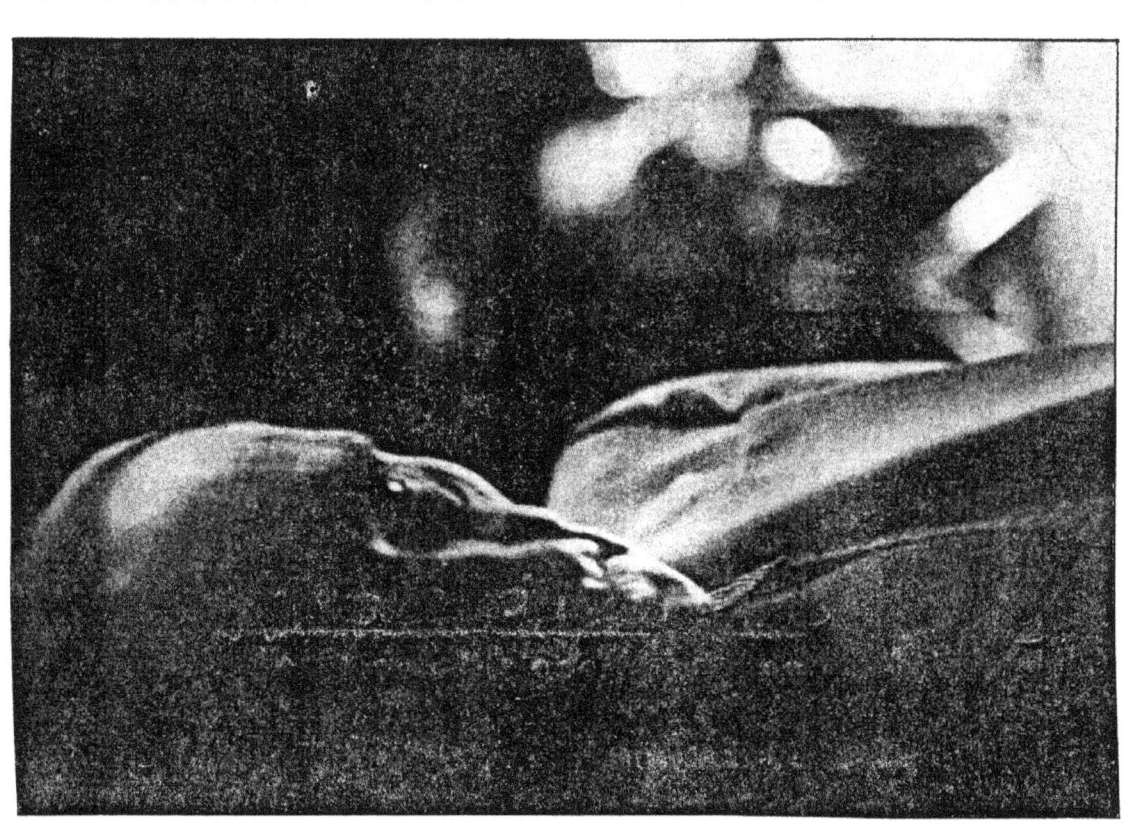

## Interview: Burroughs and Ginsberg

*Before a joint appearance, William S. Burroughs and Allen Ginsberg participated in a radio interview. The following is some excerpts from their conversations. This is the first half with the conclusions coming next issue.*

Jim Schwada: Good afternoon. This is KJHK, Lawrence. My name is Jim Schwada and I'm very pleased to have in the studios with me this afternoon two living legends of American literature--poet Allen Ginsberg and author William S. Burroughs. Opening the show we heard a bit of William S. Burroughs called "The Day I Stopped Wanting To Be President." Just a little bit more background information: Allen Ginsberg is the author of some of the most powerful and important poetry of the twentieth century; works with names like "Howl", "Kaddish", and "Reality Sandwich." William S. Burroughs is responsible for some of the most amazing works of social satire ever written. His books, Naked Lunch, The Soft Machine, Nova Express, and others, are visionary masterpieces that offer hilarious and frightening pictures of man and his existence. His autobiographical work, Junkie, the story of his addiction to narcotics, stands as the frankest account yet of drug addiction and life on the fringes of the underworld. Both of these gentlemen will be reading from their works tonight in downtown Lawrence and have taken a few moments from their busy schedule to come in and talk about their lives and work. Joining me in the studio is Eric Schindling, editor of Talk Talk magazine, who will be helping out in this interview. Gentlemen, I really appreciate you coming down to talk to us.

Allen Ginsberg: Well, thanks for inviting us.
William S. Burroughs: Thank you.
AG: We are holding in our hands an uncorrected proof galley of Mr. Burroughs' latest novel, Cities of the Red Night, with a lavendar-pink cover. What else does it say?
Eric Schindling: "A Boys Book."
WB: "A Boys Book" is going to be removed because I did not want to have the idea that this was...
ES: For children?
WB: Well, for any particular audience, like saying a womans book. It limits it.
AG: What did you mean by a boys book to begin with?
WB: I do not...uh...I was opposed to it.
AG: Whose idea was it?
WB: I do not remember.
AG: I am opening it up to page 182. "The lizard boy now leads the way, setting the fastest pace. As he moves, his body changes color to blend into the landscape."
WB: That is enough. I do not feel it is fruitful to just dip in.
JS: When will it be out?
WB: In January or February. I may try to arrange it to come out on my birthday, which is February 5.
JS: As I was giving the introduction, it appeared to me even as I read it how trite the "living legend" seems to be. But it really seems to fit. Not only have you been immortalized by your own works, but also your characterizations in the works of Jack Kerouac, many of his novels feature other groups of your friends who became known as the Beat generation in the 50's. How did you first meet?
WB: Well, let me see. I met, uh, I forget if I met you first or Kerouac. I think Allen and I met first.
AG: On Christmas, 1943. I think

TALK TALK 177

# Interview: Burroughs and Ginsberg

WB: This was through Lucien Carr who came from St. Louis. He was going to Columbia where he had met Allen. And I met him and through Allen then in turn I met Jack Kerouac.
AG: Well, I think what happened was that I had never been to Greenwich Village and Bill had an apartment down there and another friend of his.
WB: On Bedford Street.
AG: So we went to visit Lucien's other friend.
WB: Ah, David Camera.
AG: Yes. He was not around, but you were. So we were introduced. I remember the first thing I heard Bill say was sort of a description of a fight in a gay bar between a lesbian and somebody else had gotten drunk and bit her ear off. And Bill said, "Tis too starved an argument for my sort." That was the first time I heard Shakespeare quoted in a funny way. It sounded like something worth listening to.
JS: The period that you first came to meet and when a lot of your early works were done—The 50's—to someone who was not alive then like myself seems like quite a repressive time—The Cold War and McCarthyism. But you were very open in your use of different drugs and your admission of homosexuality as a lifestyle. Did you ever feel a danger in doing so back then?
WB: Well, I was not at all at that time in the public eye. Remember, I did not publish until 1953. That was under another name and I was not in the States at the time.
JS: The first book was Junkie.
WB: I got into quite a bit of trouble through the use of drugs. It was not a question that I was advocating anything about these publicly because I did not have any public to talk to.
JS: You all have experimented with several different varieties of drugs. Do you find them useful in writing?
WB: Well, I find, I have always found, cannibas a useful drug because it seems to stimulate the whole associative process and the process of visualization. Other drugs...I have never talked to a writer who is able to actually write when they were using alcohol or actually drunk.
JS: Last night in Mr. Ginsberg's reading, you read a poem—a sort of Wordsworthian poem that you had written under the influence of LSD.
AG: Yes. I am glad you remembered that. It is called "A Whale's Visitation." But that is rare indicational poem, specifically attempting to see if I could bring back from an LSD state anything as particularly detailed and concrete as a description of nature that might communicate to others the same sensations I had when I was high. So it was an attempt to look outside my subjective sensations and see what I saw with my eyeballs and describe what was outside of myself and make "objective correlative"--T.S. Eliot's phrase, and object correlate my feelings that might correlate with other people's awareness and intelligence and get them to get a glimpse of the same state or space I was in. That was a rare poem. Then there is another one called "LSD, Mescaline, and Howl, Part II." the first notations or first twenty lines were written on peyote. And that is about all.
WB: It is my feeling that drugs are the same as any other area of experience—It may or may not be productive.
JS: At the end of Junkie, the last sentence in fact was written in 1953 and you are off to Columbia to experiment with yagé. Both of you collaborated on The Yagé Letters, I believe.
AG: Yes.
JS: The last says it could be the ultimate fix, the ultimate kick. Did you find it to be so?
WB: Ah, no. Not at all.
AG: That in itself was sort of a humorous line. It was not something to fix with anyway. It was a drink.
WB: But actually at that time there had been very little research and very little was known about that class of drugs now lumped under hallucinogens. When I went to the library to find out about yagé, there was almost nothing. Now you could fill this room with references....
JS: I have a copy of The Nova Convention record which I wanted to play but unfortunately due to FCC regulations, a great deal of it is not air playable. You had quite a bit of experience with censorship trials in the 50's. How do the 50's stack up against the 80's? We are still not able to play a lot of these.
WB: Well, there has actually been a certain amount of retrograde. I remember that Pacifica stations were able to play literary material like Burroughs' and mine all during the 60's and early 70's. Then I think there was an FCC decision or temporary ruling when a program manager discussed the seven deadly words—the blue words that were not supposed to infiltrate the airwaves. He did a humorous discussion of them and that was rated illegal. But I do not think any literary text has yet been ruled illegal. And I think it never could be ruled illegal because the standard is and always has been if it has to do with free speech and criticism of society such valid, useful social description or criticism...
WB: Redeeming social significance.
AG: Obviously, what you just played by Mr. Burroughs which was a critique of the psychology of the Presidential ambitious characters would have redeeming social significance. That is covered by the First Amendment. The First Amendment is absolute about this. Congress shall make no law prohibiting the free exercise of speech. This is not an ambivalent area. It is a real area of political speech. So I do not think anyone who challenged you would be unAmerican and an unconstitutional character.

# Interview: Burroughs and Ginsberg

JS: Censorship is another form of control and control forms is quite a subject in the works of Mr. Burroughs and also in your work, Mr. Ginsberg. In The Job, a 1969 interview, there was quite a bit of talk about the impending police state. Do you find the police state firmly in place now?

AG: Well, I think you just turned off that criticism of presidential ambition in the midst of an election when everyone in the country is totally disgusted with both the candidates for president and realize the whole thing is a scam and nobody wants to vote for anybody and everybody is scratching their head and Bill is giving a psychological description. WB: I do not see any approach to what could be called a police state without so extending the definition of police state to become meaningless.

AG: Well, wait a minute, Bill. A few years ago, I remember you saying the functioning police state does not need police. You do not need the police hanging out in every radio station.

WB: It depends on what you mean by a police state. What we mean is secret police arresting people in the middle of the night, suspension of habeas corpus, and all that sort of...

AG: We had a mild form of that ten years ago here in Lawrence.

WB: Yes, but a mild one. Very mild compared to the real thing. When people talk about America being a police state, I say they are talking nonsense.

AG: I do not think so. We had the fall of the President to check that tendency...

WB: Absolutely. It was checked. I say there has been a terrific improvement in the whole atmosphere of America since Watergate.

AG: I think so. But internal vigilance is the price we have paid for...

WB: I do not think I would agree with that.

AG: I would agree that we are not anywhere near the police state I will find when I go to Moscow next month. Because that is really heavy police state.

JS: The danger lies in being too complacent and not speaking out by the people more so than the police state being put in place by political figures.

AG: I would say that we have some kind of surveillance state or military authoritarianism. The image that has been coming to me more and more recently is, not only America but the whole world, of being a kind of Jonestown, ever since December when the President announced limited nuclear war was one of our political options and military options in the Middle East. Now they had threatened that secretively, Ike in Korea, before, but never acknowledged it publicly to prepare the country to take the kool-aid of nuclear war at the orders of above, like Jim Jones, from above. It seems there is some sort of parallel there. The entire nation is completely inert.

JS: Mr. Burroughs, some of your work is based on the cut-up method. Would you care to explain that a little bit.

WB: Well, it is simply applying a montage method which is pretty old hat in painting to writing. It was not my idea, but Byron Gysin's idea who is a painter and a writer. He simply said writing is behind painting by 50 years.

JS: It appears for the first time in Naked Lunch?

WB: No, it never appeared in Naked Lunch. Oh, there is a spider. Is it a Brown Recluse?

AG: No, do not kill! He is alright.

WB: No, there are no cut-ups in Naked Lunch. The first cut-ups were in Minutes To Go. I mean there were no cut-ups in the sense of actually taking a pair of scissors to a page. The first cut-ups were in Minutes To Go, published in 1959, which was a pamphlet, a small little booklet.

AG: Well, there was a little cut-up there where we were in the middle of a subject and Bill's eye caught the spider. Then an immediate transition.

WB: Life is a cut-up. Any time you look out a window or walk down the street your conscience is constantly cut up by random factors, like the spider here. So it is simply making explicit something that goes on all the time.

JS: Last night in your performance, I enjoyed very much the musical pieces you did, especially the one about anti-smoking where you suggest we should give up cigarettes and take up oral sex.

AG: I was using that as if you need a placebo in the 24 or 48 hours after giving up smoking you should get in bed with your favorite person and every time you want to put a cigarette in your mouth you put some meat in your mouth instead.

WB: You are not being serious.

AG: I found it worked for me a couple of times when I wanted to quit smoking. It really does. The delight of making love is stronger than the yen for a cigarette.

WB: I dare say.

AG: Given also the pain of smoking. See I got to the point of getting high blood pressure and when I smoked I got a headache. So I had this negative reinforcement. And I was suggesting this positive reinforcement if you could find anybody cooperative who is sufficiently interested in getting you off tobacco and willing to get in bed with you and offer their bodies as oral pleasure.

WB: It is a poor substitute.

AG: No, it is not a poor substitute. You are getting old, Bill.

## Johnny Winter

Live: October 20      Lawrence Opera House

"Well, Sherman, let's get in our time machine and turn the clock back a few years."
"Sure, gosh, Mr. Peabody, where to this time?"
"The year 1970, Sherman."

And it seemed just about that on this cool Wednesday night, as I pushed my way through the bearded, Harley t-shirted, Southern Comfort and Jack Daniels guzzling crowd. When I arrived at The Opera House, the warm up band, whose name escapes me now (thankfully), whose style seemed to be derived from the deep South, southern fried boogie band school of music, was just finishing.

During the hour between the end of the warm up act and the beginning of Johnny Winter's set, I stood in awe as I watched drunks stumble by me and three people get gently but forcibly removed from the premises for unknown causes (though they did appear falling down drunk). Everywhere I went I could see or hear sleepy, slurred voices offering the crowd, "Acid, Hash?" The thought that kept going through my head was that these youth and semi-youth were the future of America (how depressing).

Finally though, the lights were dimmed and, with a long drawled out "Yaaaa", Johnny Winter hit the stage. He was in a form that night that fit what the audience wanted. Lots of guitar solos, too many bass and drum solos, but an energy and experience that is missing from too many shows altogether nowadays. Johnny blazed through his old hits (Rock and Roll Hootchie Coo) and selections from his new record, Raising Cain. The crowd loved him and so did I. No matter how old I get there will always be a special place in my heart for this albino Texan. Like the old blues masters, Johnny will survive. --VS

James Brown Live and Lowdown at the Apollo, Vol. 1 (Solid Smoke:8006)--When this Lp came out on the King label in 1962 it was immediately hailed as "the greatest live show ever recorded." Well, a lot has happend since then, and although Otis Redding's 1967 performance at Monterey is stiff competition for the title, this is still a red hot disc. J.B. and his famous Flames are caught here at the peak of their powers, belting out such favorites as "I'll Go Crazy", "Night Train", and the ever-popular "Please.(+)

## Burroughs/Ginsberg/Thumbs

Live: September 30
Lawrence Opera House

The evening opened with Allen Ginsberg playing some selections and reading from his works. Later William S. Burroughs gave an entertaining reading. Local band Thumbs ended the night with a set of rock.

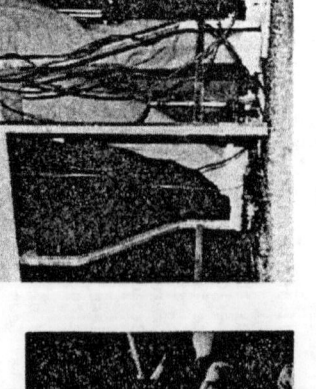

*Left: Allen Ginsberg plays his hand-held keyboards and sings, accompanied by guitar. Above: Martin Olson provides the keyboards for Thumbs. Below: guitarist Kevin Smith, bassist Carl Hoffman, vocalist Steve Wilson, and drummer Dede Mosier. Photos by Christopher Lucas.*

## Album Reviews

Prince Far I Jamaican Heroes (Trojan:TRLS 190)--Jamaican Heroes is basically the straight version of the Daddy Kool release, Cry Tuff Dub Encounter-Chapter III. The tracks are the same but the vocals are different. Cry Tuff III has been my main record for a couple of months now and this Trojan release shows a more restrained sound with less dubbing. The cover is great especially as an introduction to the heavy sounds inside. The Prince demonstrates a new vocal style at times, which is surprisingly very full compared with some of his occasional yells. A good album to have--get it and the dub version. --WB

Toots and The Maytals (from p. 16) project was a flying success. The energy level is high, the quality crisp and invigorating, the selections outstanding choices. As customary, Toots opens with "Pressure Drop", one of my favorites. "Sweet and Dandy", "Monkey Man", and "Get Up Stand Up" with the rich harmonies of The Maytals outfront. The inner rhythms in Toots voice during "Monkey Man" demonstrate why he has remained so popular. There is real conviction captured here with the rhythm and blues influences easily noticed. Side two opens with "Funky Kingston", acclaimed by some critics as the highpoint of the album. The show closed with "Time Tough." An encore number, "Hallelujah", is a new song of Christian praise. --WB

James Brown (from p. 25) Please, Please, Please." Volume Two of this set has just been released on a European label, and if there is enough interest Solid Smoker will probably release it, too. Superbad! --DCool

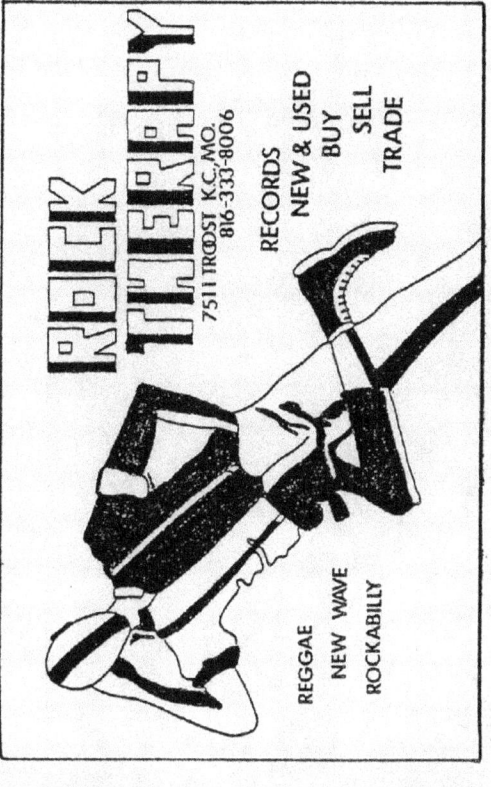

Oct 31 - Nov 1    The Lotions
November 5        Texan Reggae
November 8        Clox
November 14-15    The Secrets
                  Son Seals Blues Band
November 17       XTC

TALK TALK

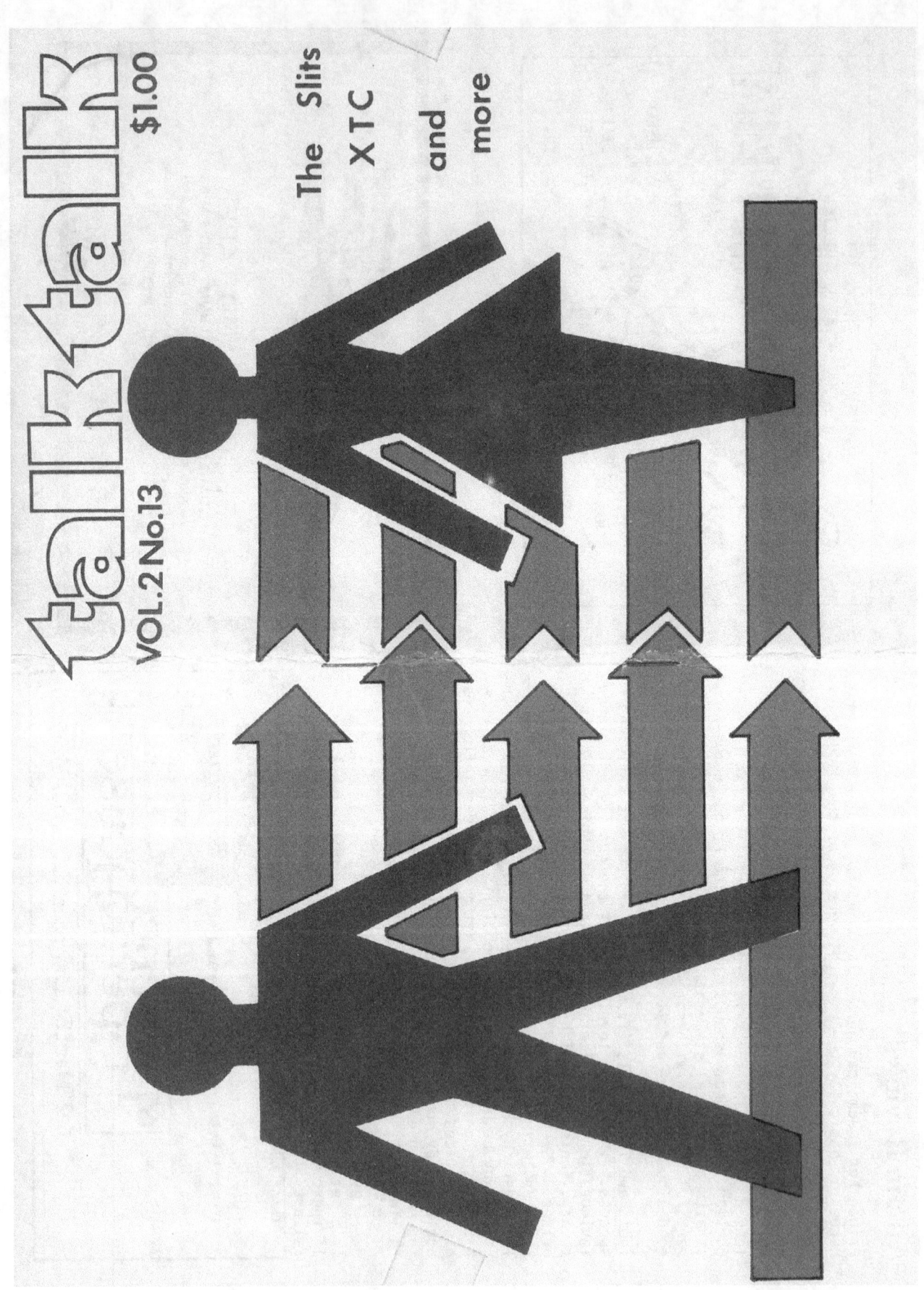

TALK TALK

Vol. 2 No. 13    December 1980    $1.00

The Midwest American Rock and Reggae Magazine

## Table of Contents

Awards.................................3
Concerts: XTC..........................4
Album Reviews: Comsat Angels,
  Simple Minds, XTC....................8
Public Image, Bauhaus..................9
Orchestral Manoeuvres in the
  Dark, Rockpile, Colin Newman........10
Killing Joke, The Tear Drop
  Explodes............................11
Concerts: Abuse.......................12
Psych. Furs, Wall of Voodoo...........13
The Slits.............................14
Reggae Reviews: Mikey Dread,
  King Tubby, and Rod Taylor..........20
Black Slate, Augustus Pablo...........21
Single Reviews: Mo-dettes,
  Imports, Neptune's Car, 999.........22
Buzzcocks, A Certain Ratio,
  Walter Steding, Nash The
  Slash...............................23
Interview: William Burroughs
  and Allen Ginsberg..................24
Concerts: Aagarns,
  Embarrassment.......................28

### TALK TALK

Editors:
Bill Rich
Eric Schindling

Contributors:
Rick Hellman
The U-Man
Jim Schwada
Mark Gilman
Bobs
WB, DC, VS

Photography:
Christopher Lucas
Bill Rich

Cover Design:
Christopher Hunter

Layout and
Production:
Bill Rich

Typesetting:
Joan McCabe Moore

# *Talk Talk* Proudly Announces
# The 1980 Awards For Excellence

# KJHK - FM 91
### Radio Station of the Year

# Rock Therapy
### Record Store of the Year

It is not easy to live in the Midwest and try to keep up with the music scene. You can try to find out what is happening by reading the English press weeklies (if you can find any) or some of the commercial music monthlies and then decide on your own what to believe. Or you can just see what the corporations are pushing. One of the reasons Talk Talk was started was to provide opinionated information on new bands, new sounds, and local action. But reading is not even close to actually listening to music. Because of this, we are all fortunate to have a decent radio station in Lawrence, KJHK is the only place one can hear new releases. Although operated by the University of Kansas, their "sound alternative" keeps you informed of the music scene and they will play your requests. So, if you are wondering what something sounds like before you shell out the bucks, chances are good you can find out.

If you want to buy a record or just want to see what actually is available, the place to go is Rock Therapy, at 75th and Troost in Kansas City, Missouri. They are stocked with the latest releases, plus you can hear and talk about it. Sometimes they might only get a handful of records that go quick, so do not wait forever! Although this small shop has only been around less than a year, they have established themselves as the record store in the area.

All contents copyright 1980 by Talk Talk Publications, PO Box 36, Lawrence Kansas, 66044. All rights reserved. Any opinion expressed is solely that of the writer and not necessarily that of this publication. Subscription rate is $6 for six issues. Articles, reviews, and pix submitted for editorial consideration are welcome. Not responsible for unsolicited material. Address all correspondence to Talk Talk Editors, PO Box 36, Lawrence, Kansas, 66044, USA.

# XTC

**Live: November 17, 1980 — Lawrence Opera House**

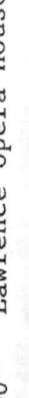

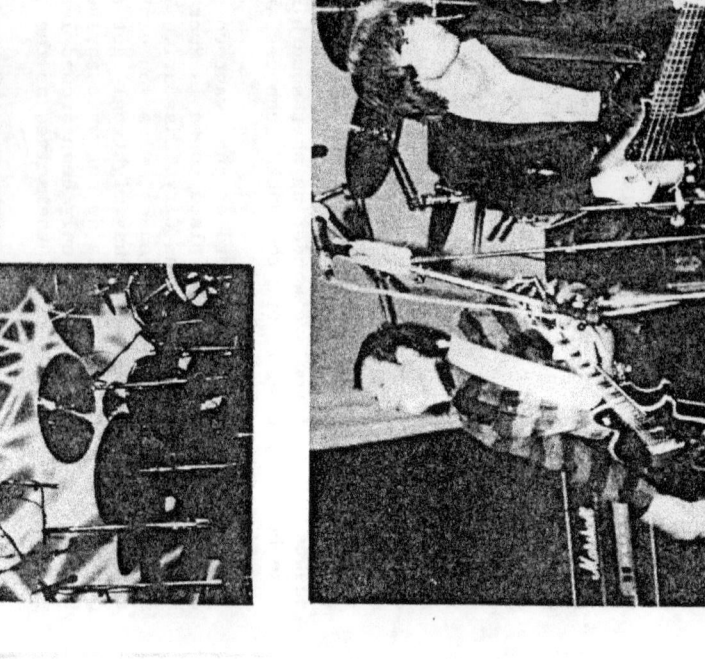

It was a good sized crowd that made their way into the Opera House to attend the second visit of XTC to Lawrence in less than a year. The show started fairly close to schedule, with the opening act being Thumbs. This was the first time I had seen them in quite a while and they handled their end of the show with energy and commitment. One thing is sure—they are never satisfied with past achievements and for that they should be respected. After a short break, XTC made their way on stage and immediately tore into a medley of hits off their Drums And Wires Lp. Songs like "Helicopter" got the audience off and the crowd that already thronged the stage steadily grew as the night went on. The stage presence of the band was more confident and aggressive than the previous time. But along with this new found assurance, there seemed to have been something lost. On stage they no longer seemed to be taking any risks. Their moves are more polished. One thing that I missed from this new show was the lack of non-commercial songs. Their (→6)

XTC are: Andy Partridge, vocals, guitar; Colin Moulding, bass, vocals; David Gregory, guitar; and Terry Chambers, drums.
Photos by Christopher Lucas

# XTC

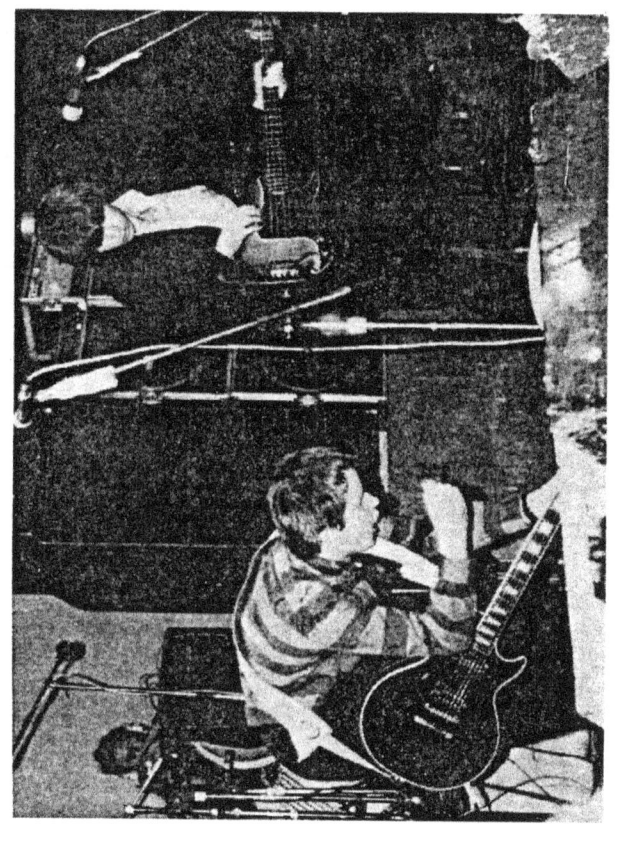

(from p. 4) playlist this time seemed more rigid. When a friend of mine asked for a playlist that was hanging off a monitor, he was told he could not have it because they did not want to copy a new one. Now do not get me wrong, I still enjoyed the show and band even with these obvious shortcomings. They still seem to care about their fans, unlike so many other bands, who seem to be getting beyond the people who pay to listen and see them.

## Album Reviews

**The Comsat Angels Waiting For A Miracle** (Polydor Super 2383 578)--At last the debut Lp from one of the brightest new bands to hit the current music scene is now available. The only complaint I have, and it is a minor one at that, is that four of the ten tracks on this record can be found on the Made In Britain compilation. Other than that this record is fantastic. Like the communications satellites from which they derive their name, these boys are able to seemingly look down at the earth, breeching all barriers and focus upon life's complexities no matter how insignificant they may seem. This is how they go about gathering data for their songs, which are neither doomy-gloomy nor condescending. They are full of pathos. Musically, they are very complex and create a variety of sounds without the use of any effects or synths. It is kind of a refreshing change of pace. To put it simply: this is some of the most sophisticated pop music that I have ever heard and I, for the most part, loathe pop-type-stuff. Best songs: "Monkey Pilot", "Real Story", and "Map of the World". Afterthought: Too bad they did not include "We Were". --U-Man

**Simple Minds Empires and Dance** (Arista: SPART 1140)-- There is just too much clutter and electronic excess on this third attempt from the simpletons. It is as if these guys sat around one day and listened to Gary Numan, John Foxx, Bowie's Lodger, et al., and then, in a moment of insipid inspiration, said, "Let's sound like this." This is nothing more than a conglomeration of other people's ideas. The lyrics are cliche and seemingly borrowed directly from other material and the music is simply electronic fluff. An eminently forgettable record. --U-Man

**XTC Black Sea** (Virgin: VR 1-1000)--Well, these sugar pops go down well enough but they do not snap and crackle like they used to. XTC (read Andy Partridge) are treading a tricky line between being clever enough and being too clever. Like most of us, sometimes they succeed and sometimes they do not. Colin Moulding seems content to contribute his two songs per Lp and here they both rate. "Generals and Majors" at first sounded cloying and (→29)

## Album Reviews

**Image Publique S.A. Paris Au Printemps** (Virgin: V2183) --Seven old Public Image songs performed live last spring in Paris, in one of the few public appearances the band had made before playing a few shows in America. This is better than the bootlegs, with a pretty good mix. Wobble's bass and Aitken's drumming seem pretty straightforward and constant and are supplemented by the synthesizer and guitar work created by Keith Levine. While the instruments do not always follow the songs as the originals, Lydon's vocals pull it all back together. This recording is Public Image as they used to be, as they are now without Wobble or Aitken (although he has done some studio work on the new material) and with Janette Lee playing a more important part alongside Lydon and Levine. So I am still waiting for some new material to surface and we will see if Public Image retain their throne. --WB

*Public Image, in Chicago, May 1, 1980, showing the same lineup as their live album recorded a few weeks earlier. They are: Keith Levine, John Lydon, Martin Aitken, and Jah Wobble. Photo-by Bill Rich*

**Bauhaus In The Flat Field** (4AD: CAD13)--After a string of excellent singles, the first album from these four guys has been awaited with anticipation. It was a surprise to find nine new and different songs with little link to such classic sounds found in "Bela Lugosi's Dead" or "Terror Couple Kills Colonel". After being aware of that, the album does indeed sound like the characteristic Bauhaus in terms of vocals, buildups, peaking drums, and overall tone. So listen to this one and get the full feel of Bauhaus. If it is too extreme for you, check out their new and fourth single, T. Rex's "Telegram Sam." Now that sounds like the classic Bauhaus. --WB

## Album Reviews

Orchestral Manoeuvres in the Dark Organisation (Dindisc: DID 6)--I have never been impressed by OMD. Some people, who seem to be in the dark as well, actually consider this stuff new and that is a puzzler. If you want Muzak or atmosphere, why not listen to Tangerine Dream, Cluster or some of the other originators of the teuto-electronic thing. The only difference between OMD and these German groups is that the krauts were about ten years ahead of them and what took them sometimes over ten minutes for a single composition OMD does in just about half the time. That is so you can hear their horrible lyrics. This stuff is sterile and blasé. When I want this kind of schlock I will hang out at a shopping mall, grocery store, or call some business firm and have them put me on hold. --U-Man

Rockpile Seconds of Pleasure (Columbia: JC 36886)--Rockpile--the most-recorded band that never made an album--until now, that is. Their debut Lp, Seconds of Pleasure, proves it was worth the wait. This album delivers everything you have come to expect from its principals, Nick Lowe and Dave Edmunds--catchy songs and classic R & R, respectively. A pleasant surprise are the lead vocals second guitarist Billy Bremner is allotted in this format. The album is split between Lowe originals and obscure covers no doubt unearthed by Edmunds, but the single "Teacher Teacher" is not the best song here. That title has to go to "When I Write The Book", which sounds like a countryish "My Girl" only better. If there is anything wrong with this album, it is that no new ground is being broken. But, hey, that is not what these guys are about. If the Lowe/Edmunds axis has caught your ear before, they will no doubt grab it again with Seconds of Pleasure. --RH

Colin Newman A-Z (Beggars Banquet; BEGA 20)--Another solo product from another member of Wire. This one features, besides Mr. Newman, both Wire's drummer, Robert Gotobed, and Wire's producer, Mike Thorne. This Lp is entirely different than B. Gilbert and G. Lewis's Dome Lp. A-Z, in fact, could be the fourth Wire album. It has got everything that one associates with them: cryptic lyrics, complex sounds, and frenzied delivery. --U-Man

## Album Reviews

Killing Joke Killing Joke (Malicious Damage, EG Records: EGMD 5-45)--The stark cover of youths running and performing mysterious deeds on a wall set the tone for this album. Killing Joke serve to us with a disturbing yet extremely likable Lp. The sound is very electric. The band treads a fine line musically. They literally take their music to the edge of that line and so at times you keep wondering if they will step over that line on a dare and into the realm of Heavy Metal. "Requiem" and "Wardance" are on this disc but in a different form. "Wardance", in particular, is striking with its mutating vocals. The entire package is unsettling. Soon though, I would not be surprised if the Heavy Metal crowd embrace this band to their heart. My recommendation is to play this record very loud! --VS

The Teardrop Explodes Kilimanjaro (Mercury: 6359 035)--Following the release of three singles and the search for a record label, The Teardrop Explodes have finally released their long-awaited first Lp. They are one of three bands from Liverpool that are currently very popular. The other two are Pink Military and Echo and The Bunnymen. There is somewhat of a rivalry between The Teardrop Explodes and The Bunnymen, primarily because Ian McCulloch (of The Bunnymen) was once in The Teardrop Explodes. Anyway, that is the scenario. Unlike the cynicism of The Bunnymen, the "this is the world and the way things are and you better see it as we do" kind of stuff...The Teardrop Explodes deals more with the exploration of life and seems to possess a more inquisitive outlook on things. Musically, this Lp is very diverse, through the use of trumpets and keyboards. Four of the eleven songs are taken from their singles but they are treated a bit differently. There is possibly an underlying current of competition between Julian Cope and Ian McCulloch and, hence, the two bands, as well. Right now, The Bunnymen seem to be getting all of the attention, perhaps I am helping to perpetuate the myth, too, but The Teardrop Explodes is building to a critical mass...an emotional tide. --U-Man

# The Psychedelic Furs
# Wall of Voodoo

Live: October 18, 1980
Whiskey A Go-Go, LA

On the strength of their first Lp, I figured The Furs would be great. They plodded through the songs like it was a 9 to 5 job and the singer could not hit any of the notes. He was an intense poseur as well. They had trouble ending their songs and had no rapport with the audience, who did not seem to care much anyway. The real stars were Wall of Voodoo, an up and coming local bunch. They are definitely the most unique and interesting wave band around. I do not care what people say about Devo, B-52s, Talking Heads, etc., these guys are it. Joe Nanini, formerly of The Eyes, and Black Friday, plays electronic rhythm, African percussion and a drum set made of pots and pans. The singer plays a doctored Farfisa, the rhythm player a moog synthi, the keyboardist assorted synthis and bass, and there is a most unconventional guitarist. They have a self-produced Ep available soon. Get it. You will not believe your ears. I was getting fed up with music until I heard WOV. —The Gill Man.

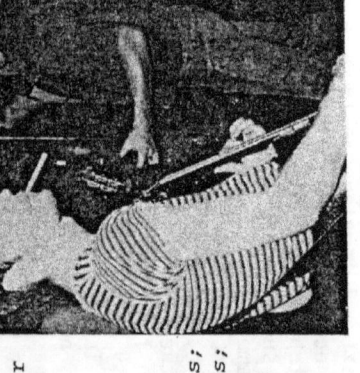

# Off The Wall Hall

Live: November 14

Abuse are a three-piece rock band similar to the Johnny Thunders/Sid Vicious school of hard beats. Although they are young, their progressively improving sound puts them at higher levels of expertise than earlier.

*The band is composed of: Clay Galbraith, bass, vocals; Chris Garner, guitar, vocals; and Willy McNeil, drums. Photos by Christopher Lucas*

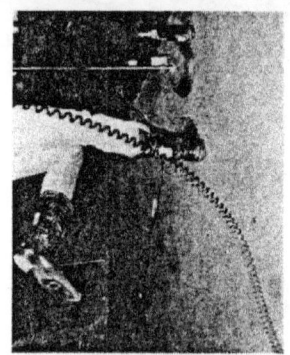

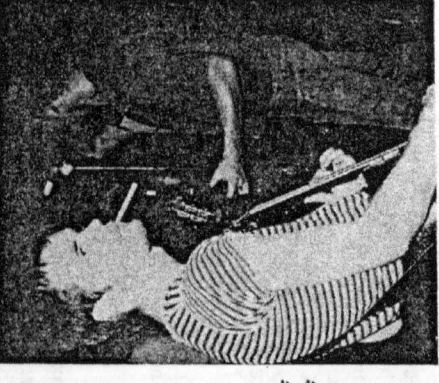

# The Slits

Live: November 7, 1980    Waves, Chicago

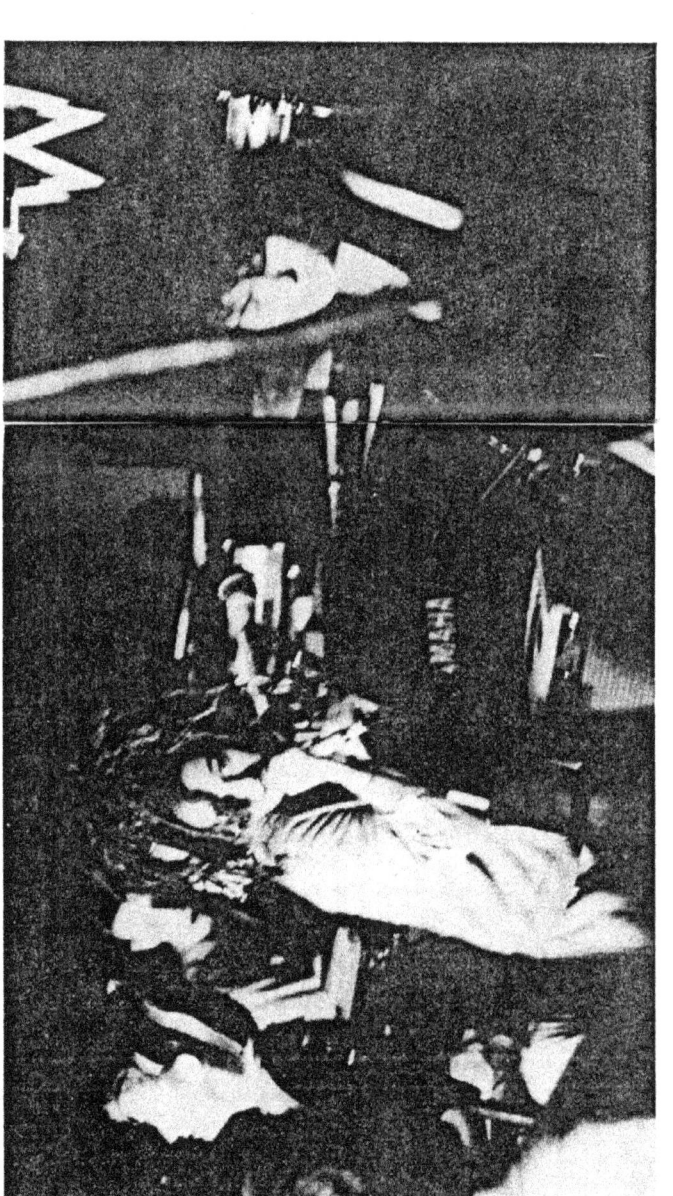

After making a debut American appearance last New Year's Eve at Hurrah in New York, the Slits are on tour. Concentrating on the northeast section of the States and Canada, they have been playing shows to appreciative audiences. The touring band is made of six musicians--three females, who are the original core, and three males. Although The Slits have been labeled as "not playing music, just rambling along", their show was definitely a musical experience with many of their songs, like "Typical Girls", "Grapevine", "Man Next Door", played in a more dynamic way. The band relies heavily upon rhythms and the individuals take off from each other and create additional rhythms (→)

# The Slits

(from p. 15) Tonight it worked wonderfully with the crowd easily flowing from one rhythmic derivation to another. To some degree, it is dangerous for a performing band to be as spontaneous as The Slits were. And no doubt some shows do not result as successfully as a straight rock approach might. But The Slits have always played this way, perhaps allowing for more inter-coordination to(→) surface. At one point, a song ended but vocalist Ari Up was still singing and chanting. She paused to say, "I'm not finished yet" and then continued her solo until its end. The band works with a variety of sounds, including cheap noise maker gadgets they find in out of the way stores. Keyboardist Steve can be seen at times whirling a stringed whistle around his head and the drummer (→28)

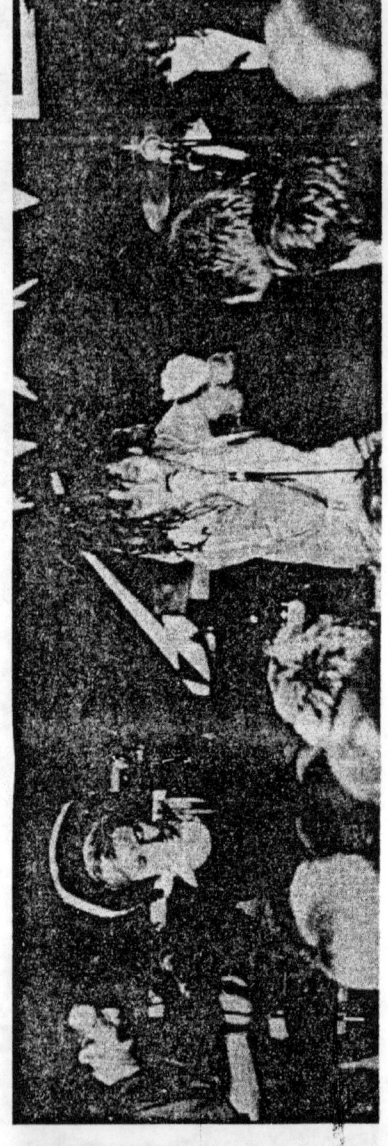

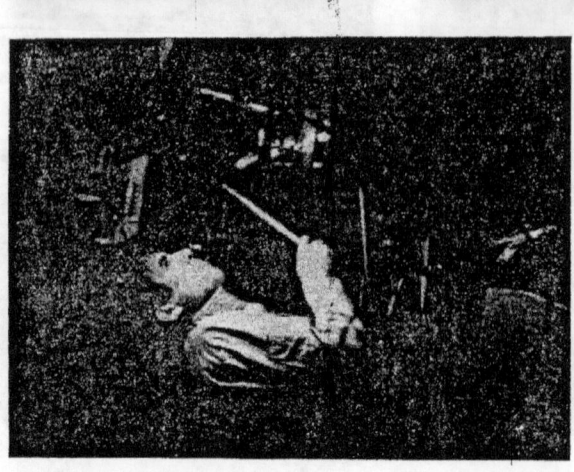
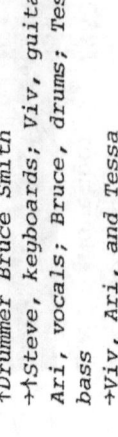

↑Drummer Bruce Smith
↑Steve, keyboards; Viv, guitar; Ari, vocals; Bruce, drums; Tessa, bass
→Viv, Ari, and Tessa
All photos by Bill Rich

# Interview: The Slits

*Talk Talk spent some time before the sound check interviewing The Slits members who were present--Ari, Viv, and Steve. They talked about touring and their feelings on performing. The following are some excerpts from these discussions.*

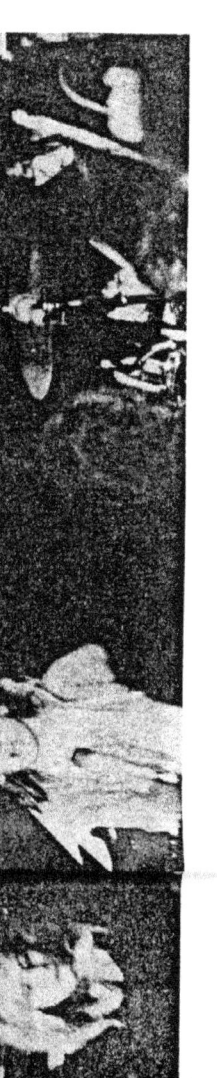

Viv: Were we just a curiosity at first? We always had big audiences from the beginning. That was because we were girls, I think. But, obviously,.we were not just any old girls...It was kind of half and half really--half because we were girls and half because we were interesting.

*The Slits started out as four girls. Palmolive, the original drummer, left before their album was released. Now, Bruce Smith, from The Pop Group, is the drummer. A keyboard has been added, as well as Dave Lewis as guitar, bass player. They talked about their album.*

Viv: It sold quite well in England. We really do not know, though, because we have lost contact with the record company...of course we did not get any money from it.
Ari: It is deleted now.
Viv: Collectors' item. We should probably buy them all up.

*They did not want to talk about what they have been doing or offer any explanations of their labels.*

Ari: Do we have to talk about all this again? It gets like machinery. We try to get away from this machinery rap...In America, their god is technique. All they want to talk about is technique. I mean it bores me to talk about that.

*The conversation turned to food and Ari took a stand.*

Ari: I am not really a vegetarian. I just want normal food, right? Most food is so sick you have to buy your health. That is why they call it health food, instead of normal food. It is terrible. You just buy your health or if you cannot buy your health, then you are just out wanting on the side streets.
Steve: It is just that it should not be an effort.
Ari: If you do not eat the right food, it is like not getting enough sleep. Sleep and food are vital to the spiritual and physical survival on this earth. Especially in earth parts where there are hardly any earth left. In the cities you really have to watch out for food, otherwise you get your body all spotty--not spotty in the way normal eruptions come. But you get ill, so your spirit gets ill.
Viv: We have done pretty well so far (in eating right on the road).
Steve: Very well.
Viv: Every day we made sure we have eaten health foods.
Ari: Yes, because usually when you do not, it will mess you up. In England we stop on the motorway and after two days we were ill. It is much worse in England.

*The band was a little upset at the foot-high stage at the club.*

Ari: I hate this place. I hate being pushed into the "New Wave" bag. I am sick of it.
Steve: Everybody in the world will say, "we are individuals and we are totally different." But whether they are or not...

*When asked what types of clubs in England they play at,*

Viv: We normally play college halls --something that is a modern wooden hall, very clean with good acoustics built quite recently with a high stage. Up north we play some clubs ...But we do not consider ourselves part of rock and roll with its dingy red and blue lights in a little black underground cavern. We want to take music back out into the open more in the fresh air where it came from.

*The Slits have two new singles coming out or already out. Although they did not want to talk about any of it at all, some facts came out.*

Viv: It is called "Animals Face", released on Human Records. It is a 12-inch. Get it.
Ari: We are influenced by everything around us. The negative we try to push off. And the positive we just take in. It could be from anywhere. So our music is universal.
Viv: People are always saying, "what are your musical influences?" Everything that happens to you is an influence because your songs are just a reflection of you and your influences. It may go through the lyrics or a certain feeling or come out in the way you do a rhythm in a song. So everything you hear--it is not just music that influences you. It is everything.

## Reggae Reviews

**Mikey Dread and King Tubby** *Love The Dread/Internal Energy* (DATC) **Rod Taylor and Mikey Dread** *Behold Him/Parrot Jungle* (DATC)--Just over two years ago, Mikey Dread or Michael Campbell had the only reggae radio show ever on JBC. His late night "Dread at the Controls" was taking the Kingston ghetto by storm. But, alas, his ideas were a bit too original for the management and he got the boot. Fortunately for us, he landed in the studios and his Dread at the Control (DATC) label was born. Always trying and coming up with the new and original, the Dread's dub style set the trend with imaginative use of sections of the board others had long forgotten. Mikey's imagination turned treadworn rockers into bounding rhythms and bouncing dub exclusives. These two 45s are prime examples. "Love The Dread" was the premier for his DATC label and it finds the musing Mr. Dread in top toasting form. He enters with a series of Mother Goose roots ditties and catchy phrases and then adds an extended tribute to King Tubby, who is across the glass at the board. The dub is aptly titled "Internal Energy" and starts off with a great melodic hook by the organ and guitar. Following that and not far behind is a vicious bass line and a manic guitar riff climbing over top. Bouncing tom toms and a touch of Tubby's secret ingredient equalize out the dub chemistry, providing even the most jaded brain with fresh reorganization. "Behold Him" marks Campbell's first production exclusive for another artist, something he has continued to do, notably with the likes of Jah Grundy, The Ovations, Edi Fitzroy, Dave Richardson and Michael Israel, all standouts. Rod Taylor is a roots hero and premier vocalist. He is a solid bet on any of his various discs and "Behold Him" is a stunning example of how the man can break through with sincerity and power. Strictly from the other side, a demention of pathos, emotional certainty, and spirit. This one ranks high as a tribute to Jah then up surfaces the wicked militancy of The Revolutionaries and backing mix from Mikey. Bouncing rockers again, sure fire treat for those avid dub patrons when issued originally in '78. The writing was on the wall here and it is something to be reminded of when now Mikey Dread stops the show to...take it from the top, because this one is the original style. --BOBS

## Another Outbreak of the Reggae Wars

### Off The Wall vs Opera House
### New Era vs Blue Riddim

Once again, local promoters have booked out of town reggae bands for the same weekend. It is hard enough to find one decent show a week--whether rock or whatever. But when two bands compete against each other at the two local concert halls, everyone--ends up suffering. What does the audience do? Go to one show one night, the other show the next night? Go to both on the same night? Try to decide which one will be more fun? Stay home and listen to records? No matter what happens, people should tell the promoters and the band members that they are unhappy with such arrangements and try to end these wars. Our advice is to go see both bands. They are both quite excellent and deserve your support.

**Black Slate** *Black Slate* (Alligator: 8301)--This debut Lp by yet another gang of English/Jamaican dreads is pleasant enough, but...it boils down to the same old sound with a new name--listenable but repetitious, much like most of the things done by Steel Pulse. On the bright side, Black Slate is the first reggae release by Bruce Iglauer's Alligator label, a small Chicago-based outfit who are responsible for most of the worthwhile blues releases coming out today--most of the Alligator roster of artists do the Lawrence circuit, and hopefully Black Slate may do the same--perhaps they will be more entertaining live. --DCool

**Augustus Pablo** *West Abyssinia Dub* (Cha Cha Records: 12-inch 45)--Another satisfying dub offering from the elusive Mr. Pablo. His trademark, Eastern sounding melodica, is enough to charm the snakes in any disco. --DCool

*There were not a lot of new releases this month, so there are not a lot of reggae reviews. More next issue.*
*--Ed.*

## Single Reviews

Mo-Dettes Dark Park Creeping/Two Can Play (Decca: DET2)--Mo-Dettes once again lay claim to the title of best girl group around with this bouncy, elastic tune. As their last single, "Paint It Black" made clear, their sound is not far removed from that on early Beatles' and Stones' records. Straight imitations, though, do not suit them and, as such, this is a nice comeback. Ramona's limey soprano is quite charming atop the clanging guitars and frenetic drum beat. The B-side is more in line with "White Mice" with spoken/sung vocals and repeated guitar and bass figures. It works, too. These girls combine the bumbling charm of The Raincoats with enough musical sense to make it play. Now if they had not stiffed Lawrence on their U.S. tour. --RH

The Imports Side One/Side Two (Cirkle Records)--An impressive debut from this Chicago-based band. They sound like they have been listening to Joy Division for a while. Side One goes on a little too long, but on Side Two the band really show what they can do. A moody song that leaves you wanting more. It is worth your while to check out. --VS

Neptune's Car Baking Bread/Lucky Charms (Koolie Records)--This band hails from Ohio and is at the moment one of my favorite singles. "Baking Bread" is a great song that has the sound of The Beatles meet Television. Both songs have a frantic wall of sound that makes you want to reach for the volume knob and turn it up. Sitting in on drums is Scott Kraus of Pere Ubu fame. Hopefully, this is just the beginning of a long career for this fine band. --VS If you can not find it in your local record shop, order it from Koolie Records, 250 High Street, Chagrin Falls, Ohio, 44022.

999 The Biggest Tour In Sports (Polydor: PD1-6307)--This special six-song EP recorded live somewhere on their spring tour does not shed any of the old conceptions people have of this band. They play fast and loud with a strong bass line always drilling itself in. "Homicide" fills up the first side, while the flip holds the rest. They give a good performance on "Emergency". Overall, a solid record from 999. --VS

## Single Reviews

Buzzcocks Are Everything/Why She's A Girl From The Chainstore (IRS: IR 9017)--The first piece of new vinyl from these boys in quite a while. On the whole, it is a slightly different sound. I am sure part of it has to do with the band's direction and partly the man with the hand in everything, Martin Hannett at the control room knobs. The sound is more layered than the Buzzcocks past efforts. The songs basically speak for themselves (their titles say it all). On the sleeve it says Part One. I am waiting now for Part Two. --VS

A Certain Ratio Blown Away/Flight/And Then Again (Factory: FAC 22)--A 12-inch single produced by Martin "Zero" Hannett for the currently top Factory band. This single catches the band in a melancholy mood and Hannett works his typical production magic as the spiritual sound of Joy Division is resurrected. "Blown Away" and "Flight" are two unreleased songs, while "And Then Again" was originally released on the Factory Benelux Product (FAC BNL-004) as a B-side to "Shack Up." Need I say more? (Yes. You forgot to mention the jungle beat that draws one in further than is safe. Ed.) --U-Man

Walter Steding Walter Steding (Red Star Records: RED 101) Nash the Slash Dead Man's Curve b/w Swing Shift (Cut Throat Records: WRC3-1173-A)--You want slagging, well here it is. Neither Walter Steding nor Nash the Slash live up to their advance billing and both offer potent reasons for disliking synthetic muzik. First, let us dismiss Nash out of hand. I cannot fault his invisible man visuals, but this single, at least, leaves me cold. This is a particularly insipid re-working of the old Jan and Dean classic and the B-side, "Swing Shift", does not. We can only hold out hope for the future. Walter Steding is not quite that bad, he just does not raise one's blood pressure at all. The first side offers some fairly interesting Eno-esque drivel called "Woke Up Mixed Up" and the wacky single "Hound Dog", along with a couple of other listenable tunes. Side 2, though, is a total waste of vinyl. This is the noodling of dilletantes --like David Bowie with no soul. Another album that was better left a single. --RH

**TALK TALK** 193

# Interview:
# William S. Burroughs and Allen Ginsberg

*William S. Burroughs and Allen Ginsberg were both recently in Lawrence, where they gave a joint reading. Beforehand, the two gentlemen were interviewed on the college radio station, KJHK, by Jim Schwada. Last month's issue contained the first half of the interview, where they explained how they met, talked of their lives and works among other things. Talk Talk would like to thank all those involved in this project and we believe these two still remain important literary figures influencing the current state of affairs.*

*Video stills by Christopher Lucas and Mark Goodwin*

Jim Schwada: KJHK is known around here as the rock and roll station. When I told people I was going to interview you two, one of the questions they wanted me to ask Mr. Burroughs was, a lot of groups have taken inspiration from your work, do you have any interest in rock and roll?
William Burroughs: Well, yes, I do. I am not very knowledgeable about music. Moroccan music I like perhaps more than any other genre. And old-time jazz. Indian music. I am not at all knowledgeable about rock and roll.
Allen Ginsberg: Bill has met or worked with a lot of musicians.
WB: I have talked to some of them.
AG: Jagger, we met together in '67 in London. David Bowie you had...
WB: I met Bowie a couple of times.
AG: Dylan, you met.
WB: A couple of times.
AG: Patti Smith.
WB: That is true.

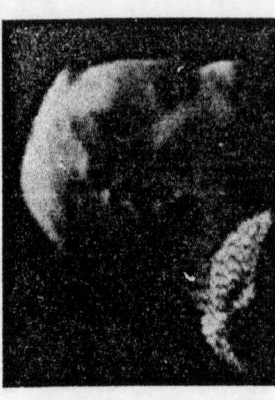
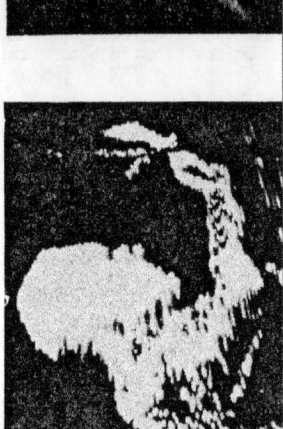

AG: And there are a lot of bands named after you. The whole phrase, heavy metal, you used the first time in...
WB: Yes. The Heavy Metal Kid in Soft Machine or The Ticket That Exploded. I cannot remember.
AG: 1960ish.
WB: Yeah, Heavy Metal Kids, Insect Trust, Steely Dan, Soft Machine; all phrases...
AG: Also a lot of the genre of costume and psychological attitude of punk where you have people making transitions to Lizard boys, things like that. Or people dressing up as mutants--the notion of the human mutant and the mutant hero. The mutant musician, or mutant wild boy. I think that notion you introduced.
WB: Oh, yes.
AG: As part of the imaginative literature. Probably sort of a science fiction understanding.
JS: About a month ago, a group called Throbbing Gristle came into town working on a project. Are you involved with them, or are they doing it just with your approval?
WB: Oh, yes, indeed I do know about it. I've known these people for years. What they are doing is taking a number of selections from the Nova Convention, some readings, and some old tape experiments that I did ten and fifteen years ago and making an Lp. I would be very interested to hear it.
JS: What about film? At one time there were plans to do Junkie.
WB: There was, but it never came to completion. Eventually the financing was withdrawn and the project collapsed.
JS: Would you like to make a film of "The Last Words of Dutch Schultz?"
WB: There were about seven or eight years where we attempted to make a film of this. At one time Elliott Gould was going to play the part of Dutch Schultz and it fell through. This happened again and again.
JS: I wanted to ask you about one of the subplots in Cities of the Red Night involving a Utopian colony that was set up in the 1600's or 1700's.
WB: Yes, I think it was late, 1690. About a hundred years before the American revolution.
AG: Where was this at?
WB: It was set up off the coast of Madagascar.
JS: It was set up with slavery abolished and sexual freedom was recognized. A lot of the things you say in the book, your chance to do what you want to, died a hundred years ago.

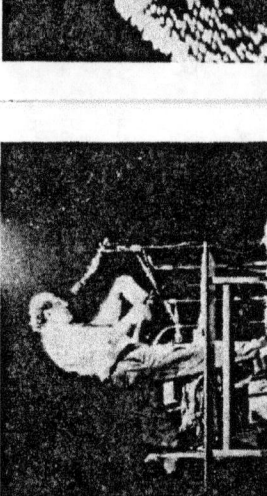
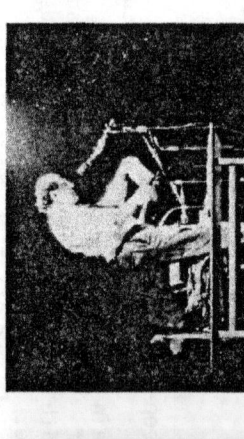

# Interview:
## William S. Burroughs and Allen Ginsberg

WB: More than a hundred years ago. Well, Captain Mission set up the Articles as I said in the book. No man may be imprisoned for debt, no torture, no death penalty, people have the right to any sort of religious belief or expression. His colony was wiped out by natives, probably suborned by British Intelligence. So the whole thing collapsed.

JS: He never had the opportunity to express to the natives the kind of life they may have been able to lead if they had followed him. Let us talk a little about a project you are both involved in, The Naropa Institute in Colorado, School of Poets?

WB & AG: The Jack Kerouac School of Disembodied Poetics.

JS: How would one go about attending some seminars or finding out a little more about it?

AG: You can write to them for their catalogue. The school will be in session from January, it has been for seven years. In the fall we are off. It begins again in January, 1981, and runs for three terms, winter, spring, summer. March 15 will be the beginning for spring when I will come back and teach a course called Literary History of The Beat Generation to the 50's. I have already done the 40's a couple of years ago. You can write to Naropa Institute, 1111 Pearl Street, Boulder, Colorado, 80302. And they have a big catalogue.

ES: Were you ever heavily influenced in the past by the pulp? I see influences like Edgar Rice Burroughs, Chandler, Hammett, the way your novels progress?

WB: Oh, yes. I read them all. I read <u>Amazing Stories</u>, adventure stories, short stories when I was a kid. Burroughs was never one of my favorites.

AG: I remember when we first met in the 40's, you were reading a lot of Raymond Chandler and John O'Hara. What was called in that day the hard-boiled school of detective fiction.

ES: I notice in your works the way you structure the chapters with the cliff-hanger where you jump with a time warp. Not just a different scene but you time warp back and forth. That is sort of set up like the pulps were—get people interested then they have to wait awhile while something else is going on.

WB: That was certainly not confined to pulp. That was the very essence of the 19th century novel with the chapter always leaving the characters in some situation of suspense. Then you have another chapter. So that was the structure of the novel.

AG: Just like present day television and soap operas and radio-suspense serials. Those were written for newspapers. Dickens used to write for newspapers and he would have to get his characters and Dostoevsky too. They would have to leave everybody in a pickle and then get them out of it in the next chapter or next paper.

JS: You both have traveled extensively. Do you find that you are better appreciated outside of the United States?

AG: No. We are pretty well known wherever English translations are read. With the exception of China, where there might be quite a bit of underground interest. Bill has many, many books in German. I have eight or so. My own poetry books, I have a great translator in Italian so they are the best selling poetry. There is a great deal of attention if we give readings abroad. Two summers ago we were in Rome for a reading outside with a crowd of ten to fifteen to twenty thousand people depending on which newspaper you read, for a big international poetry reading with a lot of Nairopa poets. Burroughs, myself, Corso, Waldman. We were asked to come back last summer. I find if I go reading in Germany and if Bill reads there, there is quite a bit of attention. I was interested to see last night at the reading here that I gave with a guitarist, there were quite a few people. There were about 400 chairs and they brought in another 150 and lots of people were standing. And they stayed for three hours to the end, including some silent meditation practice. Or most stayed, over three-fourths, for a long, long time. And I think we will have a good crowd tonight. It is the first reading we have done together around here.

JS: Tonight when you give your reading, there will be those who later sit down at their Smith-Coronas and attempt to write something.

AG: Good!

JS: What advice do you have?

AG: Keep your eye on the ball and write about minute particulars. Kerouac said details are the life of prose. William Carlos said no ideas but in things. Ezra Pound said the natural object is always the adequate symbol. What do you say, Bill?

WB: Well, I think you have said it all.

AG: Keep your eye on the ball. Specifics, and do not get hung up on writing a lot of gush about visionary heaven abstraction and do not go ladeda about something...

WB: Never write on paper anything you could not draw a picture of.

JS: Gentlemen, thank you.

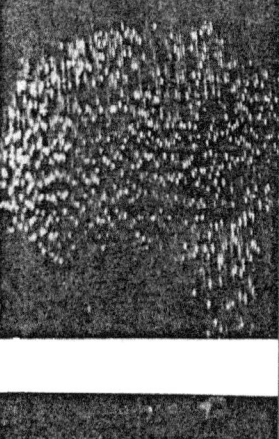

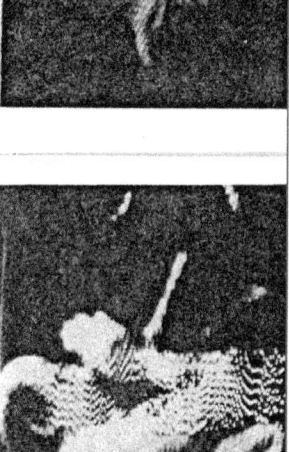

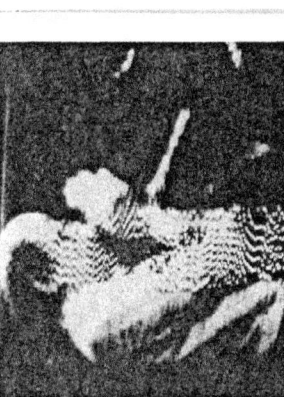

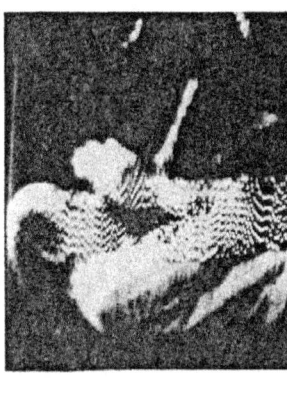

## The Embarrassment    The Aagarnes

Live: November 21, 22, 1980    The Downliner
Kansas City, Missouri

Both bands are back again and stronger than ever. The Embarrassment continue to grow in both quality and sound. The four of them work well as a whole—building tension and building momentum. My particular favorites during their two sets were "Chapter Twelve" and a remake of the Chambers Brothers' classic "Time Has Come Today." The Embarrassment are a band hindered by their geography. Nobody likes to take anything from Kansas seriously.

Part two of the show was filled by another Wichita band, The Aagarns. This five-piece band are fairly new and at times showed a lack of direction. Right now they are in the dance band faze of their development, performing mostly covers with an unsteady original thrown in here and there. The best way to describe them would be to say that they strive for melodic dissonance. I had a good time and I will keep my eye on them. Something could develop here.
--VS

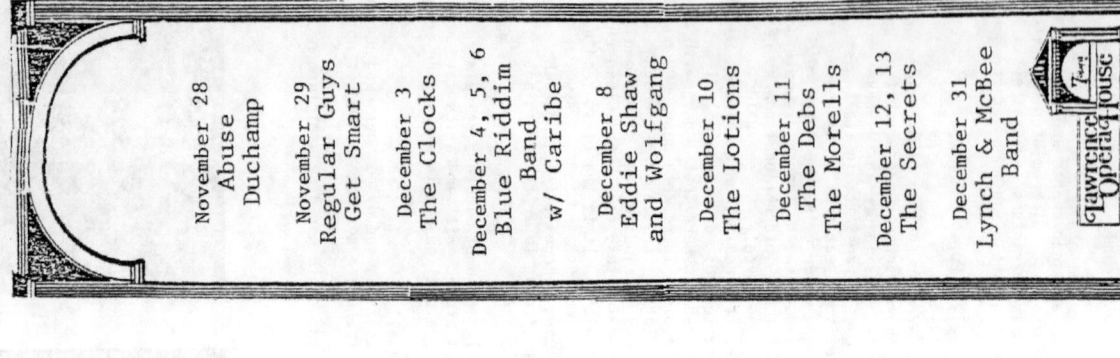

November 28
Abuse
Duchamp

November 29
Regular Guys
Get Smart

December 3
The Clocks

December 4, 5, 6
Blue Riddim
Band
w/ Caribe

December 8
Eddie Shaw
and Wolfgang

December 10
The Lotions

December 11
The Debs
The Morells

December 12, 13
The Secrets

December 31
Lynch & McBee
Band

Lawrence Opera House
7th & Mass.    842-6930

XTC (from p. 8) cutesy-pie political but on further hearings it pans out and allows you to enjoy the hook. No such problems with "Love At First Sight." It has got the most straightforward hook on the album and it is a sidewinder reminiscent of "Set Myself on Fire." The rest of the Lp is Partridge's and he seems to be somewhat the worse for recent wear. "Living In Another Cuba" was an immediate pick but after a few listenings it has gotten too cute and I want to skip it. There are a handful of good, interesting tunes here but in other places the sound is beginning to wear thin and the loss of keyboardist Barry Andrews is more evident than ever. Dangerous strains of pop/disco synth creep in and, coupled with vocal phrasings that threaten to become standard, one has to wonder. Perhaps the saving grace of Black Sea is the closer "Travels in Nihilon." It is a descent into the maelstrom as weird as anything yet from Mr. Partridge. The message is clear: do not look here for answers. --RH

Slits (from p. 17) might have an object in his mouth or even be standing on stage away from his drums programming a type of rhythm generator or playing a melodica. And with Dave backing up the guitar, Vivian can concentrate on singing without an emptiness in sound resulting. So, although they might appear at first glance to be just another rock and roll band, The Slits do work with a variety of techniques in presenting their performance to the audience.

The band talked about how everywhere they go, people ask what sort of message The Slits try to get across. They hate questions like that. But their final song of the night was one of the most impressive things I have heard from them. It was a very rhythm oriented juxtaposition of the traditional "Chicago" song with the Glaxo Babies "Limited Entertainment." Since The Pop Group does the last song also, it began with the drumming being more Pop Group than Slits. The funk beat was there and the lyrics concentrated on "sell your soul for a bag of gold, twenty-four hours a day" and later "don't sell your soul like the rest of Chicago." A message to the audience, who will remember The Slits.

**ROCK THERAPY**
7511 TROOST K.C. MO.
816-333-8006

RECORDS
NEW & USED
BUY
SELL
TRADE

REGGAE
NEW WAVE
ROCKABILLY

**LOVE**

RECORDS AND TAPES
GUARANTEED USED ALBUMS AND TAPES
We also carry a large selection of posters and t-shirts. Bring your good used albums in for cash.
OPEN 7 DAYS A WEEK

15 W. 9th St., Lawrence, Ks.   7222 W. 75th St. Overland Park, Ks
(913) 842-3059                 (913) 384-2499

# FREE

# BUTTON

Talk Talk Publications   PO Box 36   Lawrence, Kansas, 66044   USA

Dear Talk Talk, I would like:
( ) To subscribe for 6 issues @ $6.00
( ) Information on Advertising Rates
( ) Information on Consignment Sales
( ) Free Button (Enclose SASE)
( ) Back Issues: No. _____ @ $1.00

Enclosed is $ _____

Name _____
Address _____

# Talk Talk

Vol. 3 No. 1     January/February 1981     $1.00

Reggae Reviews
  Errol Scorcher, Revolutionaries............4
  Linton Kwesi Johnson, Morwell
    Unlimited, Jah Bunny, Jack Ruby........5
  Pablo Moses, Ras Midas
  Prince Jazzbo........................................6
Concerts
  Jimmy Cliff, Third World.......................7
Album Reviews
  Basement 5, Specials, Industry............12
  Bow Wow Wow, Sex Pistols, Fleshtones...13
  The Clash.............................................14
  Velvet Underground, A Certain Ratio...15
Concerts
  New Era Reggae Band..........................16
  Iggy Pop, Abuse..................................18
  The Morells.........................................19
  Duchamp, Get Smart............................20
  Get Smart, The Clean..........................22
Small Labels...........................................24
Single Reviews
  Cabaret Voltaire, The Slits,
    A Certain Ratio................................25
Concerts
  Laurie Anderson..................................26
Single Reviews
  Throbbing Gristle................................28
  DAF.....................................................29
Local Scene.............................................30

**Editor**
Bill Rich

**Editorial Staff**
Marc Burch
Scott Epsten
Rick Hellman
Christopher Lucas
Dave Stuckey
Jim Schwada
Daddy Cool
U-Man
WB, NN, SK

**Photography**
Christopher Lucas
Bill Rich

**Layout**
John Lee

**Typesetting**
Joan McCabe Moore

**Cover**
Rick Schneider

*All contents copyright 1981 by Talk Talk Publications, PO Box 36, Lawrence, Kansas, 66044. All rights reserved. Any opinion expressed is solely that of the writer and not necessarily that of this publication. Subscription rate is $6 for six issues. Articles, reviews, and pix submitted for editorial consideration are welcome. Not responsible for unsolicited material. Address all correspondence to Talk Talk Editors, PO Box 36, Lawrence, Kansas, 66044, USA.*

## Beginning Our Third Year

*Welcome to the 1981 Talk Talk. Yes, we know we are a little late with our third year debut but at last it is finished! The new year will bring a lot of changes and uncertainty for Talk Talk's future. But we are planning big things so keep on the lookout! Besides keeping everyone updated on the worthwhile records released, we plan to emphasize more local bands. We got a letter that said it was great how we ignored the local scene and focused on international acts and import records. Well, we never intended to slight any one or most of all, ignore the local scene! This issue includes reviews and photos of area bands, including Get Smart, Duchamp, The Clean, with an emphasis on reggae—Jimmy Cliff, Third World, New Era Reggae Band, and lots of dub reggae reviews, plus our usual witty opinionated comments on everything. If you see something you like or dislike, drop us a line. We could use some more contributors and feedback. Now on with the issue. --BR*

## Coming Up Next Month
## Expanded Size
## Free Abuse Flexi-disc

This issue has been typeset and pasted up at the offices of Patterson, Theis, and Lee, for which Talk Talk will remain forever thankful.

## Reggae Reviews

Errol Scorcher Roach In A De Corner (Scorcher Music)–I first heard Errol Scorcher a few years back singing on a Revolutionaries album. Since then, he has received some acclaim from his singles and the hit 'Roach In A De Corner.' The album begins with Errol singing, 'This is the brand new Scorcher.' As he races through the nine songs on this showcase album, you get the feeling it is a new Scorcher, better and improved. He does all the arrangements and productions and then fits his voice in ever so carefully. A good record.

Sensimilla Dub The Chariot Riders (Crystal Records: 1009)–There are a few familiar rhythms here or at least some fleeting bits and pieces. Channel One does it again! The production is by Derrick Harriott, who proves that he knows what he does. Maybe to some people these tracks are old. You almost expect the booming voice of Big Youth to break through. But it does not. Instead, the beat just goes on. This album is not too spacey sounding, but I would not call it calm either. Just right for a chariot ride.

King of Dub (Clocktower Records: CTLP 0101)–'. . . Dub-wise bass and drum rhythmwise.' From Brad's Records in the Bronx comes this collection of ten of the hardest rhythm tracks. Recorded at Channel One and mixed with the help of King Tubby, this release does have 'the right sound and effect,' as claimed. The bass of Robbie Shakespeare and George Fullerwood keep this thing going. Very upfront but not the kind to blow your speakers out.

The Revolutionaries Dutch Man Dub (Burning Music: BV 1002)–Clear vinyl from London and outstanding graphics combine to make you want to put this on the turntable. The sound is a bit calmer than I prefer. Pretty homogenized. The bass is pretty faint and the rhythm guitar highlighted. The drums are locked into a stationary beat.

And News. Robbie Shakespeare, who was recently held by Jamaican authorities on charges of firearm possession at his home, has been released. It seems the situation is related to tension and conditions related to the killings by the authorities of the singer/DJ/toaster General Echo and several others. General Echo will be missed. His oftimes ribald lyrics and the combined rhythmic flow of his recordings will be missed. Although a new government is still talking control in Jamaica, there is still continued injustice, and as before, it remains that the 'poor can't take no more.'

Linton Kwesi Johnson LKJ In Dub (Island: ILPS 9650)–Finally, an album of dub by The Poet. These eight cuts are versions of songs contained on the Forces of Victory (from 1979) and Bass Culture (from 1980) albums that established Linton Kwesi Johnson as a major spokesman for the black youth in England. It is produced by Dennis Bovell, the great dub-master. But it does not sound like a Matumbi release, which it is not, of course. The tunes and rhythms are all LKJ's. What is a little strange is the exclusion of lyrics or phrases. Only a few cuts have any vocals, and vocals are Linton's trademark. So we have an LKJ album with little LKJ evident. Big deal. His presence remains, nevertheless. This album is great and a nice companion to his 'un-dub' work.

Morwell Unlimited A-1 Dub (Trojan: TRLS 193)–This album is produced and mixed by Blacka Morwell. He is a new one to me. It comes from Channel One but it is not exactly in the Channel One mold. Most of the air space is split between blast of ear-splitting guitar chords and the use of random drum beats held together with a heavy rhythm from the deep bass. A few cuts have vocals fading in and out. And there are lots of other instruments audible in spurts. Overall, sort of another laid back LP of A-1 dub.

Jah Bunny Dubbs Internation (JAH: LP001)–Lloyd Donalds n really shines here. Better known as Jah Bunny, the popular producer, he not only composed, arranged, and produced this but also played all the drums. A master with the tapes for sure. Dubbs Internation is quite upbeat and bright sounding. As a product from London, it is interesting to note the similarity with Blackbeard. As Jah Bunny says, 'if you feel like go deh, den go deh.' This one will make you feel like it.

Jack Ruby Hi Fi (Clapper Records: CLPS 1981)–A showcase album of various artists who have recorded at Jack Ruby's Studio in Jamaica. Most of the names are unfamiliar and a bit trendy, outside of Ken Boothe, who sounds better than he has for years. The songs cover a wide range of reggae styles. Like most showcases, a version follows the song. So there is a lot of good dub here along with the original sound to compare. That helps it all move along nicely. This collection is proof that Jack Ruby still can do it.

## Jimmy Cliff

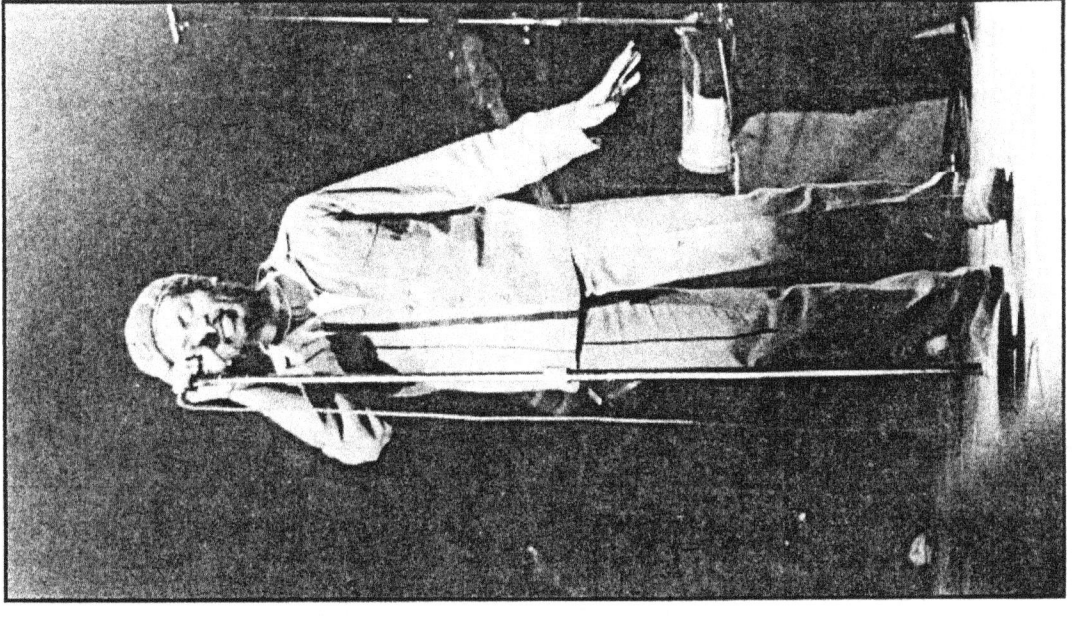

Bill Rich

## Reggae Reviews

Pablo Moses A Song (Mango LP)--Relatively unknown outside of Jamaica, where his song 'Blood Money' was a hit a few years back, Pablo Moses' latest A Song is a pleasant, if not potent, showcase for the singer's sweet soulful voice and above average song- writing ability. The LP boasts an impressive array of sidemen, from keyboardist/wailer Earl 'Wire' Lindo to saxman Glen Costa, but overall the energy level is low and Mango Records has already slated Pablo for the cut-out bin, which is where I found mine. Fave cuts: 'Dubbing Is A Must' and 'Music Is My Desire.' -D. Cool

Ras Midas Rastaman In Exile (SKEJ Productions: SKE 7023)--I had never heard of this singer until I found this record. The many musicians involved made it seem like a safe bet to buy. Upon listening, Ras Midas sounds very similar to Bob Marley. The band is tight and the two female backing vocalists develop the sound to perfection. Marcia Griffiths, of the I Threes, fills such a need here that it almost sounds like The Wailers. Reggae music has become more well known compared to an earlier time when everyone thought any reggae they heard was Bob Marley. But this record does resemble such a style. Perhaps Ras Midas has been overlooked because of his similarity or maybe he has tried to appeal to the same market. Beats me. See what you think.

Prince Jazzbo Ital Corner (Clocktower Records: CT 0103)--This is a newly released album but the material might have been setting around for a while. Prince Jazzbo is a classic Jamaican DJ who pops in and out of the scene from time to time. His voice has the right edge in accenting phrases so that you believe in the intensity and urgency he provokes. And the production by Lee 'Scratch' Perry puts the clamp down on any doubters. My favorites are on Side One, although Side Two's 'Coming on Strong' is another great one. The 'Prophet Live' and 'Prophet Dub-Satta' are the two outstanding cuts that have become a vital part of my energizing songs used to keep on going. I should point out that the dub cut was mixed by Brad Osborne, whose company released this album. So look for that label when you shop.

TALK TALK 201

# Jimmy Cliff

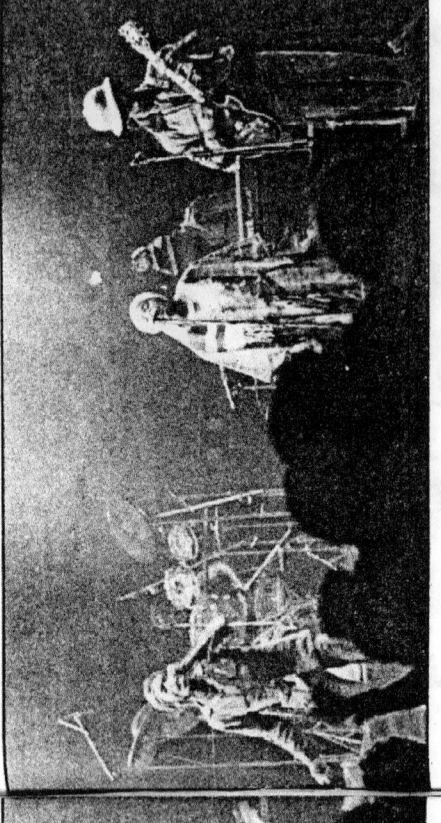

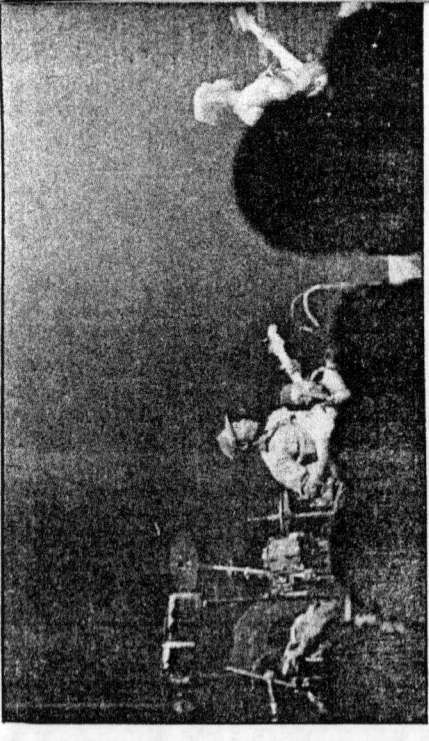

The Band: Sidney Wolfe, percussion; Kofe Ayivor, percussion; Roger Maclean, rhythm guitar; Senyah Haynes, bass; Jimmy Cliff, vocals; Specks Bifirimbi, drums; Barabara Jones, vocals; Checore Ramacon, keyboards; and Earl 'Chinna' Smith, guitar.

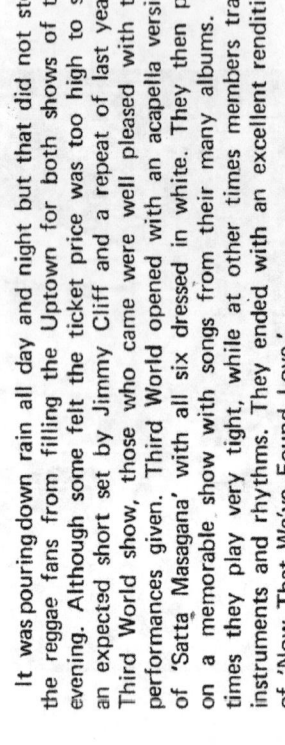

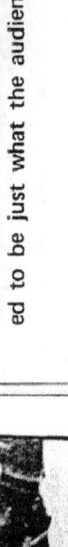

Photographs by Bill Rich

**Live: December 7 Uptown Theater, KC, MO**

It was pouring down rain all day and night but that did not stop the reggae fans from filling the Uptown for both shows of the evening. Although some felt the ticket price was too high to see an expected short set by Jimmy Cliff and a repeat of last year's Third World show, those who came were well pleased with the performances given. Third World opened with an acapella version of 'Satta Masagana', with all six dressed in white. They then put on a memorable show with songs from their many albums. At times they play very tight, while at other times members trade instruments and rhythms. They ended with an excellent rendition of 'Now That We've Found Love.'

After a short break, Jimmy Cliff began his show with 'Bongo Man Is Alive.' He has just finished filming 'Bongo Man.' A lot of time has passed since his first film, 'The Harder They Come', and Jimmy Cliff has lost some of his momentum, which boosted him into stardom. But his show tonight, featuring his early hits, seemed to be just what the audience needed and wanted.

# Third World

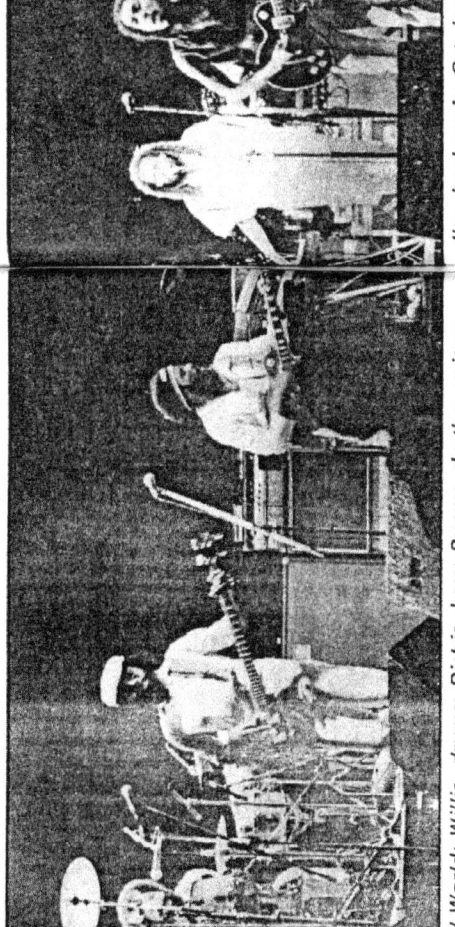

*Third World: Willie, drums; Richie, bass; Bunny, rhythm guitar;*

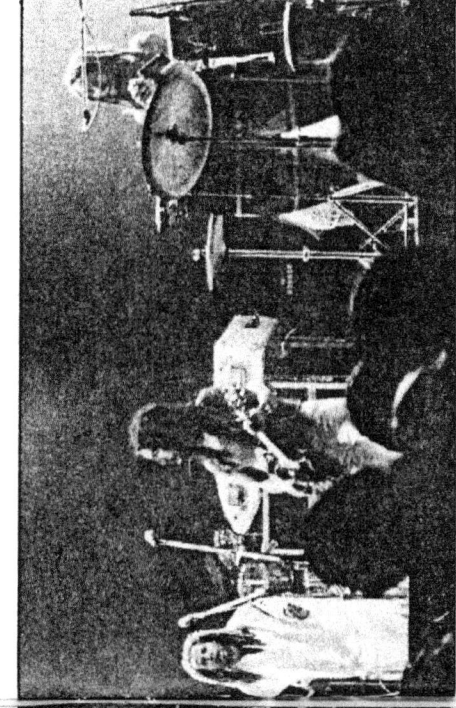

*Ibo, keyboards; Cat, lead guitar; Carrot, percussion.*

Photographs by Bill Rich

## Album Reviews

Basement 5 1965-1980 (Island: ILPS 9641)–Wow! I have to admit this album caught me off guard. After hearing their recent dub releases, I put Basement 5 into a more hardcore reggae category. But on this, their debut album, the band comes across as the latest punks with vocals in the vein of Angelic Upstarts and maybe The UK Subs. Maybe it is just the chanting vocals and steady drumbeats. Whatever it is, I like it! In fact, I have liked these guys since the first single, 'Silicon Chip,' And I think Basement 5 will rank in the very top of 1981 bands. I have heard that they do not quite equal in live performances their technical mastery. But I still want to see them. Go buy this one now! Some people say they are dated with such militant or negative ravings. I guess that depends what sort of time clock you punch nowadays. Their slogan says it all: 'Stay Cool –Hang Loose–Admit Nothing.' –WB

The Specials Rude Boys Out of Jail (Centrifugal Records–possible bootleg)–Instead of reviewing the new album, we bring this live recording to your attention. It is a double album of a show last year (1-30-80) in Boston. The songs are from the singles and debut album. They sound a bit different than the earlier releases, but convey the live frantic excitement The Specials generate. I can think of few bands that really create such an intense concert experience as these guys. The Lawrence community has been waiting for the group to return to America as a local show has been tentatively planned for ages. Of course, when they do tour America again, they will probably be concentrating on their latest album. All the more reason to get this record. The worst part is there is very little low end to this pressing; almost 'tinny.' But this can be overlooked once the action starts. And The Specials are an action band–something you must see to understand. -WB

Industry Industry (Metro Records: MET-1-40001)–I am not sure what this is all about. The basics are that this is a 12-inch 45 with five songs by two New Yorkers who spent days (actually years) overdubbing and creating some music. I say music because it is not electronic noise but music. Granted, it all goes by rather quickly, and undoubtedly you will not see Industry at the local venue. It took work and I hope it was worth their time to them. –NN

The Sex Pistols The Heyday (Factory: FACT 30)– A little late for The Sex Pistols you say? By the way, did you see the reissue special packaging of six Sex Pistols singles? If you want music, then get that. If you want to complete your collection of interviews, get this. Why did Factory enter the Pistols market? Maybe they had the tapes. I was told that this release offered nothing new. It is interviews with the band–or part of it. But after listening to it and having everything they have released, I cannot recall, for instance, Sid Vicious explaining about how he fraudulently claimed to be a peaceful person, etc. I have not read anything about this, but parts of it occur after the big split. This is a cassette that is too short for me. But I like it. Another perspective and more light for the historians who have not figured out what The Sex Pistols were about or are unsure of what they helped begin. –SK

Bow Wow Wow Your Cassette Pet (EMI: WOW 1)–Eight songs in twenty minutes on a cassette packaged in a cardboard box like a deck of cards or pack of Marlboros. Malcolm Maclaren does it again! One thing about him, he does progress. I mean, this is quite a trendy little job. So it is neat to have, but the ingredients are somewhat incomplete. In many ways, it is good that Adam Ant is not associated with such products. I do find the female vocalist whose name escapes me sort of exciting. And the original Ant band are pretty good. The drumming does seem to be pretty mechanical. Overall, the whole thing moves along pretty quick. And that is all I have to say. –SK

The Fleshtones Up Front (IRS: SP 70402)–On this, their initial effort for IRS Records, The Fleshtones present themselves to the public in a somewhat shaky light. On one hand, their Go-Go/surf sensibilities (evidenced in the music and the fab cover art done by vocalist Peter Zaremba) are totally commendable. The big problem occurs when you try to listen to the lyrics without wincing. That can probably be overlooked for the moment, however, in view of the 'atmosphere' of the record (especially on the best cut, 'Theme from "The Vindicators"', an instrumental in the best Gary Glitter head-banging tradition will have you careening off the walls in no time . . .). Anyway, they seem to be on the right track since this 12-inch EP is much better than either of their cuts on the 12' x 5' compilation LP. –Stuck

# Album Reviews

The Clash Sandinista (CBS: FSLN1)-- The question everyone seems to ask lately is what are The Clash up to? The year ended with the release of their triple record set containing 36 songs, presented in a new way for the band. Gone is the fierce rebellious attitude which established this early punk band as the ultimate. This disappoints some hard core fans and causes the listener to continually evolve to unknown areas of musical appreciation. I think a strong case can be made that a bigger sell-out would have been if the band kept their beginning feelings and continued to rock out in cliques of the punk movement. After all, this is 1981 not 1977. Sandinista shows The Clash to be more versatile than early on. In many ways, this release creates a similar feeling to the release of London Calling. I remember seeing The Clash over a year ago, before London Calling was completed but the songs were developed and performed. Hearing the Willie Williams' classic, 'Armageddon Time,' I was spellbound by their newly-exposed intensity. I recently found the original single finally and treasure it because this song (or sound) helped open the way to enjoy the new direction The Clash had taken. And the new album shows several more steps. While I commend the band for this, many people are worried. Some feel that, having so many more songs in their repertoire, the energy and force which used to be high-lighted will fall aside to a more lighthearted, easy-going, and nonsensical atmosphere. Others are glad that all these songs are out and that the band can now go further. The Clash have never been ones to stop developing and there seems to be little evidence that they will become stuck playing Sandinista cuts. But it would be hard to ignore the many excellent tunes which are included. The home-tapers will have a field day picking their favorite sounding songs. Maybe that is how the public should approach this. For there are many outstanding songs here as well as some that just do not do much for me. Being a supporter of the great Mikey Dread, I am particularly impressed and enjoy the cuts which he has mixed. And, by the way, his association with The Clash has helped his Dread At The Controls label to have an outstanding year with unique 12-inch 45's. In many ways, this is the team-up of the year. I look forward to having much more released soon.

While it might seem that I think this is a cheery, happy release, as one listens to it, the lyrics and mood point to the current injustices in today's existence--war, ghettoes, suffering, etc. The Clash have not lost their emphasis on social commentary, but now have gone beyond screaming their frustrations to letting their musical sounds create visceral moods. The result is a deeper communication and an accomplishment that few realize.

The Velvet Underground (Plastic Inevitable Records: First 1) Lou Reed Rock and Roll Diary 1967-1980 (Arista: A2L 8603)-- For several years, Lou Reed was my rock hero. It seemed that as time progressed, his releases had less and less of an impact. Arista has compiled this two-record set of previously released meaterial to keep Lou Reed from falling into obscurity and to reacquaint listeners to the sounds that did have a large impact on the development of rock. When it comes down to the bare facts, I bought this because my Velvets albums were getting too scratched. I could do without the second record actually. And I would recommend finding the newly released--for the first time--pre-Velvets collection, Velvet Underground-Etc, which has ten cuts of exceptional material. Too bad Lou is not as hep as he was. Some of this is from 1965, some from 1967, and some from 1969. Lou Reed will always be one of my heroes because of what he did, not what he is doing or might do. --NN

A Certain Ratio The Graveyard and the Ballroom (Factory: FACT 16)-- An innovation from Factory and Martin Hannet. Over 40 minutes of propaganda that one can carry concealed and then introduce to various cassette slots, thus infiltrating parties, your parents' autos, and other behind-the-times music venues. The 'Graveyard' side is material taken from the studio and the 'Ballroom' side is live from the Electric Ballroom. Each side gives a different insight into the band and the sound quality is excellent. Although two of the 14 songs are found on both sides of the tape, this is not a repetitious or tedious work in the least. The best side is the 'Ballroom' side because of its spontaneity and rougher electronic edge. There is also a bit of humor on this side. The band drop some hints about what they think of the fact that many critics and fans alike have labeled them as the heirs to Joy Division. Case in point: between 'Choir' and 'The Fox,' the lead vocalist says matter- of-factly, 'It does sound like Joy Division, doesn't it?' After this, the very same singer goes into 'She's Lost Control' and then he chuckles either to himself or at stupid comparisons. Musically, there is a lot of synth work, guitar effects, and echoing trumpet but no jungle drums on this one folks. There is nothing at all primitive on this. It is technology at its best. --U-Man

# The New Era Reggae Band

Live: January 12 The Downliner, KC, MO

New Era have been busy. They played at Off The Wall Hall early in December, then at Parody Hall later in the month, and came back again to appear at The Downliner. Probably one of the smallest clubs they have played, it was here that their sounds seemed to really flow out. I have seen this band too many times to blindly rave on and on. Of course, at times their harmonies might be a bit off key or off beat, or the solos verging towards self indulgence.

But, opposed to earlier times, they now play quite a few of their original songs that match anything coming out of Jamaica today. Signing to a major label will soon be a reality.

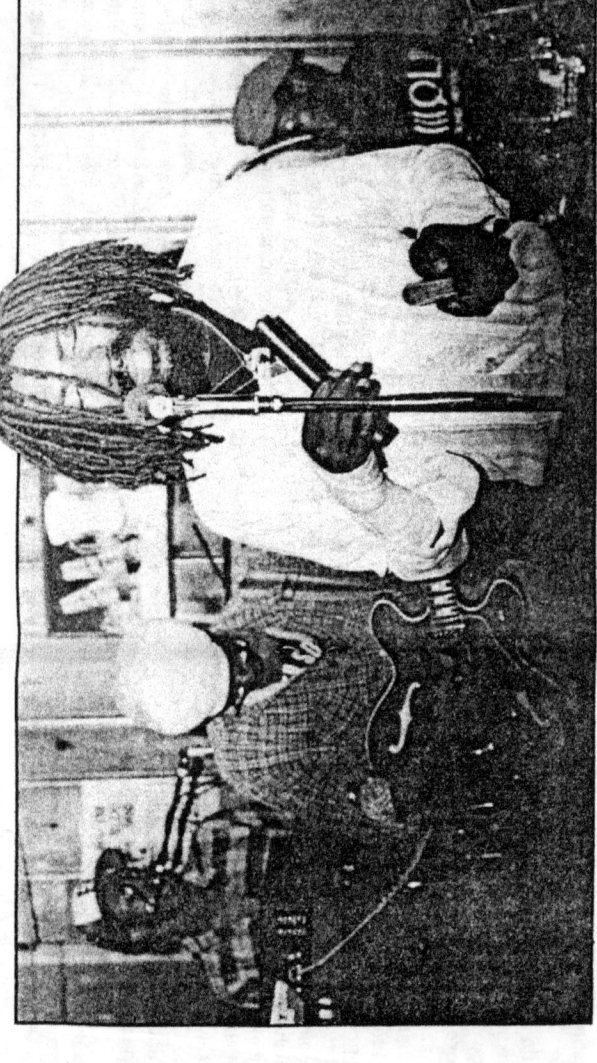

Photographs by Bill Rich

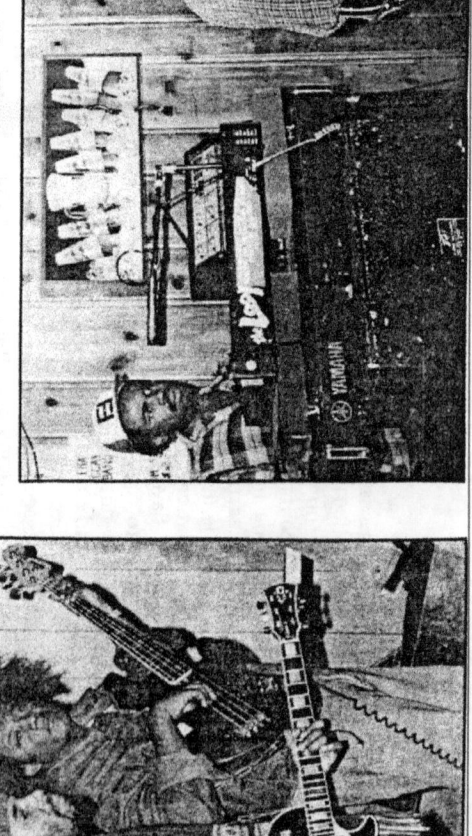

The Band: Donny Johnson, keyboards; Steve Blair, rhythm guitar; Bunny Martin, drums; Greg Barnes, lead guitar; Aswad Greggori, percussion; Chris Rose, bass.

## Iggy Pop

Live: November 29 Gateway Hotel Ballroom St. Louis, MO

After a semi-rousing/ear-splitting set by a group of 14-year-old St. Louis punks called the 'Ooz Kicks', Iggy took the stage. With not as much intro fanfare as the Lawrence show, Iggy ripped into "TV-Eye". What followed was a series of early songs including 'Raw Power' and 'Search and Destroy'. A rare treat, considering he did nothing like this in Lawrence. The crowd was large and wild, which was surprising as this was, of course, St. Louis! Iggy looked better than ever in his new haircut and destructive mood. Never a dull moment, The Ig kicked over mike—stands and generally made a Rock 'n Roll nuisance of himself. Unlike the Lawrence show, he was actually believeable (as opposed to his 'posing.). Not a tune was played from New Values and only one from the recent Soldier ('Knocking Them Down in the City').

He did a few unknowns and kept a fast pace throughout. And then (Yes!), 'Louie, Louie'. You pays your money and you gets your choice! No one threw eggs or bottles, but it was terribly exciting nonetheless.

After a few more drinks, I began to lose track of the trivialities like song titles, band members (who seemed to be the same ones from the Lawrence show), and encores (at least two that I am sure of). It was a fabulous show with a newly revitalized Iggy Pop. --SE

## Abuse

Live: January 23, 24 Off The Wall Hall

The main action this weekend was Abuse. Friday night had the trio with Dalton Howard and The Go-Cats, who were billed as The Buzzcats. On the second night, the opening act ,was The Hitler Youth in their Lawrence debut. The Youth seemed a bit calmer and conservative, as opposed to some of their gigs which have resulted in their being baned from many venues. They play loud and hard with few of the vocals being understood. The two nights showed quite a contrast, but Abuse shone through at each. It is evident that they practice daily, with few errors in timing or progression. A complete story and photographs will be included in the next issue, plus some surprises.

## The Morrells

Live: December 12 & 13 The Downliner KC, MO

Guaranteed true conversation between one guy in wrap-around shades and another with no sideburns: 'Punk is just a bunch of dummies playing fast 'n loud noise.'

"Yeah, that's why I like New Wave. Punk's not fashion-oriented enough for me.'

Against a backdrop ranging from skinny-tied wavers to fat, bearded Willie Nelson look-alikes, The Morrells invaded KC's favorite (and only) punk watering hole, The Downliner, and won over the audience with their good rockin' sounds. From the worst kind of dyed-hair-and-leather poseurs to preppy-looking tourists, The Downliner attracts them all. Add to that a few bikers, bartenders, and nondescript others and you have a pretty interesting crowd, if a bit obnoxious.

Anyway, The Morrells have got to be the grooviest band in the four-state area. Their catalogue of obscure covers has earnd them the monicker of the human jukebox. I could not tell you what half the titles were, but they ripped through the set with a rockabilly fervor that Robert Gordon would sell what little soul he has for.

The Morrells (formerly The Skeletons, formerly The Symptoms) are no spring chickens. Lou (b&g) and Marilee (k) could be your parents from the looks of them, but there is no way your folks could rock like this.

On Saturday, they tended to lapse into country (I especially dug Lou's improv vocals on 'Folsom Prison Blues') but paced the set well, even including a reggae (?) tune 'about a punk rocker from the Midwest who goes to England but has really terrible breath.'

The whole thing is held together by the stinging guitar of one D. Clinton Thompson. Sure, he is short and wears penny loafers, but he can play as tough as anyone you would care to name--and he's got that surf/rockabilly sound DOWN. I mean, you have just got to move.

And to show they do not live entirely in the past, The Morrells unveiled 'the first car song of the 80's', a perfect expresion of pre-apocalypse Midwestern decadence, 'Trans Am' ('gonna' ride a-round while we still can, in that damn Trans Am'). Quite simply, one of the best shows I have seen in ages. This band is hot. Join The Morrell Majority now !--RH

# Duchamp
# Get Smart

Live: January 16, 17 The Downliner, KC, MO

A weekend of music by what some consider 'art-school' bands. While much of the crowd might be 'art school' related, the groups themselves are quite dissimilar and do not fit in such a category. Duchamp are more theatrically oriented in their extensive costumes and presentation. It seems some people love it, others are embarrassed and still others do not care. So, I will leave it at that. They are all young musicians and have three singles out. I would rather see them live than listen to their records. Duchamp usually produce some energy in their shows and the crowds love them. One of their strengths is changing the pace--just when a song seems to be slowing down to a welcomed death, they pick up the tempo and save themselves.

Get Smart are one of the encouraging developments in the local music scene. Emerging at the end of 1980, they have attracted more attention and positive responses than anything for ages. Their repertoire is surprisingly quite extensive for such a new band, only performing minimal covers, including Gang of Four, Elvis Costello, and Public Image. The vocals seem to be reminiscent of the B-52s in tone or inflection. Outside of that, other influences are basically absent. Get Smart have a unique sound. Go see them.

*Duchamp: J. Scanlon, guitar; Tom Cat, drums; F. Frenge, guitar; Bill Scanlon, vocals; D. Mink, bass. Right--Get Smart: Marc Koch, guitar; Frank Loose, drums; Lisa Wertman, bass.*

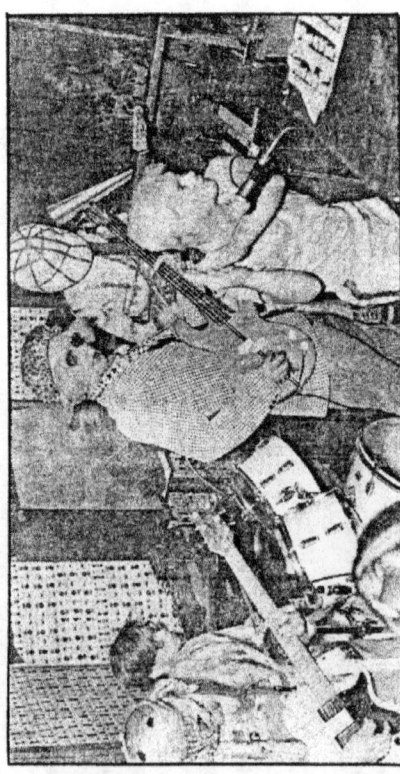

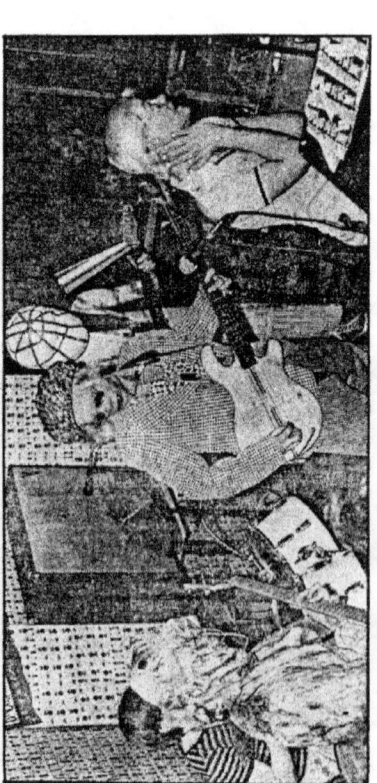

Photographs by Bill Rich

# Inaugural Ball with Get Smart and The Clean

Live: January 20 Off The Wall Hall, Lawrence, KS

The nation was in celebration--not because of the inauguration but because the hostages were free. And Mohammed Ali talked a guy out of jumping off a building. The weather was nice also, so the hall was packed with people ready to dance and have a good time. Get Smart opened the evening with a long set, including favorites 'Modern Boy' and 'Ankle Deep In Mud.' The Clean headlined the bill. The band has made some drastic changes in their aproach, as has been witnessed the last few times they have performed. They have added more new material. Their overall tone, not so cheery but not gloomy, is more towards influences such as The Doors. Some new instrumentals resemble Magazine and they have been listening to Sandinista for sure. Each member has improved, which adds up to a big boost for this local favorite.

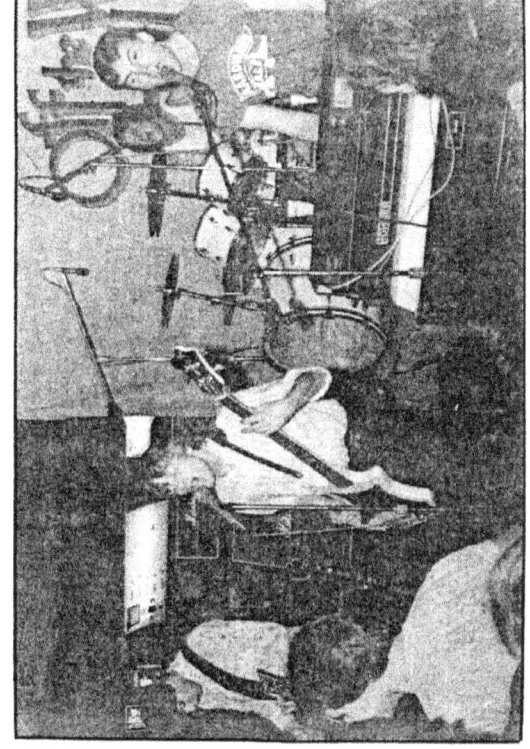

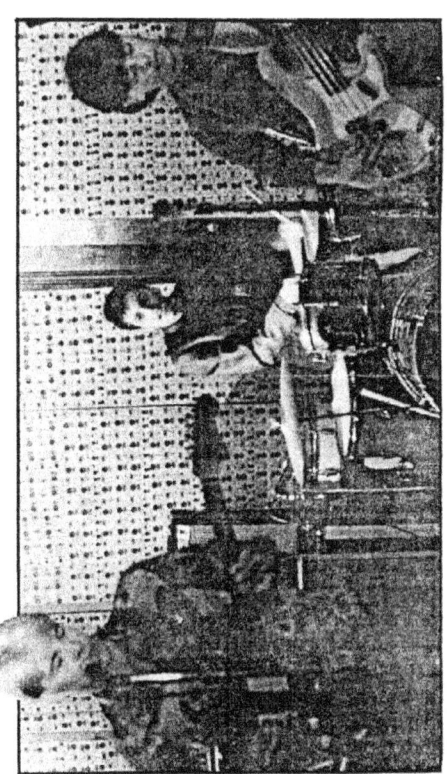

*Get Smart: Marc Koch, guitar; Frank Loose, drums; Lisa Wertman, bass. The Clean: Jay Francis, guitar; Todd Kitchen, bass; Jim Slocomb, drums; Shawn Kelly, keyboards and vocals.*

Photographs by Bill Rich

## Small Labels, Independents, and more.

Lots of small timers this month. Most were not so hot but encouraging anyway. Picked up some independents in New Orleans. The Producers' 'You Won't Let Me In/Nobody But Me' sound like a de-Spectorized girls group (Zareba Records, 417 S. Salcedo, New Orleans, LA, 70119). The Cold do not come off as good as live on 'You/Three Chord City.' Both groups use female lead vocals, two guitars, bass, and drums. The Manic Depressives EP (Vinyl Solution Records, 4304 James Dr., New Orleans, LA, 70003) are more to my primitive punk mentality.

Going west to Texas, The Vast Majority score a hit with 'I Wanna Be A Number/God's Groin/Throwdown' on Wild Dog Records (PO Box 35253, Houston, TX, 77035).

Skudder, a band from Omaha (Box 14533, Omaha, NE, 68124) have their second release out, an EP which reminds me of The Stranglers. They also have a live cassette out with more originals.

Waldo Records (c/o Another Record Store, 5 W. Charlton, Cincinnati, OH, 45219) are off to a good start with an EP by the newly formed News. It is fast paced and an all-around alternative to the typical Ohio sound.

The single by Nuance, 'Having A Good Time/Stay', seemed to appeal to the Tom Jones type listener. Maybe their forthcoming LP will disprove that, but I doubt it (San-Lyn Records, Box 46, Calvin Station, Syracuse, NY, 13205). I sort of liked them anyway.

The Beakers, who claim to be the favorites of The Gang of Four, have a single out and contribute to the Life Elsewhere album (Mr. Brown Records, Box 445, Olympia, WA, 98507). They sound a bit like an Uberized Contortion clone with a funk swing. Also on Mr. Brown are The Macs, whose single 'The Cowboy Song/Walking Down The Street' really has grabbed me.

I guess that is about it for this time. I cannot find anything on the floor or in the trash, so, if I did not mention something you sent, it either got tossed or ripped. More next month, if anything comes. --The Blind Reviewer

## Single Reviews

<u>Cabaret Voltaire Seconds Too Late/Control Addict</u> (Rough Trade: RT060)--This is CV's most accessible piece of vinyl to date. It is good but not that exciting. The most noteworthy thing about the A-side is the use of drums. They play an integral part in this song and really stand out. The B-side should have been the theme song for Ronald Reagan's inauguration. It has a catchy cowboy clippity-clop death valley daze to it. Here comes the nuclear roundup from Hollywood. CV have anticipated the event. --U-Man

<u>The Slits Animal Space/Animal Spacier</u> (Human Records)--With three new releases, The Slits seem to be more prolific than in the past. Their latest single is a disappointing mish mash that is hard to do anything with--listen, dance, ignore, etc. Maybe it will become less irritating with time. A three-song 12-inch, offers new versions to the A-sides of some of their singles. 'Man Next Door' is done with an interesting excursion into tape mixing. 'In The Beginning' has a different approach to the same rhythm. Good production. The flip has 'Animal Space' but I have not figured out how similar it is to the original version--either the straight side or dub side. A nice surprise was finding the Rough Trade release of The New Age Steppers doing the reggae song 'Fade Away'. It is definitely The Slits and is also one of the songs they perform live. Everyone knows these girls and guys, since half the band are male, whether the public knows it or not, can make great music. Let us hope that they continue. --NN

<u>A Certain Ratio Do the Du - The Fox/Shack Up - Son and Heir</u> (Factory, US: FACUS 4)--An American release, with Rough Trade assistance, that shows another side to this complex band. I like this better than the Factory tape. Listening to it, I do not remember what time it is or what time is. Oh, yes, this is another 12-inch 45 in the A Certain Ratio vein with the usual use of white space, small photo on the left and minimal information. And this is a very minimal review, which should not reflect upon the band, just on the reviewer. But it is a good, enjoyable release--a little haunting, maybe a little irritating. I think you can handle it. I think you will like it. --NN

# Laurie Anderson

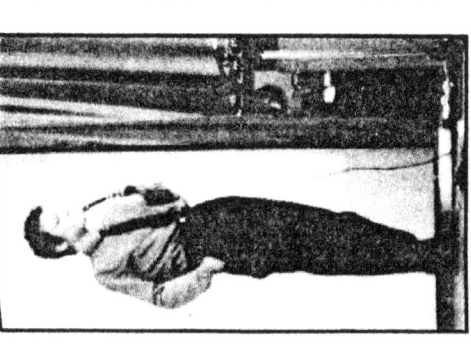

### Live: January 15 Kansas City Art Institute

The rhythms and images laid down by Ms. Anderson proved that she could extend to a space and audience avant garde expression without compromising her work.

Although she only played fragments of her seven-hour piece 'United States' she pushed, pulled, and wooed her audience with a variety of electronic sounds and physical images. The music, while at times sounding like Throbbing Gristle, was more diagrammatic, more pure, than recent TG. Ms. Anderson compared her electronic sounds to a saxophone alive with human breath and tone. She enjoys electronics, saying, 'One is always aware of the imminent possibility of electrocution.'

Her rhythm tapes and voice treatments were literally electrified by feedback and strumming of her violin. She loves her violin and performs brilliantly with it.

Laurie Anderson is recognized as an outstanding performance artist in New York. Her pieces, which combine talk, gesture, film, slides, audiotape, music, and childhood, have in recent years been performed at the Kunsthalle, Basel; the Walker Art Centre, Minneapolis; the Museum of Modern Art, The Whitney, and The Kitchen, New York; the Bienale in Paris; and Dokumenta 77, Kasel.

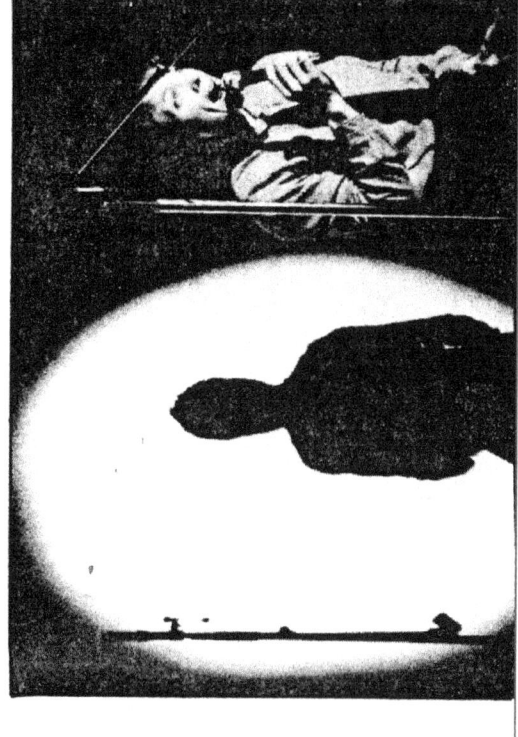

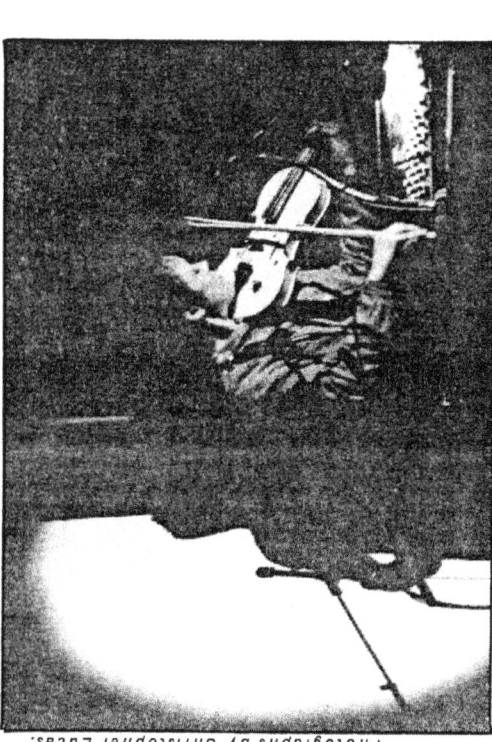

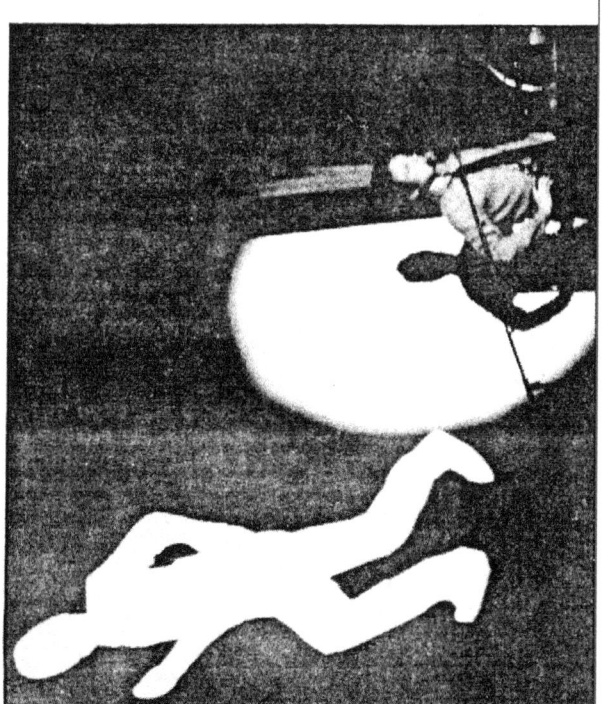

Photographs by Christopher Lucas.

# Single Reviews

**Throbbing Gristle** Subhuman/Something Came Over Me (Industrial Records: IR0013); Adrenalin/Distant Dreams (Part 2) (Industrial Records: IR0015)--These two singles were originally scheduled for release September 3rd, commemorating the anniversary of WWII. In keeping with this, TG has packaged these singles in camouflage outer sleeves. It is quite effective, as it successfully conceals the four photos on the actual record jackets. IR0013 is more music from the Death Factory. Both 'Subhuman' and 'Something Came Over Me' deal with typical TG fetishes, perhaps a better word is pastimes, in which they prefer to indulge.

'Subhuman' begins with some seemingly ordinary violin and guitar and then erupts into abrasive chaos. Our hero, Genesis P-Orridge, screams out the lyrics in primal frenzy. He wants to stamp the subhuman out. What is the subhuman? He is probably talking about people who do not appreciate Throbbing Gristle or maybe he is another Pol Pot and it is all the third worlder-types he loathes and their impoverished existences that they want to ease by erasing. This is a classic in the vein of SPK.

'Something Came Over Me' is a hymn to the glories of masturbation, which basically says, if it feels good, do it. It opens with keyboards, followed by a strong percussive rhythm that one can stroke along with. It is musical porn with whining synths and violin. GP-O says this is the message for today from Jack.

'Adrenalin' is a very fast moving song about being elsewhere and having an expletive good time. This is an example of TG's 'happy' music. Disco drums and handclaps play a big role in the makeup of this song. It has an explosive ending, as the singer is consumed by his own energy. 'Distant Dreams (Part 2)' is the most musical of the four. Opening with a synth loop, TG go into what sounds like a soundtrack. Music for hydrocarbon-powered vehicles. It makes excellent driving music. Genesis sounds very foreboding as he explains reality in his terms: we are not real. It is as simple as that. --U-Man

**Deutsch-Amerikanische Freundschaft** Tanz Mit Mir/Der Rauber und Der Prinx (Mute Records: MUTE 011)--Rallies are being held in Nurburgring once again. The youth of the west revel in excess. A modern day masque of the red death. If you play this single, your perception of life's futility will be awakened. Not being able to understand die deutsche sprache will not help a bit. You will be compelled to listen. DAF have latched onto a truth, one as revelatory as Nietzche or Mein Kampf. A driving pulse-like bass starts the ritual. The singer, Gabi, his voice feverish . . . he knows the inevitability of it all. We must dance. He makes it a point to we are unable to forget. . . . we are the human machine. We too are steel and liquid. Framework supporting framework. A screaming guitar beckons, the dance begins. Life is fast/Life is hard. The human race dances and completes the body circuitry. A celebration of life's uncertainties. Man sagt oft: there is no permanence. So what, there is now . . . the moment. A negative piece of music? No, it stimulates thought. This song is so dramatic that it is captivating. It flushes the body in its emotional scope. Youth rallies shall be held. This is the anthem. We are the victims, the causation of these days, the celebrants of life. Dance and enjoy enventually it will end.

The Bandit and the Prince is very synth oriented, a bouncy sounding song about a romance between a prince and a bandit. All in all, a rather strange fairy tale. This single is for those of the PLUS ULTRA and it is the best. --U-Man

OFF THE WALL HALL
737 New Hampshire
(913) 841-2266
In downtown Lawrence

Off the Wall Hall can accommodate your party. We also have affordable rehearsal space for bands. We book many bands from the tapes we receive. If your band has a demo we would like to hear it. Please send demos to Post Office Box 91, Lawrence, KS, 66044.

January 30--Caribe
January 31--The Clean
February 6 & 7--Get Smart and The Regular Guys
February 13--The Deal
February 14--Valentine Party
March 6 & 7--The Embarrassment
March 27 & 28--Tony Brown Reggae-Band

## Local Scene

Thumbs have finshed a first stage in recording for their next album. Around thirteen songs have been basically laid down with more time required to develop the sounds. Their debut album last year has become one of the best received independent works to date in America as well as in the midwest and especially in Lawrence. Reviews in New Musical Express, The Village Voice, and Rolling Stone among many others brought a lot of attention and pressure on this local band. Although without a major label, they continue to negotiate with numerous record companies. It looks like right now, Thumbs plan to develop and put their own finishing touches on their latest album and will go from there.

The other major attention-getter around here last year was the four-song EP by The Regular Guys. In fact, Trouser Press recently included it in their Underground Top Ten singles of 1980. A hearty congratulations and a tip of the hat to TP for their taste.

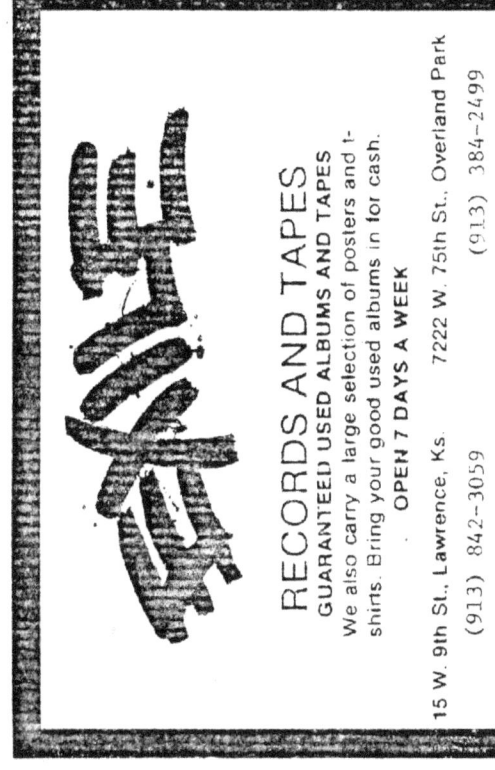

RECORDS AND TAPES
GUARANTEED USED ALBUMS AND TAPES
We also carry a large selection of posters and t-shirts. Bring your good used albums in for cash.
OPEN 7 DAYS A WEEK

15 W. 9th St. Lawrence, Ks.   7222 W. 75th St. Overland Park
(913) 842-3059                (913) 384-2499

Leon Russell
February 4

Blue Riddim Band
February 5, 6, 7

Maynard Ferguson
February 13

Sir Douglas Quintet
Thumbs
February 14

Larry Coryell
February 18

The Secrets
February 20, 21

Morrells
February 25

Glory Boys
February 27, 28

Lawrence Opera House
7th & Mass.   842-4930

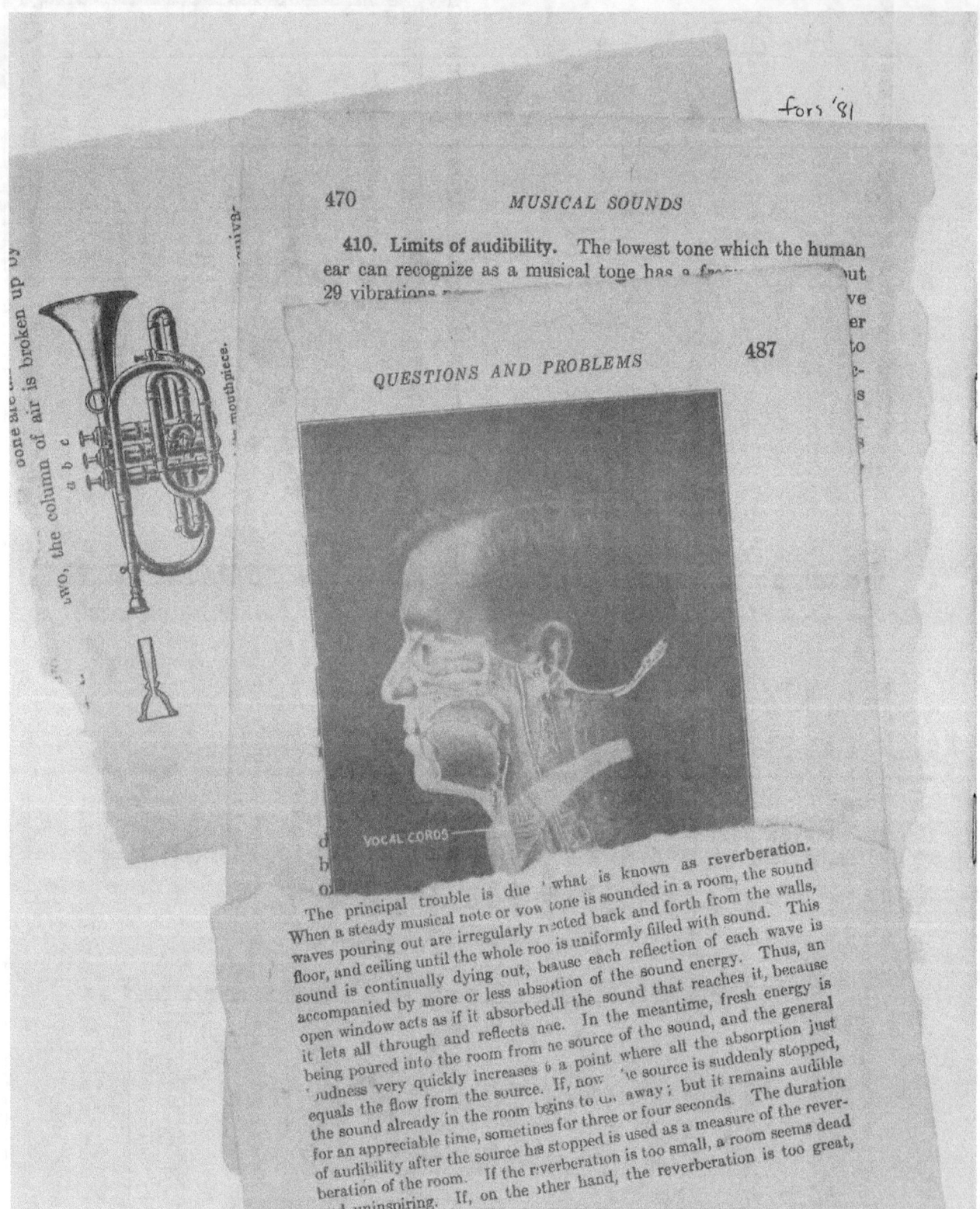

# TALK TALK
## The Midwest American Rock and Reggae Magazine

Vol. 3 No. 2   $1.00

# Talk Talk

Vol.3 No.2　　　March 1981　　　$1.00

INTERVIEW:
  Bunny Clarke of Third World ...................... 4
REGGAE REVIEWS:
  Max Edwards, Bunny Wailer ...................... 5
  The Equators, Mikey Dread,
  The Selecter, Madness .......................... 6
  Augustus Pablo, Dance Craze ................... 7
INTERVIEW:
  Robert Zohn of The Blue Riddim Band ......... 8
SMALL LABELS' INDEPENDENTS
  AND MORE ....................................... 12
NEWS AND VIEWS ................................. 13
LIVE:
  Oingo Boingo, Jon and The
  Nightriders, The Blasters ...................... 14
  The Regular Guys .............................. 15
INTERVIEW:
  Abuse ........................................... 16
CENTER:
  Fresh presents Abuse .......................... 16
ALBUMS:
  The New Age Steppers, Lewis and Gilbert,
  Thomas Leer and Robert Rental ............... 20
  Der Plan, Magazine ............................ 21
LIVE:
  Get Smart ...................................... 22
  Hitler Youth ................................... 23
ALBUMS:
  Adam and The Ants, Black Flag,
  The Zantees .................................... 24
  Circle Jerks, Ian Dury ......................... 25
SINGLES
  San Francisco Underground No. 2
      SINGLES:
  San Francisco Underground No. 2,
  Crispy Ambulance .............................. 26
  Crass, Stranglers .............................. 27
PRINT:
  Volumne ........................................ 28

**Editor**
*Bill Rich*
**Editorial Board**
*Marc Burch*
*Rick Hellman*
*Steve Kemp*
*Jim Schwada*
*Dave Stuckey*
*Harold Thorn*
*Rick Schneider*
**Photography**
*Christopher Lucas*
*Bill Rich*
**Layout**
*John Lee*
**Typesetting**
*Joan McCabe Moore*
**Cover**
*Nate Fors*

All contents copyright 1981 by Talk Talk Publications, PO Box 36, Lawrence, Kansas, 66044. All rights reserved. Any opinion expressed is solely that of the writer and not necessarily that of this publication. Subscription rate is $6 for six issues. Articles, reviews, and pix submitted for editorial consideration are welcome. Not responsible for unsolicited material. Address all correspondence to Talk Talk Editors, PO Box 36, Lawrence, Kansas, 66044, USA.

# Third World

In between shows at the Uptown several months ago, I talked with Bunny Clarke of Third World. Although a bit late, there were some interesting things discussed, some of which follows.

Talk Talk: What about the new government in Jamaica?
Bunny Clarke: You mean Seagua being elected? Well, you know Third World's views on politics. I'm not really interested in who is holding office. The people elected Seagua, you know.
TT: What about marijuana? I hear that he is going to legalize it?
BC: Seagua said the ganga trade has been keeping Jamaica alive for a long time and it will continue to.
TT: Back to the government. Will people be able to find work and be able to eat? I know a lot of Third World's efforts are devoted to planning for the future to make it better for people growing up.

*Bunny Clarke*

BC: And that is what he (the new Prime Minister) said he would do. Provide that they have food and shelter for the folks. It should get better. The people are the ones that decide. Not a person but the people. Another question, brother.
TT: This is the last date on the tour. Have you been opening for Jimmy Cliff every show?
BC: It is equal billing. But we decided to open. So when we are finished, we get a chance to go . . . so it is not really opening. We finished about fifty shows now.
TT: How is your film doing? (Prisoner In The Street)
BC: Well, it opened a while ago. We have been getting good vibes, good reports.
TT: Are you planning any changes in your new material?
BC: Dance, rockers style.
TT: Do you ever let your locks down on stage?
BC: Yeah, man, sometimes. They kinda get in the way sometimes.
TT: Has Third World as a band been helping any other new bands lately?
BC: Well, this tour (with Jimmy Cliff) and the last one with Toots and The Maytals, we were really concentrating on a kind of package deal. And this will be the last of it. But it was important for us to show booking agents, field managers, promoters, printers, and all the others, who needed to find out and know that reggae groups can go through a program that has been set up months before without any copping out or . . . .Reggae needed to build back that confid so the mission of the last two tours . . .
TT: Has been successful.

BC: It is. Especially this last one had turned out even much better than we thought it would, you know. The reception turned out good. We plan in spring to do another tour of mainly college dates. Right after our new album is finished. We are going into the studio now.
TT: CBS?
BC: We have not signed any contract yet.
TT: But at the beginning of the show they announced that Third World were CBS recording artists, right?
BC: We are not with anyone right now. We are still negotiating. We have not made up our minds.

# Reggae Reviews

MAX EDWARDS Still Alive/Rockers Arena (Epiphany EDS-02) THE FABULOUS TITANS (Epiphany EEP-003)--Epiphany Records of San Francisco, which recently released LPs by The Soul Syndicate and Earl Zero, continues to spotlight new reggae talent, coming out this month with a 12-inch single by Max Edwards and a 5-cut EP. Max Edwards is a talented vocalist and songwriter in the style of Greg Isaacs--'Still Alive' is concerned with his survival in the mean streets of Trenchtown, while 'Rockers Arena' is a straight ahead dance tune presented in both original and dub version on the B side. No musician credits are given, but it would not surprise me if it was The Soul Syndicate, who seem to be Epiphany's house band. The Fabulous Titans, Epiphany's other reggae related release this month, are five gentlemen, four white and one black, who play in a style reminiscent of the English Beat--pleasant danceable rhythms with a taste of 'California style' dub thrown in--they have even got a sax player nicknamed 'Rico'--with a little luck and hard work it is easy to see them enjoying the success of the E. Beat, The Specials, or Bad Manners.
--D Cool

BUNNY WAILER Sings The Wailers (Mango LPS 9629)--The big news this month is the return of Bunny Wailer, the most mysterious and least commercial member of The Wailers, the band which gave us Bob Marley and Peter Tosh. Bunny's latest effort is a tribute to the original Wailers sound, the sweet soul music that made them as many critics have said, 'the Beatles of Jamaica.' The emphasis is on music Bunny himself wrote (when he was known as Neville Livingstone)--tunes like the beautiful 'Dancing Shoes,' 'Burial,' (a better version than on his Blackheart Man LP) and the defiant 'Walk The Proud Land.' Also included is 'Hypocrit,' a tune written by Wailer influence Percy Mayfield, and a dub heavy interpretation of Peter Tosh's 'I'm The Toughest' that blows Tosh's version out of the water. If you are a Wailers fan who thinks reggae music began with 'Natty Dread,' you owe it to yourself to check out Bunny Wailer Sings The Wailers. For a taste of Bunny's contemporary sound, try the Protest LP.
--D Cool

# Reggae Reviews

**THE EQUATORS** Baby Come Back/Version (Stiff: BUY-IT 95)--This is a new group for me. The song is by Eddie Grant, who also produced this 12-inch English release. The first thing you notice on listening is the straight rhythm guitar and keyboards which sets the beat along with the bass drum. Secondary rhythms are created by the bouncing bass and cymbals. The vocals glide along nicely. These things are what you hear on the original cut. The version side is a really enjoyable echo excursion. Both move along in the up tempo tradition of real rockers. It is an easy record to continually play and get a charge from. --WB

**MIKEY DREAD** The Jumping Master/Break Down The Wall Dread at The Controls: DREAD 1)--These two cuts are the openers on the World War III recent release. They are a good choice for single releases as they capture the new intensity of sound of today's Dread. Both cuts are in the fine tradition of Mikey Dread. Each has the dub tag at the end, something which adds quite a bit of meat to the feast. 'The Jumping Master' lists some of the great masters of reggae production. I did not catch that until a few plays. The song is really captivating. 'Break Down The Wall' is a plea for unity in breaking down the walls of Babylon that surround and separate us. Such thoughts are part of Mikey Dread's message to the people. The thing that makes this 12-incher valuable are the dub cuts--an area that has always shone brightly from the Dread at the Controls. --WB

**THE SELECTER** Celebrate The Bullet/Last Tango In Dub (Chrysalis: CHS S2)--The first release since leaving Two Tone and changing the bass and keyboard players shows The Selecter as powerful as ever with a new twist. 'Celebrate The Bullet' is a fine display of Pauline Black's vocal style. The use of a minor key riff of the guitar, along with the horn section, provides additional imagery not associated with the ska/dance usual. 'Last Tango In Dub' has that spacey blue beat influence with an exceptional mix. The Selecter prove once again that there is more to their music than explained through terms of calypso dance. It looks like they have become stronger and not locked into a dated mold. --WB

**MADNESS** The Nutty Boys In The Return of The Los Palmas 7 (Stiff: BUY-IT 108)--The latest single comes on a 12-inch with four songs. The title cut is a lengthy instrumental with a Latin flair. It is followed by 'My Girl.' The B-side starts with 'That's The Way To Do It,' a nice new tune. 'Swan Lake' ends this release in a live version taken from the 'Dance Craze' movie which is not on the soundtrack Lp. Not bad at all. --WB

AUGUSTUS PABLO Rockers meet King Tubbys in a Firehouse (Shanachie 43001)--These people seem to meet everywhere. This time they are down at the firehouse. Maybe that is a good place since some of these cuts really start burning. This release is a classic dub production. There are no vocals. Augustus Pablo supplies the keyboards and in many cases one cannot hear his presence, although it is felt. The bass and drums create an atmosphere that makes you feel like being in a cave surrounded by strange walls and barriers. The guitars float like bats zipping past.

DANCE CRAZE Various Artists (Chrysalis: CHR 1299)--The soundtrack from the movie Dance Craze is a documentation on the Two Tone-ska movement. This release is destined to be the top compilation of the year. There are three songs each by The Specials, The Selecter, The Beat, and Madness, plus two by Bad Manners and one by The Bodysnatchers. Since these are all recorded live, each song is different from the earlier studio versions which have fed the ska-starved. Instead of spending a fortune buying all these groups' records, you can go out and for five or six bucks buy this 5-song collection. That is our money saving tip. But if you do not have many of the ska releases, this one will probably result in spending more to get them. The Specials open with an energized 'Concrete Jungle' and end with 'Nite Klub,' which has a jazzy blues intro, just like you were in one of those sleazy laid-back joints.

Walt Taylor, editor of Top Rankin', has written to fill in some gaps in our knowledge of Blacka Morwell in response to last issue's dub album review. He writes, "Blacka Morwell a/k/a Morwell Esq. a/k/a M. Wellington is one of the true Madmen of Dub Production. He produced the relentlessly crazy 'Humble One' LP for Jah Lloyd, and also has produced Ranking Joe among others, and his own vocal group 'The Morwells.' The Morwells have an excellent LP called Cool Running that is a really rough-hewn roots gem. I have a single on the 'Sir Jessos' label called 'Don Morwell' by The Morwells b/w 'The Killer-Bass and Drums' that is one of my all-time favorites."

# Interview: The Blue Riddim Band

Talk Talk: Let us start by finding out what the band has been doing and the story on the album.

Robert Zohn: We have been in Chicago and playing around. We were playing in Minneapolis and have gotten a pretty good toe-hold there. We played in a little place there called The Seventh Street Entry, which is kind of a little new wave club with graffiti written walls in a cellar dungeon. It is right next to Sam's, a big joint there. It has taken about four times there to finally break that town. Next time we are going into Sam's, which is a huge nightclub.

TT: How soon will that be?

RZ: Whenever we get back there. Probably late spring or early summer. At Madison, Wisconsin, we finally got to be headlining at Merlins. It took us a few times. But we have mainly been breaking in areas. Being in Chicago, our New York thing got thwarted. We had the Tramps gig booked there. They had the ads out and everything. We had Ones booked. When we got done with this whole last tour, we could not afford to go to New York. We did not even have the gas money, plain and simple. So, the next week we just made use of the time by going into the studio. We had a week off and got the studio dates. We had Prince Jammy come in. We found him in New York.

TT: What was he doing?

RZ: He was in New York doing some kind of business. He has a friend in Kansas City and Duck (the drummer) was able to run him down and got him to come to Chicago and mix the album and to have his vibe there. He added an awful lot as far as the . . . He sang back up on one of the cuts. He is on 'Restless Spirit' singing backup harmony.

He had a lot of ideas like 'let's put a piano here, let's do this here, let's do that.' It really figured into the thing. We left and it was mixed when we left. My wife

Blue Riddim Band: Howard Yucon, guitar; Scott Korchak, trumpet; Andy Meyer, bass; and Jack Blackett, saxophone.

*Robert Zohn, guitar;*
*Pat Pierce, keyboards*
*Howard Yucon, guitar;*
*Scott Korchak, trumpet.*

stayed and Jammy and Freddie Brightberg, the main engineer. He engineered the first four cuts we did at Curton. All of it was recorded at Curton--Curtis Mayfield's studio. A lot of Alligator (Records) stuff is done there. It all started with us doing the Lonnie Brooks time. And then Flying Fish became interested. It was Flying Fish and Alligator and we did not know which it was going to be. Then Bruce from Alligator was kind of hesitant. It could be because he does not have any white acts. I do not think he wanted to buck tradition with his label. We ended up going with Flying Fish because they were ready, willing, and able and they had booked us some time and gave us a budget and we went in and did it. We did six more tunes. We are using all six--a total of nine of the ten on the album. We are really just waiting on the artwork now. We are looking at April 1 or possibly March 15 if we get it done in time. We might have it out early.

TT: Is there going to be a tour with the album?

RZ: I guess it is beginning now. There has been some talk about us going on tour with Black Slate. We do not know when they are getting here. Since they are on Alligator, and Alligator is still interested in The Blue Riddim Band, they just did not want to spend any money on it. We might go to New York, play about seven dates there, then hook up with Black Slate and do about 35 one-nighters around the country. So, we might be doing that around April, but it is almost a rumor now until those guys get something concrete down like when they will get over here. As it stands now, we are going to a bunch of places in Texas. And then our plan is to stay south . . . go through Alabama and go to Florida for the Easter vacation. So, we are trying to get down there and be perched on the East Coast when the record comes out and go to New York. They want us in Chicago for a week when the record comes out. I do not know if that all is going to firm up or not. We are trying to cover ground and break as much territory as possible instead of just running a tour.

TT: What is the lineup on the album?

RZ: Well, we did not really switch anything. Andy is playing bass on everything. Drew put trombone on a couple of tunes we don't usually have trombone on. There are some extra things we don't have live usually. There is pianabout five tracks and synthesizer on one song. There will be two long versions of original tunes, 'Cuss Cuss' and 'One Love, One Heart' or 'Rocket Sisters,' as it stands now. We will have the

# Interview: Blue Riddim

dub tag on the end which Prince Jammy did. The rest is all kind of sweet, positive, upbound, with the exception of 'Cuss Cuss' and 'Restless Spirit,' which are both in a minor key and bluesy. We wanted something mean in there because the whole thing was coming off real sweet. It is pretty representative of what we do and pretty modern as far as reggae goes. It is a pretty honest album. I feel good about it. It will get to a lot of people. I think we came up with something a little more asessable and a stronger identity and a better focus than the Mango thing would have been We haven't done any calypso here. There are two ska tunes, 'Twisting the Night Away' and 'The Jokes On You.' Everything else is reggae.

TT: What do you label the band as playing?

RZ: Rock and soul reggae. Or rock reggae soul music. We kind of let it go where we have gotten a little more funkier. A little more than the Jamaican or West Indian stuff we play. We kind of jam out a little occasionally. We have played the songs so much that instead of just going through the motions we try to find new ways to interpret them without wrecking the roots. I think we have gotten a lot more r&b influence in the band. James Brown, we occasionally play one of those tunes. To get our funk off, we almost have to play it in the context of reggae. It is integrating more with some of the drum beats. Reggae music is played with more open drums today. Instead of the closed stick and the knock. This has opened the door for us.

TT: You have been playing around to a lot of different audiences and areas. What sort of reaction do you get as white musicians playing reggae? Or do they consider it more of a blend of reggae, soul, and rock?

RZ: I wonder, really. When we are playing in an area, there is usually someone there from somewhere else. So, if you are playing in Indiana and thinking well what do these people know and you hear someone from Washington, D.C. say, 'this band is unbelievable.' I don't think that people know that they are not hearing just reggae. I don't think that they stop and think that there is a lot of other elements. They are just responding to it and maybe not knowing why. But we are not making a big deal about us being a white reggae band. I know we have been having a lot better response than some of the black reggae bands. I mean there are those who like to hear black people play reggae. To them, this is credibility, when they see a black face and dreadlocks. We don't even have our black percussionist, David Lawrence, anymore. In a way, we miss the repeater and Jamaican percussion. I think what is important is that we have guys who really like reggae music and my theory for the past ten years has been that for reggae to be successful you need to have white people seeing white people play it and seeing them play it honestly and with some reverence and rock it a little bit--that would open the door and I think that it has. I know that in certain areas where reggae is big they are dying for it. People want to see it. I think it makes it easier to get to because we are not Rastafarians and there is not this doctrine and rhetoric coming down even though this is spiritual music. We are not playing on that so much. Rather let's have a good time, let's enjoy ourselves, let's live right. We do not play anything that is really evil, just a positive experience--reggae rock gospel music. I think the white thing has probably helped us. I have heard people say that we are lucky to be white and doing this because there are not many white reggae bands in this world. I feel lucky and glad that I am a white reggae musician. If I was a black one, I would probably be playing new wave.

TT: The Blue Riddim Band seems to be the one opening up new channels. Do you think there will be more bands in the future?

RZ: Yes. Everywhere we go, we hear that there is a band here, a band there, they keep popping up. There are more white bands playing reggae, even if it be something like The Selecter or The Specials.

TT: Whatever happened to your plans to get to Jamaica?

RZ: Well, once again, if we couldn't get to New York, how could we finance going to Jamaica? We are talking about going down there in summer. We always talk about going about six months later. So possibly, if we get some type of reaction out of this (the forthcoming LP) here, I think, since we are kind of connected now with Prince Jammy and he wants to

*Scott Korchak, trumpet;
Steve McLane, drums;
Jack Blackett, saxophone.*

do a dub album, we could wind up working with him in a number of places. I personally feel we could do as good of tracks in New York as in Jamaica, as long as you have the engineer there and he knows what he is doing. Even though it probably would sound better in Jamaica. But if we have Prince Jammy we could go do it in Kansas City. I think the atmosphere is real important. But we are about due to go down there. It is a question of finances. If we get down to Florida we might be able to pull off a trip if we have a good week. Right now it is a semi-massive undertaking. We would have to have quite a few bucks in order to go down there and live. Because we cannot work there. We could not make any money, I think. So we would have to finance the trip for about ten people.

TT: Do you have anything lined up with Prince Jammy?

RZ: As of right now, he has been talking about doing something in April. In April would be the first time we could work on this dub album. So we have to work out the fine points, I guess. Let this first album come out and let the dub album kind of eek out. We don't know what kind of arrangements we can make. It will probably remain an independent. If Jammy can get the time to do a dub album, we will have it. Probably have to do another couple of tracks. He was going to be here for these gigs. But he had a death in the family and he wound up not coming. We were half counting on getting some versions here. But that did not pan out. We are in touch with the guy, though. We definitely want to get some stuff in dub. To tide us over we will have those two cuts on the album so everyone gets a little sample.

## Small Labels, Independents, and more.

Tot Rocket and The Twins have their second release, a four-song 7-incher, available now. They are a New England-based four-piece with several years of experience. Their recordings are upbeat rock and roll that move along briskly--not fast or rushed, just brisk. At times, like on 'Employment Line,' the vocals resemble Tom Robinson in tone. They have a clean sound that is well polished. Write to them at P O Box 3483, Grand Central Station, New York, NY, 10017.

From Virginia comes an experimental single by Zack Swagger. 'Empty Highways' uses sounds recorded driving down the road. He is working on new material entitled 'Standard Appliance.' Write to him at Box 7332, Arlington, VA, 22207.

From Des Moines, Iowa, comes news of The Law. They have recently released a four-song EP entitled 'King Size Cigarettes plus three other Big Hits.' They claim to be out basically for fun, with their shows being big dance parties. Fighting apathy, they recently staged a showcase night called 'Music For No-Man's Land,' which was not as successful as planned. The five guys in this band are young and their songs rough, while having a smoothness that keeps you listening. 'Hole In My Heart' is the standout. Available from Fly Girl Records (2313 33rd. Street, Des Moines, IA 50310).

Gulcher Records (Box 1635, Bloomington, IN 47402) has a puzzling release by a group named The Panic. This three-song EP was recorded half a year ago and their info says they had been together four months before disbanding. So do they exist today? I do not think so but since these four are in their teens, this record is probably just the beginning of their various careers. And, hopefully, they will get better. Even while covering a Gizmos tune (another biggy on Gulcher) the rawness is close to being too much to handle.

TAPE 1--featuring Information, Mofungo, and Blinding Headache--I could come on spouting Beefheart and Ubu all over these recordings out of NYC, but that would not be fair. Sure, they take their cues from the aforementioned sources but these bands (they all share members to some extent) are no mere imitators. This is a one-hour cassette of listenable, experimental sounds that are never weird just for the sake of weirdness like so many avant-garde bands these days. The songs are generally short and their textures are varied. You would do well to hear it yourself and I am not loaning out my copy. Try to get one yourself from Information member Chris Nelson, 259 East 10th, No. 7, New York, NY, 10009, only $2.50.

# News and Views

*For the last year, the main weekend club in Kansas City has been at 47th and Troost. For various reasons, the spot has moved to the corner bar, The Music Box. Some-thing-Tu-Du Productions, operated by Craig and Pam Travitts, have been the two who have arranged for new bands to play and the crowds to enjoy the music. The new club has plans to remodel the basement, which will hold around 400 people. In the meantime, shows are being performed upstairs. Last weekend The Clean played along with Home Improvements.*

*A major plus is that since The Music Box has a food license, all ages are admitted. No longer will the under-21 crowd be excluded from enjoying some of the best bands. Although a great deal of the plan is yet to be implemented regarding the basement opening, this is surely a positive sign.*

*In case you did not know, Off The Wall Hall has changed their programming to be new wave and reggae. No more bluegrass or country.*

Let us talk about the recording industry with all the built-in support systems for dinosaurs and executives. A great deal of blame for the near-collapse of the industry which exists today is placed on the 'home-tapers' or those who buy blank tape and then record from borrowed records or from the radio. In England, the situation is such a severe problem that a special surcharge tax, to pay for lost royalties, is being pushed for immediate law. The legalities of the issue have yet to be established. A bit of a boring subject, you say? Well, to add a little life to the matter, Island Records has released a series of cassette tapes with an album on one side and blank tape on the other side so you can use their tape to record something else. An interesting market deploy. Island's 'One Plus One' series has included some Bob Marley and The Wailers albums on their initial conquest.

# Live:

**Oingo Boingo**
**January 30**
**Whiskey A Go-Go**

Once known as 'The Mystic Knights of Oingo Boingo', they have shortened their name, and expaned their set to the point where they need a full-time roadie to shift the various instruments they play. A debut EP containing four poppy tunes is good and exciting, but does not match what this offbeat crew does live. The eight-man lineup consists of a three-piece horn sectioncomprised of what look like stereotype grade school band teachers; flat tops, skinny ties, Casper Milquetoast-look. They also double on congas, chimes, cymbals, and keyboards. The rhythm section has the standard guitar/bass/drums/keyboards line, and singer Danny Elfman rounds out the band with his vocal ability reminiscent of old Devo. The horns are staccato, the drums anywhere but on a regular beat, the guitars meander around all points of the scale and the synthis buzz. The opener was a rousing version of 'Auld Lang Syne,' followed by mostly new material and yet another version (though unrecognizable) of the Kinks 'You Really Got Me.' Oingo Boingo are heart machines gone mad, a bet that is out of control. Unfortunately, they are headed for commercial success. See them before it happens.
–The Gill Man

**Jon and The Nightriders/ The Blasters**
**January ll**
**Whiskey A Go-Go**

Surf met rockabilly for a frantic night of pure rock and roll. The Nightriders took the stage and Jon Blair, the group's leader, said, 'Back in the 60's, dance bands used to play instrumentals. Here's a few.' They launched into 'Mr. Moto' and followed that with most of their LP, 'Surf Beat '80.' Their renditions of 'Walk, Don't Run,' and 'Hawaii Five-O,' rivaled the guitar work of Bogle and Tyalor from The Ventures (who, incidentally, are performing again after ten years of silence). Visually, however, they were somewhat dull. Blair had on a blue Nehru jacket and the rhythm player had an authentic Mosrite Ventures guitar, but that did not make up for the fat that the bassist resembled a Molly Hatchet refugee. Nonetheless, some very impressive guitarwork from Blair, illustrating a style that is seldom used anymore, but difficult to master just the same. Most of the crowd (a strange one at that) came for The Blasters. Resembling a cross between an aging biker gang and a bunch of haggard cowboys, we heard a lot of standards from these guys. Several Elmore James, Carl Perkins, and some songs closer to c/w. The appeal to a diverse audience, but were very hot and accomplished musicians. They closed their set with a knee-slapper, 'Marie, Marie,' a cout from the Teenage Cruisers soundtrack, a great rockabilly sampler. They put down their No-Namo guitars and left the crowd wanting more. A jumpin' night at the Whiskey.
–The Gill Man

*One of the local rockers, Dave Stuckey, is seen accompanying Abuse on a few tunes. Besides being a member of The Regular Guys and The Go-Cats, Dave can be found guesting with The Debs and others.*

*The Regular Guys: Brad Reid, Dave Stuckey, John Chiarello, and John Odell.*

# Interview: Abuse

Talk Talk: How did Abuse form? How did you meet each other?

Clay: I was Mr. College. He had hair down his back and I had short hair. I was a waiter and was walking through the kitchen.

Chris: I was making something one day and this character walks by wearing a little bowtie and a gangster suit and says, 'Man, what are you making? That looks bad. Let me taste some of that.'

Clay: It was a nightclub where the waiters had to dress up in costumes.

Chris: Later I heard him talk about a concert he had been to. We started talking about guitars and found out we both had the same type. That same night we decided to get together and jam. →

C. LUCAS

Vol. 3 No. 2

# FRESH FLEXI 001

B. RICH

FRESH RECORDS BOX 36, LAWRENCE, KANSAS 66044 USA

FRESH FLEX 00I

Release date: March 1981

Artist: Abuse

Titles: No Money, In America, Love Is Alright

Speed: 33 1/3 rpm

Size: 7 inches square

Color: Black vinyl

Willie McNeil--Drums, vocals Army brat born in Germany. Started playing drums in 4th grade. Lived all over, in Topeka last five years. Graduated from high school last year, works in a record store. 18 years old.

Clay Galbraith--Bass, vocals Born in LA, moved to Topeka. Moved to Las Vegas. After high school, returned to Topeka. Gambling spirit. 22 years old.

Chris Garner--Guitar, vocals Born in Wichita. Moved to Topeka when 10. Went to boarding schools and subsequently ran away for several years. 20 years old.

# Interview Abuse

And so Abuse started to form in late 1978. The next year Chris and Clay practiced a lot and tried to find a drummer. After a few different drummers failed to hit it off, they heard about Willie.

Willie: We kinda met and at first we did not have any style at all. Chris played a Marshall at about 10 and that was about all I could hear. And Clay played bass and sang real high without any control at all. Then all of a sudden things just fell together.

Chris: Willie used to come in. He is a real fancy drummer. We played these songs and he hit all these drums all the time.

Willie: So you decided to stick with me. Plus I could sing.

Clay: And you drove a Cadillac so we figured you had to be cool.

Willie: The only thing I had to haul my drums with was my mom's car.

Chris: We pulled up to our first gig and parked it next to the stage.

Clay: Early on, we did not play, just practiced a lot. Then we got serious.

Chris: We set up goals of where to play around.

Willie: In March we played at a big show in Topeka. And then we played at The Downliner. That was the first time it really freaked me out. All these people hanging out in leather. I did not know what was going on. We stayed at Dave's house of Rock Therapy. He had a bunch of parties. We played around the next few months and started building up our name, getting into bigger places. Now we have a much better idea of what we are doing.

Chris: The whole time we had done it on a little pawn-shop PA system. We did not know anything about lights or anything, about actually setting up a show. Now we know a lot more.

## Album Reviews

THE NEW AGE STEPPERS The New Age Steppers (On-U: LP 1)--The New Age Steppers are basically The Slits plus friends. The album has many types of songs on it. At first I liked it, then later I was not too impressed. But now I think it is quite good. It starts off with the strongest cut, previously released as a Rough Trade single, 'Fade Away.' The next cuts are electronical or something. Then a Pop Group sounding song with vocalist Mark Stewart closes the side. In addition to Bruce Smith, four other drummers are credited with playing on the album. So it is a little hard to identify everything. Side Two is more basic dub and gimmickry that is enjoyable tones. The star of the album is Steve Beresford, keyboards. I would not be surprised if The New Age Steppers replace The Slits as the operating organization for their future activities. --WB

LEWIS AND GILBERT 3RA (4AD Records: CHD 16)--
Lewis and Gilbert have really mastered the art of using tapes and studio facilities. Side One with 'Barge Calm' and '3.4 . . .' give you the most incredible feeling of machinery, like large metal objects clanking endlessly. They glorify the machine image with sound, much like the sounds David Lynch created for his movie, 'Eraserhead.' Lewis and Gilbert have taken a tremendous step forward in creating imaginative images through sound. I have never heard anything so visual as this. Side Two with 'Barge Calm (Part II)' and 'R' gives you an ethereal feeling of detachment from conventional space and time. When you listen to 'R' you should feel nothingness like one hand clapping. It is obvious that Lewis and Gilbert (members of Wire) are looking forward in their music rather than backwards. Even the art they use for their cover is minimal in concept and explains the contents very well. If you are not a conceptualist, you might not like this record. --V2

THOMAS LEER AND ROBERT RENTAL The Bridge (Industrial Records, Ltd., 1979)--This album was recorded on two eight-track tape machines provided by Industrial Records, owned by T. G. It is interesting because they use domestic appliances for sounds which are intrinsic to the music. But do not get me wrong--this album is not noise. Having been recorded at their home, they have captured everyday sounds and processed them for their own needs, like taking a found object and using it for a collage. Side One has vocals with some experienced synthesizer work on songs like 'Attack Decay' and 'Fade Away.' Most percussion is created by rhythm generators and tape recorded sounds. Side Two uses mostly tape loops which sound a bit like Fripp and Eno's first album, Evening Star, having a flowing ambience. This album is pleasing and can sorely be listened to more than once. Leer and Rental are to me another step forward into the future of Industrial Music. More Industrial Music for industrial people. --V2

DER PLAN Geri Reig (Warning Records: Warning 003)--Another band from Dusseldorf, the same locale as DAF, makes it onto vinyl. In fact, one of the members of Der Plan, Pyrolator, was an original member of DAF. The similarities between these two bands end here. Der Plan, in case you have not deciphered the meaning, translates to THE PLAN. What is it? Their credo is to make the most with the least; to use ingenuity, no synths, no hi-tech in any form. All that is needed for 'Geri Reig' is the mental facilities to create. Yet, they hardly conform to their own maxims as synths and electronix abound on this Lp. But in the spirit of PLUS ULTRA, Der Plan takes the necessary steps to be different in the utilization of their instruments. In a way, they are very similar to the d-d-movement of the early 20th. There are quite a few terms I could employ in the description of what Der Plan is and what their purpose is. But in an attempt at not being arty-farty, I will simply allude to them. Their music does possess a ready-made quality to it, once again demonstrating a link to -a-a. By this I mean, the easy accessibility that ideas can be obtained and used. This Lp deals with all manner of current topics: world revolution, urban terrorism, religion, love, medicine, etc. The way in which these subjects are handled brings to mind both ab..rdist principles and ex..ten....ism. Each of the 15 songs evokes a fearful ambiguity. You are never really sure how to react to this music. Whether one should laugh along with the chipmunk voices that say the world is terrible or cry for the forlorn Hans, who becomes a mass murdering general-field marshall for the sake of lost love. And what about all of you dangerous clowns strolling along out there? What is behind the mask? What is in your balloon-heads? Nitrous or Zyklon-B? After listening to this disc, you begin to wonder about the sanctity of the herd; about the violence that lies just below the surface. We are all potentially dangerous and Der Plan are making use of this. --U-Man

MAGAZINE Play (Virgin: V2184)--Here we have an excellent sounding Lp of live material from Magazine. It was recorded on 9/6/80 in Melbourne, Australia, and is basically a 'greatest hits' record, as the material is taken from their three previous Lps and singles. Besides that is the way most concerts are anyway, they hit you with familiars. John McGeoch's replacement, Robin Simon, is the featured guitarist. This is the last recording of Magazine with Robin Simon. He has since left the band. Howard Devoto is caught at his wittiest, as he introduces most of the songs with a thought or two. My personal favoriate is 'Model Worker,' as Devoto changes, 'I know that Carter will look after me,' for 'I know that Reagan will look after me.' He must have some foresight. Devoto even throws in a little French to further impress us in 'The Light Pours Out of Me.' An even extra bonus is the unidentified saxophone on 'Twenty Years Ago.' This Lp is a must for Magazine subscribers. A definite state-of-the-art live recording. --U-Man

*Get Smart:
Lisa Wertman, bass;
Frank Loose, drums,
and Marc Koch, guitar.*

*Drum drum boys--
Frank Loose
of Get Smart
and Bill McMillian
of Hitler Youth*

*The Youth: Bill Mauer, guitar; Bill McMillian, drums; Mike Cahill, vocals; and Kevin Ink, guitar.*

# Album Reviews

**ADAM AND THE ANTS Kings of the Wild Frontier (EPIC: NJE 37033)**--The third album by Adam but the first with The New Ants lineup. You remember Malcolm McLaren became their manager last year then dumped Adam, while keeping the others in the band and using their tunes with a female singer as Bow Wow Wow. At one point, Adam told the ex-Ants that he was still going to use the new material they had developed. Subsequently, there are similarities in the two bands, most noticeably the snare drum rolls. Adam and The Ants have been around since 1977 but this album has proved to be the most successful effort so far. Released in November as an import and in February as a domestic, this record became number one in the charts and three top ten singles have been drawn out--'Ant Music,' 'Dog Eat Dog,' and 'King of the Wild Frontier.' Always fashion oriented, Adam's current dress takes in elements of early colonialism and Indian regalia. The audiences love the shows and the press labels him New Artist of 1981. So that is what Ant-mania is about. --SK

**BLACK FLAG Jealous Again (SST Records: SST003)**--A major release for these West Coast faves. Black Flag are known for their wall of noise presentations, which are often accompanied by some form of destruction. But a lot of the violence at gigs is due to other factors, not withstanding the attitude of the audience. It had looked like Black Flag would play in the area when they were on their 'Creepy Crawl' tour in December. Although it did not occur, chances are good that they soon will. Now, once you listen to their latest release, you might not really want to see them. Granted, this type of music is not for everyone. The 12-incher contains six songs, all of which zoom by too fast. Side A is over before you can hardly turn around. I guess after all this time, I expected more length and more meat. It seems that they have not quite reached a point of reflecting their energy on vinyl as well as live. It should be interesting to see what will happen next. --SK

**THE ZANTEES Out For Kicks (BOMP Records: BLP 4009)**--Now these guys have the right idea! This New York-based quintet are currently the only ones in the whole batch of so-called rockabilly revivalists (except maybe Billy Zoom) that have captured the spirit of the original genre. Plenty of howlin' vocals and up-front drums. And heck, out of the 13 songs here, eight of them were penned by guitarist Paul Statile. Most importantly, the whole thing was obviously recorded in the spirit that no matter how solid the playing got, it might fall apart at any second. (This release, coupled with the new Stiv Bators and Jon and the Nightriders' LPs, shows that BOMP is once again on its feet and a contender.) Ray Campi, eat your heart out. --Stuck

CIRCLE JERKS Group Sex (Frontier: FLP 1002)--Their title is the most titallating aspect about this new band. The novelty soon vanishes and one is left to associate the album's intensity with their beat and not words. Vocalist Keith Morris left as singer for Black Flag after their first single and formed this band with guitarist Greg Hetson, bassist Roger Rogerson, and drummer Lucky Lehrer. The two bands have similar sounds and some sort of rivalry which carries on down to their audiences. I think the Circle Jerks are one of the best bands to come out of LA. (Of course, The Dead Kennedys are the top West Coast band.) This album contains 14 cuts, ome of which are very short. How do they play so fast? One interesting note on the hostility felt by Black Flag. One cut: 'Don't Care' was actually a Black Flag song which surfaced as 'You Bet We Got Something Against You,' tagged onto their Jealous Again EP. They have made quite a big deal of this incident but The Circle Jerks seem to maintain their coolness and aloofness. For a taste of what is happening today, listen to this. --SK

IAN DURY AND THE BLOCKHEADS Laughter (Stiff SEEZ 30)--Hooray: Ian Dury is back from self-imposed disco exile. The ugly little Brit you love to feel sorry for has compensated for the loss of his band's music director, Chaz Jankel, and produced an album much closer in feel to the '77 classic 'New Boots and Panties' than 79's funk-infected 'Do It Yourself.' Not that funk is out of the scene all together. The opener, 'Superman's Big Sister,' is funky enough. It is done with a humor and rollicking style that was not always evident on the DIY album. Jankel's absence forced Dury to add some random sounds like a string section or Don Cherry's trumpet here and there. Guitarist Wilko Johnson fits in well with a new, light-fingered touch and reedman Davey Pane is a definite plus. We are treated to the drunken, raging sort of 'Uncool-ohol' and a bunch of yobbos singing much too loudly at a bar in another one. 'Over The Points' is a jittery ride through the English countryside with Dury the conductor. That is what I like best about his records, they are like a trip to the Britain of movies and books, led by a foulmouthed Tiny Tim. --RH

# Single Reviews

SAN FRANCISCO UNDERGROUND NO. 2 (Subterranean Records: SUB 10)--Four songs by four bands brings us up to date on the SF scene. The Spikes open with 'Life Is Hell.' It sounds like it. Lewd's 'Mobile Home' shows more enthusiasm and style remin cent of 999. 'Title Role' by Society Dog is the fastest paced, guitarwise, of all but not too memorable. Undead try to build a song around 'Hitler's Brain' being in a jar in the USSR. They change pace quite a bit but seem to get back into the flow of things. Overall, a nice release from Subterranean.
--HT

CRISPY AMBULANCE Not What I Expected/Deaf (Aural Assault: FAC 32)--There are a lot of bands that either try to imitate or derive inspiration from Joy Division. This is one of them. A debut single by a relatively good band. The A-side is very JD sounding, using basically the same sort of phrases and sounds to create a melancholy atmosphere. The vocalist croons in a somewhat familiar tone as he sings about something that is 'unsightly and serene.' The other side is a bit weaker and sounds an awful lot like Brian Brain, albeit in a serious manner.
--U-Man

CRASS Nagasaki Nightmare/Big A Little A (Crass Records: 421984)--I was very surprised to find myself liking this record. Although the Crass fans are numerous, their rough style and anarchial attitudes put a lot of people off. Is this their attempt at crossover or have they just progressed to a higher quality of music? The lyrical message is the same as always so the main thing different is that the listener can enjoy what he hears. I have thought for a while that if Crass could pull off what they do on this release, they will soon fill in the existing gaps in the music world left by early punk bands. Crass are going straight up. --HT

THE STRANGLERS Thrown Away/Top Secret (Liberty Records)--This is the latest single release by The Strangers. Side One, 'Thrown Away,' sounds almost discoish with the keyboards cooled down a little. It is still evident though that these are the Stranglers. They have not died yet. They all seem to have mellowed a little. This single is not as heavy as their earlier material. Side Two, 'Top Secret,' is a very good tune, very mechanical, like their earlier songs from their most recent album, The Raven. I am pleased with this single because The Stranglers have not lost their songwriting ability. If you enjoyed their earlier work, you are sure to like this one. --V2

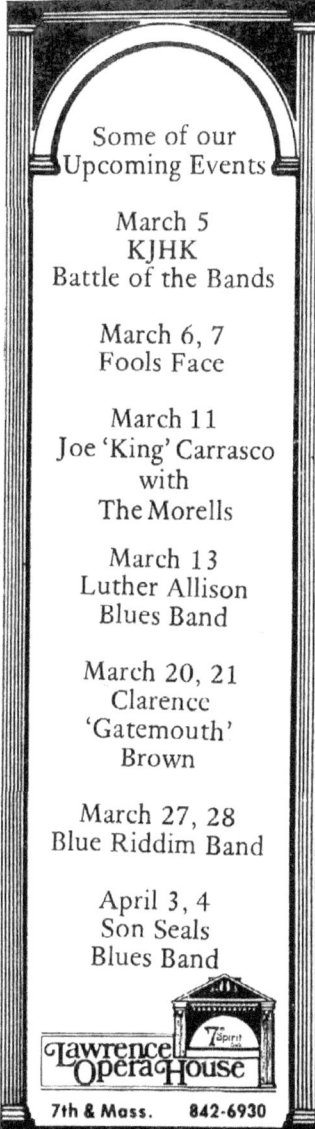

Some of our Upcoming Events

March 5
KJHK
Battle of the Bands

March 6, 7
Fools Face

March 11
Joe 'King' Carrasco
with
The Morells

March 13
Luther Allison
Blues Band

March 20, 21
Clarence
'Gatemouth'
Brown

March 27, 28
Blue Riddim Band

April 3, 4
Son Seals
Blues Band

Lawrence Opera House

7th & Mass.   842-6930

# Print

A couple of months ago, those busy-bodies at One Ten Records (110 Chambers Street, NY, 10007) released their long worked on directory of records, labels, distributors, stores, publications, clubs, and radio stations. The orientation is towards punk-related concerns or new wave, if you wish. A few years in the making, Volumne is the most complete and interesting book on the scene. You can look up records and groups to check their lineup or releases. You can get addresses of distributors and small labels. You can check out an area to find a good club or radio station. And you can get information on fanzines, including Talk Talk. But even if they had not mentioned us, this book still deserves a rave review. Concerning their faults: of course seomthing as massive as this would have some outdated information. Specifically, if you plan to go to city X and check out the listings for it, there is a chance that the best clubs changed or a new hot spot has developed. One-Ten knows this and asks for updates to be sent to them. They plan trelease Volumne II in September. So check it out, write them a letter and help Volumne become more of a phenomenon. You should be able to buy this at your favorite bookstore or record shop. If not, ask them to order it. The retail price is $8.00--maybe a bit steep, but remember that this book was done by noncorporate interests who have gathered together more facts than any others have ever assembled, especially anything related to new music.

If you want a coffee table book, check out

---

Off The Wall Hall
March 3--Sunflower Alliance Benefit
March 5--ERA Benefit
March 6, 7--The Embarrassment
March 12--The Morells
March 13--Nightshift
March 14--Regular Guys w/ Get Smart
March 20, 21--Abuse
March 27, 28-The Tony Brown Reggae Band
April 1--April Fools Costume Ball w/ Thumbs
April 4--Grassroots Art Association Benefit
April 9--Banastre Tarleton
April 10, 11--The Dog People
April 24, 15--Gypsy Fari Reggae Band

OFF THE WALL HALL
737 New Hampshire
(913) 841-2266
In downtown Lawrence

Off The Wall Hall can accommodate your party. We also have affordable rehearsal space for bands. We book many bands from the tapes we receive. If your band has a demo we would like to hear it. Please send demos to Post Office Box 91, Lawrence, KS, 66044.

The Rock Yearbook 1981 (Grove Press, $12.00). It is a thick glossy covering the rock scene (which means there are numerous mentions of the hit makers) from late 1979 to mid-1980. There are some good photos and articles with some new perspectives on the music business. If it was not good, it would not be mentioned.

There was a movement, now defunct in San Francisco, which tried to establish a nationwide communication system. They put out a few issues entitled New Youth Productions. Their original idea, I guess, was to develop a network which would assist bands traveling across the continent to find clubs and areas where they could play--basically to help strangers who had common musical interests to work together. They eventually stopped their efforts. But the same kind of information is in Volumne. The only way this type of communication can be furthered is if all those interested help out. A few years ago, the Copeland brothers shocked the established corporate moguls by setting up a network of clubs, radio stations, and involved people by asking and digging for information and trying out their new contacts. The result of this has been the emergence of Frontier Booking International and The International Record Syndicate as the tops in their fields.

We all have benefitted from their discoveries and development. It can happen--the people do have some power. While I am not advocating total anarchy, I do want to stress that we control our destiny.

On Sundays

Tune Your Radio to FM-91-KJHK

'The Soul Shakedown Party' with Jim 'Daddy Cool' Schwada
Reggae 4-7 p.m.

'The Rebellious Jukebox' with Marc 'U-Man' Burch
10 p.m.-2 a.m.

'The Death Disco' with Rick 'V-2' Schneider
2-6 a.m.

Brought to you in part by Talk Talk Publications

KJHK, 217 Flint Hall, University of Kansas, Lawrence, Kansas, 66044, USA

# Talk-Talk Publications

P.O. Box 36  Lawrence, Kansas 66044

Back Issues Still Available
Vol. 1 Compilation--Early record reviews, Interviews with Miles Copeland, Brian James, Fashion, Ultravox
Vol. 2 No. 1--London Calling, Metal Box, Ultravox photos
Vol. 2 No. 2--Reggae special, Local record stores, Thumbs photos
Vol. 2 No. 3--XTC interview
Vol. 2 No. 4--Clash, Iggy Pop, Jam, Madness, XTC photos
Vol. 2 No. 5--Singles Special, 999, The Dickies, Iggy Pop photos
Vol. 2 No. 6--Summer Mini-Issue, Regular Guys feature
Vol. 2 No. 7--Tourists, Squeeze, New Era, Selecter interviews and photos, Public Image photos
Vol. 2 No. 8--New Era, Toots and The Maytals, Third World, Blue Riddim Band, Thumbs photos
Vol. 2 No. 9--American Exclusive: Reggae Sunsplash: 18 pages of photos and reviews
Vol. 2 No. 10--Dexy's Midnight Runners photos, Throbbing Gristle, Cramps, Magazine interviews and photos
Vol. 2 No. 11--The Beat, Blue Riddim Band interviews and photos, Throbbing Gristle
Vol. 2 No. 12--Ultravox, Burning Spear, William Burroughs, Allen Ginsberg
Vol. 2 No. 13--XTC, The Slits, Burroughs and Ginsberg, FREE BUTTON
Vol. 3 No. 1--Jimmy Cliff, Third World, New Era, Duchamp, The Clean, Get Smart, Laurie Anderson
Vol. 3 No. 2--Abuse Flexidisc, Blue Riddim Band, Hitler Youth, Regular Guys, Get Smart

Enclosed is $_____ for :

___ 6 month Subscription.

___ Back Issues @$1 each.
     [Please state no.]
___ Free Button.

___ Ad and Sales Information.

Name_____

Address_____
       _____

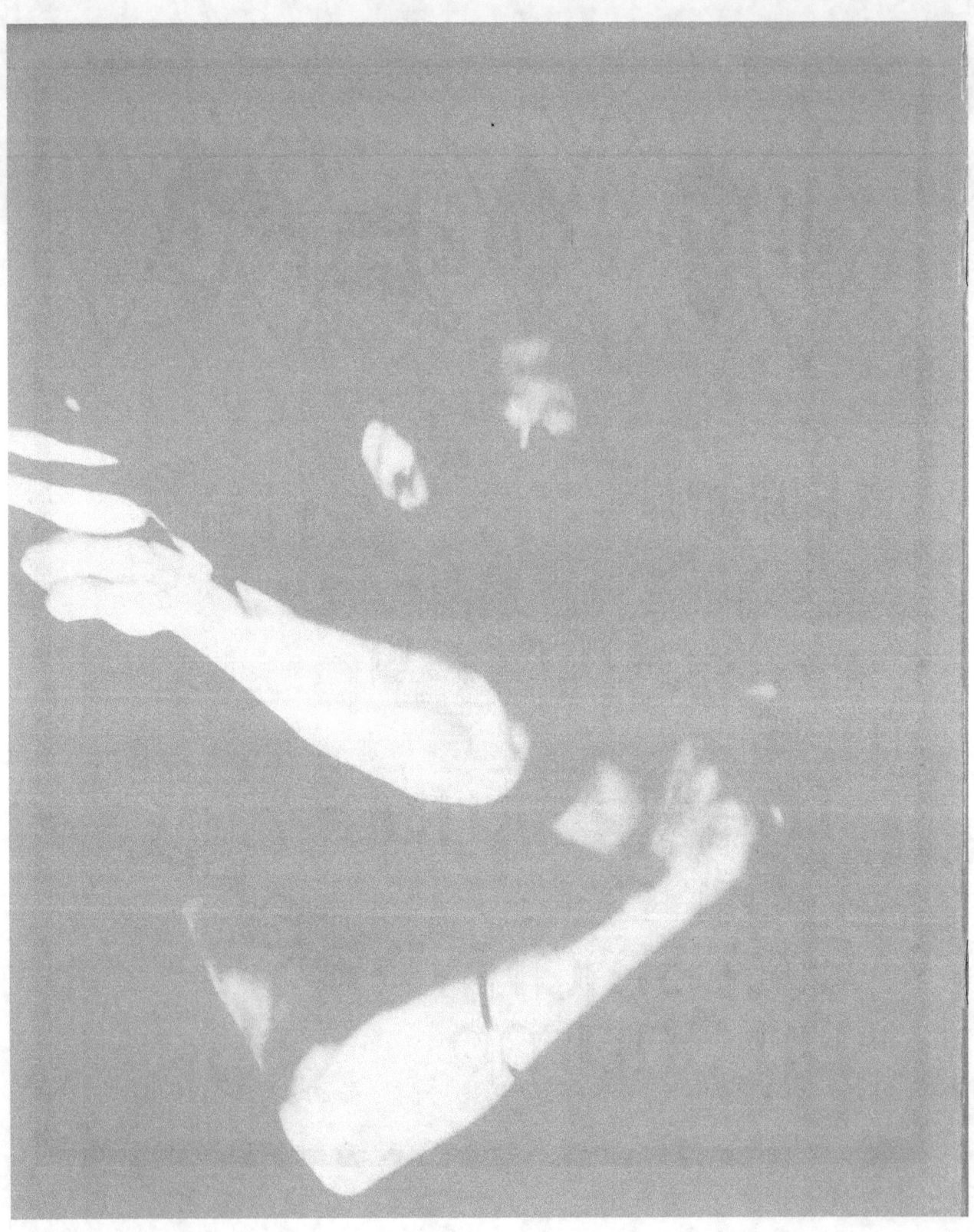

The Midwest American Rock and Reggae Magazine

# TALK TALK

Vol. 3 No. 3   $1.00

**BAUHAUS**

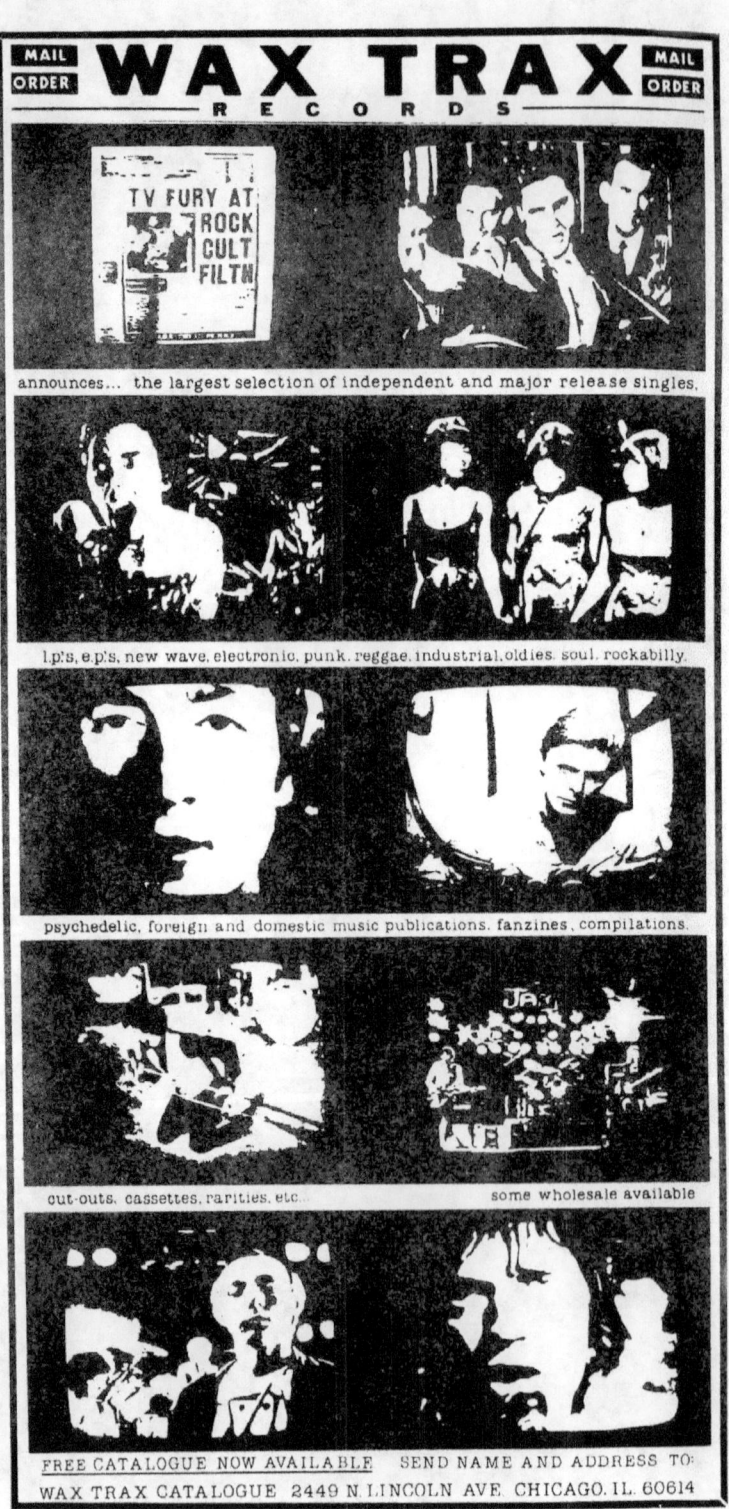

# TALK TALK

Vol.3 No.3  April / May 1981  $1.00

**LIVE:**
Wiliam S. Burroughs ..........................4
The Embarrassment.........................6
Secret Affair ...................................7
West Coast Report........................8
**INTERVIEW**
Ian Page of Secret Affair ................9
**SINGLE REVIEWS:**
Mass, Buzzcocks,
Cabaret Voltaire, Colin Newman ..........10
**ALBUM REVIEWS:**
Blurt, Gang of Four,
The dB's, The Raybeats......................12
Negativeland, Factory Quartet..............13
**INTERVIEW:**
Tony Brown ........................................14
**REGGAE REVIEWS:**
The Mexican, Dennis Brown,
The Night Doctors, Inner Circle
The Equators, Sheila Hylton................16
**ALBUM REVIEWS**
Stray Cats, Eno and Byrne ..................17
**LIVE:**
Bauhaus .............................................18
**SMALL LABELS, INDEPENDENTS
AND MORE** ........................................25
**LIVE: THE MUSIC BOX**
The Yanks .........................................26
The Gear, Home Improvements.............27
**ALBUM REVIEWS:**
The Fall, The 101ers .........................28
James Chance ....................................29
**LIVE:**
Abuse .................................................30
**SINGLE REVIEWS:**
Pere Ubu, The New Order ...................31
PiL, Bauhaus......................................32
**REGGAE ROUNDUP**...........................33
**ALBUM REVIEWS:**
The Lounge Lizards,
Heartland USA ...................................35
**LIVE REGGAE EVERY NIGHT** ...........37

**Editor**
*Bill Rich*
**Editorial Staff**
*Marc Burch
Rick Hellman
Robin Kyle
John Lee
Christopher Lucas
Rick Schneider
Jim Schwada
Buzz Spencer*
**Photography**
*Robin Kyle
John Lee
Frank Loose
Christopher Lucas
Bill Rich*
**Layout**
*John Lee*
**Typesetting**
*Joan McCabe Moore*
**Cover**
*Bauhaus' Peter Murphy.
Front: Tuts, Chicago.
Back: Bookies, Detroit
Design by
Frank Loose and
Christopher Lucas
Photos by Bill Rich*

All contents copyright 1981 by Talk Talk Publications, PO Box 36, Lawrence, Kansas, 66044. All rights reserved. Any opinion expressed is solely that of the writer and not necessarily that of this publication. Subscription rate is $6 for six issues. Articles, reviews, and pix submitted for editorial consideration are welcome. Not responsible for unsolicited material. Address all correspondence to Talk Talk Editors, PO Box 36, Lawrence, Kansas, 66044, USA.

# William S. Burroughs

William S. Burroughs is once again in the celebrity spotlight. The noted writer has been on 'The Red Night Tour' in celebration of the much awaited Cities of The Red Night, his latest novel, which has been acclaimed the best of his career. During his performances, Mr. Burroughs reads portions of the book, along with some older works and some newer works from an in-progress novel.

The show at Tuts was very outstanding. John Giorno also performs on this tour. He is a well known New York poet who started the Dial-A-Poem operation. Mr. Giorno also has a

*Terry Southern and William S. Burroughs*

*John Giorno & Burroughs.*

*James Grauerholz.*

record company which features numerous noted poets. Part of his intense performance uses some recorded tapes of the same piece he reads. The combination of hearing him speak along with hearing the tape simultaneously is a unique and memorable experience.

William S. Burroughs and (manager/agent) James Grauerholz proceeded to Lawrence, KS, along with John Giorno, for a few days before continuing the tour in St. Louis, MO, the hometown of William S. Burroughs.

The long-awaited album put out by Throbbing Gristle's Industrial Records label of tapes from the 50s and 60s, featuring William S. Burroughs has finally been released. If you are a fan of the cut-up method you will be unable to not buy and continually listen to this record. Certain small passages will remain forever in your minds. Well, don't they already?

Not much of it is intense music-just basic voice transmissions of Mr. William S. Burroughs. The shortness of each segment definitely increases its intensity. There must be several hundred bits of tape spliced together to make this an outstanding and, dare I say, sane recording. In fact, it is great! Buy this, demand this, get with it, man.

# The Embarrassment

*The Embarrassment, March 7 : Ron Klaus, bass ; Brent Giessmann, drums ; John Nichols, vocals ; Bill Goffrier, guitar.*

This show featured a contrast between the distinctive-sounding band from Wichita, The Embarrassment, and the winners-of the KJHK Battle of the Unknown Bands, Waiting for the Coup. Things were off to an energetic start, with the Coup moving steadily through a series of familiar new wave covers. This band was rumored to have formed somewhere in the catacombs of the KU dorms. This rumor seemed to be verified by the large crowd of dorm residents/fans who started dancing at the first guitar chord and kept it up right through 'til midnight.

The Embarrassment picked things up after a short break and held everyone's attention with their refreshingly original set. The lead singer's drone-like delivery against a complex back-up is developing into a very consistent sound for this band. In addition to their standards, 'Sex Drive' and 'Patio Set', the boys from the Air City managed to further Embarrass the crowd with a few new numbers from their recently-released EP. --JL

# Secret Affair

Ian Page and Dave Cairns

Dennis Smith

Sunday, March 22, about 300 people turned out at Pogo's for what had to be one of K.C.'s most interesting culture clashes this year, Mod meets Johnson County. Secret Affair, London's premier mod band, played a tight enthusiastic set to an audience consisting largely of under-18-Johnson County-teenyboppers, definitely a Styx-Reo stronghold.

What might have proved too much for a lesser band, showcased Secret Affair's professionalism and charismatic appeal. Starting off with 'Shake and Shout', it was obvious that Secret Affair had risen to the top of the proverbial heap on the English Mod Scene for good reason. They kept the dance floor full throughout the set, performing music mainly from their first LP, GLORY BOYS, with a few covers like 'Going To A Go-Go', 'Get Ready', and 'Road Runner' thrown in as a tribute to the American artists that so heavily influenced their music.

Focally, the band is-the epitome of the British Mod movement--sharp, slick, mohair and two-tone suits. Ian Page is the perfect front man and focal point, aggressive and self-assured; the compendium of mod-smart and neat. The sound was superior, the vocals and brass coming through with precision and clarity.

The Regular Guys, Lawrence's power-pop trio, were excellent as usual. Their clean, bouncy sound combining well with Secret Affair's brassy arrogance for an evening of upbeat fun.

After the show, Talk Talk was able to talk to Ian Page, Secret Affair's volatile lead singer.

## West Coast Report

It is a great compliment to the Go-Go's huge local following that they sold out this Friday night show at Perkin's Palace, a revamped movie theatre in Pasadena, Cal. That, however, is not always a good thing, as the theatre was a little too big and too confining (no dance-floor, crummy sound system)—to get to 'know' the immediately likable Go-Go's. As the culmination to a thrill-packed week with the Gill-Man, I was looking forward to the Go-Go's, who have shown so much with just one single, not to mention Jon and The Nightriders, favorites of hodads and D. Clinton Thompson. It was not to be--for a-while at least. After a nondescript set by an East L.A. band, The Brat, The Nightriders took the stage to the accompaniment of crashing waves. As it turned out, they were performing for the first time with a new drummer. As a result, everything was way too fast and again they suffered from the large hall, a lack of stage presence, and doing too many well known covers ('Pipeline', 'Walk Don't Run , ad nauseum). They did, however, manage to save the show with a smash-up cover of The Packards' 'Squad Car' and 'Rumble at Waikiki', an original. But it was these five girls from L.A. that the crowd, largely composed of under 21-ers, had come to see, as they hysterically recieved each (obviously recognized) tune. This may be due, in part, to a four or five song demo tape that has been receiving considerable airplay in the Los Angeles area. The band's material on that tape includes a great cover of 'Cool Jerk' and 'Surfin and Spyin', an original that, incidentally, is slated to be The Ventures' comeback single A-side. Their stage presence and rapport with the crowd were both very relaxed. Given the size of the hall, pretty impressive. Aside from their own material, they also covered the Shangri-Las' 'Walking in the Sand' and encored with Wanda Jackson's 'Let's Have a Party'. I really wished I'd seen them before they had become so popular. No small halls again for these girls, it appears. They also took the opportunity that evening to announce to the frenzied throng that they had just been signed to IRS records. Be still, my beating heart!
–BS

Sure it's 1981, but the punk scene in Los Angeles shows no sign of letting up. Of course, there are a few more weekend punks and assorted poseurs in attendance. Oh well, a small price to pay . . . This time found The Starwood, site of almost weekly closings and reopenings by the police, hosting L.A. punk vets X. Opening act Fear from San Francisco seemed reasonably tame (maybe anticipating more trouble getting gigs as they have in the past) and basically not very interesting. Anyway, they were much funnier in 'Decline of Western Civilization' ('Here's some money. Would you like us?')
When X took the stage, it was clear why they were the headliners. Their totally unique synthesis of early rock-and-roll, punk, and somewhat psychedelic elements were absolutely captivating. They immediately rocketed into 'Your Phone's Off The Hook (But You're Not)' from their debut LP and then proceeded to showcase material off their forthcoming release, 'Wild Surprise', including 'Adult Books', and early B-side, and the excellent 'Beyond and Back', also on the aforementioned 'Decline' soundtrack. They did, however, choose to omit their latest single, 'White Girl' from performance. And they managed to make it through the set despite the skinheads hurling themselves off the stage every 30 seconds or so (cries of 'sell out!' by some of the more hard core L.A. punks are so laughable they don't even merit discussion here). Out of the dozens of bands on the West Coast, X seem to be the only ones going anywhere. Here's hoping they will. --BS

# Interview

**Talk Talk: Are you billing Secret Affair as a 'mod' band on your American tour?**

Ian Page: In America the term doesn't mean anything, there's nothing for any American to relate it to. But what underlines every kind of fashion and evey kind of music that comes along, is that basically it still has to maintain the same quality. Whatever the name, or classification of the music, whether it's ska or early rock and roll, jazz or classical music, it still has to maintain the same element of quality that can appeal to people, and communicate a message, which is our most important underlying fact, as opposed to what it's called from one country to the next.

**TT: Is 'mod' still fashionable in England?**

IP: Well, obviously, it's been so panned by just about everybody, that those that were involved in it have been keeping a very low key. We haven't gigged in England for something like six months and we came to America because we felt unless we could ride on a hit single in England, there's no point in playing there. We couldn't maintain the same standard, the same attendance at gigs. So we came here because it's unbroken territory, we felt we needed the diversity, the new direction, something else to appeal to, we're much better as club, live band than as a concert hall band.

**TT: Is this your first time in America?**

IP: No, I was here and I spent quite a few weeks in New York. Then we came here later on and did just kind of a taste tour-NY, LA, and San Francisco, just to see how we went down and it was OK. We'd been planning this (tour) obviously for a very long time. We did another tour in England, but it wasn't what we were happy with, so we decided to come here on the basis of that. In the meantime, we lost Sire Records, so there was even greater motivation for coming at this time, it was really crucial.

Ian Page

**TT: What happend to Sire?**

IP: Initially, we signed to Sire because they were an independent, but had all the major corporate workings as Warner Brothers, who subsidized their label. When Warner Brothers took over Sire, absorbed it, sacked a lot of their people, it wasn't the same record company. So we split with them. That was just prior to releasing our second album in England, so we're going to try and chase another deal on this tour. See if we can get another album out.

**TT: Has the direction of the band changed much from its inception?**

IP: I don't think there's any musical change in what were doing. We're still using the same concept as before--the 3-minute record that has everything in it, including the sax solo, the backing, and stuff like that, but is also different from everything else in the charts at the time.

**TT: What sort of music have you been listening to lately?**

IP: The contemporary band that I listen to most is U2. We're going to be doing some gigs with them in fact. I think their album is really superb, it's perfect in every way. Steve Lilywhite is probably the best producer in the world. Certainly better than any American producer.

All the other people I listen to are Black Americans. I think all the basis of everything that anybody ever played comes from there. Which has all sorts of directions, The Stones, all that stuff is based on Black R and B.

# Single Reviews

**MASS You and I/Cabbage (4AD Records)**-- This is the debut single of a new group on 4AD Records, who are Danny Brionet, Cary Asquith, Michael Allen, and Mark Cox. Mass is a group who definitely have their fingers pointed at idiots and the misguided, and it shows in their songs. The A-side, entitled 'You and I', is obviously directed at the stupid cocaine user and how he deals with his friends and reality, with lyrics like 'You shift the blame', 'Can't take much more of your animosity', and 'Elleviate the pain with your cocaine!' The B-side, entitled 'Cabbage', is even more ominous. Who is the cabbage? I'm sure we all know at least one. 'Cabbage' is a cut with a lot of verbal harassment directed to all subhuman vegetables in much the same vein as Throbbing Gristle's 'Subhuman'. Mass either wants to destroy these creatures or merely wants to bring them to our attention. Nevertheless, Mass are a powerful group in much of the 4AD tradition. If you're looking for something with guts, this record will definitely suit your tastes. --V2

**THE BUZZCOCKS Parts 1-3 (IRS Canada: SP 9701)**-- A 12-inch release that has the last three singles was inevitable. If you did not get all three as they came out, you might want this. Anyway, it is a lot more filling to play several Buzzcocks' songs in a row. You can see similarities and differences of this series with earlier material. 'Are Everything' opens things. It is one of their stronger songs. 'What Do You Know' is probably my favorite. Pete Shelley is in classic form with a sliding vocal outpour. A more orchestrated number for sure. Since Pete Shelley has quit the band, this might be their final release. No doubt there are many more tapes on shelves. In many ways The Buzzcocks helped stabilize and legitimatize the original movement of a few years ago. And they will continue to influence. --SK

**CABARET VOLTAIRE Three Crepuscule Tracks: Slugging for Jesus, Your Agent Man, Slugging for Jesus (Part II)**-- This is the newest material by Cabaret Voltaire released through a new record company, Burit Essential. Cabaret Voltaire are definitely on their way to something new and unique. Side One of this 12-inch single is entitled 'Slugging for Jesus'; it's like win one for The Gipper. It is composed of a speaker at a religious telethon or seminar telling people to donate their money and slug for Jesus, 'We want sacrifice!' 'Slugging for Jesus (Part Two)' is an example of the outward exploration which Cabaret Voltaire possesses and is a culmination of that talent. With a satirical visionary morality much like Throbbing Gristle, it is at times a frightening reality with lyrics like 'radioactive afterbirth'. Another cut on Side Two is 'Your Agent Man', who is working for your greed service. He will save you, he's the man in the control position for you. Cabaret Voltaire is one of the few groups who actually use their conceptual vitality. Their ability to use their electronic skills has reached an ultimate high on this record. Cabaret Voltaire has reached a point of utterly apocalyptic concerns. The result, if you will, is a work of art. --V2

**COLIN NEWMAN Inventory/This Picture (Beggar's Banquet: BEG 52)**-- The A-side of this single is taken from Newman's solo LP, A-Z, and is one of the best tracks from that. It displays his ability to create an aural picture by blending both sound and word, usually random phrases and arriving at an exciting product. The flip captures Newman in a more cryptic and somber mood. The rhythms generated by bass and percussion are strongly pronounced; but it's that lonely piano and background vocal track that keeps this single, like his other material, on my turntable. --U-Man

# Secret Affair

Dave Winthrop  Ian Page

TT: How did you become interested in R & B?

IP: I had an older brother who was into it. I used to go with him to a market, a thing in England, a place just outside the East end of London, called Petticoat Lane. They sell lots of secondhand records and stuff. I used to go and help him steal all these records and by the end of it we suddenly found we had this complete British collection of Tamala/Motown records. So I got to hear all of them and I really like them.

TT: Who are some of your favorites?

IP: I like a guy called R. Dean Taylor, who is in fact one of the very few white artists on Tamala/Motown, in fact, there were only two white artists on Tamala/Motown. Kiki Dee, she started out there. 'The Day Will Come Between Sunday and Monday' the song was called. And R. Dean Taylor, who was called Motown's blue-eyed soul brother, that's what it said on his press handouts. He had the records 'Got To See Jane' and 'Indiana Wants Me'. And he did a couple other ones. I like him a lot. The Temptations are always good, even the later stuff with Norman Whitfield--The Psychedelic Shack album and 'Just My Imagination' and 'Smiling Faces'. I like just about all of it, all of that period.

TT: Do you think appearance has a lot to do with success?

IP: In absolutely everything, and especially in rock and roll, no matter what anybody says, Rock and Roll artists from Rush to Motorhead to Styx to Led Zeppelin to the Beatles, always chose a specific image that they want to relate to the audience at concerts, every single one of them. People who say they don't contrive the way they dress are contriving the way they appear, because they chose to wear that when they go out on the stage. You can't be anything other than a public figure when you walk out on a stage. The public judges you, and everything about you by the way you dress. The way you initially present yourself.

# Album Reviews

**BLURT In Berlin (Armegeddon Records: ARM 6)**-- Blurt is a three-man from Stroud, who are Pete Creese on guitar and trombone and the Brothers Milton (Ted: vocals and sax and Jake: drums and vocals). This debut LP is a live recording from the rock against junk concert in Berlin. Although most of this material has been presented elsewhere, 'My Mother Was A Friend'. . . 'Get' on their first single and from the Live Factory Sampler, it possesses a freshness to it. The sound is much clearer and more enjoyable. A lyric sheet is included so you can understand the entire thing. This isn't punk-funk, because there's no bass. In no way does it resemble the Pop Group or James White. It's more like the Glaxo Babies or Pere Ubu, but comparisons stop here. This is one of the best records released this year. The prime cuts on it are: 'Puppeteers of the World Unite', 'Dyslexia Rules', 'Cherry Blossom Polish', and 'Ubu'. This is a tribute to Alfred Jarry's creation. Inside us all there is an Ubu waiting to conquer . . . do the ubu, uber alles, join the comic march with no direction NSEW dominate. --U-Man

**GANG OF FOUR Solid Gold**-- The Gang of Four have become a very progressive group with this second album, Solid Gold. It's obvious that they are serious about what they do and that they don't want to do it twice. The key to this album is their meaningful songwriting ability and their new sound. Their songs on this album deal more with everyone's own political and commercial helplessness and what we can do about it, if we can do anything about it. Songs like 'Paralyzed', 'Why Theory?', 'The Republic', and 'Cheeseburger' convey this idea very efficiently. What really makes this album extremely successful is their new sound. It's more slowed down and treated than their first album. The song that best describes this is 'History's Bunk' on their new single. But The Gang of Four are by no means weak. This is their best album to date and I'm sure that they will only get better. --V2

**THE DB'S Stands for deciBels (Albion Records: ALBIo5)**-- On their first trip out, the dB's have produced a powerfully subtle pop-rock album that belies their relative inexperience. In fact, it is probably too good to ever garner the American exposure it so richly deserves.

It is not surprising then that the group had to travel to Britain to find a record company to release their debut LP. Appropriately, though, the dB's specialized in an English-sounding style that reminds one of those Anglophiles, the Flamin' Groovies, without that band's studied classicism.

Songwriters Chris Stamey and Peter Holsapple tease your memory a la Nick Lowe, ripping off the odd lick or vocal phrase and integrating it perfectly with their own compositions. But what sets the dB's apart from such Beatle imitators as the Romantics, the (US) Beat, et al., is a willingness to incorporate some idiosyncratic and often strange-sounding touches into their music.

This is a good band with two strong song writers and a personality all their own. Watch for big things from the dB's. --RH

**THE RAYBEATS Roping Wild Bears (EP) (Don't Fall Off the Mountain Records: Y4)**-- You've heard the hype, now hear the record. Roping Wild Bears is the 80's equivalent of a Booker T and the MG's or Ventures album. Rocking instrumentals with touches of surf, soul and funk--in short, perfect for your next party tape.

Jody Harris' slinky guitar figures are buttressed by Don Christensen's rock solid drumming and Pat Irwin's cool sax and keyboards are certainly preferable to mentor James Chance's uncontrolled squawking.

This is good stuff, but one can only wonder what The Raybeats must have sounded like with George Scott on bass. As it is, RWB negotiates a fine line between nostalgia and innovation. Docked a point for matching blue suits, though. --RH

# Album Reviews

**NEGATIVELAND** Points (Seeland Records: OPT-LP-002)-- An electronic band from California, much in the tradition of Throbbing Gristle and Cabaret Voltaire. Like these bands, N-land is heavily dependent upon tapes of random or collected conversations as a primary source of lyrics. This record is less musical than either TG or CV, in that there simply isn't much presence felt by any musical instruments; be it synths, guitars, bass, etc. Only taped fragments seem to be used throughout the record. The subjects that N-land seem to enjoy are mundane when compared to TG's fetishes. But N-land take CV's Voice of America one better because they actually seem to capture the idiosyncracies of today's American public. Material for this project was gathered from 'typical' relatives, TV game shows, religious speakers, personal letters, a salesman at a county fair, and children at a BBQ. This is stuff that we have all taken part in and yet when presented by N-land it has a very strange quality to it. It's the fishbowl environment of America that is the subject of Points. --U-Man

**A FACTORY QUARTET** Blurt, The Royal Family and The Poor, The Durutti Column, and Kevin Hewick (Factory: FACT 24)-- The verdict on this two-sided record art gallery? One great side, two fair, and one horrible.

Of course, Blurt's four tunes stand head and brawny shoulders above the rest of the crowd. Sax/word man Ted Milton is a firm believer in the Coltrane-Coleman-Beefheart-Chance school of honking, and he does it with such a passionately amateurish fervor you cannot help but love him. Milton proves you do not have to learn the system to tear it down. A true punk.

Next best are The Royal Family, who, at best, plunge to the Stygian depths of PiL or The Fall but more often drone and shout monotonously.

Vini the C's side is pleasant enough, even if he is just treading water.

Kevin Hewick, though, is totally without socially redeeming value. I will not even waste your time putting down this pathetic folkie.

And there you have it. Three dogs and a diamond in the rough. Still, I am glad I bought it. The Blurt side might be worth the $12. --R H

---

**KJHK FM 91**

On Sundays
Tune Your Radio to FM-91-KJHK

'The Soul Shakedown Party' with Jim 'Daddy Cool' Schwada
Reggae 4-7 p.m.

'The Rebellious Jukebox' with Marc 'U-Man' Burch
10 p.m.-2 a.m.

'The Death Disco' with Rick 'V-2' Schneider
2-6 a.m.

Brought to you in part by Talk Talk Publications

KJHK, 217 Flint Hall, University of Kansas, Lawrence, Kansas, 66044, USA

# Interview: The Tony Brown Band

Jim Schwada: You're listening to KJHK in Lawrence, Kansas. This weekend is a reggae weekend with not one but two very fine bands playing downtown. One of the bands making their first appearance here is the Tony Brown Band. We have Mr. Tony Brown in the studio and he is going to talk with us about his music. Thanks a lot for coming down, Tony.
Tony Brown: Irie.

JS: Lawrence was able for a while to support its own reggae band. What's the scene--you're from Madison, WI, originally?
Tony Brown: Yes. Well, not originally but that is where we are based now. I consider Madison one of the three cities in the U.S. that has a very large reggae West Indian community. Every major tour that goes through the country goes there. Also tours that have not gone in the whole country come to Wisconsin. In Madison, similar to here, they have several radio stations that play reggae.

JS: So there is quite a bit of interesting stuff in that part of the country. Sort of like isolated pockets with interest in reggae.
Tony Brown: It's really strange but it is spread all over. Most people don't find it because they don't expect it to be there.

JS: How long have you been writing?
Tony Brown: About 22 years.

JS: What inspires you?
Tony Brown: Life.

JS: We were talking earlier about positive music.
Tony Brown: Positive music. You can sit back all the time and look at all the craziness and get completely vexed with it to death. But it doesn't do you any good until you can give them something to help them through it. If you can at least acknowledge it and verbalize it, then your verbalization, in a positive fashion, is going to help somebody a lot more than your frustration and venting in a negative fashion.

JS: You are a follower of the Rastafarian religion for ten years, you say? That is something that can confuse people who listen and are not familiar with it. What are some of the major tenets of Rastafarianism?
Tony Brown: Number one is to enlighten everyone and make them aware of the truth. Or make them themselves search for the truth in their lives. Also for a group of people that have very little but have the whole world to have at their hands. Why deny yourself the truth? And to confront all the negative and craziness going on right now not with violence but with the truth. And with the feeling of coming from a place of love not hate. That is just as bad as confronting it with violence.

JS: You are originally from the U.S. but you have lived in Jamaica?
Tony Brown: Yes. Not for a few years.

JS: What do you find when you go there?
Tony Brown: A lot. I find a lot there, man.

JS: Do you want to go and live there again someday?
Tony Brown: I'm making some plans to do that. Some plans in the near future.

JS: When we were talking earlier about rock and roll bands--especially stuff coming out of England these days has quite a bit of reggae techniques sound to it. The Clash have Mikey Dread doing dub on their album. Do you think it is going to help? Will people who hear it pick up records by the original artists?
Tony Brown: I think what it will do is give people the basis to understand--not a different

music because people have already heard the music except they have not heard it come from Jamaica. People have heard the same beat that is in reggae ten years and twenty years ago in this country. It was all involved a basis or type of music that people have heard since the existence of music. Now what is happening is that the United States has kicked out all this muisc and now it is coming back not only as music but as a pure form of a way of living within music. It is very hard for people to take that. We come from a basis of a higher level than most people in the world. In actuality our moral level and our spiritual level is not as high because we have a very lot materialistically, whereas some people, all they have is their relationship with God and Earth. And the music that they convey, there has to be brought about that identification for everybody so you can grasp, number one, the things for those to hear.

JS: It is hard to understand . . .
Tony Brown: It is not meant for everyone.

JS: It is hard to understand when you have so much what people that have so little are . . .
Tony Brown: And to find the basis of liking a music. That is one basis that you find that you identify with. That also reenlightens you culturally. And makes you think about what you have been doing with your life. That makes you want to search for something a little better. I mean, it is a very small thing but it is a very large thing. It is like an amoeba —it is very small but a very important thing in existence in the world because it is a living organism. So just that one little facet of music that you might get in hearing new wave bands that makes you want to hear something more positive, you see. A lot of times, as we said before, what comes across is negative. They take the technical end of it and put it into a musical and negative nature. But if it is good, it is good music long enough to get across. So people search out that clip.

JS: More than the sum of its parts, it's a whole thing.
Tony Brown: Yeah.

JS: Talking about reggae music, originally they were hearing a lot of soul music from Miami radio stations and things like that. And then took it into their own musical stylings. Who influenced you? Not only reggae but any kind of music?
Tony Brown: It is an endless list. Anyone who I have listened to has influenced me.

JS: Anything that is positive . . .
Tony Brown: There are certain things that are positive just in the way they convey, like blues singers. They sing about bum times. But the way they sing it is positive because they at least express it. But some singers that yell at you are singing about love. And they yell at you. I can relate to a person giving themselves an expression of self and of their relationship. It is a spiritual given.

JS: The intensity of the performance means a lot
Tony Brown: Seen.

JS: We are really looking forward to your first visit here. You said you were in Lawrence ten years ago?
Tony Brown: Yes, at the Red Dog Inn, with a 12-piece R & B band.

JS: It sounds real, real good. I'd like to thank you for coming down. Is there anything you want to tell everybody
Tony Brown: Jah love.
JS: I think that about covers it. Alright. Thanks again, Tony.

# Reggae Reviews

**THE MEXICANO** Trial by Television/Jamaican Child (Stiff: BUY 93)-- I thought this was more Tex-Mex trash until I finally played it and found it to be pretty pure reggae. Nice release which probably has been overlooked. Look for it. --WB

**DENNIS BROWN** Foul Play (A & M Records: SP 4850)-- A finely tuned LP from the most popular artist in Jamaica (next to B. Marley), very soul oriented and featuring backup from Sly and Robbie and guitarist Willie Lindo--better than Marley's latest, too bad they did not dub it up a bit more. --DC

**THE NIGHTDOCTORS** Just Enough/Hit and Miss Affair (Race Records: RB 001)-- The first release of Race Records, owned by Specials manager, Rick Rodgers, shows great potential. It is produced by Brad, the ex-Specials drummer. The sounds are classic reggae to groove on. Don't know much about the band itself. Sure we will see more in the future. --WB

**INNER CIRCLE** We Come to Rock You (Mango: MPLS 7787A)-- Once again a sampler from an upcoming LP with a hot A-side and a forgettable flip . . . 'We Come To Rock You' is a jumper from start to finish, driven by a powerful guitar beat and anchored by typically fine Inner Circle vocals . . . some of their best since the death of Jacob Miller. --DC

**THE EQUATORS** Baby Come Back/Georgie (Stiff: BUY 95)-- The Equators' earlier single is noteworthy if you like their 12-inch reviewed last issue because it contains their original cut, 'Georgie'. It is the only other song they have released so far. But with the success of the recent 'Son of Stiff' tour, an album is due out soon, along with an American tour. --WB

**SHEILA HYLTON** Beds Too Big Without You (Mango: MPLS 7788A)-- This time reggae borrows from rock. Sheila Hylton shows off her considerable vocal talents on this extended version of a song originally written and performed by The Police . . . produced by Harry J and arranged by the ubiquitous Sly and Robbie, this is a good intro to a soulful lady whose first LP should be out soon-as to the B-side, 'Give Me Your Love'--forget it . . . . -DC

# Album Reviews

**THE STRAY CATS** (Arista: STRAY 1)-- Who'd a thunk it? Just a month ago, it seemed that The Zantees had the whole bop-cat scene about sewn-up, but not three weeks later in steps Brian 'Alka' Setzer, Slim Jim Phantom, and Lee Rocker with a new release threatening to out rock anybody and everybody this side of Levi Dexter. All under 21, these guys make no mistake about their affiliations when they rip it up on this debut LP. After two knockout singles, the pressure was on for the Cats initial long-player. And, with almost no exceptions, they came through with flying colors. Besides the two singles and one B-side, standout originals include 'Fishnet Stockings', 'Rumble in Brighton', and 'Wild Saxophone'. Dynamite cover choices include Warren Smith's 'Ubangi Stomp', Eddie Cochran's 'Jeanie, Jeanie, Jeanie', and Gene Vincent's 'Double Talkin' Baby'. Apparently, Setzer remixed some of Dave Edmunds' production, but it's a minor point at best. Except for some of the more obvious lyrics ('Storm the Embassy' in particular), Setzer seems to have a good start on his songwriting. Now, if only this temporary rockabilly craze doesn't suffocate these guys . . . Like, man, my ears are smokin'! --BS

**BRIAN ENO AND DAVID BYRNE** My Life in the Bush of Ghosts (Sire Records: SRK 6093)-- Dive head-first into this simmering stew of funk and found sounds, of sultry Arabic motifs and humorous juxtapositions.

BUSH OF GHOSTS is Eno's best (read most accessible) work in years and Byrne seems to have struck a creative spark in the old baldy with his fascination for Afro-American rhythms.

Using an innovative method of put and take, the two of them construct collages of sound that envelop the listener. Voices sing and talk like a broken five-band radio bouncing through the funk-wash of the backing tracks.

Although reminiscent of REMAIN IN THE LIGHT, BUSH is a superior record because the ratio of Byrne to Eno is more even and its sonic experiments are more daring. We are treated to Eno's third-world desert wind, some water music, even a devo-esque talk show host decrying America's lack of will.

This is a heady brew that satisfies all the months of expectation. It is an experiment that succeeds marvelously. It is one-world music. --RH

TALK TALK PUBLICATIONS
PO BOX 36
LAWRENCE, KANSAS. 66044 USA

Name
Address
Enclosed is check/money order for $_____ for the following:
6 Issue subscription at $6.00
Back issues at $1.00 each
(Please add .$.50 per item for P&P)

# BAUHAUS

Bauhaus have recently ended their first American tour and are back in Britain watching the climb of their latest single. TALK TALK followed the band for three dates to get a look at one of the top British groups making rapid steps on the way to stardom. For some, Bauhaus are already considered the best. Their first single, 'Bela Lugosi's Dead', was released two years ago by Small Wonder and became an instant hit. 'Dark Entries' was their second single and their first release on the 4AD Records label. This was followed by 'Terror Couple Kills Colonel'.

Late last year, Bauhaus released their first album, IN THE FLAT FIELD. It did not contain their earlier singles and, for some, lacked the cohesion of earlier material. Although it reached No. 1 on Alternative charts, the established press unmercifully attacked it for being too pretentious and gloomy. It is an intense album for which many were not prepared. Following it, they released 'Telegram Sam', a T-Rex cover with a sort of offbeat, cheery mood. The 12-inch version includes John Cole's 'Rosegarden Funeral' and a song about their work called 'Crowds'. A video of 'Telegram Sam' has been made, which gives a visual taste of Bauhaus.

Their latest single has been released on Beggars Banquet, 4AD's parent company. This will allow a better distribution to result. In their live shows, Bauhaus do several unreleased songs, which will surface on their next album. Presently, they are finalizing an agreement to begin American distribution and their releases will soon be available domestically.

Bauhaus was formed in late 1979. Peter Murphy and Daniel Ash got together and wrote some songs. Brothers Kevin Hastings and David Jay had played with Daniel earlier and they got together. Kevin plays drums, David plays bass, Daniel plays guitar and saxophone. Peter provides vocals, movements, and an occasional keyboard and bongo drums.

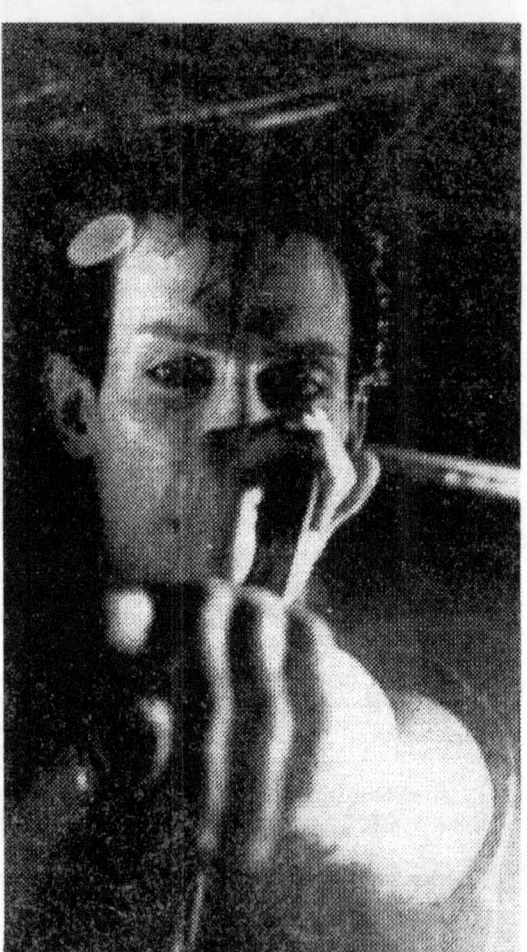

*Peter Murphy at Bookies in Detroit*

Bauhaus should be witnessed live. Their music can be very haunting and forceful. The stage show is one of the most forceful presentations for ages and probably today's top. There is little gimmickry involved aside from stark white blinding lights. Black and white is the emphasis. The band takes command of the audience. Peter Murphy covers the space available with both smooth and frantic movements.

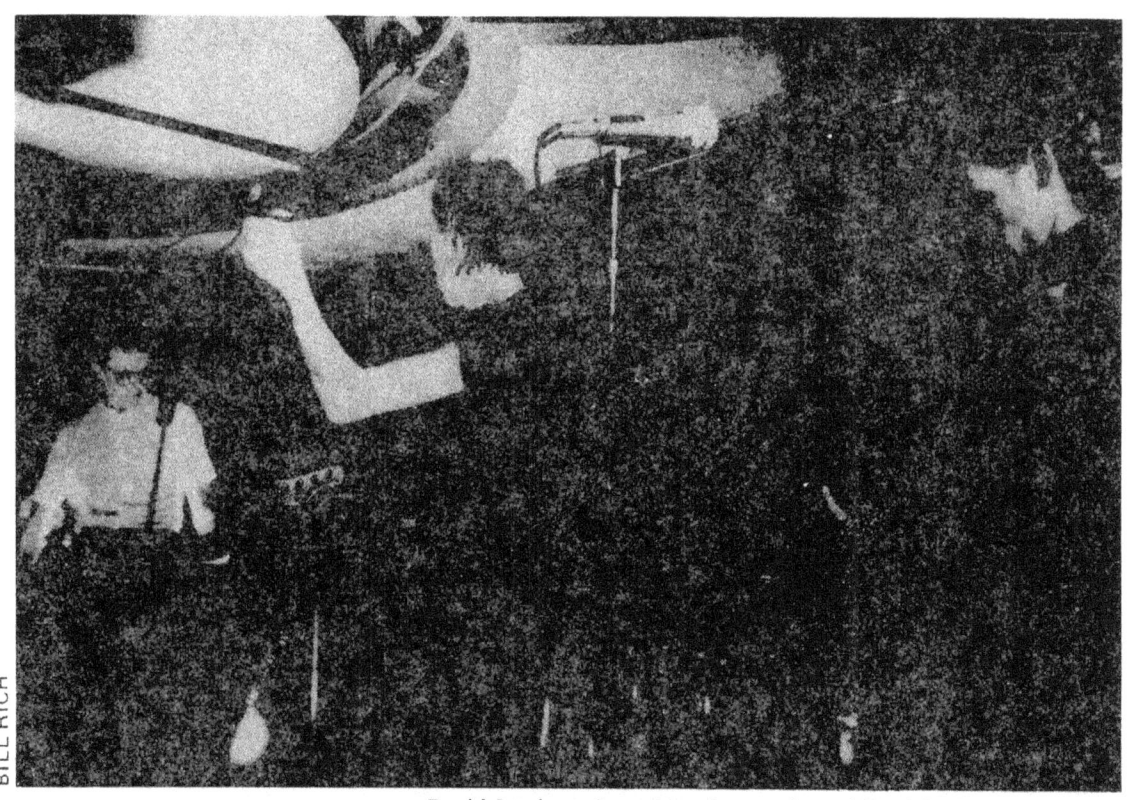

*David Jay, bass; Peter Murphy, vocals; and Daniel Ash, guitar at Tuts.*

My first experience with Bauhaus was in Detroit at Bookies, a famous hot spot. The crowd was small--no more than 200. But the streets were very glazed this evening and traffic was crawling. Opening was L7, who could be classified as a nihilistic group of guitar, bass, drums, and sax/keyboards, fronted by a dead acting female zombie droning in a minor key. Although they individually were good musicians, together it sounded like a practice session. Their stale sound was further supplemented with comments such as 'You could have danced to that one.' L7 probably have played with better crowd reception but overall are probably victims of the blase Detroit attitude.

When Bauhaus came on, the small crowd in front stood almost disinterested in the show but fascinated by the awe of the spectacle. The sound was deafening. A little less volume would have greatly increased everyone's enjoyment. I expected to hear comments on Murphy's similarities to Iggy Pop in regard to appearance and stage movements. Although Bauhaus are great Bowie fans, they do not speak of Iggy. But the movements of Murphy are rooted in the artform created and made famous by Detroit's own Iggy Pop. The set began with a recording of the B-side of their new single, 'Saturi,' a moody instrumental.

# BAUHAUS

The four members of the band approached the stage and began playing the title cut of the album, IN THE FLAT FIELD. This is about the only album cut they did. The most receptive responses came from their singles, 'Bela Lugosi's Dead', 'Terror Couple Kill Colonel', 'Telegram Sam', and 'Dark Entries', which is their closing number. There were also four or so new songs, including the latest release, 'Kick In The Eye'. They performed no encore, as they prefer to limit encores to special occasions when the audience really wants it rather than the customary, obligatory additional song.

On the name Bauhaus:
As Peter explains, "the name is from the school from Weimar, Germany. We are getting sick of this labeling, this link. At first, we saw some links--very simple approaches, very basic frameworks. But we don't embrace the overall scheme. We just thought it made for a good name.'

# BAUHAUS

BILL RICH

Bauhaus made their American debut several months ago in New York and Chicago. The people in Chicago were ready for their return. They played two nights with the first show being at The Space Place, an empty warehouse in the meat packing section of town. There was no bar and no age limit. Although tickets were originally limited to 300, there were close to 500 crammed into the small room. Naked Raygun opened the evening and helped loosen up the crowd. The Men followed, offering their insults

# BAUHAUS

to the audience along with their brand of music, resulting from the lineup of vocalist, bass, synth/rhythm machine, and celloist, with an occasional saxophone. Supposedly, they usually perform better. Some consider The Men to sound like a mix of Tuxedo Moon and Blurt. But like the previous night's show at Bookies, the excessive negativism of the opening acts did nothing but cause a drop in esteem for these local bands. They acted like that was what they wanted and that was what they achieved.

Then Bauhaus came on to perform their hour set. Peter Murphy had stated that no matter how big the stage is, he covers all of it. The Space Place offers a big stage-its only redeeming feature. And Murphy was continually moving. With a flying cape and extensive makeup, which accented his lean facial features, his charm and control became the focus of attention.

All too soon, their set ended. The announcer stated that Bauhaus had already left. So ended the evening.

The following day, Bauhaus played at Tuts. At the beginning, Murphy announced that they would be performing a different set than the night before.

Bauhaus brought over their own equipment for this tour. The electronic generators require a special converter, which might have caused problems for club owners. But it worked wonderfully each of the three shows I saw.

Daniel Ash, on guitar, did incredible things to get the sounds that set the mood. Quite an accomplished musician.

They played a different type of show. Peter never touched his small drum setup. 'My hands get so sweaty, the sticks fly out of my hands', he explained. He did use a portable keyboards more, along with flashing a mirror at the audience which caught many blinding rays. Lots of visual excitement helped to make this their best show I had seen yet. Next time they are in America, you can count on me being there.

FRESH FLEXI INFO
Next Issue
Get Smart Flexidisc

# Small Labels, Independents, and More...

This column is dedicated to first timers both in the reviewed recording being the first release of the group but also the first releases of the record companies. It seems like a good topic for support. Leading it off is Touch and Go Rekords, an offshoot of Touch and Go, the Lansing fanzine often in questionable taste, devoted to new music and a supporter of early punk attitudes. In fact, I think Touch and Go had the first printed review of TALK TALK for what that is worth. Their first release is The Necros (Box 421, Maumee, OH, 43537), with local punter Barry Henssler on vocals; they have come up with four short songs of the 'faster and louder' style of the finest West Coast spirit. 'Better Late Than Never' is a great conceptual cut. 'Police Brutality' could become an anthem for many. Maybe it already is.

The second release is the Fix with 'Vengeance' and 'In This Town'. This record really moves. There are frantic guitars and drums with a wall of bass. The vocals sink in on top of it all. (Available from Touch and Go Rekords, P.O. Box 26203, Lansing, MI, 48909.)

The TV Babies have got a lot of good press on their four-song EP, which shows a diversified and competent band scanning many influences and attractions. The saxophone fits in with the jazz mood. And the added versatility of both female and male vocalists helps. (Available from Rockin' Horse Records, 13 E. 17th. Street, New York, NY, 10003.)

Charlie Pickett and The Eggs have a single out with 'Feeling', a blues oriented original, on the A-side and a cover of 'White Light, White Heat' on the flip, which is its redeeming quality. It is the first release of the popular record store, Open Records, 'where being warped is no defect'. (901 Progresso Dr., Ft. Lauderdale, FL, 33304)

From Iowa, comes Roz with 'All the Day' and 'Whippin' Junior Into Shape'. This young band does have a good sound, at least on this high quality recording. Their many influences and steals are on the tip of my tongue. They do put it together very nicely. (Contact Roz through Randy Van Hosen, 1125 25th Street, No. 2, Des Moines, IA, 50311.)

Identity Crisis have their first single out on Chicago's Cirkle Records. (Definitely not the first Cirkle Records release, since they are the home of such as Epicycle and the (now defunct) Imports. But which such success, their inclusion is warranted). It is not a major breakthrough for rock and roll though. 'Pretty Feet' sure seems to be a slow, repetitious stanza. The other side has a Monochrome Settish vocals that really add to the overall basicness. It was recorded nine months ago and a new sound has been born which will be forthcoming on their next release. (Contact Identity Crisis at PO Box 429, Park Forest, IL, 60466.)

That's it for now. Hope I didn't destroy too much. Keep 'em coming in! –The Blind Reviewer.

## Action At The Music Box

*Not everyone appreciates the new bands that play at The Music Box as shown by this 'regular'.*

### The Yanks

BILL RICH

The Yanks: Jeff Ritchie, bass; Mark Roberts, drums; Randy Shiling, guitar.

# The Gear

*The Gear: Mike Flanagan, guitar; John Ingram, drums; Abe Haddad, bass.*

The Music Box has jumped out to a major lead in the race for the best club. Shows are still being held in the ground floor bar area. The basement continues to be remodeled and let's hope that they continue to work on it. In the meantime, the couple of hundred people who can fit in have been enjoying some of the best shows to be happening. Venture down to 4701 Troost and check it out yourself.

## Home Improvements

# Album Reviews

**THE FALL Grotesque (After the Gramme) (Rough Trade: ROUGH 18)**-- This is one of the most venal scraps of vinyl I've ever heard. Mark Smith and Company actually expect people to buy this record after they so vigorously and thoroughly attack the music industry from all sides? Every song is a treatise on this or a related subject. The LP opens with 'Pay Your Rates', which is a lesson to be learned. If you fail, it's off to the debtors' estate. From here, such things as Two-Toners, the international radio conspiracy, DJs, journalists, and the peasant-fans are openly dissected and seen for what they are or at least how M. Smith views them. There are four main oratories on Grotesque (After the Gramme): 'CnC S. Mithering', 'Impression of J. Temperance', 'Gramme Friday', and 'The NWRA'. 'Cash and Carry Stop Mithering' is the anti-peasant song. Mark Smith goes into the origin of the new scene in his sing-talk style, accompanied by acoustic sounding guitar and tin pan drums. He expounds on the modern fans, who have as much taste as waved food. The peasants who have a new favorite with every purchase; a new allegiance, spouting their driveling opinions in search of converts. The onslaught continues as The Fall go into the peasant-fans' fascination for hanging out with their modern favorites. 'I like your new single yuh yuh great', they say. Synth groups are shelved by Mark Smith. He believes that the conventional is the experimental and that sums up what The Fall are trying to do; by utilizing what could only be described as discordant folk music and these scathing lyrics to derive at something different. 'CnC S. Mithering' concludes with further digression on California, sex and death. 'Impression of J. Temperance' and 'Gramme Friday' both deal with another constituent of the scene, that thing that slices the brain, TUBOS. 'IJT' is a tale of an abstinent dogbreeder and the horrible transformation he undergoes after the gramme is laid out by the two who did not hate him. This song should require a disclaimer. A chopping military drum sets the mood for this. GF describes what lurks in the mind of the working youth/peasant-fan. We all have our hungers on Friday. The record closes with The NWRA (?) that revives the supposedly deceased R. Totale. It is through him that Smith hints to some kind of inevitable revolution. Perhaps, the fall of the 'scene' is prophesied. This record seems to be Mark Smith's soapbox, just as The Fall seem to be his vehicle. The material here may disgress in a somewhat unrefined manner, but that is the way The Fall have always conducted their affairs. --U-Man

**THE 101ERS Elgin Avenue Breakdown (Andalucia Records and 101)**-- The years 1975 and 1976 were pivotal ones for the British music scene and the 101ers were at the forefront of the change from pub rock to punk.

The bootleg-quality sound on some of Elgin Avenue Breakdown's cuts only serves to enhance its smoky, small club feel. Of course, the real reason for buying this record is to hear Joe Strummer on vocals and rhythm guitar and even casual fans of The Clash leader should not be disappointed.

On songs like 'Keys to Your Heart', 'Let'sagetabitarockin', and 'Junco Partner', Strummer and the band attain a cohesive sound strong enough to equal some of the best Clash stuff. Not that the rest of the tracks are bad. Quite the contrary, they're good, sloppy R&B.

This is Strummer before he became famous and political and had all those impossibly great expectations laid on him. Turn back the clock and kick up your heels with the 101ers! —RH

## Album Reviews

**JAMES CHANCE WITH PILL FACTORY (ZE Records: 45T); THE RAYBEATS Roping Wild Bears**-- One, two, three . . . Pill Factory are James Chance, Bradley Field, Arto Lindsay, and George Scott; The Raybeats are Pat Irwin, Jody Harris, Danny Amis, and Don Christensen. The two bands have many things in common, starting with George Scott. George cowrote many of the songs on both records, he plays on the Pill Factory, but not on the Raybeats. George Scott is dead, he lost his life to a hard city drug last summer. This makes the Pill Factory release old material. The Pill Factory is material from Diego Cortez's soundtrack, 'Grutzi Elvis', from the summer of '79.

The Raybeats (excluding Danny Amis, who replaces Scott) are all ex-contortions from the NO NEW YORK days, in fact, everybody (except Amis) was on the No New York album, either in the Contortions, DNA, or Teenage Jesus and The Jerks.

The Raybeats are into a cool movie soundtrack rhythm, perhaps they are writing a score for television, there are no vocals. Their music sounds dated but modern studio techniques abound. The image they have with their blue velvet suits is like a dinner club band, any requests?

The Pill Factory starts out with George Scott rapping out the bass line to 'That's When Your Heartaches Begin'. James Chance really has a heartache, Arto Lindsey steps in with his mannered guitar style (insects walking on strings) and brings the song to a climax and an abrupt end. 'Schleyer's Tires' and 'McGraw Army Base'/'Muncher' are spacious, eastern drumming tracks, with Bradley Field drumming and hitting time much in the vein of Teenage Jesus, without the lunch. The last track, 'Theme from Grutzi Elvis', is an all-out blow, but our hero keeps time to the marching rhythm, without missing a step, left-right, left-right, left-right--classic stuff. --CL

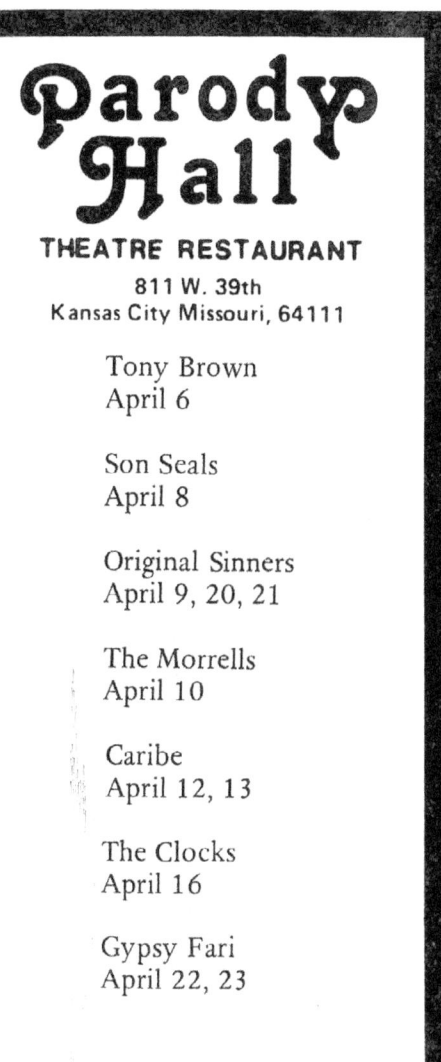

**Parody Hall**
THEATRE RESTAURANT
811 W. 39th
Kansas City Missouri, 64111

Tony Brown
April 6

Son Seals
April 8

Original Sinners
April 9, 20, 21

The Morrells
April 10

Caribe
April 12, 13

The Clocks
April 16

Gypsy Fari
April 22, 23

# Abuse

# Single Reviews

**PERE UBU Not Happy/Lonesome Cowboy Dave (Rough Trade: RTUS 004)**-- When first heard, this immediately brought to mind 'It Feels Like Heaven'. David Thomas asking the listener why we can't all be happy like the birds and bees in (of all places) South America. Why we can't be happy like he is. With every mention of one of Jah's creations, David impersonates it with that cartoon voice of his. And is that Tatoo going, 'But, Boss . . . But, Boss'? Allen Ravenstine treats us to some excellent synth work as well creating what sounds to be electromaraca waves. Something about this ditty makes me feel good. The B-side is Pa Ubu Cowboy in the saddle again. David introduces himself like a modern Paul Bunyan and then goes into a bigger than life description of his cowboy outfit. A hat the size of Oklahoma. Boots like Florida and he's galloping along on a horse as big as ? going yip, yip, yo. The bass and drums get this one moving. Mayo Thompson's guitar and an occasional neighing synth add to the comic western. --U-Man

**THE NEW ORDER Ceremony/In a Lonely Place (Factory: FACT 33)**-- The New Order consists of all the remaining three members of Joy Division, plus one new member on keyboards. Both cuts are previously written material by Joy Division. The B-side, 'In a Lonely Place', is actually sung by the late Ian Curtis, giving this song a feeling of the next dimension. It is nice to hear Ian's voice again, maybe for the last time. 'Ceremony', on the A-side has that nice, pure, always welcomed, sound of Joy Division. This is a great single with that Joy Division sound. If you loved everything else by Joy Division, you will love The New Order. --V2

Some of our upcoming shows

The Secrets
April 10, 11

Shangoya
April 15

The Clocks
April 16, 17

The Specters
featuring
Glenn Matlock
April 17

New Era Reggae Band
April 24, 25

The Stranglers
April 25

Steel Pulse
May 4

Lawrence Opera House
7th & Mass.   842-6930

# Single Reviews

BILL RICH

BAUHAUS Kick in the Eye/Saturi (Beggars Banquet: BEG 54)-- A strong release of original songs which will show the way to a more rhythmic Bauhaus sound. 'Kick in the Eye' grabs you like 'In A Flat Field' or 'Dark Entries'. The B-side is an instrumental. As Peter Murphy explains, 'We did that song in about 10 minutes, really quickly in the studio. We were trying to capture the very essence of the lyric which is about the search through life. And it worked.' --BR

PUBLIC IMAGE LTD. Flowers of Romance/Home Is Where The Heart Is (Virgin: S397)-- 'Now it is summer. I could be happy or in distress sent you flowers, you wanted chocolates instead' --Flowers of Romance. Moving forward into the summer of '81, PiL is moving away from the metal box that they existed in, that contained, stored the music of their lives. Now the company is three, John Lydon, Keith Levine, and Jeanette Lee, with the absence of a well known bass player, the three seem to be able to portray their work personally, clearly, complete, and they are vulnerable. The birds are singing, women are crying, there are flowers, the daily paper is on the carpet, things are psychedelic. Relying on themselves--they have gleaned the most out of voices, drums, guitar, and a very minimal bassline to come up again with music worth spreading over the world. --CL

# Reggae

**REGGAE ROUNDUP**

The influence of reggae music on rock and roll (especially the English product) is definite and pervasive, but it seems that reggae itself is destined to remain an acquired taste here in the U.S.

As host of the local reggae radio program, I am often asked by listeners about a track they have heard or to suggest the best recorded example of a particular artist . . . with that in mind, here is a highly subjective and selective 'buyer's guide' to the sounds of JA. Keep in mind that there are literally hundreds of singles and LPs from Jamaica and England (where many top reggae artists now reside) that may never reach the U.S. or may be years old when they do--most of the following LPs are either American releases or easy to find imports.

Bob Marley and The Wailers are easily the most popular and best known reggae artists, and a suitable starting point for a reggae collection . . . their 1974 release, 'Natty Dread', was my introduction to island music and it is not sentimentality that causes me to recommend it as their best work. Although Peter Tosh and Bunny Wailer had left the band by the time it came out, excellent studio versions of classics like 'No Woman, No Cry', 'Bend Down Low', and especially 'Rebel Music' more than make up →

REGGAE REGGAE REGGAE

**TONY BROWN BAND**

APRIL 6th — **PARODY HALL** — KANSAS CITY
MAY 1 & 2 — **OFF THE WALL HALL** — LAWRENCE

WORLD RECORD REPRESENTATION MADISON, WI 608-257-6651

REGGAE REGGAE REGGAE

# Reggae

for their departure... The Wailers' live sound is best captured on the two-record set, 'Babylon By Bus', which was recorded on the band's 1978 tour of America. Seeing The Wailers live is always a rewarding experience, and the versions of 'Stir It Up', 'Concrete Jungle', and 'Kinky Reggae' on this album are indicative of the intensity they can reach. Music from the original Wailers, with both Tosh and Bunny W. is heard best on 'Shakedown', a dynamite piece of work often found in the cut out bin. Solo efforts by es-Wailers Tosh and Bunny Wailer are also worth seeking out, Tosh's magnum opus being 'Equal Rights', a hard driving and militant record predating his limp efforts with Jagger and Richards. Bunny Wailer, he of beautiful voice and mystic temperament, can be heard to best advantage on 'Protest', his finest contemporary effort and 'Sings The Wailers', his latest, a tribute to the original sound of 'The Beatles of Jamaica'.

If you are attracted to reggae's soulful sound but the heavy political/religious content leaves you cold, the music of Toots Hibbert and The Maytals might be just the thing. Toots, at 40, one of reggae's oldest superstars, has taken the best of American soul and island roots music and synthesized it into a sound all his own. His recorded output spans the years of ska music up to the present, with most of his albums worthwhile. The essentials include 'Funky Kingston', with its dynamite title track and reggae version of 'Country Roads', 'Just Like That', his extremely danceable studio effort of last year, and 'Toots Live', a just released concert recording done in 1979 at England's Hammersmith Palais, featuring many of his finest songs, presented before a super enthusiastic crowd.

Reggae's most hypnotic and spiritual performer is Winston Rodney, better known as Burning Spear. Spear's albums literally drip with dread, and his followers are among reggae's most

*Toots Hibbert.*

fanatical. No Spear collection would be complete without the 'Marcus Garvey' album, with its must-hear versions of 'River Jordan' and 'Slavery Days' and the companion dub album, 'Garvey's Ghost'. Others of note include 'Social Living' and his latest, a tribute to Haile Selassie, called 'Hail, H.I.M.'

As mentioned in the introduction, this listing is highly subjective and not everyone will agree with it, but, hopefully, it will help familiarize you with the best works of worthwhile reggae artists. This is only the first installment, and in future issues we will cover dub, DJ, ska, and the English scene... do not forget, Reggae Got Soul! --Daddy Cool

# Album Reviews

**THE LOUNGE LIZARDS** The Lounge Lizards (Edition: EG)-- Well, man, it's about time somebody crossed 50's jazz with the NY Art/New Wave scene. Looking back before their childhood, the band covers Thelonius Monk's 'Well You Needn't' and 'Epistrophy' and choose Teo Macero as their producer (producer of many Miles Davis albums). Throw in some more Miles, T. Monk, some John Coltrane, a little Carly Bley, and some jaded cynicism and we have a very cool sweaty record which one can file next to all those great black jazz performers. --CL

**HEARTLAND USA** Various Artists (Prairie Sun: PS101)-- Prairie Sun is a free weekly music newspaper operating in the northern Midwest area--Illinois, Iowa, and Minnesota. They cover various timely topics and musically their concentration is more towards the country, soft, laid-back rock orientation in demand today. So one might expect that a recording they sponsored would lean toward their tastes. Well, it is not my kind of music and I probably should not be writing about it. In closing, there are ten bands performing effectively who no doubt will gain from the exposure. And probably too many people will like it. --SK

# Live Reggae Every Night Of The Week

Within the last year, reggae in the Midwest has made tremendous progress. Several new bands have been creating cross-country circuits of small clubs, where people are starving for more reggae. Chicago has become a big center of activity. The Wild Hare Club, at 3530 N. Clark, features live reggae shows seven nights a week and claims to be the only club in America that does. Currently there are about eight or so bands that regularly play there.

The club is booked by Jam Rock Productions, who began with the favorite, The New Era Reggae Band. New Era are six Jamaicans who formed in Chicago a few years ago. One Love, another Jamaican band, was another early formed band. Although there is a growing Jamaican community, the majority of the 300-plus who pack in on the weekends are white.

An earlier band, Traxx, have split into two groups--the calypso funk Gypsy Fari and Earthquake. A unique sound is the combination of Ethiopian melodies and reggae rhythms provided by Dallol, Ethiopians attending college in Chicago. Sterio is a reggae band from Belize who are gaining a following. Nyan Como is another Jamaican band. Heavy Manners are more ska oriented than the others. Most of these bands stay in the Chicago area. The Tony Brown Band from Madison travel a different circuit but they are professional musicians.

The Blue Riddim Band travel around with their rock soul reggae blend. Their debut album, on Flying Fish Records, is due out soon and was produced by Prince Jammy. They are the only white reggae musicians in the area but they believe that seeing white musicians playing reggae will help reggae to become more popular. And who can deny that reggae is the music of the 80's?

---

April 10, 11--The Dog People

April 14--Congo Song

April 15--Storm

April 16--Suitcase Sympson

April 17, 18--Abuse and Get Smart

April 22--Ram

April 23--Beth Scalet and Method

April 24, 15--Gypsy Fari Reggae Band

April 29--Idol Threat and Days

April 30--Caribe

OFF THE WALL HALL
737 New Hampshire
(913) 841-2266
In downtown Lawrence

Off The Wall Hall can accommodate your party. We also have affordable rehearsal space for bands. We book many bands from the tapes we receive. If your band has a demo we would like to hear it. Please send demos to Post Office Box 91, Lawrence, KS, 66044.

## TALK TALK PUBLICATIONS
## FRESH RECORDS

New Address
Editorial Office
2 East 7th Street
Lawrence, KS, 66044

**Free Button**

P.O. Box 36   Lawrence, Kansas 66044

Back Issues Still Available

Vol. 1 Compilation--Early record reviews, Interviews with Miles Copeland, Brian James, Fashion, Ultravox

Vol. 2 No. 1--London Calling, Metal Box, Ultravox photos

Vol. 2 No. 2--Reggae special, Local record stores, Thumbs photos

Vol. 2 No. 3--XTC interview

Vol. 2 No. 4--Clash, Iggy Pop, Jam, Madness, XTC photos

Vol. 2 No. 5--Singles Special, 999, The Dickies, Iggy Pop photos

Vol. 2 No. 6--Summer Mini-Issue, Regular Guys feature

Vol. 2 No. 7--Tourists, Squeeze, New Era, Selecter interviews and photos, Public Image photos

Vol. 2 No. 8--New Era, Toots and The Maytals, Third World, Blue Riddim Band, Thumbs photos

Vol. 2 No. 9--American Exclusive: Reggae Sunsplash: 18 pages of photos and reviews

Vol. 2 No. 10--Dexy's Midnight Runners photos, Throbbing Gristle, Cramps, Magazine interviews and photos

Vol. 2 No. 11--The Beat, Blue Riddim Band interviews and photos, Throbbing Gristle

Vol. 2 No. 12--Ultravox, Burning Spear, William Burroughs, Allen Ginsberg

Vol. 2 No. 13--XTC, The Slits, Burroughs and Ginsberg, FREE BUTTON

Vol. 3 No. 1--Jimmy Cliff, Third World, New Era, Duchamp, The Clean, Get Smart, Laurie Anderson

Vol. 3 No. 2--Abuse Flexidisc, Blue Riddim Band, Hitler Youth, Regular Guys, Get Smart

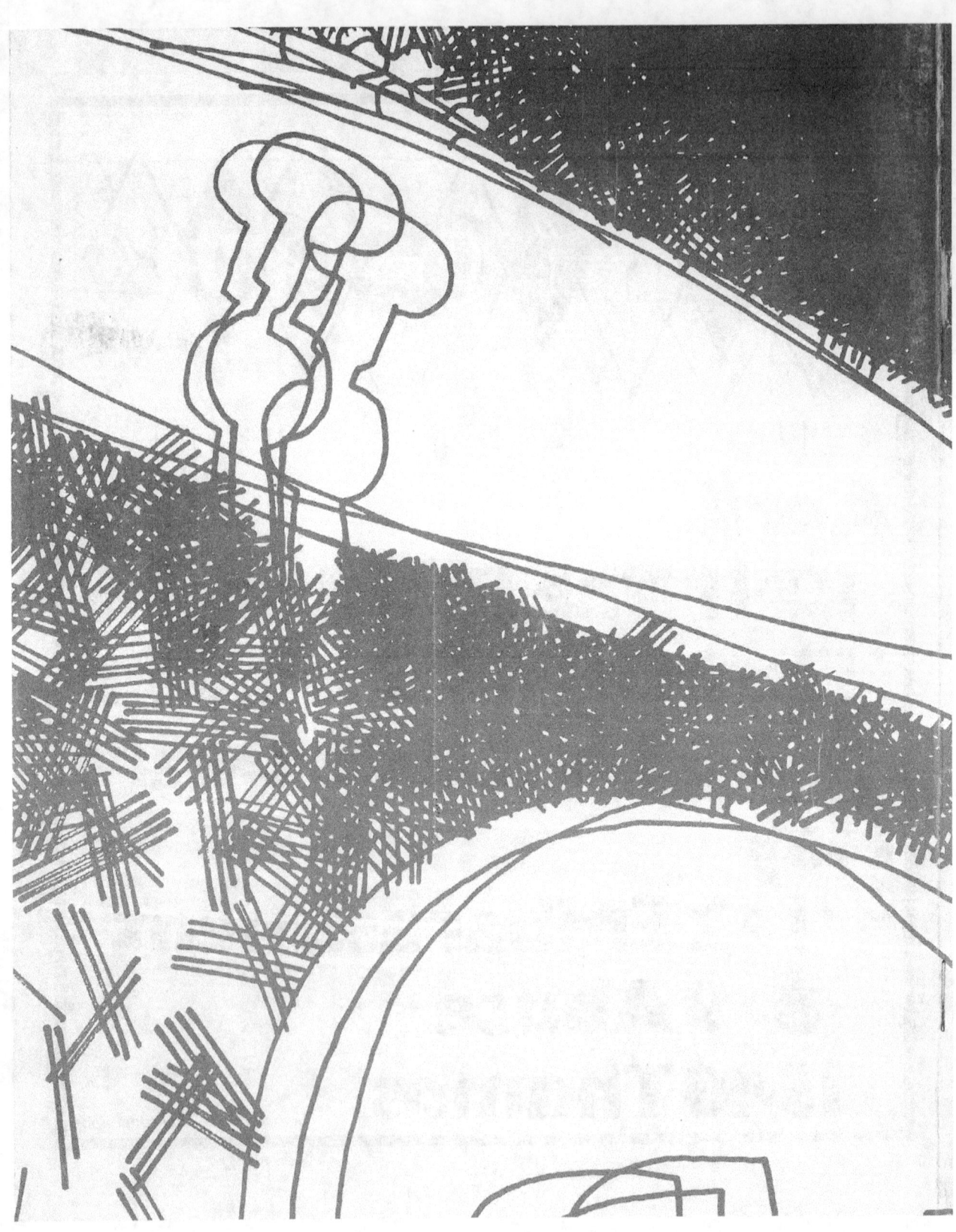

# TALK TALK

The Midwest American Rock and Reggae Magazine

Volume 3 Number 4

$1.00 SPECIAL

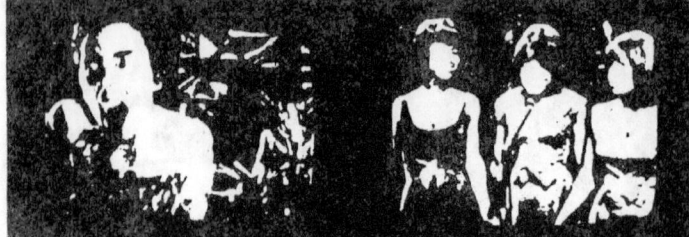
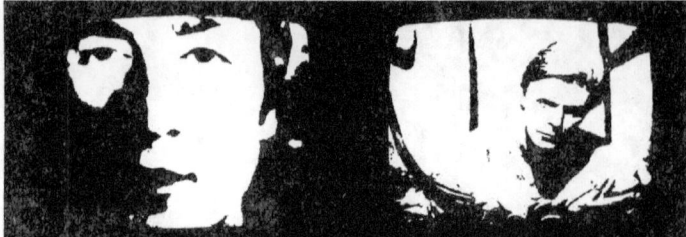
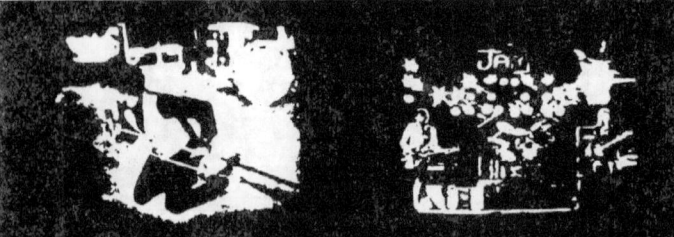

# TALK TALK

Vol.3 No.4          June 1981          $1.50

INTERVIEW: Dennis Brown .................... 4
LIVE: Steel Pulse ............................. 6
REGGAE REVIEWS: Rico, King Kong,
    N    Kojak ................................ 8
NEWS AND VIEWS: .......................... 9
LIVE: U2...................................... 10
INTERVIEW: U2 ............................. 10
LIVE: The Spectres ......................... 12
INTERVIEW: Get Smart! .................... 14
INTERVIEW: Lee 'Scratch' Perry ............. 20
REGGAE REVIEWS: Black Ark, Jah Thomas,
     Barry Brown, Majestarians, General Saint .... 21
LIVE: The Stranglers ........................ 22
SINGLE REVIEWS: Laurie Anderson, The Names 26
WEST COAST REPORT ....................... 27
ALBUM REVIEWS: The Cure, Pere Ubu, Stiff
     Little Fingers, Metal Urbain, Tuxedo Moon .. 28
     Cramps..................................... 29
     Declaration, DAF .......................... 30
     Ramona Open House ...................... 30

**Editor**
Bill Rich

**Editorial Staff**
Marc Burch
Robin Kyle
Mark Gilman
Sharon Mayer
Dave Stuckey
Mel Cheplowitz
Rick Hellman
Ivan Hough

**Photography**
Doug Cunningham
Robin Kyle
Frank Loose
Bill Rich
Rick Schneider

**Layout**
John Lee

**Typesetting**
Joan McCabe Moore

**Cover**
John Lee

**Office**
Linda Slaper

All contents copyright 1981 by Talk Talk Publications, PO Box 36, Lawrence, Kansas, 66044. All rights reserved. Any opinion expressed is solely that of the writer and not necessarily that of this publication. Subscription rate is $6 for six issues. Articles, reviews, and pix submitted for editorial consideration are welcome. Not responsible for unsolicited material. Address all correspondence to Talk Talk Editors, PO Box 36, Lawrence, Kansas, 66044, USA.

# Interview: Dennis Brown

*Dennis Brown has recently signed with A & M Records with Foul Play being the initial release. He was recently in LA and A & M arranged this telephone interview.*

TALK TALK: Hello, Dennis. This is Bill Rich from TALK TALK. Let's start out by getting some background information on your history and then move to current things.

Dennis Brown: That sounds cool.

TT: You started singing when you were quite young–when you were nine in 1967?

Dennis Brown: 67 and 68. Yes.

TT: Were there any recordings made then?

Dennis Brown: Actually, I made my first recording when I was 13. The first album was called NO MAN IS AN ISLAND, NO MAN STANDS ALONE, which was for Sir Coxonne Dodd.

TT: I thought you started out with Byron Lee.

Dennis Brown: Oh, yes. That was way back, way back. That was like doing shows. But recording-wise, it was for Downbeat, Coxonne Dodd.

TT: About 1970.

Dennis Brown: Yes

TT: How does your story compare with today's opportunities. I expect you had a hard time, being so young with certain people backing you or pushing you to do recordings. Are there opportunities like that today?

Dennis Brown: Well, no. My experiences were very different than other artists'. I was with this band called Falcon in Kingston. I was the lead vocalist. The manager knew Coxonne and we did a demo recording of an American song called 'Love Grows' by the Hollies. Downbeat was impressed with this sound and thought it would be best to go ahead and do an album.

TT: What do you have out now-about 17 or 18 albums out?

Dennis Brown: No, about 14. The 13th was FOUL PLAY.

TT: What about SPELLBOUND–is that 12th or 14th?

Dennis Brown: 12th.

TT: How is that one going?

Dennis Brown: It has been successful in both Jamaica and England. But I think FOUL PLAY will be even more successful.

TT: I didn't realize you were so young. Being around so long, I thought you were middle-aged.

Dennis Brown: I am 24 now.

TT: A lot of people would think that is quite young to have achieved such a high level of success. Do you get much resentment from the other older reggae musicians who have been around as long and not achieved your stature? Is that much of a problem?

Dennis Brown: No, not really. You see, I am glad to say that I am one of the most respected artists in the industry in Jamaica. I have had no problems with anyone.

TT: OK. You are in America now getting a tour together?

Dennis Brown: Yes, we should start in June or July for about eight weeks.

TT: I saw you last July at Sunsplash with We, The People as your backing band. A lot of people considered your performance, which closed out the Sunsplash show, to have been the highlight of the week. Are We, The People or Joe Gibbs and The Professionals or Sly and Robbie going to be backing you on this tour?

Dennis Brown: I am not too certain about Sly and Robbie but there will be some Professionals there. Some A-class musicians, like Earl Chinna Smith and probably Lloyd Parkes on bass and some of the best musicians there.

TT: What are you doing in your shows now?

Dennis Brown: A mixture of old and new. I will give them a bit of my new stuff and mix it with some of the old stuff.

TT: I was a little surprised on FOUL PLAY, which seems to have an emphasis on personal relationships. Isn't that more prominent here than on other albums?

Dennis Brown: Yes. You see, what we were trying to do on FOUL PLAY was to vary the music and the sound. The songs like 'On the

Rocks' and 'Come On Baby' and even 'Foul Play' are very different and I have never done anything like that before.

TT: Are you going to continue along that same line?

Dennis Brown: Hopefully, hopefully. I'll be doing songs that I think will be accepted by the majority. My main interest is to get across to the Americans because I am fairly new here.

TT: I guess, to the general public at the moment. I still think that JOSEPH'S COAT OF MANY COLORS and LIVE AT MONTREAU 1979 are my favorites.

Dennis Brown: You see, JOSEPH'S COAT is one of those albums that is a protest album . . . more protest than anything else.

TT: So, are you trying to get away from that or how do you explain it?

Dennis Brown: What I am trying to do is get these people involved in Dennis Brown before venturing on to any other direction. An album like JOSEPH'S COAT would be too hard for them to get into.

TT: I really love the John Holt song, 'Man Next Door'.

Dennis Brown: Well, 'Man Next Door' was one of my favorite songs and like I did that song mainly because I loved it and I wanted to sing it. I think I will be doing more of those songs soon.

TT: There is an English band, The Slits, who have also covered that song. What do you think of all these rock bands doing reggae like Blondie's 'Tide Is High'?

Dennis Brown: I think they are doing a good job. Such as The Police are helping to get reggae more established.

TT: Do you think that is the correct way to go about it? Some people don't.

Dennis Brown: Well, some people don't but we must face facts. They are more established than any other reggae artists, you know. They are trying to do reggae and they are only making reggae music more acceptable to a wider audience. I, personally, would not put them down but give them credit for what they do.

TT: OK. Let's talk about labels for a minute. The DEB label (Dennis Brown's own company).

Dennis Brown: No, it does not exist anymore.

TT: What about Laser?

Dennis Brown: I'm not contracted to Laser anymore. The reason for that-Joe Gibbs and Laser--I was only appearing on Laser through Joe Gibbs and that contract has expired now. I am only recording for A & M now. I will not be recording with Joe Gibbs anymore.

TT: Are you still friends with them?

Dennis Brown: Yes, but now I am with A & M.

TT: How did that happen, anyway?

Dennis Brown: Everything started happening through Larry Maxwell (his manager).

TT: Is A & M going to pick up any of your old albums?

Dennis Brown: Yes, I think they will start handling the whole catalogue of Dennis Brown.

TT: You must have five or six labels that you have been on

Dennis Brown: Right. But most albums are mine and have been self-produced.

TT: So, no problem in getting them out again.

Dennis Brown: Right.

TT: How long have you been in America?

Dennis Brown: I left Jamaica on Friday (4/24) and will leave Wednesday for Kingston.

TT: What is it like in Jamaica now?

Dennis Brown: Everything is smoothing out now--less violence now. Things are changing.

TT: Is anything getting any better regarding anyone getting money to eat?

Dennis Brown: Yes, things are changing now since the new government has taken over.

TT: How about new sounds in reggae music?

Dennis Brown: What is really happening is the sound of Sly and Robbie. Everyone is searching for that sound.

TT: OK. I want to thank you for taking the time out.

Dennis Brown: It has been a pleasure.

# Steel Pulse

LIVE: Lawrence Opera House May 2

Steel Pulse remain the frontrunners of reggae bands emerging from England. The six musicians have been to together four years and have released three albums. The first, HANDSWORTH REVOLUTION, was the top release of 1978. The follow-up, TRIBUTE TO THE MARTYRS, in 1979, showed a tighter sound. The message of praising those who were victimized by society was upfront but the music was still the focus. Their latest release, REGGAE FEVER or CAUGHT YOU, depending on where you live, is in a different direction with a touch of a disco orientation. The band and their label, Island, have parted company, mainly a result of Steel Pulse's frustration at the lack of promotion and distribution. Like many bands, they have been checking out record companies while on this tour, now three months along and drawing to a close.

Their performance in Lawrence was the best reggae act to appear at the Opera House. The crowd was large enough and enthusiastic. Fortunately, it was a cool evening, with the proper ventilation, a welcome relief from the heat Steel Pulse create. They are perfectionists and their practice proved to pay off.

They performed songs from all three albums, including the early hits: 'Handsworth Revolution' and 'Ku Klux Klan'. Several live dub interpretations were done, including 'Biko' 'Reggae Fever', and 'Drug Squad' from their latest release and 'Soundsystem' were other outstanding selections. The sound was almost identical to their recorded productions with the added sensation of an impressive stage presentation. David, lead guitar and vocals, was the focus and Steve on drums kept everyone going with his creation of several rhythms occurring at once. Since the show was videotaped for cable television, there was plenty of emphasis on lighting, along with cameramen running around the stage I can't wait to see that. And as soon as the band finds a suitable label, they will be recording again.

BILL RICH

# Reggae Reviews

**RICO That Main Is Forward (Two-Tone: CHRTT 5005)**-- Rico Rodriguez is, of course, the top trombonist, whose career became rejuvenated when he joined the young English ska band, The Specials. This album has been anxiously awaited for years. And no one will be disappointed. Now, maybe some might be surprised at finding covers of songs by Charlie Parker and Lionel Hampton, but when they came out in the late '40s and early '50s, Rico was playing them in Jamaica to who knows what kind of audience. There are two sets of musicians on this album, who together form the cream of the crop of reggae. It was recorded at the legendary Joe Gibbs Studio in Kingston. As one might expect, Rico's trombone is continually the focus. The whole brass section is extremely outstanding. Those of you who enjoy the trombone will get hours of enjoyment from this. --WB

**THE KING KONG COMPILATION (Island: IRSP 12)**-- Leslie Kong was one of the most respected producers of reggae throughout the '60s, when reggae was in its early stages. The success of many reggae artists was a direct result of his belief and dedication to this musical form. This album contains some of the best cuts of the musicians he helped, including Toots and The Maytals, Desmond Dekker, The Pioneers, Ken Booth, Delroy Wilson, Ansell Collins, The Melodians, Tyrone Evans, and Bruce Ruffin. They represent work done in 1968 to 1970 before his untimely death in 1971. KING KONG contains 16 songs-- some hits and some obscurities--that give the genuine feel of early Jamaican reggae music. There are some great liner notes by Rob Bell, who, along with Warick Lee, selected the cuts for this excellent compilation. Right now I think that KING KONG is the best compilation of the year. So look for this one in the racks and take a look at it. You'll probably carry it to the counter and to your turntable. --WB

Kojak in Kingston last summer.

BILL RICH

**KOJAK AND LIZA Showcase LP (Kojak: NKLP 001)**-- At long last, an entire album has been released by one of the new breed of Jamaican singers. There are six songs along with their versions which give the listener a good taste of new sounds in Jamaica. Most songs use a female backing vocal toaster--two different Liza's are used. The hit, 'Penitentiary' is reworked to fit into the overall feel of this release. It was originally recorded at Joe Gibbs, but Kojak has moved on to other pastures. Besides writing all the cuts, he produced it all. Good work. You'll be hearing more from this character to be sure. --WB

# News and Views

The police paid a visit to Kansas City's Music Box about midnight Saturday, May 2, and, although the club survived the courtesy call with only minor inconveniences, it looks like there are some changes in store for the club. Specifically, it will be a 21-and-over club for at least the next few months.

According to the authorities, the visit was prompted by a large crowd milling about outside the club at 47th and Troost during a break by The Embarrassment. Some of them were drinking, including a 14-year-old female (is that you, Annabella?), who appeared rather intoxicated.

About seven officers moved into the club and began randomly checking IDs. Because the club has a food license, people under 21 are allowed in but can't drink. Everyone checked had proper identification, but one poor soul, mistaking a female officer for a fellow patron dressed as a cop, put his arm around her. The officer, not taken by the chap's friendliness, removed him from the club.

The police then started checking the club's wide assortment of licenses. After asking for and examining one license, the police would walk outside and caucus before returning and asking for another license. It all took about 45 minutes, during which The Embarrassment dutifully played away. Eventually, they came to a license that couldn't be found and the club was closed.

Promoter Pam Travitz, wary of antagonizing the police, said although she would have preferred a more abbreviated procedure, 'They didn't harass anybody. It was a very non-violent police action. Nobody flipped out.'

One more oddity about the license check: a week earlier, police had checked the bar's papers and found everything in order. A spokesman for the Kansas City Police Department said it was a matter of policy whenever there was a disturbance at a tavern.

'If it's a place with a continuous problem, or a place where we think it may become one, we'll check them,' the spokesman said.

Travitz said this was the first time the club has had problems with the police. Jim Crawford, the owner, hopes it's the last.

Crawford said the city 'has been down on us with the under-21 crowd' because the club is too crowded to make sure the youngsters aren't imbibing.'

And that gets to the root of all this evil. On most Fridays and Saturdays, the Music Box bears a striking resemblance to a can of sardines. If you want a breath of fresh air, or for that matter to even exhale, you have to walk outside. If you happen to have a beer in your hand, you're breaking a city ordinance.

Although the club has planned to expand for a long time, that move is still in the unforseeable future. So, as a temporary measure, the club's kitchen will be removed within the next week and converted into an area for bands. That will provide an additional 150 to 200 square feet of dance floor.

But, because of that, club owner Crawford voluntarily surrendered his food license, which means no more under 21ers will be allowed in the club.

The club had originally planned to expand downstairs, but Crawford said 'I've run into so many little things you've got to do, it's just been a flat headache.'

Now the club has two options. They can still expand downstairs or there's a possibility it can expand sideways, taking in the building next door, which is expected to be vacant soon. As for now, Crawford said, all plans are up in the air. He can get his food license back, and thus the under-21 crowd, depending on the final setup of the club.

The missing license was taken care of and the club reopened on the Monday after the police dropped in. Because the food license is gone, it will no longer be open on Sundays. But Crawford says he hopes the temporary expansion and the eventual remodeling will relieve the overcrowding and remove any future incentive for police action.
--Ivan

# U2

LIVE: Uptown Theater, KCMO April 6

U2 stress their individuality. When approached about the image they wish to project, they reply that they don't consciously try to project any image, they are individuals. They don't fit into any of the popular musical categories. U2 has amazing crossover potential, which their show proved by the diversity of the audience.

If U2 project anything at all, it's enthusiasm and optimism, their live show is a joyful experience, something fresh and lively, compared to the nihilistic feeling so chic among young bands today. Bono was constantly on the move, the vast stage almost too confining for his bouyant vocals. Bassist Adam Clayton and Drummer Larry Mullen provided a stead bottom along with the added razor sharpness of The Edge's guitar. --RK

Bono Vox

*TALK TALK wishes to thank Ellen from Island (Warner Brothers) for setting up the following interview with Larry Mullen, U2's drummer.*

TALK TALK: Give us a little basic background on U2.

Larry Mullen: We started about five years ago, in school, I put a note up on the school board asking for musicians who wanted to join a band, cause I had a set of drums. The Edge, Bono and Adam came out of that. We played in school for about two years, just messing about, just learning to play, and learning to play together. When we all left school, we just sort of carried on from there. None of us were working just sort of messing around, trying to get things together.

TT: I've heard that Adam was sort of a driving-guiding force behind the band in the beginning.

Larry: That's a good one--Adam came along and we were just sort of learning how to play. Anyway, Adam comes along with his bass guitar and he was using words like 'gig' and 'fret', things we hadn't heard cause we were still young, in school, you know. And we thought, 'Well, this guy must be able to play.' So he joined, we were having some trouble working things out and a friend came along to practice to see the band, she said to turn down our sound and let Adam play and we found out he was just poking along, messing about, he couldn't really play a bit. We soon changed that.

TT: Is the band all of the same religious persuasion?

Larry: No, Bono and The Edge are Protestant, I don't know what Adam is, and I was brought up Catholic.

TT: Does that cause any tension?

Larry: Not at all, Ireland is a country of many religious attitudes, ,and religion doesn't actually come into our work. Besides we're from the South, in the North they fight about it, in the South they talk about it.

TT: Do you think being Irish has changed your approach to the music business?

Larry: Being Irish has made a difference in everything, from attitudes to just everything, but especially musically, cause in Ireland we sort of grew up and learned to play first, we were then asked if we wanted to go to England to play. We went in with a very, very open mind, but knowing what the whole music business was like. It seemed because we were Irishmen, and removed from the whole scene, that we could see things more clearly. Whereas, a band that was right in the sort of middle of it, say from London, who sort of before they've grown up, before the band's even a year old are swallowed up by the British press and chewed up and spit out, before they know what's happened. We had a chance to grow up and see all of this happen before we were exposed to it and that's really important.

TT: Your song lyrics deal a lot with growing up psychologically.

Larry: Yes, basically that's what it's all about. Because we were all sort of 15 or 16 when we started off, we've gone through this together, as friends. Seen it all happen together and Bono felt it more than anyone else. So that's what his lyrics are about--they deal with growing up mentally---everybody goes through it, it's just people are usually afraid to write about it.

TT: Who's really big in Ireland? Besides U2.

Larry: Lot's of British bands. Let's see, who's really enormous--ABBA, Boney M, Rod Stewart--those are the people who sell a lot of records. The Police are enormous, they're probably the biggest right now.

TT: What do you listen to?

Larry: Again, we all have very individual tastes. Myself, if I want to sit down and learn, I listen to Joy Division, Wire, Magazine, Talking Heads, that's if I want to learn something. But, if I want to relax, I listen to anything from The Sex Pistols to ABBA. Actually, my favorite song at the moment is 'Wishing On A Star' by Rose Royce. I think it's an amazing song. I don't put myself in any box musically, neither does anyone in the band. Everybody's very open with the music they listen to.

TT: Do you find yourself being lumped musically into the 'New Wave' category?

Larry: We were at the beginning and we were trying very, very hard not to be. Because we were never a 'New Wave' band, never ever, never said we were. Then the press started trying to put us in with Echo and The Bunnymen and The Teardrop Explodes, in with the psychedelics, that's even worse. Obviously, they try and categorize us becauseit makes a journalist's job much easier, if he can say, well this is this and that's that. We don't fit any categories. We're individuals.

TT: Are you ever criticized for being too commercial?

Larry: No. We've been very lucky cause we haven't had a single in the British charts, therefore, we've never been a Top Of the Pops band. So, we've never been accused of selling out, we've always taken things on our own level. We didn't get on TOTP's on that sort of thing because we weren't prepared to make commercial singles. The record companies say, 'Well, you'll have to make some changes if you want to make it in the charts' and we say, No way.' We're not changing for anybody and I tell you, it's worked a lot better. Cause if we'd had a single in the charts, we would have come over here and done maybe eight tates and would have left. Whereas this time we have to work hard because people haven't heard us.

# The Spectres

BILL RICH

Most bands touring the Midwest are fairly conventional. Not so in regard to The Spectres. To begin with, they are an English band who decided to try to break America by touring without any record contract or support. It can be hard enough to achieve success when the big bucks are there to bail a band out of jams. When you are on your own, you have to work harder and risk more. The Spectres seem to be doing alright. Working from the West Coast to the East, the five band members, along with manager and roadie, travel by car from one city to another.

Among the memories of their performance will be the unconventional lineup of drums, bass, guitar, saxophone, and accordion. The accordion is the keyboard element and Bill McCabe gets his share of stares, which he takes advantage of by providing entertaining facial expressions.

The Spectres are, of ,course, Glen Matlock's band. Glen Matlock is remembered, first of all, for being the bassist and songwriter for The Sex Pistols. He was kicked out (and replaced by Sid) for being a fan of The Beatles, rumors say. No doubt more was involved than than. He formed The Rich Kids, who released some singles and an album with a sound which was a bit soft or melodic and poppy. Nothing much hapened and they finally dissolved. Then Iggy Pop picked him up for a tour and an album cutting ,project. Matlock tired of being on a payroll and formed his own band with him as frontman. The Spectres have changed their lineup over their short existence several times. An unexpected change happened a few weeks ago, when drummer Graeme Potter broke his leg. Dolphin Taylor is acting as replacement, which brings to three the number of ex-Tom Robinson Band members that have played with The Spectres. Mick Hanson joined the band as guitarist in January. Arthur Collins has been blowing his various saxophones since the beginning and Bill McCabe on accordion has been a member for quitsome time.

The band released their first single last June and their second single in December. They are waiting for a recording contract to finance their future recordings.

Anyone expecting to hear Pistols influenced songs were disappointed. If any comparisons with previous Matlock bands are to be made, it would be with The Rich Kids. They were a poppy, cheery sounding bunch of musicians.

# Interview: The Spectres

TT: Let's talk about how The Spectres ended up in Lawrence, Kansas on a self-supported tour taking a gamble.

Glen Matlock: Well, it's not just a gamble. We are talking to record companies. But mainly instead of just playing a few showcase gigs with A & R promo men who think they know it all standing around at the bar, I'd rather go out and play for the kids. So, this is what we are doing. We are trying to approach this American thing as an American band would... The problem in England is that we don't fit into a category and I would rather have a primal individual approach about it. It is a bit like banging your head against a brick wall in England at the moment for us. So, we decided to bring the whole thing, lock, stock, and barrel, over to the States and take it from here. American bands don't just do showcases, here and there. They play. So that's what we do.

Mick Hanson: Americans are a lot more responsive than England.

TT: Where did you play at first, anyway?

Glen Matlock: We just played around England. Then one of our sax players left because it was getting into more of a keyboard driving sound.

TT: I can't think of any bands that use an accordion.

Glen Matlock: Bill Haley. And a band in 'The Girl Can't Help It'.

TT: That was 1958 or so?

Bill McCabe: It's coming back in.

TT: It's sort of amazing in a way. Since no one else does it. You probably get a lot of mixed reactions.

Glen Matlock: It's been surprising, actually.

Bill McCabe: The thing I have heard is that a lot of people regard it as a novelty and that is a worry.

Glen Matlock: In a way, yes. It's a novelty that fits in. It's not a five-minute run but rather an integral part of the sound.

TT: So, do you talk about The Pistols anymore?

Glen Matlock: Interviewers and DJs always bring it up. But it is in the past. I just forget about it. It's no big deal to me. We're The Spectres.

Bill McCabe: In America it is a great thing to claw to, to grab. In England, now, they have gotten over it all. They recognize The Spectres as what they are.

# Interview: Get Smart

TALK TALK: We are talking tonight with Get Smart--Frank Loose, Lisa Wertman, and Marc Koch. What made you decide to form a band?

Marc Koch: Actually, to take it back when we first started talking about a year ago, I had just come back from taking a year off school. I was in another local band here who did two public appearances. It was a three-piece and both of the other members were quite aware of my frustration throughout the whole experience because I had a lot of originals in my head and a lot of ideas. During that whole experience, we (Get Smart) sat around and talked about how stagnant a band like that was and how stagnant bands were getting in this area. Throughout that whole time in 1980 there was a section of time where nothing was happening. We started talking about some concepts and what would be nice to hear and deal with. Why aren't people producing music we want to hear or anything interesting? Why is everyone still content with cranking out old covers and relying on new wave as a source of regenerating old '60s music?

Lisa Wertman: Or even cranking out old Ramones songs in the late '70s.

Mark Koch: Yeah, like this is the '80s. Why not something new?

Frank: It all comes to we were tired of the same old garbage...

Marc: Well, it's not garbage.

*DOUG CUNNINGHAM*

Frank: . . . garbage. Anyway . . .

Marc: There was a lot of good music.

Frank: We weren't hearing what we wanted to hear. And we knew what we wanted and we were the best ones to do it.

Marc: I think all of us, being artists in some form or shape, weren't really worried about what makes up a good song or anything. More of being creative in music, developing . . .

Frank: Taking chances.

Marc: And experimenting and creating a certain sound. At some point, I said . . .

Frank: 'Buy a drumset, Frank.'

Marc: Yeah. I just said, well, why can't we form our own band? We have all these good ideas and have been working together. I've dealt with beginning players before and I consider myself a beginner since I don't have a ton of experience. Why couldn't we do it ourselves? I was willing to give it a lot of time. It was a long shot but we went out and tried it.

Frank: A lot of times we hear three-chord cover songs that get boring after a while. We didn't want to do that. Some of our early songs are in that vein.

Marc: We had never discussed any innovative bands or delved into what was happening at that time. It was a real naive want to create something new. It was sincere, not like we wanted to jump on the bandwagon of being innovative.

Frank: Even now much of our music is naive but it has a very sincere message. I don't want to get too specific but it comes out of our name. People who go out and get excited about this type of music and go out to form a band-- don't form a three-chord band. Form a band that will use their heads. Don't use tired lyrics or burnt-out cliches, worn out hooks, worn out chord changes. Throw in some dischord. Forget about harmony. Forget everything you know and just try to . . .

Marc: . . . I've basically forgotten all I knew about rock and roll quitar playing with this band. Their approach to their instruments is totally from an untrained form which with a rock and roll guitarist doesn't fit.

Frank: A real drummer would probably laugh at my style because it is so offbeat. It's definitely very rock steady but the way I play them is sort of different.

Marc: One of my goals all along was to develop my own guitar style, which is happening. I've never seen another rock and roll guitarist play like me and be proud of it.

Lisa: When you talk about messages and all that, one article said that we tell audiences to wise up They put a quote in our mouth and said we are trying to influence people. It is a selfish thing I guess because I get so much pleasure out of it. It can be a real pain and disillusioning a times. You have to be growing in it. When you stop growing, that's the time to stop.

Marc: Also we are very aware of new music and things and we are always making ourselves do something newer and not being afraid of coming up with something totally off the wall.

TT: How do you come up with stuff like that?

Marc: Just sitting around and playing. I've never sat down and listened to something and thought, oh, there's a neat riff, I think I'll take off on that or there's a neat set of lyrics . . . I get most of my ideas from . . .

Frank: We really never figure out anything by ourselves but together. When one person has something going and lets the others figure out something that will go with that. The lyrics always come fast. The lyrics always come first.

Marc: The words are usually written about something that has happened to us or just a basic feeling that has been building up for a long time.

Frank: It usually goes in spurts. We write a whole bunch of lyrics and then that inspiration will stop and it will take a while to build up momentum. The lyrics are ahead of the music, which is good because it gives things a chance to settle down and we forget about the words and get the music.

BILL RICH

TT: How did you get together?

Marc: I came to school here and was painting my dorm room. I was playing The Sex Pistols. The record ended and I heard this pounding on the wall, 'Turn the record over.' It was Frank next door, who I had just met. He came over and we listened to some new music.

Lisa: I lived three floors below. I went to this party and met Frank and then Marc. And we just hung out together.

Marc: After that we were in constant contact and talking about music all the time.

Lisa: It (the new music) didn't swing me at first. I had no exposure to this but started listening to KJHK.

TT: Where are you from?

Lisa: I grew up in New York and came here from St. Louis. I feel like I am from Lawrence but I identify more with the big city.

TT: Where is Get Smart from?

Frank: Get Smart is from the United States. Lisa is from St. Louis and New York. Marc is from Chicago and I'm from Florida. We are probably Midwest-East Coast oriented rather than West Coast.

TT: How did you three end up at the University of Kansas?

Frank: We each have a different story. It wasn't one unified thing. I wrote to a bunch of graphic designer schools and was recommended to come here.

Marc: I was working in a hotel and had set up a meeting room for the KU recruiter who talked me into filling out an application which she took back and get me admitted in the Art and Design School.

Lisa: I wanted to be an actress and chose an affordable college in the Midwest since I didn't really know what I wanted.

T : You re 20, right, and Marc's 20 and Frank is the old man at 22?

Lisa: Yes.

TT: What about 'Ankle Deep In Mud,'?

Marc: I was playing with a band in Chicago in 1979. The drummer, Vance Lyon, came to practice with the lyrics and the song was written then. I played drums, the drummer screamed through the lyrics and two guitarists played. And I brought it to Get Smart! We cleaned it up and made it a lot more listenable, much more subdued. It's a much more swampish sound now.

TT: What is it about?

Frank: It's about anything stuck in the mud. It could be music, politics, people, in general . . . We apply it to the music industry.

TT: How about 'Numbers and Colours'?

Marc: It's an antiwar song.

Frank: Antimilitary more than antiwar.

Marc: The numbers can refer to anything associated with war . I wrote the lyrics last summer when I had to register for the draft. The colors are military ones.

TT: So how did the flexi get done?

Frank: It was recorded at Ramona Recording Studios.

Lisa: Karl Hoffmann engineered it and Dave Stuckey produced it. It took a couple of hours.

Frank: Dan Swinney was assistant engineer.

TT: How did these songs end up here?

Frank: We've been playing regularly since last October, after we started playing professional gigs. All along there were favorites or classics that we've wanted made available and we have been working on a seven-inch EP for a while.

Marc: The chance came up to do this flexidisc first and we decided to put the top choices of our songs which wouldn't be on our EP, because it will contain our newer songs.

Lisa: So this flexi was a good opportunity to release some of our early songs.

BILL RICH

# Get Smart

TT: What about the music scene?

Frank: Lawrence can be boring at times. The US in general can be good in the metropolitan areas.

Lisa: I'd rather be in a band now more than any other time.

Marc: I would really have hated to have been in a band in '74 or '73 when the whole mediocrity was going.

TT: You think it is a good time?

Frank: There are a lot of small labels putting things out and that is good. Overall among the regular music companies, nothing has really changed. There are little things happening that are good. People that are hip to what's going on can find things like Blurt, The Fall, In Camera, Mass, and other bands-non-hype bands that are offering things that are good and different. Pere Ubu, PiL .

TT: What are your plans as a band?

Frank: Do it!

Lisa: Basically, we are tyring to work out money-wise and transportation-wise a way to play as many places as possible this summer. The main thing is to go other places and get other feedback.

Marc: To get another idea of what we really are. Now, we have dealt mainly with the colege sort of atmosphere. A college town will basically, no matter what type of music it is, accept faster something which is new whereas in other parts of the US they are more set in their ways about what they like to hear and what they consider good music. It will be interesting to see what will happen when we venture into these areas.

Frank: We've got problems. It's up to us at this point whether we make it or break it-whether we can take it and push it and push it and shape it and get smart and keep it at the same level--keep it high energy and say things and not repeat things and try to find new ways to say it. People go out and say this song is about blah, blah--it has been said before so why say it again? We need to find new things to talk about and new ways to express it. Otherwise it is boring and useless. You can go back and find an album in the past that says the basic same thing. You can't rely on old things.

Lisa: A new song is never completely written until we have played it. There are cues I take off an audience. I get edgy when people expect the same all the time. Like I had to stop the screams in 'Ankle Deep In Mud' because people would come up and say why didn't you scream. What fun is that if you expect it-it's like hearing the same song over and over again every week. The same thing goes with 'Numbers and Colours'. I've changed the beat so people won't know how to clap at the end.

Marc: You get a lot of good feedback that way. People come up and say it was great to hear the changes. We changed 'Modern Boy' to 'Mixed Up Boy'(now 'Typical Boy) and got quite a few comments.  It's more fun to keep people off guard.

TT: When did you start?

Lisa: We started practicing together in late August (1980). We played for some parties . . .

Frank: Our first professional gig was on Halloween.

DOUG CUNNINGHAM

TT: How do you think people label Get Smart!?

Marc: Something that has been happening that I have noticed in the last six months even with popular music or unpopular new music-is that people have accepted the fact that bands can exist without labels. B the time we make any type of break, they won't be as quick to make a label, put a label on us.

Lisa: Of course, it is nothing against you, but it is a tired question. And for want of anything else to say, you say nothing.

Marc: Yes. But I think even if we were searching for a label for ourselves that would almost limit ourselves to something we might possibly do. I think the only thing we have ever reached upon as far as a label for our music which can last, I think, for a while, is Frank's 'excessive minimalism', which I think is a real good term. It's a lot of nothing. It's a lot of simplicity because we are a very simple but structured but complex band. It starts out very simple but becomes something very complex, because . . .

Frank: Structurally, what we are into are patterns and weaving-where you will have a guitar part and a bass part and a drum part and they are all going along. At one certain point, maybe the bass and the drum part will cross paths and then it will be drum and guitar. There are times when they are all very separate and times when they are close together.

Lisa: When we were talking about our sound and minimalism, a lot of time I think of this image of filling in holes since we are a threesome. I think of taking a thin piece of cloth and stretching it over a box with a corner always showing no matter how much you try to stretch it. A lot of times if I quit playing for a minute it sticks out. Sometimes that can be fun. We are real aware of that--with very little, creating a complete sound.

Frank: It goes back to why we are a three-piece. There is a very good tension going on in a three-piece. If one is off, it's very obvious. There's always the threat that the whole thing will fall apart at any moment. And in fact it does occasionally, which is good because it makes it fresh if you are not perfect.

BILL RICH

# Interview: Lee "Scratch" Perry

*Lee Perry has been in New York the past few months, where he has been very busy working. There is a whole new vibration going on with reports that 'Scratch' is, for the first time in over four years, writing, singing, recording, and planning for his rightful recognition. Readers of TALK TALK know that Lee Perry gets special space whenever we run acros a Scratch related release.*
*It seems the majority of these recordings are done without Lee Perry's knowledge. A new one BLACKBOARD JUNGLE is a pirated AFRICAN HERBSMAN. He was feeling inspired and called to relate his displeasure and explain his current projects.*

*Scratch and The Terrorists are out to hijack the Universe. He has dropped his Pipecock Jackson manifestation and now is the Gorilla Priest, with recordings out soon. A recent film has been completed entitled 'Sea Bat Cloud 9 . . . (Plants, flowers, water, and sunlight)'. Scratch is also The Sea Bat, out to get the villains.*

*When asked about some recent 'Scratch' material, which has been released, he explained:*

'I know nothing about it. This is the first I've heard. I have something to tell you about those ————. They are parasites, using my name, using my studio, and using my music. If you knew the things they do to me, you would cry. They keep using me and they won't stop using me. . . . It's a terrible surprise. What is happening to me could happen to anyone. They want to eat me like going fishing. One of these days the fishes will come out and hook men. It may be a mystery. Some people can slip into a flat rock . . .

TT: When are you coming to the Midwest?
Scratch: As soon as possible, man. We are working on it now. I'm hiding from parasites. I.m pulling myself together with some new youth. I'm working with white men.
TT: So you like the people that you are working with?
Scratch: Yes, they are The Terrorists and I am Doctor Sea Bat here to bless the good and to curse the evil.

TT: What happend to Pipecock Jackson?
Scratch: Pipecock Jackson? He took a rest.
TT: Already?
Scratch: Yes, he was the executor. That is another form of him. Well. He's a man in exodus. He changed form. Do you know how many changes he had?
TT: No. How many?
Scratch: He had four million billion billion trillion different faces.
TT: That's quite a few.
Scratch: That's a lot of faces. Ha, ha, ha . . .
TT: When is Lee Perry going to open a studio.
Scratch: Soon.
TT: Why did you leave Kingston?
Scratch: I left Jamaica to come to New York and find some crooks.
TT: You think things will get better in the world?
Scratch: Things will bet better when people get justice. I am the Black Arkian General. Now is my time to collect. How about that? My music is roots music.
Scratch: I am not one of the reggae fanatics.
TT: What are you?
Scratch: I am the supreme creator. I'm putting out a double album in the next six or seven weeks.
TT: People are waiting.
Scratch: They'll soon get something from me. This is a masterpiece, they will keep forever.
TT: Do you go out much in NY?
Scratch: When I go out it is something important because I have a message.
TT: Are people listening to the message?
Scratch: I am saying to the poeple love and truth. It's the key to eternity. So I am asking the people of the universe to stop stealing, stop telling lies, stop being hypocrits, stop being parasites--that's a special message and a special warning. And stop being deceivers and deniers. When they do all that, they will get the blessing of the most high.

# Reggae Reviews

**BLACK ARK IN DUB (Black Ark: BALP 4000)**-- The musical credits refer only to the Black Ark players. Although recorded in Lee Perry's studio, no mention of him is made. A few of the ten cuts are dubs of material on THE RETURN OF PIPECOCK JACKSON and various singles. Much of the album is presented in an original sounding form. Probably most cuts have been released in other forms earlier and the comparisons might be made if someone studied each one and all Upsetter-associated projects. For all I know, a complete documentation is already well known. But that is all I know--I saw the album advertised and I ordered it. The version of 'Lion In The Winter' has made any questionable value of the release insignificant-And with Scratch singing on this as well as on others you know where it is coming from. A new one for you to look for. --WB

**JAH THOMAS Dance Hall Stylee (Daddy Kool: DKLP 16)**-- With The Roots Radics Band, Jah Thomas takes off on an upbeat excursion into the dance hall style of reggae. You get rhythmic vocals, deep bass, upfront percussion, and overdubs that take a grip in your brain. Some of the lyrics are repetitive and nonsense syllables or phrases. That's the style. It is quite easy to get in the groove. The ten songs can blend together in one body motion. If you can listen to this without jumping and skanking, you better listen again and let it settle into your bones. Of course, some of the riffs grab you more than others. For instance, 'Love Pon Corner' uses the W. Williams' Armageddon Time' melody with Jah Thomas singing about not justice but sex. 'Jah Jah Guidance' has a great guitar, horns, percussion (and bass probably which means a great sound) that really attacks you deep inside--another example of how reggae is a music of spirit and feeling. --WB

**BARRY BROWN AND RANKING TOYAN Peace and Love/JAH THOMAS AND THE ROOTS RADIC BAND Adapter Chapter (Daddy Kool: DKR 124)**-- Barry Brown might be unknown in America but he is quite familiar elsewhere (re.: England and Jamaica). 'Peace and Love' is based on the Dennis Brown song, 'Immortal Tribulation'. Halfway through Ranking Toyan takes over and toasts to the end. Great stuff! The flip doesn't seem to be related to the same song. Maybe it is. Listen to it and find out. --WB

**THE MAJESTARIANS So Many Times/Flute On Fire (Daddy Kool: DKR 126)**-- You have probably never heard of this new group. They recorded this 12-inch single at Lee Perry's Black Ark Studio and Scratch, himself, did the outstanding mix. And if you are even half the fanatic Lee Perry devotee I am, you will love this one. As often the case, the B-side version is the most outstanding experience of the release. But it is nice to listen to the A-side with the vocal harmonies, and piercing organ. It has a great tempo to keep you rocking. The Majestarians, a new band, have made quite an impact already. Let's hope that their future releases retain the high standards so far. --WB

**GENERAL SAINT AND CLINT EASTWOOD Tribute to General Echo/Two Bad DJ (Greensleeves: GRED 49)**-- The subject of this release is the murder by the Jamaican authorities last fall of General Echo. The technique used, as well as the message, is in the General Echo-DJ style. Clint Eastwood is the relatively new DJ and General Saint is an unknown to me. They do a great job, especially with the backing help of The Roots Radics Band. 'Two Bad DJ' has some familiar melodies and the fullness that two toasters can create. --WB

# Interview: The Stranglers

**Burch:** You stayed in California for a while when you made Nosferatu.

**Cornwell:** Yes, I've shot back and forth a few times. I also produced an LP that Pearl Harbor was on and OUIDA AND THE SNAKES and I knew the Ready Mades quite well and hung out with DEVO. I had some nice friends over there, so I used to bomb backwards and forwards.

**Burch:** What's your long term goals?

**Cornwell:** Well, personally, I suppose if you think you've got any talent for expression you just want to be recognized for it really.

**Burch:** What's your long term goals?

**Cornwell:** Well

**Burch:** Do you want to branch out or just do music?

**Cornwell:** Oh, no, I'd like to do some acting and some film work.

**Burch:** Is the MENINBLACK your opinion of the world?

**Cornwell:** Well, it's a good point to start from inconsidering human failings, human follies, human endeavor, and the limitations of the human being and the way it's (religion) developed so far. It's an enigma. Religion is an intangible subject and to see how the human mind copes with the intangible is quite funny. That's why there's a lot of black humor in the MENINBLACK LP. People say it's depressing, in fact there is a lot of humor in it.

**Cornwell:** If you look at the way human beings deal with the intangibles. It's funny, the things they come up with to explain things. I mean you get a book like this (reaching for a Gideon Bible) in every hotel around. All that human folly is rather funny.

**Burch:** When we were going to interview you, I was really kind of leary because of the stigma behind The Stranglers. You were booked here to play about a year or so ago, they had it on the marque and then changed their minds because they were told that The Stranglers tear things up and incite riots.

**Cornwell:** We're just educating people to the truth. People are always paranoid and frightened about us, until they meet us then they realize what they read before about us is a lot of rubbish. The press and media, most of them exist to make money and the only way they can make money probably is to create sensations. With a name like The Stranglers you've got a sensation already.

**Burch:** How did you come up with that name?

**Cornwell:** We just came up with it. It was a joke. We tried out a few names and we'd ring up agencies for gigs and today we would say, 'We are The Stranglers.' One time we called ourselves, Bingo Nightly and the O.A.P.s. An O.A.P. in England is an old age pensioner and bingo nightly is an expression you see on dance halls. It's a game, every night there's bingo. So one week we would be called that and one week we would be called The Stranglers, just to see what these agencies with the gigs would say. We would ring up an agency and say, 'We're The Stranglers.' And they'd say, 'I can't possibly book you with a name like that.' 'Don't you know what music we're playing?' 'No, I don't want to know.' And then they'd put the phone down and we'd think, 'God, that was a bit of a reaction.' Then we'd ring up another agent and he'd say, 'Oh, I've got to give you a gig just on the strength of that name. It's a great name.' So, immediately, you get this polarizing of the name. They either like it or they don't.

**Burch:** Your music has changed, you used to be more personal with violence with songs like 'Tank' and 'Death and Night and Blood' and now you've progressed to 'Who Wants the World' and 'Shah Shah A Go Go', you've gotten into the global aspect of violence.

**Cornwell:** The reason for that is because it's a natural progression, first we were living out of each others' pockets, squatting in England living on almost nothing. So we were living in streets. We wrote about what we saw in the streets and what happened to us. Then we got a recording contract, started flying ... jetting off to Japan, Australia, America and your mind starts expanding. You see situations you hadn't dreamed existed in other parts of the world. So you start writing about what happens to you.

Burch: What do you think about censorship? I read about your T-shirt incident a few years back in England aren't they a little more restrictive there? You had a shirt on that had The Word on it.

Cornwell: Yeah, they said take it off or stop playing. I took it off then I got really cold, so I put it back on again. They they switched the power off.

Cornwell: The people who did that are called, The Greater London Council. They control the licenses at the spur of the moment. They can say, 'The noise coming out of here is too loud. You've got to stop playing for tonight.' And that's it. They put a court order on you. You see, they've got the law behind them.

Burch: Well, Hugh, we had better wrap this up, so we can get up to the station (KJHK) and get this on the air. Is there anything you want to tell the listeners?

Cornwell: Yeah, this country of yours is a fascinating place. It's got the capacity to be the most enlightened country in the world and yet it's full of paradoxes which exist side by side. I'm surprised that the hip people amongst you don't do anything about it.

Burch: Thank you very much, Hugh Cornwell.

# Interview: The Stranglers

Burch: Hello, my name is Marc Burch and I'm here speaking with Hugh Cornwell of The Stranglers, who will be appearing in Lawrence tonight.

Hugh Cornwell: Hello, is that working?

Burch: How long have you been touring?

Cornwell: We have been touring since the middle of March. We've done about a month-- five weeks.

Burch: Are you going north from here?

Cornwell: No, we're going west. We've done the northwest . . . New York and the states around there and the south. We've just come up from Texas and we're heading for Colorado. Boulder and then on to LA, up the West Coast, then to Canada and any towns we've missed out.

Burch: What's the purpose of this tour? Is it to promote your new LP?

Cornwell: The purpose of it is to play to as many Americans who want to hear us. This is the second tour we've done in six months here, and we should be back in the fall for a third one. We are prepared to make sure that America doesn't forget The Stranglers. When we split with A & M, we couldn't come over and everyone thought we had split up, you know.

Burch: I can remember back a number of years reading in one of those English rags. It said or one of your members said that you wouldn't ever come to America.

Cornwell: When was that, before we had ever come?

Burch: Yes, it was before you had ever come here.

Cornwell: You see, being Englishmen, when we came to America we got culture shock. If you were spoon fed in European culture since an early age, I could understand building up a certain resentment for American culture. And that is exactly what happens in Europe. We're spoon fed, about 75 percent of everything we see on our TVs originates in America. A certain resentment builds up. It's unavoidable, that some sort of resentment builds up. You've got no choice in the matter. So the first couple of times you come to the States, you have to work that out of your system. Then you can see through all that aggression you've got and can see through it. You start meeting some nice people and start finding some towns that you like . . . you know things like that. So, I say when most people come to the States it's just a culture shock.

Burch: On your previous tours you played mainly the coasts.

Cornwell: Well, that's due to A & M's lack of understanding of the band. They said, 'right, you're going to do a small northeast coast tour.' Which we did. We did about 15 dates in three weeks. Then we went back to England and then in the summer we came back and did a coast to coast tour, which consisted of a date in San Francisco, a date in LA, and one in New York. That coast to coast tour took ten days and that was it, the extent of our touring. So, then we parted with A & M the following year and came back last autumn for a more realistic tour of the States. We did about 45 dates, I think, and this one's over 50.

Burch: How have the receptions been for you?

Cornwell: Superb, it's been great. Most of the places that we are returning to from last autumn there are about four times as many people as before.

Burch: You are an established band, one of the first bands I started listening to of the new music scene.

Cornwell: Yea, we were the first 'new wave' band to appear on any sort of scene in England. We were playing in '74. All the bands that formed in '76 came down to check us out and learned all their tricks off us. All the bands, you have The Pistols, The Clash, all these guys would be in our audience.

Burch: What were you all doing before you became The Stranglers?

Cornwell: I was in Sweden working in a hospital on a biochemistry research and playing music at night. Sort of burning the candle at both ends, so I couldn't keep that up for very long.

Burch: You had to make a decision.

Cornwell: Yea, make an incision. What was I saying? Oh, yea, we haven't even got a major US deal at the moment. We've got this one off deal with Stiff because of THE GOSPEL ACCORDING TO MENINBLACK, should be released this week. But, it's not a major deal and we're probably the only band from England of any reputation that hasn't got a deal in the States.

Burch: The MENINBLACK is from the myth about the men from space who come in all black suits and they had brand new Model Ts.

Cornwell: That's right. They could have come from space. They could have been earthly in origin and they have been warning people who have seen too many flying saucers.

Burch: Their third finger is longer than the others.

Cornwell: Everyone seems to have their own bit of information about it. It's very interesting. If every bit of information that everyone had got about them was put together you would probably find out the answers to all the questions about them.

The Stranglers: Jet Black, J.J. Burnel, Hugh Cornwell, and David Greenfield.

# Single Reviews

**LAURIE ANDERSON O Superman/Walk the Dog (One Ten Records: OTR 005)**-- If one thinks about the human voice, how advanced sounds are, or how modern or whatever, we must think about Laurie Anderson's voice and music. Laurie Anderson does not release very many records. She spends most of her public time performing 'visually'. One Ten Records has just released her new record, a 7-inch EP, with Anderson on vocals and violins, and other performers playing farfisa, casio flute, sax, whistle, and drums. We have a pulsing language of syncopated rythms and sounds. Fifteen minutes worth. 'Walk the Dog' contains some excellent drumming by Dee Sharpe, combined with Anderson's high-pitched voice, the sound is a forced driving rhythm, too electronic to be primitive, perhaps a fetish of personal sounds amplified. Well, my language is not hers, listen to it yourself. --BS

**THE NAMES Speak Your Language/Night Shift (FACTORY: FACT 29)**-- It's easy to underestimate the originality of this single on first hearing. This is not just another syntho-pop cut with a catchy beat, but is so much fun that it takes a couple of listenings to sink in. The Names apparently have a healthy respect for melodic line and know how to work it up with a most danceable drum and tantalyzingly vague but not vapid lyrics. Fresh and optimistically romantic, it's a welcome change from almost everything. The songs: 'I Wish I Could Speak Your Language' and 'Night Shift' (Factory) make an interesting, but not imitative, comparison to New Order's 'Ceremony'. Although 'Wish I Could Speak' has a hook, 'Ceremony' never dreamed of, both carry you along in a pleasantly pulsating state, at once haunting and exhilarating. --SM

May 15--Abuse
May 16--Abuse, Get Smart!,
    THE TEARDROP EXPLODES
May 19--Bel Airs R & B from Columbia, MO
May 22--Go-Cats & Gear
May 23--No Exit
May 25, 26--Blue Riddim Reggae Band
May 27--Flatland String Band
May 28--Dancing Cigarettes from Bloomington, IN
May 29, 30--Dallol--Ethiopian reggae
June 5, 6--TBA
June 12, 13--Thumbs
June 19, 20--Tony Brown Reggae Band
June 26, 27--Embarrassment

OFF THE WALL HALL
737 New Hampshire
(913) 841-2266
In downtown Lawrence

Off The Wall Hall can accommodate your party. We also have affordable rehearsal space for bands. We book many bands from the tapes we receive. If your band has a demo we would like to hear it. Please send demos to Post Office Box 91, Lawrence, KS, 66044

# West Coast Report

Live: Offs 4/12/81 Keystone, Berkeley

The Offs returned to the Bay area from New York City to open a series of dates for Steel Pulse. As far as the Steel Pulse fans were concerned, they shouldn't have bothered. The reggae fans seemed proud of either sitting on their hands or hissing. As one Offs fan said to me, 'What a bunch of snobs.' It's a shame that the closed-minded elite failed to appreciate an awesome performance by one of the most remarkable bands ever to come out of S.F.

The Offs music falls into the category of 'Punk Funk', but a fascinating combination of influences is present. There are elements of James Brown, Early Motown, Augustus Pablo, Rock Steady, and DJ Style. The lead singer, Don Vinyl, physically translates the music into a dancing frenzy.

The Offs performed two completely different half-hour sets but left out 'Johny Too Bad' and 'I've Got the Handle', apparently afraid of pushing the reggae purists too far. The first set ended with a great version of 'You Fascinate Me', easily one of 1980's best singles. The second set included a cover version of Mary Wells' 'Bye Bye Baby' and their original 'Everyone's a Bigot', which seemed unusually appropriate. They closed with a long show-stopping version of 'Why Boy', with an excellent melodica solo and Vinyl's hot toasting which makes U-Roy sound like he's on ludes.

The Berkeley date was the last of a six-city tour with the group headed back to their current base of New York. How 'bout an album, fellas? --MC

Live: Fear/The Cheifs 3/31/81 The Starwood

Will the Starwood ever die? I doubt it. It continues to pack them in night after night and is probably the most exciting club in Hollywood. When the music begins, stand back. Tonight was no exception. The Cheifs (that's 'EI'), a band that has been on the local scene for about two years, opened the show with a tight set of very fast originals. They seemed to have complete control over the crowd who were actually drawn into listening to the music instead of diving off the stage for a change. Their following has grown very large in the past few months, possibly on the strength of a three-song Ep released a while back. I like the Cheifs because they walk on and play. China White was due to play on the bill later that evening, but after watching them set up and tune for over an hour, I lost interest and left. I hate showmanship. Within only a few minutes after The Cheifs, Fear created mayhem with their brand of humor and cynicism. A few weeks earlier with X, Fear presented a very tame show; saying nothing to the audience and playing fairly accessible songs. They were just kidding, folks. Singer Lee Ving has more charisma than J.F.K., and speaking of Dead Kennedys, Fear bears more than a passing resemblance to the outrageous combo both musically and lyrically, although Fear seem to have more rage and power that the D.K.s have lost through becoming too popular. The best thing about a Fear show is between the music. Derf Scratch and Philo Kramer chide the audience into a frenzy of violent reactions and then lean back and laugh their butts off as bottles, insults, and spit fly on the stage. Soaked with gob, Derf takes a poll; 'How many people's mothers out there are lesbians? Come on, raise your hands.' Kramer tells a lengthy joke about retarded people and fights break out on the floor. They rip into another song and skinheads throw themselves from the stage and beat each other doing the skank or the pogo or whatever it's called nowadays. Are Fear saying anything about their audience? The constant accusations of being homos and acting like retards sure looks true as you watch these skinheads touching each other on the dance floor. There are never any girls. When Fear invokes such a violent reaction to their chides and slags, it seems as though the crowd is defending itself. It's amazing how stupid you can make yourself look by shaving your hair to the scalp. Look at a marine some time. We need bands like Fear to point out what is base and stupid in mankind while playing some great music on the side.
–Gill Man

# Album Reviews

**THE CURE Faith (Fiction: FIX6)**-- The Cure surfaced two years ago and established a certain style of playing that has been continued. This is their third album release on Fiction. There has been a small lineup change with vocalist/guitarist Robert Smith supplying the keyboards as the band reverts to a three-piece. Laurence Tolhurst remains as originally on drums and Simon Gallup who appeared on the second LP, SEVENTEEN SECONDS, provides bass. The Cure build a pervasive sense of melancholy with exceptional use of voice reverberation. All eight cuts seem to be of their slower style, unlike 'Jumping Someone Else's Train' and 'A Forest'. --SK

**PERE UBU 390 Degrees of Simulated Stereo (Rough Trade: ROUGH US 10)**-- Yikes! What a treat! An authorized bootleg from punk hall-of-famers Pere Ubu, recorded during their stylistic peak from 1976 to '78. I don't know about you, but I much prefer the old Tom Herman/Pere Ubu to the new Mayo T. version. These tracks fairly ooze with all the tortured emotion and electric spark missing from their last studio LP. Particular highlights are the unreleased tunes, 'Can't Believe It' and 'Over My Head', featuring the late Peter Laughner on guitar. Required listening. --RH

**STIFF LITTLE FINGERS Go For It (Chrysalis: CHR 1339)**-- In many ways, this album is the best since their '79 debut, which means better than their second studio LP or the live one. SLF still have their intensity but the reggae rhythms and general feel are the strongest yet, something I get off on. They have finally come up with a new set of material, a bit more sophisticated than the earlier raw sounds but still as intense. Good to see that SLF still have it. --SK

**METAL URBAIN Les Hommes Morts Dangereux (Byzz: CEL 2-6569)**-- Metal Urbain aka Doctor Mix and the Remix. The question is: Is this a debut LP or not? I guess, it depends on how you look at it. I think of it as a debut. Why? Because it's got 16 original songs, whereas the WALL OF NOISE was simply cover versions. The title, when translated, means Dead Men Are Dangerous. That's about as far as my French goes. What's really surprising about this record is the strength of the vocals. I've always thought that French was unsuitable for rock music. It was just too wimpy sounding and not guttural enough. You'll know what I mean if you've heard Plastic Bertrand. French is simply too high pitched or breathy. Not so with these metal boys, the vocals have a definite edge to them. This LP is less abrasive and possesses a more refined sound to it than the WALL OF NOISE. It's as if they've mastered their studio gimmickry and have enslaved it rather than being slaves to it. The majority of the songs have references to anarchy and fascism. It's a shame a lyric sheet was not provided. Best songs: 'Lady Coca-Cola', 'Snuff Movie', 'Anarchie au Palace', 'E 202', and 'Creve Salope'. --U-Man

**TUXEDO MOON Desire (Ralph: TX8104)**-- The long awaited second LP from one of America's premier bands. Like the first one, HALF MUTE, this one starts out as an instrumental, too. The first three songs: 'East', 'Jinx', and '***' all seem to flow together like a musical triptych of silent film scores, jazz, and skating music. The music picks up with Music No. 1. This track sounds like something from Pere Ubu's 'Dub Housing'. The last two on side 1, 'Victims of the Dance' and 'Incubus' (Blue Suit) display TM's technical and artistic virtuosity. The flip side continues where side 1 left off. It's this side that spends a lot of time on my turntable. Every song is a gem worthy of praise, as is each member of Tuxedo Moon. Here is a band that is able to blend together seemingly incompatible musical styles and arrive at something unique and enjoyable. --U-Man

## Album Reviews

**THE CRAMPS** Psychedelic Jungle (IRS: SP 70016)-- Um . . . What else can you say? Not only is it spring, but the new Cramps album is out. Unrelated events, to be sure, but yeah, these rockin' ghouls are back. Unaffected by two personnel changes, the band actually seems all the better for dumping Alex Chilton as their producer, too since the band's own production gets to the heart of the matter without so many distractions. Psychedlic Jungle is at once scary and hilarious. The tempos of the songs have all been slowed down, so the band positively seethes through the LP's 14 cuts, including the Groupie's 'Primitive', Randy Alvey's 'Green Fuz', and the Nova's 'The Crusher' (where do they come up with these covers?). But, if anything, these slower tempos serve to increase the ominous tone of the LP. Kid Congo seems heir apparent to the Bryan Gregory -wall-of-noise-fuzz-guitar-throne and Ivy is evidently handling most of thylead guitar work now. Nick Knox continues to be one of the coolest drummers known to human or inhuman and Lux is again in fine form as he is the catalyst for The Cramps. Don't let the title fool you, though. Not a lot of psychedelia here, unless it's in the garage band sense. The key word here is jungle beat, and The Cramps more than fill the bill in that department. (Aw, gee, I forgot to say, 'Voodoo-billy'.) --Buzz

**RECORDS AND TAPES**
GUARANTEED USED ALBUMS AND TAPES

We also carry a large selection of posters, t-shirts and buttons. Bring in your good used albums.

OPEN 7 DAYS A WEEK

15 W. 9th St.
Lawrence, Kansas
(913) 842 - 3059

7222 W. 75th St.
Overland Park, Kansas
(913) 384 - 2499

## Album Reviews

**DECLARATION OF INDEPENDENTS (Ambition/Stiff: YANK 2)**-- By now you're probably familiar with this compilation LP of material culled from various independent singles released in '79 (although the collection itself was released about eight months ago) by this New York based label. What you may not know is that two of the best tracks on the album are by (almost) local boys. D. Clinton Thompson (of Springfield's Morrells) knocks the Venture's socks off with his version of 'Drivin' Guitars' and Jim Wunderle (of The Dog People, also from Springfield) gives The Seeds a run for their money with his cover of 'Pushin' Too Hard'. Some of the other groups featured (Pylon, Robin Lane, SVT) have gone on to a success of sorts, but the album as a whole is a bit uneven, as can be expected when presenting a wide (and I do mean wide) spectrum of 'American' music. As one might guess, the problem here is focus, but tough showings are made by Razz, Tex Rubinowitz, and Bubba Lou and The Highballs. Incidentally, Ambition chose as their follow-up single a repressing of three cuts by the Symptoms-Wunderle and Thompson's previous joint venture. Yeah, they know what they're doing. --Buzz

**DEUTSCH AMERIKANISCHE FREUNDSCHAFT Ein Produkt (Warning: WR001)**-- The very first LP by DAF is now available. This one features one-time member, Pyrolator, who has now gone on to Der Plan. This record is entirely instrumental. There are numerous tracks, but no titles are given. Some of these are simply fragments and others are vaguely recognizable instrumental renditions of songs that would later apear on Die Kleinen und die Bosen. I prefer this LP to the above mentioned one as it has a more spontaneous and frantic air to it. It seems more urgent and possesses the quality of 'geri reig' that Der Plan would eventually incorporate. --U-Man

## Ramona Open House

Ramona Recording Studios officially opened its doors to the world at an open house April 26. The studio survived the minor ravages of the crowd of well wishers who turned out for the event and soaked themselves in beer and wine provided by the benevolent managers of the establishment, Dan Swinney, Karl Hoffman, and Kelley Mascher.

The three began working on the studio in February while working on the initial phases of the upcoming Thumbs album at a makeshift studio at the same location as the new studio.

'During that time,' Swinney said, 'we realized we could get loans, finish the Thumbs album and have something to keep working on.'

And thus, a studio is born.

Although Swinney said the studio isn't interested 'in any certain market other than people who want to make records,' they will naturally attract local bands.

'We're confident enough about the local scene-- that there are enough good local bands around-- that people will record here,' he said.

Their first project will be to finish the Thumbs' second album, which will involve a few overdubs and some mixing. The planned eleven-cut album is not expected to be released until around September, perhaps under a new label.

The only other definite undertaking at press time was Get Smart's EP, containing four songs.

The completed version of the studio is an eight-track facility. The basic rate is $35 an hour, which Swinney said should make the studio very competitive with the five or so other recording facilities in the Kansas City area.

Although only two projects are lined up at this time, Swinney said the busines' financial status is 'very stable'. And that, of course, is where we all want to be.

The studio will do some advertising, but will rely heavily on word of mouth. So, for those of you who want to immortalize yourselves in vinyl, you should write to Swinney at Ramona Recording Studios, 724 Massachusetts Street, Lawrence, KS, 66044 or call 913/842-9955.

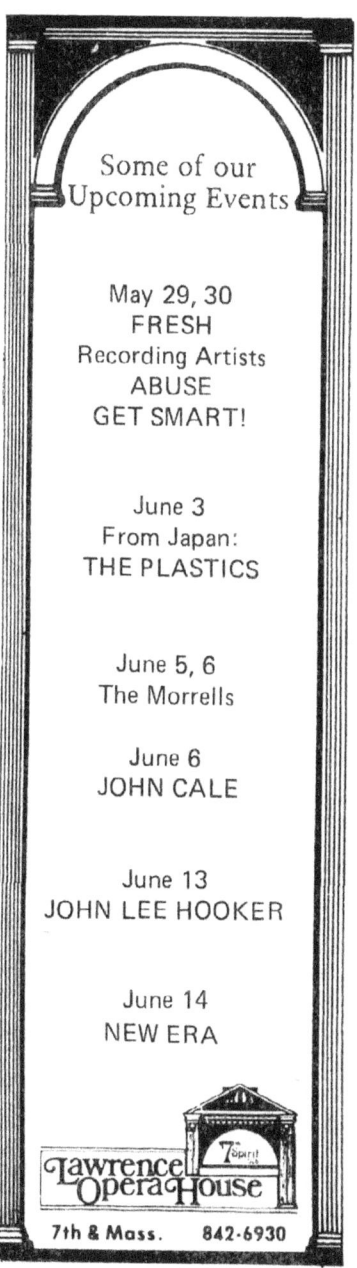

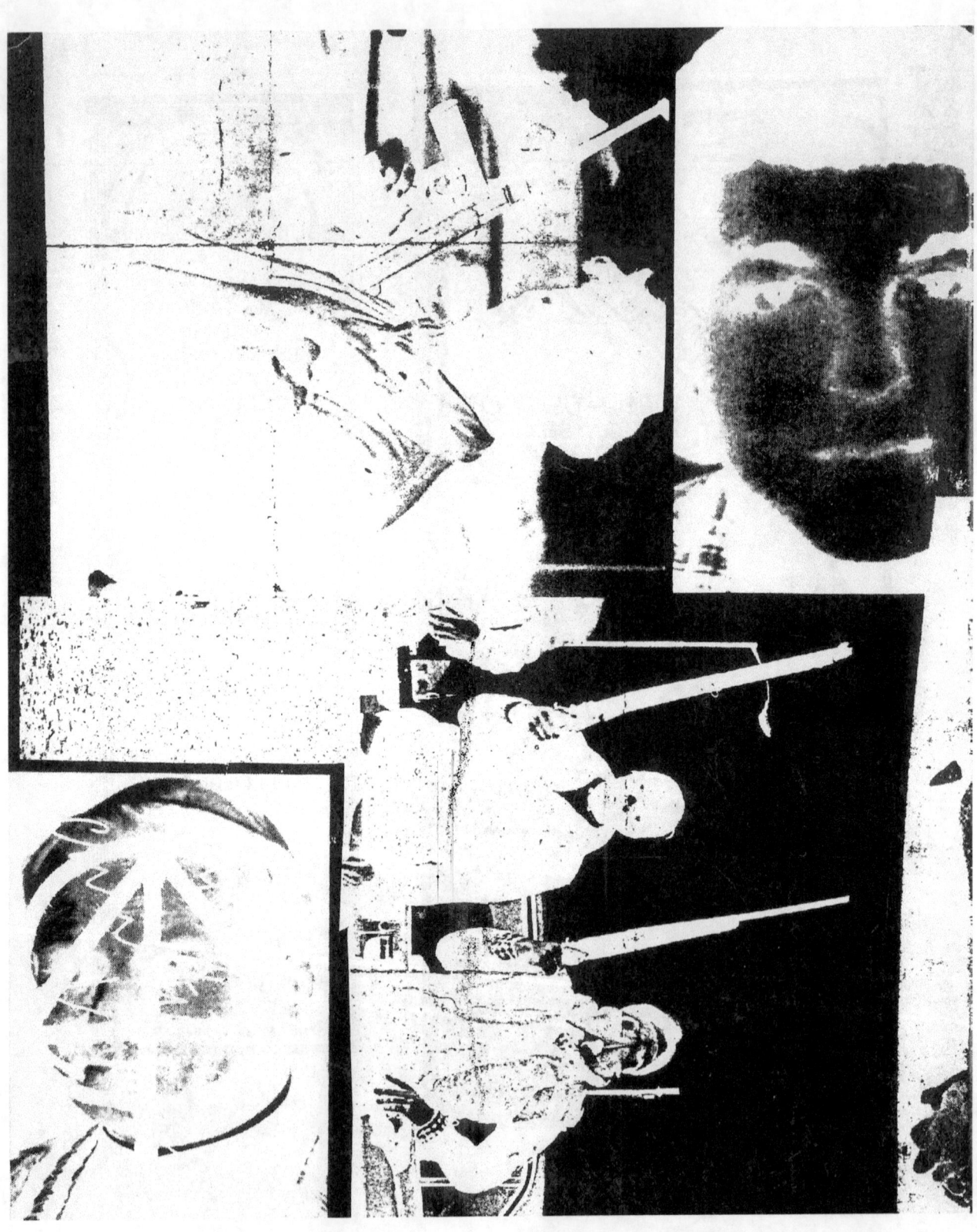

318  TALK TALK

## The Midwest American Rock and Reggae Magazine
# TALK TALK

Vol. 3   No. 5   $1.00

# TALK TALK

Vol.3 No.5             July/August 1981             $1.00

| | |
|---|---|
| Bob Marley | 4 |
| INTERVIEW: The Plastics | 6 |
| LIVE: John Cale | 8 |
|    The Teardrop Explodes | 10 |
|    The Blue Riddim Band | 12 |
| INTERVIEW: Fad Gadget | 13 |
| LIVE: West Coast | 14 |
|    Abuse, Get Smart! | 15 |
| INTERVIEW: X | 16 |
| LIVE: The Clash | 18 |
|    Throbbing Gristle | 20 |
| INTERVIEW: Throbbing Gristle | 22 |
|    SPK | 24 |
|    Colin Newman | 26 |
|    The Morells | 30 |
| REGGAE ROUNDUP Part 2 | 32 |
| REGGAE REVIEWS | |
|    Gregory Isaacs, Upsetter, Matumbi, Dennis Brown | 33 |
|    Blue Riddim Band, Bunny Wailer, Peter Tosh, Max Romeo, Equators, Third World | 34 |
| SINGLES REVIEWS | 35 |
| ALBUM REVIEWS | |
|    Rough Trade, The Fall, Start Swimming, The Beat, The People | 36 |
|    DAF, DEVO, ESG | 37 |
|    Iggy Pop, Magazine, Phantom Limb, Offs & Zero | 38 |
|    SPK | 39 |
|    C81, James Chance, 8-Eye Spy, Ludas, Packards, William Burroughs | 40 |
|    Epicycle, Typical Girls, Jody Harris/Robert Quine, Liquid Liquid, Au Pairs, Non, Psych Furs | 41 |
|    SMALL LABELS | 42 |

All contents copyright 1981 by Talk Talk Publications, PO Box 36, Lawrence, Kansas, 66044. All rights reserved. Any opinion expressed is solely that of the writer and not necessarily that of this publication. Subscription rate is $6 for six issues. Articles, reviews, and pix submitted for editorial consideration are welcome. Not responsible for unsolicited material. Address all correspondence to Talk Talk Editors, PO Box 36, Lawrence, Kansas, 66044, UUSA.

**Editor**
Bill Rich

**Staff**
Marc Burch
Rick Hellman
Rick Schneider
John Gleason
Frank Loose
Christopher Lucas
James Grauerholz
Sharon Maier
Dave Stuckey
Mark Spencer
Jim Schwada
Blake Gumprecht
Andrea Rosenthal
Stephen Graziano
Steve Kemp
Rory Houchens

**Photography**
Frank Loose
Christopher Lucas
Lowell Stewart
Rick Schneider
Nancy Schneider
Teri Bloom
Jo Stone
K. Larson
Russ Battaglia
Kate Simon
Ugene Merinov
Christopher Hunter
Bill Rich

**Layout**
John Lee

**Typesetting**
Joan McCabe Moore

**Cover**
Christopher Lucas
*'Contemporary Problems for Contemporary Music'*
Special thanks to Linda S., Louise G., Vale, Phil F., and PTL

# Bob Marley: The Lion Rests

Vol.3 No.5

On May 21, 1981, The Honorable Robert Nesta Marley, O.M., was laid to rest in Jamaica. On the left is Bob Marley at Hoch Auditorium in Lawrence, KS, from November, 1979. Above are his wife and mother, Rita Marley and Cedella Booker.

# Interview: The Plastics

TT: Let's talk about music in Japan and how everything came about.

Toshi: There are many new wave bands in Japan now, maybe a hundred or two hundred.

TT: Are there places for them to play?

Toshi: Yes, they play in small clubs. We formed the band in 1976 playing 50s and 60s style music. We have been changing.

TT: You have gone on tours with The B-52s and Talking Heads and get compared a lot to them . . .

Toshi: Because we have the same agency, same offices. That's why we played together and we love them--personalities and their music.

TT: Did you have that style before you played with them or did you try to incorporate some aspects of their vocal presentation?

Toshi: That's how we were before. Ask them

TT: You use English lyrics on your records. In Japan do you use English or Japanese words?

Toshi: Oh, even in Japan we sing in English.

TT: Do they know what you sing?

Toshi: Yes, but even if you sing in Japanese, maybe the people wouldn't understand. Sometimes we sing in Japanese but I can't understand the lyrics. When you go to concerts, you maybe only hear a few phrases.

TT: What are the bands you listened to earlier?

Toshi: The Beatles. I used to listen to Japanese bands. There was a very big movement in the 60s called Group Sound. It's a category. There were a lot of groups with sounds like Beatles, Stones style. For example, The Tigers, The Tempters . . . Tigers were the most popular in Japan in the 60s, and then Tempters were more of Stones and just trash sounds. The Janitors, the Carnaby Beats, a psychedelic group.

TT: Has the scene kept going on?

Toshi: Oh, yes. But better now.

TT: What's a typical evening out for a show?

BILL RICH

Toshi: Yes. In Europe it is called Welcome Back, Plastics. Here just PLASTICS. We just had it pressed here. We just came over from Europe and played a few US shows then went to Canada and have done a few more dates in the US up to now. American audiences are more fun than in Japan. They enjoy it more--dancing and having fun. It is good feedback. Canada was more quiet, like Japan.

Chica: They were nice people.

Toshi: Nice people, but quiet.

TT: How was England?

Toshi: London was OK. Northern England I did not like. We were billed as a punk band and we are not. The people wanted to fight.

Chica: They were living with the ghost of Sid Vicious.

Toshi: And people were shooting with slingshots. Narrow-minded. They wanted to fight.

TT: How did you get together?

Hajime: I was on the beach hunting for octopus when I met Toshi and Chica. That's how we got together. I went hunting octopus and found them. Then later we formed the band as it is now.

Toshi: Oh, maybe on weekends we go to the discos. No pubs.

TT: Not go see the bands?

Toshi: Oh, I don't want to see bands. You can't dance. It is not allowed to dance at shows. The security police make you sit down al the time. It's no fun. You can get English records at the shops. And even minor groups use small obscure labels to get things out.

TT: Your album is a combination of your two earlier Japanese releases?

# John Cale

John Cale finally made his Lawrence appearance on his current tour promoting HONI SOIT, his first studio album in several years. The live show was similar to the SABOTAGE/LIVE album. The backing band appear to be young New Yorkers who worked in the studio and can play some of the early Cale material. There were a few oldies, such as 'Pablo Picasso' with the majority of selections from the current release.

At 40, John Cale is a bit of an old dog. As the center of attention, some expected him to generate more excitement. Yes, they did rock out at times, but when Cale sits down at his organ for a slower-paced piece, as he did often, the crowd sits also. Many people were certain that

throughout much of the set, Cale's guitar was turned very low or even off. Of course Cale wasn't the lead guitarist anyway--Sturgis Nikides was. The drumming and backing vocals by Robert Medici filled important holes to give a great sound. It was a hot night, the band had a rough day on the road and the tiredness showed on occasion.

To some extent John Cale still concentrates on the theme of upcoming war, although the last few years have not produced the total destruction of which he sings. The encore, 'Mercenaries', was performed brilliantly and the crowd cheered at the thought of 'going to Moscow'. A bit sick if you ask me. But it did demonstrate that John Cale can still sing/scream with the same fervor as befc  This guy is far from washed up.

## The Teardrop Explodes

Lawrence witnessed a part of the Liverpool psychedelic revival when The Teardrop Explodes gave an outstanding performance to a capacity-full hall. People were turned away at the door, but it was too crowded to enter anyway. Even if one could not see more than an occasional-topof a head, the sound system filled the air with the sharp and distinctive music being played. It seemed that all the songs were love songs. Selections from their recordings were performed along with newer material. Their newer songs are different sounding, partly a result of the new line-up in the band. No one really mentioned the personnel changes much, but leader Julian Cope and drummer Gary Dwyer are the only original members left. Whereas Cope supplied vocals and bass to their recordings, he is now the total front man since Alfie Angius joined as bassist. The new guitarist, Troy Tate, and the new keyboardist, Jeff Hammer, provide for new excitement. The band covers the older songs well, hitting the licks as originally recorded plus adding new effects.

CHRISTOPHER LUCAS

BILL RICH

The evening opened as Get Smart! played an hour set to the already overflowing crowd. After a short break, The Teardrop Explodes entered the stage amidst the dense smoke/fog from the only gimmick of their presentation. I guess that this was the first time I had seen a smoke machine used at a show, since I normally don't go to the type of shows that use them. This time it only added to the overall excitement. --Bill Rich

# The Blue Riddim Band

BILL RICH

LIVE May 25, 26 Off The Wall Hall

The Blue Riddim Band returned to town bringing with them their debut album, RESTLESS SPIRIT. They had just returned from New York, where their shows brought praises and enthusiasm from critics and audiences. The Hall was packed both nights as the band played to the crowds of local BRB fans. They played tighter and more relaxed than regularly probably a result of the combination of playing at a familiar hall again and the relief of finally getting their record out to the people. It has been a struggle for them, but it will soon pay off. Look for The Blue Riddim Band to be internationally well known soon. --Bill Rich

# Interview: Fad Gadget

*Fad Gadget of Mute Records and one of the most popular electronic bands around was recently in country, playing several gigs along the East Coast. While here, he called the offices of TALK TALK from New York and arranged for an interview via telephone. Here is that interview between Fad Gadget and TALK TALK, who was represented by Marc Burch.*

TT: How extensive a tour are you on?

Fad Gadget: We're doing mainly New York then along the coast: Boston, Philadelphia, and Washington, DC.

TT: Nick Cash and Robert Gotobed both play drums on this tour. How did you manage to acquire Robert?

FG: A friend of mine knows him. He was out of a job also, now that Wire has split up.

TT: Are you the head of Mute Records?

FG: No, Daniel Miller is the head of Mute. Fad Gadget is just Fad Gadget.

TT: Are the Silicon Teens still together or is that just another incarnation of Fad Gadget?

FG: I've helped them along and wrote one of their songs, 'TV Plaything', which is on their album. But, it's mainly Daniel.

TT: On the Fad Gadget LP, how are a lot of those background rhythms created?

FG: Through a sequencer and synthesizer link up.

TT: Do you collect sounds?

FG: Sometimes I do, usually I recreate sounds in the studio.

TT: Do you find it fascinating that now with the advent of micro-electronics that electronic oriented bands are able to tour now; whereas a couple of years ago they were limited by the bulk of their equipment?

FG: Yes, things are a lot better now. They're making things smaller, but they haven't quite taken it far enough. It seems that Casio is going in the right direction.

TT: What inspired your new single, 'Lady Shave'? TV?

FG: TV is a source for inspiration, but it mostly comes from everyday life.

TT: 'Newsreel' is one of the most gruesome songs I've heard with its references to shooting mothers, babies, and afterbirth.

FG: That's to do with the media. The way they cover things with a sensationalistic attitude.

TT: How do you manage to perform or carry out your various duties? You play synthesizer, tapes, electronic percussion and sing. Are you trapped behind a console?

FG: I only play electronic percussion live. I have musicians to play everything else.

TT: Who are these musicians?

FG: Peter Balmer, ex-Ski Patrol, on bass. David Simmonds on keybaords. Nick Cash and Robert Gotobed on drums.

TT: A lot of people wish you were coming out here to Kansas.

FG: Maybe next time. We can't afford to travel much this time around.

TT: Is Fad Gadget the main band on Mute Records?

FG: The Normal and Fad Gadget were the first two Mute bands.

TT: Has DAF left Mute?

FG: Yes, they've gone to Virgin.

TT: Do you like the German music scene?

FG: Frankly, there's not much going on there. I like Der Plan, but I don't like DAF. They're not very nice people.

TT: Well, I better let you go now.

FG: OK, next time when we come over, perhaps we could meet.

# West Coast Report

*The Little Bears From Bangkok*

From Seattle, WA, the message arrived that TALK TALK needs to look further than LA for the West Coast. Kirby Saad Mohammed writes of two important bands on the scene, 'The Little Bears from Bangkok, three females and one male bassist, are reminiscent of early Mekons or The Raincoats, while having two bassists like Delta 5.

The Three Swimmers are built out of the remnants of The Macs and The Beakers and use layers of rhythms.'

*Three Swimmers*

# Abuse                                    Get Smart!

Abuse as a four-piece: Allen Wolfschlaegal Chris Garner, Willy McNeil, Clay Galbraith     A TALK TALK Production.

Get Smart! : Marc Koch, Frank Loose, and Lisa Wertman. Both bands performed 5/29&30 at the Lawrence Opera House

# Interview: X

*On the occasion of X's last gig in their Great Tour of the Midlands June 6 at Misfits in Chicago, Talk Talk sat down with the band to discuss their climb from obscurity in the beach ghettoes of LA to what some say is their present status as the Last Great White Hope for American Music. Of course, not everyone sees it that way. Although Tom Carson recently wrote in the Village Voice that X is the best band in America, other critics and listeners have written them off as just another LA punk band.*

*But whatever the evaluation of X, there is little doubt that they are at the forefront of a rather dilapidated American music scene.*

*A brief note of explanation is needed before we get down to business. Although TALK TALK interviewed the entire band, Exene, the band's enigmatic lead singer, was busy fleecing the roadies in a nickle and dime poker game and thus didn't join the conversation until she had earned enough money to finance her next pinball spree.*

*The interview began with John Doe, bass and vocals, Billy Zoom, 1956 Gretsch Silver Jet guitar, and Don Bonebrake, drums, discussing the 12-city tour, which began May 16. The band seemed almost surprised by the number of X fans they found in the Midwest, saying the smallest crowd they played to was 250. The Misfits crowd that night proved to be no exception, turning out in full force even though the show was moved at virtually the last minute from the recently closed WAVES. X didn't let anybody down, either, as they pummeled the crowd from the opening 'Sugarlight' to the encores of 'The World's A Mess' and 'Johnny Hit and Run Paulene', with emphasis on material from the recently released 'Wild Gift'.*

*The following are edited excerpts from the lengthy interview.*

TT: With all this relative success, have things changed at all with the fans in LA?

John: Um . . . a little bit. What I think basically went on was that there were maybe 500 people who supported us at first. Then after our record came out (LOS ANGELES, released in 1980) there was this whole new audience, this record buying public, and some of the original people who came down to see us didn't come 'cause it was a real hassle to go 'cause there were so many people. Now what's going on is a lot of the, like, skinheads are comin' round and making it real unpleasant for people. I think it's sort of evening out now . . .

TT: Have you gotten any negative comments from them yourselves?

John: Yeah, yeah, they don't like us. They think we're establishment. You have to understand that the bands themselves are pretty good; they're open minded and stuff like that but some of the audiences are real narrow minded and as soon as

NANCY SCHNEIDER

Black Flag or the Circle Jerks or Adolescents or any of 'em gain any success their audience is going to say, 'Aw, they sold out.'

TT: So, in other words, for them, you have to not sell many albums and not have anybody at your concerts?

John: Right. I was reading somewhere, . . . um. I can't remember who said it, but someone was saying it's stupid to play for 30 people so they can feel like they're the coolest ones.

Billy: Their definition of selling out is a band who appeals to anybody but them.

TT: So it's kind of an elitist attitude?

John: Right. Oh I know who it was. It was John Waters and he called it 'reverse snobbism'. He was talking about his first movies, like 'Mondo Trasho' and 'The Diane Linkletter Story.'

John: We got two letters before we left. One guy was saying, 'What the hell is wrong with you guys. You used to be a good band,' something like that. And obviously from the handwriting and just the attitude it was this 15, 16-year old . . .

TT: Was it in crayon?

John: No. He was saying how we should be a punk band. He wasn't even there. He's trying to tell US how to play punk music?!

John: And another letter that came the same time, this person who went on and on with some pretty intelligent things, 'but it's too bad I can't come to see your shows because the skinheads beat me up.' What a weird situation. You have one person that really likes ya and they can't go because the person who doesn't like you goes and beats 'em up.

TT: When you're on stage, how do you handle that?

John: Just yell at 'em.

Billy: We kick 'em in the face occasionally if it gets out of hand.

TT: I noticed the night I was at The Starwood (in Hollywood) and saw you guys in March, there was heavy skinhead activity until you, Billy, got so pissed as to throw a guy off stage.

Billy: Good show.

John: Yeah, that was real good. Another thing is that if someone throws something at you, all you can say is 'no, no, no' (shaking his finger in the air).

Billy: Problem is, you never see who threw it. You stare at the audience for 20 minutes, look away for a second and something flies.

John: The problem is, if you ever preach to an audience you sound like an idiot, so you just try to handle it as cool as possible. Or if someone is getting hurt in the audience and they're close to the stage, one of our roadies will pull them onto the stage and set them back.

TT: Sorta' nice to get away from that a little.

John: Yeah. You see, in LA, I'd say a year and a half ago, there were these little clubs, the Hong Kong and the Club 88, that were the only clubs we could play at. They were small and sweaty and fun. And that's good.

Billy: I think it's mostly young kids that weren't old enough a couple of years ago to be around the beginning and they see Black Flag and read a couple of fanzines and they think, 'Oh, yeah, that's great.'

TT: Certainly X has, head and shoulders, gotten the most media response...

John: I think that's mostly because we've got a record.

TT: Think so?

Billy: A lot of it is 'cause we're the only band from LA that's been able to make a real record on a reasonable budget. There's a few bands that produced their own records for a few hundred dollars.

John: And most never sound that good. They may be good in spirit, but it's hard for people to get past the poor recording.

Billy: Studios are expensive and it takes time to do a good recording.

TT: Did you spend a lot of time on LOS ANGELES for a first album?

Billy: We spent about 100 hours in the studio.

John: Yeah and we took about a month on the new one, took a bit more time. The first was $10,000 compared to, say, $250,000 for a major label. And the second one was $15,000, or $18,000 or something like that. We found we had sold 20,000 in two weeks, at least we had gotten orders for that. I know it's going to go good.

TT: Some critics have said the second album is a little more accessible, maybe partly because of the production. Was there any conscious effort in that?

John: I really wouldn't know what to do to make something more commercial.

TT: So I take it that you're pretty happy with Slash and the way that's working out?

John: Yeah, they give us a lot of freedom and give us a lot of good input as far as what to do on certain things... like suggestions and stuff. They know what we want to do. We got some offers from A&M and Capitol and they were just really lame, and...

TT: Probably wind up going into debt.

John: Yeah. They wanted us to change producers, they wanted us to become more commercial...

TT: Were there things they specifically wanted you to do, or did you ever get that far in it?

John: No. I was just glad they came right off and said it. Like Billy said, they get points for honesty but they lose them all for saying the wrong things. Slash also tried to get some distribution deals but the major companies, again, screwed 'em over. They said they'd give them 14 percent of the sales and they would keep the rest.

Billy: And we get 10 percent and Ray gets 2 percent and that leaves Slash with 2 percent to run a record company on.

TT: Great deal.

Don: It seems that everyone gets screwed over. Most of the bands that have signed in LA that we've known... they're in debt, sometimes the record company will kick out members of the band...

TT: You're kidding! So who would be the first to go in this band? Did they finger anybody? (laughter)

John: Probably Billy. (more laughter)

Billy: (Silence)

TT: That's wild. So you're going to Europe soon?

Billy: In September, yeah. England, France, Germany and maybe Italy.

TT: What did you think of your response when you went over there

*Continued on p.28*

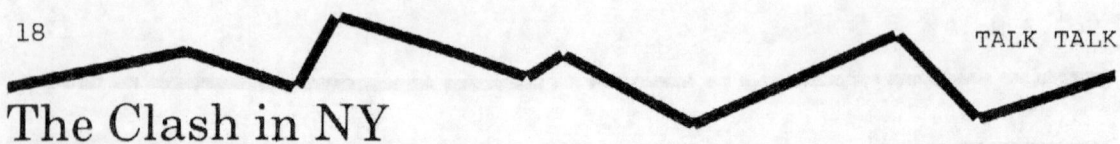

# The Clash in NY

It was an ambitous plan from the start: The Clash would play an eight-night run, in late May and early June, at Bond International Casino in New York, promoting the show entirely independent of CBS/Epic, their record company, and forcing loyal fans to travel, like the mountain to Mohammed, to New York if they wished to see this 'only American appearance' in 1981. And from the start, the plan was plagued with problems. Kosmo Vinyl, the band's aide and creative advisor, and Bernard Rhodes, their recently re-joined manager, visited New York early this Spring to decide on a venue, after Epic Records refused to give tour support to a scheduled 60-date US tour booked to open April 28th, forcing its cancellation. Instead, the band played a reportedly very profitable European tour, and Kosmo and Rhodes decided on Bond after visiting a Ramones gig there with an audience of about 4,000 or capacity-plus. At that rate they could play to about 32,000 people in all, and avoid the distancing effect of playing in a room the size of the Garden or the Coliseum. With ticket prices at about $10, and no cross-country touring overhead, this 'US tour' looked like a sure thing.

At the end of the first night's show (May 28), with about 3,700 in the audience, the New York Fire Department pulled a surprise inspection and ordered that henceforth the club's legal limit of 1,752 would be the max, period. As all eight of the original shows had already been sold out to about 4,000 Clash fans for each night, the band and the management of Bond had to add seven more shows. Two nights later, the New York Building Department put in their two bits, placing a vacate order on the club for allegedly unsafe exits, etc., and this touched off a small riot. Eventually a compromise was reached and announced at a press conference, two more nights were added, and the show went on. Bernard Rhodes was later quoted as saying, 'It was definitely down to club wars,' alleging that another, unnamed, club had tipped off the City.

An unexpected side benefit of all this was a storm of media attention, and I think it is safe to say there were about 1,700 paid admissions for each of the 16 shows after the first, overcrowded one. Also noticed in the press was the perceptibly racist response of the lumpen-white audiences to one of the black opening acts: Grandmaster Flash and The Furious Five were literally booed off the stage. Oddly, another of the openers, Funkapolitan, were also a rap band but went over smoothly on a different night; the latter band is British and—mostly white. The last I heard, plans for a couple of 'Aftershock' evenings, featuring the most popular of the various opening acts, were being cancelled due to previous commitments by Bond. (One such commitment, 'Aluminum Nights,' two evenings scheduled by The Kitchen as a benefit for that art/performance/music space's tenth anniversary, was to feature John Giorno, Philip Glass, The Raybeats, Zev, Laurie Anderson, The Bush Tetras, Rhys Chatham, Funky Four Plus One More, The Lounge Lizards, and several other guests, announced and 'surprise'. At last word, David Byrne, Robert Ashley, and VEDO (DEVO) were pulling out for one reason or another, an unfortunately typical situation for such benefits.)

I went to Bond with poet John Giorno and photographer Kate Simon, on June 11, the third-to-last night. We hadn't made any press-pass arrangements, but as an old friend of the band, Kate was recognized at the press door and shooed right in. We were given sticky-back back-stage passes and told 'this will get you to the sound booth, your friend Allen Ginsberg is there already.' We set off in search of the sound booth, a slightly difficult task since for all of us this was a first visit to Bond, and the building was formerly a giant clothing store, complete with escalators, curving marble stairways in the air, and various blind alleys. Seated at the foot of one of these stairways was an official-looking guy who looked at our passes and kept them, saying, 'I'll return these when you come back down.' Of course, he was an impostor, and only Kate had the sense to hang onto her pass.

We found ourselves on a mezzanine balcony with the spotlight operators and the usual cross section of New York's hip: leopardskin stoles, silver lamé pants, pointy shoes--all the accoutrements necessary to give oneself a feeling of successful fashionability, and distinguish one from the middle-class kids from Long Island and New Jersey (and, presumably, the 50 States) down there on the dance floor like so many rounds in an ammo box. The opening act, whoever it was, were finished, and presently we heard a deafening music from the sound system: it was a grandiose Hugo Montenegro theme with an 'Also Sprach Zarathustra' feel. Ready for anything, I watched The Clash take the stage to the screams of the audience and tear into 'London Calling.'

It was a great show; especially notable was Paul Simonon's 'Guns of Brixton'. While the band played, four or five slide projectors threw giant images on a screen behind them: Irish demonstrators, Cambodian/Kampuchean refugees, screamer headlines from the N. Y. Post, London Star, and other yellow tabloids.

During one song about El Salvador, in which Joe Strummer with heartbroken voice screamed the nation's name a dozen times and a dozen times again, sheets of paper began to issue from holes in the high ceiling of the main space, swirling down by the hundreds and hundreds. I picked up a boot-soiled copy of the page later: it was a leaflet from CISPES, the Committee in Solidarity with the People of El Salvador, a group also in evidence at the entry-doors, where they sold T-shirts showing the same clenched fist as on the 'Sandinista!' album. Unfortunately, the Nicaraguan revolution was, apparently, more successful than the current El Salvadorean struggle: the Carter Administration's policy on Central American people's insurgencies has been completely overturned by Reagan's people.

Eventually we went down to the main floor, where the view was better, really, and stood near the sound-mixing board. After another two or three songs, the band ended and left the stage. There was the inevitable clamor for an encore, and the wait was so long I began to wonder if there would be one. Then the band ran back on, and Joe Strummer grabbed the mike to yell: 'ALLEN GINSBERG!' I could hardly believe my eyes: there was Allen, with whom I had just had a modest dinner at his Lower East Side apartment two days before, taking the mike to sing his 'I Don't Like CIA' song. And what's more, he looked--and sounded--great. The Clash's steadily rising backup to his simply-chorded song gave it an effectiveness I have never heard in it before not when he played it with harmonium and acoustic guitar in Lawrence last fall, not even when Dylan played backup on some 1973 tapes that will soon be released by John Hammond Records through Columbia. He was magnificent, and the crowd threw up a roar and a sea of clenched fists when he ended. Then the Clash forged into three more songs before leaving the stage.

A lot has been written about The Clash's sympathy and support for various left-wing causes, and many have found it easy to take a shot at them for the contradictions in their stance. A friend of the band, with no criticism implied, estimated each member was earning about $3,000 a night during the shows. From my point of view, the sneers at their rhetorical overkill laced with a certain naiveté, or the cheap shots aimed at their (only recent) commercial success, are irrelevant. The Clash are a great rock and roll band; they give a great show, and they make records that, whatever their flaws, advance the political consciousness of their audience. And there is a lot of room for advance with the kids that came to these shows; as we left the club, around our feet swirled dozens of the CISPES tracts on the floor, abandoned. --James Grauerholz

# Throbbing Gristle: The Final Performance

On May 22, 1981, at Veterans Auditorium in Los Angeles and May 29, 1981, at Kezar Pavilion in San Francisco, Throbbing Gristle, one of England's most striking industrial groups, made their American debut and their last performance as a group. Throbbing Gristle, consisting of Genesis P. Orridge on bass guitar and violin, Cosey Fanni Tutti on guitar and cornet, Chris Carter on keyboards and Peter Christopherson on tapes and rhythms, were the founders of Industrial Records Ltd., an independent record label which worked through mainly mail order distribution.

Eighty percent of Throbbing Gristle's material is recorded live on stage because most of their live gigs are improvised, giving each member of the group more freedom to do what they want and it keeps them original every time. Each gig is different, so they record every concert. Throbbing Gristle has 35 cassettes recorded live, plus a TG briefcase full of cassettes and these last two gigs in America will make 37.

We were lucky enough to attend Throbbing Gristle's final performance as a group at Kezar Pavilion in San Francisco (a large basketball court with bleachers all around). After a gruelling hour of distortion from a San Francisco local band, Throbbing Gristle took the stage, each member setting up their own equipment, which was contained in premade cases which were simply opened and ready to function, no amplifiers were used.

Chris Carter, TG's electronic whiz kid, builds most of TG's equipment, especially for this tour, making everything compact and easy to transport. This is a fine example of Throbbing Gristle's idea to do things right and independently.

Throbbing Gristle aren't a synthesizer group, Chris Carter used a small Casio keyboard, Peter Christopherson used small, hand-held Sony stereo cassette machines, run through a small control keyboard unit designed by Peter and built by Chris, equipped with rhythm generator. Cosey played her guitar through a number of gadgets, fuzz, wah wah, etc., and Gen. did the same with his bass, which was equipped with a built in string resonator that obtained an incredible roaring sound.

A Throbbing Gristle concert can be described as a live sound laboratory,

PHOTOS BY RICK SCHNEIDER

many of the generic punk rockers who push fighted gaily at the warm-up group were awed or stupified by the power of TG's music. Many people who intended to see TG listened attentively, letting themselves be susceptible to the sounds they created. TG played for an hour, using improvisation yet still as a cohesive single unit. Towards the end of the concert they did their latest release, 'Discipline', as Genesis frantically sang vocals while running from side to side, beating the microphone stand against his head.

The audience was writhing in primal rhythms as Genesis grabs a swooning gay and gave him a wet kiss with lots of tongue which drove the poor boy wild. Throbbing Gristle functioned symbiotically, giving the audience music to feed on and they,

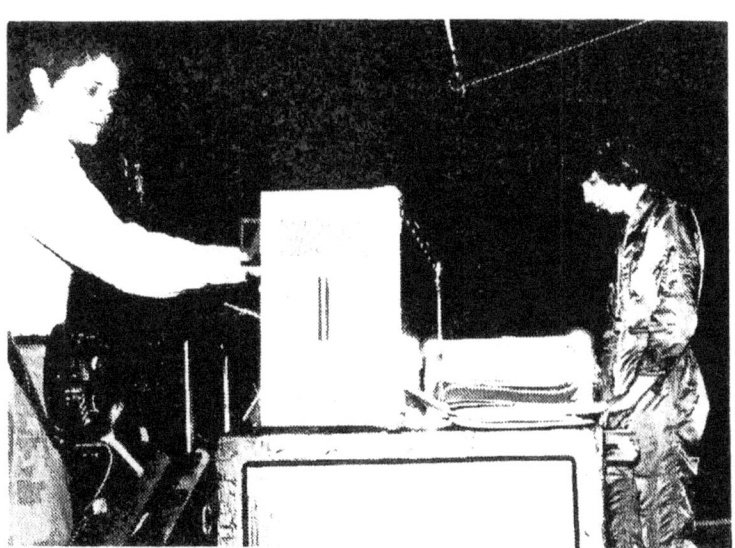

# Interview: Throbbing Gristle

in turn, feeding from the audience's reactions. No one mixes their show, which gives them complete control of what is happening on stage.

Soon the hour was up and the gig was over, after we had talked to Peter and Cosey it was confirmed that Throbbing Gristle, along with Industrial Records, are separating. Cosey Fanni Tutti and Chris Carter are going to continue producing music and Genesis P. Orridge and Peter Christopherson are planning to do video to be broadcast on late night British television, when all other stations have gone off the air. Genesis and Peter have also released NOTHING HERE BUT THE RECORDINGS, an album compiled from tapes located here in Lawrence, Kansas, in the William Burroughs archives, utilizing the cut up method of writing created by Brion Gyson and experimented with by William Burroughs.

Throbbing Gristle are breaking up mainly because they have become more popular in the past few years, maybe too popular. They feel pressured to do more material because of that popularity Throbbing Gristle won't do what they don't want to do and they also won't do it unless they can do it right and independently the way they want, which is the reason why they formed the record company. They feel that they need to separate to continue with their individual ideas rather than as a whole. And they feel it's time for a change. We're sorry to see TG break up but I'm sure they will go on individualy to do bigger and better projects done the right way. Goodbye, Throbbing Gristle, and Good Luck with the future. --V2

Cosey Fanni Tutti Interview
May 28, 1981
Kezar Pavillion
San Francisco

*In the aftermath of the final performance of Throbbing Gristle, the individual members of the group were not as elusive as expected. All four were in a great rush to accomplish the work usually done by roadies--tearing the equipment apart and packing it up. The cases into which the equipment went were all designed to be loaded by the group themselves, with a minimum of time and effort. This is just one demonstration of Throbbing Gristle's unparalleled independence. They rely on themselves for virtually everything. They waste no time accomplishing their goals. And, they don't do anything they don't want to do.*

*Cosey Fanni Tutti is the group's coronet player and lead guitarist. She is the only female member of TG and she is undeniably the most ravishing woman the British Isles ever produced. We cornered Cosey in the middle of her pack-up work as it was our only chance for an interview.*

TT: Congratulations on the end of Throbbing Gristle. Peter told us that he and Genesis were forming a video production company. What are you and Chris going to do?

CFT: Chris and I are going to work on some tapes-do an album for Rough Trade.

TT: When will that be ready?

CFT: We've got to go back and send them some tapes and just see what happens.

TT: You do a lot of work for your Industrial Records label yourself, don't you?

CFT: What usually happens is that when we do music I arrange the position on the tapes--get rid of the irrelevant stuff. Chris does a lot of the tapes. He's the one that figures it all out really. He does all the background tapes and everything.

TT: What will happen to Industrial Records?

CFT: We won't know 'til we get back. We'll decide what happens then.

TT: Will people still be able to order the briefcase of tapes?

CFT: That'll carry on for a bit longer. It won't just stop immediately when we get back. I only just got one myself. Chris doesn't even have a copy of Second Annual Report.

TT: How soon will tapes of the two California gigs be available?

CFT: A couple of months or so.

TT: So some of the deleted albums will be available from Japan now?

CFT: Yeah. They're also doing a 'greatest hits' with one new song.

TT: I can't believe there won't be any more new TG singles.

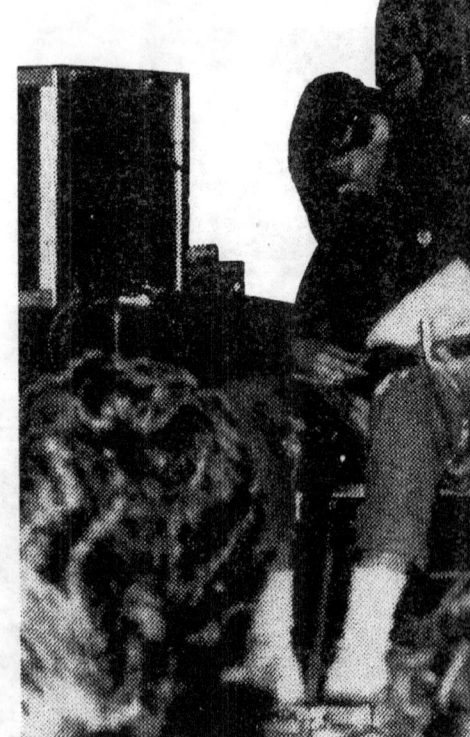

CFT: The new single's out.

TT: Why the mono recording? Is it older material?

CFT: No. That's just how we recorded it. Sometimes because of the places and equipment we just have to record in mono.

TT: I think it's interesting that the only female member of TG is the guitar player. The group's sound doesn't focus on the guitar, but it's still an integral part. Is it just all those gadgets you use on stage to get that sound?

CFT: I don't tune it either.

TT: So it's just a percussion instrument.

CFT: Yeah. I just use it as a percussion instrument. A lot of people just use it to play a melody over the rhythm or drums or whatever's going on.

--John Gleason

PHOTOS BY RICK SCHNEIDER

# Interview: SPK

*SPK performed their first show in the United States on May 16 in San Francisco. The day before, this radio interview was conducted at KALX with Operator and Tone Generator of SPK, along with members of Factrix.*

TT: People always thought your name was Surgical Penis Klinik and then we've found out that it has been System Planning Korporation all along. Is that true?

Operator: No. It was originally the Socialist Patients Kollektiv and then we changed it to Surgical Penis Klinic, which was something we thought up the morning we released the single on Industrial.

TT: The morning? Must have been a pretty quick cover job.

Operator: The morning I sent the artwork off. At this time we have changed it to the name of the U.S. Chemical and Biological Weapons Division, the secret division.

TT: The middle one, the story was that that was the name of a German group of mental patients that blew themselves up in . . .

Operator: No, that was the Socialist Patients Kollektiv.

TT: That was the first then. Where did the second one come from?

Operator: Out of my head. And it sold a few singles.

TT: Did the drawings come out of your head, too . . . Who was in charge of the graphics? I've seen the swell poster for the gig tomorrow night.

Operator: Joseph of Facrix did that.

TT: What led you to do graphics like that. Were you in control?

Operator: Yes. Our guitarist in Britain has had a similar operation so it is very close to home.

TT: Your guitarist in Britain? So are some of you from Australia and the rest from Britain?

Operator: That's the illusion we'd like to keep up. Sometimes we're from Australia.

TT: Who is actually from the group and what are their names and are they here?

Operator: Operator's here. Tone Generator is here, he's from Australia as well.

Background: Gee, this is swell.

TT: It is indeed.

Operator: And Wilkins is the guitarist. He had to remain in Britain but we are going back there next year. And he'll start playing again.

TT: OK. Let's go with another rumour, being the leader of the band, which might be yourself, was once a male nurse in a psychiatric ward.

Operator: That's right. And one of the originals was a certified schizophrenic.

TT: What happened to the originals? Were there two that are gone now?

Operator: There were three, one died and two became popular musicians.

TT: Popular musicians? With who?

Operator: A group, called Secret Secret, in Australia.

TT: How did you end up getting signed to Industrial coming from the outback?

Operator: I went to England and rang up Throbbing Gristle and in a very confusing five minutes he said he'd already heard our stuff, some idiot had sent it to them from Australia and they just offered to do it. It was actually a re-release of something we'd already done.

TT: But the new album is on your own label, Side Effects?

Operator: Yes. We split from Industrial--a mutual consent because Industrial have performed a very useful experiment of setting up an independent company. What we are trying to do is do it completely without any normal reviews, all by word of mouth or mail. And so far it is working really well.

TT: I understood there were going to be two gigs in America. Did one fall through?

Operator: There were going to be none to begin with and then there was one.

TT: How did it happen? Did you fly here specifically for this gig?

Operator: No. We were just on our way back to Australia to do another album, from England.

We're just passing through here. And Vale said while we were here we might as well do a concert.

TT: Are you going to put out other bands on this label?

Operator: We're beginning to produce a group in Australia called The Crush working on a totally different idea we've heard on tape. But any group we have anything to do with will have to be extremely odd musically.

TT: Well, you're having something to do with Factrix. Do you consider them to be odd?

Operator: Extremely odd people, yes. We don't get along at all.

TT: The sides on the album are the Ultra-face and the Hyper-face. What's the difference between Ultra and Hyper?

Operator: Well, Ultra is the manic face and Hyper is the depressive face. I don't like the Hyper-face.

TT: You don't like it and you did it?

Operator: Of course, we don't do just anything we like. We do things scientifically.

TT: What kind of scientific background did you have to do the job you were doing--giving drugs to patients...

Operator: And restraining them. I'd like to do it again. It's the only physical labor I enjoy.

TT: Why?

Operator: Because it is a great no-win situation. You are acting like a prison officer or security. There is no way out for these people once they get in.

TT: I thought the system was working well. That's what they told us.

Operator: That's what they told me as well. But one or two people don't seem to be able to hack it.

TT: Did you come in idealistically...

Operator: Yes.

TT: Wanting to help the afflicted?

Operator: Still do. You help them by oppressing them. That's the only choice you have.

TT: What equipment do you use?

Operator: We use two synthesizers: EMS synthesizers from England.

TT: Are they an unusual brand?

Operator: Yes, quite unusual. We don't have keyboards or anything like that.

TT: There's just knobs and settings?

Operator: Yes, and patches and a lot of devices which are quite difficult to use.

TT: Do you ever find your patch chords getting misplaced or you can't provide a certain affect because you don't have nine patch chords you only have eight?

Operator: No, we use patch pins. We're just so professional we never have any trouble.

TT: So we expect the gig tomorrow night to come off smooth and perfect?

Operator: No, not smooth, but perfect. Messy. I hope.

*Reports of the show support the messiness resulting from the four skinned goat heads which were used in the performance. It was only the fifth time SPK have performed-the earlier shows being two in Australia and two in Britain. A long table was set up with two microphones, cassette decks, synthesizers, a power drill and other power tools. A high point to some was witnessing Operator split one of the bloody goat heads with a cleaver, reach inside for a handul of brains and eating them. The crowd was small--around 250. The sound was very loud and rhythmic with screams. They also used a low-toned rhythm track which was pleasant to hear as one watched the two covered with blood in their Israeli army gear. Definitely a happening in the performance art tradition.*

## Interview: Colin Newman

*Colin Newman*

A rainy Spring morning on Spring Street in Soho. Manhattan is veiled in mists that temper the tone of all surroundings to an even shade of gray. Secluded, and sheltered, I sit in my room with Colin Newman as I work on an 11 a.m. Bud and try to explain my theory of punk psychedelics and how they apply to the musics of today, and especially to that of my guest; both as a solo artist and with textbook clarity in his previous (and future) band, Wire.

The previous week in New York had seen Newman's return here for live performance after an absence of two years. His only previous stage outing here was one night at CBGB for the debut appearance of Wire. What a packed house of maybe two-hundred folks witnessed that night was a jet-lagged band stumbling on stage direct from the airport, starting their set two-hours late, well after the opening band, the since re-risen Student Teachers, had gone home to bed, hitting the stage with amps turned on ten as if in the hopes that the sheer power of the volume of the music would give them the strength to make it through their set. They left the audience a mite unsatisfied but definitely shell-shocked.

Never a band to cater to accessibility, Wire showcased material from their as of yet forthcoming second lp, though in drastically different form than actually was recorded, 'Outdoor Miner' indeed, bringing it all back to earth with occassional forrays through PINK FLAG. Newman as principal vocalist, thugh not at stage center, held the major part of the audience's attention (Wire was always anti-image) with his stark, stop-action poses, tight- rawn facial expressions, all framed by intensive white, glaring stage lighting.

The New York Newman returned to is unrecognizable from the one Wire visited. The scene has exploded, venue-wise, one-hundred major shows every week. At the same time though it has lost its center, its focus, its forward momentum. New York's price for success is stagnation. There are no more local heroes. Everywhere bands are told--draw hundreds or we'll find someone else. And everyone has a band. There are five-thousand local bands and thirty visiting British outfits vying for gigs every week. Celebration has given way to spectacle. Into this atmosphere Newman brings this year's version of the continuing story of (though he hates the term) 'acid-punk'.

On stage, Newman's perverse humor and expectational analysis comes to the fore. The house lights go off and the stage stays dark. The band files on and launches into their first song. The only light is supplied by flashlights taped to microphone stands, pointing downward, illuminating set lists and feet. The players' faces are dark. With a bank of effects boxes at his feet, Newman launches into an easy chord progression that runs over and over. Second guitarist Desmond Simmons begins his own complementary progression. Lyrics: 'Everything they say seems so insubstantial...We've come to see what's left of you.' Which turns out to be an apt description of the audience-performer relationship from one of the dozen of (only) unrecorded songs that he plays.

Tempos change, guitar sounds shift, different vocalists take turns, all variations on the same theme. Across the back of the stage, and occassionally over the performers a black and white film of flashlights

*Continued on p.33*

UGENE MERINOV

# Interview: X

*Continued from p. 17* the first time?
Billy: It was pretty good.
Don: The reviewers hated us.
Billy: Yeah, the English press doesn't like American bands much. But the crowds, the response was real good. I don't think they knew much about who we were since the first album had just come out. We just played around London.
TT: I would think it would be a kind of expensive venture. Do you guys have to finance it or . . .
Billy: I don't know how it's going to work out. Slash is going to pay our way over and back.
TT: Then you're on your own?
Billy: We're going to be playing a lot bigger places and we have a lot better distribution for the second album than we did for the first. So it beats me, I don't know.
TT: So tell us a little bit about the Flesh Eaters.
John: In a nutshell, Chris D. wrote the songs and we, the band, arranged them. Dave (Alvin) from the Blasters did some of the songs, I did some of the others. We put 'em together, rehearsed about two weeks. And Chris, since he worked for Slash, had talked to Bob Biggs (Slash president) about putting out the record of it if we got it finished and it sounded good and everything, and he said yeah. So we tried this one live recording and it didn't work. We just set up in a big ol' hall and just took everything at once, vocals and everything. But you couldn't hear the instruments. 'Satan Stomp' worked, so we used it. We went into a studio and finished it, it took about a month.
TT: Are we going to hear more from the Flesh Eaters, ever?
John: Well, Pat from The Germs replaced the Adolescents' guitar player, so now the Adolescents' guitar player is going to be in the Flesh Eaters.
TT: I like the idea of things like WILD GIFT coming out so close to when it was recorded. Cut it, get it out fast. That's really neat.
John: Yeah. I don't think the band could imagine working on a record for more than about maybe two months.
John: The studio that we used, Bruce Springstein mixed that monster record he just put out. He was there for six months mixing the stuff. Could you imagine? How could you be objective about anything? And Bob Dylan is using that studio now (laughter).
TT: I would also think you would start losing interest in the things you'd done six months ago.
John: Yeah. Yeah. Maybe that, and also it's just even mixing for a week straight, you're hearing it all the time and you can't get any distance from it.
TT: Yeah. Perspective.
John: Perspective? Yeah, good word.
TT: John tells us that you are working on a project possibly with Lydia Lunch? Could you tell us a little bit about that?
Exene: We have three things. One is that we might do a record together, the second is that we might write a book together, and the third is that we might do a photography thing together. I mean, what else can you do?
TT: How about the album? Is she still in the Devil Dogs, is that still together? Would it be with them?
Exene: We don't know. It's still just something we're trying to figure out. Well, then I had to leave (for the tour) so I don't know what's going on. We can ask a lot of different people to be on it because most people are our friends. . . .
TT: Is it pretty tightly knit among musicians in LA?
John: Yeah, it's always been that way.
Exene: People mistake it for a clique sometimes. You were talking about the surf punks earlier. I think the thing is that they're still at that age where peer pressure and being in, even as much as they are out, they obviously like to be in because they are all very similar in the way they dress. So I think they think of Hollywood as a clique that wouldn't let them in and now they're getting revenge, which is ridiculous 'cause I never laid eyes on them until very recently.
TT: So, Exene, when you sit down to write a song, I realize you just don't sit down and say, 'I think I'll write a song tonight' but how is . . .
Billy: Yeah, she does. That's exactly it. 'I think I'll write a song . . . let's see, um . . .'
John: Like, 'I'm going to eat dinner at six so I better get going on it . . .'
TT: But with the relative success of the band and things like that, have things changed from the songwriting aspect?
Exene: I think writing is independent of anything else you do. It's based kind of on what you do, but if I wasn't in a band I'd probably be writing the same amount. I don't know how that sounds . . .
TT: As far as what you write, like maybe the attitude in it, and how things have changed for you, you know, two albums out now . . .
Exene: Are you saying it may be harder to write now?
TT: Well, no, maybe the kind of things you write about being a bit different, or the attitudes . . .
Exene: No, no it's all pretty much the same. I've got so much stuff written now anyway from the past that I don't think I'd have to worry about it. I'd like to do some more different topics because most of my songs are real love songs or songs about drinking or something and I'd like to kind of get away from that. But George Jones can do it, so I guess it's alright, that's what his songs are all about.
John: I think if anything does change in the things you write about, if that does change, it

happens so gradually that you don't even notice it. Like maybe the Rolling Stones realized five years after they'd gone in a certain direction that, Oh, we've created a Frankenstein. Actually, they were probably groovin' on what was going on, but you could look at it that way. If you did change, it's real gradual and you don't really notice it. The Doors were a real good example of that. Their last record, 'LA Woman' is really down to earth and street-level lyrics, and recording, too. They had gone to 24-track on 'Soft Parade', I think it was, and then they went back to 16 to do 'LA Woman'. So it doesn't have to be that if you get more famous you get removed from stuff.

TT: The vocal stuff you do seems to be more intuitive than any figured intervals.

Exene: Yeah, that's right. When I sing my little harmonies with John, I just keep singing it out until I like it, then I usually keep it and change it around when we play live.

TT: It's something that you just worked out?

Exene: It's just pretty made up. We've been compared a lot to Jefferson Airplane and the Mommas and the Papas, which I think is because they had male and female singers and each band was from California.

Their harmonies were really like classroom harmonies. I don't know about the Jefferson Airplane because I'm not familiar with them but the Mammas and the Papas' hits were, well, I couldn't do that even if I wanted. I don't understand any of that.

TT: There were keyboards a couple of times on the first album, any particular reason that didn't happen this time?

John: Because everybody in all these live gigs we were doing on the East Coast and in England and even in the Midwest they were always going, 'Where's Ray?' It was not this thing where we planned for him to be in the band, he just played on some songs. So we made a conscious decision for him not to play on the second one. Partly because people's attitude that if it's on the record it should be done live. We are a four-piece band, we're not a five-piece. It's fun to hear those sounds on the first album.

TT: I'd heard someplace, Billy, that maybe some band you were involved in earlier had played with Gene Vincent on his last tour.

Billy: I played with Gene Vincent.

TT: Was this his last tour, was it in England?

Billy: No, it was on the West Coast, we toured for five or six months.

TT: When was this?

Billy: It was in '71 right up to about the time just before he died. It's all true

TT: One last question. Who do you listen to?

Exene: Top Jimmy and the Rhythm Pigs, The Blasters, and The Cramps.

TT: The Cramps, yeah. Any English groups?

Billy: We don't listen to foreigners much.

TT: Why?

Billy: They don't have any sense of rhythm. Foreigners can't play rock and roll because they don't have any sense of rhythm.

NANCY SCHNEIDER

# Interview: The Morells

Fun. Remember Fun? Hot fun in the summertime? Fun as a reason to rock? Yes, Virginia, some folks still believe in the power of fun in the face of the daily crises that confront us. They are The Morells from Springfield, MO and the best time you ever had legally.

Talk Talk spent the day with The Morells during their last three-day stand at KC's Parody Hall and got the lowdown on the group's storied history, financial status, and future recording plans, among other bits of trivia.

For the uninitiated, the group consists of Lou Whitney on bass and guitar, Donnie (d. Clinton) Thompson on guitar, drummer Ron Gremp and Maralie on keyboards. All four sing, but Lou is the focus, cracking jokes between and during songs and mugging away on stage.

Born 38 years ago in Phoenix, AZ, Whitney 'attended' Eastern Tennessee State U. where he played in various r&b bands.

Lou: We all had guitars and we'd sit around and play at parties. We needed a bass player and I was probably the worst guitar player, so . . . that and the lure of four strings.

Lou graduated and came to Springfield to take a job in real estate (no kidding) but that only lasted a year or so before he quit and got back into music.

Lou: I met Donnie in 1971 or two when he was working in a music store. We had a bar job in Columbia, MO, and we needed a guitar player so Donnie came up and we've been playing together since then, off and on. Mostly on since 1977. The Symptoms were the first band we ever started together.

The Symptoms were the current Morells plus vocalist Jim Wunderle. Though now defunct, their legend lives on, through booster Gary Sperazza and a recent 'hit' with the posthumously released single 'Double Shot (of my Baby's Love)'. They pressed 500 of the albums from which the single tracks were taken. 485 were sold and 15 were given away. Lou and Maralie have only one copy for themselves, and Kim Fowley has been calling and begging for one. Several companies have offered to re-press the record and Lou says he'd do it if guaranteed a thousand advance. After The Symptoms break-up, Lou and Donnie recorded the 'Driving Guitars' single at home. It has since been included on the 'Declaration of Independents' compilation. They claim to have received $134 in royalties so far.

Next up for the two was The Skeletons, an outfit with guitarist Randle Chowning and drummer Bobby Lloyd. They didn't last too long but recorded 'Gas Money' as Bobby Lloyd and The Windfall Prophets and 'Trans Am' has been a minor hit on both coasts.

After The Skeletons broke up, Lou and Donnie re-recruited Maralie and Ron to form an as-yet unnamed band.

Maralie: We were driving in from practice one night and trying to think of a name and I came up with The Morells . . . it's kind of like The Shondells or The Shirelles . . . but people always misspell it.

As The Morells, they have consolidated all the best parts of the previous groups and have honed their act to perfection. They can rockabilly with the best of them yet claim to be 'the only band in Missouri that does a slow song.' They score political points with their version of J. Richman's 'Government Center', their own 'Trans Am' and 'Sour Snow'. 'People can't categorize us and that scares them,' Lou says.

They are not getting rich by any means. They do it for the fun of it. There's that word again They want to be successful, but not at the expense of fun.

Donnie: You can either sit back and do your own thing and hope somebody recognizes it or you can kind of force it . . . and then you end up having to do a lot of things you don't really want to. I mean, we're doing our part, we hope somebody on the other side does their's.

Their satisfaction has come from small victories. Like the 'Double Shot' single, on whose strength they made an East Coast swing. 'Driving Guitars', they tell me, is the background music for WNEW's concert line.

They simply enjoy resurrecting rock and roll obscurities from the scrap heap and making them their own.

Lou: It's like follow-up songs. Do you remember 'Let's Dance' by Chris Montez? We do a song called 'Some Kind of Fun', being the typical follow-up song of the day ... everybody would say, 'Oh, it's too much like 'Let's Dance'' but, really, it's a better song ... so, consequently, no one ever heard of it ... but years later, a good song is a good song. Period. That's it. It doesn't matter when it was done or whether it was a hit or not, it's still good.

Lou: I like records that sound like they were recorded in a room, you know? Nowadays, you can hear every string, every note ...

They don't think much of current trends.

Donnie: I liked reggae before marijuana. I guess it always had it, but it seemed like it got real stoned and all slowed down, like 70s rock slowed down.

Lou: I'll tell you, it's getting pretty bad. Four years ago it was pretty easy to find an independent record you liked and wanted to buy but now you've got to shuffle through about 300 of them.

Nevertheless, The Morells have plans to make a record under their own name, probably this summer.

Donnie: We might just take a two-track down to where we play and do it live ... it might be studio, it might be a combination ... It's not like we've got a week booked in New York at The Record Plant.

Lou: The record industry is geared to handle the 12-inch size, they don't have bins to fit these little ones.

Donnie: Even in the collectors' stores, the specialty shops, they've got 'em in a box up there on top of a shelf.

Lou: Maybe a one-sided album, sell it at a budget price ... --Rick Hellman

# Reggae Roundup Part 2

At it's best little can compare with the soulful rapping of an inspired Reggae Deejay. Deejay Style has its roots in the old sound system days, when Jamaican deejays would vie for crowds' attention by talking over popular dance tunes. Ewart Beckford, better known as U Roy, is credited by many as being the man who made deejay an insitution in Reggae and many creative young artists have expanded the genre to the point where it is being eumulated by popular rock 'n roll musicians. U ROY debuted in America on DREAD IN A BABYLON, an excellent album worth having for the cover alone, which depicts the star, glassy-eyed and smiling in a thick cloud of Ganja smoke. Others of note include JAH SON OF AFRICA, NATTY REBEL, (with a fine dj version of Bob Marley's 'Soul Rebel' as its centerpiece), and VERSION GALORE, a long out of print collection of his early work reissued by Virgin Records in 1978. VERSION is a dj textbook containing the definitive version of John Holt's 'Tide Is High'.

I ROY 'Hello, all you teeny boppers, this is your musical poppa!' begins one of Roy Reid's most inspired compositions. Reid, who calls himself I Roy, has based a long and successful career on his uniquely soul oriented delivery. His best work can be found on THE GENERAL, which included a free dub LP with the record, and WAP 'N BAP'N, one of the most danceable LPs ever recorded. Also worthwhile if you can find it is TEN COMMANDMENTS, a colored vinyl picture disk containing his versions of ten Bob Marley tunes.

THE BIG YOUTH Unarguably the most visually striking performer in Reggae, his massive locks set off by a mouthful of diamond-studded teeth, The Youth has recorded several superb records. His material ranges from the heavy religious stuff that characterizes the music to off the wall versions of tunes by Ray Charles and Marvin Gaye. SCREAMING TARGET is his early best, as hard-hitting as the name implies. Other essentials include NATTY CULTURAL DREAD, with its tribute to Youth influence John Coltrane ('JIM SQUASHY') and HIT THE ROAD JACK. The Youth's interpretation of the title track is amazing, as is his rendition of the aforementioned Mr. Gayes' 'What's Going On?'

DILLINGER Dillinger had a huge hit with a funky nursery-rhymed track called 'Cokane In My Brain' a few years back. The album CB 200 on which it appears is now a hard-to-find classic. My other favorites include the righteous paen to the future BIONIC DREAD, and the funky and filthy FUNKY PUNK a French album.

The above 'big four' are by no means the only DJs worth hearing but they are the most prolific. Others of note include:

TRINITY THREE PIECE SUIT is some of the heaviest dub I've ever heard. The chipmunk refrain on 'Muhammed Ali' must be heard to be believed. DON'T STOP TILL YOU GET ENOUGH is a 12-inch single from Joe Gibbs studio that finds Trinity teamed with a fine singer named Derrick Laro, a fine roots workout on the Michael Jackson disco number.

DR. ALIMENTADO BEST DRESSED CHICKEN IN TOWN, a winner all the way from the bizarre effects to the impassioned preaching and wailing of the Dr., pictured on the cover in his best Bermudas, zipper rakishly at half-mast--what kind of a doctor is he, anyway?

PRINCE FAR I MESSAGE TO THE KING, the Prince's raspy meditations have a soothing quality and a righteous message, especially on 'Commandment of Drugs'. DUB ENCOUNTERS CH.III features less of the Prince but several big names from English bands like The Slits and The Flying Lizards. 'Shake The Nation' is terrific.

TAPPER ZUKIE MAN AH WARRIOR, magnificent holy music, great cover. Listen to 'Message To Pork Eaters' and shudder, infidels. LIVING IN THE GHETTO early, contains anthem 'Oh, Lord'.

LINTON KWESI JOHNSON Although not really a Deejay, LKJ is a poet who uses music as just another vehicle for his apocalyptic messages. His style is brooding, with a violent edge just under the surface. Listen to 'Two Sides of Silence' on BASS CULTURE and see what I Mean. --Daddy Cool

# Reggae Reviews

**GREGORY ISAACS The Early Years (Trojan: TRLS 196)**-- I had forgotten how smooth the voice of singer Gregory Isaacs was until listening to this new collection of early songs. There are at least three, separately-produced segments here But no information on when the recordings occurred. The last few years have seen a flurry of Isaac albums-out representing both old and new. Some of these cuts are available elsewhere, but not all of the 12 are. If you are looking for some soothing, basic reggae, then THE EARLY YEARS are definitely for you. --WB

**THE UPSETTERS AND FRIENDS The Upsetter Collection (Trojan: TRLS 195)**-- A new compilation of early Lee Perry presents some new sounds from the Upsetter label. Although the great keyboardist Ansell Collins is not mentioned, it seems that his organ playing is the most predominant sound on this release of 16 cuts. The songs are instrumentals with an occasional 'Scratch' introduction of sorts. These rhythms are from 1969 to 70 and 1972 to 3, an exciting time in the creativeness of this wonder producer. Good beats and very enjoyable skanking inspirations. --WB

**MATUMBI Matumbi EMI: EMC 3355)**-- More slick sounds and smooth harmonies from this English bunch. This is a good album in the melodic reggae style, no heavy dub passages here. Still, it's not quite as satisfying as last summer's magnificent POINT OF VIEW LP. Not earthshaking, but if you're a Blackbeard fan, you won't be disappointed. --R. Hellman

**DENNIS BROWN Money In My Pocket (Trojan:-- TRLS 197)**-- Although this is a new release, it is not the latest sound but some of the older cuts Dennis Brown has done. The song, 'Money In My Pocket', has been one of my favorites. This cut has the dub tag at the end by The Big Youth, a treat indeed. --WB

---

*Continued from p.27*

with wavers. Very Monochrome Set-ish, I think. Colin later tells me that he did the film with one of the M.S.ers and that he has been asked to produce their next album-Now there's a band with Colin's sense of humor. The New York crowd seemed listless, maybe because of the low energy-level, since the performance was positively-laid back, and the late hour. No weekend healiner goes on util :30 a.m. at least. Sincehe uses no stage lights, Colin claims to dispose of the 'Tyranny of the Stage', but left to their own devices most of the audience was lost. One thing that the dark stage did allow was for the band to see the audience clearly.

My set list had since disappeared, but Colin said that the names of his own songs weren't important since he wouldn't be recording them anyway. At least not in their present form. They could be working drafts for upcoming ones. Future projects do include an album of instrumentals (probably now completed), and more from Wire once someone (anyone) offers them enough money so they can afford the studio time.

In the meantime, Colin is looking toward America. He is positively overwhelmed by the potential of greatness and space of this country. 'I can't understand everyone's fascination with Europe', he says. 'Europe is nowhere. They're struggling with a 500-year-old culture they can't understand.' He also sees signs of cultural decay in New York, and I'm inclined to agree with him in the observations that he makes. 'There's something wrong in a city where people have to wait around for the band to go on at two o'clock in the morning. They're not there to hear the music. They're in the club for the sake of being there, that's the place to go, the band is secondary.' He dismissed New York's lack of enthusiasm for his gigs by citing Toronto-which was sandwiched in between some NYC shows. 'The kids there were really into it. They're more receptive to new ideas; ready to be challenged. They got the encores. They loved the shows. Maybe it's because they are closer to the heartland.' –Stephen Graziano.

# Reggae Reviews

**THE BLUE RIDDIM BAND Restless Spirit (Flying Fish: FF255)**-- Even though I have seen this band play live countless times the past few years, this album has really thrown me for a loop. The intensity and perfection displayed on this, their first release after years of planning, approaches the category of being unmatched in today's recording industry. Sort of strong talk you say, but I think it's on the mark. Readers of TALK TALK are no doubt aware of this band and their activities the past few years. Now you can get their music, listen to it yourself, and decide on your own their worth. The album opens with The Supremes' 'Come See About Me' and moves into 'Shoo Be Do'. Right off you find this is not a strictly reggae band as the soulful tunes abound. Next is the title track 'Restless Spirit', a bluesy number, followed by 'One Love, One Heart' complete with the dub track. Side two opens with another original, 'Rock It, Sister', one of my favorite cuts. 'Cuss, Cuss' has a dub tag mixed by Prince Jammy. 'Twisting the Night Away' uses more of the horn harmonies, moving at a fast continuous beat. The close harmonies of the vocalists on the sweet 'Oh Babe' make this sound like an old classic, although it is another original. The closing original, 'Joke's On You', demonstrates the soulful reggae feel of The Blue Riddim Band along the vein of Toots Hibbert. A fine achievement and more of a door opener for the band than a statement of their sound as far as future breaks occurring. They have had it rough but these musicians have kept it together and finally have their album out with more plans for the next several releases, including some 12-inch 45s. Get this while you can and keep posted for more. --Bill Rich

**UB 40 Present Arms (DEP International: LPDEP1)**-- A very fine album. Carrying on in the tradition of their debut SIGNING OFF, there is also a 12-inch 45 along with the eight-cut record. UB 40 are, of course, an English, racially-mixed band that play with a reggae-oriented, self-formed style. They haven't become 'real big' yet but continue to grow in popularity. The eight musicians create a slow and heavy sound that at times is almost so jazzy and light that it becomes floating reggae, going to the clouds. If this doesn't grab you at first, the closing cut, 'Lambsbread', will definitely bring you in. The 45, with 'Don't Walk On The Grass' and 'Dr. X' is more of a dub encounter, quite easy to listen and groove in on. --WB

**BUNNY WAILER Arab Oil Weapon/Lifeline (Nighthawk Records: NH1001)**-- With the death of Bob Marley and the decline of Peter Tosh, Bunny Wailer, the third member of the original Wailers, continues to churn out righteous roots music. 'Arab Oil Weapon' is a 12-inch 45 rpm preview of his soon to be released LP WISER DREAD, a scathing indictment of Middle Eastern energy politics. 'Lifeline', the flip, is an ethereal dance tune. I can't wait to hear the album. --Daddy Cool

**PETER TOSH Wanted Dread and Alive (Rolling Stone/EMI America: SO 17055)**-- No doubt many will be disappointed with this release. Maybe it doesn't stand up to his early solo work but it is an improvement over some of his recent work. Quality music from quality musicians. Sly and Robbie back up Tosh to create that special sound. Eight new cuts and the A-side of the latest single are here with some better than others. Listen to it yourself. --WB

**MAX ROMEO Holding Out My Love To You (Shanachie: 43002)**-- Max Romeo possesses one of the finest voices in reggae next to the late Bob Marley and he's made some excellent LPs (especially WAR IN A BABYLON with Lee Perry). Unfortunately, HOLDING OUT MY LOVE TO YOU is overly slick and superficial and the blame for this must rest in a large part with Keith Richard, who helped produce, mix, and plays lead guitar on it. Most of the album reflects the disco-reggae trend and the title track is especially jive. Best cuts: 'Bell The Cat' and 'Smiling In Your Face'. --Daddy Cool

**THE EQUATORS Hot (Stiff America)**-- The debut LP from this English sextet, HOT reminds one of The Beat with an emphasis on keyboards rather than sax. Fine vocals and deft use of the melodica make this one a winner. The Equators single 'Baby Come Back' also on Stiff is not included and also worth a listen. --Daddy Cool

**THIRD WORLD Rock This World (CBS: FC 37402)**-- What, another album already? These fine musicians don't mess around much. With a new label (CBS from Island) Third World once again demonstrate why they are one of the top reggae groups in Jamaica and the rest of the world. Their strength lies in the personnel: six talented rastas who know what they are doing. 'Let's rock the world with music', they sing, and they do. Some think Third World have 'gone disco' but there is no evidence of that on this. They do have a multiple of layered sounds and rhythms, but close to roots music. I've only listened to this a few times so far, but I like what I hear. --WB

# Single Reviews

**KATE FAGAN** Don't Wanna Be Too Cool/Waiting for the Crisis ((Disturbing Records) **STRIKE UNDER** Immediate Action EP (Wax Trax Records)-- These two releases from the Chicago area show that the local scene theryis finally beginning to live up to its potential. Kate Fagan, who is currently in Chicago based ska band Heavy Manners, offers a great side about some of the more trendy aspects of any local 'scene'. With just bass, guitar, and rhythm box, it sounds anything but what she's doing now, although the band does a ska rave-up of the song live. Look for a Heavy Manners single soon. STRIKE UNDER, while definitely more in the punk mode, doesn't seem to draw from any readily apparent influences, which is nice. Infectious stuff, which keeps finding its way to my turntable. Fave cuts are the semi-instrumental 'Closing In' and 'Sunday Night Disorientation'. The five-song EP is the initial release from Wax Trax Records. Excellent start. --Buzz

**MEDIUM MEDIUM** Hungry, So Angry/Nadsat Dreams (Cherry Red Records: CHERRY 18)-- Medium Medium are mediocre. These guys could be singing 'I love you baby' with the same effect as 'so hungry, so angry'. Despite a wailing sax on top of a funky beat there are no feelings of hunger or anger in the cut. 'Nadsat Dream' has more emotion in its gruff vocal style but ultimately it goes nowhere, too. (Nadsat means teenage, re: Clockwork Orange). Instead of a saxophone, Hendrix guitar style is added for decoration--but it is only a decoration. The nadsat dream is neither fantasy nor a nightmare. It isn't even boring enough to put you to sleep. --A. 'Enthal

**POLYPHONIC SIZE** Nagasaki Mon Amour/Hiroshima 1945 (Sandwich Records: No. 22580)-- Polyphonic Size isn't really a group. It's Strangler J. J. Burnel and his textured synthesizer work. The cover of this record is in Japanese and the 'group' name is hidden at the end of the credits so it's an easy record to overlook unless you're specifically looking for it. 'Nagasaki Mon Amour' (no relation to Ultravox's 'Hiroshima Mon Amour') is all in French and the best word to describe it is 'pretty'. B-side, 'Hiroshima 1945', is a killer. This is more art and poetry than rock, with church-organ- synthesizer, mellow repetitive riff, recitations in French-accented English and an endless atom bomb blast. Personal gripe: A-side plays at 45, B-side plays at 33. Neither side is labeled for speed. -A. 'Enthal

**THE DIAGRAM BROS.** Brick/Postal Bargain (New Hormones: ORG9)-- Two of this band's favorites from the John Peel shows they've beenfeature d on. So they have some fans plus an earlier single, 'We Are All Animals' (Construct Records). 'Brick' has a minimal presentation with good rhythm. 'Postal' is not quite such a bargain. --SK

**FIVE OR SIX** Another Reason/The Trial (Cherry Red Records: CHERRY 19)-- Those who like Pink Floyd's DARK SIDE OF THE MOON might also enjoy Five or Six. 'Another Reason' is an electro bossa nova with mellow vocals that gives the feeling it is an edit from a longer work. 'The Trial' is a gloomy raga with scattered conversations and a moaning choral arrangement reminiscent of 'Brain Damage'. --A. 'Enthal

**ZEITGEIST** Touch/Yellow Fidgets (Human: HUM 7)-- I don't know anything about this English group except they have two good singles out. The earlier four-song EP (Human: HUM5) sounds like early Ultravox or John Foxx singing with a female vocalist following his lead. 'Yellow Fidgets' is great listening with several melodies and verses going at once. These people sure sound like a lot of others--Joy Division, Ultravox, A Certain Ratio, etc. Is there a connection? Something seems fishey. Probably all new musicians really. They've got something here. Soon to be big.

**THE PLAGUE OF TOADS** Born Again Christians (Inc. Records: 10-4-1240)-- Owing a debt to the work of Daniel Miller ('TVOD', 'Warm Leatherette'), the Nealous brothers, under the name of Plague of Toads, tell a tale of being accosted by Jesus freaks at a bus stop. Just as infectious as the Normal though the riff is slightly more complex. B-side is the same song backwards. --A. 'Enthal

**POSITIVE NOISE** Charm/. . . And Yet Again (Statik Records: STAT 4)-- Positive Noise make pulsating pop. 'Charm' features a handclap-like beat, horns (and no doubt a forked tail). Bits of radio garble add an avant garde touch but never interfere with the flow. '. . . And Yet Again' is a jazz influenced, rather than guitar-based, love ballad but both sides are definitely rock. --A. 'Enthal

# Album Reviews

**WANNA BUY A BRIDGE? (Rough Trade: RTUS 3)**-- Anthologies, samplers, and compilations are usually a good buy— collectors find them invaluable, cheapskates love 'em 'cause they offer the widest selection of entertainment for a reasonable price, and they make it easy for the average record fancier to decide what may or may not be an artist worthy of future investments. WANNA BUY A BRIDGE?, one of the first Rough Trade releases in this country, is a collection of 14 single cuts by relatively obscure English and Irish music makers.

Despite the annoying simplicity of Television Personalities and The Pop Group's abrasive chaos, the first side is salvaged by The Slits' mysterious 'Man Next Door' and the catchy contributions of Delta 5 and Essential Logic.

And side two is about as good as this sort of album gets. Starting off with the marching pop of Spizz Energi, right on through the irresistible quirkiness of girl groups, Kleenex and The Raincoats, up to Cabaret Voltaire's industrious, electronic pulse beats. The Young Marble Giants, the U.K.'s latest rage and already temporarily disbanded, mix vague gothic and olde English influences for a colorless, but pleasing, hybrid, while Scritti Politti's avant-folk favorite, 'Skank Bloc Bologna', conjures up memories of Richard Thompson, Peter Gabriel and (gasp!) King Crimson's earlier works. But the single most memorable moment on the album comes at the very end with Robert Wyatt's chilling 'At Last I Am Free'. He has taken Chic's disco romp and transformed it into an optimistic, but eerie, declaration of hope and liberation.

Without half of side two, WANNA BUY A BRIDGE? would still be a bargain, but the inclusion of the Robert Wyatt tune alone makes its possession a necessity. Rough Trade —Rory Houchens

**THE FALL Slates (Rough Trade:-TRADE 3/10)**-- This is without a doubt the record that will finally do it for The Fall. The one that pushes them over the top and into the platinum stadium-rock stratosphere occupied by mythical creatures like Styx and REO. But seriously, this is a good product from The Fall-and it may help them broaden their stateside audience. This six-song, 10-inch has just the right amount of patented Fall drone music. Sure, vocalist Mark Smith trots out someoverworn phrases but the songs seem to have more zip than previous outings. Of all the punk/wave bands, The Fall have stayed closest to their original intent. It's about time they caught on. —R. Hellman

**START SWIMMING (Stiff America:- SINK 1)**-- 'A taste of New York for the crowds in London' describes this live album of five American bands who went over and played The Rainbow, February 20, 1981. Some of the immediate English musical-press seemed overly-critical of the shows but from the album, it must have been quite extraordinary. We get two songs each from favorites Raybeats, Bush Tetras, The Bongos, Fleshtones., and the dBs. The Bush Tetras' affect on 'Cold Turkey' will become a classic. Not to be overlooked are the opening cuts, 'Telephoto Lens' and 'In the Congo', by The Bongos, which included three-fourths of Throbbing Gristle (no P. Christopherson). In fact, the whole album will be viewed as a classic 'international exposure' document in the near future. That's what I think. Wish I would have been there. --SK

**WHA'PPEN? The (English)—Beat (Sire: SRK 3567)**-- In which The Beat beat the dreaded second album jinx and confirm their status as the best band to come out of the whole Two-Tone crop. Easy-rocking reggae tunes like 'Doors Of Your Heart' and 'Monkey Murders' are along the same saxy lines as the first LP and the single, 'All Out to Get You' is included but my favorite is 'I am Yur Flag'. It's got a honey of a horn chart and a pertinent lyric. Anything on the second side is pure gravy. -R. Hellman

**THE PEOPLE Musical Man/Sons & Daughters (Race Records: RB003)**-- Since leaving Selecter, Charlie Anderson, bass, vocals, and Desmond Brown have re-teamed with guitarist John Hobley, who they had played with four years A drummer finishes the lineup. The People add another dimension to the Coventry Ska/Two Tone impact. Race Records was recently founded by those formally once associated with The Specials. As earlier releases on the label, this is a good reggae single. Calling themselves 'one of the hardest reggae/rock bands around,' The People prove to be promising. --WB

# Album Reviews

**DEUTSCH AMERIKANISCHE FREUNDSCHAFT Alles Ist Gut (Virgin: V2202)**-- With the release of this third LP, it appears as if DAF have undergone some kind of re-evaluation. DAF is now simply two people: Robert Gorl (music) and Gabi Delgado Lopez (words and voice). From this change in lineup comes a slight reduction in the intensity of DAF's overall sound. Gone is the explosiveness or musical terrorism that they originated. This aspect of DAF will be missed. Instead, what they have done is an apparent revolutionary approach to electronic music. They have abandoned totally the sense of aloof alienation or cold unfeeling detachment that is so often present in this type of music. DAF have created a kind of electronic primitivism that seems genuinely inspired and full of spirited emotion. It is this emotion that is the key to DAF's success on ALLES IST GUT. There are ten actual songs on this record, instead of fragments and untitled tracks that are found on their previous two LPs. These songs are similar to most of their other material, being short and to the point, verse that's built around a series of synth hooks that really grab the listener's attention. Their music isn't overly complex, it simply possesses some kind of emotional energy that is a rarity for electric music. This emotion is further expressed by Gabi's lyrics and vocal delivery. Gabi sings with a sense of urgency or vitality and this is what really sets DAF apart. He seems to want to relay his message with an intensity that is nearly exhausting with its erotic sensuality. DAF songs are a blend of politics, romance or heart-felt sensuality and dance. Gabi is able to collate socio-politico images and then adapt them to the image of the dance. There are two subjects that the songs on ALLES IST GUT deal with: romance/politics and the dance/the struggle. Five on each subject: 'Rote Lippe', 'Mein Herz Macht Bum', 'Als War's Das Letzte Mal', 'Alles Ist Gut', 'Der Rauber und der Prinz' all are related in the imagery of the color red, be it love, blood, or communism. 'Sato-Sato', 'Der Mussolini', 'Ich und die Wirklichkeit', 'Verlier Nicht den Kopf', 'Alle Gegen Alle' all deal with the ideas of factionalism and the struggle between right and left, the black and the red. These are things that compose German expressionism to an extent and these are vital components of DAF. DAF have demonstrated that so-called 'Drone Music' can have emotion or spark as well as intelligence. --U-Man

**DEVO Live (Warner Brothers: MI-NI3548)**-- What can you say about the average live album? It's usually a two record set? It can be melted down into an attractive and trendy door stop? It has all the excitement and spontaneity of a 'Dragnet' rerun? Well, friends, it is a six-song 12-inch, mini-album. The performances, when not totally lackluster ('Gates of Steel' and 'Planet Earth' reach new heights of plodability), rarely rise above a lukewarm tedium. The exceptions are a particularly enthusiastic execution of the spud-boy's 'big hit', 'Whip It', and a sweat-inducing, heart palpitating version of that ever popular, Darwinian anthem for the common homo erectus, 'Be Stiff'.

There's nothing here that will make you pack up your best vinyl jumpsuits and enlist in Akron's rubber army, but if you find it hard to stay on your DEVO diet until album number four rolls around, then splurge a little bit with this bundle of live band-aids. It's low on calories and contains the minimum daily requirement of synthetic vitamins and minerals. I bet your mom will even say 'Good for you!'
--Rory Houchens

**ESG (99 Records: 9904/Factory: FAC 34)**-- ESG are a five-piece, one guy and four sisters band that have a very deceptive record out. It is simple and straightforward enough for the most traditional of tastes, yet the sounds and textures that are happening have got to be admired by even the most finicky of music fans. Specifically, ESG use drums and bass in very simple, rock 'n roll-funk manner. They just don't play though, ESG has SOUL! This record jumps. Side One, produced by Martin Hannett, consists of three songs---'You're No Good', 'Moody', and 'UFO'. On all the songs the drums have a reverby-feedback quality that makes them sound very unique. The bass drum almost isn't a sound at all; it feels like a punch in the chest. Probably the most important instrument on the album is the bass; it throbs, sets the tone for all the songs and provides the framework for Renee's great cat/bird vocals. Which gets us to why ESG is so great. They create a very heavy sound emphasizing rhythm and pulsating bottom notes, then pierce it with Renee's high voice. ESG uses very little middle sounds, just the tension between Renee's voice and the bass/congas/drums. Very soulful, indeed! Side Two is a live recording of three more songs: 'Earn It', 'ESG', and 'Hey!'. Live, ESG almost gets instrumental in a funky-dub way. The vocals are kept to a minimum and rhythms to a maximum. They add a little more of guitar, too. The songs sound much different than the studio side but are still very good and, I would say, better. ESG has great potential and sound-wise I can think of very few comparisons. The drums sound a little like The Fall on the live side; but that is certainly where that comparison stops. ESG are fun. Maybe if The Plastics had been born in Brooklyn though... --Frank Loose

**IGGY POP Party (Ariola Benelux: 203 806)**-- The latest progression of Ig's career a step further from SOLDIER. Thom Panunzio, who mixed SOLDIER is the producer for the bulk of the album. Producer Tommy Boyce (of Monkee's fame) has the honors for the last three which include two old covers, 'Sea of Love' and 'Time (Won't Let Me)'. The other production, also on the single is 'Bang Bang' a great, steady beat, rocker. The three are a bit more (Iggy) 'pop' oriented.

Lyrics have always been an important aspect for this performer. He is one of the best song writers around. This time, Ivan Kral co-wrote the eight originals. The themes are basic rock and roll oriented with rock and roll clubs, emotional relationships, trying to have fun; all with a degree of cynical satire. He has used experiences from his last tour such as being at the Mardi Gras and at the Lucky Number in Chicago. The geographic orientation gets carried further with 'Houston Is Hot Tonight'.

PARTY starts out with-mentioning what it all is about: 'Pleasure'. The sound is powerful, fast-paced, and energetic. Horns are used on several cuts. Backing harmonies are used in choruses. The band is the same as the tour. Besides Ivan Kral, who is more or less in charge, there is Robert Dupree, Michael Page, and Doug Bowne. Basically, the drums keep a steady 4/4 beat, the bass repetitive and low volume, and keyboards follow the vocals similar to the guitar, although there are some guitar solos stuck in occasionally. The music itself is quite enjoyable. But make no mistake about the fact that this is Iggy Pop, the singer, whom you hear first and the band is his band.

This album was released by Arista Records' Holland branch, Ariola Benelux, and also in France and West Germany. Arista UK got cold feet but they will probably issue it soon. There are no US or domestic release plans . . . so far. There should be. --BR

**MAGAZINE Magic, Murder and the Weather (Virgin/IRS: SP70020)**--- The fourth studio album from the recently disbanded Magazine continues along with some of their trademark distress and anxieties. It seems front man Howard Devoto felt it was time to end the Magazine experience, regardless of this release and the newly-found attention they would have (and still will) received. --SK

**PHANTOM LIMB Admission of Guilt**-- The recent popularity of flexi-discs has made available to consumers a lot of music that ordinarily would go unrecorded. Local groups with little money can scrap together a couple of hundred dollars, rent or borrow a decent 2- or 4-track tape recorder and be in business. It then becomes possible to send them to clubs, radio stations, fanzines, friends, etc. They wear out quickly and, therefore, are perfect for rock and roll.

Phantom Limb have their flexi, 'Admission of Guilt', available through The Offense, a fanzine out of Columbus, OH. You can also get it through Limbo Party Music, 280 E. Hudson, Columbus, OH, 43202. It is worth having a copy.

The whole song has an early Siouxsie and The Banshees feel. At times it is as heavy as anything Siouxsie has done. The introduction is real smooth and progresses into a nice break before the vocals begin. The other breaks throughout the song are good also--one of them features a psychedelic guitar riff that is slightly short of stunning. Turn it up loud and you can feel your spine crawl. It really makes the song. Overall, there is a feeling of paranoia or unknown, lurking threats. The lyrics are good too: 'I've been a taker of tests/ I have not conformed/ I've dabbled in lifestyles/ Are you of the norm?/ The sounds you create/ The pages you tear/ Symbolize resistance to art.' Not a bad piece of plastic. --Frank Loose

**EARL ZERO VS THE OFFS/THE OFFS VS ZERO (Epiphany Records: ED8 04)**-- How this 12-inch, 45 came about is probably an important story, of which I have heard nothing at all. The Offs are an American white boys' band that has a partial hard-core reggae orientation. (This is shown by their single of a few years back with 'Johnny Too Bad'. Also TALK TALK recently reviewed a concert where they opened for Steel Pulse in California.) Earl Zero is a Jamaican reggae artist who has worked with Epiphany in the past.

One might assume that perhaps Zero just influences a hip band by producing them. Probably not, since this was produced by Rough Trade's Allen Sturdy, himself. What it sounds more like is an overall combined effort with The Offs not afraid to reggae-out.

Parts of both sides seem separate but most blend together. Although each is around ten minutes, it ends too quickly. Hey . . . put out an album!

Side One opens with 'Wild Boy' performed by The Offs, sounding the closest I've heard to England's The Members in vocals and rhythm. It closes with a mix-mastered version. The second side has a continual reggae song. --BR

# Album Reviews

System Planning Korporation "Information Overload Unit" (Side Effect, ser01)

System Planning Korporation aka the Surgical Penis Klinik aka the Socialist Patients Kooperativ were three people involved in music as psycho therapy. These three members have since departed ie one has died and the other two have gone on to become popular musicians! Three new members have been recruited to expose the lurking global maddness: Operator, Tone Generator, and Wilkins. IOU is a record that describes the state that man has fallen to. We have become overloaded with information. Facts that for the most part have proven/will be proven to be harmful to mankind are what SPK dwell on. Their aim, as stated in Dokument #1, which is included with this record, is to expose the listener to various levels of mental disturbances. This is "sonics for manics". Sex and death (of the violent sort) comprise most of their material; which are collected tape recordings of lectures on methods of torture, the effects of nerve gas, criminal confessions and pornographic fragments. It is combined with some of the most violent and disturbing sounds I've ever heard, ie the drill press lobo sound is present in every song. Life to SPK must not be very enjoyable or precious as seen in such titles as SUTURE OBSESSION, MACHT SCHRECKEN, RETARD, STAMMHEIM, TORTURKAMMER, and KALTBRUCHIG ACIDEATH. What results when one listens to this over an extended period of time? Perhaps, you'll become one of those solitary shoes on the edge of the road or the accompanying body in the HEFTY bag.

U-Man

*The proper study of mankind is man.*
Alexander Pope

# Album Reviews

**NME/ROUGH TRADE C81 (Rough Trade: 001)**-- Quite an accomplishment by these heavies in the new music world who compiled 24 separate songs from the current charts. Everyone has probably heard about this by now, but here it is again. Some highlights include the first side with Scritti Politti's 'Sweetest Girl' opening, followed by The Beat in 'Twist and Crawl Dub', then a new Pere Ubu cut, Wah! Heat, Orange Juice, Cabaret Voltaire, DAF live, Specials and the last Buzzcock's tune. The other side, with Raincoats, beginning, doesn't have quite the punch as Side One. But a great collection indeed and one that will be available in shops soon. --SK

**JAMES CHANCE AND THE CONTORTIONS Live in New York (ROIR: AA100)/ EIGHT EYE SPY Live (ROIR: A101)**-- These are the initial releases on this cassette tape only company, Reach out International Records (611 Broadway, No. 214, New York, NY, 10012). None of the material has ever been on vinyl, so this is the only way to get it. So what is it? The Contortions' tape mixed by James Chance has an hour's worth of cuts from late 80 and early 81 from shows at the Peppermint Lounge and the Eighties. It shows Chance and Contortions continuing on as before; soul, jazz, wild sax/vocals and bizarre sounds all around. Absolutely great! The Eight Eye Spy tape, collected from many shows, between January and August, 1980, can be a bit much to take unless one is familiar with their style and Lydia Lunch. The liner notes (yes, casettes can have liner notes, too) refer to the sound as American Sex Voodoo. The opening, 'Diddy Wah Diddy', is exceptional and can be used by judging their departure from the original, as a guide to their sound. Hard to explain but easy to classify after hearing. Both groups are part of the same scene as most people probably know. It is very good to see these groups forge out into new territory, i.e., live, cassette only releases. --SK

**LUDAS Pickpocket (New Hormones: CAT1)**-- New Hormones, the label the Buzzcocks set up, have branched into cassette with their initial release of a six-track cassette with magazine of Ludas, who have just finished their third single. There are three people in the group, with Linder being the focal point and vocalist. So what does it sound like? Well, there's lead guitar and percussion going up and down the scale, light airy vocals, quick little ditties. If one was real frizzed out, it might not help to play this. But maybe it would. PICKPOCKET does have a continual rhythm and beat. Good work. --SK

**THE PACKARDS Pray for Surf (Surfside 001)**-- This 12-inch, eight-song release heralds the now burgeoning Southern Cal surf revival, although no neophytes, these Packards. They're led by one Paul Johnson, the impetus behind the Belairs (who later turned out to be The Challengers) way back in the 60s. They had a minor hit with 'Mr. Moto', which is redone here, plus other Johnson compositions. Cool stuff, although the absence of reverb on the guitars is somewhat disquieting. The remake of The Belairs' 'Squad Car' is the personal fave here, as it fulfills the main requirement of instrumental music, that it sounds (as Karl Hoffmann puts it) like the theme to a bad, bad movie. Trash rules. (THE PACKARDS can be ordered from Surfside Records, Box 3564, San Clemente, CA, 92672). --Buzz

**From the Archives of William Burroughs NOTHING HERE NOW BUT THE RECORDINGS (Industrial Records: IR0016)**-- The LP illustrates the Gysin-Burroughs cut-up method. It is not intended to be art or a substitute for literature. This is simply an attempt at utilizing the cut up method in a different medium, the spoken and recorded language. Then again, it could be an audio time capsule that has been prematurely heard. Through Orgones, drugs, libidinous magic or sheer will, Burroughs has seen the future and has revealed it to us, the unwary. The persona of Hassan Sabbah, thyold man of the mountain, assassin supreme, is Burrough's vehicle for warning all life forms, be they dead, alive, unborn or Outside, of the inevitable end. On earth, global violence reaches virulent levels. Recorded newscasts from different eras merge into one timestream. Newscasters, generals, presidents, the members of the boards and syndicates strive to make this epidemic none of our concern. From Outside, phantom recordings infiltrate our sphere. These are recordings that inexplicably appear on tape machines, even though the machine has been running in an empty room devoid of sound. How can these exist? A rupture in space/time continuum? Bits and pieces of Burroughs' works click in and out. This is as frightening as HP Lovecraft's horror story, 'The Whisperer in Darkness' with its alien recordings. Listening to this makes one feel awfully helpless, as if the event has been pre-planned. If so, then we are helpless. The intriguing thing about this record is the question of randomness. 'How random is random?', asks Burroughs. This record is the answer to that. You must listen. What made me write this? Why'd I say that? --U-Man

# Album Reviews

**EPICYCLE Epicycle (Circle Records: CST1111)**-- Epicycle are a Chicago teenage band, who have been playing for a couple of years. They have been a local favorite since their early appearances and have put out some EPs in the past. Always energetic and modish in the tradition of The British Invasion bands, Epicycle further establish their mark on the new music scene with the release of their debut album. The twelve songs, written by the four members, convey a variety of influences and moods. In general, the tracks have a layered fullness with melodic harmonies. The vocals are clearly pronounced so one hears the lyrics, mainly short comments directed to 'you'. That's pretty minor though compared to the overall packaging--well, it's basic in design, yet attractive and informative. The production of the tracks are surprisingly exceptionally clean--something unexpected in general today with the lower budget operations or small scale labels.

**TYPICAL GIRLS Live in Cincinnati and San Francisco (A Basic Bootleg)**-- This is part of two live shows from The Slits' last tour. As reported earlier (Vol. 2, No. 13) their live shows are much better than their recordings, largely due to the backing musicians and tribal spirit they generate. Most of the cuts are well known, although two new ones are included. The first side starts with 'New Town' with 'Man Next Door' being the outstanding song. The other show starts with a great version of 'Heard It Through The Grapevine', in fact, the best one I've heard, then continues with 'Typical Girls', 'Fade Away', 'In The Beginning' and a new one ends the side. The fidelity is high on both versions of the album out but the thinness makes it ideal for warpage. So put it on tape and get the feeling of a Slits concert. --WB

**JODY HARRIS/ROBERT QUINE Escape (Lust/Unlust: JMB 236)**-- These two New York guys have created a masterpiece of sound and effects with guitar, bass, and electronical percussion that has a continual low melody line layered into guitar chords and riffs. You can slink around with the beats from these five songs forever. It sticks into your mind. Vocals are not used making it more a mental trip. Fun listening, too. --SK

**LIQUID LIQUID (99 Records: 9907 EP)**-- Another new release on 99 Records of New York City, LIQUID LIQUID is a five-man percussion band, playing such instruments as marimba, rototoms, metal phones, congos, melodica, bass, drum kit, very little guitar. Over the top of these is Salvatore Principato chanting (perhaps ethnic) scary and threatening noises. The music, while sounding simple, contains many complicated rhythmic symptoms at times dreamy, slow deliberate rhythms slosh around like the ocean with swells and lulls. After listening to the recorded album (one side live, one studio), Liquid Liquid would be a very exciting group to see. --CL

**AU PAIRS Playing With A Different Sex (Human Records: Human 1)**-- At last, a group that focuses on unabashed anti-sexism for its lyrics! Au Pairs has followed their single with a surprising album. Not only do they sing out with some thoughtful ideas, but they make it lively and energetic, just the way I always thought cultural revolution could sound. 'It's Obvious' has been sharpened and wired up for the album, and all the instrumentals are more innovative than expected. Not unlike Gang of Four meets Talking Heads. Beautiful cover, provocative lyrics, groovy music; I rate this one nine out of ten. --Sharon Mayer

**NON Pagan Muzak LP or 45** On a seven-inch record in a twelve-inch sleeve are 17 looped grooves that revolve around two holes that can be played at two, or three different speeds depending on your turntable. If that doesn't make sense, neither does the latest release from Non, Pagan Muzak. Non is Boyd Rice, some Californian out to get people physically involved in his music without making them dance. He has recorded 17 'sounds' ranging from rather pleasant to God-awfully irritating. The whole effect is like taking your house key and scratching very deeply into The Flowers of Romance, SPK, or Throbbing Gristle. Talk about endless fun! This is hardly music, but it is good. You can find a groove you like, play it all night, 15 seconds, or whatever length of time your mood desires. Some of the rhythms are just incredible, and then, some of the loops have no rhythm. One of the two holes is slightly off center so that when you play it there is an added bit of distortion going on. The whole effect is like standing on a corner and having a car with its stereo blasting go by. This is an incredibly conceptual record; it's anything you want it to be and more. Don't let the concept scare you out of buying a copy though. --Frank Loose

**THE PSYCHEDELIC FURS Talk Talk Talk (CDS: 84892)**-- For their second album, the Furs continue on with this semi-established sound that has been so widely accepted and enjoyed. Not quite the impact of the debut but very close to it. --SK

## Small Labels, Independents and More...

The last few months have brought many independent releases to TALK TALK. Some have been quite good records but too many are mediocre at best. This column will very briefly mention most of the releases. It's hard to go into much detail when all you have to go on is the record itself and minimal-information. Onward. THE BRONCOS (Terminal Records, Box 17388, Cleveland, OH, 44117) recorded this EP last summer before breaking up. Hope they have improved from their loud, abrasive approach. THE TENANTS (Rent's-Due Records, 819 14th St., No. 9, San Francisco, CA, 94102) have been around bout a year and have got a lot of attention for their single with lots of airplay. A bit basic. THE SKUNKS (1007 S. Congress, No. 354, Austin, TX, 78704) have a great single although at times it is hard to defend the emptiness. MODERN WARFARE NO. 2 (Bemisbrain Records, 200 Termino, Long Beach, CA, 90803) is very fast, good neopunk music. THE WOLVARINES (Tom Records, 70 Lundys Lane, San Francisco, CA, 94110) seem to be doing well with this 45. Their lineup includes ex-DK drummer Bruce and ex-Zeroes bassist Hector. Sweet and slow love songs. DA (Autumn Records, 2427 N. Janssen, Chicago, IL, 60614) have their first single out now. They are one of the up and coming Chicago bands with one male and three females in the lineup. They will also be on a new Chicago live compilation LP out soon... check it out. OTTO KENTROL (Control Records, Box 95, West Hurley, NY, 12491) is an interesting character who plays all instruments on the Learn Greek in Greece LP with similarities to Contortions' style. THE ROCKING CLONES (Record Service, Inc., 605 E. Green Street, Champaign, IL, 61820) have a pretty basic single out similar in tone to Phil Ochs at his wimpyist. THE FLAMING OH'S (Flame City Records, 324 N. First Street, No. 9, Minneapolis, MN, 53401) concentrate on organ as lead. Not bad overall. THE MELODIC ENERGY COMMISSION (Energy Discs, 2936 W. 4th, Vancouver, BC, V6K 1R2 CANADA) have an interesting sound as they deal with energy as melody. Violin very prevalent.

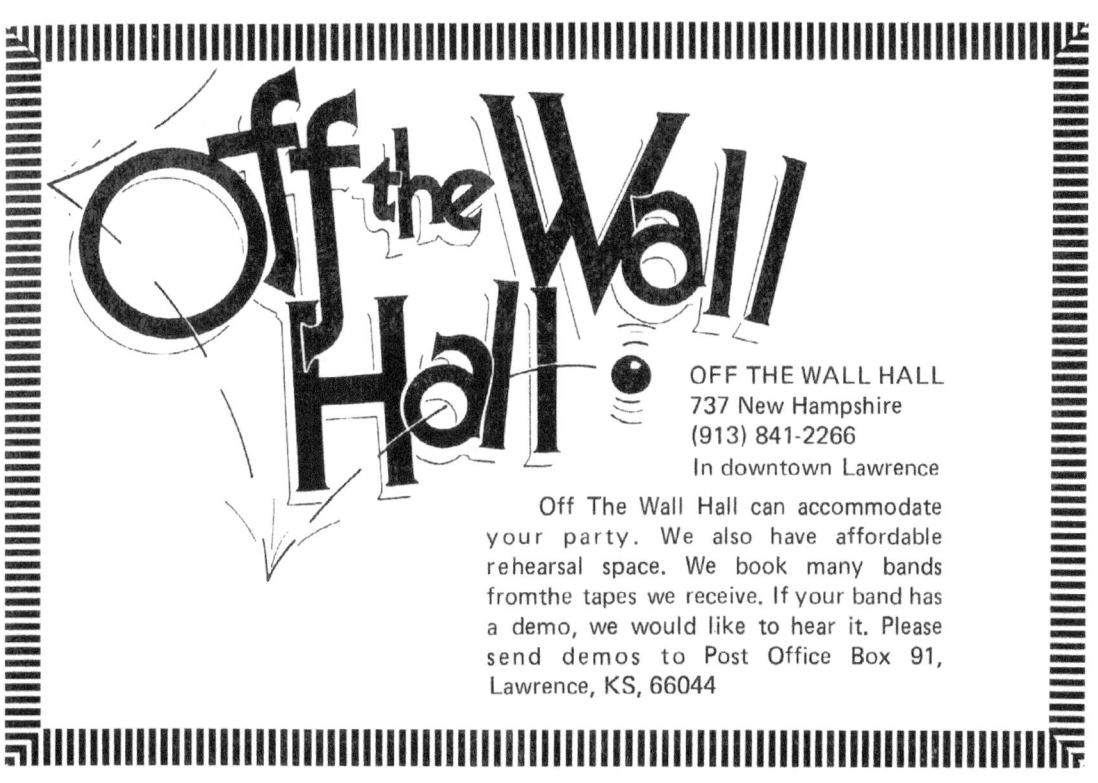

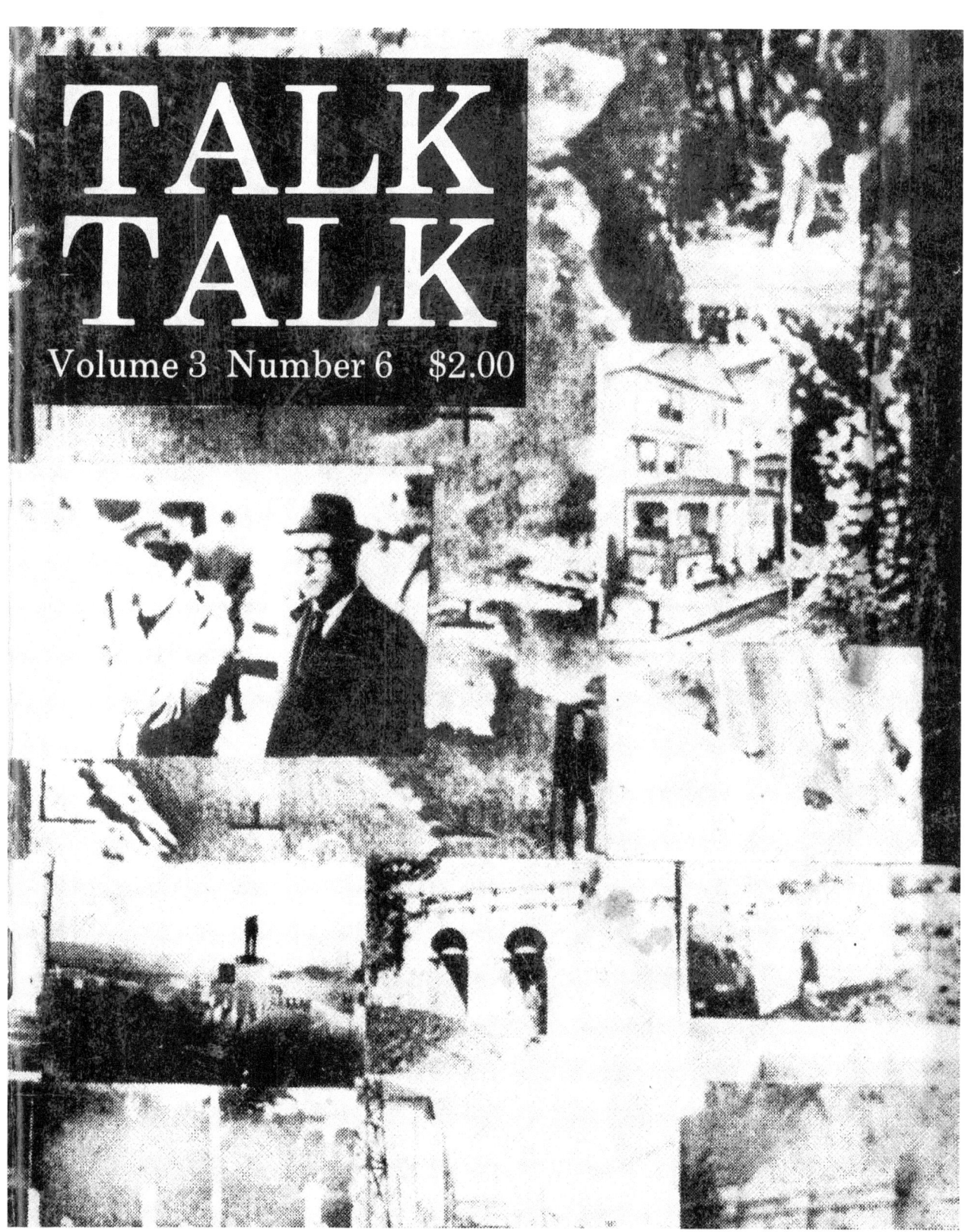

# TALK TALK

Vol.3 No.6  Autumn 1981  $2.00

**Editor**
Bill Rich

**Staff**
Frank Loose
Rick Hellman
Marc Burch
Andrea Rosenthal
Martin Olson
John Gleason
Dave Cade
Jim Schwada
Steve Kemp
Mark Gilman
Dave Stuckey
Mel Cheplowitz
Sharon Maier
Tom Hoyt
**Photography**
Frank Loose
Lowell Stewart
Jo Stone
Eric Schindling
Bill Rich
**Layout**
John Lee
**Typesetting**
Joan McCabe Moore

| | |
|---|---|
| LIVE Peter Tosh | 4 |
| REGGAE REVIEWS | 6 |
| LIVE Abuse, | 8 |
| Sunsplash, Ventures | 9 |
| INTERVIEW | |
| Psychedelic Furs | 10 |
| LIVE The Fall | 12 |
| INTERVIEW | |
| Billy Idol | 14 |
| Iggy Pop | 15 |
| William Burroughs | 18 |
| LAWRENCE | 24 |
| GERMANY | 25 |
| TAPE REVIEWS | 26 |
| RECORD REVIEWS | 28 |
| LOCAL SCENE | 37 |

TALK TALK is published by Talk Talk Publications, PO Box 36, Lawrence, Kansas, 66044, USA. All contents copyright 1981 Talk Talk Publications. No portion can be reproduced without written authorization. Subscriptions are unavailable. Distributors include Rough Trade and Systematic.

**ABOUT THE COVER:**
In 1964, William Burroughs prepared to return to the United States from Tangiers. On New Year's Day, he was back home in St. Louis, commissioned to write a piece for *Playboy*. He was interviewed by Conrad Knickerbocker for *Paris Review*, which also ran the story, 'Return to St. Louis'. He was working on scrapbooks of clippings and typed passages, making conceptual messages. Several pages were given to Knickerbocker for inclusion. Three were not used. The manuscript materials are now in the hands of Tom Knickerbocker, the interviewer's son, who lent them to TALK TALK. The page reprinted here shows many of the themes of that period when *The Nova Express* was printed. The block of photographs are from Tangiers, Europe, and South America. The cover is a blow up from this.

We asked Mr. Burroughs to identify what photographs he could.

Mr. B.: OK, TALK TALK, upper right hand corner is your reporter with a single barrel 16-guage shotgun in the jungle outside Pucallpa, Peru, 1953.

Just below that is a boarding house in Atlantic City, taken from a picture. One of my characters, sort of a burglar, is slinking out at the extreme left-hand corner.

Below that you will see a young man standing in a strange position. The police were looking for a murderer in London seventeen years ago. So they dressed up a young man that looked like the victim--I don't know what they thought they were doing. But anyway, beneath him was 'Stand in For Mr. Who.'

Just to the left of that is myself and Ian Summerville. Ian had just shot a bullseye and they took a picture of us.

Below the young man is the old arch which is 1899. And in the lower right hand corner we see the same arch. This was in Gibraltar and it was torn down.

Just above the arch in the corner is a picture of a vacant lot, taken from my house in Tangiers.

There are several pictures of the arch. Underneath the one with the boy going through is another picture of Gibraltar.

At the extreme lower left hand corner (of the front) is a picture of the French Consulate taken from the Cafe de Paris in Tangiers. That's one page.

On the other side, at the extreme upper left corner you see a boy and his dog taken in Pucallpa, Peru, with a view acros the Urubamba River.

Just to the right is a staircase in Panama City. I took them in 1953.

Most of the others are various shots of the Cafe de Mexico in Tangiers. The angular shots are taken from my balcony.

The lower left hand corner is Tangiers--apartment buildings. I think there is a picture of the American Consulate in 1964. There are some I can't identify and some are moon shots.

This was a jumble of photographs--a montage. I just put them on the table and took the picture. The Nova Express page was done shortly before the publication of Nova Express in England in 1964.

# Peter Tosh

**PETER TOSH Agora, Dallas, Texas**

It was standing room only as The Steppin' Razor, Peter Tosh, strode onstage at The Agora, Dallas, for the fourth and final Texas date of his 75-concert 'Dread and Alive' tour of America.

Tosh, aka The Bush Doctor, thrilled the capacity crowd with an hour-and-a-half of roots reggae that had the predominently white audience skanking to the beat as if they were born to it. Backed by the skintight Word, Sound, and Power band Tosh showcased material from his latest WANTED DREAD AND ALIVE album and infused new life into old crowdpleasers from each of his previous three LPs.

Singing well, but playing little, Tosh opened with 'Pick Myself Up' from the new one, followed by 'African,' 'Coming In Hot,' 'Walk and Don't Look Back,' 'The Poor Man Feel It,' and 'Rastafari Is.' Although the lead guitar duties for most of the evening were discharged by the very talented Donald Kinsey, Tosh did pick up his axe for 'I'm The Toughest' and contributed a fiery conga break to the aforementioned 'Rastafari Is.' Taking things back a few years, Tosh paid tribute to his late comrade Bob Marley with 'Mystic Man' and the well received classic 'Get Up, Stand Up' before closing with 'Legalize It,' as the assemblage cheered and waved a forest of smouldering spliffs.

Tosh, heir apparent to the title of No. 1 Reggae Performer, after the death of Bob Marley, is quick to take issue with the comparisons between them. In an interview in the Dallas Times Herald, he said simply, 'Bob Marley is Bob Marley, I am I.'

If the Dallas show is any indication, that is more than enough. -DCool

*PHOTOS BY LOWELL STEWART IN LAWRENCE, KS.*

# Reggae Reviews

**THE PARAGONS (Mango)**-- The notion that each of reggae's predecessors, be it ska, blue beat, or any other, needs its own revival is wishful thinking on the part of some shop record execs. The fact is that it takes many people a long time to learn the differences between them. And just because a white pop act like Blondie can achieve high sales figures with a disgustingly lame version of the Paragons' classic, 'Tide Is High' doesn't mean there will be a rock steady revival. That song was just one in a lengthy string of Jamaican number one hits the Paragons had when they helped originate the rock steady beat in the mid-60s. Most of them were penned by lead singer John Holt. This album contains new arrangements of ten of those hits sung by the original trio of Holt, Tyrone Evans, and Howard Barrett. Those ubiquitous revolutionaries, Sly Dunbar and Robbie Shakespeare, provide the arrangements and rhythm. It's great to hear the Paragons sing together again--this time with modern recording quality and fine musical backup. Whatever that ephemoral quality is that makes a Jamaican group great, the Paragons still have it. However, if producer Lister Hewan-Lowe's intention is to re-popularize rock steady, as the album notes suggest, the slightly retarded tempo of these versions does not present a very realistic idea of that style. In fact, the pace is slowed just barely enough to drive me up a wall. In contrast, the rhythm works well on two songs, 'Riding High' and 'Man Next Door', giving them power and conviction. The latter goes out with a bit of that world-famous Revolutionaries dubwise sound to great effect. This record is a must for Paragons fans and will make a fine addition to any collection not containing the hard-to-find originals. --Ja Nittu Bahd

**FELA ANIKULAP KUTI Black President (SPART 1167)**-- With over 50 records to his credit, Fela is one of the most popular and influential musical artists in West Africa. He is the originator of the Afro-beat style of music and is probably one of the most progressive forces in music today. Fela is a revolutionary in every sense of the word--an Ivan who relentlessly challenges the regime in control of the Nigerian government. His music reveals a passion for truth and a defiant stance against the 'Powers That Be' rarely found in music today. BLACK PRESIDENT is one of his latest works and is one of the few Fela albums to reach the U.S. market (via Arista Imports, England). The music on this album features distinct and driving rhythms similar to contemporary Latin, reggae, funk and jazz. There are three songs on BLACK PRESIDENT--'Sorrow, Tears and Blood', 'Colonial Mentality', and 'I.T.T. (International Thief Thief)'. All three songs have an agressive and upbeat style. If you liked the latest Talking Heads and Eno efforts, you should buy this record--they got those polyrhythmic licks from Fela!

During the 1970s, Fela and a few ardent followers established a community called Kalakuta, outside the Nigerian capital of Lagos. The Nigerian Army raided Kalakuta in 197. Fela's mother, a long-time political activist, was killed in the raid--thrown out a window by Nigerian soldiers. Kalakuta was burned to the ground. Fela was exiled to Ghana for a year.

Fela's music was so popular in Nigeria that upon his return from exile, he was officially barred from running for President in the 1979 election. The next election is in 1983. Fela says he plans to run. (There is an excellent article in Volume Three of RE/SEARCH magazine about Fela and his legendary role as an activist in Nigerian politics. Suggested reading for all.)

Fela and the AFRICA 70 band are great. There is an uncommon sense of identity with the masses evident on this album. This is rebel music, akin to the type the late Bob Marley and Linton Kwesi Johnson have been known for. A lot of people sing about it, Fela has lived it. A quote from the liner notes, 'According to the estimation of Africa's riches, every black man should be a millionaire. Why are we so poor? It is time to investigate!' Africa is hot, so is Fela! --Dave Cade

**BUNNY WAILER Dubd'sco Volume 1** is one of the most underrated albums ever. The reason for this monumental oversight can be traced to one of the worst album covers ever. In fact, this ugly green cover with some black printing on front andback looks more like a 12-inch 45. It's too bad that the cover is confusing because this LP is really Bunny Wailer's greatest hits in dub. Seven versions in all, including such Bunny Wailer favorites as 'Rasta Man,' 'Fig Tree,' and 'Dreamland.' The versions here are not the ones that appeared as dub sides of the singles. Echoing vocals dominate the spacey mix, which includes an inordinate amount of phase shifting. The percussion reverberates with lots of drumming on the rim as horns weave sinuously in and out. Weird effects abound. It's obvious that Wailer has learned a lot from working with Lee Perry. Don't let the cover fool you, this LP is one of the great masterpieces of dub. --MC

**BRAIN DAMAGE Dennis Bovell (Fontana, British)**-- YO! Don't jump off that cliff! Check out my vote for album of the year. Here's a record that can add a little meaning into the life of any broad-minded fan. When LKJ predicted two years ago that England would soon take the leading role in reggae music away from Jamaica, I laughed. With the release of this album I am convinced that it is only the large number of people involved in the Jamaican reggae industry that ensures its lead. Dennis Bovell, aka Black Beard, is the kingpin of reggae in England. The list of British chart hits he has produced and/or mixed is very long. To this country's disgrace, only a handful of those records have been released on American labels. And the chances for this one are slim. BRAIN DAMAGE, Bovell's third solo album and his first as Dennis Bovell, branches out from strict dubwise to present a cornucopia of musical styles. Ska, calypso, and funk are performed with proficiency as well as a knock-out rock n' roll number. Bovell even shows us his deejay talents. on one number. The subject matter on BRAIN DAMAGE is as diverse as the musical styles. It ranges from politics on 'Bettah', to love on 'Our Tune', to sheer comedy on 'Bertie'. Bovell handles all the vocals on the album as well as a majority of the other tracks. But he finds room for several friends including Aswad members Angus Gaye and Dan Forde. Laura Logic's sax helps make 'Bettah' one of the album's standouts. And, to make sure Bovell's solid dubwise fans who picked up on the two Black Beard albums aren't left out, there's a 'free' dub album included in the $14 price. Those same fans won't be surprised by BRAIN DAMAGE's short total length. All four sides fit on a 60-minute cassette with room to spare. It seems Bovell wants to get rid of his 'man-behind-the-man' image and prove to the world that he can do anything. He does so admirably. Watch out Scratch-- there's somebody a comin'. --Jah Nittu Bahd

**AFRICAN DREAMLAND Jah Message (AYD Records: 121880)**-- A three-piece reggae band based in Nashville who are heavy on the dread in words and print but play surprisingly enough a form of blues on vinyl. After hearing a purer style of reggae for years, this release can catch one off guard. They play the way they feel it should be. Aashid A. P. Himons is the leader, the dread in control. Along with Darrell Rose and Mustafa Abdul-Aleen, who basically are percussionists, African Dreamland present an alternative form of Jah music for your listening pleasure. --WB

**BABYLON Various Artists (Takoma)**-- If this movie is as good as its soundtrack album, we reggae fans have much to look forward to at the cinema this year. The album is blessed by not having any Island Records standards for filler as did HARDER THEY COME and ROCKERS. It is probably the first American release for several of the artists, including Yabby U, Cassandra and Dennis Bovell. Side One has the vocal tracks and Side Two is strictly dubwise. As in most collections with an I-Roy number, it is the standout. But all of the songs here have hooks. The dub side is the most fun for me. The idea of using a lot of dub for a soundtrack is long overdue. It doesn't have any lyrics to get in the way of the dialogue or important action. Congratulations to Takoma Records for such a fine release as they branch out into the reggae business. --JG

**THE TERRORISTS with LEE PERRY Love Is Better Now (Splif Records)**-- Let's hope that this record is the final nail in the coffin of the idea that white people can't legitimately play reggae music. Jah music is like Jah herb. It is one of God's gifts to man. Sooner or later whitey's got to catch on just like he did with blues and jazz and rock & roll. LOVE IS BETTER NOW is a solid groove. Fine performance by the four-piece Terrorists. Haunting backup vocals and a trombone are added for the perfect touch. The B-side is Scratch's toast over the same song. Perry's association with these American reggae hopefuls seems to have given him new energy that just wasn't there on a lot of the stuff on the Pipecock Jackson album. More new Lee Perry stuff with American bands like The Majestics should be out before long. And if it's as good as this, the Upsetter probably has plenty of productive years left in him. --JG

ROUGH TRADE inc.
mailorder
1412 GRANT Ave.,
SAN FRANCISCO,
CA 94133

# And Other Shows

Since July 1, it has been illegal in Kansas to sell what has been termed paraphernalia. The standard 'head shops' have been closing and a new dialect has been established in referring to smoking and snuff accessories. Some accessories continue to be sold with law enforcement agencies apparently waiting for a court decision. An organization of merchants, KRTC (Kansas Retail Trade Cooperative) had a benefit one weekend at Off The Wall Hall with Abuse and The Tunes one night and Kelly Hunt and The Kinetics the next. Proceeds went toward the mounting legal fees. There are several issues involved here, including the right of free enterprise and also the assumption that all accessories banned are for illegal drug use.

*The most objectionable quality is the inherent inability to define paraphernalia. No statutory listing could possibly proscribe all the items which might be used with an illegal drug. Any attempted listing, no matter how long, must thus be viewed as incomplete.*

*Secondly, and of more importance to the newer statutes like that in Kansas, is the presumption contained in the law that any person who purchases or possesses any of these items intends to use them with some illegal drug. This presumption seems to me to eliminate the possibility of any tobacco-related or decorative purposes for these items, and creates a presumption that the purchaser is, in fact, an illegal drug user. In this context, the statute seems patently unconstitutional. It creates a presumption of criminality and is both vague in its terminology and overbroad in its application.*

*Those are the legal arguments and on top of that we must consider the wisdom, or lack of wisdom, involved in this prohibition-type approach to the issue. I think it obvious that the billions of taxpayer dollars spent in the effort to curb marijuana use have been wasted. No conceivable law enforcement policy can stop the use of a recreational drug used regularly by nearly 30,000,000 Americans.*

*The new paraphernalia statutes are founded on the same ill-conceived notions as that effort, and thus constitute an impractical and unenforceable statute that also undermines our few remaining constitutional protections.*

THE VENTURES Live at the Palomino, North Hollywood, August 22, 1981

The Ventures at the Palomino? Yee Haw, as they say in cowboy talk. I felt like I had taken a time machine back to Lawrence as I sat with the hard-core cowboys both urban and real. It was a far cry from the usual rowdy skinhead crowd I was used to. Excuse me, but I thought cowboys were supposed to get rowdy and have a kickin' good time. Not one of them moved even through the opening set by house band Palomino Riders. The stiff atmosphere in the place deterred me from even going to the bathroom for fear of being asked to sit down. In my brief chat with guitarist Nokie Edwards before the show, I discovered that he had been in the hospital for a bit and had no idea what they were going to play that night. He was waiting for the song list. I kept my fingers crossed that they wouldn't pander to the cowfolk with c and w, and told him that they better play some hits. Boy, did they play some hits! 'Walk Don't Run--1960' opened the show, followed by a string of greats like 'Apache', 'Slaughter on Tenth Avenue', 'Caravan, with a drum solo', 'Telstar', 'Walk Don't Run--1964', and their latest single, 'Surfin and Spyin', penned by the Go'Go's. I think I heard all my faves in the hour set they did which included three encores and a walk through the audience. I'll never learn though. Outside, lined up for the late show were the Ventures fans. Not a cowboy hat could be seen. The Ventures continue to play a style they helped to create in the early sixties. And even though they've been playing the same songs for 25 years or more, they still have a great time and constantly amaze me with their virtuoso guitar technique. Ram-Bunk-Shush! –The Gill Man

# Reggae Sunsplash

Reggae Sunsplash IV was held in early August at Montego Bay. The four-night festival is the annual reggae showcase for both Jamaicans and visitors. This year it was moved back to the tourist resort area and away from last year's inner city compound. There is a new government in power and new directives regarding the portrayed image of Jamaica. So, while the tourists were not exposed to the seamier side of existence, it still is there and things are not good. Yes, they are supposedly improving and everyone hopes conditions will continue to improve. Sunsplash itself was quite successful. And with any festival of its size, certain foul-ups occur and certain announced acts did not perform--such as Toots and The Maytals, as was announced the first night. Steel Pulse were wildly received, the first English band to play Sunsplash. Sly and Robbie's Taxi Production provided the bulk of the remaining performances, including Jimmy Riley, The Tamlins, Black Uhuru, and Culture.

The second night was highlighted by performances by Judy Mowatt, Freddie McGregor, Gregory Isaacs, and The Radics.

The third night had Third World headlining with Stevie Wonder as guest. He was there in memory of Bob Marley. The whole festival had a Marley memorial feel to it. The final night was especially designed for this, as The Wailers and the I-Threes and The Melody Makers and other Tuff Gong acts were the bill. The show continued on until morning.

# Interview: Psychedelic Furs

THE PSYCHEDELIC FURS Park West Chicago July 17th

Opening the show was some promoter's idea of the 'perfect' new wave band called Take Me. Composed of one Stray Cat, one Split End, one Jam, etc., they were well-rehearsed and totally devoid of excitement or originality.

Then The Furs came on to supply the missing passion. Richard Butler strode onstage with a loose-limbed grace, in suit and shades, exuding a drugged, hazy sensuality. Several writers have commented on the resemblance between Butler and Johnny (Rotten) Lydon and the thought crossed my mind, too. Perhaps a touch of Howard DeVoto as well.

The band was tight, reportedly a change from their first U.S. tour. They started with 'Into You Like a Train' and all the new material sounded great, including 'Pretty in Pink,' 'Mr. Jones,' and a hauntingly beautiful 'She is Mine.' The group played in front of a white screen onto which were projected patterns of colors, words, and pictures, a lone concession to the 'psychedelic revival.'

The only possible criticism of this show was that it was too much like the records. While it's true that there were only a few, undramatic departures from the norm, we're talking about the recreation of two outstanding albums here. The second show was better for sound clarity but Duncan Kilburn's sax was still mixed too low for my liking.

With a strong second album out and growing instrumental self-confidence the P. Furs have the potential to be a force for a long time to come. And with the (recent) disintegration of Magazine and The Talking Heads, there's a gap in the field of thinking man's rock. Look for The Furs to fill it. --RH

After nearly having been kicked out of the plush Park West, between shows, we managed to have a chat backstage with Richard (Rep) Butler, lead singer of The Psychedelic Furs. Thanks are due to Marilyn Laverty of CBS Records and The Furs' road manager, Mick Angus.

TT: The new album, TALK TALK TALK, seems to be different from the first album both musically and in the subject matter...

Butler: I think it's more melodic. I'd say the music's more melodic and I'd say the lyrics are more concentrated. On the first album we were striking out at a lot of things. It's basically very angry and then...well, you can slow down for a bit, we've got a few albums to go yet and I decided to make this album about love. So it's more concentrated on different attitudes and viewpoints you can have about love.

TT: On the first album you dealt with a lot of different things like in 'We Love You...'

Butler: I'm always slagging religion and marriage and politics all in one song, you know talking about India, but it was too diverse and a bit undisciplined. The first album was really raw anger, if you like.

TT: It lacked focus, in other words?

Butler: Yeah, it was just anger, whereas this one is...I'm getting more focus on things now.

TT: That's what I like about your band, that you can treat love in one song and something angry and cynical in the next moment and it's all homogenous.

Butler: Yeah, it's all part of a philosophy, an attitude, you know?

TT: What attitude is that?

Butler: The Psychedelic Furs' attitude. Who's to defend?

TT: Why do you think you wrote more about subjects of love this time, are you not quite as angry as before?

Butler: No, it was something that was going on in my personal life made me want to examine it...I write to find out about myself as well. It was one way to find out about that time. I think I'm wiser for having written the stuff I did then and I'm hoping when people listen to it that they're going to get a bit wiser and it may do other things for them, as well.

TT: I guess The Psychedelic Furs got together, with the exception of one member, about four years ago. How have things changed musically in as far as competence and the things you deal with?

Butler: We're now aware that we have an audience, which, when we started, we weren't and that gives you a lot of confidence and matters a lot...You're aware of X amount of people that want to hear certain types of things and you just...take them along with you.

TT: But how have things changed musically?

Butler: We can play. We've learned our own limitations and we can play better.

TT: As far as the style of your music, has that changed?

Butler: It changes all the time. Every time you learn a new chord, it changes something else.

TT: Do you play any musical instruments?

Butler: Well, yeah. I write the tunes.

TT: What do you write on?

Butler: The guitar.

TT: How come you never play in concert?

Butler: I like to just sing. I don't like to have an instrument strapped around my neck.

TT: I guess a few people have charged that some of the songs in TALK TALK TALK are sexist or something. Could you go over that?

Butler: I don't really want to go over it, no. They just are simply not sexist. Things are said from a male point of view but the reason why we put it on the album, we had a big discussion when we were doing it and we decided that girls could say the same things as well, so it's not sexist. I've had girls come up to me and just saying, 'I want to sleep with you' and that's it. You get groupies every time, lots of those things, lots of girls in all walks of life. If you send Robert Redford into an office block, there's going to be X amount of girls who are willing to sleep with him. They wouldn't want to have a long conversation or anything, they'd just take him home for a night.

TT: So it's basically stupid to say that's sexist then?

Butler: Well, yeah. Of course. It's denying libido in human beings and I'm really into sex.

TT: Well, who isn't?

Butler: I'm not into denying libido.

TT: You have said that The Psychedelic Furs, coming up at the time when punk was so big in England, combined the energy and aggression of punk with the psychedelic aspect of the 60's. Could you explain that?

Butler: Yeah, have you got a cigarette?

TT: To me, the psychedelic tag is just an attempt to make another fad.

Butler: Yeah, it's just been invented. And it's been invented by the English music press. All that thing about the psychedelic revival is absolute bull.

TT: But you have said that your music is somewhat of a merging of those two sides...

Butler: No, I've never said that, I've been misquoted.

TT: Well, I've read that some of your favorite bands are The Seeds and The Velvet Underground.

Butler: Yeah, and Edith Piaf and Frank Sinatra.

TT: And The Supremes?

Butler: No, not too much.

TT: Isn't that in the song ('We Love You')?

Butler: Yeah, but that song is a bit tongue-in-cheek.

TT: What do you think are, and I hate to use the word, the main influences in your music?

Butler: We've got so many influences I couldn't begin. We're all individuals and we all play together and when we go into the stuido we just start playing riffs. And Vince, our drummer, likes things that I abhor.

TT: For instance?

Butler: I don't want to give you any for instance, he just likes things that I hate and vice-versa.

TT: I seem to hear a little Roxy Music in your sound. Was that a favorite of yours?

Butler: No. Roxy Music I dislike intensely. Their first album was good in a way but everything since then I don't like at all.

TT: What are some of the bands playing today that you like a lot?

Butler: I can think of a couple, Heaven 17, Killing Joke a little bit, some of their stuff not all of it, about 50 percent. U2, about 50 percent...

At that point, a company of satin-jacketed 'security' goons entered the dressing room and forced us to leave. I don't hold them personally responsible. After all, they were only following orders....

# The Fall

NAKED RAYGUN/DA/THE FALL Tut's Chicago July 16th

We arrived in time to catch the last half-song of Naked Raygun, who were, indeed, naked save for strategically placed guitars. The only one with guts was the bass player who had a clear-bodied instrument.

The next act, Da, were quite an improvement. The female lead singer and bassist was cute, though clothed and an engaging front person. Da's music is fresh and original. This group must have sent away for the Charles Atlas 'Dynamic Tension' method. Snatches of Siouxsie, Gang of 4, and funk could be heard but comparisons are odious and don't do the band justice. Da kept the focus shifting from guitar to guitar to singer to drums and showed some controlled use of string-hacking distortion, especially when compared to the Raygun's pervious inept performance. The license to be ugly is a dangerous thing in the wrong hands. No such problems with The Fall. The keyboards weren't working this night so two guitarists were employed. Mark Smith came on looking as far from a New Romantic as one could possibly get and what followed was an hour-plus of uncompromising rock music as only The Fall can do it.

I recognized few of the songs and the words to more familiar ones were changed. Smith sang with his back turned to the audience 50 percent of the time, while the band sweated and kept the churning, jagged riffs rolling. All the songs melted into one with the highlights of 'Totally Wired' and 'No Christmas for John Quays.'

The Fall aren't easy on the ears or the mind, which could explain their relative lack of popularity. They are one of the most consistently challenging groups in a decadent scene, more and more content to dress up and fall into line. Maybe these really are the last days before the Fall. --RH

PHOTOS BY ERIC SCHINDLING
IN OKLAHOMA CITY, OK.

# Interview: Billy Idol

Five years ago, Billy Idol was practicing with his group, Generation X. The punk music scene had not really begun and things had not begun to be torn down. The band played songs that were enjoyable and energetic. Hits such as 'Ready Steady Go', 'Wild Youth', and 'Your Generation' helped fuel the minds of other musicians and fans. As the years continued on, two albums and various singles later, the band split.

The last year, Billy Idol has been living in New York, where he continually pops up at 'happenings' as sort of the visiting celebrity in residence. A single, 'Dancing With Myself', has seen chart action and dance club support. It has been followed by another single, 'Mony Mony' and 'Baby Talk'. A 12-inch 45 with 'Dancing With Myself', 'Mony Mony' and 'Baby Talk' and remixed 'Untouchables' is out now, a release which provides an updated collection of current Billy Idol. He recently explained what he was doing.

'I am getting a band together of New York people and will be out touring in November and December, after we put tracks down to get the feel of what we're going for.

The whole point in moving to New York was that I needed a new feeling. I wanted to find out about America before I began making any sort of records. I wanted to learn the subway and walking about the streets, meeting Americans face to face. I've got more of an idea now than from just watching movies.

TT: Several years ago during the early punk rock days, bands like Generation X and Alternative TV were putting out dub-mixes of songs. That was the first exposure for many to this reggae technique. It seems that rock dubs didn't catch on very much.

BI: I still use the same idea now. With 'Dancing With Myself', the longer version is basically like a disco dub. We took it another step and integrated the reggae dub into the music. That's what the style of the last Generation X album was about--integrating the spacey, loose feeling of reggae with rock and roll. With 'Mony, Mony', I think I've integrated it even more, although it is harder to detect. On the 12-inch, the long middle section is influenced by reggae. We dropped everything out. But I think now we are doing it in a way that is less distinguishable. So it's not so obviously a gimmick. That's what I'm aiming for. I don't want to make gimmick records, I want to make things that integrate the styles together.

TT: Do you touch the controls?
BI: I've got to admit that I do push the controls at times. It's usually the dusty parts of the board that the engineers don't like to touch.

But a lot of the sound for the EP is because we don't have a full band (together) yet. But we will for the album. So it will be the same band that will go out on the road.

TT: I read a long time ago that you have albums worth of material of dub to release. What happened?
BI: A lot of people don't think it is commercially viable. I'm going to wait until I have enough money to finance it myself. I definitely will be doing some dub remix of most of the stuff, maybe even old Generation X stuff. At the moment, I'm really concentrating on getting this new thing together.

TT: How did you get started?
BI: Purely by listening to reggae. It makes you realize just how cluttered rock and roll has become. It lost a lot of its sense of humor. People became overly serious about guitar sounds and the style of the record and putting classical music with it. One of the things people forgot was that if you drop some of the instruments out and let more space and let the real melodies and feelings come through, you get a lot more interesting a track out of it. Listening to reggae made us want to do it. I feel the whole of punk rock was about taking away-- too many instruments and a million people, you know the things they got on the record. Instead of people realizing that they are human and that they don't always play brilliant stuff and if it isn't brilliant it shouldn't be on there.

The reggae people used a sense of humor. Even on a very sad track they would have some deft noise. It was exciting and rhythm music. And that's what punk rock was and is--rhythm music.

Vol.3 No.6

# Interview: Iggy Pop

Iggy Pop and his band returned to Lawrence in late August. The following interview was done at KJHK-FM by Tom Hoyt.

Talk Talk: Where are you living now? Berlin, New York, Houston?

Iggy Pop: I left Berlin, I was drifting about Houston but really I don't have a home anymore. I gave up the one-- the flat in New York in early summer. I've been on the road now since the beginning of June.

TT: Where did you start from?

Iggy: Denmark--Copenhagen. This will be over in September. I plan to go back to New York City. I don't know what I want to do after that.

TT: Are you still working on projects with David Bowie?

Iggy: No, we haven't been working on anything really.

TT: There's a rumor that you might be working on a movie script with Bowie.

Iggy: Yes, I won't mind doing that. He's had a couple of ideas for a while. But he's working on something called Ba'al, the play about a guy who drives all his friends crazy and finally has to commit murder to satisfy his evil lustings. He's been doing that for the BBC.

TT: You've been in music since 1968 with the first album produced by John Cale.

Iggy: Yes, he was the babysitter. It was more or less my style.

TT: Are you influenced much by his music or the Velvet Underground?

Iggy: Probably much more by Lou Reeds' work than John's, although John was very instrumental in their sound. I like John's work much better since then, perhaps better than what Lou Reed has done.

TT: Do you think Lou Reed mellowed too much?

Iggy: Well, no. It's a problem that I have also in my work, when there are a lot of different styles you dig and can do this or that. Sometimes you can veer off the point.

TT: In 1977 there were four album releases by Iggy Pop that were very much varied. THE IDIOT, LUST FOR LIFE, TV EYE, and KILL CITY.

Iggy: I'll tell you what I want to do--be a shepherd in Wyoming. I.m really sick of this whole phoney game anyway.

TT: You want to get out of the music business?

Iggy: Yes, it takes the cake. You

# Interview: Iggy Pop

talk about a concentration of creeps in one business--all the way from the DJs to the performers to the record company owners. It's somewhere between a home for geeks and just plain dishonest people, you know. The ones that aren't dishonest are all brain-damaged or they have ego problems or something. There's a wonderful opportunity to become shepherds in Wyoming. I read about it in the Wall Street Journal. They'll train you-- send you to the University of Wyoming for a year to learn to be a shepherd. I'm thinking seriously about it on days like this.

TT: You prefer varied sounds for your albums?

Iggy: It really is not by design. One reason is that I rely very heavily on collaborators. When you have a different collaborator, you have a different sound.

TT: You like changing your sound every album then?

Iggy: No, I haven't done it on purpose, really. It's just one of those things that happens. People who like what I do, they'll get to digging what I'm doing and then they'll go, 'Hey, you changed on me over here. What are you doing, this is terrible music. I thought you were the punk rocker, now you are making this crooning sound'. And my mother is going, 'this is a nice song'. She likes my new album, the song about the happy man. Meanwhile, some angry young journalist goes, 'that Happy Man was a particularly failing attempt at reggae-influence ska' or 'Mr. Pop Shows us what we have known all along--that he has no talent' and la de da. You can't please everyone.

TT: Do you think there is a future in the club scene?

Iggy: I think the club scene is the best thing that has happened to America for music in history. If it wasn't for what's happening in the clubs, I would definitely be out of music today. When you are born, they teach you what you're supposed to do is grow up and work very hard and get your sack full of money and then you get to buy a rainbow. That isn't how I see it. The important thing for me is what am I doing with my time right now. And music has always been a way of life to me as something that is supposed to result in a record or something. I believe the process is just as important as the result and that's what I would do anything for. I certainly wouldn't live my live my life just doing the often very dull things that you do in a studio. Studios can be very dull. It's all very dull except playing the

"You talk about a concentration of creeps in one business-all the way from the DJs to the performers to the record company owners. It's somewhere between a home for geeks and just plain dishonest people, you know. The ones that aren't dishonest are all brain-damaged or they have ego problems or something."

gigs. That's what I enjoy. And I like hanging around nightclubs, that's just the way I am, what fits me. I like a job that gives me a lot of time to read and loaf. I have been going out less lately than I would have. If you have enough friends on your side, they conspire all sorts of ways to make you work, to get you to work. I know they're being my friends and la de la. Too much work, I think, is very bad for you. I don't think people were meant to work in the first place. The best records I have made have been the ones that I've spent a great deal of time planning. I must be truthful. I would say RAW POWER and FUNHOUSE; the second and third albums--actually the first three are probably the most important.

Generally, when you are dealing with an innovator, which I am, it's obvious that if it's someone who has had 22 years to save up all their ideas and then let them go, generally the first few albums are going to be the best ones and the others are going to have, oh, well you can learn little tricks, like how to get on the FM radio and little polishes. Basically, if you think of any innovators, the major statement they had to make which really changed the face of music at the time they came out, gets made in three albums. The Stones, Beatles, David Bowie. It's the same for me, just about everybody. If the importance of what you are doing is based on its dissimilar aspect to the broad picture of what's going on, then you can be sure that your importance will fade after about 25 tracks. That's about how many you have.

> "If the importance of what you are doing is based on its dissimilar aspect to the broad picture of what's going on, then you can be sure that your importance will fade after about 25 tracks. That's about how many you have."

.... Maybe that's one reason my recordings have gotten so erratic in the sound in the last seven years. Maybe I'm searching for a second innovation. Maybe I want so badly to find a second way to play music that no one has done yet. Sometimes a different sound--for instance, THE IDIOT, was near that, a minor innovation. I think I might join a band again, that's the other thing I may do. Be in a band instead of my band. So I wouldn't have to answer all the questions and do all the things. It's starting to get tedious, seeing myself in People and everything. So I don't know. I'd like to start a sex cult, a kinky sex cult. Something that I could be the guru and get my own TV show.

The performance that night was very energetic and smooth. Earlier reports of lackluster shows on this tour definitely were not substantiated. The songs were predominately from the last two releases, SOLDIER and PARTY. Several encores were delivered to the hungry crowd. The show was quite a bit more exciting than last year's. The main difference in the band is the absence of Ivan Kral and the addition of Gary Valentine and Richard Sohl.

Since the review of PARTY in the last issue, Arista has released the album both in England and America. Actually, they claim it was first released in England and then in Europe, although at the time no one could find the British pressing.

PHOTOS BY BILL RICH

# Interview: William S. Burroughs

PHOTOS BY BILL RICH

*One of the most influential American writers is William S. Burroughs. His impact upon the Western world is unmeasurable but immense.*

*His main medium is the written word. Fictional accounts of alternate realities in strange deformed environments are combined with addiction, sexual activity, control, and destruction.*

*Lately, he has been giving public performances of readings from his works, concentrating on rock and roll clubs with a warm-up band. He is also close to finished with a long-time pet project--a western novel.*

*TALK TALK, through contributor and friend James Grauerholz, have established a history of coverage of his activities. Mr. Burroughs was recently in Lawrence for June and July, where he was working on the finale to a new novel. Bill Rich had the opportunity to spend time with William Burroughs and taped some conversational interviews. The topics were diverse, concentrating on his new book, his personal life and activities, theories on time travelling, and other strange little known facts.*

TALK TALK: Today's Bastille Day, how long have you been in town.

Mr. William S. Burroughs: I will have been here six weeks on Monday. I think I got here about the 12th (of June). I wanted to get out of New York and get a new ambience.

TT: I looked through the 60-some pages you've written here. They are numbered 330 on. So you have all the others done?

Mr. B.: Oh, yes. This is the end.

TT: It didn't seem to be a western...

Mr. B.: Well it isn't a western anymore. At this point he has left the west and is going back...back to the big shootout, which will take place in Boulder. I could hardly be expected to write a completely conventional western.

TT: Is Kim Carsons based at all on Kit Carson?

Mr. B.: Not at all. Kit Carson was back at the beginning of the 19th Century and this is way after that, the end of the 19th, beginning of the 20th Century. He has nothing in common with Kit Carson.

TT: How has your trip been?

Mr. B.: I did what I came for. I wanted to see how the end would work out. Now I've found out.

TT: Can you tell me about it?

Mr. B.: Well, it's in there. James showed me a picture of an orange-looking monkey that happened to be a creature from outer space, the missing link to the human species. Now in the end, my hero retraces his steps back.

TT: How? How does he go back in time?

Mr. B.: Well, it's what the whole thing is about--time travel. It's quite a complicated procedure. He does it. Having gone forward in time, he starts backwards in time. In doing so, he's upsetting the whole order of the universe and he leaves a series of disasters behind him--earthquakes, riots, stock-market crashes, because he's leaving an empty space behind him--very much like a tornado because he's leaving a low pressured area where he was.

TT: How is he doing it? What mechanism?

Mr. B.: He's going back in time on associational networks. Actually time travel is something all of us do. You just have to think about what you were doing an hour ago and you're there. There's an interesting book out called EXPERIMENT WITH TIME by John Dunne, who found that his dreams consisted not only of the past but the future as well, which is possibly easier than travelling into the past as you are bucking your whole past karma, a particularly dangerous operation. He drew from this concept of the observer universe. You are observed by an observer who is observed and so on to infinity. They only reason you are stuck there is that you are used to seeing time in a certain way. Simply a convention that you use because you have accepted it.

Potentially, you can move both into the past and future. So I did a lot of experiments with this and wrote down dreams and found that, indeed, he is correct and a portion of dreams refer to future time, often to quite unimportant incidents. If you're traveling on your own time track, it isn't...If you have a dream of an earthquake and it does happen, what you see is not the earthquake but the moment you become conscious of it by the newspaper because it's your time track. In other words, you haven't lived up there and seen the earthquake, you have moved forward in time to the moment you have heard about it. And traveling back in time is trickier than traveling forward. The Mayans did a great deal of backward travel. They computed, made computations on their calendar of the past, back to 400 million years ago. Oddly enough, they didn't make any computations into the future, just the past. They did have a definite idea that time starts and time ends. They realized that time is a resource, like coal or gas, and there is a time when time runs out for a person, for a nation, for any operation. And time can run out before other resources run out. We are squandering time and time is running out. We must conceive of time as a resource. That is one of the concepts central to this book. Another is that people are living organisms as artifacts made for a purpose, not cosmic accidents, artifacts created for a purpose.

TT: What are some of the purposes?

Mr. B.: Space. Leaving the planet. We are here to go. This first chapter shows you the concept of living beings as artifacts which is developed much more in the rest of the book. Artifacts created for a purpose, just like arrowheads.

TT: Have you decided on a title?

Mr. B.: Oh, yes, Place of Dead Roads...The planet earth, place of dead roads, dead purposes.

TT: You said there are 40 more pages to go?

Mr. B.: Yes. The end is already written. The end was written the same time the beginning was written, about a year ago. Then I had to find out how he got there. At the end he is back on the mesa and has had the shootout with Mike Chase. Well, you don't know about Mike Chase yet.

TT: What about all the physical hours spent while going in the future and coming back?

Mr. B.: You see, we think of time as having a measurable meaning, but it doesn't at all.

TT: Has he aged?

Mr. B.: He's a clone of a clone at this point. He's cloned himself a number of times. Of course, if people could travel they would likely never age. These terms don't have much meaning. Even the speed of light only has meaning with reference to human measure. You say light travels at the speed of 180,000 miles a second. Well, it does so with respect to human measurements. Nobody's been able to crack Einstein yet but the black holes may do it because in a black hole all physical laws are invalid.

TT: But still, did he age? He had all these experiences.

Mr. B.: Of course physically not aging is one thing. Say he's a clone. Suppose I had a clone made of me.

TT: Do you?

# Interview: William S. Burroughs

Mr. B.: Well, I don't have one, no. The clone would have all his experiences but be physically young. The physical youth is not as important as everyone thinks. Say if someone was actually 500 years old but occupying the body of an 18-year-old, you would not be an 18-year-old boy, no matter how much you might want to be.

Time is obviously limited time, with no meaning without a limit. The only reason time has meaning to you is because you have limited time. You are going to die, you're getting older. If you had unlimited time, it would have no meaning.

TT: The human body does wear out and age.

Mr. B.: Yes, but you can trade it in on a new body, like a new car. You aren't your body, you are simply an occupant of it. However, if you remain locked into three-dimensional concepts, you have not gained anything-you gain time perhaps to get beyond the physical body. People who say they want to live forever are talking nonsense because forever is a time word and time is something that ends--you missed the plane, you're getting older. They simply mean they want to live a long time. This is quite possible. You see brain transplants, a much cruder idea, are within the reach of modern technology. They made the startling discovery that there are no rejection syndromes in brain transplants done in rats.

There is a location in the brain which might be said to correspond to the ego, your conception of yourself. So you take it out and slop it down in a young healthy body.

Mr. B.: You were asking about time travel, backward and forward and how it is possible. It is all explained in the text. But briefly, you have someone called God, which might not mean anything except he is the director of a certain section of human film. He decides

when this guy is going to do this and when he will do that, just like a film producer.

The only thing not prerecorded or prephotographed and, of course, the whole concept of human destiny being prerecorded is very old.'Mektoub', it is written. So we have this director in charge of a certain time segment and he can do anything with it he wants--slow it up, run it backwards, this and that. The only thing not prerecorded in a prerecorded or prephotographed universe is the prerecordings themselves. So my hero, Kim Carsons, begins tampering with the pre-recordings. In other words, he cuts in on God's monopoly. And that is one of the things the book is about and how he is able to move about--backwards and forward in time under certain very tringent terms.

TT: Once Kim goes into the future and stops and then comes back, he doesn't go forward again?

Mr. B : I don't exactly remember. I know he went into the future and got into this very involved situation and then came back but then he finally disappeared and made another trip. A Russian scientist said we will travel in space and in time as well, which mean that when you travel in space, you travel in time.

TT: What about a person travelling in time who comes back to before the point of departure. Would he find himself?

Mr. B.: You possibly put more emphasis on the self than it deserves. As the Buddhist say, there is no such thing as the self. It changes from second to second. No, he would not find himself as he was then. He might find something else.

TT: Do you think that has been done yet?

Mr. B.: Who knows? Perhaps.

TT: Where would you prefer to live?

Mr. B.: I live in America by preference. For one thing, it's my country. If you live outside of America for as many years as I have, you realize that it means

# William S. Burroughs

## Abandoned Artifacts / On The Nova Lark

FRESH FLEXI 003 William S. Burroughs
Abandoned Artifacts/On The Nova Lark
Produced by James Grauerholz and Karl Hoffmann
At Ramona Recording Studios, Lawrence, KS
Percussion on Abandoned Artifacts by Martin Olson

### Abandoned Artifacts

A processed version which combines three separate overlapping readings along with a rhythm track. Original recordings courtesy of James Grauerholz from performances at The Edge, Toronto; Tuts, Chicago; and Keystone Korner, San Francisco. Another reading of the same piece from New York is contained on the newly released double album featuring William Burroughs, John Giorno, and Laurie Anderson, entitled "You're The One I Want To Share My Money With". "Abandoned Artifacts" is a selection from Chapter One of Burrough's upcoming western novel, The Place of Dead Roads.

### On The Nova Lark

This selection was recorded by William S. Burroughs in the early 60's in London or Tangiers. It is a passage partially contained in The Nova Express. The background music is probably bleeding backwards from an instrument.

This recording was a press run of 2,000, available only in TALK TALK, Vol. 3, No. 6, September/October, 1981.

# Interview: William S. Burroughs

something to be in your own country where if you have a beef with the landlord, you have the same rights as he does. This is very important. Besides America is the freeist country in the world, no doubt about it. You have more freedom here to do what you want without police interference than any other country. There's no heat here on personal use of drugs, no worry about police coming at 3 in the morning to drag you out and blow your brains out, the way it happens to 1,400 people a year in Argentina. You're running your TALK TALK magazine and they don't like it and one day the just come kick your door in and drag you out and shoot you. This happens all the time in the Latin American countries. We don't realize the horror going on. It's no myth, it's true. This doesn't happen here.

TT: Talking about oppression, don't you have a certain worry about people out there who don't like what you have done?

Mr. B.: Well, Bill, you have the same worry. I've gotten in the position of Reagan or John Lennon or anybody else. As soon as you are a public personality, you are a potential assassination target. Of course, I think about it.

TT: So what do you do to stay out of that situation? In New York everyone wants you to be at their event.

Mr. B.: I can handle the New York scene very well--just cut it off. I don't go to parties or gallery openings. There is no doubt that everytime I get up to give a reading that it is quite possible some nut will be there. So far as that goes, you just take your chances.

TT: You wouldn't recommend to anyone to become timid and not do what they want?

Mr. B.: I think this is always a mistake to back up. I got a lot of nasty reviews on 'Cities'. Although I got a lot of good ones, too. I got a lot of people mad. It's completely anti-Christian and the next book will be even more anti-Christian and coming to America, anti-Protestant. Well, now for me to sort of hide? No, no, instead I go on a Red Night tour. As Napoleon said, 'Dastardly and more dastardly and more dastardly is the sequence of success—you never retreat.' But you do know that you are laying it on the line.

I'm pretty good at picking up trouble, seing where it could come from and avoiding it.

TT: Let's talk about Denton Welch.

Mr. B.: I am writing an introduction for a German translation of 'In Youth Is Pleasure'. I've been running through it and underlining certain passages. I'll just read some at random. He's such a marvelous writer, the way he can make anything into something. Writers who complain that they don't have anything to write about should read Denton Welch and see what he can do with practically nothing. Like this, he borrows a boy's bicycle.

'Oh, yes,' said the Stowe boy in his most tired voice, 'you can borrow it for as long as you like. I loathe riding it. The saddle seems specially designed to deprive one of one's manhood; but perhaps you won't mind that.'

Orvil was too happy to be pricked into any retort by the intended insult..,

Orvil wished passionately that he had no body so that these remarks could never be applied to him. He felt ashamed to be in a position to be deprived of his manhood.

His tears made damp, chocolatey lumps out of the feathery dust.'

'The whole surface of the river bristled with a fir of hissing raindrops, sharp as bullets.'
What a mind!
Denton Welch is actually Kim Carsons in the new book. I sort of kidnapped him to be my hero. And so much of it is written in the style of Denton Welch. It's table tapping, my dear. He's writing beyond the grave and I should certainly dedicate the book to him.

TT: Denton Welch used different characters, didn't he?

Mr. B.: He's only got one character and it's always him. Well, there are other characters, yes. But the main character, what it all pivots around is an eternally 15-year-old boy. His writing was all done after his accident. He had this accident when he was riding his bicycle and some woman ran into him from behind. That happened when he was 20 and he was an invalid the rest of his life and died at the age of 31 from complications.

BR: I like his journals.

Mr. B.: I love his journals. I like everything he wrote. I've read every word I could get my hands on. He started out to be a painter. He was in art school when he had the accident. He has a terrific style with the choice of one word or another or a sentence that no one but Denton Welch could have written. I compare him to Jane Bowles because she had the same faculty for writing a sentence that no one else could conceivably have written. And there, again, her completed work is 500 pages or so. People ask me about influences. I would say that he is the strongest influence on my work-stylistically certainly.

TT: When did you first read him?

Mr. B.: Back in 1947 or 48 when he was still alive. Kerouac read him. I thought he was great. I didn't realize the extent to which he had influenced me or the extent to which the character Audrey Carsons was derived from Denton Welch until I reread him in 1976 in Boulder. Cabell, who I was sharing an apartment with, had found someone who was a Denton Welch fan and had all the books. So I reread them and read some I hadn't before, like the Diaries. I was even more impressed. Some writers reread well and others don't. He does. And another writer I was influenced by was Joseph Conrad.

BR: What do you think about the usefulness of the music industry?

Mr. B.: In a way, of course, it is thy oldest industry in the world. It is quite probable that singing came before talking. The things that are new are the huge amounts of money being made and the fact that mass performances are held. If you would remember in the 1920s, the jazz performers would play in a club for about 100 people. This Seha Stadium bit is almost unprecedented in the history of entertainment. Perhaps the gladitorial combats or Hitler's games and rallies are the only comparisons that come to mind of the tremendous mass audiences.

TT: I've been reading the new book WITH WILLIAM BURROUGHS by Victor Bockris.

Mr B.: It isn't my book, although I had to go through and correct it word for word. When people take dictation from conversations they misread words and just get a meaningless mess. So I did a lot of work on correcting it. For another thing, I wrote the end. I have mixed feelings about it. There are some good photographs in it. But I could have lived without it.

TT: It does have a lot of information available nowhere else.

Mr. B.: Yes, this is true

TT: Do you keep up on current events?

Mr. B.: I read the papers every day and most days I cut something

out. I think it is very important for a writer to maintain his input from newspapers and magazines Often times, I don't know where the next chapter will come from and I pick up the paper or turn on the television or someone will drop over and I'll get it. People who say they are going to go lock themselves away in a cabin and write the great American novel-it does take that sort of concentration, yes. But if you cut your input, you're making a great mistake.

# Looking At Lawrence

*I was recently solicited by an American music monthly to write a story on Lawrence, KS. I began in earnest and then became involved in other things. A rough draft was rewritten, one deadline passed and then another. I threw out half of the information, then expanded some parts. When showing it to others for advice, it was pointed out that Lawrence is no Utopia. Parents do not feel safe letting their children walk around. There are dangers here as everywhere. In fact, I have personally been attacked at some concerts and there are the death threats. So where do I get off praising this city? Other people pointed out that there are no jobs available. Those who go to the University and obtain training and then stay in the city cannot find work in their trained field. So many stay and get minimal jobs. So, anyway, I finally realized that maybe I should print the article here. After all, I haven't been hard at work the last few years putting out TALK TALK to just give away an exclusive area report to a paper that has not once even mentioned TALK TALK in its pages. For the readers in the local area, most of this will be common knowledge already. But many people are not familiar with the unique situation which is found in this city when compared with hot and hip places today.*

Lawrence, Kansas, USA. The liberated oasis of the fundamentalist midwest. For over a hundred years, individuals have swarmed here to escape the isolation of the prairie plains. A diversity of attitudes prevailed from its inception and continues strongly today. Outside of the coasts, Lawrence is where it is at. Why it exists and what it is like are hard things to explain.

Historically, Lawrence was settled by abolitionists and western-looking pioneers. The University of Kansas was founded, bringing academia and cultural influences. The first theater west of the Mississippi was built and successfully served the region. An appreciation and interest with the traditional arts from the general public helped the city grow and develop. This strong, early orientation continued along with the years.

With the reputation of being a liberal and exciting city, the University continues to draw more students. After experiencing the tolearance for diversity and the attitude of freedom here, many stay after college years, helping Lawrence remain a self-sustaining town. Diverse attitudes are recognized without suspicion. New ideas come out and experimentations away from traditional thought occur.

In the 60s, Lawrence became a hot spot in the nation for antiwar, antiestablishment activities. These days, things are calm with well channelled activism.

In the late 70s, there were punk bands here and people were well aware of the punk rock movement. There was no catch-up necessary, except in regard to the new young arrivals. A necessary survival item, a good radio station, strengthens the new music scene. University-run KJHK plays new releases and imports. They recently were rated in the top seven stations by CJM.

So where is this place? 45 miles from Kansas City. Also, 600 miles from Chicago, 1,200 miles from New York, 1,550 miles from Los Angeles and 1,800 from San Francisco.

In Lawrence itself, there are only two clubs where bands play. The larger and more ornate one is the Lawrence Opera House, where all international acts play--although recently the smaller venue, Off the Wall Hall, presented The Teardrop Explodes. There is not live music every night here and, of course, sometimes the live shows are worthless. At other times, there are several worthwhile performances at both places and in Kansas City as well. Shows always start before 10:00, most before 9:00. By 1:00, everything is over.

The summers are slow but the scene picks up when the 25,000 students return and shows are booked. But there is not nearly enough live music. There are lots of local and regional bands.

Some residents would like to keep Lawrence unknown. Although they feel secure in living here and not ashamed to tell others, they do not want the general public to think that this is a cool place or somewhere desirable to live. Author William S. Burroughs has just spent several months in town finishing up a new novel. 'Lawrence is nice and quiet and safe. It's a lot like Boulder'. Although often compared to Boulder, CO. 'there are no mountains nearby to escape to' as James Grauerholz, Burroughs' manager, who resides here, pointed out, 'and there is little chance that the city could become overrun and destroyed like Boulder.'

It is not all rosy, either. For example, back at the hotel bar after a highly successful performance in late August, Iggy Pop found himself with a cut cheek and black eye, the result of a 300-pound drunken redneck who did not like the way The World's Greatest had sneered at him. This is an exception, no doubt. Or is it? I guess anything can happen anywhere at anytime. And a person has to be ready for it, no matter where.

# The German New Music Scene

Since the arrival of DAF and Der Plan on the new music scene, a lot of attention has been directed to this new German music. This phenomena just didn't happen overnight or over the past couple of years. It has been going on for some time--circa the mid-70s. It simply wasn't receiving any attention until the release of EARCOM No. 3, which featured DAF. Where is the central location for this new German music? It's either Dusseldorf or Hamburg, both are relatively industrial and a cloistered almost stifling grayness hangs overhead. Perhaps it's this atmosphere that serves as a source for inspiration for desperate youth, as was the case for Cleveland or Akron? This music needed something to broaden its venues, since it was only being heard on the Continent and in England. Something was needed that would give it wider access to the world--that would bring it to America. Thus, from Hamburg came Rip-Off Distribution and ZickZack Records. Here was a means for various German bands to broaden their listenership. Most ZickZack records have a raw garage sound to them. The only discrepancy with them is that the vinyl they use isn't of the best quality. There are a lot of pops and hiss on some of their products. Not all of the music presented on ZickZack is electronic, actually there's quite a diversity of sounds coming out of the BDR. ZickZack isn't just another small label out to make some quick Marks. They are committed to making this music readily available to the world. They aren't a label that possesses a single style or sound like Factory or 4 AD and this is one of ZickZack's main assets. ZickZack Records has brought the varying sounds that are in Germany together and made them all available to the public through their catalog, which is quite extensive. They have made other European labels available through this catalog, as well, such as: Rondo, Monogam, Atatak, and Pure Reude. Music from Belgium, The Netherlands, and Switzerland is also available through ZickZack.

**Vertrieb**

The most popular ZickZack band is Abwarts (who toured throughout Europe with The Cure) and have their share of hits. ZZ head, Klaus Maeck recently passed through town after arranging distribution by Systematic. He was headed to New York to work on a tour for Abwarts, the first independent German band. Other popular bands are: Front and Geisterfahrer, two bands that sound slightly like ACR but much more powerful and not as redundant. My personal favorites are the more electronically oriented bands: Andreas Dorau--a sixteen-year-old whiz kid--whose single, 'The Laughing Pope', was quite successful. Look for it. Another one-man band is Mathius Schuster ie Konnekshen. His single, 'Im Namen des Volkes', is really powerful. Spielverderber and Katastrophentheorie are two bands that utilize tapes extensively, creating a secretive type of music. This music

## ZICKZACK
### Platten

is presented entirely in German, but the language barrier is transcended--the message can be received. I highly recommended ZickZack and commend them for their successful attempt at exposing a guilt-free Germany on vinyl.

And speaking of Vinyl. There is a fanzine called VINYL coming out of Amsterdam. It's a very current magazine with lots of photos and interviews with such notables as: Blurt, Pere Ubu, This Heat, LKJ, ACR, Fad Gadget, as well as local bands from around the European Continent. The entire thing is written in Dutch, except maybe an article or two is written in English for some reason. There have been four issues released, each one containing a flexi-disc of very good music. No. 1 features Mekanik Kommando. No. 2 is new music from Pere Ubu, with D. Thomas singing in French; No. 3 and No. 4 present local bands: Minioon, Zuge Horigkeits Gefuhl, Signal(s), and Z'ev. Obviously some financial backing and intelligence is behind this. All of this is a good reason for learning another language, my fellow 'mericans. --U-Man

# Cassette Tape Reviews

**THE DICTATORS Live (Reachout Int. Records: A102)**-- In case you don't know, The Dictators were an early group in the New York punk scene who played raw, uncultured, heavy metalish music for many years before breaking up. This tape was recorded live at a reunion show last winter. From this recording, one can detect the same spirit as earlier days--the same songs also. OK, so it is neat to hear Handsome Dick Manitoba babble to the audience and the band saving themselves by rocking out in the right places. But there still is this feeling that this tape should be put away somewhere. It just doesn't do much new, more of the old, recent sounds in rock and roll. And right, if ROIR hadn't released this, no one probably would become reacquainted with The Dictators. --SK

**SUICIDE Half Alive (ROIR: A103)**-- Since beginning ten years ago, Alan Vega and Martin Rev have gained a certain degree of respect for their form of music. People might not play their material but probably are aware of how some of it sounds. This tape could widen some horizons. There is a mixture of time influenced work here, from home recordings in 1974 to late 70s' performances. While this is not their 'commercial release', it is listenable, especially if one starts with Side Two's cover of 'Sister Ray' and then thinks about synthesizer-art bands as the tape continues. --SK

**FAST FORWARD Cassette Magazine**-- For the last year, a small group of radio people in Australia have been putting out cassettes of interviews, music and information on the Australian scene. Working with an FM station, 3RRR, they have combined the highlights of broadcasts and additional scene coverage and some humour. Speaking of humour, maybe they are a little too dry. (Even if TALK TALK does present a somewhat boring or lack luster image, at least we don't inflict such torture to your ears.) Actually, I think I like their approach to relating aspects of the music scene. In the latest release, No. 6, there was not a familiar name among the 12 groups featured in song or word. So to broaden your horizons, check this out.

Each issue comes in a packaged case with a small pamphlet fanzine which allows one to connect the sounds to images. The latest also has a short 'how to do it' insert on making cassettes and as always, an original, music crossword puzzle. Highlights of earlier issues include interviews with Gang of Four, Pere Ubu, Birthday Party, John Cooper Clarke, and NME editor Neil Spencer. To subscribe, the cost is $17 for three issues airmail, from FAST FORWARD, 251 Fitzroy, Victoria, Australia, 3065.

**Capitol Punishment Benefit. A Tape of Lincoln, NE area bands.**

Capitol Punishment is a fanzine out of Lincoln NE. A tape of some of the local underground bands was released with one of their latest issues. Recorded at a benefit for CP, the quality is not that great, but the sheer energy of most of the bands makes the tape worthy. It is also informative. Although some of the bands are not together now, a glimpse of the music scene in Lincoln turns out to be much like other areas of the states. Specifically, a lot of really young kids getting together to thrash their way through songs that are politically and socially motivated.

The End (Pope Patrol) have two songs on the tape, 'Anastasia' is good; it has lots of energy. Better though is 'Don't Damn Me', a great song that complains about everything but offers no solutions.

Dick Tracy are now called Coloring Books. They've had a few personnel changes since the tape, I think. 'Feeling My Walls Close' is very good, but of the six songs they do 'Another World' is definitely the best.

I've seen Coloring Books live and they are much better than the tape suggests. Sara Kavonda fronts this five-piece band of drums, bass, organ, and guitar. Their sound is very full, never quirky, but always powerful. My favorites on the tape were The Youngsters. 'We Need People Who Must Grow' has a good bass line and broken up/atonal guitar that seems to follow no particular rhythm pattern. Great lyrics, too. 'Bedrock Twist' would definitely be on the charts in some of California's D.K. enclaves. It has funny lyrics and a captivating guitar piece.

D.K.ed Willies were the loudest in getting their message across in 'Manipulation Tool'.

This Machine Kills Fascists were pretty unintelligible. I couldn't understand anything so I don't think I'll say anything.

I liked the idea of getting to hear what bands in other areas are doing—Maybe some other fanzines will get some bands together for a compilation tape of area talent. It certainly couldn't hurt.

**MINISTRY OF FEAR Two Separate Incidents (Tape)**-- These are long songs. Fortunately, they do not drag. Neither do they rumble, convolt or race. They pulse, wind, and casually progress to a logical end. Although the songs take their time, they are powerful sounding.

Effects exist on almost every level. Sometimes this is annoying when the vocals aren't clear. M of F use vocals in a very rhythmic manner though--repeating lines and meters to create another texture to their very layered sound. The sound is good and on a whole, above average and definitely uncommercial except to most people inside the new music scene. --FL

**PRIMITIVE ROMANCE (a tape on Dot City Records)**-- Technology, in the right hands can be used to create some very original and creative sounds and styles. Primitive Romance try very hard to use echoplex and phase shifters to create their special brand of rock music. Somehow, though, they seem to just cover up a very good street-punk sound. This is especially evident on the guitar parts.

Primitive Romance have a lot of energy, especially where the basics are concerned. The phase shifters only distract, not emphasize this. The use of echoplex on the voice, I feel, is a bit more successful. Probably because it is more consistent.

All the songs (five in all on this tape) show promise, and the lyrics are pretty good. Different production could give them the unique and energetic sound they deserve. At least they aren't afraid to experiment a bit. --Frank Loose

**THE NEW WAVE BROTHERS (Tape)**-- New, original music in Kansas (and most of the Midwest) is usually like a trek through a desert. Sooner, but usually later, an oasis is reached where there is a small pocket of inspiration and talent. Wichita is one such oasis. We are all familiar with The Embarrassment, who have a new EP out, but most have never heard of the New Wave Brothers (Jim, Britt, Court, and Alex).

These guys are probably the only synthesizer band in Kansas.

They are also very prolific. Each song is very unique and always has something to say, either by irony or allegory. If there is one subject that seems to be a favorite one, it would have to be love and human relationships. To the New Wave Brothers both seem to be a series of conflicts that inevitably lead to end of the relationship, not because of chauvinistic attitudes; they just try to point out human weakness.

Musically, the group is very abstract and show very few influences except when satirizing pop hits. Sometimes it is ambient, sometimes driving--always witty and simple. Silly lyrics are out. After listening to two of their tapes, I'd say they have at least a good double album's worth of material. This probably will never happen, thanks to tapes, though there will always be New Wave Brothers to listen to -Frank Loose

**MUSIC FOR NO MAN'S LAND (Flygirl Records: CT001)**-- A live cassette of eight bands who played at a two-night event in Des Moines, IA, promoting new blood. The bands are young and not totally polished. The shows must have been an enjoyable experience, according to accounts and the enthusiasm conveyed to tape. It seems that only two bands, The Law and The Edge, had ever played to the general public. So one might expect some roughness. Wait awhile and see where they go. Although Des Moines is referred to as Dead Man's Land, the people there pulled this thing off for the second year. TIME'S UP, a local fanzine, put it together and have the 50-minute taped highlights for a reasonable $3 (P.O. Box 65592, W. Des Moines, IA, 50265). --BR

**RADIO SWEAT (New Hormones: CAT 2)**-- An entertaining half-hour cassette release depicting a radio broadcast created by C. P. Lee of Alberto Y Los Trios Paranoias, who were a performing group known for their parodies of various musical forms a few years ago. RADIO SWEAT is a parody of radio with six songs alongside DJ comments, advertisements, call-ins, news, jingles, and more comedy. The musical selections, themselves, are similar to basic country music, although the first one is a takeoff of 'Shot By Both Sides' with Pete Shelly on guitar (New Hormones is/was the Buzzcocks organization). The tape is packed in a bag along with other goodies including a program guide. One of the more funny comments is a radio show plug for the station's one-hour a week reggae show when U-Boat, the host, starts ranting about one lousey hour a week. There are safety tips for nuclear incidents.

# Record Reviews

**MINUTEMEN** Joy, Blacksheep/More Joy (New Alliance Records, P.O. Box 21, San Pedro, CA, 90733)-- Here we have some swift-paced black and white melodies. Borderline 'Contortions' without droning into monotonous ego rapping. Edgy but intense percussion with no hesitation. (Just isn't time in less than a minute..)--MO

**(MEAT) PUPPETS EP** In A Car/Big House/Dolphin Field/Out In the Gardener-Foreign Lawns (World Imitation Records. % Thermidor, 912 Bancroft Way, Berkeley, CA, 94710)-- While listening to this release, I closed my eyes...All I could imagine was three angry hamsters. --MO

**THE TIKIS** Surfadelic/Junie (World Imitation Records)-- Roamin' thru the foam! Madras shirts, chinos and ponytails, a'go-go...good clean-cut fun in the Beachin' 80s. (Can the vocals, please!)--MO

**RED BEAT** See/Survival (Manic Machine Products, Dist. by Rough Trade)-- Anger and forboding seethes from the grooves of the vinyl as the worm we call the future eats what is left after the nerve gas warfare of my mind.. wahahahaaa! ...gimme some air!! --MO

**ZOUNDS** Demystification/Great White Hunter (Rough Trade)-- Vocals and percussion play off one another with a minimum of other instruments in order to rally at the climax of 'Demystificstion'. A straightforward, unified band with no frills. --MO

**PRIMITIVE ROMANCE EP** Time To Talk/Everything Means Nothing Anymore/Hearts and Flowers (Dot City Records, 1000 Kossik Road. Zephyr Hills, FL, 33590)-- Gothic romance meets the phase shifter under a palm tree. A little too cliche to get off the ground. No peaks--no valleys in this land of the lost. --MO

**PUPPIES** Mechanical Beat, Atmosphere (Stiff Records: Tees 7.03, Fan Club, 3859 John Street, San Diego, CA, 92106)-- Pop! Pop! Pop! Love the lyrics, hated the words...slick as a whistle, etc. Financial backing for these guys and gal! Put 'em on tour with The Plastics! --MO

**LOS REACTORS** Dead In The Suburbs b/w CULTURE SHOCK/PREGNANT GIRLS (Cynykyl Records)-- Delightful keyboards with predictable guitar and drum noises. Sassy pubescent vocals with an all too prevalent Doomsday inflection. Head- bangers and low riders will love this! --MO

**LOG-A-RHYTHMS** Logs/Coffee (Curve Records, 1614 W. Thorndale, Chicago, IL, 60660)-- Kell excentrique! 7/4 rhythms! Violins! Bitchin' vocals all add up to...well.. .an overdraft of the senses. One might wonder what brand of caffeine this group endorses. I couldn't tear this one off the turn table fast enough. -MO

**SPORT OF KINGS** Every Night/The Same Breath (Sport of Kings: SOK-11131)-- A group with some guts! A seductive intertwining of human rhythms, urban sounds, and some insightful lyrics keep this new release coming back to the top of my stack. A good, solid, modern sound with an edge to it. --MO

**STRANGE CIRCUITS** Industrial Living/3000 (WaxTrax Records, Creative Soundz, Bos 8022, Chicago, IL, 60680)--So many keyboards--so little time! Actually just a little busy for the engineer to keep track of--not awful, just busy. The vocals need some depth, filling out, keep plugging away! --MO

**NAKED SKINNIES** All My Life/This Is The Beautiful Night (Naked House Records: 10345)-- Post J.D. type vocals with pleasant enough instrumental backing. Chord progressions are a bit long in the tooth. It's been my experience that this style of composition works better in front of an audience with intense sympathies toward the music. --MO

**THE YOUNG PROFESSIONALS** Your Eyes/Looking Sidewise (E. Q. Records, Div. of Decade Productions, 821 N. Taylor Street, Arlington, VA, 22203)-- A spirited group with a unique sound mix on 'Your Eyes'. At first your ears are bent toward the speakers attempting to find the vocals, once acclimated, however, it's there and reaching through. Good keyboard sound without being ostentatious. Very danceable. -MO

**THE ERECTOR SET Inside Out/No Room for Comfort (Erectunes)** -- The Erector Set are a dance band from Cincinnati, Ohio. Judging by this single, they appear to be the Ohio equivalent of our own Blue Riddim Band. They play a mix of rock, ska, and soul in a very upbeat and energetic fashion, much like the English beat. It's the full and forceful singing and playing that cary this single. The songs are good but seem to be consigned and limited to style. Enjoyable soul nontheless. For a copy, send $2.50 to Dan-O Management, 2145 Sinton, Cincinnati, OH, 45206. --DC

**HUMAN HANDS Trains vs. Planes/Blue Eel (IRS/Faulty Products: FP02)** -- This quintet is from Los Angeles. They claim their music has punk origins, yet their music has little in common with the X and Black Flag Speed Rock that has evolved in that area. Treason, you say? No, it's just that their music has moved in a direction toward a more eclectic and cerebral style. The B-side of this single demonstrates this point. It's a hard song to listen to, but also hard to ignore. 'Trains vs. Planes' is a good song, reminiscent of the Urban Verbs' 'Subways' but I found it a bit too long on tune and short substance for my taste. Not the best single in the world, but worth the effort. One others can learn from. --DC

**SPEEDIES Something On My Mind/Time (Speedy Delivery)** -- Sugar-coated pop cum punk. 'Produced by Clem Burke' is about the only interesting thing I found on Products, 145 Kane Street, Brooklyn, NY, 11231. --DC

**THE DANCING CIGARETTES Puppies in a Sack/Mr. Morse/Pop Doormat/Best Friend (Gulcher: 007A)** -- This bares a strong resemblance to the Human Hands in style; rhythmic drive, T. Heads influenced, etc. 'Pop Doormat' overshadows most of the other cuts on the EP. The only problem with this disc is in the vocals. Michael Gitlins singing is a bit too much -- a David Byrne clone with matching warps, woops, and quivers. This is what kills 'Puppies in a Sack'. The DCs are a good band, they appear to have a sense of purpose and style. I expect they will have better stuff out soon. --DC

**MARK LANE Love Is So Aggravating/They Call It Game/Mystery Hero (Artwerk Records)** -- This one comes from Ventura, CA. 'They Call It Game' is a great cut, it has rhythm and drive. All the songs on this 45 have recurring themes, which to Lane's credit do not come off as overdone or overtly repetitive. They synthesizer sleeper of the month. --DC

**SLIVERS Restraint For Style (New Alliance)** -- This is a five-song 45. Captain Beefheart meets the residents. Interesting but not outstanding. New Alliance, PO Box 21, San Pedro, CA, 90733. --DC

**WILD KINGDOM Roma-Destiny (No-Mag Flexi)** -- This one has an interesting circus organ riff floating on a fast paced Dead Kennedys type of rhythm. It's the Jello Biafra-roller coaster vocals that hurt this one. --DC

**THE JETSONS Suicidal Tendencies/Genetically Stupid/Killing (Gulcher)** -- Just as good as the Speedies. From Indianapolis Gulcher, PO Box 1635, Bloomington, IN, 47402. --DC

**THE VERTIBRATS Jackie's Gone/Diamonds in the Rough ((V.B. Records)** -- Pop from Champaign, Illinois. PO Box 1446, Champaign, IL, 61820. --DC

**THE IRRITATORS Voodoo Boogie/Whack The Dolphin (Robey Records: ROb 2S-A)** -- Combining influences as diverse as Sea World and Indian tabla, the appropriately named Irritators manage to create a record as weird as anything put out on the Ralph label, but delightfully still in the music-for-listening rather than noise-as-anarchy camp. 'Voodoo Boogie' is a flowing instrumental with nasal synthesizers and a saxophone lead. 'Whack The Dolphin' opens with a child's delighted squeal and bounds along through tape loop nonsequitors and tickling synthesizer blurts, over a drum beat more commonly heard on ragas. What sets this record apart from the self-produced efforts of other art school bands is its musicianship. There's no feeling of being taken on a trip through somebody's term paper, or listening to a kid discover fourths. I have no doubt these guys could play serious jazz or even that perverted stuff you hear in elevators. Luckily they don't want to. (Robey Records, Box 808, Newhall, CA, 91322) --AE

# Record Reviews

**DIVINE Born To Be Cheap/The Name Game (WaxTrax Records, 2449 Lincoln Ave., Chicago, IL, 60614)**-- Well, here we have inimitable star of stage and tarnished screen--Divine--putting her licks and feet (spikes first) into the recording industry. Only slightly out of 'her' element in a sound studio, Divine drops us a couple of crusty crumbs of camp cacophony. At least, I would hope, Divine doesn't take 'herself' as seriously as 'her' peers--Sylvester and Jayne County, no contest...(not many similarities, either, on second thought). Fun!! --MO

**IAN HUNTER Short Back & Sides (Chrysalis Records, 9255 Sunset Boulevard, Los Angeles, CA, 90069)**-- Being an admittedly sporadic listener/follower of Ian Hunter, I can say that I haven't enjoyed any work of his better than his newest release. Quite possibly his collaboration with studio superheroes Mick's Ronson and Jones, as well as Todd Rundgren was the boost Ian needed. The results are an incredible turn of the ear. Noticeably absent is Hunter's tediously incessant eighth-note keyboard jack-hammer. I'm not sure how successful his dabbling with Jamaican rhythms is, but the dub-style mix works well on this new effort. --MO

**SURFACE MUSIC Slim Boy/I Am A Janitor (Suitcase Prod., P.O. Box 1256, Lafayette, CA, 94549)**-- A talented group with some diverse background that doesn't seem to get too well on this effort. Songs that don't sound the same all the way through or have no logical turning points are too difficult to pay attention to. There are too many needless departures from the origional theme to provide a cohesive unit. --MO

**ICE HOUSE (Chrysalis Records, 9255 Sunset Boulevard, Los Angeles, CA, 90069)**-- The aloofness of the production/ engineering on and of Ice House renders them precariously perched on that edge close to untouchable. But, somehow there's a thread of life woven into this group that beckons the listener and keeps one's attention. The sound here is not unlike the finesse one might find on a Procol Harum album mixed with the more satiny approach of latter Gary Numan (at his very best, of course). Ice House is worth looking past their 'hit' single--'Sister'. --MO

**RED SNERTS The Sound of Gulcher (Compilation)(Gulcher Records, P.O. Box 1635, Bloomington, IN, 47402)**-- All in all a fairly lively collection, I would like to go on to say that with 16 groups represented I thought I would hear a little more diversity. At times the engineering quality could have something to do with that. I know for a fact that'The Dancing Cigarettes' are a lot more exciting live. I certainly wouldn't mind a musical visit to Bloomington soon! --MO

**OBSERVERS Observing Observables (Hardly Music, P.O. Box 55365, Indianapolis, IN, 46205)**-- Obviously oblivious to modern trends of embellishment, the 3-0 band has pared down the the bare essentials of self entertainment. No need to disturb. --MO

**SCRITTI POLITTI The Sweetest Girl/Hons After Slumber (Rough Trade, London)**-- Soothing dub-style vocals with keyboards/ percussion awash with echo. Smart, smooth, and relatively harmless melodies. Oh, so Eighties. --MO

**NOMMOS: CRAIG LEON (Takoma Records, dist. by Chrysalis Records, Inc.,9255 Sunset Boulevard, Los Angeles, CA, 90069)**-- Overall a very well produced album. Craig Leon has learned his lesons well from recent masters (Eno, Froese, etc.) in this future primitive genre. One thing that certainly adds to the interest and freshness is that it is recorded live at the Lone Star. (Even though there is little audible evidence of an audience.) For the most part, the compositions are minimal. Keyboard (synthesizer, organ) sounds dominate with wonderfully etherial percussion as a foundation. -MO

**ROKY ERICKSON AND THE ALIENS The Evil One (415 Records, P.O. Box 14563, San Francisco, CA, 94114)**-- One of the 13th floor elevators, for you psychedelia buggs, Roky Erickson is still boiling over with inthusiasm. His foundation is as stable as the Rock of Ages. THE EVIL ONE indeed is reminiscent of the 60s without being bogged down, and is as exciting as any music you'll hear today. --MO

**BPEOPLE You At Eight/Weather to Worry/M.P.C.D. (IRS/Faulty Products, P.O. Box 2853, Pasadena, CA, 91105)**-- Jazz, funk, and 'art school' all come to mind while pondering the BPeople. There is no reason to shy away from this record if you are adversely affected by any of these because these elements and more have been suitably homogenized to suit these artists. Give 'em a listen. --MO

**ELODIE LAUTEN** Orchestre Modern (Rockin' Horse Records, 13 E. 17th Street, New York, NY, 10003)-- ORCHESTRE MODERN has some intriguing metallic moods woven together with one of the most androgynous voices in music today. Elodie Lauten has succeeded in side-stepping artistic labelling by placing this production firmly in the future, hermetically sealing the arrangements to protect from excess and influences. Those of you looking for something in a well-tailored vein might enjoy this one. --MO

**HENRY BADOWSKI** Life Is A Grand . . . (IRS Records)-- Having no rough edges to catch, one tends to allow this album to slither right by. Either this boy spends a lot of time with a pocket mirror and headphones listening to Visage or I'll eat my make-up. Imagine Bette Midler telling you just how 'tasteful' this album is . . . --MO

**JOSEF K** The Only Fun In Town . . . (Postcard Records of Scotland) -- This band reminds me of a wide angle lens with nothing in particular to focus on--nothing even threatens to come to the foreground. Maybe if I turn it down it would be ambiguous enough to fade into the wallpaper. --MO

**CHUNKS COMPILATION** (New Alliance Records, P.O. Box 21, San Pedro, CA, 90733)-- With such distinguished guest artists as Black Flag, STains, Nig-Heist, and Nine Other Assaults--the one thing I could find to be happy about was that this disc plays at 45 rpm. The one group present I do have a soft spot for is Minutemen. They'll probably never be invited to be on another compilation as a result of my support. Tough break . . . --MO

**MONOCHROME SET** Ten Don'ts for Honeymooners/Straits of Malacca (PRE Records: PRE18)-- This record is something of a comeback for the Mono Set after two disappointing singles and a label change.

The droll humor and deadpan vocals of Bid mark the A-side along with a bouncy backing track. The B-side is a bit of a departure for The Set, utilizing as it does acoustic guitar and a swing rhythm. Good stuff. --RH

**BUSH TETRAS** Boom/Das Ah Riot (Fetish Records: FET007)-- A big improvement over their first record. This one makes the city-jungle connection stick and nails it to a beat that just won't quit. 'Boom' is built around a slinky riff buttressed by tin-pan percussion worthy of Pere Ubu. 'Das Ah Riot' is a bit more standard but still better than their icy, earlier efforts. --RH

**LANDSCAPE** Einstein A-Go-Go/Japan (RCA Records)-- A spirited pastiche of rhythms, textures--vocal overlays resembling Byrne-Eno's latter work at times. Other references to Bill Nelson or John Foxx without drowning in lengthy keyboard droning. --MO

**THE FLESHTONES** All Around The World/The World Has Changed (IRS Records)-- Rockin' in style! A modern, urban savvy comes on strong with this big band sound. Good harmonica fills to beef things up. The Fleshtones are firmly rooted with something worthwhile to say. --MO

**BRIAN BEVERLY** Eleven It Ends (Takoma Records, dist. by Chrysalis Records, 9255 Sunset Boulevard, Los Angeles, CA, 90069)-- Brylcreem vocals, high-gloss finish, steady beat, all evoke visions of Roy Orbison or Tommy James and Co. Basically the writing has some original twists (e.g., guitar sound on 'Till I Changed'), but like so many bands of this ilk, once a new 'hook' or 'riff' is discovered it tends to become overused. To those whose staple diet is REO, this will seem a delightful change. --MO

**GG ALLIN** Always Was, Is And Always Shall Be (Orange Records, Ltd., 639 Broadway, Box 902, New York, NY, 10012)-- Look out! Here's an angry, raving leftover from that 1977 Max's-CBGB family tree. If this is the music of the streets, I'm staying on the sidewalk. Gong Show contestants. --MO

**HEAVY MANNERS** Flamin' First/Old Man Bates Is Dead (Disturbing Records, PO Box 11463, Chicago, IL, 60611)-- A refreshing ska band. Undoubtedly cashing in on the hip-white reggae club circuit-but if you've got it... B side lyrically a bit confusing along with the composition. Nice sax! --MO

**NADIA KAPICHE** Bitches and Bastards/Africa (Vinyl Child Records, 2005 Cheremoya, Los Angeles, CA, 90068)-- A poetic and pensively gripping approach to today's music. Heartbeat percussion with vocals that don't let go combined with some haunting tribal drums on 'Africa'. 'Bitches and Bastards' makes ya wanna stomp! --MO

# Record Reviews

**THE RAYBEATS** Guitar Beat. (Don't Fall Off The Mountain: X7)-- . . . In which we find the oh-so-hot New York Raybeats, the last hope for instrumental music today, falling victim to the ever-enticing demon OVER-PRODUCTION. Aside from the ethical implications of including three of the four cuts from their debut EP (all except 'Flingel Blint', which is on vinyl a second time on the live set START SWIMMING anyway), 'Roping Wild Bears' and both A and B sides of their single, the Beats suffer from the inexplicably Muzak-like production of Martin Rushent, who mixes the drums way up front and buries everything else to the point of ineffectuality. (A talent he did not display on the previously produced EP and single) The three songs previously mentioned that were so good on the EP are just so much mush here. Even the studio version of 'International Operator' (debuted on START SWIMMING), which promised to be great, is disappointing. And how many times are live instrumental cuts better than the studio?

And for cryin' out loud, somebody take that cowbell away from Don Christiansen! --Stuckey

**THE RAYBEATS** Guitar Beat (Don't Fall Off the Mountain Records: X7)-- More cool sounds for hot summer nights from your favorite ex-Contortions in matching suits. Heck, I don't even mind if three of the four songs from the EP are included here. Not with such gems as 'Calhoun Surf' and 'Holiday Inn Spain' lurking in the tracks.

This record is authentic down to the sand in your hotdog but still has that NYC edginess that makes you wonder if everything is as serene as it seems. As far as value for money goes, it's a short album from an American band at an import price.

Even so, GUITAR BEAT is the perfect accompaniment for the dog days of summer. Now where's good car radio when you need it?--RH

**DELTA 5 See The Whirl (PRE Records: PREX6)--** On their first album Delta 5 continue a progression from their early Gang of Four oriented sound into the more funk-influenced style of their later singles. They've obviously been woodshedding and it shows.

Heavy bass and drums are the springboard that these songs bounce off with chopping guitar still present, though in smaller and subtler doses. The best thing about this record are the brassy, braying horn sections. They skitter around, on top of and against the melody as punchy as anything this side of Dexy's. Very interesting use is also made of pedal steel guitar and movie soundtracks.

This funk-rock sound is much the same as the one now being explored by Talking Heads, Pigbag, Bush Tetras, and others. A solid instrumental base and engaging female vocals make Delta 5 worth checking out.--RH

**THE RAINCOATS Odyshape (Rough Trade Records: Rough 13)--** The Raincoats deinitely exist outside of popular musical tradition, playing with a female sensitivity of very primal origins. This is music from the heart and bones; music hidden in some labyrinth of the inner ear, almost a racial memory. The Raincoats are an anomaly, the best of both primitive and sophisticated. They create music in the true sense of creation --I can't imagine anyone doing a cover of any of their songs.

They do not hesitate to break and change rhythms; vocals and violins fly off in unexpected directions, all done with the confidence of musicians playing by intuition. Gina lays down a fluid, loose bass line, a clear dark pool rippled by Ana/Gina's vocals. Vicky Aspinall has some way to curl time and space around a musical passage. There are moments in 'Red Shoes' and 'Dancing in My Head' when I can only sit, breathing suspended, waiting to be released from the spell of Vicky's violin. All instruments and vocals exist in a happy symbiotic state; nothing dominates, nothing competes.

The Raincoats are singular in modern music for their sanity and lyricism. They play powerful, sensitive, and genuinely beautiful music, matched in my mind only by qualities of sufi singers, of certain gamelon music, of the best of Laura Nyro or Kay Gardner. If I were making music, this is the music I would like to make. --SM

**MEN WITHOUT HATS Folk of the 80's (Stiff Tees 12-01)--** Men Without Hats are a Canadian group from the French-speaking city of Montreal, who play Germanic technopop on an American subsidiary of a British label, but their global influences don't contribute a thing to their sound. 'Modern(e) Dancing' is new romanticism at its most repetitive. You could dance to it, if you don't mind repeating the same step for 4 minutes, 12 seconds. There's nothing to listen to. 'Utter Space' is an utter bore-- more technodisco. Only 'Security' has any life with swooping syndrums, pulsing beat, delicately enunciated vocals and intermittent heartbeat drumming. Kraftwerk, Suicide, Tuxedo Moon, The Plastics, and even David Bowie did this better before. --AE

**YOU'RE THE GUY I WANT TO SHARE MY MONEY WITH** Laurie Anderson, William S. Burroughs and John Giorno (Giorno Records, 222 Bowery, New York, NY, 10012, Giorno PSR: GPS020-021)-- A very nice double album with recent works of three important artists. Each presents one album side and all share the fourth, which has three concurrent grooves. Where you put the needle down will determine which groove you hear. The combination of these three performers works well together. Laurie Anderson can perform numerous styles of music. Here is a mixture of jazz-rock instrumentals and her usual voice manipulations. Her usual visual presentation of images to accompany the music is missed. John Giorno performs by himself, releasing intense emotion in delivery. Some electronical magnifications are skillfully used. William S. Burroughs gives a straightforward recitation which cannot be duplicated. This state of the art combination really documents a segment of American life. -WB

**BC GILBERT AND G LEWIS Ends With The Sea/Hung Up To Dry Whilst Building An Arch (4 AD: AD106)**-- Gilbert and Lewis have been moving progressively away from 'machine' electronic music and towards something less artificial. Theirs is a search for elemental rhythms that can be expressed musically and still retain some of its original power. With this single, the feat has been realized. The struggle between land and sea is impressed upon the listener. The sensation of actually experiencing this birth-death continuum is generated by the almost tidal qualities ,of bass, piano and assorted percussions. The B-side further displays G & L's interest in primal sounds by resurrecting long forgotten racial memories and creating tribal electric music. The effect is supernal. --U-Man

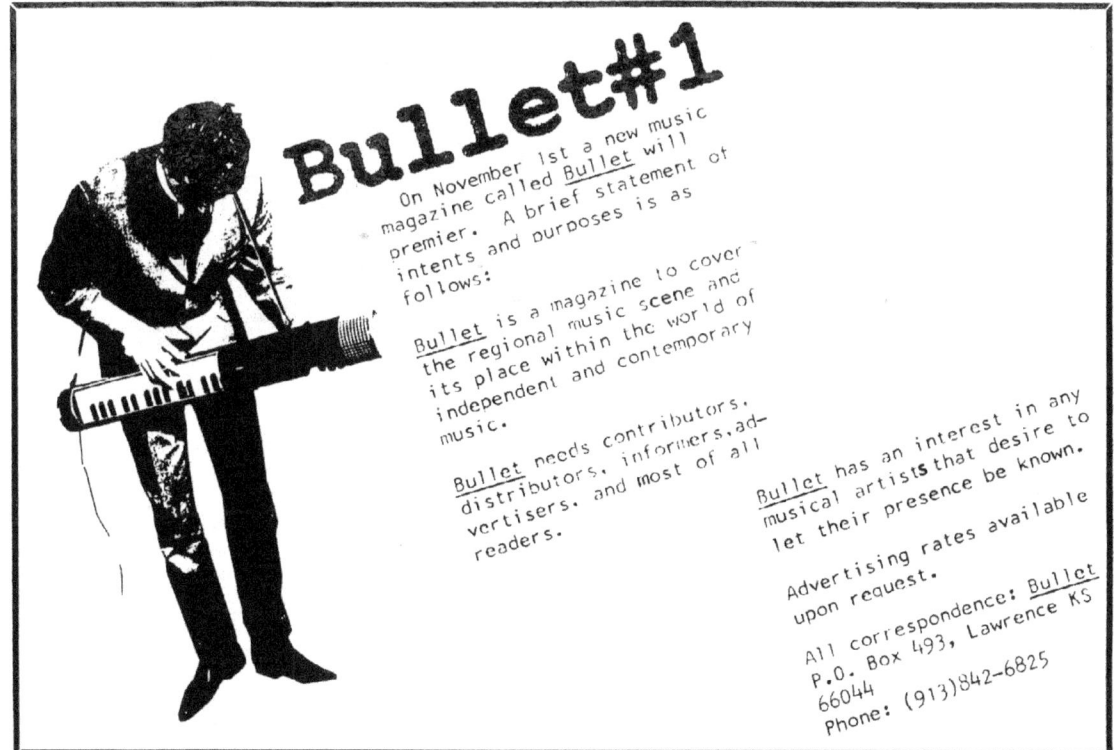

# Record Reviews

BILL RICH

**GET SMART! Words Move (Syntax Music, PO Box 493, Lawrence, KS, 66044)**-- Earlier in the year, TALK TALK released the first recording of this three-piece as a flexi. WORDS MOVE, a four cut EP, shows a positive progression from my favorite band. Since my views cannot be considered objective, this subjective rave has a message. BUY THIS ONE. Actually, Get Smart! are a new band that continue to grow and improve, unlike many. Limitations to the sound available from just guitar, bass, and drums are viewed as an asset to create new dimensions. The basic, sparce approach to rock is used as a tool for communications. They are trying to project a new feel to the listener and do succeed. The record opens with 'Disillusion' which has a punctual rhythm from bass and drums and sharp vocals. 'Where Did This Week Go,' one of the two with bassist Lisa Wertman singing, is my favorite. The other, 'Eat Sleep A Go Go,' is a bouncy, upbeat number. Frank Loose's drumming keeps the trio together as they move along. The closing, 'This Is Style,' has guitarist Marc Koch heavily enunciating with some special effects. The production on a whole is very clean, crisp, and clear. --WB

**THE EMBARRASSMENT EP (Cynykyl Records, Box 293, Wichita, KS, 67201)**-- This band had some problems and could write a book on the pitfalls a new group might come across in getting a record released. The final form is a 12-inch 45 with five originals. The two-song side, entitled the happy side, is definitely an outstanding example of the style of rock The Embarrassment have popularized in the midwest. 'Don't Choose The Wrong Song' has a bass line that never stops. The guitar produces such frenzied bursts that it can only be wizardry. The drummer is one of the best and he shows it. The vocals are presented in an off key, maybe minor or flat which sets the whole sound just a bit separate from the usual expected rock & roll which is one of the band's strengths. The smooth-moving 'Wellsville', with references to passing by a highway exit sign, or by analogy, passing something by, seems destined to become a hit. It already is with the live performances, as are all these five ongs. The other side, the snappy side, has 'Celebrity Art Party,' 'Elizabeth Montgomery's Face,' and 'I'm a Don Juan.' I'd always thought the first was about a sadistic party . . . and still do. The next two are further statements on life and continue showing more diversity and control which The Embarrassment have. Lively paced music for today's and tomorrow's rock world. This is their second release, aside from the cut on a Bomp collection. Current plans include work on the album. This band has improved by leaps and bounds and know no limits. --WB

**THE FALL Early Years 77-79 (Step Forward/Faulty Products: COPE 2)**-- This compilation consists of material which was originally released on singles and albums, which has caused some to think it unnecessary. However, to have a domestic release with part of the greatest songs The Fall have created is indeed both delightful and convenient. There's no filler here in the 11 tracks chosen and I bet another LP could be assembled of other great hits. Although the personnel changed many times, it is still Mark Smith who defines the fine sound of The Fall--both in the earlier days and today. This band gets mixed reviews. Their recent American tour won them many new fans. This record is for them. --SK

# Record Reviews

**MISSION OF BURMA Signals, Calls and Marches (Ace of Hearts Records: AHS 1006)**-- This six-song, 12-inch EP starts off with a bang in the magnificent 'That's When I Reach for My Revolver.' It's a rocking little number with a 60's flavored chorus that holds up to the best of X. The Burma's line-up is standard bass, drums, and guitar, but it's used in an unorthodox way which they make seem as natural as worn-in blue jeans. Other highlights include 'Fame and Fortune' (is a stupid game) and the instrumental 'All World Cowboy Romance.' Slick cover, great sounds, a picture of the band inside, what more could you ask for? --RH

**JOEBOY In Rotterdam/San Francisco (Backstreet Backlash: BBR 004)**-- Sometimes a mystery is more interesting than its solution. In November, 1980, Praxis, a Chicago-based art magazine, issued a flexi disc 'Urban Leisure Suit Part IV', never outrightly identified as the work of Tuxedo Moon, though it came coupled with a Tuxedo Moon interview and listed the members of Tuxedo Moon on the label. Since then, fans have been wondering, if that was part IV, where were parts I, II, and III? The answer can be found in Holland, on a disc cryptically identified as being Joeboy (the name of Tuxedo Moon's first single, plus Martin Van Der Leer and Peter Groute, produced and recorded by (Tuxedo Moon vocalist/visual artist) Winston Tong. This is not a bootleg but it's not rock either. About a dozen loose experimental electronic pieces run across side one's nearly 23-minute face. Side two includes the full 'Urban Leisure Suite', a fusion jazz composition, and 'Wild Boys', a soundtrack of spliced conversation bits, sirens and narration about a character somewhat like De Niro played in Taxi Driver. So why all the secrecy and intrigue? What were Tuxedo Moon trying to hide? Nothing really. This is art-sound, not rock, that might disappoint Tuxedo Moon fans. Only the very patient or very avant garde will get to the end of both sides. From P. O. Box 632, 3000 AP Rotterdam, Netherlands. --A. 'Enthal

## Can't Find Reggae?

Our new reggae mail order catalog lists hundreds of English, Jamaican, and American reggae releases at reasonable prices.

For a free copy, write:   Shanachie Records
Dept. PK
Dalebrook Park
Ho-Ho-Kus, NJ 07423

**GARY CHARLSON** Real Live Gary! (Titan: EP 8100, P.O. Box 5443, Kansas City, MO, 64131)-- For those of us who were aware of its existence the wait has been a lengthy one. This was a wise move on Gary's and Titan's part to record live in the studio. This technique allows the band to flow together as a spontaneous unit (as in performance) and takes advantage of the detailed recording that only a studio can provide. Charlson's crisp renditions of 'No Matter What' (Badfinger) and 'My Back Pages' (Dylan ) blend effectively with the pop origins of the band. --MO

**SCARS** Author! Author! (Stiff Records)-- A solid, rock-steady sound grabs you from the moment the needle hits the groove. What one gets is a good blend of hard-hitting vocals with an 'anvil chorus' percussion backdrop. Guitamelt down the roughness without denying us any urgency. --MO

**LUXURY EP No. 1** (Angry Young Records, 3701 Carpenter, Des Moines, IA, 50311)-- Everything about this EP is so 'pretty' it's difficult to figure out if Luxury is really anything to work toward. I'm not sure if these guys have ever been angry. They, however, have certainly listened to Devo. --MO

**THE SMASHCHORDS** (Rough Trade, 1042 Murray Street, Berkeley, CA, 94710)-- With all the spontaneity of a teenage boy with a new Marshall amp or the firt time behind the wheel without Dad--is it a blender?--or a runaway van?-No, it's the Smashchords' own brand of blue cheer sans vocals (Thank God!). Aural vampires unleashed!! --MO

**ATILA** Would Be Mothers / Chinese (Fish Ranch Records, P.O. Box 973, Santa Monica, CA, 90401)-- Anarchy unleashed. Go back two steps. Forget you heard this. Don't collect. --MO

# EXILE

## RECORDS AND TAPES
### GUARANTEED USED ALBUMS AND TAPES

We also carry a large selection of posters, t-shirts and buttons. Bring in your good used albums.

**OPEN 7 DAYS A WEEK**

15 W. 9th St.  
Lawrence, Kansas  
(913) 842 - 3059

7222 W. 75th St.  
Overland Park, Kansas  
(913) 384 - 2499

## Local Scene

The Embarrassment have played some good shows here lately. Their off key, drone vocals are a trademark. Thetempo is always close to frantic with fast paced melodies.

Lately they have been using The Buckthrusters as an opening band. They are a new group also from Wichita. Besides the guitar, bass, and drums, there are two keyboard players at each side of the stage. Their sound is full and layered. Greg Cowper also plays accordion in addition to synthesizer. Jim Skell operates the other keyboards. The rhythm from the bass and drums provided by brothers, Jim and Britt Rosencutter keeps everything flowing and moving along. The band is fronted by guitarist Stacie Stull. She definitely adds a new twist to the overall force The Buckthrusters present. An up and coming band, for sure. One that will become area favorites.

The Oil Capital Kings were in town this summer, playing with The Wilsons, a new local group. Both bands are fairly new to the performance field, but make up for any lack by their sheer enthusiasm. The Oil Capital Kings are from the Oil Capital, that being Tulsa, OK. They are a three-piece group with Dale Lawton on guitar and vocals, David James on bass and vocals, and drummer Murry Gray. David and Dale were in The Vindicators and just formed this group weeks before their appearance. The chances are good tha they will be back at Off The Wall Hall soon.

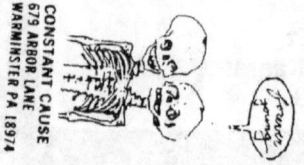

CONSTANT CAUSE
679 ARBOR LANE
WARMINSTER PA 18974

# FRESH

A Fresh Compilation of Sounds on Cassette Tape featuring area artists

## FRESH SOUNDS

announces the upcoming release of a series of cassette tapes featuring predominately regional artists. We bring you the best of the new sounds, including artists such as:

Get Smart! /
The Embarrassment /
The New Wave Brothers /
The Mortal Micronauts /
Color Entertainment /
The Yardapes /
The Buckthrusters /
William S. Burroughs /
Monte Montclaire /
Remains Nonviewable /
C. Lucas Experience /
plus many more

# FRESH SOUNDS FROM MIDDLE AMERICA
## TALK TALK TAPE TALK

TALK TALK TAPE TALK is a cassette-only special courtesy of Talk Talk Publications. Portions may be reprinted in conjunction with tape reviews.

Copyright 1982 Fresh Sounds, Inc., Box 36, Lawrence, KS, 66044 USA. Special thanks to the members of the bands, PTL, Dan Rouser, and Bill Craven.

## FRESH SOUNDS FROM MIDDLE AMERICA

**TAPE 101**
**SIDE ONE**

### GET SMART!
In The Dark/Face/One More Circle/They Walk In Pairs/That's What They Tell Me

Marc Koch  Guitar, vocals
Lisa Wertman  Bass, vocals
Frank Loose  Drums, vocals
All songs ©℗ 1981
Syntax Music / BMI

P.O. Box 493
Lawrence, KS, 66044
Produced by Get Smart!
and Kenny Fulk
Engineered by Karl Hoffmann
Recorded at Ramona Studio

### THE MORTAL MICRONOTZ
The Controllers/Blonde Haired Ghost/Individuality/The Police Song/Daydream/Subterfuge

Dean Lubensky  Vocals
John Harper  Guitar
David Dale  Bass
Steve Eddy  Drums

1209 Tennessee St.
Lawrence, KS, 66044
Produced and Engineered by
Marc Koch and Kenny Fulk

All songs ©℗ 1981 Mortal Micronotz / BMI

**SIDE TWO**

### THE YARDAPES
Playing With Snakes/Living On Welfare/Your Pretty Face/The Long Walk/Jungle Rots/Never You Mind

Elisa Hodes  Vocals, percussion
Chris Fowler  Vocals
Devin Snell  Vocals, percussion
Ron Achelpohl  Guitar, bass, vocals
Bruce Eddy  Bass, guitar
Lisa Vader  Synthesizer
Steve Beai  Drums

406 E. 43rd St., No. 3E
Kansas City, MO, 64110
Recorded at Chapmans
All songs ℗© 1981
Yardco Entertainment/BMI

### THE EMBARRASSMENT
Dino In The Congo/Godfrey Harold Hardy/D-Rings/Chapter Twelve/Jazz Face

John Nichols  Vocals, keyboard
Bill Goffrier  Guitar, vocals
Ron Klaus  Bass
Brent Giessmann  Drums

Box 293, Wichita, KS, 67201
Produced and Engineered by
The Embarrassment & Jim Skeel
Recorded at Skeel's
All songs ℗© 1981
Embarrassment Songs/BMI

## Get Smart!

Get Smart! are a three-piece band who met and formed while at college in Lawrence just over a year ago. Their first release, 'Numbers and Colours/Ankle Deep In Mud', was a flexidisc in TALK TALK (May 1981). They have a cut on the SUB/POP cassette and plans for other compilations. The recent four-song EP, 'Words Move', has received high praise.

Talk Talk: Say something about your songs on the tape.
Frank: 'In The Dark' is one of our earlier songs. It's always been one of our favorites.
Marc: So we decided to get it out. 'Face' makes Lisa cry. My mom likes it.
Lisa: It makes me feel like crying.
Marc: One of our better achievements.
Lisa: One of our newer ones.
Frank: Along with that, one of my favorites is 'They Walk In Pairs' which is simple but effective.
Marc: I think everyone should hear that before they die.
Frank: Lisa wrote that when she was depressed.
Lisa: Yes, a song about talking and not saying anything. It deals with how feelings guide your actions, and words often don't mean anything at all.
Frank: And how you get into trouble because of it. And 'That's What They Tell Me' that's my angry song.
Lisa: Frank's singing debut.
Frank: It's definitely a song out of anger and frustration.
Marc: I think we got better recordings this time than with the EP.
Lisa: When I wrote 'They Walk In Pairs', I didn't know what I was writing about. That song is definitely about me and how I react to things. I still haven't learned from it.
Frank: That's so strange, too. We can sit there and write a song out of one feeling. And we're so human that we just turn around and do it again. Most of our songs are about human failures. I think we're getting more introspective. Our first songs seemed to be more about what we see outside and now they are becoming more introspective as we look into ourselves more and writing out of a personal type of feeling rather than what we see.
Marc: I think we've learned how to handle the outside world and it's now the inside world . . .
Frank: That we're trying to tackle.
Talk Talk: Is your band going along the way you thought it would?
Marc: We never wanted it to go any particular way but naturally the way it goes.
Frank: If someone had told me a year ago that we would have had reviews all over the world for a record, I would have gone, 'sure'. I don't even know how to play this stupid thing. So it's a big surprise.
Lisa: I feel that we are positively in control now of what we're doing. It's a feeling I didn't have when we were constantly traveling. It wore me and the others. We had these dates planed and they just kept coming and coming-a feeling of being out of control.
Frank: I felt that we were becoming a circuit band that was . . .
Marc: Forced happiness.
Frank: There's been pressures for us to jump back on. But we've been writing more songs. We've written six or seven songs

BILL RICH

## The Mortal Micronotz

The Mortal Micronotz are a four-piece group of high schoolers from Lawrence. Basically, a group of friends who started playing last year, the band has become local legends at their early stage.

Talk Talk: How did the band form?
Dean: John and David had been playing together. I was going to be the guitar player but John had the money for it and I didn't. So I was going to be the manager. Then they got me drunk one night and made me sing.
John: That was last year.
Steve: I wasn't in the band then.
Dean: We had a heavy metal drummer who left us for his girlfriend who he thought was pregnant.

Steve: Who stole the PA and everything.
Dean: Don't put this in the magazine about the abortion and selling the PA to pay for it. A bad experience.
John: Well, that's not why he quit the band.
Dean: Now we buy band contraceptives.
Steve: He was just trying to get the PA back to quit. He's a preppie now.
Dean: It's hard going to school and playing. David really has it tough because he has a job he has to do to live also.
John: And Dean's parents never let him practice because he flunks all his courses.
Dean: The main thing holding us back are our parents and our age.
David: The thing I think about is that this band was together before we could ever play. We learned to play after we were formed. Everybody pretty much knew what they were going to do.
Steve: They've been together since the third grade.
Dean: We've always been into music and close friends. Everybody else was either on the football team or playing basketball. We were the weirdos who were into real strange music that no one else knew.
John: We probably would be too if the band wasn't semi-successful. People seemed to like us and we thought maybe we should keep doing this for a while.
Dean: It was also fun being liked for a change.
Dean: Everybody seems to have better equipment than us because we don't take money super seriously. When we make money we go out and get wopped.
John: Buy tacos.
David: After a gig you can usually find us at Taco Grande.
Steve: We almost didn't get to Wichita. We ate away the money to rent a trailer.
Talk Talk: What are your plans? To play more?
Steve: And eat less.
Dean: The whole idea of the band, the reason we came to do this is because of Phil, the fifth Micronotz.
John: The legendary fifth micronotz.
Steve: Is there something I don't know?
Dean: He's distributed in five places in David's house.
John: He inspired us.
Dean: He's one of the little toy micronauts.
David: He got smashed by a guitar.
Talk Talk: Was that before or after you picked the name?
Steve: After, kind of a ritual in our happiness of name-picking.
Talk Talk: Why Mortal?
Dean: We're just human. We're small but human.
Why did you form a band and spend all your time on music?
Dean: It was destiny. If it wasn't this, it would be something else we'd be doing together.
Talk Talk: How did you decide on what covers to do?
Steve: We bought SID SINGS. It was all we could afford.
David: Are you kidding? I worked for weeks to get that.
Dean: It was the only punk record we had besides ROCK AND ROLL SWINDLE. . . And some 45s.
John: And Ramones.
Dean: In Search and Destroy, I sing totally different words because I hadn't heard the original.
John: All we heard was SID SINGS. We couldn't figure out the words so we made our own.
Talk Talk: How do you describe your music?
David: It's mostly been described as regressive rock.
Dean: It's just rock. We're not a practiced punk band or new wave or artsy.
David: Kansas plains.
John: Kansas music.
Steve: Cowboy punk.

PHOTOS BY BILL RICH

Dean: Everything we write basically sounds the way we feel, the way we are.
John: Happy rock for little sailors.
Talk Talk: What are you trying to get across?
All: Have a good time.
John: The music doesn't count as much as the attitude.
Dean: The music has a lot to do with the title in that it's stupid and silly. If people can accept that as part of being young and youthful, part of being a kid.
Talk Talk: What grades are you in?
Steve: David and I are juniors and John and Dean are sophomores. Dean was just 14 when it started. David is 17, I'm 16, John is 16 and Dean is 15.
Talk Talk: Do you keep up with what's going on?
John: Most just what we hear on the radio, KJHK.
Steve: We can't afford to buy records.
Dean: I buy TALK TALK so I can read up about bands and records, just so I don't feel stupid. I don't think we're affected by a lot of other stuff played now. We like a lot of the old music and a lot of people think that is a mistake but good music is timeless.
Steve: If anyone comes to see us and we mess up, just laugh, don't throw anything. That's all we're doing - we really loosen up when we get on stage. It would be nice to play everything perfect but we don't expect to and when we mess up we pass it off. We scream at each other a little bit and then pass it off.

## The YardApes

The YardApes are a seven-piece group from Kansas City. With three vocalists and alternating on instruments, they are a fun band to watch.

Talk Talk: Where are you all from?
Lisa: We're all from the K.C. area.
Talk Talk: When did the YardApes begin?
Lisa: The YardApes started in June of '81, but we have been in bands with each other before. Several of us started our first band in high school, the Implications. A few songs that the Apes play now were written then. Our band also includes people from bands like The Office Supplies and Last Rites. When Ron was in school in New York, we all wrote letters to each other about how we wanted to be all together in a band. We ended up with more singers than anything else. We decided that might be a pretty cool situation to work with.
Talk Talk: You don't play covers, do you?
Devin: We've only played one so far.

Ron: The main reason we don't do many covers is because we have such a backlog of our own material to work on.
Lisa: Everyone except Steve sings and almost everyone plays the guitar. Several can play keyboards or synthesizer.
Talk Talk: How many configurations of the band do you have? Four or five?
Ron: Every song is different, but basically I play guitar; Bruce plays bass.
Lisa: I play synthesizer and Steve plays drums and Chris, Devin and Elisa sing.
Chris: Elisa does a lot of the percussion, too.
Talk Talk: Do you find it hard working with such a large number of performers, to trade off and change?
Devin: Actually, I think it's easier than other bands I've been in. Everyone has something to add. Even when Elisa just dances, that adds to the feeling. When you cramp us into a small space, the movement

is incredible.
Chris: The element of confusion definitely adds.
Lisa: We've injured each other bodily on stage several times.
Chris: That's why we are YardApes.
Lisa: It's more fun to play with more people.

FRANK LOOSE

# The Embarrassment

The Embarrassment are a four-piece band from Wichita, KS. They are viewed as the veterans or examples to be followed by many new bands in the Midwest. Releases to date include their first single, 'Sex Drive/Patio Set', a track on the Bomp collection, BATTLE OF THE GARAGE BANDS, a cut on the SUB/POP tape and their new, highly acclaimed five-song, 12-inch EP. Current plans include working on their debut album and heavy touring.

Talk Talk: Let's talk about the songs on the tape. How do you write songs? For example, how about Godfrey Harold Hardy?
Bill: Well, Brent wrote the lyrics.
Brent: Sometimes it happens that a person will have the lyrics and a few musical ideas. But the band is responsible for the arrangement. There's also the points where the band will have an idea while we're together and work it out.
Ron: Brent was taking a math class.
Brent: There was this family tree of mathematics and he was on it. I looked him up in the library because he interested me. From a very early age he was a mathematician.
Bill: I like it because it seems to be about someone accomplishing something. And they're pretty happy about it, telling you what they've done. It's kind of got that glad sound.
John: It has a good beat, you can dance to it. Give it a 93.
Brent The important thing is the group is anxious to get their hands on new material like 'D-Rings,' Bill had the lyrics and just vaguely gave an idea of what he wanted musically. Between John and Bill, there was a lot of experimenting around.
Ron: Coming up with the musical part is what takes longest. Someone will come up with a line or riff they like and we'll play off it. It's just a development that goes on. It works well, if I have a bass line, Brent and Bill can play off of that. If Bill has a guitar line or Brent has a drum rhythm I can usually come up with a bass line pretty easy. I like to have a strong bass line.
Bill: Sometimes the guitar line turns into the bass line and we build on top of that.
Ron But there's no definite way we write songs, no formula we follow.
Bill: We have to wait a long time until something unexpected finds its way in or somebody misunderstands somebody's idea. And that might turn out to be what was needed. But nobody thinks of it that way on their own. John might try to explain an idea he has and we interpret that our own way and apply it to the song. It's not what he had in mind and none of us thought of it, but we put it in, it works OK and we know we have something a little different and unique to that song. It finally happened that way with 'Godfrey Harold Hardy'. For a while it sounded like 'Lewis and Clark', then something happened, but 'D-Rings' goes back years ago.
John: Back during the Voyagers Mission.
Ron: When they went past Saturn. That's what this is about, the D-rings of Saturn.
Talk Talk: These are from one session?
Ron: We selected these songs to record for you and went down and did it in three nights.

Talk Talk: How is it living in Wichita?
Ron: It's hard to get a job playing. No matter what kind of music people just don't come out to support live music. The biggest contingent are the heavy metal bands. But even at that, there aren't many good ones. In that sense, we're doing pretty good to get a couple of hundred people to hear what they might consider obscure music. There's not much of anything that gets a bigger crowd. Live music is pretty poor.
Talk Talk: Are you pretty satisfied with being based in Wichita?
John: We get to do pretty much what we want to without too many . . .
Bill: Distractions or influences.
Brent: That's important. No distractions or influences. The only competition is in Lawrence and Wichita.
Bill: Our competition and influences and how we have our entertainment is usually all within our circle of friends; musicians like The New Wave Brothers, The Buckthrusters, the old Aagarns, all the people we know who are trying to get something going. That's our entertainment and that's how we learn.
John: The sad part is wanting to play for a new audience, we have to drive so far.
Talk Talk: You had plans for a big East Coast tour that has been delayed.
Ron: Not by choice. The record plant put us three months behind, we could have had the ball really rolling by now but they stopped us cold in our tracks. And with winter weather, we have to wait.

## Get Smart!—cont. from p 4

lately and decided to only keep three of them. That's exciting to be able to sit there and go, oh, there's no pressure, we don't have to keep those, let's just forget them! Before it was like, 'here's this new song, let's force it and get it out'.
Lisa: That's what you felt.
Frank: We all felt it to some extent.
Lisa: It was mainly rehearsing for gigs in tension.
Frank: It's a much more relaxed, creative atmosphere now and it's going along very well. We're improvising more, playing a long time, running through riffs, picking out beats or notes or chords.
Marc: I don't think it happened before. Lots of bands sit and 'jam' and that's what is happening now. We're able to do more.
Frank: Everyone keep those cards and letters coming, especially from West Germany. But we feel that there isn't much more new to say. We're following in the original concept and continuing on that.
Marc: To have a lot of energy when we perform. Try to have spontaneity.
Frank: Make people dance but also think.
Marc: Evoke some sort of feeling.

# FRESH SOUNDS FROM MIDDLE AMERICA
## TALK TALK TAPE TALK

TALK TALK TAPE TALK is a cassette-only special courtesy of Talk Talk Publications. Portions may be reprinted in conjunction with tape reviews.

Copyright 1982 Fresh Sounds, Inc., Box 36, Lawrence, KS, 66044 USA. Special thanks to the members of the bands, PTL, Dan Rouser, and Bill Craven.

---

**FRESH SOUNDS FROM MIDDLE AMERICA**
TAPE 102
SIDE ONE
**THE BUCKTHRUSTERS**
Blu Lite Special / And It Is / The Drive / The Moment / Ha! Ha!
Jim Rosencutter Bass
Britt Rosencutter Drums, vocals
Staci Stull Guitar, vocals
Greg Cowper Accordian, synthesizer, vocals
Jim Skeel Keyboards, synthesizer, vocals
©℗ 1981 Buckthrusters / BMI
1708 N Vassar
Wichita, KS, 67208
Recorded and Produced by Jim Skeel, Greg Cowper, and The Buckthrusters at Skeels, Wichita, KS.

**THE NEW WAVE BROTHERS**
New Wave Brothers Rap / I'm The Best / DNA Monsters
Jim all instruments, vocals
Britt all instruments, vocals
Alex all instruments, vocals
Court all instruments, vocals
1708 N Vassar
Wichita, KS, 67208
©℗ 1981 New Wave Brothers
Recorded at Hellbirds

SIDE TWO
**COLOR ENTERTAINMENT**
Instrumental / Come On! / Plants / Fruit Of The Womb
Fred Skellenger
Kathi Inukai
©℗ 1981
Color Entertainment,
815 E 48th Street, No. 6,
Kansas City, MO, 64110

**MONTE MONTCLAIRE**
Period Piece
Monte Montclaire
Produced by Monte Montclaire. Engineered by Karl Hoffmann  Recorded at Ramona
©℗ 1981 Monte Montclaire, PO Box 701, Lawrence, KS, 66044

**THE C. LUCAS EXPERIENCE**
Silliness / Art / Sincerity / Indulgence / And Acting Out
Christopher Lucas all sounds
©℗ 1981 C. Lucas, Box 1357
Lawrence, KS, 66044
Fresh Sounds Music / BMI

## The Buckthrusters

*The Buckthrusters are a five-piece Wichita band with members from several earlier groups popular in the area. Their use of two keyboard-synthesizer set-ups allows for additional sounds to be created.*

The Buckthruster, a device comprised of a hydraulic arm attached to a magnetic cumberbund worn by willing band members. The arm rhythmically elongates to first project a musician up, out, over, and into the audience, then withdraws returning the player to their stage position. *Wichita, Lawrence, Kansas City, MO/hydraulic arm into the audience/ thrustin thru the shows yea yea yea, Buckthrust!* The Buckthruster is a noteworthy alternative to glitter and flash pots and an elaboration of it might be the singer who hovers over the crowd in a cherry picker.

The Buckthrusts formed in the fall of 1980 as a quartet drawing members from the seminal alternative Wichita bands the Aagarns, the Inevitable, and Dr. Doom and the Victims of Circumstance. The first incarnation of the band found Staci switching between bass and guitar, Greg and Jim playing keyboards and trading key bass responsibilities, and Britt holding down the drums. The addition of Jim Rosencutter on bass guitar tightened-up and pushed the music into new dimensions. It was during this middle period that Greg added more accordion to live performances and the period from which these five songs were drawn. By the fall of 1981 the band had run its course, the guitarist had left, and the Buckthrusters played their final gigs again as a quartet, the instrumentation having evolved to synthesizers, sox organ, clavinet, bass and drums.

The divergent musical histories of the Buckthrusters-rock'n'roll, folk, art-rock-culminated in a novel, varied, layered, and infrasonic new music. *Love's the wreckless car/Love's the deadest she/Love drives on forever and ever/ Love you cannot keep, you cannot keep*

All songs © Copyright 1981.

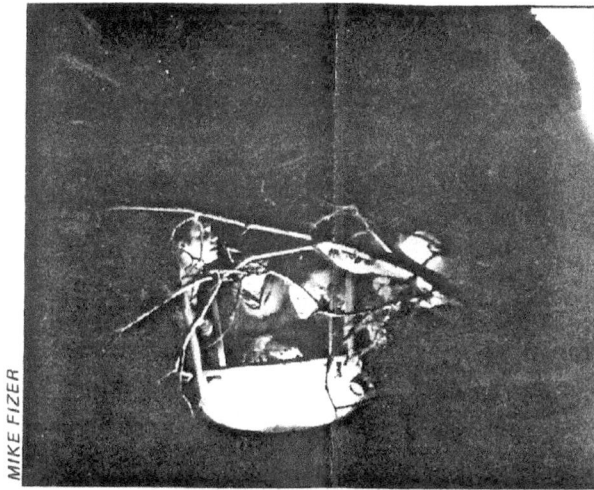

MIKE FIZER

## New Wave Brothers

*The New Wave Brothers are a four-piece group that play a loose-flowing, post-industrial freeform rock. While not wanting to be perceived as a joke band, they do add an element of comedy to their performances.*

'Tired of the music scene, we decided to get together and change the approach and pretentiousness of it and eventually the world.'

Starting off with 'New Wave', as it was the most expressive mode of music at the time, they carved out a place in music history to be remembered.

'Cute lyrics are out', they said together, as they did everything together. This is not to say that they were not handicapped by their background. For obvious reasons, this stunted their capacity to be open to different thoughts.

Then the Hellbird came into our lives and with his inspiration, Hellbird Studios evolved. Our first project, BAND BY MAIL, shed light on the obvious beginnings, an instrumental called A NEW DAWN FOR MAN or THE EPIC POEM: The History of Materialism. The music that we've written since is not scripture or any kind of heavy statement, it's simply dance music for the brain.

We feel that people don't use their minds as much as their biases, their brains as much as their bodies. They'll jog ten miles a day but they won't read a book in a month.

Hellbird Studios 2 is now born and the/our transition is now underway. 'Don't underestimate the powers of sin' CTB

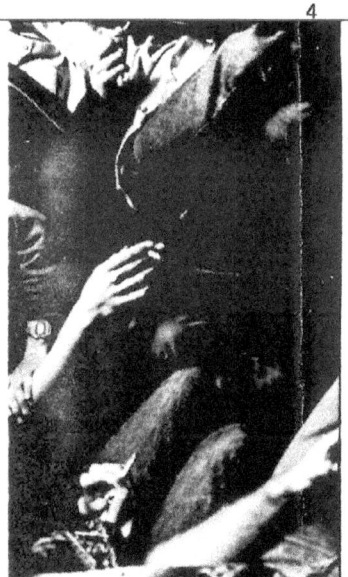

PHOTO BY MIKE FIZER

BILL RICH

## Color Entertainment

*Color Entertainment present a multimedia show with a background of slides and movies for two performers playing along with a prerecorded tape and miming. They are from Kansas City and have played only a limited number of shows to date.*

Talk Talk: How did you get started?

Fred: Color Entertainment started about four months ago when Kathi came back from New York, where she had been in a band. She wanted to combine music and visual things to create atmospheres, feelings, and get across ideas. We decided to do it and make tapes, just to see how it would come out. The songs on the tape are from the first show we did.

Talk Talk: What sounds do you like to use?

Fred: We've changed our set totally now. It is almost all recorded and we're doing more theatrical things. The main format of a song is on tape and I play saxophone in peak spots. We show a movie now and lots of slides and are changing our clothes with the songs. We have a space now to change into to use on stage that contains al our things.

Parts of our new songs are very repetitious that don't involve rock and roll like drums and bass or even saxophone. We can always do our first set but we have this new one prepared also, which is a lot more electronic noises and rhythmic sounds.

PHOTOS BY BILL RICH

8

We try to be interesting to both ourselves and to audiences. People want to see new things.

Talk Talk: Are there other performers similar to you?

Fred: In New York. I like the fact that there is not a lot of it, because that makes it unique when someone does see it. They don't know what to think of it and maybe they don't like it. It's kind of dangerous for us, because we could get in situations where people expect something totally different, like in a leather jacketed, punk crowd or even with totally New Wave rock and roll expectations.

Talk Talk: How do you come up with your concepts?

Fred: Basically, I'll be playing some music that will make me feel something or see things in my head. Kathi has been doing some other things. My work is pretty easy to understand.

Talk Talk: Do you both have theatrical experience?

Fred: I took one course in high school but not a lot of training. Kathi has been doing ballet and modern dance for a few years.

Talk Talk: How does she write material?

Fred: Usually she will have a concept of some sort and will follow it up until the end. She's working on some video and one of the new songs is for video.

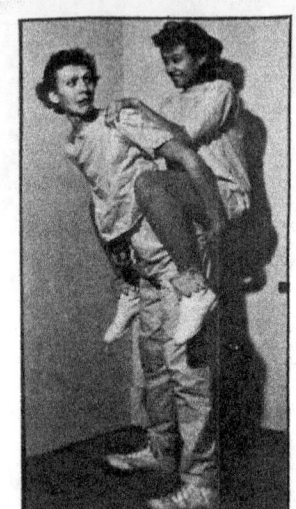

9

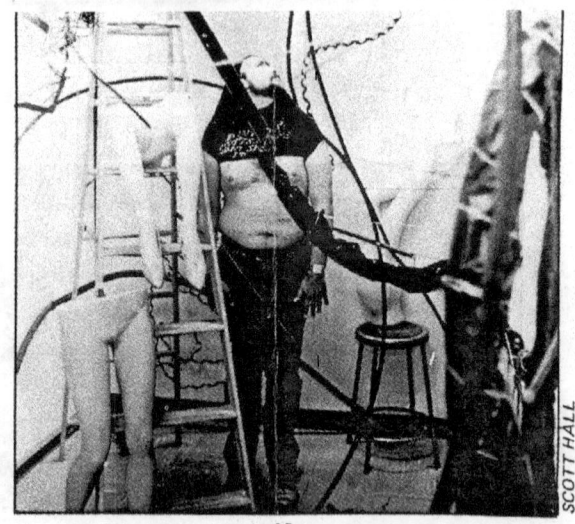

SCOTT HALL

10

## Monte Montclaire

*Monte Montclaire is a local artist/musician who created 'Period Piece' recently in the studio.*

ENTITY IN SEARCH OF QUALITY. PRODUCT OF A GENRE OF VICTIMS. DRIVEN BY LUST, ECONOMICS, AND THE MOVEMENT AT THE EDGE OF VISION. LIFE AROUND THE CORNER. ACHIEVEMENT IS ALL TO STRIVE FOR.

"PERIOD PIECE" ENVELOPS THE DECADE IN WHICH THIS ENTITY ESTABLISHED HIS METHODS OF REFLECTING AND EXPRESSING HIS EXPERIENCE. WINTER 1981

BILL RICH

## The C. Lucas Experience

*The C. Lucas Experience is the work of local artist Christopher Lucas. Up to now, his music has only been heard between sets at local clubs.*

Talk Talk: Please explain yourself.
Christopher Lucas: The C stands for Christopher and the experience is in Kansas.
Talk Talk: 'Acting out'?
CL: I have fears and I act my emotions out partly in everyday life, partly making visual situations and partly with sounds. I'm sure glad I'm not deaf or blind.
Talk Talk: Do you like pleasure? Do you like rhythm? Do you like winter? Do you like women? The question really is do your sounds provide pleasure to anyone else?
CL: We will see. I like pleasure. My tapes -my sound expression-is a pleasurable sensation to create. I hope people will listen to my sounds and will attempt to make their own tapes. Sometimes pleasure is pain.
Talk Talk: What is your approach to music?
CL: I like collecting sounds, counting rhythms, systems...
Talk Talk: Systems?
CL: Yes, like holding a guitarneck, playing one note, then moving away from that position to another location, then playing that note which is found there. I try to play instruments visually, creating a system in which to move around. My scale is a physical one. Sometimes I wish I could play the piano, read music and write movie soundtracks, get married and have children.
TT: Do your musical sound tapes and artwork, such as at your recent show, Kansas Objects Religious Inexperience, go together in any way?
CL: Yes. My art objects are more personal than the sounds on my tapes. I look at my objects a lot--I have them around my house. But I don't leave my tapes playing in the background. Sometimes I make tapes and never listen to them again, they are a vestige of a specific location, emotion, time, which may or may not require listening to. For some reason, I feel a sense of wholeheartedness with my eyes but not with my ears. It would be OK to be deaf--a shame. But blind--I would die.
TT: What do you want other people to think about your music?
CL: To conclude that there are sounds all around and each person can make noise, play instruments and experience this as their own emotion, and of course, music. Just like the children at work counting and singing with me, it's their music.
TT: What are you currently doing.
CL: Making tapes with a friend who sings about cheese.

---

"It is quite probable that singing came before talking."
--William S. Burroughs (TALK TALK)

With this thought in mind, one can realize the importance that communication through music and song has had upon the human race. In an evolutionary scenario, early humans might have sat around warbling to each other. Later, specfic phonetic sounds gained meaning and short utterances became the language. Somewhere in the forgotten, unused sections of the brain are centers that respond to tones and pitches and melodies. Perhaps todays music lovers actually have a greater experience than realized when listening to music. Musical sounds do cause a hard to explain enjoyment.

Two important points regarding this project are the medium and the content.
Cassette tapes are making a big impact on the music industry. With skyrocketing record prices and less purchasing power, more consumers tape borrowed records or songs. The cassette deck is as standard to the sound system as the FM tuner. Portable units and car stereos blast out cassette sounds at every corner. Truly the new medium.
The content demonstrates that new music is being created all over--not just in England or the American coasts, but in the center as well. -- Bill Rich.

# INDEX

101ers, The, 274
11th Street Rhythm Method, 12
20 of Another Kind (*compilation*), 40
4" Be 2", 31
8-Eye Spy, 358
999, 193
A Certain Ratio, 193, 205, 210
A Factory Quartet, 259
Aagarnes, The, 196
Abuse, 85, 152, 188, 207, 230-233, 276, 334
Abwarts, 387
ACR, 387
Adam and the Ants, 238
Adverts, 18
Allen Ginsberg, 180, 194-195
Alligator Ball, 56
Andreas Dorer, 387
Angelic Upstarts, 15, 24, 99
Arthur Kay, 24
Arthur Kay's Originals, 112
Atila, 399
Au Pairs, 359
Augustus Pablo, 192, 221
B-52s, The, 159
Babylon (*compilation*), 369
Bad Manners, 98, 112
Barrington Levy, 128
Barry Brown, 63
Barry Brown and Raning Toyan, 307
Basement 5, 119, 134, 204
Bauhaus, 76, 77, 147, 186, 264-270, 278
BC Gilbert and G Lewis, 395
Beakers, The, 210
Beat, The, 32, 35, 70, 107, 155-158, 160, 354
Big Youth, 63
Black Ark, 95, 307
Black Flag, 210
Black Slate, 192
Black Uhuru, 62, 63, 96, 122, 142
Blackbeard, see Dennis "Blackbeard" Bovell
Blasters, The, 228
Blue Riddim Band, The, 23, 96, 111, 129, 160, 166, 222-225, 330, 352
Blurt, 258, 387
Bob Andy, 119
Bob Marley, 322-323
Bob Marley and the Wailers, 6, 23, 119, 163, 279
Bodies, The, 71

Bodysnatchers, The, 70, 162
Bomis Prendin, 162
Bongo Herman, 126
Boomtown Rats, The, 17
Bow Wow Wow, 147, 204
Boys, The, 36
Bpeople, 263, 392
Brian Beverly, 393
Brian Brain, 147
Brian James, 16
Broncos, The, 360
Buckthrusters, The, 400, 416-417
Bunny Wailer, 176, 219, 280, 352, 368
Burning Spear, 75, 92, 124, 174-175, 280
Bush Tetras, 173, 393
Buzzcocks, The, 5, 21, 23, 25, 31, 35, 37, 193, 256
C. Lucas Experience, The, 406, 409
C. P. Lee, 389
C81, 358
Cabaret Voltaire, 19, 53, 100, 144, 210, 256
Cairo, 63
Can You Hear Me? (*compilation*), 113
Capital Letters, 134
Capital Punishment Benefit (*compilation*), 388
Carlene Davis, 124, 128
Charles Bukowski, 65
Charlie Pickett and the Eggs, 273
Chelsea, 62
Chiefs, The, 313
Chrome, 90
Chunks Compilation (*compilation*), 393
Circle Jerks, 239
Clash, The, 3, 7, 29, 31, 40, 50, 59, 64, 105, 171, 205, 336-337
Clean, The, 32, 71, 73, 158, 165, 209
Clint Eastwood, 97
Club Ska '67 (*compilation*), 96
Cockney Rejects, 12, 24, 61, 68, 105
Cold, The, 210
Colin Newman, 187, 256, 344-347
Colin Winski, 133
Color Entertainment, 406, 408
Comsat Angels, The, 147, 152, 186
Craig Leon, 392
Cramps, The, 145-146, 162, 166, 315
Crass, 241
Creation Rockers (*compilation*), 50
Crispy Ambulance, 240

Cult Hero, 26
Culture, 12-13, 126-127
Cure, The, 14, 68, 89, 98, 101
Da, 360
DAF, see Deutsch-Amerikanische Freundschaft
Damned, The, 24
Dance Craze, 221
Dancing Cigarettes, The, 391
David Bowie, 151, 153
David Isaacs and Jah Thomas, 50
DB's, The, 258
Dead Kennedys, The, 172
Debs, The, 106, 121, 131, 151
Declaration of Independents, 316
Decorators, The, 83
Delroy Wilson, 124, 125
Delta 5, 31-32, 84, 394
Dennis "Blackbeard" Bovell, 92, 322
Dennis Brown, 49, 51, 63, 70, 128, 129, 262, 290-292, 351
Der Plan, 235
Derrick Laro and Trinity, 176, 387
Desmond Dekker, 148
Deutsch-Amerikanische Freundschaft, 74, 134, 212, 316, 355, 387
DEVO, 355
Dexy's Midnight Runners, 63, 70, 137-139, 160
Diagram Bros., The, 353
Dickies, The, 30, 69, 74
Dictators, The, 388
Dillinger, 63
Divine, 392
Dome, 143
Dr. Alimantado, 63
Dr. Mix and the Remix, 52
Drinking Electricity, 113, 114
Duchamp, 132, 208
Duchamp-Duchamp, 77
Duke Reid (*compilation*), 111
Durutti Column, 40, 77
Earcom (*compilations*), 20, 71, 387
Earl Zero, 356
Earth and Stone, 41
Echo and the Bunnymen, 120, 143, 173
Egg Hoover and the G.E. Three, 18
Elodie Lauten, 393
Elvis Costello and the Attractions, 55, 61
Embarrassment, The, 18, 84, 106, 112, 161-162, 167, 196, 252, 397, 400, 402, 405
English Beat, The, 354
Epicycle, 359
Equators, The, 220, 262, 352
Erector Set, The, 392
Errol Scorcher, 200
ESG, 355
Essential Logic, 12

Fad Gadget, 77, 331, 387
Fall, The, 17, 62, 99, 147, 274, 354, 374-375, 397
Fashiön, 10, 15
Fast Forward (*cassette magazine*), 28
Fast Product, 36
Fear, 313
Feelies, The, 134
Fela Kuti, 368
Five or Six, 353
Flaming Ohs, The, 360
Fleshtones, The, 204
Flowers, The, 43, 112
Front, 387
Front Line 3 (*compilation*), 17
Gang of Four, 5, 20, 98, 258
Gary Charlson, 399
Gear, The, 273
Geisterahrer, 387
General Echo, 81
General Saint and Clint Eastwood, 307
General Smiley and Poppa Michigan, 124, 125, 128, 129
Get Smart!, 208-209, 236, 300-305, 333, 396, 402, 403
GG Allin, 393
Gladiators, 35-36
Glaxo Babies, 90, 152, 171
Glenn Branca, 163
Graham Parker and the Rumour, 56
Gregory Isaacs, 34, 63, 163, 351
Growling Tiger, 148
Guns for Hire, 112
Heartland USA (*compilation*), 281
Heavy Manners, 393
Henry Badowski, 393
Heptones, The, 128
Hitler Youth, 237
Holly and the Italians, 70, 76, 106
Home Improvements, 273
Hottest Hits (*compilations*), 21, 111, 118
Human Hands, 392
Human League, The, 12, 20
Human Switchboard, 43
Ian Dury, 239
Ian Hunter, 392
Ice House, 392
Identity Crisis, 271
Iggy Pop, 16, 20, 48, 56-57, 67-68, 76, 80, 207, 356, 377-379
Image Publique S.A., see Public Image, Ltd.
Imports, The, 84, 85, 90, 193
In Camera, 173
Industry, 203
Inevitable, The, 18
Infinite Sensuality, 124
Inner Circle, 77, 262
Intensified (*compilation*), 11
I-Roy, 11, 12, 41

Irritators, The, 392
Ivan Kral, 57
Jack Ruby, 200
Jah Bunny, 200
Jah Lloyd, 21
Jah Message, 325
Jah Thomas and the Roots Radic Band, 307
Jah Wobble, 91, 101, 143
Jam, The, 24, 58, 73
James Brown, 180-181
James Chance and the Contortions, 159, 165, 358
James Chance with the Pill Factory, 277
James Grauerholz, 140, 164, 165, 252
Jetsons, The, 391
Jimmy Cliff, 133, 176, 201-202
Jimmy Riley, 122
Jody Harris, 359
Joe Gibbs, 12, 13
Joe Gibbs and the Professionals, 62
Joe Higgs, 17
Joeboy, 398
John Cale, 24, 83-84, 326-327
John Foxx, 42, 48, 52, 76, 120
Johnny Winter, 180
Jon and the Blasters, 228
Josef K, 393
Joy Division, 26, 32, 77, 84, 120, 132, 147
Junior Murvin, 12-13
Kate Fagan, 353
Ken Boothe, 125
Kiddus I, 126
Kidz Next Door, 31
Killing Joke, 50, 187
King Kong, 296
King of Dub, 200
King Tubby, 192
KJHK (*radio station*), 183
Konnekshen, 387
Kurtis Blow, 172
Landscape, 393
Laurie Anderson, 211, 312
Lee "Scratch" Perry, 142, 152, 306, 369
Lene Lovich, 51, 58
Leroy Sibbles, 128, 129
Lewis and Gilbert, 234
LiLiput, 173
Linton Kwesi Johnson, 75, 92, 101, 200
Little Bears from Bangkok, The, 332
Little Queenie and the Perculators, 56
Liquid Liquid, 359
LKJ, see Linton Kwesi Johnson
Lloyd Parks and We the People, 124, 128
Log-A-Rhythms, 390
Lone Ranger, 62
Lori and the Chameleons, 27

Lounge Lizards, The, 281
Love of Life Orchestra, 83
Ludas, 83, 358
Luxury, 399
Lydia Lunch, 43
Macs, The, 210
Madness, 18, 42, 58, 70, 160, 201
Magazine, 61, 73, 98, 105, 114, 149-150, 234, 356
Majestarians, 307
Manic Depressives, The, 210
Mark Lane, 391
Mass, 256
Mathius Schuster, see Konnekshen
Matumbi, 352
Max Edwards, 219
Max Romeo, 352
Meat Puppets, 389
Medium Medium, 353
Mekons, The, 12, 36, 75, 151
Members, The, 84, 195
Men Without Hats, 394
Merton Parkas, 26, 27
Metal Urbain, 314
Mexicano, The, 262
Mi-Sex, 62, 90
Michael Rose, 123
Michael Smith, 128
Mighty Diamonds, 126-127
Mikey Dread, 81, 104, 192, 220
Mikey "Mao" Chung, 123
Miles Copeland, 9, 11
Minioon, 387
Ministry of Fear, 389
Minutemen, 390
Mission of Burma, 398
MnMs, 106
Mo-dettes, 42, 120, 193
Modern Warfare No. 2, 360
Moderns, The, 90
Moebius and Plank, 65
Monkey Business (*compilation*), 111
Monochrome Set, 19, 83, 100, 147, 171, 393
Monte Montclair, 406, 408
More Intensified (*compilation*), 96
Morells, The, 207, 348-349
Mortal Micronotz, The, 402, 403-404
Morwell Unlimited, 200
Mr. Isaaccs, 13
Mr. Partridge, 56
Music for No Man's Land (*compilation*), 389
MX-80 Sound, 84
N. O. Experience Necessary (*compilation*), 56
Nadia Kapiche, 393
Naked Skinnies, 390
Names, The, 312

Native, 124
Negativeland, 259
Neon Boys, The, 84
Neptune's Car, 193
New Age Steppers, The, 234
New Era Reggae Band, The, 64, 96, 97, 103-104, 114, 152, 206
New Irish Movement, The (*compilation*), 96, 101
New Order, The, 277
New Wave Brothers, The, 389, 406, 407
News, 210
N Kojak, 63, 130, 294
Nightdoctors, The, 262
Nightriders, The, 228
Nine Nine Nine, 39, 70, 72, 75
Non, 359
Observers, 392
Offs, The, 313, 356
Oil Capital Kings, The, 400
Oingo Boingo, 228
Oku Onaru, 122
Only Ones, The, 89
Orchestral Manoeuvers in the Dark, 64, 187
Original Mirrors, 64
Otto Kentrol, 360
Pablo Moses, 201
Packards, The, 358
Paragons, The, 368
Pat's Blue Riddim Band, see Blue Riddim Band, The
Pauline Murray and the Invisible Girls, 167
Penetration, 13, 40, 43
People, The, 354
Pere Ubu, 18, 21, 144, 277, 314, 387
Peter Gabriel, 107, 121, 131
Peter Tosh, 122, 123, 280, 352, 366-367
Phantom Limb, 356
PiL, see Public Image Ltd.
Pink Military, 104
Plague of Toads, 353
Police, The, 10
Polyphonic Size, 353
Pop Group, The, 35, 88, 104
Positive Noise, 353
Pretenders, The, 24, 43
Primitive Romance, 389-390
Prince Edwards, 128
Prince Far I, 63, 181
Prince Far-I and the Arabs, 142
Prince Jammy, 41, 91
Prince Jazzbo, 201
Producers, The, 210
Professionals, The, 173
Protex, 26
Psychedelic Furs, The, 26, 98, 188, 359, 372-373
Public Image Ltd., 5, 30, 79, 94-95

Puppies, 390
Pylon, 104, 114
Rachel Sweet 35
Radio Sweat, 389
Raincoats, The, 20, 30, 394
Ramones, 40
Ras Midas, 201
Raybeats, The, 258, 275, 394
Reactors, Los, 390
Rebel Music (*compilation*), 11
Red Beat, 390
Red Snerts, 392
Regular Guys, The, 4, 12, 18, 42, 44, 82, 121, 131, 213, 229
Revolutionaries, The, 10, 16, 41, 49, 51, 126, 127, 200
Richard Hell, 84
Rico Rodriguez, 41, 178, 294
Robert Quine, 359
Robbie Shakespeare, 122, 123
Rock Against Racism (*compilation*), 163
Rock Therapy (*record store*), 183
Rockers (*compilation*), 11
Rocking Clones, The, 360
Rockpile, 187
Rod Taylor, 192
Roky Erickson and the Aliens, 392
Roots Radics Band, 91
Roy Reid, 148
Roz, 271
Saggitarius, 126
San Francisco Underground No. 2 (*compilation*), 240
Scars, 399
Scratch on the Wire (*compilation*), 17
Scritti Politti, 392
Secret Affair, 24, 26, 36
Section 25, 125
Selecter, The, 12, 55-56, 83, 92-93
Sensimilla Dub, 200
Sex Pistols, The, 204
Sham 69, 7, 12, 83, 118
Sharp Cuts (*compilation*), 107
Sheila Hylton, 262
Sid Vicious, 30, 36
Signal(s), 387
Silicon Teens, 61-62
Simple Minds, 198
Siouxsie and the Banshees, 120, 132, 172
Skanking Lizards, The, 64
Skeletons, The, 131, 134
Skudder, 210
Skunks, The, 360
Slits, The, 5, 73, 89, 132, 189, 210
Slivers, 391
Sly Dunbar, 34, 122, 123
Sly and Robbie, 119, 130
Sly and the Revolutionaries, 91

Smart Pills, The, 18
Smashcords, The, 399
Snakefinger, 26-27
Soul Syndicate, 176
Specials, The, 12, 17, 50, 112, 204
Specials, The, with Rico, 57-58
Spectres, The, 298-299
Speedies, 391
Spielverderber, 387
SPK, 173, 342-343, 357
Sport of Kings, 390
Squeeze, 64, 100-101
Start Swimming (*compilation*), 354
Steel Pulse, 17, 133, 289-290
Stiff Little Fingers, 7, 19, 61, 68, 117-118, 147, 314
Strange Circuits, 390
Stranglers, The, 241, 308-311
Stray Cats, The, 263
Subway Sect, 19, 106, 113, 118, 134
Sugar Minott, 128, 129
Suicide, 388
Surface Music, 392
Surgical Penis Klinik, see SPK
Susan Springfield, 113
Swell Maps, 19, 159
Swinging Cats, The, 162
Sylvain Sylvain, 48
System Planning Korporation, see SPK
Talking Heads, 172
Tamlins, The, 122-123
Tappa Zukie, 75, 81
Tea Set, The, 61
Teardrop Explodes, The, 73, 74, 187, 328-329
Tenants, The, 360
Terrorists, The, 369
The, The, 173
Third World, 87, 97, 103, 163, 166, 203, 218, 352
This Heat, 44, 387
Thomas Leer and Robert Rental, 234
Three Swimmers, The, 332
Throbbing Gristle, 112, 140-141, 163-165, 212, 338-341
Thumbs, 4, 12, 18, 37, 39, 44, 85, 115, 180, 213
Thunderbirds, The, 139
Tikis, The, 390
Tom Robinson, 52
Tony Brown Band, The, 260-261
Toots and the Maytalls, 75, 87, 92, 103, 176, 181, 230
Tourists, The, 88-89, 99, 101
Traxx, 121
Trinity, 74, 75, 124
Tuxedo Moon, 90, 314
TV Babies, 271
Typical Girls, 359
U2, 296-297
UB40, 63, 176

UK Subs, 13, 24, 32, 64, 73, 99
Ultravox, 21, 23, 25, 27, 37, 119, 159, 169-170
Undertones, The, 5, 83, 105, 114, 119
Upsetter, 351; see also Lee "Scratch" Perry
Upsetters, 41, 210; see also Lee "Scratch" Perry
U-Roy, 81
Vague, The, 65
Velvet Underground, The, 213
Ventures, The, 372
Vertibrats, The, 391
Vic Godard and the Subway Sect, 106, 113, 118, 134
Visage, 21
Voids, 64, 65
Wall of Voodoo, 188
Walter Steding, 193
Wanna Buy a Bridge? (*compilation*), 354
Wild Kingdom, 391
William S. Burroughs, 163-166, 194-195, 250-251, 358, 364-365, 380-385
Wilsons, The, 400
Wire, 21, 22
Wolvarines, The, 360
Word, Sound and Power, 122-123
X, 113, 334-335, 346-347,
X-O-DUS, 75
XTC, 17, 47, 52-53, 59-60, 71, 184-186, 196
Yanks, The, 272
Yard Apes, The, 402, 404
Young Marble Giants, 132
Young Professionals, The, 390
You're the Guy I Want to Share My Money With (*compilation*), 395
Zantees, The, 238
Zap-Pow, 126, 129
Z'ev, 387
Zeitgeist, 353
Zounds, 390
Zuge Horigkeits Gefuhl, 387

*Photo by Bill Rich*

*Photo by Bill Rich*

www.ingramcontent.com/pod-product-compliance
Lightning Source LLC
Chambersburg PA
CBHW080722300426
44114CB00019B/2465